Shadow Banking in China

To my parents, my wife Jin Xin and my daughter Yixi

Shadow Banking in China

Risk, Regulation and Policy

Shen Wei

Shandong University Law School, China

Edward Elgar
PUBLISHING

Cheltenham, UK • Northampton, MA, USA

Published by
Edward Elgar Publishing Limited
The Lypiatts
15 Lansdown Road
Cheltenham
Glos GL50 2JA
UK

Edward Elgar Publishing, Inc.
William Pratt House
9 Dewey Court
Northampton
Massachusetts 01060
USA

A catalogue record for this book
is available from the British Library

Library of Congress Control Number: 2016931792

This book is available electronically in the **Elgar**online
Law subject collection
DOI 10.4337/9781784716776

MIX
Paper from responsible sources
FSC® C013056

ISBN 978 1 78471 676 9 (cased)
ISBN 978 1 78471 677 6 (eBook)

Typeset by Servis Filmsetting Ltd, Stockport, Cheshire
Printed and bound in Great Britain by TJ International Ltd, Padstow

Contents

Figures

Tables

About the author

Professor Shen Wei, PhD (LSE), LLM (Cantab), LLM (Michigan), LLM & LLB (ECUPL), Attorney-at-Law, New York, is Dean and Professor of Law at Shandong University Law School, KoGuan Chair Professor of Law at Shanghai Jiao Tong University Law School, and Global Professor of Law at the New York University School of Law. He practiced law for a decade, mostly in Hong Kong, on foreign direct investment, private equity and mergers and acquisitions prior to joining academia. His main research interests include financial regulation, corporate governance, international investment law and international commercial arbitration. Professor Shen has published more than 130 articles in Chinese and English journals, and is the author of the books: *Rethinking the New York Convention – A Law and Economics Approach* (Intersentia 2013), *The Anatomy of China's Banking Sector and Regulation* (Wolters Kluwer 2014), *How Is International Economic Order Shaped? – Law, Markets and Globalisation* (China Law Press 2014), *Corporate Law in China: Structure, Governance and Regulation* (Sweet & Maxwell 2015), and *Investor Protection in Capital Markets – The Case of Hong Kong* (Sweet & Maxwell 2015). Professor Shen is an arbitrator with Hong Kong International Arbitration Centre, Shanghai International Arbitration Centre, Shanghai Arbitration Commission, and Shenzhen International Court of Arbitration. Professor Shen is a member of both the Moody's China Academic Advisory Panel and the Financial Markets Law Committee's G20 Steering Group.

Foreword

Since the global financial crisis, shadow banking has been growing rapidly and in some jurisdictions, including the United States, is beginning to dwarf traditional bank financing. China has a significant shadow-banking sector, approximately one-third the size of its bank-lending market. The growth of shadow banking can pose risks to financial stability, both domestically and globally. Yet the shadow-banking sector is often weakly regulated. At the international level, both the G20 and the Financial Stability Board (FSB) have raised concerns about these risks, with the FSB suggesting that major economies take appropriate mitigative measures.

Shadow Banking in China: Risk, Regulation and Policy by Professor Shen Wei is thus a timely book, presenting readers with a comprehensive and coherent conceptualization of shadow banking in China. It systematically defines shadow banking, describes how the different types of shadow banking subsectors—including wealth management products, peer-to-peer lending, local government financing vehicles, and underground lending—are growing, and examines how Chinese regulators are responding. It also explains the risk-taking, economics and behavioural aspects of each of these subsectors, revealing the endogenous market forces driving their expansion and describing how shadow banking is innovatively helping to channel funding to the cash-starved private sector and real economy.

The book frames its analysis in a valuable context by explaining how shadow banking and its regulation should fit into China's overall regulatory and economic growth framework. To this end, it discusses the law of central banking and monetary policy, the importance of risk allocation, and the nature of systemic risk and its potential impact on the real economy. It also assesses public and private regulatory frameworks in considering how regulatory reforms can be most effectively designed.

Additionally, the book provides valuable comparative perspectives, including comparing the similarities and difference between Chinese shadow banking and shadow banking in the United States and other economies. For example, China has a closer interconnection between shadow banking and traditional banks. Also, compared to shadow banking in the United States, Chinese shadow banking relies less on complex structured financial products and special purpose vehicles; and so China has, so far, seen far fewer repos, securitizations and other asset-backed financings, and money market mutual funds. In part, the relative simplicity of China's shadow-banking sector may reflect stronger Chinese financial regulation generally; but in part it may also reflect China's less developed financial markets. Because of these differences, US and other foreign regulatory precedents may not serve as ideal models for regulating Chinese shadow banking.

Since the global financial crisis, financial regulation has become an even more important subject of academic, political and practical interest. This book is an important contribution to that effort, being the first comprehensive account of China's shadow-banking sector and its regulation. Ideally, too, the book will serve to inform and inspire further research by scholars, regulators, and policymakers worldwide.

Steven L. Schwarcz
Stanley A. Star Professor of Law and Business
Duke University School of Law

Acknowledgements

This book has evolved over a number of years since the outbreak of the latest global financial crisis, and would not have been possible without the help I received from many colleagues and friends.

Thanks are due first and foremost to Professor Steven L. Schwarcz, who made helpful comments on the manuscript and wrote the foreword for this book. Throughout the course of writing this book, I greatly benefited from many fruitful discussions and exchanges about various topics and issues with – in alphabetical order – Jennifer Arlen, Douglas W. Arner, Emilios Avgouleas, Dan Awrey, Robert P. Bartlett III, Omri Ben-Shahar, Sir William Blair, Ross P. Buckley, Yun-chien Chang, Weitseng Chen, Yijian Chen, Iris H.Y. Chiu, Donald Clarke, Kevin Davis, Jacques deLisle, David Donald, Eílis Ferran, Adrian Fong, Andrew Godwin, Say Goo, Brian Gruber, Mitu Gulati, Li Guo, Paul H. Haagen, Frank Xin He, M. Todd Henderson, Liyang Hou, Nicholas C. Howson, Robin Hui Huang, Aroon Jhamb, Juha Karhu, Rainer Kulms, Saul Levmore, Chien-chung Lin, Feng Lin, Ulla Liukkunen, Dora Neo, Matti Nojonen, Eric Posner, Albert Romano, Roberta Romano, Steven J. Saxby, Mathias Siems, Beate Sjåfjell, Thomas Stanton, Michael Taylor, Robert Chang-hsien Tsai, Dicky Tsang, Frank Upham, Matthias Vanhullebusch, Jiangyu Wang, Wen Yeu Wang, Casey Watters, Sarah Worthington, Chao Xi, Dali Yang, Simon Young, Kenny Yu, Tao Yu, and Wei Zhang.

I warmly thank Gillian Pickering for her wonderful skills in editing the book and Victoria Litherland, the desk editor, for her support from the early beginning.

I gratefully acknowledge the financial support provided by the Shanghai Education Commission under the Eastern Scholarship Scheme, the KoGuan Foundation under the KoGuan Distinguished Scholar Scheme, and a research grant from China's National Social Sciences Foundation (Project No.:15BFX100). Without their generosity, I would not have been able to devote myself to this exciting book.

Chapters 9 and 12 are written and updated on the basis of two articles previously published in Banking Law Journal. I thank Lexis (the publisher of the Banking Law Journal) and Matthew Bender & Company, Inc. (the copyright owner) for granting me the permission to reuse and include these two articles in the book.

As always, deep thanks go to my wife, daughter, parents and parents-in-law for their constant support, encouragement and tolerance during my pursuit of writing this and other books.

Acronyms

ABC	Agricultural Bank of China
Big Four	collectively, ABC, BOC, CCB, and ICBC
BOC	Bank of China
Bocom	Bank of Communications
BoJ	Bank of Japan, Japan's central bank
CBRC	China Banking Regulatory Commission
CCB	China Construction Bank
CCP	Chinese Communist Party
CDB	China Development Bank
CIRC	China Insurance Regulatory Commission
CSRC	China Securities Regulatory Commission
FDI	Foreign direct investment
Fed	the Federal Reserve or the Federal Reserve System, the central banking system of the United States
FIEs	Foreign invested enterprises
FSB	Financial Stability Board
G20	the Group of Twenty
HKMA	Hong Kong Monetary Authority, Hong Kong's de facto central bank
HK$	Hong Kong Dollar, the lawful currency in Hong Kong
HSBC	the Hongkong and Shanghai Banking Corporation
ICBC	Industry and Commerce Bank of China
IMF	International Monetary Fund
IPO	initial public offering
LGFVs	local government financing vehicles
MOF	Ministry of Finance
NDRC	National Development and Reform Commission
PBOC	People's Bank of China, China's central bank
PRC	People's Republic of China, or in abbreviation, China (for the purpose of discussions in the book, excluding Hong Kong, Macau and Taiwan)
P2P	peer-to-peer lending or internet lending
RMB	Renminbi, renminbi, or yuan, the lawful currency of the People's Republic of China

SAFE	State Administration of Foreign Exchange
SAIC	State Administration of Industry and Commerce
SDR	Special Drawing Right
SMEs	Small and medium-sized enterprises
SOEs	State-owned enterprises
US$	United States Dollars, the lawful currency in the United States of America
WMPs	Wealth management products
WTO	World Trade Organisation
Yen	Japanese currency, the lawful currency in Japan

1. Decoding shadow banking: a primer

The shadow banking system attracted little attention before the latest global financial crisis which began in 2007 but turned out to be one of the main causes[1] for "the worst financial crisis since the Depression".[2] It was plausibly claimed that the global financial crisis started as a liquidity run on the repo market, which was categorized as one of the most important sectors in the shadow banking system.[3] There are two schools of thought explaining the cause of the recent financial crisis. According to the global savings glut theory, it was high savings which fueled flows of money from emerging market economies and pushed long-term interest rates down to rock-bottom levels, leading to asset bubbles in the United States and other countries.[4] By contrast, the global credit glut theory diagnosed the illness in an opposite way: it was the scale of global shadow banking that caused the trouble.[5]

The FSB indicates that, during the period from 2002 to 2007, the shadow banking system increased by US$33 trillion, more than doubling in asset size from US$27 trillion to US$67 trillion.[6] This is 8.5 times

---

[1] Jason Hsu and Max Moroz, "Shadow Banks and the Financial Crisis of 2007–2008", (2010), available 26 February 2016 at http://ssrn.com/abstract=1574970.

[2] IMF, World Economic Outlook: Financial Stress, Downturns, and Recoveries, (2008), available 26 February 2016 at https://www.imf.org/external/pubs/ft/weo/2008/02/pdf/text.pdf.

[3] Gary Gorton and Andrew Metrick, "Securitized Banking and the Run on the Repo", (2010) Yale ICF Working Paper No. 09-14, available 26 February 2016 at http://papers.ssrn.com/sol3/papers.cfm?abstract_id=1440752.

[4] Gary Gorton, *Slapped by the Invisible Hand: The Panic of 2007* (Oxford University Press 2007); Hsu and Moroz, "Shadow Banks and the Financial Crisis of 2007 and 2008" (2010).

[5] Financial crisis can be divided into three categories. The 2008 crisis came with the collapse of previously rock-solid institutions such as Lehman Brothers. The 1997 crisis was unfolded when global investors lost faith in countries and pulled their money out of Asian countries. The 2007's Northern Rock crisis in the UK was more about a public run on one or more financial institutions. For a detailed account of a variety of financial crises, see generally, Carmen M. Reinhart and Kenneth S. Rogoff, *This Time Is Different: Eight Centuries of Financial Folly* (Princeton and Oxford: Princeton University Press 2009).

[6] This is almost equal to a quarter of total financial assets of the 20 countries and the Eurozone covered in the FSB survey, or 111% of these countries'

higher than the total US current account deficit of US$3.9 trillion during the same period. It is estimated that the shadow banking system is around 25 to 30% of the global financial system and 50% of total global banking assets.[7] It was said that the volume of credit intermediated by the shadow banking sector was just as large as the volume of credit intermediated by the traditional banking system on the eve of the financial crisis.[8] The shadow banking sector has been booming since the onset of the global financial crisis in 2007 with a total amount of US$67 trillion worldwide in 2012.[9] In early 2008, the size of shadow banking was US$20,000 billion while the traditional banking system was US$11,000 billion.[10] Various attempts have been made to estimate the size of shadow banking. It has been estimated that non-bank financial intermediation accounts for 50% of banking system assets and 120% of GDP.[11] Due to the lack of transparency and the breadth and diversity of shadow banking itself, a precise assessment of the size of shadow banking may be a mission impossible.

Globally, the scale of shadow banking assets exceeds global GDP. Non-bank financial intermediation grew to reach US$71 trillion, which accounted for 117% of GDP.[12] The largest shadow banking system exists in advanced economies while the emerging economies have seen the growth of shadow banking outpace that of traditional banking systems.[13] The broadest measure of shadow banking assets tracked by the FSB grew by US$5 trillion to more than US$75 trillion in 2014 in 20 countries plus the euro area. That represented 120% of the region's GDP – approaching the high of 123.4% recorded in 2007.[14] In the US, shadow banking assets

---

economic output. "Shadow Banking – Under the Spotlight", *Financial Times*, 19 November 2012 (online).

[7] Andrew Sheng, "Left Unregulated, the Shadow Banking Sector is a Financial Disaster to Come", *South China Morning Post*, 12 November 2011, A13.

[8] Zoltan Pozsar, Tobias Adrian, Adam Ashcraft and Hayley Boesky, "Shadow Banking", (2010) Federal Reserve Bank of New York Staff Report No. 458, available 26 February 2016 at http://ssrn.com/abstract=1645337, p.65.

[9] Reuters, "Regulators Aim to Shine Light on Shadow Banking", *South China Morning Post*, 28 January 2013 (online).

[10] Pozsar et al., "Shadow Banking", (2010) pp.3–5.

[11] Tyler Durden, "Shadow Banking Assets Increase by $5 Trillion To Record $75 Trillion, 120% Of Global GDP", 30 October 2014, available 8 March 2016 at http://www.zerohedge.com/news/2014-10-30/shadow-banking-assets-increase-5-trillion-record-75-trillion-120-global-gdp.

[12] FSB, "Global Shadow Banking Monitoring Report 2013", (2013), p.2.

[13] IMF, "Risk Taking, Liquidity, and Shadow Banking – Curbing Excess While Promoting Growth", (October 2014) Global Financial Stability Report, p.65.

[14] Sam Fleming, "Shadow Banking Nears Pre-Crisis Peak", *Financial Times*, 31 October 2014 (online).

exceed the value of assets in the traditional banking sector, and exceed GDP by over three times. Shadow banking assets in emerging market economies increased from 30 to 70% of GDP from 2002 to 2012.[15] In 2014, shadow banking comprised 24.5% of financial assets, the highest share since 2007. By contrast, traditional banks' share of the sector slipped to 45.6% from a high of more than 49% in 2008.

It is fair to state that the shadow banking sector is growing in size and significance, not only in the world but also in China. China is now the world's third biggest shadow banking sector after the US and the UK. Some Chinese institutions estimated that the shadow banking size can be in the range of Renminbi 20 to 30 trillion.[16] The FSB projected that China's shadow banking assets have experienced a growth rate of 42%.[17] It was estimated by Goldman Sachs that 24% of total credit to corporates and consumers were extended through shadow banking in China, accounting for 45% of GDP in 2012.[18] The staggering figures of shadow banking assets, the unprecedented speed of its growth, and the complexity and novelty of its products have made it a rather urgent case for regulation and monitoring. The IMF has warned that China's shadow banking sector deserves particular monitoring.[19]

1. DEFINING SHADOW BANKING

It is technically hard to define shadow banking in a concise and precise manner. The term "shadow banking system" was invented first by American economist Paul McCulley in 2007,[20] and referred to "the whole alphabet soup of levered up non-bank investment conduits, vehicles and structures", "unregulated shadow banks [which] fund themselves with uninsured commercial paper [and] which may or may not be backstopped by liquidity lines from real banks" and which stand in contrast to

---

[15] IMF, "Risk Taking, Liquidity, and Shadow Banking: Curbing Excess While Promoting Growth", (October 2014) Global Financial Stability Report 73.

[16] Yingwei Zhao, "A Comparison of Shadow Banking Credit Risk Aggregation from the Perspective of Global Financial Crises in the Past", (2013) 11 *Finance and Economics Science* (in Chinese).

[17] FSB, "Global Shadow Banking Monitoring Report 2013", (2013), p.12.

[18] Goldman Sachs, "China: Banks", (2013) *Equity Research* 4.

[19] IMF, Global Financial Stability Report: Financial Stress and Deleveraging Macrofinancial Implications and Policy, (2008) 90.

[20] Paul A. McCulley, "Teton Reflections", (2007) PIMCO Global Central Bank Focus, available 26 February 2016 at https://www.pimco.com/insights/economic-and-market-commentary/global-central-bank-focus/teton-reflections.

"regulated real banks, who fund themselves with insured deposits, back-stopped by access to the Fed's discount window".[21] According to the report released by the Financial Stability Board (FSB) in November 2011, shadow banking is defined as "credit intermediation involving entities and activities outside the regular banking system."[22]

1.1 Wide Spectrum of Academic Definitions

Academic definitions of shadow banking take different forms. At one end of the spectrum is the formulary approach, and shadow banking is defined by reference to a few generalized functional characteristics. For instance, shadow banking was defined by the US Federal Reserve to be "financial intermediaries that conduct maturity, credit, and liquidity transformation without access to central bank liquidity or public sector credit guarantees".[23] Falling somewhere along the spectrum is a second approach, which lists a variety of activities which shadow banking encompasses. Ben S. Bernanke once referred to shadow banking as "the intermediation of credit through a collection of institutions, instruments, and markets that lie at least partly outside of the traditional banking system".[24] This other form of list approach is to list some subsectors in shadow banking. For example, the FSB breaks shadow banking sector into nine major subsectors including investment funds, broker-dealer, structured finance vehicles, finance companies, money market funds and hedge funds.[25] The list approach may have a different focus on entities,[26] instruments, markets[27] or subsectors. At the other end of the spectrum is the approach that looks into the nature of shadow banking. The shadow banking system is broadly defined by the FSB as "a system of credit intermediation that involves entities and activities

---

[21] Ibid.

[22] It is widely recognized that the concept of credit intermediation involves maturity, credit, and liquidity transformation which can significantly reduce the cost of credit relative to direct lending. For details, see Pozsar et al., "Shadow Banking" (2010).

[23] Pozsar et al., "Shadow Banking", (2010).

[24] Ben S. Bernanke, "Some Reflections on the Crisis Outside of the Traditional Banking System", Speech at the Russell Sage Foundation and The Century Foundation Conference on the Rethinking Finance, New York, 23 April 2012.

[25] FSB, "Global Shadow Banking Monitoring Report 2013", (2013), p.14.

[26] Stijn Classens and Lev Ratnovski, "What Is Shadow Banking?", (2014) IMF Working Paper 14/25.

[27] Gorton and Metrick, "Securitized Banking and the Run on Repo", (2012) 104(3) *Journal of Financial Economics* 425–451.

fully or partially outside the regular banking system, or non-bank credit intermediation in short".[28] The FSB intentionally cast the net wide so that inherent risks can be thoroughly addressed. While this definition characterizes as shadow banking a network that binds together shadow banking institutions,[29] it does not explain the key components of shadow banking but identifies the intermediary function of these components.

The extra-bank nature of shadow banking appears to be the commonality these definitions share. Following this line of thinking, the functional characteristic shadow banking uniquely has but regular banks do not possess is its function of non-core or non-traditional funding.[30] Although this is labeled as an "activity" concept, it is in fact a nature-based one. Financing through non-core liabilities, in contrast to regular banks' core financing through deposit-taking-and-lending,[31] is the defining feature of shadow banking regardless of the entities (either banks or non-bank institutions) that carry it out. Moulding shadow banking through this non-core financing feature can easily fit some non-bank financing activities into shadow banking. Securitization, either conducted directly by a bank on balance sheet or indirectly by an off-balance-sheet special purpose vehicle, is a typical type of non-core financing and falls into the definition of shadow banking. So do other non-core financing such as repos, swaps and derivatives.

In the end, these definitions are neither precise nor all-encompassing. Given the fact that the shadow banking system is evolving and spans a wide range of activities and entities across countries, the definitions of shadow banking are necessarily incomplete. Some of them do not specify the types of entities and/or vehicles that comprise the shadow banking system. Others may be too narrow to be used to encompass some key shadow banking features. The shortcoming of encompassing all forms

---

[28] Financial Stability Board, "Shadow Banking: Scoping the Issues – A Background Note of the Financial Stability Board", (2011) available at http://www.financialstabilityboard.org/wp-content/uploads/r_110412a.pdf.

[29] Emilios Avgouleas, *Governance of Global Financial Markets: The Laws, The Economics, The Politics* (Cambridge: Cambridge University Press 2012) p.52.

[30] Apart from its legal form or the services it offers, economic function is one criterion used to define a bank. Accordingly, a bank is defined a financial intermediary accepting deposits, offering checking accounts, and making loans that provides transaction services to customers. Richard Scott Carnell, Jonathan R. Macey and Geoffrey P. Miller, *The Law of Financial Institutions* (New York: Wolters Kluwer 2013) p.39.

[31] Ross Cranston, *Principles of Banking Law* (Oxford: Oxford University Press, 2nd edn., 2000) p.5.

of non-banking financial intermediation into shadow banking is its lack of analytic value in assessing the underlying systemic risk. Some shadow banking activities, subsectors or vehicles may not create or involve systemic risk, which justifies a narrow-down approach focusing on the subsectors of non-bank credit intermediation which pose systemic risk related to maturity and liquidity transformation and/or leverage.[32] The wide definition of shadow banking may add some value to the regulatory design exercise. In order to curb systemic risk, widening the scope of shadow banking, instead of focusing on the specifics, may facilitate a macro-prudential regulatory approach placing an emphasis on the system-wide risk.

1.2 Understanding Banks

An appreciation of the nature of banks and of banking activities is a must to the study of shadow banking, shadow banks and shadow banking activities. A proper understanding of banks encapsulates a great deal of what this book is about: facilitating financing, curbing systemic risk and regulating financial markets. However, it is only possible to skate the surface in a book of this nature.

The essential feature or function of banking is a medium of exchange with the purpose of conducting lending transactions to supply money.[33] Banks are traditionally categorized as a credit intermediary, which acts as a middle man to connect borrowers and lenders in the lending business. The process of channeling credit between lenders and borrowers through the banks is referred to as credit intermediation, which provides the depositors with necessary information, not only reducing the lenders' costs involved in screening and monitoring borrowers but also facilitating investments in a more diverse loan portfolio. Traditional banks' lending is "on-balance-sheet" financing. In this process, the depositors deposit money to the bank in return for a checking or savings account that can

---

[32] FSB, "Global Shadow Banking Monitoring Report 2014", (2014), pp.6, 40.

[33] In common law, the essential characteristics of the business of banking are defined as an instrument of society and "a financial reservoir receiving streams of currency in every direction, and from which there issue outflowing streams where and as required to sustain and fructify or assist commercial, industrial or other enterprises or adventures". *Comrs. of the State Savings Bank of Victoria v. Permewan, Wright & Co. Ltd.* (1915) 19 CLR 457, 4710–11. Statutory definitions of banks take different forms. For instance, Article 1 of the EU's Credit Institutions Directive reads that: a credit institution takes deposits (or other repayable funds) from the public and grants credits on its own account.

be withdrawn at any time.[34] The bank lends these funds to borrowers and holds these loans on its balance sheet to maturity.

Credit intermediation involves maturity, credit, and liquidity transformation, and is enhanced through the use of third-party liquidity and credit guarantees, often in the form of liquidity or credit put options. Transforming illiquid assets into liquid assets is the key function a bank is to play in modern economy.[35] The banks realize this transforming function by providing liquidity services to the clients and real economy. Through this transforming function, a depositor can invest in the bank's loan portfolio indirectly, and, more importantly, retain the right to withdraw her investment without taking a loss. As far as the real economy is concerned, this credit and liquidity transformation process enlarges the supply of capital. The enhancement of credit intermediation is usually reliant upon the public sector, such as the deposit insurance scheme and the interbank money market. A liability with public-sector-backed enhancement of credit intermediation resides on a bank's balance sheet.

Banks rely on short-term liabilities to fund illiquid long-term assets. This feature makes banks prone to bank runs and suffer from responsibility failure.[36] One technique the regulatory system relies upon to shield banks from the risks inherent in reliance on short-term funding is to grant banks access to liquidity and credit put options in the form of discount window access and deposit insurance. However, the use of put options, together with the difficulty in accurately pricing such options, promotes excessive leverage and risk-taking. The regulators in turn design the financial security net and prudential regulation to curb such risks.

Banks have a core function, that is, liquidity creation. When an investor

---

[34] Under common law, the banker-customer relationship is a debtor-creditor relationship (instead of a trustee-beneficiary relationship), which means that banks should treat money deposited with them as their own. Banks are only obliged to return an equivalent amount to depositors. *Foley v. Hill* (1848) 2HLC 28, 9 ER 1002. Cranston, *Principles of Banking Law* 131; Alastair Hudson, *The Law of Finance* (London: Sweet & Maxwell 2009) 771. The other way of interpreting the bank's title over the depositor's deposits is the nature of cash or payment, most of which is a negotiable instrument and the holder in due course is the legal owner. Mark Hsiao, *International Banking & Finance Law: Principles and Regulations* (Hong Kong: Sweet & Maxwell 2011) 334.

[35] Douglas W. Diamond and Philip H. Dybvig, "Bank Runs, Deposit Insurance, and Liquidity" (1983) 91 *Journal of Political Economy* 401, 409.

[36] Viral V. Acharya and S. Viswanathan, "Leverage, Moral Hazard, and Liquidity", (2011) 66 *Journal of Finance* 99, 103; Huberto Ennis and Todd Keister, "Bank Runs and Institutions: The Perils of Intervention", (2009) 99 *American Economic Review* 1588, 1590.

experiences a need for cash but is unable to sell assets without loss, the investor faces a liquidity risk, which inhibits the optimal allocation of capital in the society.[37] Most investments encounter liquidity risks due to information and transaction costs such as search costs, due diligence, and other agency costs. Banks supply liquidity by offering a deposit contract through which the depositor can invest his savings while retaining on-demand access to funds.[38] Depositors can withdraw their deposits at any time regardless of the long maturities of the bank loans that they finance. The liquidity-creating function played by the bank in taking deposits from its depositors is known as maturity transformation.[39] Credit lines offered by the banks provide borrowers with a source of liquidity that is incentive-compatible as the ex ante contract-based interest rate is lower than an ex post refinancing rate.[40]

Deposits have a liquidity-risk mitigating function due to their ability to reduce transaction costs. Deposits are information-insensitive investment tools compared to other financial products such as the least information-sensitive debts.[41] The lower level of information sensitivity encourages agents to produce information and discourage adverse selection when the securities are sold or traded.[42] By pouring money into banks, investors repackage their money into deposits, which are different from other risk-intensive investment projects triggering the investors' efforts to conduct due diligence.[43] In addition, deposits are essentially a share of the bank's diversified portfolio of assets,[44] and the depositors' risks are shared with

---

[37] Robert G. King and Ross Levine, "Finance, Entrepreneurship, and Growth: Theory and Evidence", (1993) 32 *Journal of Monetary Economics* 513.

[38] John Bryant, "A Model of Reserves, Bank Runs, and Deposit Insurance", (1980) 4 *Journal of Banking & Finance* 335, 338–339.

[39] Xavier Freixas and Jean-Charles Rochet, Microeconomics of Banking (Massachusetts Institute Technology, 2nd edn., 2008) 4.

[40] Bengt Holmström and Jean Tirole, "Private and Public Supply of Liquidity", (1998) 106 *Journal of Political Economy* 1, 12–14.

[41] Gary B. Gorton, *Misunderstanding Financial Crises: Why We Don't See Them Coming* (Oxford: Oxford University Press 2012) p.219.

[42] Tri Vi Dang, Gary Gorton and Bengt Holmström, "Financial Crises and the Optimality of Debt for Liquidity Provision", (2010) University of Chicago Working Paper, available 26 February 2016 at http://bfi.uchicago.edu/research/working-paper/ignorance-crisis-and-optimality-debt-liquidity-provision.

[43] Gary B. Gorton and George Pennacchi, "Financial Intermediaries and Liquidity Creation", (1990) 45 *Journal of Finance* 49, 50.

[44] Gary B. Gorton and Andrew Winton, "Financial Intermediaries", in George M. Constantinides, Milton Harris and Réne M. Stulz (eds), *Handbook of the Economics of Finance* (Amsterdam and Boston: Elsevier Science Ltd 2003) p.431, 455.

the bank's shareholders (to the extent of their equity) and the government-backed deposit insurance scheme (a guarantee against residual default risk). In this sense, banks play a fundamental role in a market economy.

1.3 How does Shadow Banking Differ from Banking?

Shadow banking was once called the parallel banking system,[45] and is sometimes termed market-based financing.[46] This means that shadow banking is parallel to the formal banking sector. There are various reasons for the appearance of a shadow banking sector. The existence of shadow banking has been a market response to the incentives created by the tight control over bank lending. It is a result of regulatory arbitrage through various channels of arbitrage employed by the traditional banks to avoid regulatory restraints and supervisory oversight.[47] The increases in traditional banks' capital reserve and liquidity requirements make shadow banking more competitive and prominent in the financial market. While Basel I tried to break down the link between risk and assets for reasons of regulatory arbitrage,[48] Basel III's enhanced capital requirements may enable shadow banks to grow even faster since traditional banks are vying for extra capital in order to meet the more stringent capital standards. In this sense, shadow banking grows organically in an arena left behind by the traditional banking networks which are often constrained by restrictions on lending or deposit rates.[49] Shadow banking businesses are therefore used to circumvent the tighter regulations imposed on banking

---

[45] Tim Geithner, "Reducing Systemic Risk in a Dynamic Financial System", Remarks at the Economic Club of New York, 9 June 2008, available 26 February 2016 at http://www.bis.org/review/r080612b.pdf.

[46] FSB, "Global Shadow Banking Monitoring Report 2013", (2013), footnote 19.

[47] The possibility of arbitrage also exists in the relative prices of assets. The fact that complex claims can be priced is owing to (i) complex claims can be decomposed into their constituent elements; (ii) the markets exist in which individual elements of a sequence of cash flows can be separately traded. Shadow banking emerges and evolves when the credit intermediary function is reallocated onto constituent elements of a sequence of cash flow and these elements can be priced separately and efficiently compared to the scenario in which the intermediary function is played by the bank only. For an account of the concept of arbitrage in relation to pricing, see generally, Jürgen Eichberger and Ian R. Harper, *Financial Economics* (New York: Oxford University Press 1997) pp.242–244.

[48] Avgouleas, *Governance of Global Financial Markets: The Laws, The Economics, The Politics*, 40.

[49] FSB, "Global Shadow Banking Monitoring Report 2014 – Annex 4: IMF Report on Shadow Banking Around the Globe", (2014), available 26 February

institutions. Regulatory arbitrage is the root motivation for shadow banks to exist. The more stringent regulation tightening risky banking activities could amplify the size of less or unregulated shadow banking activities, which in turn affects financial stability and leaves risks intact in the broader financial system. This could be a greater regulatory challenge regulators have to face while the formal and shadow banking sectors are more closely connected through stronger linkages.

The profit maximization goal pushes traditional banks to maximize their lending capacity by removing liabilities from their balance sheet. By doing so, a bank may set assets to investment vehicles. The consequence of this is two-fold. First, traditional banks and shadow banks are interconnected. Second, separating some investment functions from the bank not only creates competitive (or comparative) advantages and specialization but also some segments of the shadow banking system. A prolonged low interest rate environment and high institutional demands for assets from insurance companies and pension funds[50] also have a combined effect on shadow banking.[51] Financial innovation conducted by non-bank institutions squeezes out the profitability of essential bank functions and leads to the decline of the traditional banking model, which has become less profitable. As a result, traditional banks seek new profit opportunities.[52] Technically, shadow banking will always be in existence as long as financial innovation and arbitrage are omnipresent in the financial system.

The erosion of banks' "specialness" on both the asset and liability sides contributed to the appearance of shadow banks. The erosion took place when a group of specialized non-bank institutions were allowed to enter the financial sector in the late 1970s. In conjunction with this wider market entry, financial innovation, together with technological breakthroughs,

---

2016 at http://www.financialstabilityboard.org/wp-content/uploads/r_141030.pdf?page_moved=1.

50 E. Philip Davis, *Pension Funds – Retirement-income Security and Capital Markets: An International Perspective* (Oxford: Clarendon Press 1995) 5 (pointing out that pension funds are financial intermediaries and sponsored by non-financial companies).

51 FSB, "Global Shadow Banking Monitoring Report 2014 – Annex 4: IMF Report on Shadow Banking Around the Globe", (2014).

52 Lowell L. Bryan, *Breaking Up the Bank: Rethinking an Industry Under Siege* (Homewood IL: Dow Jones-Irwin 1988); James R. Barth, R. Dan Brumbaugh Jr and Robert E. Litan, *The Future of American Banking* (London: Sharpe 1992); John Boyd and Mark Gertler, "US Commercial Banking: Trends, Cycles, and Policy", in Oliver Blanchard and Stanley Fischer (eds), *NBER Macroeconomics Annual 1993* (Cambridge, MA: MIT Press 1993).

pushed forward the deeper involvement of other unconventional banking institutions in the financial sector. Growing competition from specialist non-banks further posed a competitive threat to commercial lenders, which then gradually shifted their financial resources to some less regulated business sectors or activities by relying on some new techniques or off-balance-sheet vehicles. The consequences of financial innovation are two-fold. First, it provides excessive liquidity to the market. Second, it plays a more catalytic role than debt accumulation. As an exogenous development, financial innovation, as argued, precedes most financial crises.[53]

Shadow banks refer to those financial or non-financial institutions that engage in the shadow credit intermediation process. Some refer shadow banks to the institutions that exclusively engage in shadow bank credit intermediation and that do not have any access to central bank liquidity or public sector credit guarantees.[54] Shadow banks can also be characterized as financial intermediaries that conduct maturity, credit, and liquidity transformation without access to central bank liquidity or public sector credit guarantees. Examples of shadow banks include finance companies, asset-backed commercial paper conduits, structured investment vehicles, credit hedge funds, money market mutual funds and securities lenders. Money market funds, finance companies, structured finance vehicles, hedge funds, investment funds, broker-dealer, and real-estate investment trusts and funds have also been included in the shadow banking system.[55] The broad scope of shadow banks indicates the fluidity of shadow banking as a whole. The coverage of shadow banking can vary from one jurisdiction to the other. The shadow banking system is often complicated as it involves structured investment vehicles, money market funds and public financial institutions such as the government-backed mortgage lender. In this sense, shadow banks form a network, which is the shadow banking system. This network is close to the credit intermediation process performed by the bank in the traditional lending system.

In the US, the government-sponsored enterprises such as the Federal Home Loan Bank System, Fannie Mae and Freddie Mac are the main

---

[53] Charles P. Kindleberger, *The World in Depression, 1929–1939* (Berkeley, CA: University of California Press 1973); Charles P. Kindleberger and Robert Aliber, *Manias, Panics, and Crashes* (Basingstoke: Palgrave Macmillan, 5th edn, 2005) p.26, 54–58.

[54] Pozsar et al., "Shadow Banking", (2010) p.11.

[55] Financial Stability Board, "Global Shadow Banking Monitoring Report 2014", (2014).

players in the shadow banking sector. In addition, the US shadow banking sector hosts a large group of external shadow banks, which originate, warehouse and securitize loans in the US but conduct maturity transformation through offshore financial vehicles. The other feature of the US shadow banking is its reliance on capital markets largely because repo and securitization markets are open to all the market players including banks and non-bank institutions such as hedge funds, money market mutual funds and structured investment vehicles.[56] As a result, the US may have the broadest definition of shadow banking, which includes not only investment banks, money-market mutual funds and mortgage brokers but also sale and repurchase agreements, asset-backed securities, collateralized debt obligation, asset-backed commercial papers, and other contracts.[57] The most distinctive feature of the US shadow banking lies in its market-based and market-driven operational system.

"Shadow banks" in the context of Western countries is quite different and refers to buy-out firms, hedge funds, venture funds and ordinary corporations which are using their investors' money and wholesale funding to hire disgruntled bank traders, engage in direct lending and escape traditional banking regulation. In this sense, the shadow banking sector may also cover insurers, private equity capital or pension funds, which may in some cases provide much needed funds to the real economy. Likely, the shadow banking exists in the form of complex chains of deals starting from securities lending or repo transactions and ending up in other investments vulnerable to investors when the underlying asset values fall sharply. The shadow banking sector therefore takes on some bank-like attributes such as using short-term assets to fund longer-term lending, which is known as "maturity transformation".

The shadow banking is somehow mixed or connected with all sorts of new forms of money such as derivatives, off-balance sheet vehicles, securitization and other debt instruments. The financial regulatory landscape in the past several years was to put priority over rebuilding bank capital and the fight to save the Euro. In terms of size, market-based sources of credit such as corporate bond sales and direct lending by hedge funds are half the size of the traditional banking sector.[58] Non-depository institutions such as private equity and hedge fund investors have been more heavily involved in some more "conventional" sectors such as the

---

56 Pozsar et al., "Shadow Banking", (2010).

57 Gorton and Metrick, "Regulating the Shadow Banking System" (2010), p.5.

58 Brooke Masters, "Call to Rein in 'Shadow Banking'," *Financial Times*, 16 January 2012, p.1.

distressed shipping industry, ranging from buying ships to purchasing loans from banks that have previously financed the sector.[59]

Shadow banking has often been viewed as a financial disintermediation process. Disintermediation occurs as depositors, borrowers and banks all want to lower regulatory and compliance costs incurred in credit intermediation. Hence, end-suppliers and end-borrowers of funds interact with each other without the involvement of traditional banks. Some specialist non-bank institutions step in and connect the wholesale financial market.[60]

Although shadow banking is a result of financial disintermediation, shadow banking itself, as a matter of fact, is a credit intermediation (or re-intermediation) process.[61] It differs from traditional credit intermediation in the sense that a non-bank institution is involved in the shadow banking's intermediation process and it is not supported by public funding or the public sector. Put differently but simply, shadow banking is the realm of lending that does not rely on deposit-taking banks using customer money to fund loans. Consequently, shadow banking's credit intermediation may actually lengthen the credit intermediation chain due to the participation of more institutions in the lending business. Multiple institutions then decompose the credit intermediary function (or the credit intermediation process) played by the traditional bank and form a vertical (or functional) slicing of a traditional bank's credit intermediation process in the form of a series of distinctive steps.[62] In a sequential order, they perform functions or discrete operations such as loan origination, pooling of loans, collateralization, securitization, repayment and debt collection. Horizontally, risks are grouped and redistributed in various tranches corresponding to each pool of loans. Some pools of loans rely on a range of typical off-balance-sheet

---

[59] Henny Sender, "Shadow Banks Tap into Distressed Shipping", *Financial Times*, 1 January 2013 (online). There has been some increasing interest over the banking sector. Private equity firms are now more willing to expose themselves to the squeezed margins of the retail banking sector by betting that banks will be forced to shed assets at discounted prices in return for government bailouts or to meet more stringent regulatory capital requirements. Banking assets in Europe for example are now more appealing than elsewhere in the world partly because of their trading at low valuations and in part due to the fact that there have been no regulatory caps on private equity ownership of retail banks. Banking returns and market valuations, pinched by higher capital requirements and low interest rates, will ultimately recover. Jennifer Thompson, Anne-Sylvaine Chassany and Patrick Jenkins, "Private Equity Bets on Retail Banking", Financial Times, 4 January 2013 (online).

[60] Richard Comotto, "Shadow Banking and Repo", (2012) ICMA's European Repo Council, available 26 February 2016 at http://www.icmagroup.org/.

[61] FSB, "Global Shadow Banking Monitoring Report 2013", (2013), p.1.

[62] FSB, "Shadow Banking: Scoping the Issues".

securitization or asset management techniques. The use of securitization enables banks or shadow banks to lower the transaction cost of lending. For banks, securitization requires less capital than if they had retained loans on their balance sheets for issuing loans. Banks are incentivized to participate in this credit re-intermediation so as to improve their return on equity.

This explains why the shadow banking system is also a credit intermediation process,[63] which is indeed more complicated than the formal bank's intermediation cycle. It is a credit re-intermediation process in the sense that traditional banks are somehow involved in the shadow banking system by separating their portfolio management functions from their core treasury function and relying on some off-balance-sheets business. The off-balance-sheet conduits gained their popularity in the 1980s when the banks faced mounting competing threats from securitization. Banks then had to switch some short-term securitization techniques in order to maintain their market share in the financial market. Securitization is an ingenious mechanism used to spread risk, reduce financing costs and obtain regulatory capital relief. It can also be used to move bank assets off balance sheet.[64] The use of securitization and other off-balance-sheet instruments helped banks to free up capital that would otherwise have to be set aside in compliance with the capital reserve requirements under domestic banking laws. More fundamentally, the use of securitization and off-balance-sheet instruments straddled the boundary between commercial banking and capital markets, thereby complicating the regulatory landscape.

However, financial disintermediation or re-intermediation in shadow banking differs from conventional financial intermediation. The key difference lies in the fact that the market players involved in these intermediation processes are not the same. Given a large number of specialist non-bank institutions, the shadow banking system relies on liquid capital markets for the working of funding, securitization and distribution of funding. These specialist institutions are not regulated as banks in the typical lending market. Rather, they are regulated as gatekeepers in the capital markets due to their professional or underwriting capacities. This creates an additional layer of fragility in the credit disintermediation process since the market is prone to systemic risk or financial crisis.[65]

---

[63] Avgouleas, *Governance of Global Financial Markets: The Laws, The Economics, The Politics* p.51.

[64] Charles Calomiris, "Financial Innovation, Regulation and Reform", (2009) 29 *Cato Journal* 65–91.

[65] Raghuram G. Rajan, "Has Financial Development Made the World Riskier?", (2005) NBER Working Paper No. W11728, available 26 February 2016 at http://www.nber.org/papers/w11728.

Unlike formal banking, in shadow banking, investors place their money with non-bank (financial) intermediaries. Money is then invested in the liabilities of these intermediaries, which offer a spectrum of seniority and duration, risk and return. Money can also be invested into other products or projects that offer higher returns. Different from a bank's credit intermediary role, the shadow intermediation process not only involves traditional funding flow such as loan processing and funding but also complex securitization.

2. FORMAL BANKING v. SHADOW BANKING

2.1 Similarities between Banks and Shadow Banks

It has been well recognized that formal banking and shadow banking share a similarity. Shadow banks were defined as near-bank entities in an IMF 2008 report.[66] They are quite similar or identical in the sense that both have three actors, that is, savers, borrowers and intermediaries. In shadow banking, intermediaries are specialist non-bank institutions. In the funding or lending process, a shadow bank performs similar functions a regular bank typically plays. As a financial intermediary, shadow banks also have a liquidity-creating function. Financial contracts supply similar on-demand liquidity in the shadow banking system.

Although the securitization-based credit intermediation process increases efficiencies, it also involves agency problems. Traditional banks' credit intermediation process, however, does not involve agency problems.[67] The unregulated agency problem can cause a much more severe impact on the entire financial market due to the interconnectedness of a group of financial institutions. The mitigation of agency problem therefore is of great help in reducing the supply of poorly underwritten loans and structured securities so as to avoid the collapse of financial markets as a whole.

Both formal and shadow banking are pro-cyclical – they tend to grow during booms and contract during busts. When the economy booms, shadow banking increases leverage, liquidity and maturity mismatches, thus contributing to the build-up of vulnerabilities. When the economy

---

66 IMF, Global Financial Stability Report: Financial Stress and Deleveraging Macrofinancial Implications and Policy, (2008) p.19.

67 Adam B. Ashcraft and Til Schuermann, "Understanding the Securitization of Subprime Mortgage Credit", (2007) 2(3) *Foundations and Trends in Finance* 191–309.

collapses and liquidity dries up, the risk-weighted capital requirement, a backward-looking model for risk assessment, contributes a pro-cyclical tendency that amplifies the economic cycle. Banks in financial distress react to avoid balance sheet insolvency through securitization by removing assets from their balance sheet. By doing so, the banks diversify investments without a guarantee of removing risk.

Shadow banks are likely to amplify pro-cyclicality largely owing to its high leverage and interconnectedness with the formal banks. The high leverage of shadow banks, resulting in an increasing availability of credit, has a high chance to heighten the risks of causing asset price bubbles. Other factors such as valuation changes in collateral assets and wide use of margins and haircuts have a combined effect on pro-cyclicality.[68] Shadow banks have an intimacy with the real sectors of the economy and tend to exacerbate business cycle fluctuations and financial sector instability. The interconnectedness of shadow and formal banks increases the fragility of both sectors. As a result, a bank crisis is likely to lead to a shadow bank crisis. This seems inevitable if the financial market is viewed as a system-wide sector in which formal banks and shadow banks are closely correlated. In the same vein, the risk in the shadow banking sector can also be spread not only across jurisdictions but also sectors. This pro-cyclicality complicates the implementation of Basel III. The counter-cyclical buffer under Basel III is used to curb bank lending during periods of excessive credit growth.[69] As this buffer does not exist in the shadow banking sector, it is inevitable to see a paradox that applying Basel III rule will lead to a more sizable shadow banking sector which worsens deleveraging in the formal banking sector and counter-cyclical efforts encouraged by Basel III.

2.2 Differences between Formal and Shadow Banking

a. Intermediation process

The formal banking sector involves conventional lending businesses. Formal banks or traditional banks refer to all forms of deposit-taking institutions, including commercial banks, credit unions, rural credit cooperatives and industrial loan companies. Shadow banks are interconnected

---

68 Markus Brunnermeier and Lesse Heje Pedersen, "Market Liquidity and Funding Liquidity", (2009) 2(6) *Review of Financial Studies* 2201–2238 (arguing that the falling value of collateral securities and increasing margins in the time of stress can abrupt deleveraging and margin spirals).

69 BCBS, "Basel III: A Global Regulatory Framework for More Resilient Banks and Banking Systems", (2010) p.57.

along a vertically integrated credit chain through a variety of securitization and secured funding techniques. The securitization and secured funding techniques convert risky and long-term assets into money-like and riskless short-term liability. In this sense, the shadow banking system is a process of securitized credit intermediation.

b. Lending model

Shadow banking activities have been in existence in the marketplace for some time. It has been recently crystallized into a sophisticated and dynamic financial system. The principal driving force behind this crystallization is a transformation of large banks from low return on-equity utilities that originate loans and hold and fund them until maturity with deposits, to high return on-equity entities that originate loans in order to pool, securitize and distribute them, through off-balance sheet asset management vehicles. Traditional banking products are often booked on the bank's balance sheets whereas securitized products are not. Banks therefore transform their conventional model from "original-to-hold" to "originate-to-distribute". In conjunction with this transformation, the nature of financial system also changed. Formal banks are traditionally involved in a deposit-funded, credit-risk intensive, spread-based process. In contrast, shadow banking is no longer the traditional loan-to-own space but is closer to loan-to-loan to fill up the gap created by the credit crunch. For example, a firm with a securities portfolio can build a shadow bank by lending it out for cash and then using the cash to make loans. Their combined credit creation and proprietary trading and hedging may account for much of the global liquidity flows. Consequently, shadow banking is a less credit-risk but more market-risk intensive, fee-based process.

The wide utility of the "originate-to-distribute" model provided the initial impetus for an explosion of financial activities in the shadow banking sector.[70] More importantly, this model changes the financial market landscape. The "originate-to-distribute" model provides little incentive to generate ongoing information on the quality and performance of underlying assets that were repackaged. The bank originates the loan as an originator but does not retain the risk of the loans. Rather, the bank passes the risk onto other financial institutions which repackage the loans. The bank in this model loses the incentive to conduct due diligence and monitor the borrowers. Oppositely, the bank is incentivized to originate more loans without due attention paid to the borrower's creditworthiness

---

[70] Avgouleas, *Governance of Global Financial Markets: The Laws, The Economics, The Politics*, p.40.

as its revenues are mainly tied to loan volume instead of loan quality (that is, the repayment rate of the originated loans or the non-performing loan ratio). Thus, the "originate-to-distribute" model is a credit disintermediation process leading to reckless lending and risk exposure. In brief, shadow banking is a securitization-based lending process whereas formal banking involves a hold-to-maturity lending.

Securitization packages bank loans into asset-backed tradable debt securities so that banks can transform illiquid assets into liquid deposits by pooling and marketing their assets (in the form of loans, mortgages or collateralized debt obligations backed by the mortgage pools underlying each asset-backed security[71]) to investors through a variety of special purpose vehicles (SPVs).[72] This re-shapes the bank-centered credit intermediation process. Banks traditionally intermediate credit by originating loans and taking deposits, which appear on their balance sheets as assets and liabilities. Securitization, however, blurs the boundary between lending and capital markets as investors now can finance loans originated by banks. Through securitization, institutional investors can finance bank loans that used to be funded by deposits.[73] Asset-based securities gained popularity in the years before the global financial crisis.[74] In the US, issuance of securitized bonds exceeded corporate bond issuance by 2005.[75]

c. Funding

Deposits gathered through banks are the key source of funding for traditional banks. The shadow banking system relies upon the issuance of money market instruments to investors for funding. The purchasers of these instruments are shadow banks' depositors.

The shadow banking system relies upon wholesale funding, which is

---

71 Steven L. Schwarcz, "The Alchemy of Asset Securitization", (2008) *Stanford Journal of Law and Business* 531, 537.

72 Gary B. Gorton and Nicholas S. Souleles, "Special Purchase Vehicles and Securitization", in Mark Carey and Réne M Stulz (eds), *The Risks of Financial Institutions* (Chicago: Chicago University Press 2007) pp.549, 550.

73 Stuart I. Greenbaum and Anjan V. Thakor, "Bank Funding Modes: Securitization Versus Deposits", (1987) 11 *Journal of Banking and Finance* 379, 379.

74 The Financial Crisis and the Role of Federal Regulators: Hearing Before the H. Comm. of Gov't Oversight & Reform, 110th Cong. 2 (2008) (statement of Alan Greenspan, Former Chairman of the Board of Governors of the Federal Reserve System, available 8 March 2016 at https://shadowproof.com/2008/10/23/greenspan-to-testify-on-%E2%80%9Cthe-financial-crisis-and-the-role-of-federal-regulators%E2%80%9D/.

75 Gorton, *Misunderstanding Financial Crises: Why We Don't See Them Coming*, p.50.

not protected by the financial safety net. The funding stems from short-term or callable deposit-like liabilities, including short-dated asset-backed commercial papers, short-term repos and money fund investments. Non-bank institutions, in the shadow banking sector, originate loans with the intention of selling them. Banks, however, originate loans and intend to hold them through maturity. The logic of this funding is the market-based pricing system and the secondary loan market.

By purchasing the collateral (in the form of a bond) from the borrower, the lender extends credit (usually to the bank first) in exchange for a small premium over the purchase price the borrower pays for the repurchase of the collateral from the lender later on.[76] Investors therefore "deposit" funds into the repo market. By tapping new creditors, the repo market and other shadow banking sectors open up new sources of funding for the banking system.[77] As borrowers rely on repos and other short-term debt instruments as an alternative source of short-term funding, these instruments are more like a substitute for insured demand deposits and play such functions as liquidity maximization and principal protection.[78] Repos' functional analogy to deposits is recognized by law, which treats repos as money-like reserve assets rather than as risky debt securities.[79]

d. Sources of risks

Systemic risk is an externality from the individual financial institution's activities. Along the intermediation chain in either formal or shadow

---

76 Kenneth D. Garbade, "The Evolution of Repo Contracting Convention in the 1980s", (2006) *FRBNY Economic Policy Review* 27.

77 Hyun Song Shin, "Securitization and Financial Stability", (2009) 119 *Economic Journal* 309, 310.

78 The legal nature of repo transactions and the role of a trustee in bankruptcy or debtor in possession in the bankruptcy of the seller have not been clarified by the judiciary. In a repo transaction, a seller (debtor) sells a security to a buyer (secured creditor) and promises to repurchase the security within a specified period of time. The buyer has the right to sell the security on the market to satisfy the liability at a higher repurchase price as the lender's interest charge for the loan. In the US, some courts held that a buyer's sale is an outright sale of a security whereas other courts opined that such a sale is a secured loan and the seller transfers a security interest to the buyer for a short term loan which will be liquidated by the seller's "repurchase". Different judicial approaches here may lead to a contrasting result when a trustee in bankruptcy or debtor in possession in the bankruptcy of the seller may assert rights against the buyer and the buyer may be regarded as an unperfected secured creditor. For details, see James J. White, *Secured Transactions: Teaching Materials* (St. Paul, MN: West Group 2000) 229.

79 Morgan Ricks, "Regulating Money Creation After the Crisis", (2011) 1 *Harvard Business Law Review* 90.

banking, an institution's failure caused by investment risk, hedging risk, counterparty risk or liquidity risk can destabilize the entire chain through an internal contagion mechanism. The concept of bank run also applies to many shadow banks such as mutual funds and hedge funds. Investors in mutual funds may redeem their shares at once. A hedge fund may have to run if no lenders are willing to roll over its repos. Repos are designed to be insulated from credit risk.[80]

The risk in the traditional banking sector stems from a liquidity mismatch in banks' balance sheets.[81] The role of banks is to satisfy investor demand for liquidity by converting illiquid assets (loans to the production sector) into liquid liabilities (demand deposits), thereby creating liquidity by pooling risks among its depositor-owners. When risk-averse depositors withdraw their money early fearing bank failure, the bank is forced to sell all the assets at a penalty to generate the cash for withdrawals. As the bank cannot meet its contractually promised payoffs, it has to declare bankruptcy. This is a Diamond-Dybvig bank run. The financial crisis occurs when the bank's excessive use of leverage intensifies.

Like regular banks, shadow banking displays some of the same vulnerabilities and poses some of the same risks. Nevertheless, in the case of shadow banks' liabilities, perceived credit quality is driven by the credit risk free nature of collateral that backs shadow bank liabilities. The credit rating is often used as a label of insured deposit to express the credit-risk free nature of deposits in the traditional banking system even though excessive dependence on ratings has been criticized as being flawed[82] violating well known principles of risk management.[83] Shadow banks still have a liquidity mismatch problem as they also fund illiquid assets with short-term liabilities. The shadow banking system is also vulnerable to runs when investors refuse to pay when the debt matures.[84] Different from traditional banks, shadow bank runs are of fundamentals rather than the Diamond-Dybvig type of bank runs. A fundamentals bank run is caused

---

80 Garbade, "The Evolution of Repo Contracting Convention in the 1980s", p.27.

81 Diamond and Dybvig, "Bank Runs, Deposit Insurance, and Liquidity", (1983) 91(3) *Journal of Political Economy* 401–419.

82 Mads Andenas and Iris H-Y Chiu, *The Foundations and Future of Financial Regulation – Governance for Responsibility* (London and New York: Routledge 2014) p.192.

83 Thomas H. Stanton, *Why Some Firms Thrive While Others Fail – Governance and Management Lessons From The Crisis* (New York: Oxford University Press 2012) p.113.

84 Gorton, "The Panic of 2007", (2008) NBER Working Paper No. 14358, available 26 February 2016 at http://www.nber.org/papers/w14358.

by a real economic defect or a liquidity crisis. Other investors' investing behaviors probably are not the key concern resulting in a domino effect even though other investors' decisions may speed up the demise. Shadow banks can be more leveraged than traditional banks which are forced to deleverage due to higher margin requirements and falling asset prices.[85] Traditional banks, in following Basel III requirements, have been undergoing a deleveraging process by scaling back the practice of extending credit to high risk consumer and business borrowers as well as tightening lending criteria. The result of this scale-back is the booming shadow banking sector.

Credit risk is always the concern so long as there is a possibility of the inability of a counterparty (that is, a borrower) to meet its obligations when they come due. Investors require protection from the risk that the borrower will fail. Shadow banks can be highly leveraged. The nature of some shadow banking businesses such as securities financing transactions is highly risky and leveraged. Rehypothecation is a clear example to manifest this riskiness – the repo collateral received in a repo deposit can be freely reused in another transaction with an unrelated third party. One attraction the shadow banking system is said to have is that shadow banks pass their unwanted credit risks onto the capital markets through securitization.[86] In other words, the advantage of securitization is to permit lenders to efficiently offload credit risk to outside investors. While it is beneficial way to diversify risks, the downside is the enhancement of contagion.

The shadow banking system is subject to minimum regulatory constraints[87] and is not protected by the lender of last resort, which may lead to a higher level of risk for customer protection even though the lender in some shadow banking instruments may incur negligible liquidity risk to the extent that the borrower is solvent or the collateral is relatively liquid. The wide use of short-term liabilities in some of the funding bases undermines financial stability in the absence of any form of deposit insurance, prudential regulation and lender of last resort facility. The agency risk[88]

---

[85] Markus K. Brunnermeier, "Deciphering the Liquidity and Credit Crunch 2007–08", (2009) 23(1) *Journal of Economic Perspectives* 77–100.

[86] Ian Bell and Petrina Dawson, "Synthetic Securitization: Use of Derivative Technology for Credit Transfer", (2002) 12 *Duke Journal of Comparative & International Law* 541, 550.

[87] Ricks, "Regulating Money Creation After the Crisis", p.87.

[88] In a typical company law context, the agency relationship exists between shareholders and directors, and as agents, directors will not act in the best interest of shareholders, as principals. Michael C. Jensen and William H. Meckling,

is likely to aggregate given the involvement of multiple intermediaries in financial intermediation.[89]

The other source of risk is the interconnectedness between the traditional banks and shadow banks through "cross-holding" and funding interdependence. Shadow banking businesses are linked to the formal banking system through a web of interconnections,[90] in the form of various financing vehicles, funding channels and risk-sharing techniques. Shadow banks' portfolios are then linked to mortgages, commercial papers, conventional bank receivables and other short-term borrowing markets as a whole. Regular banks participate in the credit re-intermediation chain led by shadow banks through a range of services such as investing into financial products, "warehousing" assets for securitization, acting as a third-party guarantor, transferring assets and providing funding. This interconnectedness creates a spillover effect. Any shock in the traditional banking sector can be transmitted to the shadow banking sector, giving rise to systemic risk concern,[91] and vice versa. The individual bank or shadow bank's failure can generate contagion and have an impact on the systemic stability in the financial market.

The interconnectedness can be a source of counterparty risk, a risk that other parties will default on payment obligations,[92] within the shadow banking system. The combination of repo-based financing and asset securitization leads to a complex chain of off-balance-sheet vehicles and structured financial transactions. This complexity can easily cause counterparty risk. The risk mitigation is not only relevant to end-borrowers but also a variety of entities involved in the intermediation process. Some disconnecting strategies can be deployed to avoid the counterparty risk. For example, a sponsor can move the loan pool off its balance sheet by transferring it to an SPV. The "bankruptcy-remoteness" of an SPV ensures that the insolvency of the sponsor, either a bank or a firm originating the loans,

---

"Theory of the Firm: Managerial Behavior, Agency Costs, and Ownership Structure", (1976) 3 *Journal of Financial Economics* 305–360. This is the cause of agency risk that is related to an agent's action in his best interest.

[89] Tobias Adrian, Adam B. Ashcraft and Nicola Cetorelli, "Shadow Bank Monitoring", (2013) FRBNY Staff Report 638.

[90] Adair Turner, "Shadow Banking and Financial Instability: Lord Turner Speech to the CASS Business School", (2012) available 26 February 2016 at http://www.fsa.gov.uk/static/pubs/speeches/0314-at.pdf.

[91] R. Gandhi, "Danger Posed by Shadow Banking Systems to the Global Financial System – the Indian Case", (2014), available 26 February 2016 at http://www.bis.org/review/r140827b.pdf.

[92] Jan Job de Vries Robbé, *Structured Finance: On From the Credit Crunch – The Road to Recovery* (Austin: Wolters Kluwer 2009) pp.21–22.

has no impact on the SPV, which means creditors of a bankrupt firm are unable to claw back assets from the SPV.[93] Consequently, the securitized loans are segregated from the bankruptcy estate of the sponsor.

The interconnectedness renders maintaining the stability of the entire system difficult. This is the same risk to the traditional banking system. The bank-centered liquidity is insufficient to cure the aggregate liquidity shortage,[94] which is the source of system-wide volatility or a collapse of the entire market.[95] As far as shadow banking is concerned, it has been argued that short-term money market instruments respond to increases in risk primarily through a contraction in quantity.[96] The fire sale of one shadow bank's underlying assets could easily exacerbate financial volatility. Allowing (or disallowing) the liquidation of counterparty collateral in the midst of a crisis encourages counterparties to race to exit from the pool of assets, which does not mediate contagion among market participants but makes the shadow banking system more vulnerable.

e. Protections

Banks' liquidity-creating function provides their depositors with liquidity insurance but makes banks absorb liquidity risks leaving the underlying assets on the balance sheet illiquid. Holding illiquid assets means that a bank may run short of cash when it has to sell portfolio assets at a discount to satisfy the depositor's claims.[97] An individual bank's failure produces knock-on effects that spread to other banks, causing a contraction in economic activity.[98] System-wide banking panics, if not rescued, can easily turn into a financial crisis. Overcoming banks' inherent fragility and bank failures' contagion effects requires a remedial solution to banks' illiquidity.

Formal banks are protected by the financial safety net, which is supposed to comprehensively address systemic risk in the banking sector.

---

93 For a general account of SPVs, see Gorton and Souleles, "Special Purpose Vehicles and Securitization".

94 Bengt Holmström, and Jean Tirole, "Private and Public Supply of Liquidity", (1998) 106 *Journal of Political Economy* 1, 5.

95 Jeremy Stein, "Securitization, Shadow Banking & Financial Fragility", (2010) 139 *Daedalus* 41, 45.

96 Charles W. Calomiris, "The Subprime Turmoil: What's Old, What's New, and What's Next", (2009) 15 *Journal of Structured Finance* 6, 24.

97 Freixas and Rochet, *Microeconomics of Banking* p.4.

98 Charles W. Calomiris and Gary Gorton, "The Origins of Banking Panics: Models, Facts, and Bank Regulation", in R. Glenn Hubbard (ed.), *Financial Markets and Financial Crises* (Chicago: University of Chicago Press, 2nd edn., 1991) pp.109, 113–115.

Regulatory responses designed to counter bank runs include deposit insurance, lender of last resort facility, suspension of convertibility, and maintaining sufficient liquidity. These measures, in particular the first two, rely on the public sector's support as a public interest is at stake. The government insures the deposits in the traditional banking system. Formal banks have a meaningful access to a lender of last resort, which is able to help avoid default by injecting the liquidity into the failing bank. This function is usually played by the central bank. Banks are subject to the capital reserve requirement, which ensures that the bank holds sufficient liquid assets.

Shadow banks lack access to public sources of liquidity. Both the liquidity facilities and interbank money market are not available to shadow banks when they face liquidity and capital shortfalls. Arguments have been made that shadow banks are well protected due to liquidity and credit puts provided by the private sector.[99] The investors receive collateral from shadow banks when depositing money, and the deposit-collateral transactions are processed in the form of repos. Shadow banks' liabilities are more broadly collateralized by most AAA-rated risk-free and liquid assets. AAA-rated assets are vulnerable to systemic risk as these assets are structured to withstand idiosyncratic risk. When all securities are highly correlated and all investors are incentivized to sell high quality assets in order to generate liquidity, there will be a liquidity crisis. As pointed out by McCulley, "shadow banks . . . may or may not be backstopped by liquidity lines from real banks. Thus, the shadow banking system is particularly vulnerable to runs – commercial paper investors refusing to re-up when their paper matures, leaving the shadow banks with a liquidity crisis – a need to tap their back-up lines of credit with real banks and/or to liquidate assets at fire sale prices".[100] A natural question is whether the shadow banking sector is able to maintain its stability in the absence of credit and liquidity support from the government. Nonetheless, offering publicly-sponsored safety mechanisms to shadow banking entails moral hazard risks as the private sector may reasonably expect to have support from the government.[101]

Shadow banks do not have credible public-sector backdrops. Shadow banks are not covered by the deposit insurance scheme while formal banks are the major target of deposit insurance. Shadow banking might be brought into the daylight with public liquidity and liability insurance, but can once

99 Gorton and Metrick, "Regulating the Shadow Banking System" (2010), p.3.

100 McCulley, "Teton Reflections".

101 Manmohan Singh, "The Economics of Shadow Banking", (2013) Reserve Bank of Australia Paper, available 26 February 2016 at http://www.rba.gov.au/publications/confs/2013/pdf/singh.pdf.

more be pushed back into the shadows while the public sector withdraws. In the financial crisis, the government bail out also applied to the shadow banking sector. The emergency liquidity facilities, lending programs, large-scale asset purchases, guarantee scheme, and deposit insurance program provided a complete backdrop as they did to the traditional banking sector.

Investment banking arms sometimes choose to become bank holding companies in order to qualify for financial assistance. Therefore, broker-deals can be protected on the same basis as commercial banks. Commercial banks create legal entities in the securitization process and these entities' assets can be taken back to the banks. These entities are termed structured investment vehicles or off-balance-sheet vehicles. When these vehicles are merged into their sponsoring banks, they are protected as banks' assets.[102]

In the repo market, which is the key source of funds for the securitization process,[103] repo lenders, like bank depositors, have the option to withdraw credit immediately. Shadow banks may avoid bank runs through the suspension of the investors' withdrawal rights. The institutional investors can choose to withdraw the money by selling the repos, bonds and other debt instruments, without going into a bankruptcy procedure. Hedge funds, mutual funds and others have implied but not legally binding obligation to redeem their own shares on demand.

f. Resolution

Modern approaches to bank resolution are quite different from those applicable to other types of enterprises or companies. Most payments to unsecured creditors in corporate bankruptcy are usually delayed until final resolution. Applying corporate-bankruptcy-style restrictions on depositors' accounts is likely to render the banking system less efficient and attractive since the depositors are forced to costly monitor banks for the sake of transaction safety. By comparison, the strategy of bank resolution is to shift losses away from banks' depositors and noteholders to other stakeholders who are less risk-averse. These stakeholders include bank shareholders, other banks, and the central bank. They either share risks with or supply backup liquidity to otherwise solvent banks that might fail due to a liquidity shortage.[104]

---

102 Kenneth W. Dam, "The Subprime Crisis and Financial Regulation: International and Comparative Perspectives", (2010) 10 *Chicago Journal of International Law* 581, 605.

103 Gordon and Metrick, "Securitized Banking and the Run on Repo" (2012).

104 Allan H. Meltzer, "Financial Failures and Financial Policies", in George G. Kaufman and Roger C. Kormendi (eds), *Deregulating Financial Services: Public Policy in Flux* (Cambridge, MA: Ballinger 1986) pp.79, 83.

This liquidity-loss-shifting strategy removes the risk that depositors are denied immediate access to the insured par value or recovery value of their accounts, leaving savings frozen in a failed bank.[105] The importance of this strategy is two-fold. First, it ensures the information insensitive quality of bank deposits and the depositors' little effort or expenditure on monitoring the solvency of the banks. Second, it safeguards the supply of capital available to the banking system. The bank resolution mechanism is a risk-intolerance strategy (that is, risk-proof to depositors).[106] However, this liquidity-rights-centered resolution mechanism does not eliminate risk. As a result of the liquidity-loss shift, other stakeholders take over the risk on claims (the deposits) from the depositors. In terms of information-sensitivity, risk-splitting and asset portfolios, risk-averse stakeholders are informed agents holding equity while risk-sensitive depositors are uninformed agents holding debt.[107]

As far as repos and derivatives are concerned, bankruptcy-law safeguards can be relied upon to protect creditors from chaotic unraveling by their counterparts when a shadow bank fails. The approach of bankruptcy law is to protect assets from inefficient liquidation so as to ensure an equitable and incentive-compatible recovery. The liquidation repayment priority rule embedded in the bankruptcy law avoids coordination problems among customers or creditors racing to seize collateral or withdraw cash. The coordination problems prevent creditors' recovery efforts from achieving an optimal allocation of a failed firm's assets and default losses. However, this protection is only relevant to the resolution of failed financial intermediaries and creditor protection. It does not address shadow banks' role as suppliers of liquidity,[108] even though the typical mechanism of bankruptcy law may allow a failed intermediary to supply customers with immediate access to funds.

Banking regulation is of little help in protecting a shadow bank from failure. Apart from the fact that banking regulation is at a distance from

---

105 Robert R. Bliss and George G. Kaufman, "U.S. Corporate and Bank Insolvency regimes: A Comparison and Evaluation", (2007) 2 *Virginia Law and Business Review* 143, 149.

106 Calomiris, "The Subprime Turmoil: What's Old, What's New, and What's Next", p.26.

107 Gorton and Pennacchi, Financial Intermediaries and Liquidity Creation", p.50.

108 Charles W. Calomiris, "Is Deposit Insurance Necessary? A Historical Perspective", (1990) 50 *Journal of Economic History* 283, 284. Little empirical evidence has been found that derivatives expand credit supply. Beverly Hirtle, "Credit Derivatives and Bank Credit Supply", (2009) 18 *Journal of Financial Intermediation* 125.

shadow banking, banking regulation is rooted in the theory that the efficiency of markets guarantees the enforcement of financial contracts provided that participants are free to transact while exposing themselves to uncertainty and delay in a counterparty's insolvency proceeding.[109] Liquidity is defined as the ability to trade an asset at minimal cost or delay.[110] The market-rooted regulatory ideology itself does not sharpen shadow banks' liquidity-generating ability. Rather, the investor's liquidation rights in the collateral are central to the deposit-like characteristics of the securitization transactions. The repo, like derivatives, permits a party to the repurchase agreement to unilaterally terminate its contract as a result of a bankruptcy filing by the other party, and to liquidate its dealings outside of bankruptcy. The legal infrastructure safeguards this unilateral liquidation right by applying exemptions to some financial contracts under the bankruptcy law and deposit insurance scheme so that repo parties are able to seize collateral and liquidate without going into bankruptcy.[111] The liquidation rights in the collateral are exempted from formal bankruptcy procedures granting repos and derivatives a bankruptcy-proof status.[112] This bankruptcy safe-harbour protection[113] makes repos analogous to deposits ensuring that a party to a repo contract would not be treated as a debtor in the bankruptcy proceedings. It is liquidation rights that offer legal protection similar to that provided by deposit insurance,[114] and guarantee uninterrupted access to liquidity.

g. Regulation

At the national level, banks are protected by a financial safety net comprised of lender of last resort, deposit insurance, prudential regulation and failure resolution. The regulators face a daunting task, through this

---

109 Robert R. Bliss and George G. Kaufman, "U.S. Corporate and Bank Insolvency Regimes: A Comparison and Evaluation", (2007) 2 *Virginia Law and Business Review* 143, 154–155.

110 Michael Aitken and Carole Comerton-Forde, "How should Liquidity Be Measured?", (2003) 11 *Pacific-Basin Finance Journal* 45, 46.

111 For example, in the US, there was an amendment made to the Bankruptcy Code in 1984 to the effect that an automatic stay provision would not prevent the depositor who held the collateral from selling the collateral without court permission. Garbade, "The Evolution of Repo Contracting Conventions in the 1980s", pp.27–42.

112 Gorton and Metrick, "Regulating the Shadow Banking System", (2010).

113 Edwin Smith, "Financial Contracts under the Bankruptcy Code", (2087) 5(2) *ABI Committee News* 536–541.

114 Gorton and Metrick, "Regulating the Shadow Banking System", (2010).

financial safety net, to reduce the incidence of bank runs at minimal cost to bank liquidity creation. The global financial regulation is soft-law based, consisting Basel I, II and III, focusing on the capital requirements.

It is difficult to prevent shadow bank runs by any existing regulation. For instance, the heightened capital requirements codified in Basel III are only applied to international banks and not shadow banking. Therefore, shadow banks are not required to possess loss-absorbing capitals against losses associated with an increase in systemic risk. There have been discussions on the possibility of setting up a global liquidity fund, a privatized liquidity provider of last resort to shadow banks, supplementing the existing liquidity channel centered on the network of central banks.[115] Opponents to this proposal argue that, aside from strong political outcry, this favoritism towards the wholesale financial services industry and additional liquidity provision would not prevent the causes leading to a systemic crisis in the banking sector.[116] Put simply, offering a secured liquidity source to the shadow banking sector reinforces rather than curbs moral hazard.

Compared with the formal banking sector, shadow banking presents more challenges to regulators in terms of its novelty, opacity and complexity. The risks associated with non-bank-centered financial intermediation are beyond the reach of public policy tools and regulatory instruments. Regulators may not have clear targets on their radars. In addition, they lack sufficient judgment and expertise to deal with such challenges. The novelty underlying the shadow banking sector is partly a result of deregulation of the formal banking sector.[117] Segments of the shadow banking sector and fragmented regulatory oversight undermine the effectiveness of prudential regulation in the formal banking system.

Shadow banks are subject to limited regulation. This appears the chief concern to the FSB, which pointed out that shadow banks are in an environment where "prudential regulatory standards and supervisory oversight are either not applied or are applied to a materially lesser or different degree than is the case for regular banks engaged in similar activities".[118]

---

115 Steven L. Schwarcz, "Controlling Financial Chaos: The Power and Limits of Law", (2012) 3 *Wisconsin Law Review* 815.

116 Emilios Avgouleas, "Comment on Professor Schwarcz's Article 'Controlling Financial Chaos'", (2013) 1 *Wisconsin Law Review Online* 1, 3.

117 John C. Coates IV, "Cost-Benefit Analysis of Financial Regulation: Case Studies and Implications", (2015) 124 *Yale Law Journal* 882, 905.

118 FSB, "Shadow Banking: Scoping the Issues", p.3.

In response to novel shadow banking, regulatory designs should be responsive and creative. Some efforts have been made to regulate shadow banking activities or shadow banks. The Dodd-Frank Act makes an attempt to apply a centralized regime to regulate some shadow banks. For instance, hedge funds must register with the SEC, and some of the over-the-counter derivatives trading is to operate in the exchanges and clearing houses. Other shadow banks will be included into the regulatory ambit for regular banks. Typical examples are those systemically important institutions and retail finance lenders which will now be regulated by the Federal Reserve and the Federal Reserve's Consumer Financial Protection Bureau.[119]

These regulatory experiments suggest that the principles and instruments in traditional banking regulation can be inferred for and transplanted into the regulation of shadow banking. In other words, regulating shadow banking may be largely modeled on traditional banking regulation. In this sense, shadow banking regulation may be eventually bank-type regulation.

Table 1.1 is a summary of key differences between shadow and formal banks based on the above analyses.

2.3 Causes of Shadow Banking

The causes of the shadow banking's popularity are manifold. The growth of shadow banking has come about due to the technical innovation and regulatory changes in the past several decades. For instance, traditional banks have been under pressure to exit the regulated sector and rely on money-market-funds, securitization and repo for more profits.[120] Investors are struggling to find places to use their money in a profitable manner. Regulatory pressure and costs may press investors to find a sensible way to get around legal or regulatory restrictions. Apart from its weaknesses and shortcomings, shadow banks also provide diversification for the financial system and resilience. From consumers' perspectives, shadow banks offer more investment options and efficient pricing for consumers and businesses. Shadow banking facilities go for higher returns at the cost of introducing riskier financial instruments. In the Chinese context, the emergence of wealth management products and shadow banking facilities are shaking up a system that has relied on channeling funds to state entities.

---

119 Gorton and Metrick, "Regulating the Shadow Banking System", (2010).
120 Gorton and Metrick, "Regulating the Shadow Banking System", (2010).

Table 1.1 Key comparison between formal and shadow banking

Perspectives	Traditional Credit Intermediation	Shadow Credit Intermediation
Function	Liquidity creation	Alternative funding channel
Core	Bank-centered	Securitization-based
Parties	Depositors, borrowers and banks	End-suppliers, end-borrowers, and (possibly multiple) non-bank institutions (shadow banks)
Role of balance-sheet	On-the-balance-sheet financial activities	Off-balance-sheet activities
Source of funding	Deposit-funded	Wholesale-funded, pool of investment
Cash flow	Originate-to-hold	Originate-to-distribute
Term	Long-term	Short-term
Key products	Loans	Money-like instruments
Lending	Hold-to-maturity	Securitization-based
Termination	Maturity	Withdrawable on demand (like a demand deposit)
Credit risk	Intensive credit-risk Liquidity risk	Less credit-risk
Regulation	Heavily regulated	Little regulation
Impact of regulation	Undergoing a de-leveraging process by tightening lending criteria and scaling back the practice of extending credit to high risk consumer and business borrowers	Increasing the size of shadow banking
Intermediation	Credit intermediation	Credit disintermediation (or re-intermediation)

2.4 Benefits of Shadow Banking

The shadow banking system, as an important alternative channel, provides sources of inexpensive funding for credit as well as the real economy. It also facilitates credit extension to some cash-starving sectors, in particular, those firms that are restricted from normal bank loans. The injection of additional credit protects the broader economy from the dangers of a collapse in the supply of credit. Non-bank institutions are specialized in some functions or perspectives, which lend efficiency into the financial sector. Shadow banking also provides effective means for risk diversification and efficient channeling of financial resources.[121] The maturity of non-banks' liabilities, compared to banks' liabilities, better matches the borrower's maturity needs.[122] Shadow banking can provide banks and investors with a range of tools for liquidity, maturity and credit risk management. This means that regulating shadow banking needs to maximize those benefits and minimize potential risks.[123]

The popularity of shadow banking is dependent on the novelty and adaptability of such financial products offered by shadow banks. These financial instruments arise to mitigate the effects of information and transaction costs.[124] On this view, shadow banking can be treated as markets or institutions.[125] Neutering a vibrant and multi-layer capital market is still a feasible solution to remedy market failure, regulatory failure and responsibility failure.[126]

2.5 Disadvantages of Shadow Banking

The beneficial side of shadow banking is not the complete picture. There has been growing recognition that shadow banking can be destructive and pose greater systemic risk. Shadow banking itself is a credit intermediation chain and exposed to the same instability and failure traditional banks face. Lack of regulatory oversight can lead to a regulatory vacuum. Maturity and credit transformation in the shadow banking system contributed significantly to asset bubbles in residential and commercial real estate markets.

3. CROSS-BORDER COORDINATION AT THE GLOBAL LEVEL

At the Seoul Summit in November 2010, the G20 leaders identified shadow banking as one of the remaining issues of financial regulation that

---

121 Edward F. Greene and Elizabeth L. Broomfield, "Promoting Risk Mitigation, Not Migration: A Comparative Analysis of Shadow Banking Reform by the FSB, USA and EU", (2013) 8(1) *Capital Markets Law Journal* 6, 11–13.

122 FSB, "Global Shadow Banking Monitoring Report 2013", (2013), p.43.

123 Steven Schwarcz, "Regulating Shadow Banking", (2011) 31 *Review of Banking and Financial Law* 619.

124 Ross Levine, "Financial Development and Economic Growth: Views and Agenda", (1997) 35 *Journal of Economic Literature* 688, 689.

125 Douglass C. North, "Economic Performance through Time", (1994) 84(3) *American Economic Review* 359, 360.

126 Steven Schwarcz, "Regulating Shadows: Financial Regulation and Responsibility Failure", (2013) 70 *Washington & Lee Law Review* 1781.

warrants attention. The FSB, at the request of the G20 leaders, has formulated recommendations to strengthen the oversight and regulation of the shadow banking system in collaboration with the IMF and the World Bank.[127] The FSB in 2011 released policy papers to report its recommendations.[128] Thereafter, the FSB released shadow banking monitoring reports on an annual basis.[129]

Shadow banking takes vastly different forms from country to country. However, an array of identical strong driving forces are pushing regular banking activities into the shadows: ongoing tightening banking regulation, strong financing demand from investors, ample liquidity conditions, low investment returns, the combined effect of which fosters non-banking activities. Apart from these common drivers, shadow banking also brings similar benefits to the real economy of these countries. It supplements a tightly regulated and less liquid banking system by expanding access to credit, supporting maturity transformation, deepening market liquidity and increasing risk sharing capability. By and large, shadow banking improves the efficiency of the financial market.[130] Similarly, these countries face similar risks owing to a growing shadow banking sector. Systemic risk is probably the major concern to national regulators even though it may not be the source of fragility to some subsectors in shadow banking. Understandably, systemic risk is likely to be the chief trigger of a wide scale of regulatory and legislative efforts drawing up responsive policy or regulatory solutions to contain inherent risks involved in shadow banking. Financial regulators and central banks in major countries have taken some initiatives addressing the rising shadow banking sector. The Bank of England has set up the Financial Policy Committee with the specific responsibility for the stability of the UK financial system as a whole. Similar bodies exist in the Eurozone and the US. The Bank of England is seeking to limit the exposures banks have to their shadow counterparts.[131] Among others, minimum liquid asset requirements are placed on money market funds to make the shadow banking system more resilient.[132] The

---

127 FSB, "Shadow Banking: Scoping the Issues".

128 FSB, "Shadow Banking: Scoping the Issues".

129 For example, FSB, "Global Shadow Banking Monitoring Report 2013", (2014).

130 Stijn Claessens, Zoltan Pozsar, lev Ratnovski, and Manmohan Singh, "Shadow Banking: Economics and Policy", (2012) IMF Staff Discussion Note SDN/12/12.

131 Brooke Masters, "We Should Find Ways to Love the Shadow Banks", *Financial Times*, 21 June 2014 (online).

132 Sullivan & Cromwell LLP, "Money Market Fund Regulation", 24 July 2009, available 26 February 2016 at http://www.docin.com/p-979673414.html.

US Federal Reserve has discussed the possibility of imposing exit fees for bond funds that could serve a similar purpose in the debt markets.[133] At this phase, it is apparent that a one-size-fits-all type of regulatory framework or devices does not fit all countries.

Coordination of financial regulation of different countries is desirable to curb potential systemic risk in the shadow banking sector.[134] Pursuing this coordinated strategy at the global level is necessary as the cross-border trading closely connects country-specific shadow banking sectors despite a significant but declining linkage, the IMF recently claimed,[135] between the US shadow banking sector and the EU banking sector as well as a consequentially weaker spillover effect in the global shadow banking system. A stand-alone regulatory approach taken by individual countries may cause a migration of shadow banking activities and risks from one country to another. However, the difficulty is that, unlike formal banking regulation,[136] shadow banking spans a wide range of sectors and effective regulation and monitoring of these sectors is a challenge even at the national level. Without a centralized registration scheme for shadow banking vehicles, it is hard to identify, control and tax key players in the shadow banking sector. Uncertainty in terms of the scope of shadow banks basically makes global regulatory attempts less meaningful. Shadow banking in developed and developing countries is not the same. Shadow banking in developing and emerging countries is less complex and opaque than its counterparts in developed countries.[137] In advanced economies, more complicated transactions or operations such as securitization, securities lending, repos, loans and other bank-like functions are involved in shadow banking. In contrast, developing

---

[133] Tom Braithwaite, Tracy Alloway, Michael MacKenzie and Gina Chon, "Fed Looks At Exit Fees on Bond Funds", Financial Times, 16 June 2014, available 26 February 2016 at http://www.cnbc.com/2014/06/16/fed-looks-at-exit-fees-on-bond-funds.html.

[134] Schwarcz, "Regulating Shadow Banking", p. 638 (discussing the rationale of regulating shadow banking to minimize systemic risk and maximize economic efficiency).

[135] IMF, "Risk Taking, Liquidity, and Shadow Banking: Curbing Excess While Promoting Growth", (October 2014) Global Financial Stability Report 86.

[136] Some more recent literature challenges the prevailing view of the efficacy of harmonized international financial regulation and claims that regulatory harmonization can increase systemic risk. Roberta Romano, "For Diversity in the International Regulation of Financial Institutions: Critiquing and Recalibrating the Basel Architecture", (2014) 31 *Yale Journal on Regulation* 1–76.

[137] Swati Ghosh, Ines Gonzalez del Mazo and Inci Otker-Robe, "Chasing the Shadows: How Significant Is Shadow Banking in Emerging Markets?", (2012) The World Bank Economic Premise No. 88.

economies usually host less complex steps and linkages within the shadow banking system. Typical operations are still conventional including leasing, financing, factoring and investment. It is clear that the level of complication and risk differs in these jurisdictions. The degree to which shadow banking requires regulation and oversight differs and therefore justifies a non-harmonized treatment. As the regulation of shadow banking endogenously depends on the degree to which it contributes to systemic risk, applying uniform policies or regulatory devices is less feasible and will generate unequal tradeoffs. In addition, coordination at the regional or global level triggers more efforts to deal with collective problems.

Here regulation by institutional charter is not the way for regulation. Regulation by function is a more potent style of regulation than regulation by institutional form. Regulation by form (that is, banks) will always be arbitraged away by banks via shadow banks. In contrast, regulation by function of credit intermediation is a more potent strategy, a hard arbitrage form of regulation.

The FSB published its consultative document which embodies a policy framework for addressing shadow banking risks in securities lending and repossessions (repos).[138] In this consultative document, the FSB set out 13 policy recommendations. Among others, these policies are targetted at improving regulatory reporting and market transparency, regulating securities financing and dealing with structural aspects of the securities financing market such as central clearing.[139] But these policies have not become global standards.

In response to a changing global economic environment, the FSB stressed a need to keep the shadow banking system "under permanent surveillance, since new risks and new interconnections are created in the global economy".[140] The FSB proposed ways to address shadow banking activities and entities by placing emphases on (i) indirect regulation, by regulating the links between shadow banking activities and the regulated banking system; (ii) extending or revising the existing regulation to shadow banks; and (iii) adopting new regulations designed for shadow banking activities and entities. FSB's approach basically applies bank-centered regulation to shadow banking. Given the apparent differences between

---

138 Financial Stability Board, "Strengthening Oversight and Regulation of Shadow Banking – Policy Framework for Addressing Shadow Banking Risks in Securities Lending and Repos", (2013), available 26 February 2016 at http://www.financialstabilityboard.org/wp-content/uploads/r_130829b.pdf?page_moved=1.

139 Ibid.

140 Turner, "Shadow Banking and Financial Instability".

formal and shadow banking, the success prospect of this approach is uncertain.

At the technical level, in order to enhance the monitoring of the shadow banking system, the FSB has been examining the regulation of traditional banks' securitization business and securities lending as well as their interactions with repo markets, money market funds and other shadow banking entities. Improving reporting standards and strengthening disclosure rules to enhance transparency of non-bank intermediaries are also included in the policy initiatives.

The interconnectedness between traditional and shadow banking can be the target of regulation preventing systemic risk to financial stability. Basel III attempts to close the regulatory gap between different treatment of trading book and banking book. Banks' capital requirements are increased for the trading book and complex securitization exposures. A stressed value-at-risk (VaR) capital requirement, and higher capital requirements for re-securitizations in both the banking and trading books are introduced by Basel III[141] in order to remove the regulatory arbitrage. However, Basel III is still unable to put an end to shadow banking.[142] The liquidity requirements and leverage framework under Basel III can stimulate traditional banks to increase leverage or circumvent their regulatory capital or liquidity requirements through shadow banking entities. By doing so, banks can lower their capital (or compliance) costs and acquire capital from the financial market so as to meet the heightened capital requirements under Basel III. Heightened standards in Basel III are more likely to compel traditional banks to undergo a de-leveraging process, and switch to the shadow banking sector.[143] The benefit of this business switch is to reduce conventional lending activities so as to enjoy higher returns.

Limiting the risk of regulatory arbitrage can be the other regulatory focus. The risk of regulatory arbitrage can be moving toward the shadows. Regulators can try to remove some incentives created by tighter controls over bank activities that are not applied to shadow banks. Reducing excessive reliance on the banking system is the other option for policymakers and regulators. The way to achieve this target is to expand the capital markets to provide alternative but reliable sources of funding to the real economy. Deepening financial markets can facilitate risk management.

Shadow banking is at best opaque, which presents the regulators with

---

[141] Emily Lee, "Basel III and Its New Capital Requirements, as Distinguished from Basel II", (2014) 13(1) *Banking Law Journal* 27, 33–34.

[142] FSB, "Shadow Banking: Scoping the Issues".

[143] Coates, "Cost-Benefit Analysis of Financial Regulation: Case Studies and Implications", p.970.

more challenges and difficulties in regulating and monitoring systemic risk. Basel III may be applauded for regulating and containing systemic risk in the traditional banking sector, but it may fall short in preventing shadow banking risks as products and services offered by shadow banks do fall in the regulatory space drawn by Basel III. Put differently, Basel III's impact on shadow banking is probably incidental. Restraining overuses or abuses of shadow banking techniques or instruments entails a thorough assessment of conventional banking regulatory tools.

4. OBJECTIVE AND STRUCTURE OF THIS BOOK

The latest global financial crisis has reshaped the financial system and financial regulation. Politically, the theoretical and practical emphases on deregulation have been shifted to "better regulation" or re-regulation. The "lighter touch" approach has wound away, being replaced by a much heavier "hands-on" approach.[144] Major forms of the shadow banking system are still evolving but regulators and policymakers need to regulate and monitor the shadow banking sector with the aim of curbing systemic risk, and improving market-based financial markets and the regulatory system. Due to the interconnectedness between the formal and shadow banking sectors, policymakers and regulators need to assess whether shadow banking should be regulated. This book seeks to come to grips with the new developments in connection with shadow banking and its regulation. It is a country-specific study of shadow banking with an attempt to understand the shadow banking system, in particular, its related risks, regulation and policy in the context of China.

Chapter 1 lays a foundation for an account of the key characteristics of shadow banking compared with the traditional banking sector. Chapter 2 proceeds to discuss China's shadow banking sector. It first raises a China myth issue by reviewing the Chinese banking sector's performance in the wake of the financial crisis and unveiling some "home-made" problems with China's banking sector, and then moves to the definition of shadow banking in the China context.

Chapters 3 and 4 attempt to investigate the institutional structure of China's banking sector. Chapter 3 outlines China's current financial regulatory architecture. Given the role of liquidity conditions in driving

---

144 See generally, Robert Baldwin, Martin Cave and Martin Lodge, *Understanding Regulation: Theory, Strategy, and Practice* (Oxford: Oxford University Press, 2nd edn. 2012).

shadow banking, an analysis of the central bank and its overall monetary policy is made in Chapter 4.

Chapters 5 to 8 discuss four major subsectors of shadow banking in China, that is, wealth management products, local government financing vehicles, P2P lending and underground lending, respectively. Focusing on these four subsectors of shadow banking follows the narrow-down approach discussed above. The choice of these shadow banking subsectors is made on the grounds of the potential severity of systemic risk. These four subsectors of shadow banking span across three categories laid out in Circular No. 107 (discussed in Chapter 2), which gives a clear picture as to how this three-tiered definition of shadow banking works in the China context. In these chapters, the focus is placed on these shadow banks' activities, funding strategies, size and the credit and liquidity backstops, risks, and, most importantly, regulatory and policy responses.

Shadow banking has showcased the inherent distortion in China's financial market and financial system. As a case study of such market failure, Chapter 9 is a follow-up discussion of how monetary policies affect financial stability (or instability) by looking into the extension of access to central bank funding and the recent credit crunch in China. Chapters 10 to 12 switch the focus onto the ongoing reforms transforming China's financial market from a repressed one to liberalized one: interest rate reform, exchange rate reform and the establishment of an explicit deposit insurance scheme. Implementing this reform strategy, the government has also set up three financial reform-oriented zones in China tasked with different reform agenda, which is the key topic in Chapter 13.

Chapter 14 concludes the whole book.

2. Myth of Chinese banks' success and shadow banking

Chinese banks appear to be outside the recent financial crisis. While their counterparts in Western countries are suffering, Chinese banks have been able to cement their position in the market place. Nevertheless, a deep look at the Chinese banks' lending practices indicates that Chinese banks are also encountering some critical problems such as policy-oriented lending and lending irregularities, which have resulted in a local governments' debt crisis. This chapter not only looks into these problems by reference to the path dependency theory but also the shadow banking sector against this background.

Section 1 raises a question mark against Chinese banks' great success by comparing the banking sector's general performance before and after the global financial crisis. Sections 2 and 3 focus on some pressing problems Chinese banks have brought up in recent years. Sections 4 and 5 touch upon the factual and analytical perspectives of China's shadow banking sector respectively, and attempt to understand the concept of shadow banking in the Chinese context. A short conclusion follows in Section 6.

1. CHINA'S COMMERCIAL BANKING SECTOR BEFORE AND AFTER THE GLOBAL FINANCIAL CRISIS

When the recent financial crisis broke out in 2008, the Chinese banking sector was in relatively good shape. Improvements have been made in the structure, transparency and oversight of financial institutions after years of government-led transition towards a market-oriented banking system. Chinese lenders such as Industrial and Commercial Bank of China (ICBC) and China Construction Bank (CCB) are at the top of the global rankings by market capitalisation and are among the most valuable and profitable banks in the world. Bank of Communications and Bank of China (BOC) are also amongst the high rankings.

In the global economic downturn, compared to their counterparts in Western countries, Chinese banks have cemented their position as the most highly valued financial institutions in the world, taking four of the top five slots in a ranking of banks' share prices as a multiple of their book values. China Merchants Bank (with the price to book ratio at 4.3), China Citic (3.4), ICBC (3.1) and CCB (3.1) became the leading banks in the price-to-book league table in 2009, all with a price-to-book multiple of more than three while the average price-to-book value of the biggest 50 banks has halved from two to one in the past six years. Based on the benchmark of 80 global banks, Chinese banks averaged 20% return on equity while those in America averaged 13%, those in Europe, the Middle East and Africa averaged 11% and those in the rest of Asia-Pacific averaged 12% in the first quarter of 2011.[1]

Shortly before the millennium, China's entire banking system was virtually on the edge of technical insolvency as a result of rampant lending to state-owned enterprises and local governments for projects that turned sour and defaulted. The Chinese government, following the principle of "too big to fail", had to overhaul and recapitalize the entire state-owned banking sector. Modeled on the US Resolution Trust Company,[2] the Chinese government transferred 1.4 trillion yuan of non-performing loans from the Big Four banks to four newly created asset management companies at full face value in 1999–2000.[3] The second round transfer of non-performing loans at a discount on face value took place in 2004–2005.[4] The government, through the Central Huijin Investment Corporation Limited, a state-owned investment vehicle,[5] has injected US$60 billion capital out of its foreign reserves into three of the Big Four since 2003. Leading state-owned banks have since then undergone radical transformation with the Big Four and Bocom listed in Hong Kong, Shanghai or elsewhere.[6] These

---

1 Richard Lumb, "Branching Out", *South China Morning Post*, 26 September 2011, A13.

2 Zhaosheng Zhou, "Experience and Reference from RTC for China AMCs to Dispose NPLs under the Goal and Responsibility Assessment for NPLs Disposal", (2004) 25 *Journal of Theory and Practice of Finance and Economics* 25, 28–29.

3 Weitseng Chen, "WTO: Time's Up for Chinese Banks – China's Banking Reform and Non-performing Loan Disposal", (2006) 7(1) *Chicago Journal of International Law* 239, 251.

4 Michael F. Martin, "China's Banking System: Issues for Congress", (20 February 2012) 29.

5 The reason for using an investment arm instead of the PBOC itself was that the PBOC Law prohibits it from owning any commercial banks. Guonan Ma, "Who Pays China's Bank Restructuring Bill?" (2006) CEPII Working Paper No. 2006-04, p.16.

6 Paul B. McGuinness and Kevin Keasey, "The Listing of Chinese State-owned Banks and Their Path to Banking and Ownership Reform", (2010) 201 *The*

moves were also made partly in response to the prospect of increased foreign competition after China's access to the World Trade Organization (WTO).[7] More fundamentally, the banking regulatory regime has been substantially reformed and legalized even though it is in the flux of institutionalization and modernization. Strengthened financial regulation and supervision, together with bank restructuring and financial liberalization, has improved the soundness of the Chinese banking system.[8]

However, China's financial system is not risk free in a sector changing at lightning speed globally. Rather, the Chinese banking sector is facing new (or old) problems which require deeper and wider reform. Concerns have intensified that a new crisis could be brewing due to mainland banks' new record of Renminbi (RMB) 9,600 billion loans in 2009 following the Chinese government's monetary stimulus package in 2008–2009. The International Monetary Fund (IMF) also rang warning bells in its inaugural report on the Chinese financial system – *People's Republic of China: Financial System Stability Assessment* (2011),[9] carried out jointly by the IMF's first Financial Sector Assessment Program and the World Bank.[10] According to the IMF's assessment, China's financial system was facing a steady build-up of vulnerabilities. The major risks, stemming from the growing complexity of the system and the uncertainties surrounding the global economy, include distortions in capital allocation dictated by the government, the rise of shadow banking, tight control on interest and exchange rates, hidden deficits and unexpected contingent liabilities.[11] These risks continue to negatively affect the efficiency of the system, which has been a long-standing and persistent problem with China's banking system.[12]

China Quarterly 125–155.

[7] Wendy Dobson and Anil K. Kashyap, "The Contradiction in China's Gradualist Banking Reforms", (2006) 2 *Brookings Papers on Economic Activity* 10–162.

[8] Alicia García-Herrero, Sergio Gavilá and Daniel Santabárbara, "China's Banking Reform: An Assessment of Its Evolution and Possible Impact", (2006) 52(2) *CESifo Economic Studies* 304–363.

[9] IMF Country Report No. 11/321, November 2011.

[10] China is one of 25 systemically important countries that have agreed to mandatory assessments at least once every five years. The Financial Sector Assessment Programs are part of the IMF's activities in financial surveillance and the monitoring of the international monetary system.

[11] IMF Calls for Further Reforms in China's Financial System, Press Release No. 11/409, 14 November 2011, available 26 February 2016 at http://www.imf.org/external/np/sec/pr/2011/pr11409.htm.

[12] Based on semi-official non-performing loan figures released by the Chinese government, the non-performing loan ratio in China was much higher than many of its Asian neighbors throughout the 1990s. Even after the Asian Financial Crisis,

2. "POLICY-ORIENTED" COMMERCIAL BANKS AND QUALITY OF LOANS

The Big Four, namely, ICBC, CCB, BOC and the Agricultural Bank of China (ABC), along with a large number of medium- and small-sized commercial banks across the country now concentrate on lending in China's main cities for major projects on a commercial risk basis. The commercialization of the Big Four prevents Chinese banks from lending money to chronically loss-making state-owned enterprises (SOEs). Indeed, the commercialization of domestic banks and involvement of foreign investments have substantially improved the performance of the Chinese banking industry. The Big Four and other Chinese banks have continued to earn strong profits recently in spite of monetary tightening and new rules that require lenders to hold more than one-fifth of their deposits in reserve at the central bank.[13] For instance, ICBC, the world's largest bank by market value, reported a first quarter (of 2011) net profit of RMB 53.8 billion, up 29% from the same period one year earlier. ABC's net profit in the same period grew 36% from a year earlier, which was much slower than its fourth quarter growth of 83% in 2010.[14]

It is widely recognized that China has more control over its economy than other countries.[15] In reality, China can get a tight hold over the banks to finance investment projects when growth stutters.[16] Thus, the

---

Chinese banks' performance was the worst among Asian banks. Victor C. Shih, *Factions and Finance in China: Elite Conflict and Inflation* (Cambridge: Cambridge University Press 2007) p.27. Many other empirical studies confirm this low efficiency. Tarhan Feyzioğlu, "Does Good Financial Performance Mean Good Financial Intermediation in China?" (2009) IMF Working Paper WP/09/170, available 26 February 2016 at http://www.imf.org/external/pubs/ft/wp/2009/wp09170.pdf.

13 This new policy has made the People's Bank of China reserves rise to US$ 2,100 billion, which is about one-third more than the reserve balances at the US Federal Reserve. "People's Bank of China", *Financial Times*, 24 May 2011, p.16.

14 Jamil Anderlini, "Strong Profits at China Lenders Despite Tightening", *Financial Times*, 29 April 2011, p.16.

15 "China GDP – Decimal Points", *Financial Times*, 18 October 2012 (online).

16 For a long time, Chinese government targeted its economic growth rate at 8% per annum. The underlying rationale is that a lower growth rate would lead to mass unemployment which would spark social unrest. But China seemed to be comfortable with a lower growth rate of 7.6% in 2012 partly due to the fact that there have been no massive lay-offs even though the economy decelerated. Indeed, even with a lower economic growth rate, 10 million jobs were actually created in the first nine months of 2012. Jamil Anderlini, "China Confortable with Weaker Growth", *Financial Times*, 18 October 2012 (online).

Big Four and other Chinese commercial banks have never really been freed from policy-loan responsibilities. For example, BOC and others are involved in pet political projects, that is, China's spectacular railroad expansion plan.[17] Chinese banks' commercial lending activities are always influenced by the government's economic policy changes. For instance, Chinese banks have extended huge amounts of loans to local government finance vehicles, with some estimates reaching RMB 10 trillion since China started its massive economic stimulus package in late 2008,[18] equivalent to about 27% of China's economy.[19] Hidden debt by local governments through local financing vehicles poses a significant risk for the banking sector. In response to the Chinese government's attempt to slow explosive loan growth in the country, ICBC reined in lending to some borrowers.[20] Hidden government influence over privatized banks appears common in other countries such as Israel. Concentrated ownership as a result of the privatization program provides regulators with a platform for exerting informal influence over corporate decision-making such as lending and borrowing businesses in commercial banks.[21] The IMF made a policy recommendation in its *People's Republic of China: Financial System Stability Assessment*,[22] that the role of government should move away from using the banking system to carry out broad government policy goals and that lending decisions should be made based on commercial goals.

The quality of the loans on their books still ranks as the biggest challenge for Chinese banks.[23] A record surge in bank lending kept growing at a near double-digit pace, which saddled banks with a large number of

---

17 Jamil Anderlini, Andrew Hill and Paul Betts, "China's Banks Take the Train Strain, Without the Pain", *Financial Times*, 11 May 2010, p.14.

18 Reuters, "Lending to Local Banks to Decline: ICBC Chief", *South China Morning Post*, 1 June 2011, B3. The latest estimate is that total bank loans to local governments reached 14.4 trillion yuan. Lulu Chen, "Regulator Clears Bids to Raise Capital", *South China Morning Post*, 27 July 2011, B3. A large-scale economic stimulus program was to ensure 8% growth. Jamil Anderlini, "China Comfortable with Weaker Growth", *Financial Times*, 18 October 2012 (online).

19 Based on the first national audit of regional finances published by Beijing on 26 June 2011. Robert Cookson, "Resilient Asia More Vulnerable to a Global Crisis", *Financial Times*, 28 July 2011, p.23.

20 Jamil Anderlini, "ICBC to Curb Some Areas of Lending", *Financial Times*, 28 January 2010, p.14.

21 Assaf Hamdani and Ehud Kamar, "Hidden Government Influence over Privatized Banks", (2012) 13(2) *Theoretical Inquiries in Law* 567–596.

22 IMF Country Report No. 11/321, November 2011.

23 Jamil Anderlini, "Audit Lays Bare the Challenges that Lie Ahead", *Financial Times*, 14 May 2010, p.17.

loans that might go bad and kindled inflation. Chinese commercial banks indeed created more bad loans than before resulting from a government-directed lending boom in order to combat the financial crisis. Estimates of the value of non-performing loans existing in the Mainland banking sector vary but Standard Chartered's research indicates that it could be as high as 6 trillion yuan.[24] The problem is largely caused by governmental authorities or local governments which often dictate banks' lending policies or even allocate capital directly. The Chinese government has been used to push cash-rich state-controlled banks to invest and provide easy credit to the state-controlled sectors such as the railway sector.[25] Such a big expansion in lending led to a large rise in non-performing loans as many borrowers, *inter alia*, local government financing vehicles (LGFVs, which are government-backed entities in charge of funds and overseeing construction of infrastructure projects, and whose fundraising is for provincial and municipal governments), may eventually default.[26] Excessive lending to LGFVs, companies which are set up to borrow on behalf of local governments, indeed leads to concerns over systemic risks in China's banking sector. For instance, outstanding loans to LGFV at BOC were at 394.5 billion yuan.[27] China Merchants Bank's loans to LGFVs took up 7.46% of the bank's total loan book by the end of first quarter of 2012.[28] Many of these loans would have to be rolled over.[29]

A large chunk of LGFV loans incur additional transaction costs. First, the bank has to reserve more capital for possible bad loans. For example, ICBC's provision rose to RMB 194.9 billion in order to satisfy the regulatory requirement of reaching a loan loss reserve ratio at 2.5%. Second, the shareholders of the bank may have to sacrifice their dividends. ICBC cut its dividend payout by around 4 percentage points to 34% so as to push up its capital adequacy level.[30]

Mainland banks have been facing an uphill task in controlling bad loans following a lending spree during the past several years. Meanwhile,

---

24 Chen, "Regulator Clears Bids to Raise Capital".

25 Jamil Anderlini, "BOC to Invest $1.1bn in China Railway", *Financial Times*, 11 May 2010, p.14.

26 Jamil Anderlini, "Profits Jump at Chinese Banks", *Financial Times*, 28 October 2010, p.15.

27 Daniel Ren, "Bank of China Set to Slash Dividend Payouts Further", *South China Morning Post*, 31 May 2012, B3.

28 Lulu Chen, "CMB Confident on Capital Reserves", *South China Morning Post*, 31 March 2012, B3.

29 Lulu Chen, "Healthy ICBC Sees 26pc Rise in Profit to RMB208b", *South China Morning Post*, 30 March 2012, B1.

30 Chen, "Healthy ICBC Sees 26pc Rise in Profit to RMB208b".

Chinese private companies have been forced to issue bonds through offshore holding companies or special purpose vehicles and then send the money onshore in the form of foreign direct investment. While the international bond investors have loaned tens of billions of dollars to Chinese companies in recent years, foreign bondholders have been taking equity risk for a bond return.[31] What is happening in the market is very close to what went on in the West in 2007 and 2008, a liquidity-fuelled asset bubble. Chinese banks issued a total RMB 9.6 trillion of credit in 2009, nearly double the minimum target of RMB 5 trillion. In 2010, Chinese banks further granted new loans of RMB 8 trillion, exceeding Beijing's initial quota of RMB 7.5 trillion even though the Chinese government has been trying to tighten up monetary policy.[32] The data may indicate an end to a cycle of credit improvement.[33] Although the Big Four and major Chinese banks reported profit growth in recent years, sentiment has turned against these banks as investors have been concerned about the sustainability of Chinese banks' growth amid a global slowdown. Substantial increases in lending by Chinese banks may result in a rise in non-performing loans, which would exercise a further drag on operations and ultimately affect long term profitability.[34]

Mortgage lending and lending to property developers is another area of concern. The vast majority of collateral in the Chinese banking system is land or property, which is the key correlation risk to the banks. Abundant credit, a lack of domestic investment options and huge pent-up demand for housing has pushed up prices which continuously soar. The Chinese government is now trying to deflate by steadily tightening restrictions

---

[31] Robert Cookson, "Investors Warned of Chinese Debt Danger", *Financial Times*, 21 July 2011, p.23. On the other hand, the PBOC recently reported that loans had become more accessible to small firms and subsidised housing developments. New loans to small and medium sized enterprises reached 1.58 trillion yuan in the first half of 2011, accounting for 64.5% of all loans extended to companies, up 1.6 percentage points compared with the first quarter of 2011. However, the figures run counter to the experience of private firms operating outside the state-run financial system. Lulu Chen, "Central Bank Reports Rise in Lending to Small Firms", South China Morning Post, 27 July 2011, B3.

[32] Daniel Ren, "Everbright Bank Lines Up Big Guns for HK Listing", *South China Morning Post*, 1 June 2011, B3.

[33] Chen, "'Healthy ICBC Sees 26pc Rise in Profit to RMB208b". Chinese banking officials instead argued that only a continuous rise of non-performing loan ratios in several consecutive quarters may prove deteriorating asset quality.

[34] However, it has to be pointed out that the non-performing loan rate in China was only 1.14% and capital ratios averaged 12.2%, both of which are better than their counterparts in Europe and the US. Richard Lumb, "Branching Out", *South China Morning Post*, 26 September 2011, A13.

without causing the market bubble to pop, even though property loans in China so far have had a low rate of default.[35]

The domestic real estate boom has been a key driver of the Chinese economy in the past decade. The shrinking of real estate development or a steep drop in real estate prices, though good news for residents or consumers in China, is potentially dangerous for the entire Chinese economy since housing investment, as estimated, is about a quarter of fixed asset investment.[36] The central government's introduction of curbs to cool the nation's overheated real estate market has worked together with tighter credit, a crackdown on speculators and limits on purchases of second homes. As a result, price rises have slowed. In a recent banking stress test conducted by Chinese regulators in late 2011, the conclusion made that non-performing loans would rise by a small proportion even if property prices dropped by 50%. However, this clean bill of health diagnosed by Chinese regulators has triggered wide suspicion. Standard & Poor's warned as early as in 2011 that a 10% drop in sales in 2012 could be withstood but a 30% fall in sales would make developers face severe liquidity strains.[37] Analysts cast doubts largely because of omissions and assumptions which severely undermined the stress test results. The sequence of threats to the property sector envisioned in the stress test was the scenario in which prices would decline by 50% and transactions would fall by 30%.[38] In reality, what happened was that property sales plummeted but the property prices barely started to decline as the potential buyers are waiting for a further dip in the price. The methodology adopted in the stress test is also problematic. For example, banks were asked to classify a variety of property-related loans into several categories: developers,

---

[35] Reuters, "Lending to Local Banks to Decline: ICBC Chief", *South China Morning Post*, 1 June 2011, B3. It has been reported that outstanding property loans increased 16.9% in the first half of 2011 against a year earlier, down 4.4 percentage points from the growth recorded in the first quarter of 2011. New loans for subsidised housing developments in the first half of 2011 reached 90.8 billion yuan, up 54.8% from the beginning of 2011. The growth was 48.3 percentage points higher than that of total property development loans in the same period. Lulu Chen, "Central Bank Reports Rise in Lending to Small Loans", *South China Morning Post*, 27 July 2011, B3.

[36] Jamil Anderlini, "China Property Developers Start to Feel Jittery", *Financial Times*, 30 September 2011, p.6. The other source suggests that real estate investment accounts for about 13% of GDP. Jamil Anderlini, "Sombre Signs for China Growth", *Financial Times*, 17 January 2012 (online).

[37] Jamil Anderlini, "China Property Developers Start to Feel Jittery".

[38] Simon Rabinovitch, "Doubts Cast on Stress Tests' All-clear for Chinese Banks", *Financial Times*, 22 November 2012, p.4.

mortgages and upstream industries. The category of risks is not reflective of the interaction between the property sector and overall economy. More likely, the property sector may be hit first while the economy remains unimpaired. Related to the methodology is the failure to include the impact of falling land sales and prices on the value of bank collateral. The banking sector and investors have come round to the belief that a deep fall in housing prices would be traumatic for the Chinese banking sector.

In 2010–2012, the Chinese government strictly implemented its housing policies by refusing to lift curbs on the real estate boom with the aim of bringing housing prices back down to a level that ordinary residents are able to afford. As a result, the skyrocketing housing prices paused for a while. The first three quarters of 2012 witnessed a newly started floor space drop of 8.6% from 24% in the same period of 2011.[39] A lesser reliance on real estate and infrastructure investment makes the Chinese economy more sustainable in the long run. It should also benefit most residents who may enjoy faster income growth.

There were no visible signs of a deterioration in asset quality in the wake of China's post-2008 stimulus spending spree. There are several reasons for this. First, some bad loans were rolled over or moved off balance sheets. Second, interest margins were compressed as a bigger proportion of loans was repriced at lower rates following PBOC's interest rate cuts. Third, a slowing economy may result in more non-performing loans. Therefore, the true non-performing loans may edge up. In the long run, Chinese banks are at a turning point as they are making outsized profits thanks to their stranglehold on the country's financing channels. The government's move has been to nurture a more vibrant corporate bond market and more interest rate liberalization,[40] which may in the end erode the banks' dominance.

3. LENDING IRREGULARITIES

Chinese banks have been accustomed to evading regulatory requirements. In 2009 a largely unregulated market in off-balance sheet securitized loans (or informal securitization, that is, the use of lightly regulated trust companies to repackage loans and sell them back to banks for sale to

---

[39] Anderlini, "China Comfortable with Weaker Growth".

[40] PBOC's governor expressed his view to accelerate the pace of interest rate liberalization in a press conference on the sidelines of the 18th Party Congress. Reuters, "Financial Reformers Adapt Communist Party Rhetoric", *South China Morning Post*, 13 November 2012 (online).

customers)[41] proliferated as Chinese banks strained to get around the government's attempt to rein in rampant lending growth.[42] The total outstanding credit will obviously strain capitalization and loan-to-deposit ratios. CBRC has been so concerned about the rapid growth in informal securitization that it issued a temporary ban on all such transactions between banks and trust companies.[43]

More importantly, Chinese banks appear very much path dependent and unable to change their bad practices of lending irregularities. China National Audit Office recently revealed following an audit of the headquarters and 11 branches of ABC at the end of April 2010 that lending irregularities amounted to tens of billions of Renminbi.[44] The logic of these lending irregularities derives from the fact that more than 85% of profits in the Chinese banking sector actually come from the difference between government-set lending and deposit rates, a commercial reality which encourages banks to lend as much as they can in order to make more profits.[45] As a result, Chinese banks always rush to lend to a level far exceeding the Chinese government's set target. The Big Four loaned 101.7 billion yuan in the first 25 days of April 2012, and loaned a cumulative 700 billion yuan in March 2012 while a lending quota was set at 800 billion yuan in March.[46] New loans from the Big Four typically represented 30–40% of all bank loans. The huge outflow of deposits lowered lenders' loans-to-deposit ratios.

These facts forced the Chinese central bank to raise interest rates four times after October 2010 (three rate hikes in the first half of 2011).[47] This monetary tightening policy, however, had little impact on the commercial banks, which earn almost all of their income from government-set interest rate margins.[48] The Chinese central bank was then forced to increase the

---

41 Henny Sender, "Monetary Tightening by China to be Felt across Globe", *Financial Times*, 7 January 2011, p.20. The Chinese government has been very concerned with the secrutization of loans. Some few pilot projects were put on hold during the global financial crisis. However, ICBC and other Chinese banks have been promoting securitization and asset-backed security products for years. Jamil Anderlini, "China Banks Face $70bn Gap", *Financial Times*, 14 April 2010, p.15.

42 Jamil Anderlini, "Crackdown on China Banks", *Financial Times*, 11 August 2010, p.1.

43 Ibid.

44 Anderlini, "Audit Lays Bare the Challenges that Lie Ahead".

45 Anderlini, "ICBC to Curb Some Areas of Lending".

46 Natallie Cai, "New Capital Rules Put on Hold", *The Standard*, 3 May 2012.

47 Fulton Mak, "Regulator Bans Rollover of Local Government Debt", *Hong Kong Economic Journal*, 28 July 2011, p.1.

48 It has been reported that Chinese banks earn just 1.62%. The market-based alternative is to issue sterilization bills but this alternative became costly as yields

reserve requirement ratio more frequently (that is, six increases in the first half of 2011),[49] or the portion of overall deposits the banks were required to keep in reserve at the central bank. Chinese banks must now hold 20.5% of customer deposits with the central bank. Every 0.5 percentage point increase in banks' reserve requirement ratio could reduce Chinese banks, that is, ICBC's interest income by about RMB 700 million.[50]

These developments effectively remind us of the old problems and new challenges that underdeveloped and state-dominated Chinese banks may still have and face despite a decade of frenetic and large-scale reform in the banking sector. It might be still the case that Chinese banks are *de facto* instruments of the state's economic and monetary policy,[51] and that commercialization has a long way to go. Another consequence of opening up China's banking industry and the commercialization of Chinese banks is that Chinese banks are now more easily influenced by the global financial market. The recent Greek bailout is, for instance, helping the oversale of Chinese banks' shares in the market, with China Construction Bank rising 2.6%, Industrial and Commercial Bank of China up 2.8% and Bank of China 2.2% higher.[52]

Mounting non-performing loans resulting from irregular and policy lending force Chinese banks to improve their balance sheets from time to time. These banks are not afraid of bank failures, given China's "too big to fail" principle and practice, rescuing the Big Four and major commercial banks from bank runs and financial instability under any circumstance. However, the Big Four and Bocom are now facing a daunting task in meeting new global standards designed to prevent taxpayer bailouts of commercial lenders. The FSB has recently made policy recommendations to the G20 and suggested requiring global banks to hold a special debt, Total Loss Absorbing Capacity (TLAC).[53] The underlying rationale of this new policy is to make larger banks resilient enough to weather

---

on its foreign assets fell. "People's Bank of China", *Financial Times*, 24 May 2011, p.16.

[49] Mak, "Regulator Bans Rollover of Local Government Debt".

[50] Jamil Anderlini, "Strong Profits at China Lenders Despite Tightening", *Financial Times*, 29 April 2011, p.16.

[51] Patrick Jenkins, "State Lending Targets Are Grist to the Mill of History", *Financial Times*, 24 May 2011, p.18.

[52] Jasper Moiseiwitsch, "Bearing of Gifts to Greeks Gives Market 2.6pc Boost", *South China Morning Post* (Investing), 27 July 2011, p.6.

[53] FSB, Adequacy of Loss-Absorbing Capacity of Global Systemically Important Banks In Resolution, 10 November 2014, available 26 February 2016 at http://www.financialstabilityboard.org/wp-content/uploads/TLAC-Condoc-6-Nov-2014-FINAL.pdf.

economic or financial turmoil without spreading contagion to the broader financial system, and to reduce the probability of large scale government bailouts.

According to the FSB's estimation, the 30 globally systemically important banks (G-Sib) need to raise roughly €1.1 trillion in order to satisfy the TLAC requirement. BOC, ABC and ICBC together are short of €335 billion, one-third of the entire loss-absorbing debt. CCB was not included in the G-Sib list until October 2015 and is likely to need additional funding to cover the TLAC. Chinese banks are required to meet the full requirement for TLAC by 2028 (if China's corporate bond market does not expand to 55% of GDP, otherwise exceeding 55% will push the deadline forward) while developed-market banks' deadline is 2022. The TLAC rule effectively puts the Big Four at a disadvantage due to their heavier reliance on deposits and creates an extra burden on Chinese banks for their weakened balance sheets while they need to comply with Basel III, which needs the Big Four to have top quality capital equal to 11.5% of their assets, adjusted for risk, by the end of 2018. In order to meet Basel III requirements Chinese banks have already sold US$58 billion of capital bonds since 2013. The TLAC rule has a less immediate impact on Western banks drawing a larger share of funding from selling bonds, which can count towards TLAC requirements provided that bond documentation includes bail-in provisions imposing losses on investors when the bank fails.[54]

4. SHADOW BANKING IN CHINA: SOME FIGURES

The development of the shadow banking sector in China goes hand in hand with the sophistication of China's banking sector. Shadow banking in China refers to lending that is free from the same regulation as bank loans, and includes banks' off-balance-sheet vehicles, such as commercial

---

[54] By contrast, the "net stable funding ratio" concept in Basel III is more favorable to Chinese banks since it treats deposits as a better funding source than bonds. The concept is significant for banks with large short-term interbank exposures, since 10 or 15% of these will be backed by stable (primarily retail or over one year wholesale) funding. The purpose of designing this measurement is to prevent overreliance on wholesale funding which can quickly evaporate in financial turmoil, and to mitigate liquidity problems. F. Gideon, Mark A. Petersen, Janine Mukuddem-Petersen and LNP Hlatshwayo, "Basel III and the Net Stable Funding Ratio", (2013), ISRN Applied Mathematics, available 26 February 2016 at http://dx.doi.org/10.1155/2013/582707; Basel Committee on Banking Supervision, "Basel III: The Net Stable Funding Ratio" (October 2014).

bills and entrusted loans and underground lending by individuals as well as wealth management products. Trusts and securities brokerages emerged as new conduits for shadow lending.[55] Shadow banking covers loans structured as interbank assets to dodge lending caps, and investment products backed by murky pools of loans.

The way that the Chinese shadow banking system is structured is relatively simple, and basically similar to that of traditional commercial banking with a very small amount of credit created through financial derivatives, the fact of which affirms a lower level of financial innovation.[56] Due to tightly-controlled credit limits in China, there have been 81-billion-yuan domestic deposits steered from bank loans (130 trillion yuan in total bank assets) and savings into opaque, off-balance sheet, risk-laden vehicles or underground financial networks. Meanwhile, there emerged a RMB 2,000 billion shadow banking system (roughly about 5% of GDP)[57] as a result of unregulated lending fueled by small- and medium-sized firms which have been forced to look to loan sharks for working capital,[58] due to their difficult access to the formal banking sector.

A precise estimation may be difficult given the fact that the shadow banking sector includes some lending practices in the grey or even black market. Moody's Investors Service estimates that China's shadow banking may have reached US$4.7 trillion, 55% of China's GDP by 2012.[59] In 2012, two-thirds of the increase in credit came from sources other than bank loans, such as letters of credit, leasing and other informal lending.[60] Overall credit grew by about 22–23% in China in the first half of 2013, up from 20% in 2012, after a surge in "shadow" lending by trust companies and banks through off-balance-sheet vehicles.[61] China's

---

[55] Simon Rabinovitch, "Surge in Chinese Credit Raises Fears", *Financial Times*, 8 February 2013 (online).

[56] Derivatives are financial products that are involved in some of the most creative and sophisticated aspects of finance. Robert J. Shiller, *Finance and the Good Society* (Princeton and Oxford: Princeton University Press 2012) p.75.

[57] Henny Sender, "China Groups Fuel Shadow Banking", *Financial Times*, 7 September 2011, p.18.

[58] Reuters, "Shadow Bank Reform Needed to Fight Bubbles", *South China Morning Post*, 12 January 2012, B3.

[59] Victoria Ruan, "IMF Warns China of Risks in Investment Binge", *South China Morning Post*, 30 May 2013 (online).

[60] "China's Banks: Of Liquidity and Credit", *Financial Times*, 19 June 2013 (online) (citing Fitch Ratings' report).

[61] Simon Rabinovitch, "PBOC Dashes Hopes of China Liquidity Boost", *Financial Times*, 20 June 2013 (online).

shadow banking sector has financed almost half of all new credit.[62] Moody's Investors Service estimated that shadow banking assets in China reached RMB 37.7 trillion by the end of 2013, which accounted for 66% of China's GDP.[63] FSB, however, based its estimation on the narrow measure that the size of China's shadow banking sector totaled US$2.7 trillion.[64] By the end of 2014, China's shadow banking sector was estimated at a value of RMB 30.1 trillion, accounting for 53% of China's GDP.[65]

While money supply has expanded, much of the fresh credit has failed to flow into the real economy, instead being repackaged as shadow-banking products so as to avoid strict regulatory scrutiny, fueling concerns over systemic financial risks. Among all the banks directly engaged in the shadow banking sector (with more than 90% of shadow banking activities), wealth management products accounted for 7.5 trillion yuan; 5.7 trillion yuan were entrusted loans and 6 trillion yuan were bank accepted bills.[66] The situation may become worse if the Chinese government is to deflate asset bubbles especially in the real estate market. In recent years China has witnessed a fast growth in the "virtual economy" – a not very discreet allusion to the explosion of innovative financial securitization products and bubble-style investment practices, which had already precipitated the US financial crisis.

The FSB estimates that the sector represents 115% of GDP and 52% of banking assets worldwide, more than double their respective levels in China. Focusing on systemically important shadow banking activities linked to the formal banking sector, shadow banking is about 50–60% of China's GDP or about 35–30% of banking assets. As far as shadow banking subsectors are concerned, wealth management products amount

---

62 Henny Sender, "Chinese Munis Will Keep Help Curb Shadow Banks", *Financial Times*, 16 April 2014, p.20; "Keeping China's Fragilities in Check", *Financial Times*, 10 April 2013 (online). The latest statistics is that China's shadow banking system had grown to 36 trillion yuan, or nearly 70% of GDP.

63 Victoria Ruan, "China Central Bank Sees Role for Shadow Banking", *South China Morning Post*, 27 September 2014, available 26 February 2016 at http://www.scmp.com/business/economy/article/1601273/china-central-bank-sees-role-shadow-banking.

64 Victoria Ruan, "China's Shadow Banking Market Third-Largest in the World", *South China Morning Post*, 1 November 2014 (online).

65 Andrew Sheng and Ng Chow Soon (eds), "Bringing Shadow Banking Into the Light: Opportunity for Financial Reform in China", (2015) Fung Global Institute Report, p.75.

66 Bin Zhao, "A Crash in the Making?" *South China Morning Post*, 23 July 2013, A13.

to 36% of GDP or about 15% of bank assets, and the trust sector amounts to less than 8% of bank assets. A safe calculation of the much-hyped, high-risk parts of the shadow banking sector is roughly around 15% of GDP or about 6% of bank assets.[67]

China's severe economic downturn has been said to be inevitable due to the debt load, which rose from US$7 trillion in 2007 to US$28 trillion by mid-2014. China's debt is 282% of China's GDP, which is much larger than that of the US or Germany. Half of loans are linked directly or indirectly to China's real estate, and unregulated shadow banking accounts for nearly half of new lending.[68] Compared with the total credit provided by the formal banking sector, which is equivalent to 135% of GDP in China, this is a large size.[69]

5. CHINA'S SHADOW BANKING: ANALYTICAL OVERVIEW

5.1 Distinctive Feature: Strong Interconnectedness between Shadow and Regular Banking Systems

China's shadow banking has grown rapidly with its own characteristics in terms of its key components, major forms, market players, driving forces, risk profiles, government responses and regulatory instruments. In contrast to the US, China's shadow banking is closely interconnected with the traditional banking sector. Traditional banks are deeply involved in and heavily relied upon by the shadow banks for funding or financial back-up. This contributes to some distinctive features of China's financial market.

First, the financial market in China is less complicated and sophisticated compared to those in other advanced economies. Financial innovation remains at a preliminary stage largely because of an array of regulatory restrictions and the monopolistic position state-owned banks possess in the marketplace. Complicated structured financial products or tools are not widely offered. Securitization as a financial engineering technique has not gained popularity among financial institutions. The financial market is full of conventional financial products and services

---

[67] Yukon Huang, "Alarmists Overstate China's Shadow Banking Threat", *Financial Times*, 18 July 2014 (online).

[68] Andrew Ross Sorkin, "He Warned of Trouble in China", *International New York Times*, 26 August 2015, p.18 (citing McKinsey & Company's report).

[69] Milken Institute, *Underground Lending – Submerging Emerging Asia* (April 2014), p.7.

offered by traditional banks. Complex products such as derivatives, securitized loans, asset-backed commercial paper, repurchase agreements and money market funds are not offered in a large scale or amount and are in the experimental stages. The space for financial innovation is overall quite limited. Second, in terms of the source of funding, the lending market in China is far more predominant and important than other capital markets such as the stock market and bond market. Banks, compared to private equity firms, hedge funds, and money market funds, play a dominant role in possessing and allocating financial resources. Strong banks can have a crowd-effect, squeezing out other financial players and making private equity investment and securities transactions less important and weaker. As a result, the traditional banks have to be relied upon in providing liquidity, distributing financial services or products, guaranteeing credit supply and channeling funding. Third, the regular banking sector is heavily regulated. Banks are subject to loan quotas, capital requirement and cash reserve ratio, which increase compliance and transaction costs for banks. Banks have to comply with other regulatory restrictions in extending loans. For instance, banks are not allowed to lend money to corporates for working capital loans. Banks with their competitive advantages are motivated and able to participate in shadow banking. On the demand side, corporates face more difficulties in managing their liquidity and have to seek short-term loans from non-bank lenders to meet their short-term liquidity needs. Shadow banking effectively acts as a conduit connecting the supply and demand sides of funding. Serving corporates' liquidity needs through shadow banking instruments (that is, bridging loans) and vehicles (that is, trust companies or SPVs) helps regular banks arbitrage regulatory restrictions and guarantee their profit margin.

The dynamic role regular banks play in the shadow banking system leads to some characteristics of China's shadow banking sector: its interrelation with financial products and services offered by regular banks, it excessive deleverage on property and collateral value of land, its sensitivity to interest rate movements and other monetary policies.[70] Consequently, shadow banking depends on a continued influx of capital and potential exposure to excess risk when the liquidity turns out to be a serious problem. This is true when the economy slows down. The repayment pressures are not only accumulated on the asset and liabilities side of banks' balance sheets but also on shadow banks. The close interconnectedness between shadow and

---

[70] Dong Tao and Weishen Deng, "China: Shadow Banking – Road to Heightened Risks", (2013) Credit Suisse Economic Research, available 26 February 2016 at http://www.credit-suisse.com/researchandanalytics, p.6.

regular banks easily creates a spillover effect – systemic risk can spill over from one sector to the other leading to a more severe system-wide impact.

5.2 Composition of and Players in Shadow Banking

Composition and players in China's shadow banking differ from their counterparts in the US shadow banking sector. The US shadow banking sector is comprised of complex structured financial products such as derivatives, asset-backed commercial papers, securitized finance, repurchase agreements, securitized loans and money market funds. The major form of China's shadow banking activities is direct credit extension in the form of debt instruments or the first layer of loan securitization by non-bank institutions such as trust companies and brokerage firms.[71] Securitization is rare in the market even though informal securitization is available in some cases. These stark contrasts are largely due to the less developed capital market and non-bank financing market.

Trust is something which should be discussed in the context of shadow banking. Trusts take an important role in China's financial system. Trusts provide businesses which have high risks and would otherwise be completely cut off from finance with a way to finance themselves; their only real alternative would be to go to the black market. Trusts' businesses have nothing to do with "trusts" used in a common law jurisdiction. In common law, trusts are used to mobilize funds that are conservatively managed for the benefit of a third party.[72] By contrast, trusts are the widest ranging of China's financial institutions. Trusts can engage in investment banking, property lending and private equity deals – just to mention a few. Trusts package investors' loans and deals into high-yielding investment products, and to a certain extent, share a similarity with hedge funds: the risk is not borne by the trusts but by the investors. Trusts, as estimated, amount to RMB 10 trillion of assets under management.[73]

Trust loans, which have typically been given to higher-risk borrowers

---

[71] Although China has its Trust Law, the regulatory environment is a difficult one making small-scale trusts and collective civil trusts impossible. The government has been wary of the companies' desire to create new collective investment funds. This is why it is extremely rare to see large-scale trusts run by private parties for public or other interest. Stephen Tensmeyer, "Modernizing Chinese Trust Law", (2015) 90(2) *New York University Law Review* 710, 710–720.

[72] See generally, Richard Edwards and Nigel Stockwell, *Trusts and Equity* (Harlow: Pearson Education Ltd 2009), and more specifically, Sarah Worthington, *Equity* (New York: Oxford University Press, 2nd edn., 2006) 76.

[73] Simon Rabinovitch, "China Trusts Bring Contrasting Fortunes", *Financial Times*, 31 December 2013 (online).

such as property developers and mining companies, make up the largest slice of China's shadow banking sector. Shadow financing rose to account for more than a third of new credit in China in 2013. The whole trust market now amounts to US$1.2 billion. Official statistics show that entrusted loans rose to RMB 396.5 billion in January 2014, almost double the levels of the same month one year earlier.[74] Trust loans increased 78.4 billion yuan, down from 183 billion yuan one year earlier and from 106.8 billion yuan in January 2014.[75] Entrusted loans, a type of intercompany lending and a form of shadow banking, increased by 79.9 billion yuan in February, down from 396.5 billion yuan in January 2014.[76] The value of trust loans, plummeted by RMB 517 billion, was around 3% of all new credit originated in 2014.[77]

Trust financing has been an important channel for pumping funds into the economy, especially to sectors deemed too risky for traditional banks. When the government banned banks from lending to real estate developers, trusts were permitted to lend to industries such as property, coal and others with overcapacity problems, and could do so at rates of 10–15%. For example, about 75% of the property loans by Ping An Trust, the largest trust in China by assets and a subsidiary of Ping An Group, have been made to China's largest 20 listed developers.[78] Trust lending is also lightly regulated. Trusts usually plug the holes that banks are unable to fill. Ping An Trust now turns its focus to cash-strapped local governments. Local government debt, often involving trust financing, has soared to RMB 17.9 trillion, an increase of 70% from the end of 2010.

There is a genuine concern with trust companies. Unlike banks, trusts are prohibited from taking deposits but can make high-interest and riskier loans, purchase securities or invest in private equity, which they sell on to investors in the form of trust products with enticing interest rates. Trusts are a way for banks to avoid limits on their lending by moving loans off balance sheet. Recent regulation in China has restricted such activity to 20% of trust assets. A more pertinent concern is that trusts are overinvested in risky areas such as property, raw materials, local government and other sectors that banks were trying to avoid. While less than 40%

---

[74] James Kynge, "Beijing Seeks to Spear Currency Vultures with Judicious Arrow", *Financial Times*, 28 February 2014, p.2.

[75] Grace Zhu, "Lending Growth Slowed in February as Beijing Pulled Back on Reins", *The Wall Street Journal*, 11 March 2014, C3.

[76] Ibid.

[77] Gabriel Wildau, "China Shadow Bank Regulation Shows Results", *Financial Times*, 2 February 2014 (online).

[78] Rabinovitch, "China Trusts Bring Contrasting Fortunes".

of trust assets are invested in these areas, credit risks are higher for trusts than banks because they serve weaker businesses.

China Credit Trust, one of China's largest shadow bank institutions, raised Renminbi 3 billion from investors three years ago for the investment. The loan was backed by loans to a coal miner that is located in Shanxi Province and later collapsed. The "Credit Equals Gold No. 1" product was sold through the private banking arm of ICBC. ICBC refused to repay investors in the fund but many investors in trust products believed there was an implicit guarantee that they would be rescued if the investment went bad. Default was averted at the last minute after an unnamed investor took over the project.[79] China Credit Trust avoided a high-profile default by reaching a last-minute agreement to repay investors in a soured US$500 million high-yield investment trust. China Credit would sell the shares it held in Shanxi Zhenfu Energy Group, the coal miner that ran into financial trouble after its owner was arrested. China Credit has taken control of Zhenfu's shares as collateral when it failed to repay the loan. Investors are offered a deal to recoup their principal but not the remainder of their third year's worth of interest. Alternatively, investors can have shares in Zhenfu.[80]

The concern is that investors may walk away when default occurs, thereby making the whole shadow banking market into a liquidity-driven credit crisis. There have been signs that investors have reduced their appetite to park their funds with trust companies. A slowing economic growth makes a default more likely in the lightly regulated world of trust companies, the rationale of which is to get around China's artificially low rates of return for savers. A well-managed default can be a positive step towards regulating the shadow banking sector. Zhu Rongji, the then premier, shut down Guangdong International Trust & Investment Company (Gitic) in 1998. Gitic at that time raised money from investors to buy real estate and anything else it found profitable. Gitic became the first formal bankruptcy of a major Chinese financial institution, triggered by its inability to repay a US$120 million loan to a foreign lender. Its collapse was followed by the collapse of hundreds of other trust companies. When KPMG conducted the auditing, it found that Gitic's assets were US$2.6 billion with liabilities of US$4.4 billion. However, Standard & Poor's had given the group a top investment grade rating on par with that of China's finance ministry.

---

[79] Zhu, "Lending Growth Slowed in February as Beijing Pulled Back on Reins".

[80] Simon Rabinovitch and Josh Noble, "Chinese Fund Staves off Default", *Financial Times*, 28 January 2014, p.16.

Creditors in the next four years submitted claims of US$5.6 billion, including US$4.7 billion from foreign lenders. The recovery rate in the bankruptcy proceeding was only 12.5% on the dollar value.[81] The Chinese government in that case refused to bail out creditors largely due to the fact that at that point, China had a mere US$145 billion in foreign exchange reserves.

The question remains valid as to whether the Chinese government would compensate creditors when the shadow banking sector goes bad. The difference, however, is between the increased size of the problem between now and then. The other difference is that the creditors in the current shadow banking sector are Chinese citizens rather than foreign investors. Products like the ones linked to Liansheng (discussed below) are issued by trusts, which take money from investors and lend it out to fund capital-intensive projects or in other areas in which banks might be reluctant to lend. In the economic downturn, the business has been under scrutiny for signs of a major default that could ripple through the financial system.

Jilin Trust and Ping An Trust provide loans to borrowers. Jilin Trust warned investors in December 2013 that one of its products, securities backed by loans to an overleveraged coal miner in northern China was at risk of failing. Jilin Trust promised investors a 10% annual return but did not take any collateral from the miner. Jilin Trust sold an investment product backed by RMB 100 million of loans to Liansheng Resources Group two years ago, when the coal miner was heavily indebted. Jilin Trust accepted a guarantee from another coal company that is now struggling. Liansheng is now undergoing restructuring, which is attempting to pay back nearly 30 billion yuan in debt and may make itself the first significant default in the trust sector. Jilin Trust said the products cannot be repaid when they come due 19 February 2014.[82] High profile defaults have rocked the shadow banking industry. As a result, growth in trust company loans has evaporated.[83]

Amid tighter regulations, cooperation between banks and trusts has been scaled back. Potential spillover effects have declined. The trust sector amounts to less than 8% of bank assets. It is likely that only a small portion of any losses would be absorbed by the banks. If investors lose

---

[81] Henny Sender, "China's Shadow Banking Fears Revive Painful Memory", *Financial Times*, 5 February 2014, p.14.

[82] Grace Zhu and Yue Li, "Another Tremor For Trust Products", *The Wall Street Journal*, 13 February 2014, C3.

[83] Alex Frangos, "Credit for The China Slowdown", *The Wall Street Journal*, 16 April 2014, C12.

confidence in the trust market, their money will simply flow back into bank deposits because of China's capital controls. As a result, a loss of confidence in shadow banking will increase liquidity and reduce the cost of capital for banks.

5.3 Regulation and Regulatory Challenges

Regulation is the other arena showing tremendous differences between the US and China, not only in terms of tactical measures but also fundamental regulatory philosophies. The growth of the US shadow banking sector is attributable to deregulation in the financial sector during the 1980s to 1990s. The increasing size of China's shadow banking may be more related to its tightened regulation of the banking sector. The tightened credit controls, the raised bank reserve requirement ratios and interest rate controls all pushed savers to non-bank institutions and the underground lending market for higher yields. China is converging towards global banking standards by implementing Basel III.[84] However, China's attitude towards shadow banking diverges from other economies in that it tends not to completely deny the role of the shadow banking system channeling needed credit into the real economy. The PBOC pointed out that: "As mainland banks tend to favour lending to big state-owned clients with implicit government guarantees, [the central bank's targeted easing on banks' capital reserve fund] has failed to offer enough support to small- and medium-sized enterprises . . . The shadow banking system has become an important alternative channel to finance those restricted from normal bank loans".[85] Apparently, both the regulators and market players in China have been well aware of the benefits and importance of shadow banking, that is, its funding contribution to the real economy.

This pragmatic attitude is shaped by two "magnitudes". First, the magnitude of systemic risk embedded in the shadow banking sector has not yet been that severe. As the banking sector remains the key source of funding for business and the shadow banking sector involves less complicated structured products, the underlying assets are not closely interconnected. Therefore, systemic risk is less pressing and does not require a high level of regulatory attention. The second is related to the magnitude

---

[84] Bank for International Settlements, "Basel Committee on Banking Supervision", available 26 February 2016 at http://www.bis.org/bcbs/.

[85] Victoria Ruan, "China Central Bank Sees Role for Shadow Banking", South China Morning Post, 27 September 2014, available 26 February 2016 at http://www.scmp.com/business/economy/article/1601273/china-central-bank-sees-role-shadow-banking.

of the proportion of retail investors. China's shadow banking involves a high proportion of retail investors, which highlights a unique perspective of regulation. A credit default may cause social instability due to the involvement of a large number of retail investors at the grassroots level. A broader social concern to the PBOC and financial regulators is the slowing economy, which may create a damaging effect on some constituents in society. The social stabilization consideration has to be taken into account when financial regulation and policy are formulated. The shadow banking system has been viewed as the greatest risk in the financial system in the years to come.[86] Naturally, various subsectors in shadow banking have been on the financial regulators' radar. Apart from the regulatory philosophies, regulatory techniques employed by China have to be different from those adopted in other advanced economies. The IMF calls for the expansion of safe securitization in Europe to aid the credit transmission mechanism.[87] Such regulatory approach is of little relevance to China's financial market, in which neither securitization nor complex structured products are popular.

5.4 Official Definition of Shadow Banking: Rationale and Logic

Defining shadow banking in China is a challenging task. Participants in China's shadow banking sector include a wide range of non-bank market players such as trust companies, brokerage firms, microfinance firms and financial guarantee companies. Underground lending and some off-balance-sheet activities are also included. The rationale of including these into the scope of shadow banking is that these firms or activities involve regulatory arbitrage and systemic risk, which are two key concerns linked by the FSB to the shadow banking sector.[88]

The PBOC in 2013 made the first attempt to define shadow banking as follows: credit intermediation involving entities and activities outside the regular banking system, with the functions of liquidity and credit intermediation, which could potentially cause systemic risks or regulatory arbitrage.[89]

---

86 Xiao Gang, "The Biggest Risk is Shadow Banking in the Next Five Years", Everyday Economic News (in Chinese), 13 September 2012.

87 IMF, "Global Financial Stability Report", (2014), available 26 February 2016 at http://www.imf.org/external/pubs/ft/gfsr/2014/02/pdf/text.pdf.

88 FSB, "Shadow Banking: Scoping the Issues – A Background Note of the Financial Stability Board", p.3.

89 This is not an official definition but was a definition made by an official Sheng Songcheng of PBOC in a media conference on 15 January 2014, available

The State Council, China's cabinet, in 2013 issued the Circular of the General Office of the State Council on Relevant Issues of Strengthening the Regulation of Shadow banking (Circular No. 107), which indicated its preliminary but technical attempt to tackle the shadow banking sector. Circular No. 107, as the first legal or administrative document, set out an overarching regulatory framework for monitoring shadow banking in China. The Circular defines shadow banking as "credit intermediation entities and activities outside the traditional banking system". This definition is close to the one provided by the FSB discussed in Chapter 1.

Circular No. 107 took a functional approach in defining shadow banking. It classifies shadow banking into three categories, covering both traditional and shadow banks. The first category is credit intermediation entities that do not have financial licenses and that are completely unregulated, such as the so-called internet financing companies and third party wealth management entities. These shadow banks are not licensed or regulated financial businesses. The second category includes credit intermediation entities that do not have financial licenses and that are subject to an inadequate level of regulation, such as financing guarantee companies and petty loan companies. The third category includes those licensed financial institutions that have activities which are not adequately regulated such as money market funds, asset securitization and some types of wealth management products.

These three categories are divided according to their degree of institutionalization or intimacy with the traditional banking sector. The closer one category is to the traditional banking sector, the more likely it may fall into the existing regulatory space and entail documented banking rules and procedures. This definition is still quite broad, encompassing some forms of lending activities, which have not been widely recognized as shadow banking activities. Including local government financing vehicles and underground lending into shadow banking shows the regulators' anxiety about the accumulation of systemic risk and potential financial instability. Compared with other forms of shadow banking activities, underground (or informal) lending has the weakest tie with the formal banking sector, and is the least regulated subsector in shadow banking, albeit that there are some funding connections between underground lending and formal lending through letters of credit, short-term loans, discounted bills and group or residential mortgages.[90]

---

26 February 2016 at http://finance.people.com.cn/money/n/2014/0115/c42877-24126410.html.

[90] Bank of America Merrill Lynch, "Shadow Banking: Risky Business", (2012) Investment Strategy.

Circular No. 107's way of defining shadow banking or grouping shadow banking forms in China is also reflective of the level of benefits a particular shadow banking activity can contribute to the real economy. In this sense, these three categories can be placed in a spectrum ranging from credit disintermediation to credit intermediation. On the one extreme of the spectrum is the non-bank lenders, which can be categorized as the typical form of credit disintermediation without the involvement of traditional banks. The other extreme of the spectrum represents credit intermediation involving traditional banks but through off-balance sheet financing techniques. In the middle is something combining both credit intermediation and credit re-intermediation with a changing role of either a bank or a non-bank institution. This has been described as a credit enhancement layer of shadow banking[91] due to the fact that non-bank lenders channel additional funding to the borrowers which have no access to formal bank loans.

In essence, this triple-tiered framework involves a differentiated level and nature of risks. The credit intermediation process involves banks or traditional financial institutions. Therefore, systemic risk remains the key concern for this category of shadow banking. Banks' participation also determines that the regulatory instruments relied on by the regulators to address systemic risk in this section will be those regulatory tools widely used in banking regulation. The credit disintermediation does not involve traditional banks or financial institutions. Those lenders will encounter credit failure and credit risk. The disinterconnectedness among lenders may not lead to system-wide failure or collapse. In other words, systemic risk may not be the key concern for this category of shadow banking activities. Instead of bank-type regulatory instruments, resolutions or contract-based enforcement mechanisms may be more important than regulatory instruments for the purpose of containing credit risks and protecting creditors. The quasi-intermediated and institutionalized shadow banking sector presents some challenges to regulators partly because they are not heavily regulated like typical banks and in part due to the fact that they positively contribute to the private sector and small businesses. A sensible balance must be struck by the regulators between heavy regulation (in order to avoid systemic risk) and effective regulation (to ensure some benefits can still be channeled to the real economy). The

---

[91] Andrew Sheng, Christian Edelmann, Cliff Sheng and Jodie Hu, "Bringing Light Upon the Shadow: A Review of the Chinese Shadow Banking Sector", (2015) Hong Kong Oliver Wyman and Fung Global Institute Report, available 26 February 2016 at http://www.oliverwyman.com/content/dam/oliver-wyman/global/en/2015/feb/Bringing-Light-Upon-The-Shadow.pdf.

regulatory devices are licensing plus exclusion (or inclusion) rules. For instance, financing guarantee companies are only allowed to carry out licensed financing guarantee business. The banks are clearly excluded from the financing guarantee business for the issuance of bonds and negotiable instruments.[92]

Circular No. 107 outlined a regulatory framework, summarized in Table 2.1 below, corresponding to the sectoral regulatory model for regulating the financial market. It adopted a regulatory-based structure by dividing the regulatory space into three sections. Each regulatory authority has its own jurisdiction over a specific section. For instance, Circular No. 107 only briefly mentions that private equity funds are strictly prohibited from carrying on debt financing businesses.[93] This, however, is not the end of the story. The China Securities Regulatory Commission (CSRC), China's securities authority, is still relied on to supervise and regulate private investment funds, including the qualifications of the fund manager, the process of offering fund units, information disclosure requirements and the scope of financial products private equity funds can invest in. The market entry approval allows each regulator to regulate a group of shadow banks once they are incorporated.[94] Therefore, this three-tiered definition actually serves clear regulatory purposes with the aim of effectively containing risk and regulating shadow banks or shadow banking activities. Without this overarching regulatory framework outlined in Circular No. 107, monitoring shadow banking presents a challenge to the existing sectoral regulatory model. CBRC stated in its 2011 annual report that "[a]ccording to the definition by FSB, the supervision by the CBRC over non-bank financial institutions does not fall into the scope of shadow banking". This statement was technically correct in the sense that the CBRC has no jurisdiction over non-banks except trust companies. Circular No. 107 remedied this mismatch between shadow banking and the current financial regulatory framework. Consequently, shadow banking in China is also subject to a sectoral regulatory framework depending on the nature of shadow banks. For example, brokerage firms and insurance companies are regulated by the CSRC and CIRC respectively. Banks and trust companies are still regulated by the CBRC. While this regulatory framework maintains consistency with the one for formal financial market, it may leave some shadow banking activities or institutions unregulated. A

92 Circular No. 107, Article 3(6).
93 Circular No. 107, Article 3(8).
94 PRC Securities Investment Fund Law.

Table 2.1 Triple-tiered definition of shadow banking and key parameters

Tier	1	2	3
Layer	Unlicensed and unregulated financial operators	Entities operating without a finance license and under inadequate supervision by credit agencies	Inadequately supervised activities of licensed financial institutions
Coverage (major subsectors)	Underground lending, internet finance, P2P lending	Pawnshops, credit guarantee companies, microfinance companies	Money market funds, wealth management products, asset securitization
Intermediation	Disintermediation	Not typically involved in traditional credit intermediation; re-intermediation	Intermediation
Relationship with the bank	Distance from banks	Microfinance firms, which are regulated like banks	Banks or bank-type of financial institutions
Institutionalization	Least institutionalized	Quasi-institutionalized	Institutionalized
Economic benefits	Providing additional sources for funding	Existing funding channels	Formal funding channels
Potential risk	Credit risk, liquidity risk and market risk; less likely to see system-wide risk	Credit risk, liquidity risk, and market risk; possible systemic risk if the scale of lending through these shadow banks becomes large	Systemic risk
Licensing requirement for shadow banks	Unlicensed	Licensed	Licensed
Regulation	Private lending, based on contract and court enforcement for credit protection	Microfinance rules, subject to market entry rules and business scope rules	Subject to sector-based financial regulation including banking law and securities law, in particular, the financial safety net: prudential regulation, deposit insurance scheme and lender of last resort

large number of local government financing vehicles may have to be regulated differently.

Circular No. 107 applied a balanced approach to shadow banking reflecting the government's permissive stance. It recognizes both the benefits and risks of shadow banking. It is stated that the advent of shadow banking is the necessary product of financial development and financial innovation, and that as a beneficial supplement to the traditional banking system, it plays a positive role in serving the real economy and widening investment channels for businesses. On the other hand, it is also clearly recognized that shadow banking is vulnerable to systemic risk due to its complexity, uncertainty and contagiousness. For instance, Circular No. 107 is to limit off-balance sheet lending by banks and place non-bank institutions under closer scrutiny. The general tolerance showed in Circular No. 107 is to maximize the benefits shadow banking can bring to the financial sector and real economy.

Meanwhile, Circular No. 107 attempts to work out a structure to minimize the risks and negative effects the shadow banking activities may have on financial instability. It is clear that Circular No. 107's approach is to delegate regulatory responsibilities to multiple regulators based on the existing lines of financial sectors. The adherence to the traditional division of financial sectors is a clear-cut approach, matching the regulatory architecture for the traditional financial market. This regulatory arrangement may work by relying on the existing sectoral regulatory structure. Other benefits include continuity, efficiency and coherency, saving additional regulatory or switching costs for the change of existing regulatory model.

However, the defect of this regulatory or institutional build-up is clear in that the shadow banking sector is often cross-sectoral and a sectoral division may create regulatory arbitrage, overlap, inconsistency and even omission. Shadow banking involves innovative products and services which are hard to fit neatly into the typical sector or category. For instance, private investment funds[95] and financing guarantee business[96] are mentioned and regulated separately from other shadow banks which can be easily placed in existing financial sectors and regulatory spaces. Strengthening interagency cooperation is probably not sufficient to dealing with the structural fluidity or organic fragmentation in shadowing banking. This may explain why Circular No. 107 does not specify regulators for some shadow banking activities. The mismatch between the shadow banking market and shadow banking regulatory structure is likely

95 Circular No. 107, Article 3(6).
96 Circular No. 107, Article 3(8).

to affect the efficacy of regulation. In this sense, the less integrated regulatory framework outlined in Circular No. 107 is sub-optimal. As far as some cross-institution financial products are concerned, Circular No. 107 stresses contracts and contractual enforcement between the risk-bearing entity and the channel-providing entity, and the industry regulator's jurisdiction over the risk-bearing entity.[97]

It is worth noting that although Circular No. 107's regulatory framework is not optimal, it is consistent with the regulatory approach adopted by the FSB and the EU. The FSB in October 2011 made recommendations for regulation in relation to various aspects of shadow banking along with several key shadow banking sectors: banks' interactions with shadow banking entities; money market funds; shadow banking entities, securitization and securities lending and repos.[98] This sector-based framework can also be seen in the EU's Green Paper *Shadow Banking* (2012).[99]

Circular No. 107 tackles various perspectives of shadow banking. It addresses market failure by requiring banks to establish proper mechanisms for internal control, risk management and risk segregation. Banks are required to comply with the proportionality principle, that is, the business scale must be commensurate with risk-bearing capacity. At the firm level, senior management control is required to be put in place to correct agency failure.

Although Circular No. 107 represents a sound regulatory approach and constructive guidance to improving the regulation and monitoring of shadow banking, it is merely a policy document setting out broader legal, economic and policy considerations, with limited utility, clarity and details. The sectoral approach means that Circular No. 107 works only if separate financial regulators lay out their implementing rules later on. More importantly, the effectiveness of shadow banking regulation not only depends on the implementation by various financial regulators but also the re-balancing of China's economic structure as a whole. Regulators and policymakers must keep a close eye on the market so as to keep up with market developments.

---

97 Circular No. 107, Article 3(4).

98 FSB: "Shadow Banking: Strengthening Oversight and Regulation – Recommendations of the Financial Stability Board", 27 October 2011, available 26 February 2016 at http://www.financialstabilityboard.org/wp-content/uploads/r_111027a.pdf?page_moved=1.

99 European Commission, Green Paper *Shadow Banking*, 19 March 2012, available 26 February 2016 at http://ec.europa.eu/finance/bank/docs/shadow/green-paper_en.pdf.

3. Financial regulatory architecture: status quo

This chapter describes the current financial regulatory architecture in China, which is termed a one-bank-three-commission structure. "One bank" refers to the central bank, that is, the People's Bank of China, and the three commissions are the China Banking Regulatory Commission (CBRC), China Securities Regulatory Commission (CSRC), and China Insurance Regulatory Commission (CIRC), which are responsible for the banking, securities and insurance sectors respectively. In addition, the Ministry of Finance and the State Administration of Foreign Exchange play a supplementary role in the financial regulatory arena. This one-bank-three-commission architecture is indicated in Figure 3.1 below.

In parallel to this so-called sectorally-divided (also sectoral or functional) regulatory regime, there exists a Twin-Peak structure, mainly initiated by Australia, and a single (or sole) regulator model mainly practiced by the UK. There has been a large amount of literature, especially after the latest global financial crisis, discussing the pros and cons of these three models.[1] Recent preference of academics, regulators and policymakers

---

[1] For example, Eílis Ferran, "Examining the UK's Experience in Adopting the Single Financial Regulator Model", (2003) 28 *Brooking Journal of International Law* 257; Robin Hui Huang and Dirk Schoenmaker (eds), *Institutional Structure of Financial Regulation: Theories and International Experiences* (Oxford and New York: Routledge 2015); Don Brash, "Bank Governance: The Case of New Zealand", in James R. Barth, Chen Lin and Clas Wihlborg, *Research Handbook on International Banking and Governance* (Cheltenham, UK and Northampton, MA, USA: Edward Elgar 2012) pp.581–587; Ingo Walter, "Financial Architecture, Prudential Regulation and Organizational Structure", in Barth, Lin and Wihlborg, *Research Handbook on International Banking and Governance*, pp. 332–343; Thomas Oatley and W. Kindred Winecoff, "The Domestic Rooting of Financial Regulation in an Era of Global Capital Markets", in Phoebus Athanassiou, *Research Handbook on Hedge Funds, Private Equity and Alternative Investments* (Cheltenham, UK and Northampton, MA, USA: Edward Elgar 2012) pp.474–497; Christian A. Johnson, "Exigent and Unusual Circumstances: The Federal Reserve and the US Financial Crisis", in Kern Alexander and Niamh Moloney, *Law Reform and Financial Markets* (Cheltenham, UK and Northampton, MA, USA: Edward Elgar 2011) 269–305.

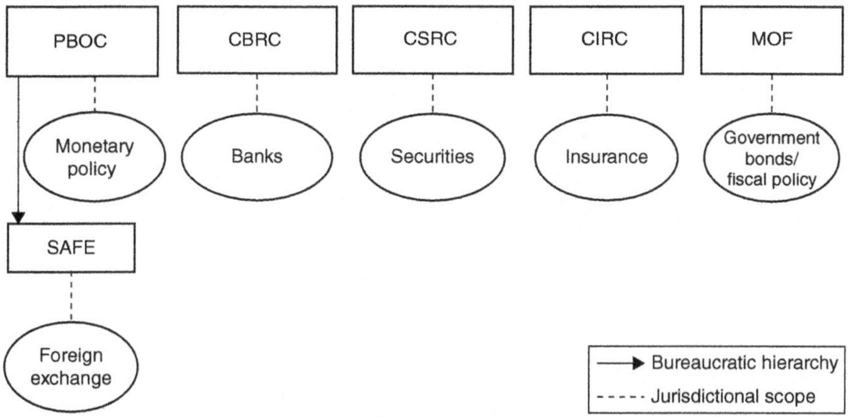

Figure 3.1 *China's financial regulatory architecture*

for the Twin-Peak model, has been indicated in the financial regulation circle.[2] It is beyond the scope of this book to comprehensively discuss and compare these three models. Nor is this chapter intended to claim the superiority of any of these three models. It is safe to say that the choice of national financial regulatory structure is largely driven by country-specific factors, and none of these regulatory models appeared to be solid enough to prevent the occurrence of a financial crisis completely. A comparison made in Table 3.1 below showing some key differences among these three regulatory models may be useful as background information.

This chapter is neither meant to be analytic nor exhaustive as a variety of institutional issues in relation to China's sectoral regulatory structure are discussed and scattered in various chapters throughout the book where such discussions are relevant to shadow banking. More historical background and theoretical arguments can be found elsewhere.[3] The purpose of this chapter is to give a quick outline of China's financial regulatory framework so that readers may obtain a certain level of familiarity to the structural and institutional issues relating to financial regulation, in particular, banking regulation. Together with the regulatory architecture

---

[2] Erlend Walter Nier, "Financial Stability Frameworks and the Role of Central Banks: Lessons from the Crisis", (2009) IMF Working Paper No. 09/70.

[3] For example, Shen Wei, *The Anatomy of China's Banking Sector and Regulation* (Hong Kong: Wolters Kluwer 2014); Wai Chung Lo, "A Retrospect on China's Banking Reform", in Hung-Gay Fung and Kevin H. Zhang (eds), *Financial Markets and Foreign Direct Investment in Greater China* (Armonk, NY and London: M.E. Sharpe 2002) pp.38–53.

Table 3.1 Comparison of three major financial regulatory models

Aspects	Single Regulator Model	Twin-Peak Model	Sectoral Model
Major countries	UK (used to be), Germany, Ireland, Switzerland, Japan, South Korea	Australia, the Netherlands, UK (moving towards this model)	US, China (large economies in terms of size)
Key feature	Unifying the responsibility for the regulation of banks, securities markets and insurance companies under one unified regulatory agency	• Prudential regulation and conduct regulation are assigned to two separate agencies • Regulatory agencies are arranged by types of regulation (objectives) rather than by the institutions that they regulate	Regulatory framework is organized along broadly sectoral lines
Regulator(s)	One regulator (apart from the central bank)	(At least) two regulators (apart from the central bank): • Australia has four key regulatory agencies with a single prudential regulator, a single conduct and disclosure regulator, a single competition regulator, and a single systemic stability regulator • The UK's new Twin-Peak model has two regulators, and makes the Prudential Regulation Authority a subsidiary of the Bank of England	Multiple regulators (apart from the central bank) in charge of banking, securities and insurance markets respectively

Suitability	It matches the market trend of financial supermarkets, which breaks down sectoral boundaries	The interaction between prudential regulation and the central bank's role as a lender of last resort of financial stability became more pressingly important post-crisis	It also matches the market trend of more sophisticated division of financial sectors
Efficiency	Efficiency (in terms of allocation of internal resources and compliance costs incurred to market players) and simplicity	• "Objective-based" model of regulatory structure with clear regulatory goals and targets • A sensible balance between two objectives: consumer protection and prudential regulation	• Less efficient as a whole due to complexity and a fragmented regulatory regime • Each regulator has its own focus • More efficient in one financial market/business line
Effectiveness	• A full regulatory "toolkit" • A more coherent and clearer mandate • Consistency in terms of enforcement • Avoid regulatory arbitrage	More responsive to the emergency of new financial markets and products that have changed the interconnections between financial intermediaries, and exposed them to systemic risks	• Allowing differentiated regulatory approaches to different financial markets • The lack of an integrated approach may create regulatory arbitrage • Involving additional coordination costs and transaction costs
Accountability	The agency cannot shift blame for regulatory failure	• Checks and balances with each other • Subject to political willingness or legislative design	• More likely to be pro-industry • Institutionally, it allows checks and balances
Potential benefits	• Achieving a fully integrated financial market • Easy resolution of conflicts between different regulatory objectives	• Clear division with clear objectives • Two agencies are equipped to deal with two aspects of financial markets	• Financial industry consolidation is over exaggerated, and a business line focused model makes sense • A clear role for the central bank to play

Table 3.1 (continued)

Aspects	Single Regulator Model	Twin-Peak Model	Sectoral Model
Potential drawbacks	• Loss of regulatory diversity due to excessive concentration of regulatory functions and powers • Oversimplification of regulation for major financial groups • Failure to apply a differentiated approach to different sectors • Concentration of captured power or vested interest	• Uncertainty over the exact role and responsibility of the agency charged with maintaining financial stability • Uncertainty over the interaction between the prudential regulatory authority and central bank • Uncertainties over the rationale of consolidating regulatory power into two agencies • Over-emphasis on banks and banking regulation but little emphasis on the macro-prudential dimension of financial markets • Conflicts between regulatory objectives in the boundary between macro and micro prudential regulation	• Easily creating regulatory arbitrage • Difficulty in coordinating multiple agencies which have different tasks and agenda • Possibly leaving a regulatory vacuum due to the fast development of financial markets and products • Likely underestimation of the importance of macro-prudential surveillance and crisis management

Source: Compiled by the author.

are macro-economic policies, which are discussed briefly at the end of this chapter.

1. PEOPLE'S BANK OF CHINA (PBOC)[4]

The People's Bank of China is China's central bank. Prior to 2003, it was not only a central bank but also a key regulator in the financial sector. The amended People's Bank of China Law refocuses and refines the role of the central bank after the establishment of the China Banking Regulatory Commission. For the time being, the PBOC's role is confined to setting and implementing monetary policy, preventing and resolving financial risk and maintaining financial stability. The Monetary Policy Committee of the PBOC has an important role in setting and adjusting macro-economic and monetary policy. The objective of monetary policy, as set forth in the law, is to maintain a stable value of renminbi and to promote economic growth.

The PBOC retains authority (somehow co-existent with that of the CBRC) to launch inspections and exercise supervision in respect of issues and transactions for which the PBOC remains responsible, for example, activities in the interbank funds market (which is managed by the PBOC); actions relating to foreign exchange handling regulations; actions relating to currency management regulations; actions relating to reserve deposit account regulations; money laundering; and so on. The PBOC also has the power to file criminal charges against persons engaged in or supporting currency counterfeiting.

Central banks in many countries are set up to help commercial banks survive financial panics as a last resort. The origins of the PBOC were different. For a long time after it was set up, PBOC was the sole lender of any kind, collecting the nation's funds and allocating the funds according to economic planning. Now, it is a national financial administrative organ and no longer a commercial lender.

Currently, the PBOC's key function is to formulate and implement monetary policy. Monetary policy refers to actions of a central bank that determine the size and rate of growth of the money supply, which affects interest rates. The 2003 PBOC Law states that the objectives of monetary policy are to maintain monetary stability, and in this way promote

---

[4] For an analytic discussion of the PBOC's role and function as well as a historical background, see Zhongfei Zhou, *Banking Law in China* (The Hague, London and Boston, Kluwer Law International 2007) Chs 1 and 2.

economic growth.[5] Part of PBOC's job is to maintain stability in the renminbi's exchange rate. At present, the PBOC targets a measure of bank credit, called M2, and instructs commercial banks about their lending practices. Other central banks play a less direct role by setting benchmark rates that offer a signpost to banks as they lend. In past decades, China's central banks ran well but banking practice has now become far too complicated.

Central banks are traditionally cursed with the responsibility for inflation, which is the most capricious of economic variables. The control of inflation is the PBOC's stated objective though it is termed in the language of "maintaining the stability of the value of the currency". Price stability is also an indicator used to measure monetary stability even though neither the central bank law nor the commercial law clarifies the meaning of "price stability". Inflation generally tends to be a self-fulfilling prophecy as an expectation of price rises will result in a demand for higher wages leading to higher prices, which means that other economic factors come into the picture simultaneously. The PBOC Law appears to suggest that monetary stability is a primary objective for monetary policy while economic growth is a secondary one, which is more closely connected to the governmental function of the central bank.

In contrast to its counterparts in other free market economies, the PBOC is more sensitive to deviations from its targets than to turbulence in the markets. The PBOC needs to take into account control of unemployment, economic growth and the balance of payments between trading states in formulating its monetary policy. The role of monetary policy has emerged as a key instrument for adjusting economic performance while central planning has become less important. Major mechanisms and monetary instruments used by the PBOC in pursuing its monetary policy goals include implementing a reserve requirement ratio, setting a central bank base interest rate, engaging in central bank lending and conducting open market operations as well as the use of other policy instruments specified by the State Council, China's cabinet. The responsibility for the formulation of monetary policy rests on the Monetary Policy Committee in the PBOC, which is vital to the macroeconomic management of the Chinese economy. The Monetary Policy Committee is only to play an advisory role but helpfully supports PBOC's role as implementer. The Committee is composed of PBOC's Governor, two Deputy Governors, a Deputy Secretary-General of the State Council, a Vice Minister of the State Development and Reform Commission, a Vice-Finance Minister,

[5] PBOC Law, Article 3.

the Administrator of the State Administration of Foreign Exchange, the Chairman of the CBRC, the Chairman of the CSRC, the Chairman of the CIRC, the Commissioner of National Bureau of Statistics, the President of the China Association of Banks and an expert from academia.

The PBOC is facing great challenges while the shadow banking sector is booming. Currently, non-bank financing has doubled since 2010 and occupies roughly 50% of total social financing. This suggests that the central bank is merely responsible for only about half of total lending in the country.

2. CHINA BANKING REGULATORY COMMISSION[6]

In April 2003, the Central Work Committee for Finance and the regulatory bodies of the PBOC combined to form a new watchdog, the CBRC with a mandate to oversee all banks and their activities in China, investigate illegal operations and punish offenders. Financial asset management companies managing systemic bad debts, trust and investment companies, finance companies and financial leasing companies are also subject to the authority of the CBRC. Currently, CBRC oversees more than 39,000 banks, financial institutions, trust companies and credit operations in China.

Being on the same administrative hierarchical level as the PBOC, the CBRC is a ministerial authority directly subordinate to the State Council and officially began its operation on 28 April 2003.[7] The main legal instrument creating the CBRC and bestowing it with its supervisory powers is the Law of the PRC on the Banking Regulation and Supervision 2003. Having assumed many of the functions previously exercised by the PBOC, the CBRC was established with a mandate to oversee the daily operation of all banks and financial institutions in China, investigate illegal operations and

---

[6] For a more detailed analytical discussion of CBRC's role and function, Yufeng Gong and Zhongfei Zhou, "Banking Regulatory Governance in China: A Legal Perspective", in Barth, Lin and Wihlborg, *Research Handbook on International Banking and Governance* pp.660–679; Zhongfei Zhou, "Banking Regulatory Law Reforms in China: A Long Way to Go Towards International Standards", in James R. Barth et al., *Financial Restructuring and Reform in Post-WTO China* (Alphen aan den Rijn: Kluwer Law International) pp.45–76; Nicholas Calcina Howson, "China's Restructured Commercial Banks: Nomenklatura Accountability Serving Corporate Governance Reform?", in Zhu Min, Cai Jinqing and Martha Avery (eds) *China's Emerging Financial Markets: Challenges and Global Impact* (Singapore: John Wiley & Sons 2009), pp.123–163.

[7] See CBRC website: www.cbrc.gov.cn.

punish offenders. Henceforth, banking market participants are required to mainly deal with the CBRC during business operations. The PBOC and the Ministry of Finance play minor roles in supervision.

CBRC describes its regulatory objectives on its website as follows:

- protecting the interests of depositors and consumers through prudential and effective supervision;
- maintaining market confidence through prudential and effective supervision;
- enhancing public knowledge of modern finance though customer education and information disclosure; and
- combating financial crimes.

Unlike the PBOC, the CBRC is not a central bank and its objective cannot be measured in the form of an explicit inflation target. Rather, the CBRC's regulatory multiple and non-operational objectives are hard to measure. The above objectives make CBRC more accountable to the general public.

On its website, CBRC indicates its regulatory standards, which include:

- simultaneously promoting financial stability and facilitating financial innovation;
- enhancing the competitive force of the country's financial industry in the international financial services;
- setting appropriate regulatory limitations and reduce unnecessary restraints;
- encouraging fair and orderly competition;
- establishing accountability of the regulators and regulatees; and
- using its regulatory resources in an efficient and economic manner.

These standards are, as a matter of fact, very close to those stipulated in the UK's Financial Services and Markets Act 2000.[8]

According to the Law of the PRC on Banking Regulation and Supervision which came into effect on 1 February 2004, the CBRC is equipped with a rule-making power. It can formulate and issue rules in relation to the regulation and supervision of banks and their businesses. The CBRC has the power to formulate prudential rules on banking operations by which banks must abide.

The CBRC is also responsible for supervision of asset management companies managing systemic bad debts, trust and investment companies,

---

[8] UK Financial Services and Markets Act 2000, Part 1, section 2(3).

finance companies, financial leasing companies and other deposit-taking financial institutions.

CBRC' s major responsibilities are to:

- formulate supervisory rules and regulations for banking institutions and banking activities;
- approve the establishment, changes, termination and business scope of banking institutions and their branches;
- vet banks' capital increases as well as identities and sources of funds of investors;
- approve all banking products;
- examine the qualifications of directors and senior managers of banking institutions;
- conduct off-site and on-site surveillance of banking institutions and penalise violations of banking law and regulations;
- compile and publish statistics and reports on the whole banking sector in accordance with relevant regulations;
- make proposals on the resolution of the risks of deposit-taking institutions in consultation with relevant authorities;
- administer the supervisory boards of state-owned financial institutions;
- enact prudent operating procedures and standards relating to risk management, internal controls, capital adequacy, asset quality, loss provisions, risk concentration, related party transactions and asset liquidity;
- systematically monitor the activities and risks of banking institutions;
- together with the PBOC and the Ministry of Finance (MOF), establish a sudden incident resolution system, designate persons, and agencies and related operating procedures; and
- perform other responsibilities delegated by the State Council.

According to the Implementing Rules for the Regulations on the Administration of Foreign Financial Institutions, amended in July 2004, the CBRC can take special supervisory measures against a foreign bank that does not satisfy the requirements for unallocated profits, exposures on large customers and fund flows.[9] These supervisory measures can be taken in the following circumstances:

- for a foreign bank branch, the sum of its unallocated profits and net losses and profits of the current year becomes negative, and the sum

---

[9] Implementing Rules for Foreign Banks, Article 95.

of the absolute value of the negative and the deficiencies in loan loss provisioning exceeds 30% of its operating fund;
- the balance of credit-granting by a foreign bank to all large customers, which are defined as customers whose balance of credit granting from a foreign bank exceeds 10% of the bank's capital or operating fund, exceeds eight times the bank's capital or operating fund;
- for a foreign bank, the cumulative amount of the funds flowing out of China exceeds the fund flowing into China in a month; or
- other imprudent operations.

The special supervisory measures include:[10]

- a verbal warning;
- submission of a written report;
- restrictions of fund outflows on businesses;
- provision of a guarantee letter;
- special requirements for risk management;
- supplementation of capital or operating fund;
- accreditation of special supervisors for a violating bank;
- senior management change within a specified period; and
- other prudential supervisory measures.

The CBRC exerts its supervisory powers in a wider range of areas than PBOC, covering business scope, capital adequacy, credit plan administration ratios, the assets or liabilities ratio, risk management, asset quality, internal control and liquidity levels. For instance, a role previously played by PBOC and now discharged by CBRC is the authorisation of new banking institutions' establishment as well as any changes or termination of the business scope of banking institutions. CBRC's enforcement powers include business suspension for rectification, withdrawal of business licence, imposition of fine and administrative penalty, prohibition on employment in banks, confiscation of illegal gains and others. The law also gives the CBRC unambiguous enforcement powers and specifies a long list of infractions and non-compliance for which penalties, administrative punishments, and referral to criminal justice authorities can be meted out.

CBRC has even wider powers to prevent the directors and senior management in direct charge from leaving China, to apply to the courts to prohibit the directors and managers from diverting or transferring their

10 Ibid, Article 96.

property or creating other rights on their property, when a credit-crisis-hit bank is in the process of being restructured.[11] The CBRC has recently issued a set of guidelines stating that banks' major shareholders should not prevent any move to raise capital, in particular, social funding, even though the CBRC does not have the authority to tell shareholders what to do. This notice was directed more towards smaller banks and could present an opportunity for private enterprises, as major shareholders of smaller banks are local governments.[12] The guidelines also provide that shareholders should allow banks to cut or suspend dividend payments if they are unable to raise capital levels to meet the minimum requirement. The rules would mainly apply to shareholders who control more than 5% of shares or voting rights and those that can exert "major influence" on the banks' decisions.[13] The guidelines indicate the extensive scope of the CBRC's authority.

According to the PRC Law on Commercial Banks, the CBRC has the power to conduct examinations at any time against a bank's deposits, loans, settlements and non-performing loans.[14] CBRC is equipped with the following supervisory measures when it conducts on-site examinations:

- to enter the location of a bank to conduct an examination;
- to enquire with bank staff, and require the staff to provide explanations on examined matters;
- to have full access to, and make copies of, a bank's documents and materials related to on-site examination, and to seal documents and materials that are likely to be removed, concealed or destroyed; and
- to examine a bank's information technology infrastructure for business operations and management.

The CBRC conducts on-site examinations and off-site surveillance of banking institutions. The CBRC is required to have approval from the responsible person in the CBRC in order to conduct on-site examinations. An on-site examination requires at least two examiners bringing legal identification and the examination notice for the site. It is not clear whether the CBRC can rely on external professionals such as auditors, accountants and lawyers for the purpose of on-site examinations.

---

11 Bank Supervision Law, Article 40.

12 Lulu Chen, "Regulator Clears Bids to Raise Capital", 27 July 2011, *South China Morning Post*, B3.

13 Ibid.

14 Law on Commercial Banks, Article 62.

However, a bank may be required to present its auditing reports to CBRC in the on-site examination.[15]

CBRC can conduct off-site examination of a bank's business activities and risk profiles, establish an information system for supervision of a bank and analyse and assess a bank's risk levels. Off-site examinations rely on the data that banks submit in their supervisory reports and on the information required by supervisors. A bank may also be required to submit a balance sheet, income statements and other financial reports.[16] Supervisors can check a bank's adherence to prudential requirements through reviewing and analysing these reports.

CBRC decides the frequency and scope of on-site examinations and measures to be taken based on the bank rating system and risk warning system according to the rating assigned and the risk level of a bank.

The CBRC can also take enforcement actions against non-compliant enterprises. In addition, CBRC conducts tests on the senior managerial personnel of the banking institutions to ensure they are fit and proper persons to hold senior managerial positions. CBRC compiles and publishes statistics and reports of the overall banking sector in promoting transparency. The CBRC is also responsible for the administration of the supervisory boards of the major state-owned banking institutions.

It is the CBRC's duty to ensure that financial institutions' business operations are in line with Chinese laws, regulations and policies. The CBRC does not necessarily grant approval to Chinese banks, even the Big Four or policy banks. For instance, it declined to allow Chinese lenders to extend rescue finance to Citigroup, a US bank, during the financial crisis in 2009. Given China's growing foreign currency reserves, the CBRC is now more anxious to encourage offshore investments to offset these capital inflows.[17] More recently, the CBRC has banned commercial lenders from rolling over or renewing credit to local government financing vehicles and ordered tighter monitoring of loans to the property sector. In addition, local financing vehicles are prohibited from moving loans off their balance sheets via trust firms, wealth management services or bill financing.[18]

The CBRC has powers to order banks to reform, alter or cease specific operations. The CBRC is empowered to enter financial institutions in order to conduct examinations, review materials and ask questions. It

---

[15] Law on Commercial Banks, Article 56.

[16] Law on Commercial Banks, Articles 55 and 61.

[17] Henny Sender, "CDB Seeks to Join TPG Stake Purchase", *Financial Times*, 23 May 2011, p.1.

[18] Fulton Mak, "Regulator Bans Rollover of Local Government Debt", *Hong Kong Economic Journal*, 28 July 2011, p.1.

has the authority to inspect the quality of management and supervisory practices and loans, investment and leasing operations of financial institutions. If violation(s) of laws, regulations and policies is detected, the CBRC can issue a warning and order the offending institution to rectify the violation immediately. In some serious cases, the CBRC can inspect the bank accounts of banks and/or persons suspected of violation of laws and regulations, stop operations and apply to the courts to freeze the assets and bank accounts of the banks and persons suspected of diverting or concealing illegal funds. If necessary, CBRC can revoke the finance permit of the financial institution. In addition, the law gives the CBRC unambiguous enforcement powers and specifies a long list of infractions and non-compliance for which penalties, administrative punishments and referral to the criminal justice authorities can be meted out.

The CBRC is also the authority in charge of implementing Basel III for Chinese banks. Basel III is the world's regulatory response to the latest financial crisis, forcing banks to triple the amount of basic capital they hold in a bid to avoid future taxpayer bail outs. Basel III norms are important for sound and competitive banks world-wide. Amidst a delay to implement Basel III in the US[19] and a possible trend whereby Europe tightened a regulatory noose around its banks,[20] the CBRC proposed strict rules on the new capital:asset ratio requirement for banks and the plan requiring all banks to comply by July 2012. Under the new rules, all banks should maintain a minimum CAR of 10.5% by the end of 2016, and large banks should have had a CAR of at least 11.5% by the end of 2013.[21] The deadline for implementing these rules was postponed so as to give lenders more time to better equip themselves. Chinese banks have been a source of concern following a RMB 18 trillion lending spree between 2009 and 2010. Fearing a wave of bad loans, the CBRC has pushed Chinese banks to replenish capital. According to the newly-passed Commercial Banks' Capital Regulations (Trial), issued on 8 June 2012, the core capital ratio – a measure of a bank's core capital including stock and cash reserves – for mid-size banks to 8.4% from the current 4%. In addition, Chinese banks will be motivated to obtain better quality credit and extend more lending

---

19 The Basel III rules are meant to be phased in from January but US regulators cast doubt on the time frame due to a flood of industry comments on the proposals. It is worth noting that there is no worldwide agreement on the implementation of Basel III rules.

20 Reuters in Gubbio, Italy, "European Banks Call on EU to Stall Basel III Rules for a Year", *South China Morning Post*, 26 November 2012 (online).

21 As a matter of fact, various Basel III norms come into force gradually up until 2019.

to SMEs as the Chinese version of Basel III lowers the risk weighting assigned to SME loans in calculating banks' capital ratios.[22]

3. CHINA SECURITIES REGULATORY COMMISSION[23]

At the initial stage, the regulatory authority over the stock market was dispersed among a variety of ministries and commissions at the central government level. A dual regulatory regime evolved. The Securities Policy Committee was the national authority in charge of formulating securities policy on a unified basis while the CSRC, which was established by the State Council in 1992, exercised specific regulatory functions. The Securities Policy Committee was subsequently made a part of the CSRC.

For a long time, the two stock exchanges, the Shanghai Stock Exchange and the Shenzhen Stock Exchange, were under the supervision of their local municipal governments, and the issuing and trading rules were set by the municipal governments with the approval of the PBOC.[24] The PBOC and other ministries issued a large number of rules on the issuing and trading of shares. The national regulatory body was established in October 1992, when the State Council established the CSRC and the Securities Commission, which was the national authority in charge of formulating securities policy on a unified basis and was subsequently made a part of the CSRC. Thereafter, the stock exchanges were under the administration of the local governments while being supervised by the CSRC.[25] This dual-regulatory model was further confirmed in the Interim Measures of Administration of Stock Exchanges in July 1993.

---

22 Simon Rabinovitch, "Beijing Puts Back Date for Enforcing Basel III," *Financial Times*, 7 June 2012, available 26 February 2016 at http://www.ftchinese.com/story/001044938/en/?print=y.

23 For a background discussion of CSRC and China's securities market, Wan Meng, "The Securities System in China", in Joseph J. Norton, C.J. Li and Yangxin Huang, *Financial Regulation in the Greater China Area: Mainland China, Taiwan and Hong Kong SAR* (The Hague, London and Boston, Kluwer Law International 2000) pp.69–156; William B. Gamble, *Investing in China: Legal, Financial and Regulatory Risk* (Westport, CT & London: Quorum Books 2002) Ch 5; Nicholas Calcina Howson, "China and WTO Liberalization of the Securities Industry: Le Choc des mondes or L'Empire immobile?", (2007) 3 *Asia Policy* 151–158.

24 Shenzhen Interim Measures for Share Issue and Trading 1991.

25 State Council, Circular on Further Strengthening Macro-Administration of Securities Markets, December 1992.

The CSRC became the sole regulator of the securities market in charge of approving and supervising the securities listing and trading in late 1997.[26] However, it was not regarded as an administrative agency until 1998 when the Securities Law 1998 came into effect and made the CSRC the sole regulator of the securities market. Thereafter, the CSRC rules were made administrative rules.

In 1998, the CSRC took over regulatory powers over the mainland securities market from the Securities Commission. Nevertheless, other ministries and commissions of the State Council may still exert varying levels of influence over a company's business operation and management. Each ministry or commission may set its own rules regulating one or more aspects of the securities market. For instance, supervision and control of market intermediaries such as securities companies, fund management companies, financial asset management companies, and trust investment companies has now been divided amongst the CSRC, the CBRC, and the CIRC. Although relevant ministries and commissions may also issue joint decrees,[27] there is no effective coordination mechanism amongst these authorities. Local government may also be involved in the share issuance and trading if the listed company is transformed from a state-owned enterprise (SOE). The very existence of multiple regulators does not necessarily improve the regulatory regime. Rather it may increase the transactional costs and harm efficiency of the securities market as different authorities may have different policy concerns, regulatory focus, legislative agenda and monitoring tools.

The principal regulatory authority regulating securities in China is now the CSRC with the support of the self-regulatory stock exchanges and securities industry association. The day-to-day supervision and regulation of the securities market is delegated to the CSRC. The CSRC is empowered to supervise and administer participants in the securities industry including securities issuers, listed companies, securities exchanges, securities companies, securities registration and settlement institutions, securities investment funds management institutions, securities investment consultancy institutions, credit rating institutions and professionals.

The Securities Law expressly confirms the CSRC's status of a centralized independent governing body. The functions of the CSRC include:

---

[26] In the primary market, the Ministry of Finance, People's Bank of China and CSRC maintain the power to approve the issuing of state bonds, financial bonds and enterprise bonds respectively.

[27] The central government issued the Memorandum of Understanding on Division of Responsibilities and Cooperation in Financial Supervision and Regulation among the CBRC, CSRC and CIRC in late 2003.

- formulating laws and regulations in relation to the securities industry and exercise of the approval powers under the laws and regulations;
- supervising and administering the issuance, trading, registration, custody and settlement of securities;
- supervising and administering participants in the industry including securities issuers, listed companies, securities exchanges, securities companies, securities registration and settlement institutions, securities investment funds management organizations, securities investment consultancy institutions, securities depository and clearing institutions, securities service institutions,[28] credit rating institutions, and professionals;
- formulating qualifications and codes of conduct for securities professionals;
- supervising the proper disclosure of information on securities issuance and transactions;
- supervising the conduct of the Securities Trade Association; and
- investigating any conduct that violates laws and administrative regulations.

It is clear that the CSRC has the dual power of overseeing and managing the securities market and of standardizing existing law and regulations on a uniform and centralized basis. This centralization movement suggests that local and municipal governments have been removed from the law-making or IPO approval and selection process.

CSRC is granted broad investigatory powers to take the following actions:

- entering premises where illegal acts have been committed to investigate and to obtain evidence;
- questioning people and entities involved in illegal acts and requiring them to make statements;
- checking and duplicating records of securities transactions, financial accounts and other relevant documents and sealing up and retaining documents and materials that may be removed or concealed;
- checking funds accounts and securities accounts of people involved in illegal acts and applying to judicial institutions to freeze or to grant "injunctions" where there is evidence that funds and securities, the subject matter of illegal acts, may be transferred or hidden.

---

[28] Securities Law 2006, Articles 122, 155, 169 and 179.

The Securities Law has apparently expanded the scope and nature of the securities coming under the CSRC's regulations, and granted more significant powers for the CSRC to exercise. The CSRC is now able to conduct on-the-spot investigations, including the power to freeze the accounts under investigation without an order from a judicial organ.[29] Nevertheless, in reality, the CSRC may have to coordinate with various authorities at different levels throughout China. In most cases, the CSRC must share regulatory authority over any potential listed company with both local authorities where the company is based and the ministry or commission in charge of the industrial sector in which the company operates. This indicates that the CSRC does lack the capacity to investigate and oversee all the aspects of the listed company's business operation, financial management and regulatory compliance.

The Securities Law also spells out a number of offences and penalties which the CSRC may impose (in conjunction with the exchanges and local authorities) on the relevant parties.[30] One commonly used sanction is to publish criticism, issued by the stock exchange on which the company is listed, against the company and/or any party found guilty of acts or omissions affecting the company's shares. Public criticism may be used together with the imposition of penalty such as a fine or other administrative penalty. The CSRC can also place the relevant company or person under judicial investigation. A company may be delisted and a professional's licence to operate in securities-related areas in the event of severe violations of law. Criminal actions have been more often used by the CSRC for combating securities market malfeasance, which may help strengthen the CSRC's enforcement.

The CSRC is granted broad investigatory powers to enter premises where illegal acts are suspected to have been committed to investigate and obtain evidence, to question people, units and individuals involved in illegal acts, to check and duplicate records of securities transactions, financial accounts and other relevant documents and seal up and retain documents and materials, to check funds accounts and securities accounts of people suspected of being involved in illegal acts and apply to judicial institutions to freeze or to grant "injunctions" where there is evidence that funds and securities, the subject matter of illegal acts which may be transferred or hidden.

---

29 Securities Law 2005, Article 180(6).

30 Securities Law 2005, Part Eleven.

4. CHINA INSURANCE REGULATORY COMMISSION[31]

In 1979, China resumed its insurance business in the domestic market. The PBOC took the responsibility of supervising the insurance industry. While the Finance Administration Department of the PBOC was in charge of supervising domestic insurers, the Bureau of Foreign Affairs of the PBOC focused on the supervision of foreign insurers. In 1995, the PBOC set up a dedicated department, the Insurance Department, to supervise domestic insurers. Meanwhile, a new department, the Foreign Financial Institutions Department was separated from the Foreign Affairs Department under the PBOC, and was responsible for the regulation of foreign insurers in China. In November 1998, the State Council set up the CIRC as the sole regulator of China's insurance market.

CIRC supervises and manages the insurance market and maintains the legal and stable operation of insurance operations in China in accordance with relevant laws, rules and regulations. CIRC is accountable to the State Council, and is a member of the International Association of Insurance Supervisors.

According to the PRC Insurance Law, promulgated on 28 October 2002 and effective as of 1 January 2003, CIRC is authorized to conduct the following activities:

- establish a complete system of benchmark indices for the monitoring of the solvency of insurance companies, and implementing monitoring and control of the minimum solvency of insurance companies;
- inspect circumstances pertaining to an insurance company's business, financial and funds utilization circumstances, and require insurance companies to submit relevant written reports and information written within specific time limits;
- inquire about the deposits of insurance companies within financial institutions;
- order the insurance company to rectify the situation within a specified time limit if it fails to allocate or carry over funds to various reserve portfolios or handle reinsurance in accordance with the laws; and

---

[31] For a background discussion of China's insurance market and CIRC, see Linbo Fan, "The Insurance Market System" in Norton, Li and Huang, *Financial Regulation in the Greater China Area: Mainland China, Taiwan and Hong Kong SAR* pp.157–193.

- undertake the direct takeover of any insurance company violating the law in a manner as to cause damage to the public interest or as is likely to imperil or has imperiled the solvency of the company.

In the case of any insurance company violating the law, the CIRC has the authority to:

- issue a warning;
- order the replacement of responsible personnel;
- impose fines;
- order rectification;
- restrict the scope of business;
- confiscate any illegal income;
- order cessation of the acceptance of new business; and
- revoke the permit for insurance business operations.

5. MINISTRY OF FINANCE

The major function of the Ministry of Finance (MOF) is to control state revenue and expenditure. Its role has overlapped somewhat with that of the PBOC, originally set up under the authority of MOF.

After the reshuffling of its functions in 1998, the MOF is now responsible for:

- drafting strategies, policies, plans, reforms and management methods for finance, taxation, state capital funds and domestic and foreign debts, helping formulate macroeconomic policies, drafting distribution policies for central and local governments and for the state and enterprises;
- drafting rules for managing the financial affairs of public finance and state capital funds, organizing international negotiations over finance and debts and signing related agreements;
- composing the annual central budget and final account plans, controlling central financial receipts, special accounts and extra-budgetary funds, and managing related Government funds;
- helping draft tax laws and regulations, planning fiscal revenue, joining international talks on foreign taxation and tariffs, and performing the daily work on the Tariff Rules Committee;
- controlling public spending of central finances, drafting Government procurement policies, controlling the non-trade foreign exchange of

Government bodies and social groups, and balancing international payments covered by the budget;
- controlling social security spending from central finance, drafting the financial management system for social security funds, and supervising the use of those funds;
- planning the issue of state treasury bonds, and representing the Chinese Government in international financial organizations;
- implementing accounting regulations created by enterprise and Government bodies, the central budget, directing auditing, and approving the domestic establishment of the offices of foreign accounting firms; and
- implementing policies, law and regulations concerning finance and fiscal revenue.

The MOF is tasked to sustain economic growth. It often pursues an active fiscal policy to stimulate domestic consumption and investment through government spending on infrastructure construction and technological upgrading in some key state-owned enterprises. Since 1998, the Chinese Government, through the MOF, has issued a total of RMB 660 billion of long term state treasury bonds. In addition, the MOF has grappled with a growing budget deficit through introducing new taxes, such as value-added tax, social security tax, environmental tax and the new tax on savings interest.

6. STATE ADMINISTRATION OF FOREIGN EXCHANGE[32]

Foreign exchange is still controlled in China. The State Administration of Foreign Exchange (SAIF) has a final say on any financial business relating to foreign exchange. All foreign-invested financial institutions, like all foreign-invested enterprises in China, are required to register with the SAIF for a Foreign Exchange Business Operation Licence within 30 days of completing the business registration procedure and receiving the business licence from the State Administration of Industry and Commerce (SAIC).[33]

---

[32] More relevant discussions are available in Chapter 11.

[33] These requirements are stated in Article 21 of the Administration of Financial Institutions Provisions promulgated by the PBOC on 9 August 1994 and the Administration of Foreign Exchange for Foreign Investment Enterprises Tentative Procedures of 1996.

7. REGULATORY AND MACROECONOMIC POLICIES

Chinese banking regulatory policies often change along with the macroeconomic policies. For instance, the CBRC initially wanted Chinese banks to achieve higher capital requirements in a shorter timeline than their global counterparts. However, given the slower economic growth in China, CBRC has softened its stance on Basel III by trimming banks' required reserves.[34] It has been reported that Chinese banks had granted 18 trillion yuan of credit in a lending spree in 2009 and 2010 to support an infrastructure-focused stimulus package from the government.[35] However, the level of new loans was surprisingly low in early 2012, with 738.1 billion yuan in new bank loans in January 2012, well below market expectations.[36] The Big Four banks' new loans totaled 101.7 billion yuan as of 25 April 2012, which only increased 700 billion, a sharp drop from 1.01 trillion yuan loans among all Chinese banks in March 2012.[37] Chinese banks' lending further tumbled due to weaker investment and slow economic growth. Presently, large SOEs suffer from weak demand in the marketplace while the small- and medium-sized enterprises have been unable to access bank loans and have been squeezed out of the lending market due to increasing borrowing costs, which in turn causes a deterioration in the real economy.

These factors have caused (i) more banks' reserve requirement ratio cuts by the central bank; and (ii) endless fresh financing demands, and in turn pushed a wave of fundraising by mainland banks such as Industrial Bank, China Minsheng Banking, China Merchants Bank, Bank of Beijing and Shenzhen Development Bank.[38] It has been anticipated that the PBOC would be likely to lower the level of reserves it requires Chinese lenders to maintain by several rounds in 2012 after the central bank lowered the reserve requirement ratio by half a percentage point to 20.5% for larger banks and 18.5% for smaller banks in mid-February 2012. The lower reserve requirement was said to release an estimated 400 billion yuan in

---

[34] Simon Rabinovitch and Paul J. Davies, "BoComm Beefs Up Capital by $9bn", *Financial Times*, 16 March 2012, p.16.

[35] Daniel Ren, "Bocom Share Offer Seeks 56b Yuan," *South China Morning Post*, 16 March 2012, B1.

[36] Reuters, "Lending Falls Far Short of Forecasts," *South China Morning Post*, 11 February 2012, B1.

[37] Lulu Chen, "Mainland Bank Lending Down Sharply in April," *South China Morning Post*, 3 May 2012, B3.

[38] Ren, "Bocom Share Offer Seeks 56b Yuan".

additional lending supply.[39] The underlying rationale of further monetary easing was to strike a balance between the mainland's economic growth and consumer price inflation. Part of the financing scheme is that CBRC has been in an attempt to use its open-market operations to inject more cash in the economy and reduce banks' funding costs.

Chinese banks are now also under pressure to attract more customers and squeeze more profitability. The pressure was less obvious with credit in short supply throughout 2011 since banks can price both traditional loans and wealth management products above benchmark rates. In such an easy monetary environment, competition for credit is also reduced. However, commercialization of Chinese banks along with tight monetary policies has resulted in more competition among commercial banks for more available funds and more attractive interest rates.[40] China's recent slowing economy has forced regulators to allow more competition in the banking sector by slowing liberalizing interest margins. Even so, that has only lead to a one-fifth rise in the earnings yields. Three of the Big Four banks showed their fairly resilient interest margins in their reported results for the third quarter in 2012.[41] Analysts had worried that a move to let banks compete more on deposit rates would cut into their net interest margins which, however, only account for about two-thirds of their profits. In reality, that effect has not materialized. In their recent third quarter financials, the Big Four banks only reported that their interest income was up 2–5% from the second quarter in 2012.[42] Large banks such as ICBC may rely on huge branch networks and close connections with large state-owned enterprises, both of which can help these banks to collect deposits. Medium- or small-sized banks may have to rely on wealth-management businesses to attract assets. The flexibility of offering more wealth management products further assists these banks to offset the higher cost of funds as medium- or small-sized borrowers are willing to pay higher interest rates for funding.

By offering interest rates that exceed the benchmark deposit[43] rate and

---

39 Denise Tsang, "Beijing Tipped to Further Ease Monetary Policy", *South China Morning Post*, 22 February 2012, B2.

40 Low interest rates provide an artificial subsidy to financial institutions so that they can borrow less expensively and then invest in higher yielding safe assets such as government bonds and property market.

41 "Chinese Banks – Business As Usual" *Financial Times*, 29 October 2012 (online).

42 Simon Rabinovitch, "Chinese Banks Face Scrutiny over Profits" *Financial Times*, 31 October 2012 (online).

43 Low rates do not necessarily increase the supply of credit. Risk aversion and higher returns on capital would encourage banks to eschew loans so that they can

providing more wealth-management products, Chinese banks can secure more funds which, however, may accumulate risks in the financial system. Most wealth-management products offer investors a yield above regulated deposit rates. In this sense, wealth management products are effectively an instrument to liberalize interest rates which are heavily regulated in China. Investors are actually channeled through off-balance-sheet vehicles to directly participate in loans while the bank can get a portion of fees for arranging the deal. Essentially, the structure of wealth management products is close to that of commercial-paper conduits or structured investment vehicles, which have been more popular in the US. The wealth management products are gaining more popularity now. For instance, wealth management products were equivalent to 10% of bank deposits in the third quarter of 2012, an increase from 7% at the end of 2010.[44] These figures suggest that funds are searching out a path for higher returns. The danger of this change is that more funds are actually leaving the "normal" financial system without monitoring. Hence, the popularity of the off-balance-sheet wealth management products is likely to erode the mainstay of profitability for traditional Chinese banks. More importantly, these products allow leverage to build unseen risks within the financial system and may trigger a financial crisis in the end because the banks may have to step in to bear all the losses and risks if the investors refuse to take in the inherent risks surrounding these products.

The choices of China's monetary policies are also influenced by other factors such as Renminbi appreciation, the fight against domestic inflation, a boost for foreign trade and the domestic economy. While Renminbi may continue to appreciate over the long term, the pace may vary subject to international political pressure, which is often tightened or loosened according to a raft of important political events such as a G20 summit, a US Treasury report on international exchange rates and US elections. The pace of Reminbi's appreciation must also be balanced with the objective of boosting China's export sector and national economy. Apart from foreign pressure, the other compelling reason that China would allow Renminbi to gradually appreciate is domestic inflation – rising inflationary level and asset bubbles. In response, China raised interest rates starting from October 2011 following its huge stimulus package and a strong rebound in growth. China is now more cautious in stimulating its slowing economies

---

put more money in government securities or property market. This is also the case in the US where banks are holding more cash and government securities than the outstanding volume of commercial and industrial loans.

[44] Tom Orlik, "Margin Call for Chinese Banks", *The Wall Street Journal*, 1 February 2012, p.28.

than in 2008, when lower inflation allowed it to unleash waves of fiscal spending and monetary easing to power the recovery. A large scale fiscal stimulus program does not seem to be on the agenda. Rather, a combination of tax cuts, support for smaller firms and increase of lending may be in the pipeline.

The PBOC's record of adjusting its monetary policy in 2006 and 2007 suggested that Renminbi appreciation would be more significant when monetary policy is tightened up. Renminbi rose 1.5% against the dollar in the second quarter of 2007, 1.3% in the third quarter of 2007, 2.8% in the fourth quarter of 2007 and 4.2% in the first quarter of 2008.[45] Renminbi appreciation has also occurred hand-in-hand with a policy of hiking the reserve ratio requirement. When Renminbi appreciated in 2008, China's reserve requirement ratio also peaked.[46] In sum, the PBOC used a combination of rate hikes, reserve requirement hikes and currency appreciation to combat rising price pressures and serve multiple economic purposes. To wrestle the economy back on to the right track, since October 2010, the central bank has raised interest rates five times and increased reserve requirements nine times. Meanwhile, it ordered banks to cap their lending below mandatory ceilings.[47]

China's banking sector has been undergoing continuous and dramatic changes as part of China's transition from a planned economy to a 'socialist market economy'. Substantial progress has been made in transforming China's banking sector during the past three decades. Banking institutions have been diversified and have made great progress towards commercialization and marketization, and, along with China's accession to the WTO in 2001, the banking market has been gradually further opened up to foreign investment. Although Chinese banks have performed better than their counterparts in Western countries in the wake of the financial crisis, they have their own path-dependent problems, which have made their high growth and attraction increasingly hard to sustain. As a matter of fact, Chinese banks are more like "fragile giants".[48]

China's banking sector, and its financial sector as a whole, is at a crossroads. The recent market developments seemed to suggest that Chinese

---

[45] Robert Cookson and Peter Garnham, "Inflation May Play Lead Role in Renminbi Appreciation," *Financial Times*, 26 October 2010, p.22.

[46] Anousha Sakoui, "Pressure Mounting on China's Currency," *Financial Times* – Investing in Foreign Exchange, 12 April 2010, p.9.

[47] Simon Rabinovitch, "Potential for Beijing Missteps Adds to Global Risks," *Financial Times*, 10 November 2011, p.4.

[48] Patrick Jenkins, Joe Leahy and Simon Rabinovitch, "Fragile Giants at the Heart of Western Hopes", *Financial Times*, 14 September 2011, p.9.

banks' lending practices are very much path dependent and are as far away from commercialization as they once planned to be. This path dependent phenomenon is largely due to the overall economy or market, which is still dominated by SOEs and heavily influenced by the government (or its corporate arms). The next round of economic reform should strike at the heart of state economic planning by pushing for more market forces in the areas of credit allocation, capital flow, liberalization of interest rates and Renminbi exchange rate. These would not only be pivotal to the future of China's financial system but also the entire economy such as increasing private businesses' access to capital and interest income for China's vast population of savings account holders. Further opening-up the financial sector to foreign investment seems a sensible move which can introduce more competitive forces into China's restrictive sectors.[49]

[49] There have been some counter arguments drawing on Hu Jingtao's keynote speech on the 18th Party Congress arguing for the preservation of and more investment into SOEs' near monopoly position. Reuters, "Financial Reformers Adapt Communist Party Rhetoric", *South China Morning Post*, 13 November 2012 (online).

4. Central bank and monetary policy

There has been widespread belief that some aspects of the conduct of monetary and credit policies contributed directly to the most recent financial crisis. It is suggested that it was the failure of the central banks that brought on the banking collapse in the financial crisis.[1] Against this background, there have been some discussions about the appropriate role for central banks and the appropriate design of their policies in the aftermath of the financial crisis.[2] Meanwhile, central banks in major economies have taken some reform initiatives or have been set on a course of some changes. For example, the Bank of Japan (BoJ) has in the past 15 years failed to defeat deflation. It has been trying to maintain its independence[3] by objecting to setting an inflation target and by adopting a more timid goal. The BoJ has also been reluctant to be seen to finance government spending directly since this would shield the government from raising taxes, cutting spending and forcing a restructuring of industry. The new Japanese government is likely to set an inflation target and to make the BoJ governor to be held accountable.[4] Setting a mandatory inflation target is no radical departure from central bank orthodoxy. The Bank of England has "imported" a

---

[1] Richard A. Posner, *The Crisis of Capitalist Democracy* (Cambridge, MA and London, England: Harvard University Press 2010) p.3.

[2] Joseph E. Stiglitz et al., *The Stiglitz Report – Reforming the International Monetary and Financial Systems in the Wake of the Global Crisis* (New York and London: The New Press 2010) 38.

[3] The BoJ gained its independence from the finance ministry in the late 1990s when the economy could have done with closer co-ordination of fiscal and monetary policy to tackle deflation. Mure Dickie, "Japan's Abe Issues Ultimatum to BoJ", *Financial Times*, 23 December 2012 (online); Jonathan Soble, "Reluctant BoJ Given Deflation-beating Role", *Financial Times*, 23 January 2013 (online). Maintaining the case of central bank independence is a less controversial principle compared with the case of independence for financial sector supervisors. Marc Quintyn, Silvia Ramirez and Michael W. Taylor, "The Fear of Freedom: Politicians and the Independence and Accountability of Financial Sector Supervisors", (2007) IMF Working Paper WP/07/25.

[4] David Pilling, "Japan Must Revitalise its Central Bank", *Financial Times*, 28 November 2012 (online).

Canadian central banker and hopefully Canadian financial stability as well.[5]

The reassessment of the latest financial crisis seems to suggest a causal link between central banks' failings in formulating effective monetary policies and the financial crisis. It is widely recognized that China should supposedly have more control over its economy than other countries.[6] Banking reform in China, however, has had its limits, which was manifested by the economic pattern affected by the monetary policy of the People's Bank of China's (PBOC), China's central bank. This chapter looks into the monetary policies of the PBOC and some aspects of China's central bank governance that may affect its formulation of various monetary policies. This chapter also tries to "rationalize" the PBOC's monetary policies and challenges in the context of the Chinese and global economy. This chapter contains three sections. Section 1 mainly investigates the monetary policies which the PBOC crafted to respond to the latest global financial crisis. Section 2 goes through major factors which affect the formulation of monetary policies by the PBOC. A short conclusion wraps up the chapter in Section 3.

1. MONETARY POLICIES IN RESPONSE TO THE FINANCIAL CRISIS

In order to fend off the financial crisis gripping the US and most of Europe, China powered through the global financial crisis in large part thanks to an explosion of credit, either through its formal banking system or a series of "shadow banks" and off-balance-sheet vehicles. The PBOC had consistently injected enough cash into the banking system through its regular bond auctions so as to maintain its money market and lending rates within its target range. The side effect of this credit spree was a remarkable increase of leverage: the overall credit to gross domestic product ratio shot up from about 115% to nearly 173% between 2008 and 2013.[7] These financial strains are all of the government's own making. This confirms the basic closed nature of Chinese banking system which is controlled by the state, and to a significant extent, by the credit crunch. The credit of the Chinese government forms the backdrop of the entire Chinese financial system.

---

5 Martin Wolf, "A Case to Reset Basis of Monetary Policy", *Financial Times*, 7 February 2013 (online).

6 "China GDP – Decimal Points", *Financial Times*, 18 October 2012 (online).

7 Gavin Davies, "China Faces a Different Credit Bubble Workout", *Financial Times*, 8 July 2013 (online).

The fiscal stimulus plan the Chinese government adopted in November 2008 has a lot to show for the money spent. Officially RMB 4,000 billion (but in fact more like RMB 11,000 billion) were spent. This figure does not include RMB 7,000 billion of local government spending, most of which went to finance infrastructure. China's fiscal program has reinforced existing economic imbalances. The government's fiscal plan is a return to the past over-investment in state-owned enterprises (SOEs) and more overcapacity leading to reinforcement of an economic model that needs to shift towards services and domestic demand instead.[8] Most analysts believe that China should have boosted consumption more rather than spending too much on infrastructure projects.[9]

The stimulus plan is often applied by the government to rescue the economy from a serious recession. The US government, for instance, introduced "the most sweeping recovery package in our history", and signed into law a US$787 billion fiscal stimulus in early 2009. The entire package of this fiscal stimulus, accounting for over 5% of US GDP, included a mixture of subsidies, tax cuts, infrastructure spending, energy investments and emergency spending for unemployment benefits, health care and food aid.[10] The governments of France, the United Kingdom, Japan and Germany all unveiled their versions of stimulus packages in various sizes and forms with the same aim of bringing the slowing economies back onto the right track. While the stimulus plan may help energize the economy and create more job opportunities, rescue operations are in part or whole financed from the public through bond sales, which may generate side effects of deficit spending and inflation.[11] Thus, the stimulus plan is said to be financed by "printing money". A host of

---

[8] The fiscal stimulus program is not necessarily helpful in the US as well. The recovery act in the US has not been a lasting catalyst for economic recovery due to the paucity of money for infrastructure in the US plan and due to the fact that the government-supported income transfers have not yielded to cuts and higher taxes. The bulk of the US fiscal stimulus went on transfer payments to state and local governments, tax cuts and an extension of unemployment benefits and programs for the poor such as food stamps. Besides, these government efforts were overwhelmed by corporate measures to preserve profit margin and revenues by laying off workers and controlling wages.

[9] This may not be true as high speed trains and subways may generate social goods, ie, reducing pollution. More money can be invested into quality healthcare and food security in addition to railways and subways.

[10] Robert Skidelsky, *Keynes: The Return of the Master* (New York: Public Affairs 2010) p.19.

[11] This logical deduction between deficit spending and inflation is based on the mainstream classical efficient market model. This neutral money axiom is asserted as a universal truth that has not been theoretically proven to be true.

unsettling issues follow and most of them may prove conducive to moral hazard on a grand scale. For example, monetary and fiscal policies infringe on the elected government's power to spend money by swapping safe government bonds for toxic assets and holding these assets on its balance sheet.[12]

In late 2008, China started its massive economic stimulus package,[13] equivalent to about 27% of China's economy.[14] Chinese banks extended huge amounts of loans to local borrowers, a legacy of the lending spree in 2009 that helped fund China's 4-trillion-yuan stimulus package. Chinese banks, with the purpose of underpinning economic growth but ignoring potential future credit risks, issued a total RMB 9.6 trillion of credit in 2009, nearly double the minimum target of RMB 5 trillion. In 2010, Chinese banks further granted new loans of RMB 8 trillion, exceeding Beijing's initial quota of RMB 7.5 trillion even though the Chinese Government has been trying to tighten up monetary policy.[15] In the first half of 2011, Chinese banks issued 4.17 trillion yuan of new loans, bringing total outstanding loans to 51.4 trillion yuan, an increase of 16.9% over the same period in 2010.[16] The PBOC released the data on its official webpage showing that total lending was set to exceed RMB 8.5 trillion in 2012, up from RMB 7.47 trillion in 2011.[17] Chinese credit issuance has risen to more than 22% year-on-year so far in 2013

Paul Davidson, *The Keynes Solution: The Path to Global Economic Prosperity* (New York: Palgrave Macmillan 2009) p.65.

[12] Noureil Roubini and Stephen Mihm, *Crisis Economics: A Crash Course in the Future of Finance* (New York: The Penguin Press 2010) pp.136–137.

[13] Reuters, "Lending to Local Banks to Decline: ICBC Chief", *South China Morning Post*, 1 June 2011, B3. The latest estimate is that total bank loans to local governments reached 14.4 trillion yuan. Lulu Chen, "Regulator Clears Bids to Raise Capital", *South China Morning Post*, 27 July 2011, B3. A large-scale economic stimulus program was to ensure an 8% growth. Jamil Anderlini, "China Comfortable with Weaker Growth", *Financial Times*, 18 October 2012 (online).

[14] Based on the first national audit of regional finances published by Beijing on 26 June 2011. Robert Cookson, "Resilient Asia More Vulnerable to a Global Crisis", *Financial Times*, 28 July 2011, p.23.

[15] Daniel Ren, "Everbright Bank Lines Up Big Guns for HK Listing", *South China Morning Post*, 1 June 2011, B3.

[16] Lulu Chen, "Central Bank Reports Rise in Lending to Small Loans", *South China Morning Post*, 27 July 2011, B3.

[17] Reuters, "China Loans Slow But Economic Recovery on Track", *South China Morning Post*, 11 December 2012 (online). It was pointed out that credit growth, as measured by total social financing, may have peaked in the second half of 2012 and may decline in 2013. Jane Cai, "Mainland Banks Face Mounting Loan Dangers", *South China Morning Post*, 16 January 2013 (online).

while nominal gross domestic product growth has dipped below 10%.[18] China's banking sector assets rose by nearly US$14 trillion from 2008 to 2012, which was almost equal to replicating the entire US commercial banking sector in just five years.[19] Substantial increases in lending by Chinese banks may result in widespread concerns over a rise of non-performing loans[20] and default risks. Monetary stimulation has seen the mainland's broad money supply, or M2, balloon by 21.1% annually over the past 27 years, fueling a long period of inflation and widening wealth disparity.

1.1 Monetary Policies amid the Overheating Economy

In curbing its overheating economy, the PBOC has used interest rates as the monetary tightening instrument.[21] In April 2011, PBOC raised interest rates for the fourth time in five months, increasing the deposit rate to 3.25% and the lending rate to 6.31%. The increase was close enough to the end of China's late tightening cycle to mitigate a key policy overhang.[22] While low interest rates can help push up asset prices, they may create economic distortions, that is, holding back economic growth and causing deflation, especially when real interest rates are low or negative. This is the dilemma which the PBOC ends up in from time to time.

The danger of low interest rates was apparent in the course of the financial meltdown of 2008. With low interest rates, investors may switch their investment to more risky projects or assets for higher returns. The consequence is an explosion of lending to poor borrowers with the risk being packaged in high-yielding structured products. To increase the interest rate will change this mispricing of capital. Although inflation rates were at a record high after 2009's bank lending binge, the PBOC was reluctant

---

18 Simon Rabinovitch, "China's Central Bank Assures Financial Markets", *Financial Times*, 28 June 2013 (online).

19 Victoria Ruan, "Tough Tasks Await Next PBOC Head", *South China Morning Post*, 30 November 2012 (online).

20 However, it has to be pointed out that the non-performing loan rate in China was only 1.14% and capital ratios averaged 12.2%, both of which are better than their counterparts' in Europe and the US. Richard Lumb, "Branching Out", *South China Morning Post*, 26 September 2011, A13.

21 Low interest rates have become seen as a panacea for economic ills in recent financial crisis. The US Federal Reserve has committed to holding rates around zero for a while and other central banks all try to follow.

22 Robert Cookson, "Chinese Equities Recover as Beijing Battles Inflation", *Financial Times*, 14 April 2011, p.22.

to raise interest rates, the rationale of which may have been not to risk the poorly performing state-owned sector.[23]

Meanwhile, the PBOC implemented the stricter loan-to-deposit requirements (the portion of deposits that lenders must lock up at the central bank) in 2011 by requiring commercial banks to lock up more of their deposits as reserves in order to tackle commercial banks' record loans in the amount of RMB 9,600 billion, a large proportion of which was rampant lending to local governments and property developers following China's monetary stimulus package of 2008–09.[24] This new reserve requirement drained an estimated RMB 380 billion from the financial system.[25] The PBOC lifted the bank reserve ratio six times in 2011. Up to August 2011, required reserves were already at a record high of 21.5% for the largest Chinese banks.[26]

Previously, the requirement had only been applicable to normal deposits but now was required to apply to margin deposits,[27] which are often used by corporate clients to obtain bankers' acceptance notes, letters of guarantee and letters of credit. Analysts forecast that the broadening of the base would mop up 950 billion yuan of liquidity.[28] The extension of the requirement to margin deposits, a vital source of off-balance-sheet lending, showed the PBOC's intention to stop lenders from finding loopholes to evade credit controls. The shift of policy focus from on-balance-sheet lending to off-balance-sheet lending matched the fact that the slowdown

---

23 Keeping low interests would negatively affect economy as a whole. Take some examples here. Low rates deter savings thereby creating a disincentive for the capital accumulation that would reduce overall debt levels, even though low rates favour borrowing and encourage substitution of debt for equity in financing structures, which increases overall financial risk. At the macro level, along with low rates, there would be low earnings on savings, which in turn encourages spending and stimulate economic activity. The preserve risk, however, is more savings and less consumption and demand. Relying on low interest rates is ineffective in addressing the real economic issues. A sustained period of low rates makes it difficult to increase the cost of borrowing. Levels of debt resulting from low rates would become unsustainable. This further reinforces the financial distortions implicit in the policy.

24 Patrick Jenkins, "State Lending Targets are Grist to the Mill of History", *Financial Times*, 24 May 2011, p.18.

25 Simon Rabinovitch, "China Repo Rate at 3-year High", *Financial Times*, 23 June 2011, p.13.

26 Simon Rabinovitch, "Beijing Signals Intent to Curb Credit Loopholes", *Financial Times*, 30 August 2011, p.3.

27 Yonnex Li, "PBOC Widens Reserve Ratio Base," *Hong Kong Economic Journal*, 30 August 2011, p.2.

28 Ibid.

of on-balance-sheet lending was offset by other forms of financing such as off-balance-sheet lending in the shadow banking sector. The less favourable external economic environment made it difficult for the PBOC to further lift the bank reserve ratio to a higher level. Although the PBOC's redefinition of the reserve requirement was applicable to all banks, it may more severely hit small and mid-sized banks which may have been more reliant on margin deposits to support loan growth. Small and mid-sized players are less competitive in the interbank chase for customer deposits.

The PBOC's monetary policy, aiming to deal with the then rapid growth in off-balance sheet activity, however, had strong side effects. The higher central bank reserve requirements accumulated unusable cash. The PBOC reserves once rose to US$2,100 billion, one-third more than the reserve balances at the US Federal Reserve.[29] The more rigid reserve requirements would squeeze commercial banks' profitability. With a higher lock-up ratio, Chinese banks' earnings were just 1.62%.[30] In addition, reserve requirements prevent Chinese banks from allocating a larger share of their portfolios to higher yielding investments. Even worse, this can be a regressive tax and disproportionately hurts small banks with weak deposit bases as well as small- and medium-sized enterprises facing a worse cash squeeze than during the global financial crisis in 2008.[31]

The consequences of such a monetary tightening policy are twofold: a shortage of credit to those who need credits most and the disintermediation of the formal banking system. China's most important gauge of short-term funding costs rose to a three-year high in June 2011 and, similarly, China's 7-day government bond repurchase rate hit 8.9%, the highest level since late 2007.[32] The reserve requirements further complicated and compromised the liquidity management of the central bank. Credit quotas, the main weapon in the PBOC's monetary policy arsenal, limits the amount that the bank can lend. In order to get around the ceiling, banks have increasingly shifted lending operations off their balance sheets through wealth management products and bill acceptances. Consequently, one symptom is a rapid rise in margin deposits. In addition, the spillover effect was obvious. The amount of money and credit sloshing around the economy strongly influenced China's stock prices. The PBOC's move to rein in bank lending or raise interest rates often hit the market hard, which

---

29 "People's Bank of China", *Financial Times*, 24 May 2011, p.16.

30 Ibid.

31 Simon Rabinovitch, "China Repo Rate at 3-year High", *Financial Times*, 23 June 2011, p 13.

32 Ibid.

was said to be the key reason for the Shanghai stock market's decline in 2010.[33]

In short, in the wake of financial crisis, China adopted "a prudent monetary policy and a proactive fiscal policy". The PBOC from time to time applied various monetary policies to sustain or balance the economic growth. The PBOC expanded the base used to calculate banks' required reserves in a move aimed at curbing off-balance-sheet lending.[34] In the battle against skyrocketing inflation, the PBOC raised the benchmark interest rate five times between October 2011 and September 2012 and increased the reserve requirement ratio six times. Stabilizing prices was once the government's top priority, outweighing the prospect of an economic slowdown amid a deteriorating global economic environment.

1.2 Monetary Policies amid the Economic Downturn

China has been experiencing its economic slow-down after the financial crisis. In a new economic downturn (a seven-quarter-long cyclical downturn in China's growth, evidenced by slow industrial output and retail sales, ended in the third quarter of 2012), the PBOC adopted various easing measures including cuts in interest rates and injecting more liquidity into the system through so-called reverse repo operations[35] so as to exert more direct influence.[36]

In response to the bad industrial figures, the PBOC lowered bank reserve ratios three times after late 2011, and cut the amount of cash banks must hold with the central bank. The cut in reserve requirements liberated existing deposits, allowing an extra 450 billion yuan to circulate in early 2012.[37] The PBOC lowered the reserve requirement ratio to 5% for smaller banks (compared to a ratio of 20% for the bigger banks) in an attempt to boost

---

[33] Cookson, "Chinese Equities Recover as Beijing Battles Inflation".

[34] Rabinovitch, "Beijing Signals Intent to Curb Credit Loopholes".

[35] The sizeable balance sheet expansion was in the official sector, that is, the central banks. The Federal Reserve targeted a US$11 trillion in asset purchases in 2013, representing a third of its existing balance sheet. The Bank of England, the Bank of Japan and the European Central Bank were all to expand their balance sheets in 2013. Mohamed El-Erian, "Beware the 'Central Bank Put'", *Financial Times*, 11 January 2013 (online).

[36] The central bank's direct influence is applied through direct market purchases and forward-looking policy guidance. Some assets however are outside the direct influence of central banks. These assets, among others, are high yield corporate bonds, equities and certain highly leveraged products.

[37] "The Air Is Thinning", *The Economist*, 19 May 2012.

credit to small- and medium-sized firms amid the slowing economy.[38] China cut benchmark interest rates twice in 2012, and made repeated, large-scale liquidity injections into the financial system[39] to underpin slowing growth in the short-term.[40] The purpose of these measures was to boost credit demand (which can be in turn injected into infrastructure projects) and energize the economy.[41] In the first seven months of 2013, PBOC continued to trim interest rates and banks' reserve requirements. Meanwhile, PBOC preferred to make ad hoc purchases of bank assets as their need for cash arose.[42] While a rate cut indicates the central bank's expansionary intent, the injection of liquidity was easier to reverse.

In its 2012 third quarter monetary policy report, PBOC mentioned

---

[38] Kwong Man-ki, "PBOC Sets Loan Reserve Ratios for Small Banks", *South China Morning Post*, 3 November 2012 (online) (quoting the official China Securities Journal's report of 2 November 2012). The Basel Committee heeded bank concerns by revising the so-called liquidity coverage ratio that requires banks to hold enough cash or easy-to-sell assets (such as sovereign debt) to withstand a 30-day funds outflow. The change is to extend the original 2015 deadline for banks' compliance. Accordingly, the banks must meet 60% of the requirements by 2019 (the time for full implementation). Brooke Masters and Shahien Nasiripour, "Basel Tries Fluid Position on Liquidity", *Financial Times*, 7 January 2013 (online). The Basel Committee gave weaker banks four more years to meet the deadlines so they would feel less pressure to pull back on lending. The Committee also broadens the definition of high quality liquid assets banks can hold. The definition now includes corporate debt rated A+ to BBB-, AA-rated residential mortgage-backed securities and certain equities, but is subject to the requirement that these assets can make up only 40% of a bank's high quality liquidity assets. The rule changes affecting run-off rates are probably the most significant changes, which will make the liquidity requirement less likely to deter financing of activity in the real economy. "Basel III: Something Like Progress", *Financial Times*, 6 January 2013 (online). Apparently, the regulator does not want to choke off the recovery by overburdening the banks. The significance of the second change is to allow banks to use some higher-yielding assets, and changed the calculation of the liquidity requirements, known as the run-off rates, for some corporate and retail business lines. But the downside of the change is that banks will still have to use sovereign bonds and central bank reserves for at least 60% of their liquidity buffers.

[39] PBOC injected 90 billion yuan into money markets through reserve bond repurchase agreements (a five-day reverse repos) on 6 January 2013. In the first week of 2013, PBOC conducted a net injection of 117 billion yuan into the market. Reuters, "PBOC Does 90bln Yuan Reserve Repos, Drains 20bln for Week", *South China Morning Post*, 5 January 2013 (online).

[40] Reuters, "Inflation Fall Leaves Beijing Room to Ease Policy Further", 9 November 2012 (online).

[41] Kwong Man-ki, "Agricultural Bank Q3 Results Beat Forecasts", *South China Morning Post*, 27 October 2012 (online).

[42] "An Understated Recovery", *The Economist*, 15 December 2013.

its priority was to ensure the recovery in the Chinese economic growth engine above other needs.[43] This was the Chinese government's priority of achieving stable economic growth and preventing a further slowdown in 2013.[44] However, a massive stimulus program was unlikely to be adopted at that point. Premier Li Keqiang ruled out a large government-directed stimulus or investment boom in 2013.[45] Short-term stimulus measures were not taken in 2014 either.[46] There were various reasons for this policy move. Part of the reason was fairly sufficient employment and lack of major fluctuations.[47] In the larger picture, the government prioritized job creation and new growth model in the medium to long run, and refrained from the massive stimulus it had revealed in the wake of the global financial crisis. A balanced and market-oriented approach seemed to be adopted to stabilize macroeconomic policies as the government was aware that stimulatory policies are difficult to sustain and may even create new problems and risks. In addition, the government was to reduce red tape and make it easier for entrepreneurs to start small- and medium-sized private businesses, which accounts for about 80% of employment in the country.[48]

In reality, however, the Chinese government each time quietly initiated a stimulus that only became fully apparent months later. At the end of 2013, China hit its growth target at the cost of efforts to cut its addiction to debt and infrastructure spending. The government was quietly taking piecemeal measures to cure the slowing economic growth, which may not only threaten the government's top priority of creating jobs but also halt support for economic overhaul plans including but not limited to reforming state-owned enterprises and liberalizing interest rates. Low interest rates suggested the injection of liquidity into the market by the central bank to stimulate the economy. The decline of borrowing costs was a result of the supply of extra cash by the central bank. The fall in the exchange rate also benefited exporters. Lining up infrastructure spending

---

[43] China's export- and investment-powered economy sunk into the seventh straight quarter of slowdown between July and September 2012 as both domestic and foreign demands waned. Reuters, "PBOC to Prioritise Economic Growth, Recovery", *South China Morning Post*, 2 November 2012 (online).

[44] Victoria Ruan, "China's Leaders Pledge to Maintain Growth Momentum", *South China Morning Post*, 29 April 2013 (online).

[45] Jamil Anderlini, "Beijing Signals Concerns at Rising Unemployment", *Financial Times*, 15 May 2013 (online).

[46] Jamil Anderlini, "China Rules Out Mini-Stimulus", *Financial Times*, 11 April 2014, p.2.

[47] Ibid.

[48] Anderlini, "Beijing Signals Concerns at Rising Unemployment".

to ease access to money was a conventional method. The government announced a series of initiatives to boost infrastructure spending to prop up flagging growth. Five railway projects were approved to spend 142.4 billion yuan, sending a stimulus signal.[49] In the first two months of 2014, China's electric grid companies increased spending by 22%.[50] The State Council decided to extend tax breaks for small and very small enterprises through 2016.

These measures, while helping to soften the growth of slowdown, may not eventually prevent growth from weakening progressively towards the 7% target after 2014 given the cyclical and structural headwinds. Chinese financial institutions slashed the supply of credit by US$90 billion in the first quarter of 2014, which evidenced the Chinese government's efforts to crack down on its vast shadow banking system. The scale of the monetary unwinding could pose a bigger threat to emerging market liquidity than the US Federal Reserve's program of reducing or "tapering" its asset purchases.[51]

While energizing the economy by taking more stimulating measures, the PBOC may have to deal with the side effect of its monetary policy – price pressures and the inflation trend.[52] Then China's economy as well as the PBOC's monetary policy may repeat its recent cycle.[53] It has been no secret that China is always caught between its worries about growth and its fears of excess. Accordingly, PBOC's policy will continue to be "prudent" and "fine-turned". The Chinese government had been fine-turning economic policy for a year to support growth. In order to ensure stable economic growth, the PBOC was to maintain the loose stance by keeping the ongoing credit loosening for a while so as to keep the economic recovery on track. A raft of measures including continuous interest rate cuts, reductions in bank reserve requirements and faster approvals for infrastructure projects were taken to implement this loose monetary policy, setting free an estimated 1.2 trillion yuan for lending as part of a year-long program of policy fine-tuning.

---

[49] Bob Davis and William Kazer, "China Takes Steps to Stem Slowdown", *The Wall Street Journal*, 25 March 2014, A9.

[50] Ibid.

[51] James Kynge, "Beijing's Crackdown on Credit Intensifies", *Financial Times*, 16 April 2014, p.1.

[52] China's consumer price inflation eased to 1.9% in September 2012 from 2% in August 2012, an expected outcome given its recent economic growth. Ibid.

[53] America is said to experience the same cycle that has followed a predictable path: recession, economic growth, boom, the Fed's hiking interest rates, and soft landing of an overheating economy. Roubini and Mihm, *Crisis Economics: A Crash Course in the Future of Finance*, p.137.

A Euro-zone break-up and monetary loosening abroad might put extra inflationary pressure on a recovering Chinese economy. In its fourth quarter monetary report of 2012, the PBOC indicated its attention supposedly to be paid to the risks from potential imported inflation amid the major economies' stepped-up implementation of monetary easing.[54] This risk was more than potential while China's service sector recorded the fastest growth in January 2013 since August 2012 with a 56.2% non-manufacturing purchasing managers' index (PMI), which indicated an expansion of business activities. Meanwhile, inflation resulting from higher commodity prices became a threat due to soaring raw material and labour costs. According to the National Bureau of Statistics, consumer prices in January 2013 were 2% higher than the same period in 2012 and down from 2.5% in December 2012.[55] The shortage of labour caused price rises in labour-intensive and service industries. If the inflation rate continued to show signs of surging again, the market expected an interest rate rise or "policy fine-tuning" in the second half of 2013.

Amid its shaky economic recovery, China's monetary policy continued to be further loosened. The monetary easing policy pushed for an increase in credit issuance which was aimed at reviving the economy while the government stepped up the pace of infrastructure investment. As a result, the banks gave a green light to provide more funding, some of which was made through off-balance-sheet channels.

Instead of quickly raising the interest rate, the Chinese authorities were more accustomed to imposing quotas on the amount of credit banks could extend. The PBOC's first tightening action was to withdraw as much as RMB 900 billion from lenders' hands in 2011. Administrative measures can bring prompt effects to cure economic problems. The government's tight grip on lending produced fast effects on inflation rates – consumer inflation was subsiding to 6.1% in September 2011 from a peak of 6.5% in July 2011. Although inflation in China edged lower in December 2011, the pace of decline leveled off and food prices picked up. However, administrative measures also have weaknesses – it is easier to circumvent them. In the credit squeeze, lending was flowing from the banking system into the informal "shadow" market. To curb explosive lending, the policymakers needed to raise interest rates so as to change the nature of cheap capital for business.

---

[54] Daniel Ren, "People's Bank of China Sounds Alarm over Inflationary Pressures", *South China Morning Post*, 8 February 2013 (online).

[55] Paggie Leung, "Mainland Inflation Down but Signs of Rising Pressure", *South China Morning Post*, 9 February 2013 (online).

A looser policy may adjust the level of interest rates and banks' reserve requirements to increase investment and in turn "heat up" the economy. Further, the continuously dipping inflation reduced the likelihood of "big bang" stimulus measures.[56] Alternatively, the central bank may keep the credit supply – the total social financing. For instance, the PBOC pumped a record US$ 60 billion into the money markets in the week of 1 November 2012.[57] Total social financing covering bank loans, trust loans, bank acceptance bills, corporate bonds and equity financing, was to hit a record high in 2012.[58] Injecting a large amount of short-term liquidity into the financial system via its open-market operations is a repeated measure taken by China's central bank to push for more infrastructure investment. Short-term cash cannot only ease credit strains but also relief concerns over renewed property and inflation risks. But the inflation rate may be beyond control. These would eventually trigger a new round of tightening monetary policies.

Flooding the banking system with liquidity to boost lending is the PBOC's conventional response to the slowing economy. The steps involve cutting the deposits banks are required to hold in reserve. The central bank resorted to the reserve-requirement reduction by cutting a half-percentage-point reduction in the reserve requirement ratio, which potentially released 678 billion in funds for banks to make loans.[59] In October 2015, the PBOC cut 0.5 percentage points of the reserve requirement ratio for financial institutions.[60] These were the third and fourth reductions in the reserve requirement in 2015. The side effect of inject-

---

[56] Jane Cai, "China's Economy Hits Turning Point", *South China Morning Post*, 10 November 2012 (online) (citing the National Bureau of Statistics' report on 9 November 2012). There is unlikely to be a repeat of anything remotely like the 4 trillion yuan stimulus package that guided the Chinese economy through the 2008/09 global financial crisis. Rather there may be smaller, more targeted spending plans that do not make cheap credit available across the country. Reuters, "Analysis: Foreign Investors Rush to Ride China Rebound", *South China Morning Post*, 26 November 2012 (online).

[57] Simon Rabinovitch, "China Pumps $60bn Into Money Markets", *Financial Times*, 1 November 2012 (online).

[58] Bank loans are only a portion of the total social financing. New yuan bank loans accounted for only 58.2% of the country's total financial aggregate in 2011. Reuters, "China Loans Slow But Economic Recovery on Track", *South China Morning Post*, 11 December 2012 (online).

[59] Lingling Wei, "China Plans Liquidity Boost to Counter Yuan Weakness", *The Wall Street Journal*, 24 August 2015, p.3.

[60] "PBC Decides to Cut Benchmark Deposit and Loan Interest Rates and Lower Reserve Requirement Ratio", 27 October 2015, available 26 February 2016 at http://www.pbc.gov.cn/english/130721/2969457/index.html.

ing more liquidity could add to the depreciation pressure on the yuan. Compared to this, the more urgent concern was the yuan funds being drained from the financial system.

Chinese data quality, a lack of a long history for many series, and the rapid institutional and structural changes that China has undergone made an empirical study of the effects of Chinese monetary policy hard. A factor-augmented vector autoregression model incorporating Chinese economic activity and inflation as latent variables is used to fill in this gap. It is asserted that increases in bank reserve requirements reduce economic activity and inflation. Changes in Chinese interest rates have substantial impacts on economic activity and inflation but changes in credit conditions such as shocks to M2 or lending levels do not create such impacts. These empirical researches confirm the similarity of monetary policy transmission channels between China and Western market economies.[61]

There have been some criticisms over the central bank's reliance on open-market operations because of the short-term nature of the instruments, with most maturing in seven days. In addition, the increased interest rate volatility has also defeated the very purpose of this use as a liquidity management tool. The counter proposal is to cut banks' required reserves as a way of generating a more long-term liquidity boost for the economy. Reserve requirement is an inefficient way to achieve protection against bank runs. Reserve requirements specify a minimum fraction of a bank's deposits, or equivalently of its assets, to be held as reserves in the form of a liquid asset. A bank must have sufficient liquid funds to meet the demand for withdrawals by depositors at any time since deposits have to be paid back on demand rather than a predetermined date. The regulators are unlikely to impose a 100% reserve requirement even though full protection against bank runs can be achieved since a bank can no longer invest any deposits in the illiquid asset, thus forgoing any returns from holding deposits. However, the required minimum reserve is supposed to be available for withdrawals by depositors in the non-bank-run equilibrium, and does not protect a bank from bank runs. The side effect of the low reserve requirements, however, is to fuel a return of inflation. In terms of the concern over inflation, the central bank can reserve its recent liquidity injections on short notice by letting the bond repurchase agreements expire. It appears that both policy tools have pros and cons.

---

[61] John Fernald, Mark M. Spiegel and Eric T. Swanson, "Monetary Policy Effectiveness in China: Evidence from a FAVAR Model", (2014) Federal Reserve Bank of San Francisco Working Paper Series 2014-07, available 26 February 2016 at http://www.frbsf.org/economic-research/publications/working-papers/wp2014-07.pdf.

2. PBOC'S MAJOR CHALLENGES IN FORMULATING MONETARY POLICY

It has been pointed out by the IMF in its report on the Chinese financial system – *People's Republic of China: Financial System Stability Assessment*[62] – that Chinese regulators use more market-based monetary policy instruments, that is, using interest rates as the main instrument to govern credit expansion, rather than administrative measures.[63] This section discusses some factors that shape the central bank's monetary policy.

2.1 Inflation

In response to a flare-up in property prices and consumer inflation, the Chinese government held off on more aggressive easing, opting to pump short-term cash into money markets to ease credit strains. Further monetary easing stimulates borrowing and bolsters the economy. But given the fact that the annual inflation had quickened to 2.1% in November 2012 from 1.7% in October 2012, easing the monetary policy was off the table. The central bank is unlikely to ease monetary policy aggressively if there is no major pressure to see a big inflation rebound. When the economic data signaled that price pressure may gain momentum, the central bank might have to tighten policy to choke off inflation in order to maintain its 4% annual target. Cutting rates, together with sluggish domestic demand, can help stem capital inflows and spur domestic demand. A modest consumer price index rise allows the central bank to ease policy by reducing rate differentials.

The PBOC could also unwind some of its earlier credit easing measures if necessary. Liquidity tightening is to help control shadow banking activities. The Chinese leadership in its annual economy conference at the end of 2012 set out a roadmap to maintain a prudent monetary policy and pro-active fiscal policy in 2013, leaving room for manoeuvre in the face of global economic risks while deepening reforms to support long-term growth.

2.2 Exchange Rate

The other critical challenge the PBOC is facing is the floating of Renminbi's exchange rate. The operation of this new foreign exchange rate regime, said

---

62 IMF Country Report No. 11/321, November 2011.

63 IMF Calls for Further Reforms in China's Financial System, Press Release No. 11/409, 14 November 2011, available 26 February 2016 at http://www.imf.org/external/np/sec/pr/2011/pr11409.htm.

to be a reform in "a self-initiated, controllable and gradual manner", is very much mixed together with China's foreign trade policy. A more balanced trade would address the main source of disruption in China's trade relations with the US and would promote the Chinese currency to appreciate at a faster pace against the dollar. Amid the global economic downturn, the rise in Renminbi has slowed to a crawl as a drop-off in demand in more advanced economies hit Chinese exports. The Chinese government has made commitments not to deliberately pursue a trade surplus,[64] which, as a matter of fact, was set to decline in recent years. For instance, the trade surplus in 2011 was about half the size of the record $298 billion in 2008, which would amount to less than 3% of GDP.[65] These data indicated that China's trade relationship with the rest of the world is increasingly balanced.

The PBOC wields control over Renminbi and is able to guide the exchange rate in line with the daily reference rate. When the PBOC freed Renminbi from a temporary peg to the dollar in 2010, it promised to make the exchange rate a two-way trade. Thereafter, the PBOC widened Renminbi's trading band in earlier 2012. Renminbi is now allowed to float within a band, up or down 1% from PBOC's daily midpoint, a daily reference rate against the dollar that is set by PBOC. The band was increased from 0.5% in April 2012.[66]

A series of appreciations after Renminbi repeatedly hit the strong end. In order to prevent Renminbi from appreciating outside the band, the PBOC was forced to buy large amounts of foreign exchange, causing the country's foreign exchange reserves to reach US$3.44 trillion in the first quarter of 2013,[67] the world's largest and roughly the size of the German economy. The PBOC has suffered paper losses worth more than US$270 billion from holding reserves dominated by US dollars during the eight years from 2003 to 2011. The central bank's tolerance to let Renminbi drift higher seems contradictory to the biggest bias of the central bank that Renminbi has been near equilibrium value given a smaller current account surplus and capital outflows.[68] Thus, PBOC's policy was to press ahead

---

[64] Kathrin Hille and Simon Rabinovitch, "Hu Commits Beijing to More Balanced Foreign Trade Relations," *Financial Times*, 12 December 2011, p.1.

[65] Ibid.

[66] Reuters, "Yuan Continues to Test Trading Edge", *South China Morning Post*, 27 October 2012 (online).

[67] Simon Rabinovitch, "China's Forex Reserves Reach $3.4tn", *Financial Times*, 11 April 2013 (online); Jane Cai, "Boost to China's Money Supply Brightens Outlook", *South China Morning Post*, 16 April 2013 (online).

[68] The contribution of the capital and financial account surplus to China's GDP rose from 0.9% in 2008 to 4.8% in 2010, and then dipped to 3% in 2011 before further dropping to 0.4% in the first half of 2012. Jane Cai, "Yuan Gains

with currency reforms to turn the yuan into a more freely traded currency while retaining yuan's exchange rate.[69] Nevertheless, the indication of flexibility was premised on an economic ground – exports appeared to be recovering. More importantly, the central bank needs to use a stronger Renminbi to lure speculative funds to China after a strong capital outflows.[70] The PBOC's strong fixing was also a response to a fall in the dollar when the Euro rose high against the dollar. The PBOC typically set its fixing more strongly in response to an overnight weakening of the dollar index, which tracks the greenback's value against a basket of currencies dominated by the Euro.[71] Inflation also presses the central bank to boost its tolerance for yuan appreciation as a stronger currency would ease price growth by lowering yuan-denominated prices for imported goods. These factors led to the PBOC being more willing to permit yuan appreciation.

The dilemma shows that China's monetary policy remains at the mercy of its rigid exchange rate system. The PBOC, unlike its counterpart in the US, does not have the ability to control an independent monetary policy. This is so because buying or selling the yuan to influence its exchange rate would affect domestic liquidity, forcing the central bank to adjust its monetary policy as a result. In the post-financial crisis decade, the PBOC had sold yuan and bought dollars to keep the yuan from rising too fast, which resulted in a massive foreign-exchange reserve and led the central bank to soak up the liquidity by raising the reserve-requirement ratio for banks.

2.3 Capital Control

Another layer of complication lies in capital flow controls. China has been on the receiving end of hot money inflows because of loose monetary policy in developed economies. There were net capital inflows to China in September and October 2012, which may not be sustained for a longer

---

Tipped to Run out of Puff Next Year", *South China Morning Post*, 31 December 2012 (online). It is getting more difficult to argue that Renminbi is substantially undervalued as the current account surplus is likely to stay low.

69 Reuters, "China Central Bank Eyes More Flexible Yuan", *South China Morning Post*, 6 March 2013 (online).

70 Simon Rabinovitch, "China Steers Renminbi Two-way Trade", *Financial Times*, 26 October 2012 (online). A strong capital outflow has been associated with concerns over China's economic slowdown and an end to expectations of one-sided yuan appreciation.

71 Other incidental factors also have some impacts. There may be a US election impact. China may be in an attempt to counter US allegations that Renminbi is undervalued as Romney has been supporting the idea of labeling China a currency manipulator.

period of time due to the more stable exchange rate for Renminbi and global economic uncertainty.[72] However, China has grappled with capital flight since October 2012. PBOC reported in March 2013 that companies and individuals sold Renminbi 684 worth of foreign exchange and bought an equivalent amount of Chinese currency in January 2013, a record for a single month.[73]

Inflows of capital are expected to generate higher demand for the yuan, which may increase the mainland's consumer inflation, and add to pressure for the yuan to strengthen. Strong inflows lead to 1.6% appreciation in the Renminbi against the dollar in the first half of 2013. Unlike the two-way movements in the yuan exchange rate or capital outflows in 2012, it is more likely that there will be greater risks of capital inflow to China largely associated with funds stemming from quantitative easing in developed economies betting on faster economic growth in emerging economies or foreign capital inflows betting on yuan appreciation.

China holds more than US$3 trillion in foreign exchange reserves and is thus particularly vulnerable to depreciation-related losses. Trade surplus and net foreign direct investment point to substantial capital outflow. Accordingly, financial institutions are keen to increase their foreign exchange holdings.[74] China has used swelling offshore holdings of its tightly managed currency (worth around 1 trillion yuan) to justify a shift in tactics to relax capital controls.[75] PBOC and Chinese commercial banks sometimes buy yuan and foreign exchange. A drop in the net purchase of Renminbi is affected by various factors. The US Federal Reserve's third round of quantitative easing as well as China's pickup in exports and rebound in economy may shrink a demand for yuan. The US "fiscal cliff" may drive more capital out of mainland China to find a safer shelter. Compared to other economies, China is better placed to withstand the impact of cross-border money flows due to its tight grip on capital controls.

The capital control rule is under scrutiny with a certain level of ambiguity and difficulty. First, China's capital account is not entirely closed.

---

72 In the first three quarters of 2012, capital outflows were net, which further deepened China's economic slowdown. Jane Cai, "Mainland Forex Regulator Warns of Big Swings in Capital Flows", *South China Morning Post*, 26 January 2013 (online).

73 Leslie Hook and Simon Rabinovitch, "China Warns over Fresh Currency Tensions", *Financial Times*, 8 March 2013 (online).

74 According to the SAFE, Chinese banks bought US$1.57 trillion in foreign currencies and sold US$1.46 trillion.

75 Reuters, "China Central Bank Eyes More Flexible Yuan".

Short-term financial investment is welcome, within limits, by "qualified" investors. Meanwhile, many unqualified investors succeed in moving capital in and out (with the help of transactional structures and the use of grey areas under current laws). A full liberalization of capital flows does not guarantee a full opening-up of capital account transactions. It may replace bureaucratic impediments to capital mobility with price-based deterrents such as taxes on foreign holdings. The net effect on the exchange rate, the cost of capital and demand may be modest. Second, outflows of capital are hard to track. For instance, inflows of foreign exchange from China's trade surplus and (net) foreign direct investment amounted to about US$108 billion in the third quarter of 2012. However, only US$28 billion showed up in China's foreign exchange reserves. Roughly US$80 billion either flowed in an opposite direction or were unrecorded.[76] Capital controls can partially block the cash flows, but can stop neither multinational companies from repatriating profits nor wealthy individuals from travelling frequently, holding foreign bank accounts and running their own cross-border businesses.

China's capital controls prevent punters from directly pouring money into domestic financial markets, but creative speculators have long devised ways to skirt these controls. One popular method was to inflate export invoices on difficult-to-value goods such as electronic circuits, in order to book speculative cash as trade receipts and convert dollars to Renminbi under the current account. Companies can understate their exports but over-report their imports so as to keep the remainder overseas. Economists at Global Financial Integrity, an American research group that campaigns against illicit financial flows, have spotted huge discrepancies between (i) China's reported exports to the world and the world's stated imports from China; and (ii) China's purchases from the world and the world's exports to China. This rampant mis-invoicing indicates that China may have understated its exports and overstated its imports by a combined US$430 billion in 2011.[77] These discrepancies partially

---

[76] According to a SAFE report released in 2012, China's balance of payments had recorded a deficit in the second quarter of 2012, for the first time since 1998. The balance of payments records two different kinds of transactions: cross-border payments for goods and services (ie exports and imports), which are recorded in the "current account", and cross-border payments for assets. Because exports exceed imports, China's current account is still in surplus. However, inflows of foreign exchange (including foreign direct investment) were outdone by a record of outflow of other kinds of capital, amounting to a net US$110 billion, leaving China's overall balance of payments in deficit. This roughly diminished China's international reserves by US$11.8 billion. "BoP Until You Drop", *The Economist*, 4 August 2012.

[77] "The Flight of the Renminbi", *The Economist*, 17 October 2012.

confirm the difficulty of curbing the cross-border flow of capital in China, a country with such a heavy cross-border flow of goods.

2.4 Export

China's exports were badly affected by slackening demand amid the European debt crisis in 2012. While China's exports were expected to turn moderately better in an improved world economy in 2013, the trade surplus in the medium or long term still declined. Foreign investment, the other key dynamic of strengthening Renminbi, was less predictable. China's attraction to labour-intensive industrial sectors will decrease with China's increasing level of labour and environment protection. The reasonable expectation is that the pace of capital inflows may slow down even though overall foreign investment may grow.

Normally a trade surplus would create appreciation pressure, as corporates sell dollars and buy Renminbi. Companies may lose confidence in the appreciation story and start holding their foreign trade receipts in dollar deposits rather than converting. Foreign exchange deposits held at onshore Chinese banks may rise. Demand for Chinese exports has been strong recently as the US economy gathers steam while imports have lagged behind on weak domestic demand. That has swelled the country's trade surplus.

2.5 Capital Markets

In response to the collapse of China's stock market, the central bank was flooding the banking system with liquidity to increase lending. The PBOC has injected liquidity into the market in order to bolster the fragile stock market since June 2015. China Securities Finance Corp (CSF), the state-owned margin lending agency, is the main conduit for injecting rescue funds into the market. CSF lent 260 billion to brokerages to support stock purchases, bought 400 billion in stock directly and invested another 200 billion in mutual funds. The government has not disclosed how much it has made available to CSF, which was estimated to have about Renminbi 2 trillion at its disposal. Among this 2 trillion, 1.3 trillion was loans from large commercial lenders, 80 billion in bonds and 100 billion in equity capital. The central bank is said to provide liquidity to CSF through relending and other channels.[78]

---

[78] Gabriel Wildau, "China Has $322bn to Bolster Markets", *Financial Times*, 7 August 2015, p.13.

Through a pump-priming exercise, the central bank poured cash into the financial system, offering commercial lenders 150 billion yuan of loans known as seven-day reverse repurchase agreements, as part of a routine money-market operation.[79] The central bank cut the banks' half-percentage-point (50bp) reserve-ratio requirements on 6 September 2015 so that banks could keep a lower share of their deposits on reserve at the central bank. This helped pump about 678 billion yuan into the banking system. Billions of yuan in funds therefore can flow from banks to make loans. The central bank cut benchmark one-year lending interest rates by a quarter of a percentage point (25 basis points),[80] being lowered to 4.6% from 4.85% previously. Meanwhile, the one-year deposit rate was lowered 25bp to 1.75% from 2%,[81] allowing lenders greater freedom to compete for business. This was the fifth time in 10 months.[82] It is rare for the PBOC to simultaneously cut interest rates and banks' reserve requirements. However, the Shanghai and Shenzhen indexes continued to sink.[83]

2.6 Economic Growth

Signs of weakness in China's domestic economy determine the PBOC's monetary policy. Government efforts to stabilize economic growth have helped to deliver a solid GDP growth rate.

Some believe that China's economy is worsening and risks from spiraling debt and wasteful investment are propelling the country towards a financial crisis. Capital flows, to these sceptics, are reflective of waning confidence. Outflows will drain liquidity from the domestic economy. Oppositely, capital outflows can be viewed as evidence showing that China is liberalizing capital controls and abandoning its mercantilist obsession with accumulating foreign reserves. The domestic liquidity concerns are unwarranted as the central bank appears to have sufficient means to expand the money supply and to replace the liquidity once created by

---

[79] Chao Deng, "Nikkei Drops but Other Asian Shares Shrug off China", *The Wall Street Journal*, 26 August 2015, p.14.

[80] Chao Deng, "Asian Shares Rise Despite Shanghai Slide", *The Wall Street Journal*, 26 August 2015, p.1.

[81] Lingling Wei, "PBOC Frees up Credit as Economic Slowdown Worsens", *The Wall Street Journal*, 26 August 2015, p.13.

[82] James T. Areddy and Lingling Wei, "World Struggles to Adjust to China's 'New Normal'", *The Wall Street Journal*, 27 August 2015, p.1.

[83] Josh Noble, "Shanghai and Shenzhen Sink Despite Rate Cut", *Financial Times*, 27 August 2015, p.18.

foreign capital flows. The trend of rising outflows reflects policy measures to facilitate outward investment and the lack of stable domestic investment opportunities.

2.7 Global Impact

The global economic environment, that is, central banks lowering interest rates world-wide, can create mounting pressure on the PBOC to follow suit. The PBOC may allow commercial banks to raise their deposit rates to up to 1.2 times the benchmark rate, which would not only push forward interest rate liberalization but also reduce the possibility of a negative real interest rate. Nevertheless, China's widening interest rate gap with Western nations has added pressure on the yuan to rise, promoting the foreign exchange regulator to tighten rules on banks holding foreign exchange assets.

The PBOC's monetary policies such as rises or cuts of interest rates now have global implications.[84] For instance, the Reserve Bank of Australia left interest rates on hold by a reference to Chinese authorities.[85] As a matter of fact, Australian currency is often seen as a proxy for Chinese growth due to strong trade links between the two countries. Australia is one of the biggest beneficiaries of China's domestic response to the financial crisis. The Australian financial market indeed followed signals from China but not so much the US. This is not surprising given the close trading relationship between China and Australia. China has become Australia's largest trading partner. The extent to which China designs and implement its economic or fiscal policies will have potential consequences that could resonate far beyond China itself, and influence growth and the price of commodities in other countries.

2.8 Renminbi Internationalization Strategy

Moving away from mercantilist currency manipulation should eliminate China's contribution to the global savings glut, one of the causes of the 2008 crash. The justification for a weaker Renminbi at this juncture is a strong one. China lost competitiveness at a time when its economy has markedly weakened while the US dollar is moving up against many other

---

[84] Internationally, low interest rates distort currency values and encourage volatile and destabilizing short-term capital flows as investors look for higher yields.

[85] Peter Smith and Geoff Dyer, "Australia Holds Rates with Beijing in Mind", *Financial Times*, 3 February 2010, p.6.

currencies. China's stock market has fallen, its exports have flagged, and its economy is undergoing restructuring. Naturally, Renminbi is included in the mix of solutions to the slowing economy.

China's move was also viewed by the market as bolstering its case for inclusion of Renminbi in the elite basket of currencies to set the value of the IMF's *de facto* currency, its special drawing rights. The IMF was due to decide in 2015 whether to include Renminbi in that SDR basket as part of a five-yearly review. The IMF staff offered a slightly sceptical assessment of China's case. The key areas of concern for the IMF have been whether China is prepared to let the market play a bigger role in determining the value of Renminbi and resist the temptation to continue to tightly manage its trading band. At the technical level, the key concern is whether or not its currency was sufficiently freely usable.

The PBOC said it would set the daily midpoint for Renminbi's trading band in line with where the currency closed the previous day, thereby handing the market the greater influence. This amounted to a response to IMF doubts and bolstered China's bid. The PBOC has effectively "defanged" potential critics such as the US and the IMF by offering just what has been asked of it – more currency flexibility. A more flexible currency regime is one of the conditions for SDR entry.

The IMF offered a cautious endorsement of China's move to let the market play a greater role in setting the value of its currency. The IMF said in the statement that China's new pricing regime was "a welcome step as it should allow market forces to have a greater role in determining the exchange rate". This could help China's attempt to win much-prized reserve currency status for Renminbi alongside the dollar, euro, yen and sterling.

Meanwhile, the IMF insisted that the changes announced by China have "no direct implications" for the criteria it would use to determine whether to include Renminbi in the SDR basket. It conceded that "a more market-determined exchange rate would facilitate SDR operations in case the renminbi were included in the currency basket". China's move is far from the last China will have to undertake if it wants to see Renminbi embraced by the IMF, which made it clear that: "We believe that China can, and should, aim to achieve an effectively floating exchange-rate system within two or three years."[86]

The IMF later deferred the particular seal of approval until 2016, and

---

86 Shawn Donnan, "IMF Cautiously Welcomes China Currency Move", *Financial Times*, 13 August 2015, p.3.

decided not to include Renminbi in its so-called special drawing rights basket, which is supposed to add to Renminbi's international luster.[87]

3. CONCLUDING REMARKS

The latest financial crisis again reminds us a central bank's key role to play in making a nation's banking system and, in a wider context, economic growth, work.[88] Among others, unsound monetary policies may open a Pandora's Box and result in a collapse of the banking system. In the Chinese context, there is no doubt that PBOC is both a referee and a player in many aspects,[89] which has created additional complexities into the regulatory regime.

Various monetary policies implemented by the central banks may have different impacts on economic performance. The Federal Reserve has encouraged more bond purchases in an unprecedented manner and kept interest rates at near zero since 2008 so as to boost the economy. Meanwhile, the Federal Reserve purchases US$40 billion of mortgage securities a month until the US labour market recovers. The PBOC raised its benchmark interest rate five times in 2010 and 2011 and then cut twice in 2012. In the interim, the PBOC increased the reserve capital requirements 12 times in 2010 and 2011 followed by three reductions in 2012. The outcome of the PBOC's recent interest rates cuts and bank reserve requirement ratios reductions freed an estimated 1.2 trillion yuan for lending as part of a year-long program of policy fine-tuning.

Although the PBOC should have various tools to ensure steady and appropriate growth in credit and money supply, the real monetary instruments are the liberalizations of interest rates and yuan's exchange rates as well as the reform of the deposit insurance system. The financial liberalization may be the instruments China can make use of or rely on to tackle these imbalances. But these necessary reforms may depress demand. Liberalizing the yuan could impede in the near term the promotion of the usage of the currency in international trade.

The new leadership after CCP's 18th National Congress adopted new policies to reform the financial market. The new policies include

---

87 Jeff Sommer, "A Short Step in China's Long Advance", International New York Times, 24 August 2015, p.17.

88 Posner, *The Crisis of Capitalist Democracy*, p.3.

89 PBOC can be viewed as a market player in a liquidity crisis for which a central bank's role as "lender of last resort" is designed. Posner, *The Crisis of Capitalist Democracy*, p.65.

liberalizing the interest rate policy away from setting deposit and lending rates to targeting short-term money market rates.[90] The new leadership after the 18th CCP focused more on boosting domestic demand, shifting from the investment and export-oriented economic development model. However, while consumption growth may grow steadily, it is difficult to expect consumption to be an independent driver of the cycle. In other words, the export-oriented manufacturing sector (or net exports) may still be the big drag for the national economic growth. Making a shift from the export-oriented to the domestically-oriented economy is not easy and requires a complete overhaul of the investment-led growth model that has been fueled by more than a decade of rapacious external demand for cheap Chinese exports. Indeed, contribution from consumption in the growth of GDP in the second quarter of 2013 fell to 2.5 percentage points from 4.3 while the weight of investment rose to 5.9 percentage points from 2.3 to reach the highest since two years earlier.[91]

The reform of the exchange rate mechanism is "relatively easy" compared with other changes such as liberalizing interest rates and opening the capital account as those carry higher financial risks. For example, the PBOC should not rush to free up the capital account as the world's central banks kept printing money to cope with a global economic downturn, which may cause a flood of capital into China. It is worth noting that PBOC's control over the banking sector is weaker than before with foreign banks surging into China and commercial banks introducing various new financial products through securitization.

The Chinese government made a proposal to set up a bank deposit insurance scheme, which lays the groundwork to accelerate interest-rate liberalization. This also serves as a signal to the market that the financial system is not risk free as the investor usually assumes that all financial institutions are implicitly guaranteed by the government. Effectively, a deposit insurance scheme may urge the banks to price their loans according to the riskiness of the borrower rather than their political clout, and lend more to the private sector at the market rate. A detailed discussion of this deposit insurance scheme is in Chapter 13.

While China's stabilizing foreign exchange reserves is a strong indicator of China's economy being well managed, the fact that China's mountain of reserves reached US$3.44 trillion (roughly the size of the German

[90] Credit Agricole Report, cited in Toh Han Shih, "Winds of Change 'to Blow Through' China's Economy", *South China Morning Post*, 27 November 2012 (online).

[91] Victoria Ruan, "China's Slower Growth Raises Rebalancing Stakes", *South China Morning Post*, 16 July 2013 (online).

economy) in the first quarter of 2013 means that China is still facing imbalances and its economy is still facing heavy and unwanted capital inflows. China's failure to tackle these imbalances will be reinforced when the global economy exits from recession. China continues to accumulate its own bubble of debt, which needs a sharp shift of policy. Otherwise China will be unable to sustain a high rate of growth in a long run.

It has been recognized that the stimulus, while reviving demand and the economy, had some damaging structural side effects to the economy: it flooded the economy with too much liquidity, it skewed the economy in favour of investment, in particular, construction projects; it made a mess of local government financing; it forced banks to serve government needs (thereby inhibiting their evolution into commercial banks); and most importantly, it delayed further economic reforms. Excessive and redundant investment (48% of GDP, far more than that needed) resulted in inflation, which basically wiped out the cost advantages Chinese products have in export markets. The failure to tackle these imbalances after the start of the financial crisis actually took China in the wrong direction. Now, China's monetary policymakers are in a tough position to balance short-term growth stability and long-term economic health. The increase of foreign exchange reserves and credit issuance has put more pressure on the Chinese government to restore balance to the economy. Ballooning local government debt and the rise of the shadow banking system have been testing the wits of regulators and policymakers. Given the side effect of monetary stimulus, the government needs to change its strategy and rely more on structural reforms through upgrading the structure of the economy across the Chinese economy, welfare provision and income distribution to achieve better quality and performance.

5. Regulating wealth management products

INTRODUCTION

Shadow banking in China refers to lending that is free from the same regulation as bank loans, and includes banks' off-balance-sheet vehicles such as commercial bills, entrusted loans, underground lending as well as wealth management products (WMPs).[1] The WMP market is the major sector in which the banks are deeply involved in the shadow banking sector. Trusts and securities brokerages have emerged as new conduits for shadow lending.[2] Due to tightly-controlled credit limits in China, part of China's domestic deposits have steered from bank loans and savings into opaque, off-balance sheet, risk-laden vehicles or underground financial networks.

The shadow banking sector has also reshaped China's financial system, which used to be less complicated (compared to its counterparts in Western economies) though clumsy. Traditionally, the bulk of savings was deposited in the Big Four and other commercial banks, most of which are largely state-owned. Chinese banks have got used to extending most of their loans to state-owned enterprises (SOEs). When Chinese banks get into trouble, they will be bailed out by the government, eventually by the taxpayers and depositors. Now, savers can choose between traditional deposits and a variety of WMPs offered by lightly regulated trust companies and asset management firms as well as banks themselves. Borrowers therefore have access to a variety of flexible sources ranging from the bond market and trust companies (making entrusted loans via a bank) to kerbside creditors. According to Fitch's statistics, traditional bank lending

---

[1] For an account of shadow banking in the US and worldwide, see generally Steven L. Schwarcz, "Regulating Shadow Banking", (2011) *Review of Banking and Financial Law* 619–642.

[2] Simon Rabinovitch, "Surge in Chinese Credit Raises Fears", *Financial Times*, 8 February 2013 (online).

now only accounts for 55% of new financing,[3] with the rest being supplied by the shadow banking sector.

Shadow banking is a complex and unregulated segment in China's financial sector. This fast expanding segment tends to create systemic and default risks. The Financial Stability Board (FSB), in its third annual "Global Shadow Banking Monitoring Report 2013" recommended that financial regulators enhance their monitoring framework to evaluate shadow banking risks and focus on credit intermediation activities that have the potential to pose systemic risks.[4] Sensible regulatory instruments need to be designed to address systemic risks. Nevertheless, plenty of ink has been spilled on the risks tied up in WMPs, and the regulatory response to this sector has been slow and ineffective.

In the past three decades, Chinese banking law has become markedly more concerned with consumer protection. Laws and regulations have been passed to require the disclosure of credit terms, protect financial privacy, police against predatory lending, limit the activities of debt collectors and penalize loan sharks. These laws and regulations are useful for the protection of consumers in the formal banking system. Financial consumers in the shadow banking sector, however, are less well protected. The question therefore is whether the government and legislature may impose "conduct of business" rules on those players in the shadow banking sector. Put differently, the question is how the regulators may step in to maintaining systemic risks in the shadow banking sector so as to protect consumers.

This chapter is structured as follows. Section 1 discusses the key structural features of WMPs while Section 2 tries to understand the reasons for WMPs' popularity. WMPs certainly involve systemic risks, and Section 3 illustrates these systemic risks by discussing three recent scandals. Major regulatory responses and instruments taken by the banking watchdog and the Chinese government are discussed in Section 4. Rationality and defects of these regulatory instruments are also discussed in this section. In terms of consumer protection in the financial sector, the necessity of having an institutional structure and reform is analysed in Section 5. The opposite argument against this proposal is also discussed. As the creation of WMPs in China's financial markets is related to the distorted interest rates formation mechanism, monetary approaches have also been put in place by the Chinese regulators to deal with the systemic risks of WMPs. This is the focus of Section 6 and leads to a discussion of China's financial

---

3 "Shadow Lengthen", *The Economist*, 13 April 2013.

4 FSB: Global Shadow Banking Monitoring Report 2013, available 29 February 2016 at https://publicintelligence.net/fsb-shadow-banking-2013/.

liberalization strategy in Section 7, which appears necessary for China to deepen its financial markets and system. A short conclusion follows at the end.

1. WHAT ARE WMPs?

The nature of WMPs can be understood from four standpoints.

1.1 Informal Securitization

WMPs are simply an intermediary or wrapper around banned or heavily regulated products, thereby constituting a pool of securities including trust products, bonds and stock funds. The cash flow of WMPs can be seen in Figure 5.1 below. A sizeable portion of these securities are repackaged into poorly documented financial products with maturities of merely several months. In this sense, WMPs have been characterized as informal securitization for proceeds.[5] WMPs are labeled as low-risk investments as they are sold through banks or other financial institutions to ordinary investors with promised returns well above government-capped deposit rates. However, around 70% of WMPs issued in China are non-capital protected products with floating earning rates,[6] unbeknownst to public investors who only assume that the profitability of WMPs is guaranteed by the banks or the state.

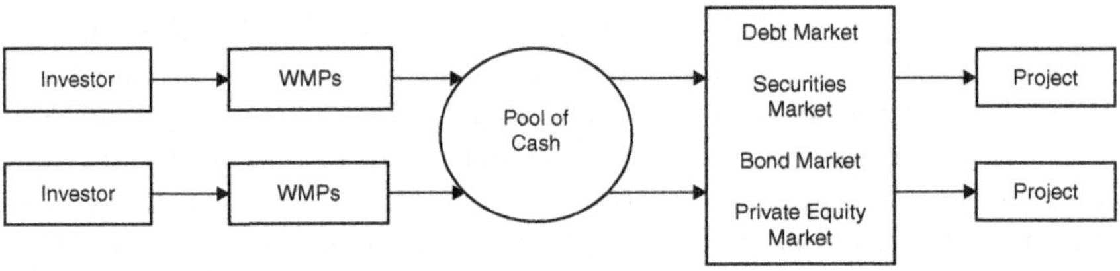

Figure 5.1 WMP's cash flow

[5] Federal Reserve Bank of San Francisco, "Shadow Banking in China: Expanding Scale, Evolving Structure", Asia Focus, April 2013, p.2, available 29 February 2016 at http://www.frbsf.org/banking-supervision/publications/asia-focus/2013/april/shadow-banking-china-scale-structure/.

[6] Wenxuan Cao, "Most Wealth Management Products in China Not Capital Protected, Says Economist", available 29 February 2016 at http://www.sino-us.com/69/Most-wealth-management-products-in-China-not-capital-protected-says-economist.html.

1.2 "Off-balance-sheet" Businesses

From an issuing bank's perspective, WMPs are divided into two categories. One is the traditional bank business that is moved off balance sheet to evade capital reserve requirements, loan-to-debt ratios and sector-specific lending quotas. This is a typical off-balance sheet channeling. The other is speculative investment products that channel funds into projects bank usually would not finance. Both categories involve maturity mismatch, a mismatch between asset risk and investor capability to manage risk, while the second category is more likely to trigger financial instability in the case that a bank has to absorb the losses.

Banks in most cases merely act as middlemen to issue WMPs to investors on behalf of the borrowers who need the funds. This means that WMPs are issuing banks' off-balance-sheet businesses as principal guaranteed products offered by banks must be counted on a bank's balance sheet.[7] Banks often provide guarantees to the trust and brokerage partners with a promise to compensate the third party for losses or to repurchase credit assets at a future date. Consequently, the bank will collect a portion of the interest income from the loans, blurring the lines between on-and off-balance sheet assets. The "stakeholders" involved in WMPs can be seen in Figure 5.2 below.

In practice, banks are on the hook for the roughly 15% of products in circulation that they have guaranteed. WMPs, however, are not backed up by meaningful assets or guarantors, and may create systemic risks

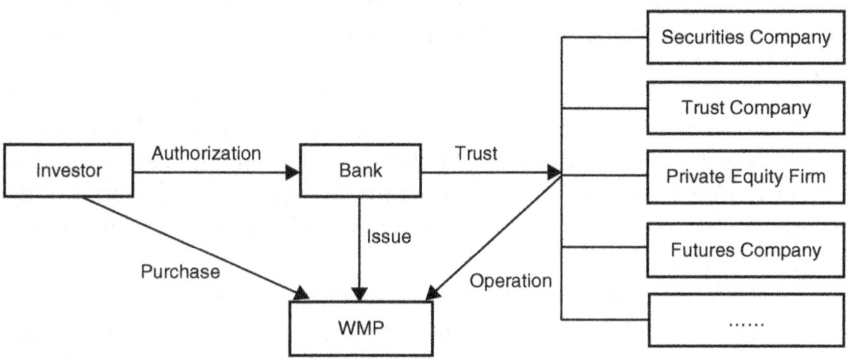

Figure 5.2 "Stakeholders" in WMPs

7 In reality, many of the assets and liabilities spend much of their life off-balance sheet. The flawed disclosure system makes this even worse.

in the end. 70% or so of WMPs are tied to bond and money markets. Technically, WMPs are likened to the collateralized debt obligation (CDO)[8] widely used in the US market. Banks may be left with packaged loans they are unable to sell when other investors stop buying CDOs and owners default. This "asset-liability mismatch" is clearly a cause for concern, and may be even worse when China's economy has slowed and the stock market has slumped. When a host of WMPs go bust, banks would be expected to cover losses and pay investors principal and interest on products. However, banks are unable to bail all the products out.

1.3 "Short Term"

Most WMPs are short-term savings vehicles, with a term of between one and three months,[9] created by third parties and issued through banks. Short-term maturity provides banks with the flexibility to move assets and liabilities on- and off-balance-sheet by choosing the suitable start- and end-dates of WMPs. A large number of WMPs are funded with short-term capital, making them vulnerable to a maturity mismatch as these products generally have a life of a few months while the projects they finance are often of much longer duration. Consequently, issuers of WMPs need to roll over WMPs continuously so as to maintain a positive cash flow.

1.4 Underlying Assets

WMPs have been used to supply high cost capital into a wide range of assets ranging from liquid and safe investments such as money market and bond funds to illiquid and risky sectors such as struggling property developers, steel mills, state-owned enterprises (SOEs) and some hedge funds that cannot borrow from the more regulated state banks. The majority of funding generated from selling WMPs could be invested in a bundle of illiquid assets or even in servicing other maturing products. In terms of the composition, nearly 40% were invested in liquid assets with relatively low

---

[8] CDOs are debt securities collateralised by conventional securities issued by named reference entities, and use credit default swaps to mimic the behaviour of the collateral pool, which is a mixed pool of mortgage loans and/or other income-generating assets owned by an SPV. Steven L. Schwarcz, "Protecting Financial Markets: Lessons from the Subprime Mortgage Meltdown," (2008) 93(2) *Minnesota Law Review* 4–5.

[9] ChinaScope Financial, "Value of Wealth Management Products Issued by Banks in 13Q3 Tops CNY 15 Tn" (22 October 2013), available at www.chinascopefinancial.com.

risks, 35 to 40% were bank loans sold off balance sheets and 5 to 10% were equity investments. Around 20% of the market is collective trusts, originated by trust companies, which probably is the category with the highest return and risk.[10] Merely 20% and 4% of WMPs target bank deposits and stock markets respectively.[11]

Demand for WMPs boost the market for cheaper credit through corporate bonds. Roughly a quarter of the WMPs are invested into corporate bonds.[12] Together with those invested into the money markets, this ratio jumps to 40%. This shows the likelihood that systemic risks may spread around as WMPs are also interconnected with other financial sectors in China. Much of the money invested into WMPs has been channeled into the shadow banking system, raising concerns among policymakers and regulators.

2. WHY ARE WMPs POPULAR IN CHINA?

WMPs have become more popular in the past five years. The number of WMPs in circulation jumped from a few hundred in 2008 to around 29,000 in 2012,[13] with the total outstanding WMPs in the amount of Renminbi 7.1 trillion by the end of 2012,[14] which further doubled to Renminbi 13 trillion as of May 2013.[15] According to a report issued by Bank of America Merrill Lynch in early January 2013, the total size of bank-distributed WMPs was estimated at 10 trillion yuan by the end of 2012,[16] (together with trust

---

10 Jane Cai, "Mainland Banks Face Mounting Loan Dangers", *South China Morning Post*, 16 January 2013 (online).

11 Cao, "Most Wealth Management Products in China Not Capital Protected, Says Economist".

12 "China Bank Results: Off the Money", *Financial Times*, 25 March 2013 (online). Funding costs for Chinese state-owned enterprises that issue bonds are 100-150bps lower than yields on bank loans. This hurts demand for loans. Consequently, corporate bonds made up two-fifths of medium and long term credit issuance in the second half of 2012 whereas commercial banks made up only 13%.

13 Reuters, "Too Big To Fail? China's Wealth Management Products Stir Debate", *South China Morning Post*, 20 December 2012 (online).

14 Federal Reserve Bank of San Francisco, "Shadow Banking in China: Expanding Scale, Evolving Structure", *Asia Focus*, April 2013, p.2 (citing the CBRC's figures).

15 Fitch Ratings, "Chinese Banks: Issuance of Wealth Management Products Moderates", 10 June 2013, available at www.fitchratings.com.

16 The latest estimate is that mainland banks have sold 12 trillion yuan worth of wealth management products. Daniel Ren, "Guarantor Repays Principal on

firms) accounting for 16.9% of overall bank loans, the largest segment in the shadow banking sector.[17] This estimated figure did not include mutual funds and insurance products.[18] By the end of 2013, WMPs had accumulated to a combined level equal to about 5% of the banking sector's assets, which stood at 133.6 trillion yuan.

2.1 Depositors' Incentive to Invest

Chinese savers have piled into WMPs in recent years and made them the fast-growing investment vehicles in the country. The popularity of these products is largely strengthened by the fact that (i) a mandatory ceiling on deposit rates (interest rates) deprives savers of the market return on their money, and (ii) inflation in China has surged past official interest rates. For example, in February 2013, the deposit rate was only 3% while the consumer price index increased by 3.2%,[19] providing depositors with a negative return for their deposits. This effectively is a system of "financial repression" that caps the deposit interest rates on offer, which are much lower than the higher returns promised by WMPs. A moribund stock market during the 2008 financial crisis left investors with few meaningful investment opportunities to turn profits. Consequently, investors are forced to seek higher returns by investing in more profitable products rather than effectively lose money in bank deposits.[20] A huge pool of hard-earned savings either runs the risk of investing in dubious products or is parked in savings accounts paying extremely low interest.

Failed Huaxia Product", *South China Morning Post*, 23 January 2013 (online). There are no definitive numbers of the size of the outstanding financing shadow banking provides. According to Deutsche Bank, it could amount to about Renminbi 21 trillion or about 40% of GDP with the wealth management products worth about Renminbi 15 trillion while Merrill Lynch estimates that the amount can be as much as 11 trillion. Henny Sender, "China Interbank Market Rates Soar", *Financial Times*, 16 June 2013 (online).

[17] Ray Chan and George Chen, "Beijing Urged to Take Quick Action on Shadow Banking", *South China Morning Post*, 29 January 2013 (online).

[18] Jane Cai, "Mainland Banks Face Mounting Loan Dangers", *South China Morning Post*, 16 January 2013 (online).

[19] Gregory C. Chow, "Stop Tinkering", *South China Morning Post*, 26 July 2013, A19.

[20] While savers are fed up with the miserable returns on their deposits and are demanding alternatives, capital is less captive. In April 2012, deposits expanded by only 11.4%, the slowest rate since at least 1998. "The Air Is Thinning", *The Economist*, 19 May 2012.

2.2 Banks' Incentive to Sell

WMPs are viewed as higher-yielding alternatives to regular bank deposits. The supply and sale of these products were initially tolerated by regulators to support the deregulation of interest rates by offering competition to low-yielding deposits. Banks, however, quickly abused this tolerance by booking WMPs as deposits or deposit-like instruments. Issuing WMPs can help banks get around the official caps on the interest rates. Unlike ordinary bank accounts, there are no regulatory caps on the rates offered on WMPs. WMPs function like a segment of the banking sector with liberalized interest rates, with yields typically 100–150 basis points higher than bank deposits.

More importantly, banks can rely on WMPs to meet loan-to-deposit ratios for further lending. Many banks often sell WMPs to investors that mature just before the end of the quarter so that the repayments are made into the bank's deposits in time for regulatory inspections. Thereafter, the funding is used in new products. The banks need to borrow the funds it repays to the products' buyers. Some of the marketing materials explicitly provide that, if the borrower does not have sufficient cash to repay the loan, the trust company acting as an intermediary will issue another loan. In this way, WMPs are used to repackage old loans and prop up risky companies and projects. Selling WMPs can bring multiple benefits to banks: enhancing market competition, shifting regulatory burdens and lowering compliance costs.

2.3 Distorted Supply and Demand Model

The economic model of supply and demand well explains the rationale of WMPs, or shadow banking system as a whole in a larger context. The supply and demand of deposits depend on the rate of interest. The equilibrium interest rate is the rate which makes the quantity supplied equal to the quantity demanded. In a market economy, the interest rate will reach this equilibrium rate. In other words, demand and supply determine price in equilibrium and leads to an efficient allocation of financial resources in the market. If the rate of interest is arbitrarily set below the equilibrium rate, the amount that the depositors are willing to supply is less than the amount that the banks wish to obtain. This inevitably results in a shortage of deposits in the market. This shortage is the source of the shadow banking system: some banks are willing to pay a higher interest rate to attract more deposits whilst some borrowers are willing to pay an even higher interest rate. The origin of this shortage, however, is the government's control (or market manipulation) over the interest rate. Seen in this vein, WMPs (or even the shadow banking system) solve the shortage problem and improve economic efficiency, which has been distorted by administrative interference.

The cause of WMPs (or shadow banking as a whole) is somehow related to the distorted interest rates system in China. The PBOC previously had set both a floor for lending rates and a ceiling for deposit rates, which guaranteed a sizeable net interest margin for state-owned banks but mispriced credit. A floor for lending interest rates provides an artificial subsidy to banks so that they can borrow less expensively and then invest in higher-yielding safe assets such as government bonds and the property market. By offering interest rates that exceed the benchmark deposit rate[21] and providing more WMPs, banks can secure more funds which, however, may accumulate risks in the financial system. The lender in a shadow banking system, built on a lattice of interlocked credit, usually borrows money from banks and other private lenders with the aim of arbitraging interest rates. A mandatory ceiling on deposit interest rates deprives savers of the market return on their money. Inflation in China which, in most cases, surged past official interest rates, made savers suffer losses. Chinese banks therefore can earn almost all of their income from government-set interest rate margins, leaving depositors with little profit and choice except pouring money into the shadow banking sector.

2.4 Small Banks' Dominance in the Market

The growth of WMPs has been phenomenal. WMPs account for nearly 10% of the largest banks' deposits and 15% for smaller banks.[22] Smaller banks have been more aggressive in their issuance of WMPs and some are already near the 20% mark.[23] In the third quarter of 2013, for example, China Merchants Bank's deposits grew 0.3% while its WMP balance increased about 40% from 2012.[24] With the growing size of WMPs, banks may have to bear higher costs in raising finance.

---

[21] Low rates do not necessarily increase the supply of credit. Risk aversion and higher returns on capital would encourage banks to eschew loans so that they can put more money in government securities or property market. This is also the case in the US where banks are holding more cash and government securities than the outstanding volume of commercial and industrial loans.

[22] Simon Rabinovitch, "Competition Puts An End To Days of Easy Profits", *Financial Times*, 27 November 2013, p.3.

[23] Simon Rabinovitch, "China to Tighten Shadow Banking Rules", *Financial Times*, 26 February 2013 (online).

[24] Ibid.

Small- and medium-sized banks are the major sellers of the products and shorter maturity dates are rising. Compared to large state-owned banks, smaller banks lack a deposit base and have to rely more on borrowing from other banks or selling WMPs to investors. They collectively have occupied a 60% share of the WMPs market, with an average of 20–30% of total deposits in WMPs.[25] These products invest into stocks and money market instruments, promising yields of 4–5%,[26] roughly 1% higher than the ceiling on deposit rates. Only roughly 4% of bank-issued WMPs are contractually guaranteed for a minimum rate of return.[27] Products with a 3-month maturity are being used to fund real estate and infrastructure projects that take far longer to finish. Part of these products offers double-digit gains by financing various projects ranging from real estate, infrastructure to car dealerships. These banks are using WMPs to secure a stable source of funding.

3. SYSTEMIC RISKS AND THREE LATEST SCANDALS

To fight for deposits, banks have been issuing WMPs in large numbers. The side effect of WMPs is that shadow banking drives the rapid growth of credit in a weakening economy which leads to a series of bank failures, including the three scandals discussed in this section.

3.1 Huaxia Bank

In December 2012, panicked investors rushed to a branch of Huaxia Bank, a middle-tier bank, after hearing the news that a WMP had stopped

---

[25] "Tight Liquidity Raises Bank Risks, Fitch Says", *China Daily*, 21 June 2013, available 29 February 2016 at http://www.chinadaily.com.cn/business/2013-06/21/content_16646437.htm.

[26] Qizheng Mao, "Measuring Off-Balance-Sheet Wealth Management Business of Commercial Banks: The Case in China", International Financial Corporation (IFC) Bulletin No. 36 (February 2013), available 29 February 2016 at www.bis.org and Credit Suisse, "China: Shadow Banking – Road to Heightened Risks", Economics Research Report (22 February 2013), available 29 February 2016 at www.credit-suisse.com. Some reports a higher rate of return up to 7–8%. Henry Sender, "Finance: Money for Nothing", *Financial Times*, 11 July 2013 (online); Simon Rabinovitch, "Uncertain Foundations", *Financial Times*, 2 December 2012 (online).

[27] Federal Reserve Bank of San Francisco, "Shadow Banking in China: Expanding Scale, Evolving Structure", *Asia Focus*, April 2013, p.3.

making payments on maturity.[28] The product offers an annual interest rate of 11–13% for one year, more than triple 3% deposit rate, the central bank's benchmark. The product was created by the so-called Zhongding Wealth Investment Centre and was to invest 200 million yuan in a pawn shop, two car dealerships and a TV production company. The product required a minimum 500,000 yuan individual investment. 160 million yuan had already been raised. The products suffered a default resulting in losses of up to Renminbi 100 million for bank customers after the borrower collapsed.[29] The lender claimed that Pu Tingting, a customer manager at Jiading Branch in Shanghai, sold the product without due authorization from either the headquarters or the regulators. A dozen investors protested outside the branch for one week. The guarantor, that is, Zhongfa Investment Guarantee, paid the principal to a total of 91 investors without a single coin of interest income.[30] The regulator did not force Huaxia Bank to pay back the estimated 500 investors hit by the default even though it has been speculated that CBRC would force Huaxia Bank to repay investors so as to avert social chaos.[31] It was reported that all the banks in China had opposed the mandatory repayment proposal due to the concern that they may have to follow suit one day.[32]

3.2 CITIC

Almost simultaneously, a trust company run by CITIC, one of China's largest financial conglomerates, delayed an interest payment totaling 74.6 million yuan due on an investment instrument offering an average annual interest rate of 10%, depending on maturity. A delay of up to three months is permitted in the product prospectus. The product was marketed to wealthy investors. CITIC Trust raised 1.33 billion yuan from investors to lend to Three Gorges Quantong Coated & Galvanized Plate, a private steel company in Hubei province. The steel company was set up in Yichang, Hubei in 2009, to take advantage of the cheap electricity made available by the Three Gorges Dam and to produce galvanized steel, which was over supplied in China at that time. The loan was guaranteed

---

[28] Kwong Man-ki, "Mainland Banks' Bad Loans Worse Than Expected", *South China Morning Post*, 19 December 2012 (online).

[29] Simon Rabinovitch, "China Investment Products Draw Complaints", *Financial Times*, 27 December 2012 (online).

[30] Daniel Ren, "Guarantor Repays Principal on Failed Huaxia Product", *South China Morning Post*, 23 January 2013 (online).

[31] Ibid.

[32] Ibid.

by a company set up by the local unit of the State Assets Supervision and Administration Commission, which provided land to serve as collateral.[33] The trust company had to work with the local government and other lenders in order to solve the cash flow problem of the steel company.

3.3 CCB

The latest in a string of scandals involved China's second largest bank, China Construction Bank (CCB). Investors claimed that a clerk in CCB's branch in northeastern Jilin province misled them into buying some underperformed products. The products were issued by Northeastern Securities through a CCB branch as fixed income products with guaranteed returns. The products were backed by a mixture of equities, bonds and money-market instruments.[34] Some investors made complaints to the China Banking Regulatory Commission (CBRC) and the China Securities Regulatory Commission (CSRC) after they suffered more than 30% loss.[35]

These scandals tainted the reputation of banks in China. These incidents fueled concerns over the safety of the WMP sector which has ballooned to nearly 7 trillion yuan.[36] These are only a tiny tip of the iceberg as it is not yet clear how many and to what extent other WMPs have or would have defaulted. But one thing is clear: if more cases come out as such and the case reaches a large scale involving a large number of investors, the failure to pay for the WMPs may cause systemic risks in the financial market.

4. RECONFIGURING THE REGULATION OF WMPs

4.1 WMPs' Moral Hazard Issue

There is a moral hazard issue here. When pressed by the regulators, banks insist any risk associated with WMPs is borne by investors. Most investors, however, have the perception that these products are ultimately guaranteed by the state. Investors have shown a tendency to invest in more WMPs as these products are, as investors have mistakenly assumed,

---

33 Reuters, "CITIC Flags Interest Payment Delay on Trust Product", *South China Morning Post*, 24 December 2012 (online).

34 Simon Rabinovitch, "China Investment Products Draw Complaints", *Financial Times*, 27 December 2012 (online).

35 Reuters, "China Construction Bank Investigates Wealth Management Product Dispute", *South China Morning Post*, 27 December 2012 (online).

36 Ibid.

insured against the consequences of the risks' materializing as these products are sold at bank counters. As a matter of fact, the majority of bank-issued WMPs are not guaranteed either for principal payments or rate of return.[37]

The regulator launched a pilot program aimed at shattering a widespread assumption among mainland investors that products (including high-yielding ones) provide guaranteed returns when offered by state-owned banks. The key change is to remove an implicit guarantee of principal and yield in the form of "expected returns" by the WMPs, making investors aware of more of the downside if investment goes bad. Currently, mainland investors treat their WMPs as tantamount to a deposit with a guaranteed yield due to the direct involvement of state-owned banks. This involves a high level of moral hazard. When a product fails to pay out a promised return, the bank would face enormous pressure to compensate investors even if they are not required to do so according to the financial documents.

4.2 Credit Tightening

While the increasing risks from off-balance-sheet businesses are leaving regulators a daunting task, regulators have been well aware of the necessity of risk management and control in relation to the WMPs market. As early as in January 2013, the CBRC ordered banks to tighten their grip on WMPs. The CBRC banned banks from selling private equity fund products. The regulatory strategy taken by the regulator seems solely focused on checks on third-party products sold through banks. This strategy is problematic as the regulator should not rely on banks alone for self-supervision. The WMPs sector faced its biggest test in early January 2014 when the Industrial and Commercial Bank of China (ICBC), the largest Chinese commercial bank in capitalization, signaled that it would not stand behind a due US$500 million issue that was distributed through its branches. This move not only made Chinese investors think twice whether WMPs are really risk free,[38] but also showed that third parties also need to be regulated while issuing WMPs. Without limits on the sector, defaults could risk contagion, which would prompt a liquidity or subprime crisis when investors flee.

---

[37] Federal Reserve Bank of San Francisco, "Shadow Banking in China: Expanding Scale, Evolving Structure".

[38] Paul Davies, "Profits Hit For Listed Lenders in China", *Financial Times*, 21 January 2014, p.14.

4.3 Pilot Program: Regulating the Pricing

Apparently, the CBRC's top priority is to prevent systemic risks, and strictly controlling off-balance-sheet businesses should be a regulatory focus. The immediate regulatory action is to force banks, trust companies and other providers of WMPs to mark the plans to market, which would reveal the actual value of the product compared to what was promised.

Under a pilot program, eleven banks are required to sell WMPs directly to customers.[39] There is no legal basis for banks to do direct financing through WMPs. The pilot scheme does not allow assigning an expected return to a product, counteracting the market perception that WMPs offer guaranteed returns. Further, banks selling these products are required to regularly publish net asset value to reinforce the idea that returns are based on the performance of the assets, instead of the creditworthiness of the bank. Banks need to identify the underlying assets, underlying project and real issuer of a product.[40] In some WMPs, the underlying asset is often an opaque trust fund or brokerage product, providing little clarity on the identity of the ultimate borrower. In other cases, the assets in a WMP are a package of loans from the bank shifting the repayment risk to investors.

The pilot scheme, akin to mutual funds, aims at turning WMPs to a pure asset-management model in which the bank connects borrowers with investors and only charges a management fee in the process but plays no role in guaranteeing returns or sharing income from the assets they manage. The pilot scheme strictly requires the banks to segregate on- and off-balance sheet funds. The initial size of the pilot scheme is small. These banks only receive initial quotas between 500 million yuan and 1 billion yuan. Chinese banks' outstanding WMPs reached 9.08 trillion yuan, according to CBRC's estimates.

4.4 Conduct of Business Rules

The CBRC deploys some conduct of business rules regulating how the WMPs are structured, and, probably more important, constructed in the

---

[39] Reuters, "Banks to Sell Wealth Management Products Under Strict Rules", *South China Morning Post*, 11 October 2013 (online). Ten lenders participating in this scheme are ICBC, Bocom, China Merchants Bank, Minsheng Bank, Everbright Bank, Citic Bank, Ping An Bank, Shanghai Pudong Development Bank, Industrial Bank and Bohai Bank.

[40] CBRC's 'Notice of Relevant Issues in relation to Standardising Investment Operations of Commercial Banks' Wealth Management Products, Article 3.

issuing banks' businesses. The conduct of business rules are put in place addressing various dimensions of WMPs.

4.4.1 Separate accounts rule

According to the CBRC, WMPs have to be managed product by product with matching assets, separate accounting and book-keeping.[41] In addition, banks need to manage WMPs with fixed incomes and those providing floating incomes under separate accounts.[42] Circular No. 107 mandates a separation between the WMPs business and other businesses of financial institutions in terms of organizational structure and accounting management. A separate department needs to be set up in the financial institution to run its WMPs business. The separate management rule is to address the possible agency failure.

According to Circular No. 107, commercial banks must separate the WMP fund from its own fund, and must not use the WMPs fund to buy its own loan products, and operate the WMPs with different risk levels in the same capital pool. These rules aim to ensure that the funding source corresponds to the funding use.[43] Banks should clearly link WMPs with the assets that proceeds are invested in. Previously, banks could pool assets in a non-transparent manner. Failure to do so may prevent the bank from issuing new WMPs. Outstanding WMPs that have not met the requirement would be viewed as regular commercial loans in terms of loss provisions and risk weights. This effectively turns these requirements to mandatory rules and penalizes banks for non-compliance by depriving banks of potential benefits packaging WMPs may help achieve. These rules are similar to the Volcker rule under the Dodd-Frank Act, with the purpose of limiting the risk exposure of traditional banks to shadow banking.[44]

4.4.2 "Haircut" rule

Banks are required to limit the number of WMPs (technically meaning investments of client funds) that are invested in "non-standard" credit assets, the other way of defining illiquid assets, which refer to assets not traded on the inter-bank bond market or stock exchanges including trust loans, bills of exchange, entrust liabilities, bankers' acceptances, accounts

---

41 CBRC, the Notice on Regulating Investment Operation of Wealth Management Business of Commercial Banks (25 March 2013), Article 2.

42 Jane Cai, "Mainland Banks Face Mounting Loan Dangers", *South China Morning Post*, 16 January 2013 (online).

43 Circular No. 107, Article 3(2).

44 Dodd-Frank Act, section 619.

receivables, equity investment with buy-back clauses and other credit products. Investments in non-standard credit assets are capped at 35% of all funds raised from the sale of the products, or 4% of the offering bank's total assets at the end of the previous year, whichever is lower.[45]

The purpose of these caps is to limit banks' exposure to shadow banking by reducing and narrowing the range of assets in which WMPs can invest, and therefore to contain lenders moving credits off balance sheet under the guise of WMPs. The "haircut" rules could limit future funding to the shadow banking sector[46] and force off-balance sheet funds into lower-risk investments, thereby potentially slowing the growth of shadow banking. Banks exceeding the limit may have to sell such assets, bring those products onto balance sheet or issue more liquid-asset based WMPs. The passing of these rules shows CBRC's bid to push for more prudent financial regulation and to reduce risks to the economy posed by shadow banking. However, these rules are not innovative and have a loophole. The effectiveness of these rules depends on the avoidance of a shift from banks to insurers and brokers, which requires insurance and securities regulators, the CIRC and CSRC respectively, to follow the CBRC's rules, since these curbs cover only banks and neglect many of the firms populating China's shadow-banking sector.

The consequence of failing to comply with these "haircut" rules is that banks could be forced to make moves that reduce their profitability such as allocating more capital to back those assets. Given mandatory rules, commercial lenders have to make a choice between, on the one hand, reducing returns to investors and risking losing market share, and, on the other hand, keeping returns and accepting lower margins. Mandatory rules are not bad by definition. When voluntary contracts cannot be relied upon to maximize social welfare, that is, contracts impose externalities or when one party is unable to make good decisions, mandatory rules can be used efficiently.

There have been some policy discussions about the possibility of imposing a cap on the number of off-balance sheet investment products

---

[45] Kanis Li, "Small Lenders Battered by Wealth Product Rules", *South China Morning Post*, 29 March 2013 (online). CBRC, the Notice on Regulating Investment Operation of Wealth Management Business of Commercial Banks (25 March 2013), Article 5.

[46] Chinese shares fell sharply after CBRC's announcement of these rules. The CSI300, an index of shares listed in Shanghai and Shenzhen, dropped 3.3%, with midsize lenders falling the most. China Minsheng Banking shed 8.7%, China CITIC Bank sank 8.9% while China Merchants Bank fell 5%. John Noble, "China Wealth Management Rules Hit Shares", *Financial Times*, 28 March 2013 (online).

that banks can issue as a percentage of their assets. Of particular relevance to WMPs, the possible rule is to have a hard ceiling on the issuance of the WMPs, for example, limiting the assets to 20% of the bank's deposit base. These policies have not materialized due to various technical difficulties.

4.4.3 Investment restriction rule

The CBRC seems more inclined to tighten its regulation over the direction of investment by WMPs to ensure such investments are in line with the state's macro and industrial policies and support the real economy. In early 2011, the CBRC required that all banks clear their "assets pool" within one month.

In March 2013, the CSRC issued rules that limit exposure of WMPs to certain risky investments. To meet these limits, banks need to convert some trust loans into regular on-balance-sheet assets. This may become a serious problem for relatively smaller banks, which have higher exposure to trust products. This is a kind of derivative that gives a bank the right to cash flows generated by loans held by trusts. China Merchants Bank, as reported, had 45.9 billion yuan of trust beneficiary rights. It had 103.8 billion yuan of loans made to other banks with trust beneficiary rights serving as collateral. Total exposure to trusts is equivalent to 70% of shareholder equity. China Everbright Bank had 263.4 billion yuan of beneficiary rights for trusts, securities companies and others on its books by the end of June 2013, equivalent to 208% of shareholder equity.[47] When trust loans were tied to off-balance-sheet WMPs, banks did not face losses as banks can pass them on to savers. Banks would have faced pressure to make customers investments good after the risks are on banks' books. The other possibility is to make it tougher for banks to funnel deposits into off-balance sheet vehicles. These new rules may lead to a slowdown in the explosive growth of China's shadow banking.

4.5 Mandated Disclosure Rule

In response to increasing concerns over mounting risks and possible defaults, the CBRC ordered banks, within a 30-day window, to provide detailed reports about all the products they had sold. Banks were required to fully disclose information on WMPs, and register WMPs with the

---

[47] Aaron Back, "Shadow Boxing With Risk at Chinese Banks", *The Wall Street Journal*, 23 September 2013, C8.

CBRC.[48] In addition, the CBRC required banks to provide greater disclosure as to their off-balance sheet activities. The new disclosure rules are wide enough to cover the size, variety, maturity and interest payment information for the products. Increasing transparency has been used by the CBRC as a key consumer protection tool. In its guidance, the CBRC mandates banks to make true statements about the nature, fee structure and major contractual terms of their products or services.[49] Without mandatory disclosure rules, very few WMPs disclosed their target investments and underlying assets.[50] As investors are unable to identify assets underlying each individual asset-backed WMP, how WMPs are backed and structured should be included in the scope of disclosed information. According to the CBRC, risk warning must be prioritized and unauthorized sales and misleading words are prohibited in sales of such products. The disclosure rule is also combined with the conduct of business regulations. For instance, in selling products, banks are not allowed to blur the distinction between their own products and those products they distribute on behalf of other institutions so as to avoid misleading consumers.[51]

These disclosure rules have been put in place to improve transparency as the use of WMPs as off-balance-sheet financing undermines the reliability of financial reporting requirements as a tool to evaluate the financial health and stability of Chinese banks. The regulator's intention is to rely on disclosure as a key regulatory instrument. The adoption of a disclosure approach to protect consumers in the financial sector is premised on the hypothetical rational consumer theory that consumers are able to make rational choices when supplied with all relevant information. The typical banking law theory is that the lack of transparency in lending arrangements carries risks for borrowers as lenders may abuse their superior knowledge as well as their control over the contractual terms including onerous terms or hidden charges. In the course of financial transactions, the transacting parties have conflicting interests and often have asymmetric information. Disclosure is a cost-efficient regulatory device which not only promotes competition but also triggers fewer political struggles.

---

[48] CBRC's Interim Measures for the Administration of Commercial Banks' Personal Financial Management Services (effective as of 1 November 2005), Articles 37 and 49.

[49] CBRC, Guidance on Protecting Consumers in the Banking Sector (30 August 2013) Article 20.

[50] Simon Rabinovitch, "Uncertain Foundations", *Financial Times*, 2 December 2012 (online).

[51] CBRC, Guidance on Protecting Consumers in the Banking Sector (30 August 2013) Article 13.

Mandated disclosure is a standard consumer protection tool to address information asymmetries, one type of market failure. The mandated disclosure rules adopted by the CBRC include standardizing information supply (including such information as the underlying assets, project, maturity, expected returns and transactional structure) and directing regulation on pricing. Specific rules on the content of disclosed information help address the concern that the investors are not aware of the identity of an issuer before buying a WMP. Nevertheless, a caveat must be made that investors in WMPs may not be the same as the conventional borrowers in the lending transactions. Therefore, while the philosophy of disclosure in the banking law, unlike the requirements of the securities law, holds some promise to counteract power imbalances and drive unfair or extortionate practices out of the marketplace, requiring the bank to disclose information about the essential terms of the transaction may not be effective or sufficient to address the systemic risks in relation to WMPs.[52]

The effectiveness of these disclosure rules deserves some deeper analysis. The literature on behavioural economics suggests that individuals often deviate from the traditional models because they have non-standard preferences, incorrect beliefs and systematic biases in their decision-making process.[53] Such biases make some financial choices less rational especially in the cases of market uncertainty or complexity. Disclosure may overload consumers, and the complexity of disclosed information may compromise the rationality of consumer decisions. Transparency, disclosure of information, and consumer education are the typical policy responses to the market failures on the consumption side. But these responses may be less effective than expected.

Effective regulatory instruments are supposed to reduce some forms of behavioural bias. One possibility is to reorganize the context in which investors make decisions (or choice architecture) so that they can overcome their cognitive biases, and then enhance their self-interest. Making financial products less complicated is such a possibility. The effectiveness of mandated disclosure rules rests on whether the disclosed information is read or understood. If the content of disclosed information is beyond

---

52 For example, disclosure may not be an efficient regulatory mechanism to short selling. See Emilios Avgouleas, "The Vexed Issue of Short Sales Regulation When Prohibition Is Inefficient and Disclosure Is Insufficient", in Kern Alexander and Niamh Moloney, *Law Reform and Financial Markets* (Cheltenham, UK and Northampton, MA, USA: Edward Elgar 2011) p.71, 102–103.

53 Oren Bar-Gill, "The Law, Economics and Psychology of Subprime Mortgage Contracts", (2009) 94 *Cornell Law Review* 1073.

most consumers' understanding or interest, the disclosure rule itself becomes artificial. The regulation of information is the most common technique in consumer protection law as the logic is that well-informed decision makers reach better, safer and more efficient decisions. Currently, the CBRC relies more on the device that mandates various affirmative disclosures, requiring the information-possessing parties to convey certain information, often in mandated formats, to all consumers. For example, banks are required to label WMPs with the standard warning: WMPs are not deposit-based products or risk-free, investors should be cautious about investment.[54] Further, banks need to inform the investor of any substantial change to the non-standard debt assets or related risks within five days.[55] To ensure regulatory effectiveness, the CBRC may consider the possibility of imposing liability on the disclosing party to assure their integrity, with causes of action against deception and fraud. The other possible regulatory device is to subdivide the customers of their WMPs, and diversify and customize their WMP services, which may help lower the level of complexity of WMPs.

4.6 Gatekeeper Rule

The CBRC mandated that all individual WMPs must undergo auditing and banks must ensure products have balance sheets, income statements, cash flow statements and other financial reports. Accordingly, banks must implement standalone accounting on financial management plans. Therefore, auditing firms are assigned to be gatekeepers in protecting consumers' interests.

The gatekeeper rule is also introduced into the regulation of WMPs. Gatekeepers refer to professional persons including auditors, lawyers, securities analysts and credit rating agencies, who provide verification and certification services to investors. They are regarded as reputational intermediaries and third party monitors with the capacity to prevent misconduct by withholding support from wrongdoers.[56] Each

---

[54] CBRC, Administrative Rules of Sale and Distribution of Wealth Management Products (issued as of 28 August 2011, and effective as of 1 January 2012), Article 18(1).

[55] CBRC's Notice of Relevant Issues in relation to Standardizing Investment Operations of Commercial Banks' Wealth Management Products, Article 3.

[56] Reinier H. Kraakman, "Corporate Liability Strategies and the Costs at Legal Controls", (1984) 93 *Yale Law Journal* 857–898; Ronald J. Gilson "Value Creation by Business Lawyers: Legal Skills and Asset Pricing", (1984) 94 *Yale Law Journal* 239–313; Ronald J. Gilson and Reinier H. Kraakman "The Mechanism of

gatekeeper occupies a special position in the market that allows for possessing more information than the investing public has about the financial products and their suppliers. This market position gives relevant gatekeepers a chance to ring the bell to the public when the information is different from that made public in the disclosure materials. According to the gatekeeper theory, a gatekeeper's failure exists when the gatekeeper, for example, verifies an issuer statement that it knows, or through reasonable effort could have known, is untrue or misleading. It is the gatekeeper's failure that reduces the reliability of the disclosure information and thus undermines the effectiveness of the regulatory institutions or means.

It has been argued that it is the gatekeeper's failure in serving as a watchdog for the public that led to an array of corporate or financial scandals.[57] Therefore, part of the solutions to cure the financial crisis or corporate failure is to improve the regulatory regime governing gatekeepers and their operational behaviours, which in turn improves corporate governance and financial regulations.[58] The problem with this gatekeeper rule rests on the uncertainty of the gatekeeper's liability for failure to monitor market failures. The effectiveness of this gatekeeper rule relies upon the scope of gatekeepers, which may be extended to other financial service intermediaries such as credit rating agencies. Some CBRC rules mention reliance upon

---

Market Efficiency", (1984) 70 *Virginia Law Review* 549–644; Reinier H. Kraakman "Gatekeepers: The Anatomy of a Third-Party Enforcement Strategy" (1986) 2 *Journal of Law, Economics & Organization* 53; Stephen Choi, "Market Lessons for Gatekeepers", (1998) 92(4) *Northwest University Law Review* 916–966.

[57] John Coffee, "The Acquiescent Gatekeeper: Reputational Intermediaries, Auditor Independence and the Governance of Accounting", (2001) Ctr. for Law & Econ. Studies, Columbia Law Sch., Working Paper No. 191, available 29 February 2016 at http://papers.ssrn.com/paper.taf?abstract_id=270944; John Coffee, "Understanding Enron: It's About the Gatekeepers, Stupid", (2002) 57 *Business Lawyer* 1403–1420; John Coffee, "Gatekeeper Failure and Reform: The Challenge of Fashioning Relevant Reforms", (2003) Ctr. for Law & Econ. Studies, Columbia Law Sch., Working Paper No. 237, available 29 February 2016 at http://papers.ssrn.com/sol3/papers.cfm?abstract_id=447940; John Coffee, "The Attorney As Gatekeeper: An Agenda for the SEC", (2003) 103 *Columbia Law Review* 1293–1316; John Coffee, *Gatekeepers: The Professions and Corporate Governance* (New York: Oxford University Press 2006).

[58] For instance, right after the Enron scandal, many countries tightened rules regulating the auditing industry even though no academic research proves a clear connection between audit and the quality of auditing work. The UK and US required firms to rotate the lead partner on an audit after five years and defined "cooling off" periods for those joining an audit client. Italy put limits on audit firm tenure. For brief historical accounts, Hughes, J., "Lehman Case Revives Dark Memories of Enron Times," *Financial Times*, 25 March 2010, p. 15.

credit rating agencies[59] but fail to identify the role and liability of credit rating agencies in packaging and selling WMPs.

4.7 Banking-type Regulation

Beginning in 2011, commercial banks were required to move the off-balance sheet assets of banks and trust companies onto the balance sheets at a rate of no less than 25% per quarter. In January 2011, the CBRC notified various banks via meeting minutes to cease offering "six categories of financial products". High-yield assets such as loans by mandate and notes financing were prohibited. In August 2011, the People's Bank of China issued a document requiring that three categories of marginal deposit for security for the bank's acceptance bill, the letter of credit and the letter of guarantee be incorporated into the scope of payment and deposit for the commercial banks' deposit reserve. These bank-type regulatory requirements show that the regulator views WMPs as part of the formal banking sector[60] and monitors them in the same way as traditional financial products sold by the banks. The CBRC vowed to tighten oversight over sales activities of these products through covert investigations.

4.8 Default as Regulatory Tool

To supplement various regulatory devices, the regulator should let small-scale WMPs be broken as, given the importance of risk awareness, domestic investors need to be educated about taking excessive financial risks in China. Absence of defaults has caused many retail investors to be stubborn in believing that WMPs have a rigid return and a limitless guarantee. Allowing more defaults can be used as a valid instrument to step up credit-risk monitoring and inject more disciplines into the market. This can also create a "knock-on" effect,[61] thereby raising yields and slowing down issuance of WMPs at a time when fixed assets investment growth is slowing.

---

[59] For example, CBRC, Administrative Rules of Sale and Distribution of Wealth Management Products (issued as of 28 August 2011, and effective as of 1 January 2012), Article 9.

[60] Scholars also view shadow banking as part of the banking industry. Richard A. Posner, *The Crisis of Capitalist Democracy* (Cambridge, MA: Harvard University Press 2010) p.55.

[61] Some commentators argued for an all-out panic, a market psychology that Chaori's failure may naturally trigger. Joseph Sternberg, "China's Quiet Lehman Moment", *The Wall Street Journal*, 13 March 2014, A13.

The regulator is changing its "zero financial failure" doctrine to accept more modest-size defaults, which may lead to capital efficiency, and more importantly, a reduction of the moral hazard problem after years of bail out.[62] Widespread moral hazard across borrowers and lenders is said to be one of the reasons that credit growth in China has spiraled out of control, with total debt rising sharply from 130% to 210% of national income in the past five years. Unlike a bank failure, a WMP or bond default is unlikely to freeze up the market. In the long run, defaults can push China to move beyond a bank-dominated framework even though these defaults may cause some volatility and disruption in the near term. After the first domestic corporate bond default, more than 30 Chinese companies have scrapped plans to issue bonds.[63] The market expects to have more defaults.[64]

Given the political reality of China's financial system, defaults would be limited for a variety of reasons. Without a certain level of control, it would be easy to have a chain reaction. Allowing one company to fail may trigger a cascade of bad loans, ultimately hurting the entire banking system. The unintended effect is a deteriorating confidence in the solvency of a wide range of borrowers, which may in turn result in a credit squeeze and more defaults. The government's withdrawal of its implicit guarantee has made lenders reluctant to extend new credit or to renew existing loans, which forces more borrowers to default. The Chinese government may then have to take stronger actions if investors stop buying WMPs en masse, since this would cause a liquidity crunch. Politically, enforcing market discipline could lead to a political backlash as retail investors come into the market based on an implicit understanding that the government may eventually bail out the failed lenders.

---

[62] It is reported that Shanghai Chaori avoided a default one year ago after a local government in Shanghai persuaded the bank to defer claims on overdue loans. Lingling Wei, "Corporate Default Heading to China", The Wall Street Journal, 6 March 2014, C3. But the difficulty for investors is to quantify the risk of default. In other words, it is hard for investors to rely on conventional tools of corporate financial analysis and economic forecasting to assess risks. Largely it will be a guessing game about which distressed company will be allowed to default based on what factors such as the size, industrial sector and political connections of the company. The usual deciding factors such as capital pricing and allocation may not have sufficient business merit.

[63] Wynne Wang, "China Firms Scrapping Debt Sales", *The Wall Street Journal*, 27 March 2014, C2.

[64] According to the IMF's Global Financial and Stability Report, problematic corporate loans could increase as much as US$750 billion and many companies may be forced to default. Landon Thomas Jr., "I.M.F. Warns of Risk From Emerging-Market Corporate Debt", *New York Times*, 10 April 2014, B3.

In China's financial system, determining which borrower can default is a political process due to the lack of market-based institutions and procedures for bankruptcy, restructuring and liquidation. The political process may choose those best connected other than the fittest borrowers to survive, that is, prioritizing private borrowers for defaults first.[65] The decision to save a troubled firm must purely hinge on economic considerations instead of the strength of its connections to the government. A more laissez faire approach towards defaults is unlikely due to the deep interconnectedness among Chinese companies. The CSRC plans to form a new division to oversee the corporate bond market, and among others, to identify default risks faster. It is said that the new division will not only put in place rules governing how defaults should be resolved but also enforce the principle that the market should be the one that decides which borrower fails.[66]

Defaults of WMPs appear inevitable. As the above-mentioned scandals showed, some of the products were sold illegally by the staff of banking outlets. Likely these products would spawn further defaults. Banks may have to compensate investors in the end if there are defaults. The risk in bank product defaults is expected to rise because trusts and WMPs, unlike the low deposit rates offered by commercial banks, provide double-digit yields for involvement in high-risk projects such as local government-backed infrastructure and credit-strapped property developers, which might go bankrupt or pay lower-than-expected returns to investors. The risk of a systemic liquidity crunch, on the other hand, seems low for the time being. This is mainly because (i) the banking system is still backed up by high household savings; (ii) the risky WMPs such as collective trusts products are only in a relatively small size; and more importantly, (iii) some banks are now creating assets pools with their WMPs – inflows from new investors are used to repay old investors thereby covering up failed investments.[67]

---

[65] It was reported that the PBOC, China Construction Bank and the government of Fenghua, a town in eastern China with a population of 500,000 bailed out Zhejiang Xingrun Real Estate Co., a defaulting real estate developer in Zhejiang, with Renminbi 3.5 billion. The company took deposits from individuals who were offered annual interest rates of between 18 and 36%. Jamil Anderlini, "China Weighs State Rescue of Developer", *Financial Times*, 19 March 2014, p.2. The company claimed its inability to repay US$600 million of bank loans. Grace Zhu, "Chinese Banks Increase Write-offs", *The Wall Street Journal*, 1 April 2014, C3.

[66] Lingling Wei, "China Tries Allowing Defaults", *The Wall Street Journal*, 26 March 2014, C3.

[67] Simon Rabinovitch, "China to Tighten Shadow Banking Rules", *Financial Times*, 26 February 2013 (online).

5. FINANCIAL CONSUMER PROTECTION AND INSTITUTIONAL OVERHAUL

Regulation of shadow banking is necessary as it touches upon both public interest and systemic risk of the financial industry. Regulation of shadow banking needs to first focus on two types of shadow banking business, that is, high-return WMPs offered over bank counters and sophisticated trust investment products. More importantly, regulation of shadow banking should go hand in hand with the reform of the banking sector, which dominates the country's financing channels. Any reform to reduce this level of dominance will eventually help reshape China's financial sector. To liberalize interest rates can help bring shadow banking back into the sunlight and rein the hidden leverage that can be a threat to financial stability. Therefore, a mid-term reform package may include more interest rate liberalization.

The new rules employed by the CBRC and PBOC merely apply to products issued by banks. In other words, other financial institutions that issue WMPs do not fall under the CBRC's jurisdiction. This raises a concern over the institutional defect in China's financial regulatory structure in relation to financial consumer protection. In some countries, the financial supervisory agencies view consumer protection as part of their mandate for financial stability and a general consumer protection agency takes on the responsibility of protecting consumers in the financial sector. The minimum requirement, regardless of the institutional structure for financial consumer protection, should have one agency for complaints and inquiries. The general consumer protection agency does not need to have expertise to deal with complicated or technical issues related to financial services. For example, Australia's so-called "three-peak" system of market regulation has a standalone regulator, the Australian Competition and Consumer Commission, in addition to the Australian Securities and Investments Commission and the Australian Prudential Regulation Authority.[68] If the financial supervisory agency takes consumer protection as part of its mandate, it is competent to address the conflicts of interest that arise between prudential and business conduct supervision, which dilute due attention necessary for consumer protection.

Currently, China has a multiple-polar (sectoral or segmental) regulatory structure for the financial sector. Apart from the central bank, the PBOC,

---

[68] Paul Latimer, "Regulation of Over-the-Counter Derivatives in Australia", in Michael C.S. Wong (ed.), *The Risk of Investment Products – From Product Innovation to Risk Compliance* (Singapore: World Scientific 2011) pp.79, 84.

in charge of monetary policy, the CBRC, CISC and CSRC are responsible for the supervision of banks, insurance companies and the securities industry. In this structure, financial regulators may have conflicting missions of ensuring the safety and soundness of their regulatory "clients". Without a specialized authority dealing with financial consumer protection, consumer protection for financial services customers is spread over several financial regulatory agencies. Where banking or insurance companies engage in distributing WMPs, the CBRC or CIRC has corresponding regulatory authority. No financial authority has focused on the whole spectrum of financial consumer protection. The State Administration of Industry and Commerce (SAIC), on the other hand, has an overall consumer protection focus but no jurisdiction over banks or financial institutions. The SAIC may even have no jurisdiction over non-bank entities that offer financial services.

There is a rising interconnectivity between the sub-markets of equity, debt, derivatives and banking in the financial markets. Interconnectivity also exists across players, institutions, jurisdictions and intermediation roles. Due to the interconnectivity, by reference to the "three-peak" model, it may make more sense to consolidate some functions in the segmented regulatory regimes,[69] which may help ensure consistent regulatory approaches hence avoiding unjustified differential regulatory instruments. This is a responsive measure to suit the increasing complexity of today's financial markets so as to improve overall administrative cohesion at the national level.

Partly imitating the doctrinal basis in the "three-peak" model, the Dodd-Frank Act created a new agency, the Consumer Financial Protection Bureau which consolidated most of the laws and regulations pertinent to consumer protection in the financial services.[70] This may be a shortcut solution to imitate. However, overhauling China's current financial regulatory structure or adding a new specialized authority dealing with

---

[69] The functional regulator model is designed to tackle four sources of market failure: unfair competition, market misconduct, asymmetric information and systemic instability in the financial industry. Each regulator in the regulatory landscape is to regulate one single function, without the involvement of other regulatory bodies. Australia's three-peak model is said to be the purest form of functional regulation. The choice of the regulatory structure depends on a large number of factors, and the market structure, the stage of market development and the range of regulatory skills all matter. Jeffrey Carmichael and Michael Pomerleano, *The Development and Regulation of Non-bank Financial Institutions* (Washington DC: The World Bank 2002) pp.41–47.

[70] Posner, *The Crisis of Capitalist Democracy* (Cambridge, MA: Harvard University Press 2010) 194.

financial consumer protection *per se* may involve consolidating and switching costs,[71] which may increase transaction costs for financial institutions and their financial transactions with consumers. In addition, the set-up of a new financial regulatory agency,[72] due to its authority over the marketing of consumer financial products, may create effects on the economics of the banking industry and become a source of new systemic risks and regulatory conflicts.[73] A less costly approach may be to craft function-based regulation with regard to various WMPs offered to the public.

One possibility is to include the issuance and management of WMPs into the PBOC's sole jurisdiction. The PBOC is in a better position to strictly control risks in relation to commercial lenders' off-balance-sheet businesses, and, more importantly, to prevent systemic risks spreading from the underground financing market to the banking system.[74] This function-based regulatory structure can benefit from the "three-peak" or Dodd-Frank's governance design in removing regulatory arbitrage that is currently in existence in the regulation of WMPs.

The way of protecting consumers in the financial sector should be differentiated from the regulatory approach to tackling systemic risks. As long as consumer protection as a doctrine is reflected in legislation and financial regulation, an institutional restructuring is not necessary. The key is enforcing consumer protection rules against anti-consumer protection businesses in the financial sector.

---

[71] Australia's three-peak system was the result of the consolidation of jurisdictions in the 1990s. Paul Latimer, "Regulation of Over-the-Counter Derivatives in Australia", in Wong (ed.), *The Risk of Investment Products – From Product Innovation to Risk Compliance*, pp.79, 85.

[72] Even in the US, regulatory overhaul and "restructuring" under the Dodd-Frank Act is not necessarily plausible. The courts have been deferential to the grant of broad regulatory authority and regulatory tasks delegated by the Dodd-Franck to agencies due to the previous failures of the prior financial regulatory regime. The focus should be placed on the understanding of more important to understand new opportunities, functions and pathologies of the evolving financial system change in designing the governance regime. Jeffrey N. Gordon, "The Empty Call for Benefit-Coast Analysis in Financial Regulation", (2014) 43(2) *Journal of Legal Studies* 351–378.

[73] Posner, *The Crisis of Capitalist Democracy*, pp.204–208.

[74] This makes no claim for the superiority of the single (or super) regulator model, which requires a unification of sectorally-divided legal regimes and tailor-made legislative framework. Eílis Ferran, "Examining the UK's Experience in Adopting the Single Financial Regulator Model", (2003) 28 *Brooklyn Journal of International Law* 257.

6. MONETARY SOLUTIONS

6.1 Lay-back Approach towards WMPs

The State Council's rules in the title of "a notice about some issues related to strengthening shadow banking regulation" indicate the government's more permissive stance towards shadow banking.[75] This so-called Circular No. 107 is China's first overarching regulatory framework, showing regulators' more coordinated approach to tackling regulation of shadow banking. The new rules formalize the role of non-bank lenders in the economy while trying to contain risks in the shadow finance sector. There are two opposite views concerning shadow banking. One is that the boom in shadow banking poses a major risk, not only fueling a surge in debt levels but also making credit flows less transparent. The other is that shadow banking represents a shift to a more diversified, market-led financial system. The new rules take a middle ground view: while shadow banking benefits the economy, it needs enhanced supervision. The growth of shadow banks is a result of financial development and innovation and is a complement to the conventional banking system as it not only enriches investment channels for public investors but also serves the real economy if guided and regulated properly. The direction taken by the new rules is to limit off-balance sheet lending by banks and to place non-bank institutions under closer scrutiny.

Circular No. 107 clarifies the term shadow banking by classifying it into three types. First, those entities which do not have operating licenses, such as internet finance companies, are not subject to regulations. The second group includes those that do not hold licences and are only partly regulated such as credit-guaranteed companies. The final batch refers to those that have licenses but face inadequate regulation such as money-market funds. Circular No. 107 indicates the government's attempt to contain potential systemic risks in the shadow banking sector. The focus of Circular No. 107 is to limit off-balance sheet lending by banks and to place non-bank institutions under closer scrutiny.

The CBRC took a laid-back approach by sending an "urgent" notice to banks and ordering them to check third party financial products sold through their branches, mainly trusts, insurance and investment funds. This approach matches the Chinese government's tolerant attitude towards the WMPs, which, in the eyes of the Chinese government, offered

---

[75] Circular No. 107. This is different from Document 9, drafted by the CBRC, with the aim of limiting interbank lending.

alternative investment opportunities and channeled credit into industries in need.

6.2 Interbank Markets

Monetary policy plays a role in implementing the government's laid-back approach largely due to the fact that the interbank market is among the most common sources of repayment for maturing WMPs.[76] The search for cash is pushing banks into some unconventional areas such as interbank funding. The interbank lending market is used by banks to borrow at low interest rates from one another to cover their short-term funding needs. Banks are using short-term interbank loans to obtain funds to make longer-term loans to borrowers. These funds are treated by regulators as risk-free capital.[77] The side effect of relying on the interbank market for funding is monetary risks as inter-bank funding may lead to higher credit, liquidity and interest (with guaranteed interest rates).

The interbank market[78] in China has seen rates soar, reflecting tighter liquidity conditions while economic growth slows and savings are being pulled from deposits into higher yielding WMPs. According to Standard Chartered, 20% or so of small- and medium-size Chinese banks' funding comes from the interbank market, up from between 10% and 15% prior to 2012.[79] The credit crunch in June 2013 witnessed a spike in interbank lending rates to double digits and market distress at mid-tier banks. Since then, the PBOC has been less willing to inject liquidity into the market, which in turn makes banks less willing to lend to one another.[80] The

---

76 "Tight Liquidity Raises Bank Risks, Fitch Says", *China Daily*, 21 June 2013, available 29 February 2016 at http://www.chinadaily.com.cn/business/2013-06/21/content_16646437.htm.

77 Chinese banks are allowed to lend no more than 75 cents for every dollar in deposits they hold. This is a constraint on their ability to expand. Interbank loans do not count toward banks' loan-to-deposit ratios. Corporate loans require banks to hold four times as much capital for every dollar lent out as for interbank loans. Disguising corporate loans as interbank loans is thus a popular way for banks to expand their lending while minimizing their costs. Interbank loans have lower risk and are subject to fewer restrictions.

78 Interbank lending is common as banks need cash in order both to make loans and to satisfy regulatory requirements.

79 Grace Zhu, Dinny McMahon and Shen Hong, "China Aims to Remove a Lending Loophole," *The Wall Street Journal*, 29 November 2013, C2.

80 Decreasing the money supply increases the value of money, and lowers the threat of inflation because less money can buy the same amount of goods and services. But this may not be a good policy option in the slowing economy. A bank's equity cushion makes a bank less likely to convert its assets into risky loans.

benchmark weighted average of the seven-day repurchase rate (a measure of interbank borrowing costs) rose to 5.94% on 18 November 2013, the highest level since the June credit crunch, and well above 3% where the market hovered earlier in the year.[81]

The PBOC switched its monetary policy by not stepping forward with fresh cash into the money market.[82] This hands-off strategy reflects a new policy stance to rein in the growth of shadow finance by constraining the liquidity available to funding new credit extension and limiting the ability of financial institutions to label corporate loans as loans between banks. The government is trying to close the door to the state-owned banks which may now have a limited but privileged access to the central bank-controlled interbank market to borrow at low, steady rates and then make risky, high-yielding investments. The new rule requires banks to count their interbank lending as part of overall loan quotas. The PBOC's tolerance towards the credit squeeze is effective to slow sales of WMPs since much redemption of such products is covered by banks borrowing in the now expensive interbank market. This demonstrates the interconnectivity and severity of shadow banking which may spread to the real economy, for example, affecting the growth of credit and the stability of smaller banks.

The CBRC planned to rein in credit growth by making it harder for commercial banks to use China's shadow-banking system to get around lending limits. Loans typically go to trust companies (or wealth management companies) that are the largest non-bank lenders in China and then are repackaged as interbank assets. A bank often makes a loan to a company through a trust company and then uses the trust asset as collateral for a short-term loan from another bank. The loan is then reclassified as an interbank asset. The network of nonbank lenders is often connected with banks, which have become adept at finding creative ways such as entrusted loan and securitization to be engaged in lending.[83]

In the Chinese context, the difficulty of combining regulatory tightening

---

Richard A. Posner, *A Failure of Capitalism: The Crisis of '08 and the Descent into Depression* (Cambridge, MA: Harvard University Press 2009) pp.196–197.

[81] Grace Zhu, Dinny McMahon and Shen Hong, "China Aims to Remove a Lending Loophole," *The Wall Street Journal*, 29 November 2013, C2.

[82] This is close to the Federal Reserve's "open market operations" through which the Federal Reserve pumps money into the economy to regulate the "federal funds" or "midnight" rate (at which banks make short-term loans to each other secured by Treasury bills), and to prevent deflation. The federal funds rate is based on the desired inflation rate and the productive capacity. Posner, *The Crisis of Capitalist Democracy* pp.21–23.

[83] Shen Wei, *The Anatomy of China's Banking Sector and Regulation* (Hong Kong: Wolters Kluwer 2014) Ch 6.

and restricted liquidity is the risk of miscalculation or an accident that might trigger the instability the regulators have been trying very hard to avoid. Another layer of complexity lies in the hybrid nature of the shadow banking sector. While it poses various challenges to financial regulation, the emergence of the shadow banking sector reflects a market demand for diversified financial products. To minimize the potential hazards, regulators should strike a balance between effective regulation and gentle de-regulation.

7. CONCLUSIONS

WMPs have shaped a market for funding, lending and investing that helps banks and other financial institutions learn to assess risks and to balance changeable costs and returns. Their role is to allow market forces to affect the borrowing costs for lenders and borrowers ahead of interest rates reform. Market players and regulators all consider the shadow banking system as a black market and all object to the shadow banking system due to the associated financial risks. The cause of this black market is the manipulation of the interest rates. The cure for this black market therefore is to let the market decide the interest rate and reach an interest rate equilibrium, which can benefit financial consumers the most. Financial risks are inevitable as risk-taking is part of efficient economic activities in a market economy. As a matter of fact, WMPs have generated a large amount of profit for the banks, and promoted the real economy by flowing back to businesses via loans, trust products and bonds.

The best panacea that can be prescribed to cure the systemic risks of WMPs is for the Chinese regulators to promote a market-based interest rate environment and establish a multi-tiered loan market. Interest rate controls have negatively impacted market-based reforms even though they support profit monopoly for Chinese commercial banks to a certain degree. More devastatingly, interest rate controls disincentivize banks' ability to innovate financial products and diversify investment risks. By contrast, the shadow banking sector becomes an active force in promoting financial innovation and growth in China. Lifting controls on deposit and loan interest rates therefore is a sensible move not only to improve the risk monitoring and control systems but also to diminish the competitive edge of the shadow banking sector. Chinese regulators must strike a balance between maintaining systemic risks in relation to the shadow banking sector and nurturing creativity in the financial sector.

6. The logic (or illogic) of China's local government debts out of control

1. INTRODUCTION

After the Greek sovereign debt crisis, Detroit grabbed market headlines for its decision to file for bankruptcy in 2013 regarding its long-term debt obligations of at least US$18 billion.[1] A possible local government debt crisis in China, at the same time, has been looming in the Chinese and global press. Local governments' huge and opaque debt, totalling US$3.8 trillion by the end of 2014,[2] has been seen as one of the significant risks threatening China's overall economy. Unfortunately, the phenomenon has yet to be understood adequately both in terms of its magnitude and its origins.[3]

This chapter is primarily concerned with the deep causes of and potential solutions to local government debts in China. An attempt is made to understand the causes of local government debts through various dynamic elements of China's public and fiscal finance, including revenue collection, allocation of government responsibility, fiscal expenditure and fiscal transfer within the central and local governments. Local governments' spending patterns reveal a deep and fundamental flaw in the overall

---

[1] Matthew Dolan, "Talks With City's Creditors Could Alter Payout for Some", *The Wall Street Journal*, 10 February 2014, A3 (reporting about US$11 billion in unsecured debt, including US$6 billion in health and other benefits for retirees; US$3.5 billion for retiree pensions and US$530 million in general-obligation bonds according to the July 2013 municipal bankruptcy filing).

[2] Andy Mukherjee, "Debt Relief for China's Local Governments", *International New York Times*, 15 September 2015, p.20 (citing the Chinese government's official statistics).

[3] There has been some literature on this topic. The angle is the prism of inadequate public service provisions in poor rural areas owing to fiscal stress. See generally, Christine Wong (ed.), *Financing Local Government in the People's Republic of China* (Hong Kong: Oxford University Press 1997); World Bank, "China: National Development and Sub-national Finance – A Review of Provincial Expenditures" (Beijing: Poverty Reduction and Economic Management Unit, East Asia and Pacific Region 2002).

governance structure, which necessitates a more comprehensive reform tackling the root problems underlying the local government debt crisis in China.

This chapter proceeds as follows. Section 2 lays some critical figures and facts about local government debts on the table and that will be followed by discussions on a few suggested pertinent risk-mitigating measures to solving the problem in Section 3. Section 4 analyses the local government debts from some law and governance perspectives with a particular emphasis on various causes to this crisis. Section 5 goes one step further by looking into the deeper political economy perspective of the crisis. Bearing these perspectives in mind, Section 6 calls for some fundamental fiscal, financial and governance reforms. A brief conclusion follows at the end.

2. LOCAL GOVERNMENT DEBTS IN THE CONTEXT OF SHADOW BANKING

Local government debts in China soared after 2008 when the Chinese government loosened borrowing constraints to implement the RMB 4 trillion-stimulus package in order to soften the impact of the latest global financial crisis. There are typically three ways by which local governments mobilise resources within China's financial system.

2.1 Local Government Approaches for Financial Mobilization

Typically, local governments establish informal financial institutions, such as local rural cooperatives and trust investment companies, through which they amass savings from local residents. A slight variation to this form of financial mobilization is that local governments act as guarantors for loans for local enterprises and other institutions. Some outstanding debt is collateralized by government-owned land that is often seriously overvalued. It is worthy to note that such financial activities are expressly prohibited under the Secured Interest Law, which stipulates that the provision of guarantees or collaterals by any governmental authority to any institutions or individuals is strictly prohibited except for borrowing from foreign or international donor agencies.[4]

Local governments also raise finance by borrowing money from banks through their financing vehicles, which are incorporated to skirt a ban on direct borrowing. According to the National Audit Office (NAO),

4 Secured Interest Law, Article 8.

more than 6,000 local government financing vehicles (LGFVs) have created a total debt of RMB 10.7 trillion by 2011.[5] Of that amount, RMB 8.5 trillion, representing roughly 79%, is comprised of bank loans, many of which would not have occurred without the backing of local governments. Due to political pressure from local governments, local financial institutions usually give in to the demand to support local government-initiated projects, many of which are potentially unprofitable or redundant, by injecting loans. If any LGFV defaults on loans, local governments are to bear financial responsibilities.[6] In recent years, these LGFVs have been primarily tasked with providing funds to construction projects associated with China's infrastructure-focused stimulus package, China's economic response to the latest financial crisis.

Issuance of corporate bonds by LGFVs is another way of raising finance. LGFVs sold RMB 283 billion of bonds in the first quarter of 2013, more than double the total for the same period in 2012.[7] Bonds issued by such LGFVs invariably receive top-tier credit ratings from domestic agencies because of governmental support. Unfortunately, most of these bonds do not have strong debt servicing abilities. Further, old debts are sometimes paid through issuance of new debts. The downgrading by Dagong Global Credit Rating Co, one of China's credit-rating firms, of the bonds issued by infrastructure-construction companies wholly owned by Chinese cities in Jilin, Jiangxi and Hubei provinces has thrown in some hints that the dominoes may have started falling, given that it is usually assumed that the government-backed bonds have ironclad credibility due to state backing.

A large proportion of funds is now raised by LGFVs through wealth management products (WMPs).[8] WMPs are simply an intermediary or wrapper around the banned products, but effectively constitute a pool of securities including trust products, bonds and stock funds. These loans are repackaged into poorly documented financial products, which are sold through banks or other financial institutions to ordinary investors with promised higher returns well above government-capped deposit rates. As a result, local government debts can be viewed as a part of the

---

5 Bloomberg, "Liaoning Missed Debt Payments, Says Caixin", *South China Morning Post*, 10 September 2011, B3.

6 Legally, local governments are not liable for these vehicles' debt but creditors believe that such borrowing carries an implicit guarantee.

7 Simon Rabinovitch, "China Local Authority Debt 'Out of Control'", *Financial Times*, 16 April 2013 (online).

8 Shen Wei, "Wealth Management Products in China: Recent Scandals and Regulatory Loopholes", (2013) 28(5) *Journal of International Banking and Financial Law* 303–305.

widespread shadow banking system in China.[9] Loans made outside the formal banking system expanded at a much faster pace than bank credit in recent years. It has been argued that governments are shadow banks because "by allowing excessive competition, providing downside guarantees and encouraging risky lending for populist schemes, governments can create periods of intense economic activity fuelled by credit booms". This is partially what the Chinese government has been doing in the market.[10] In the past several years, the shadow banking sector has nearly doubled to 25.6 trillion yuan, more than a third of total lending.[11]

2.2 Size of Local Government Debts

The precise size of local government debts is not yet clear. Local governments had incurred outstanding liabilities of RMB 10.7 trillion by the end of 2010,[12] amounting to more than 25% of the yearly GDP.[13] Local government debts had increased by almost 70% and reached RMB 17.9 trillion (US$2.95 trillion) (including contingent liabilities and debt guarantees) by the middle of June 2013 – a staggering one-third of China's GDP.[14]

NAO reported on 10 June 2013 that the debt of 36 local governments[15] had risen by 12.94% from RMB 3.41 trillion in 2010 to RMB

---

9 Shen Wei, "Shadow Banking System in China – Origin, Uniqueness and Governmental Response", (2013) 28(1) *Journal of International Banking Law and Regulation* 20–26.

10 Viral V. Acharya, "Governments as Shadow Banks: The Looming Threat to Financial Stability", (2012) 90 *Texas Law Review* 1745.

11 Reuters, "Too Big To Fail? China's Wealth Management Products Stir Debate", *South China Morning Post*, 20 December 2012 (online). Some research reports suggested that the value could reach about 30 trillion yuan, accounting for 25% of overall bank loans. Ray Chan and George Chen, "Beijing Urged to Take Quick Action on Shadow Banking", *South China Morning Post*, 29 January 2013 (online). The difficulty in clearly estimating the size of shadow banking in China is due to the vague definition of "shadow banking". On the other hand, the risk of widening the definition may hurt financial innovation.

12 Daniel Ren, "Shanghai Moves Closer to Bond Sale", *South China Morning Post*, 8 November 2011, B1.

13 Reuters, "Beijing Eyes Municipal Bond Expansion", *South China Morning Post*, 21 October 2013 (online). Depending on the definition of "local debt", Standard Chartered however estimated at that point that the size of local debt was US$4 trillion, which was 42% of GDPs.

14 Tom Mitchell, "Fears after Key China Debt Level Soars 70%", *Financial Times*, 30 December 2013 (online).

15 These include 18 provincial and municipal governments (including 15 provinces and their capitals, as well as the three municipalities of Shanghai, Tianjin and

3.85 trillion at the end of 2012 and LGFVs racked up 45.7% of that new debt.[16] NAO believes that local governments bear only a fraction of these liabilities: 19% of the explicitly guaranteed debt and less than 15% of the implicit obligations. According to the NAO, local government debt had reached RMB 18 trillion by June 2014,[17] and RMB 24 trillion by the end of 2014.[18] Nevertheless, according to the estimates made by Standard Chartered, Fitch and Credit Suisse, local government debts now account for 15 to 36% of the country's output, or as much as US$3 trillion, based on the World Bank's GDP figures in 2012.[19] The International Monetary Fund (IMF) estimated that the "augmented" general government debt, including loans to LGFVs, had risen to nearly 45–50% of China's GDP[20] and the "augmented" fiscal deficit was at 10% of GDP.[21] It has been estimated by *The Economist* that the combined debts of the central and local governments are about 50% of GDP.[22]

The conflict of these figures is largely attributed to the overwhelming proportion of contingent liabilities, perhaps to a certain degree misreporting of debt. According to NAO, local government debts (including contingent liabilities and debt guarantees) had swollen to RMB 17.9 trillion by the middle of 2013, accounting for one-third of China's GDP,[23] to almost US$30 trillion by the end of 2013.[24] This figure consists of 10.9 trillion yuan local government debts owed by the end of June 2013, several trillion yuan of debt local governments had explicitly guaranteed, and another 4.3 trillion they guaranteed inexplicitly.[25] NAO was careful not to add

---

Chongqing, and three of their municipal districts).

16 Kwong Man Ki, "Moody's Warns on China Local Government Debt, Financing Vehicles", *South China Morning Post*, 17 June 2013 (online).

17 Tom Mitchell and Gabriel Wildau, "Chinese Tycoon Sues Local Governments for Late Payment", *Financial Times*, 26 January 2015 (online).

18 Andy Mukherjee, "Debt Relief for China's Local Governments", *International New York Times*, 15 September 2015, p.20 (citing the Chinese government's official statistics).

19 Reuters, "Debt Risk Looms Large in Jiangsu", *South China Morning Post*, 26 July 2013, B2.

20 Simon Rabinovitch, "IMF Urges China to Implement Critical Economic Reforms", *Financial Times*, 17 July 2013 (online).

21 Victoria Ruan, "IMF Warns China of Risks in Investment Binge", *South China Morning Post*, 30 May 2013 (online).

22 "Shadow Lengthen", *The Economist*, 13 April 2013.

23 Jane Cai, "Local Government Debt Signals Rising Risks in Chinese Financial System", *South China Morning Post*, 30 December 2013 (online).

24 Tom Mitchell, "Fears After Key China Debt Level Soars 70%", *Financial Times*, 30 December 2013 (online).

25 "Counting Ghosts", *The Economist*, 4 January 2014, p.32.

these three figures together as debt guarantees are only contingent liabilities. Official estimates of the debt often exclude the financial liabilities of state-owned or township enterprises under the local governments' control even though local governments are ultimate debtors. The state's pension obligations and the debts of the state's policy banks are also excluded.[26] Opaque government disclosure on debt levels has aggravated concerns about the true size of the bad-debt risks.

3. MITIGATING MEASURES TOWARDS LOCAL GOVERNMENT DEBTS

Chinese government and regulators are not asleep at the switch. The central government ordered a detailed audit of the extent of the problem and tried to reform its fiscal policies to reduce the future spending burden upon cities and towns. Regulators have given the banks the go-ahead to resume securitizing assets, aiming to provide an outlet for disposing of bad loans. Regulators have permitted the creation of new provincial-level asset management companies, which are deployed as "bad banks" to deal with bad loans.

3.1 Credit-Tightening

The central government has rolled out some policies to lower the risks in connection with the local government debts. One policy the central government chose to implement was to block all new lending to local governments.[27] Ministry of Finance (MOF), National Development and Reform Commission (NDRC), People's Bank of China (PBOC) and China Banking Regulatory Commission (CBRC) jointly issued the *Notice of Stopping Local Governments' Unlawful and Illegal Financing Activities* on 24 December 2012, curbing credit to LGFVs in order to prevent risk contagion after loans (including non-bank loans) to this risky but grey sector rose to 18% of GDP.[28]

---

26 Ibid.

27 At the end of 2010, local government loans reached Renminbi 9.1 trillion. There has been no substantial increase since then. By the end of 2012, the total outstanding local government loans reached Renminbi 9.2 trillion. Simon Rabinovitch, "China Averts Local Government Defaults", *Financial Times*, 29 January 2013 (online).

28 Jane Cai, "CBRC Tightens Grip on Bank Loans", *South China Morning Post*, 16 April 2013 (online).

The tightening measures include standardizing commercial banks' lending practice to LGFVs, restricting credit to substandard LGFVs, prohibiting banks from guaranteeing bond insurances by LGFVs[29] and setting up a comprehensive monitoring system overseeing commercial lenders' exposure to the sector. Net credit is required to be only advanced to a limited range of LGFVs, including the builders of legally approved toll roads and key projects endorsed by the State Council.[30] In order to control the size of shadow banking, the Notice particularly singled out financing through use of trust companies and WMPs. On the flip side, greater scrutiny is required on LGFVs, for example capital injection into LGFVs in the form of unlawfully granted land is now prohibited. Neither can returns from reserved land be used to repay debt held by LGFVs. These tightening rules appear flimsy given that local governments may finance through shadow lenders such as trust companies and securities firms or the bond market. This may be reflective of the regulators' tendency, still, to support key infrastructure projects in order to boost economic recovery.

3.2 Rollover and Bail Out

The market consensus is that the Chinese government will provide the bail out by using its US$4 trillion foreign reserves if there is a debt crisis.[31] This solution may be simplistically optimistic for two reasons. First, reserves do not equate to the domestic wealth of the country. Second, China's total social financing (private and public debt) is close to 230% of GDP.[32] It is doubtful that the government can sustain such support of the country's debt in a long run.

---

[29] Currently, only bank headquarters have the authority to buy and hold bonds issued by LGFVs. Chinese banks are the largest buyers of corporate bonds. Shen Hong, "Risks Mount as Debt Costs Rise in China", *The Wall Street Journal*, 11 February 2014, C2.

[30] This layer of monitoring is to address the problem of information asymmetry. Records of banks' indirect exposure to these vehicles through the holding of bonds, trust products and wealth management products are useful to match assets with liabilities.

[31] Richard Harris, "China's Debt Dominoes Could Fall Fast", *South China Morning Post*, 11 July 2014 (online).

[32] Tyler Durden, "China's 'Minsky Moment' Is Here, Morgan Stanley Finds", 19 March 2014, available 29 February 2016 at http://www.zerohedge.com/news/2014-03-19/chinas-minsky-moment-here-morgan-stanley-finds (claiming that, if bank loans, corporate bonds and shadow banking are added up altogether, China's debt has increased to more than 300% of GDP). Regardless of what is

The cabinet in 2014 made it clear that it would not provide bail outs to local governments that were unable to repay their own debts, which was a clear attempt to end implicit guarantees and the associated moral hazard. The Shandong provincial government followed suit by clarifying that it would not take responsibility for debt racked up by cities and counties in Shandong. The unavailability of bailouts likely causes a race to the court room among creditors if they believe higher levels of government will not stand behind lower-level debt.

Banks have been asked by the central government to embark on a rollover of loans to local governments by extending maturities for local governments in order to avoid a wave of defaults. In terms of rollover, two criteria are imposed. First, whether a rollover is necessary and whether the project is necessary. Second, whether the investment is consistent with the new five-year plan.[33] Chinese banks have rolled over at least three-quarters of all loans to local governments, that is, at least RMB 3 trillion (of the roughly RMB 4 trillion in loans plus interest) that the local governments were due to mature by the end of 2012.[34] Figure 6.1 shows the maturity structure for corporate bonds issued by LGFVs.[35] According to Figure 6.1, more LGFVs' debts will become due and payable in the coming years. US$400 billion in debt, roughly 40% of the entire debts, became due in 2014 for cash-strapped local governments. Around US$14 trillion has been extended since 2008.[36]

Extending maturity on a massive scale to stave off defaults may help support and complete viable projects so that these projects can eventually generate revenues. Rollover may be the only sensible solution as infrastructure projects tend only to yield profits after a period often longer than 10 years. However, rollover is only a temporary postponing method as loans are not paid off but accumulated in the lending market. The

---

composed of "debt", China's national debt to GDP is probably the highest among major economies. Japan's national debt to GDP reached an astronomical 2.27 to 1 in 2010 whereas the US ratio is only 0.94 to 1. Richard A. Posner, *The Crisis of Capitalist Democracy* (Cambridge, MA: Harvard University Press 2010) p.378.

[33] Simon Rabinovitch, "Beijing to Roll Over Provinces Loan Terms", *Financial Times*, 13 February 2012, p.1.

[34] The *Financial Times* calculation was said to be based on official data. Simon Rabinovitch, "China Averts Local Government Defaults", *Financial Times*, 29 January 2013 (online). The figure is not necessarily accurate as the Chinese government only announces figures for total outstanding loans to local governments but did not publish details about interest payments or refinancing arrangements.

[35] China National Audit Office; IMF.

[36] Minxin Pei, "China Admits its Ills but Faces an Unpalatable Cure", *Financial Times*, 18 March 2014, p.7.

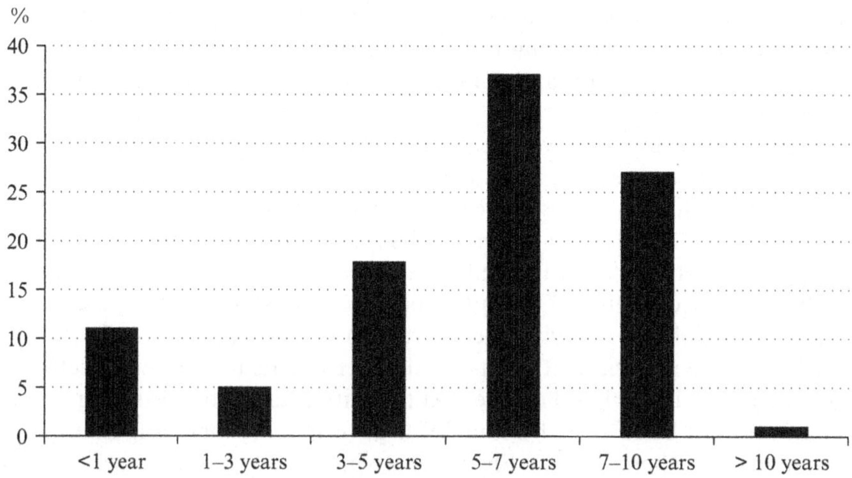

Source: China National Audit Office; IMF.

Figure 6.1 Maturity structure of corporate bonds by LGFVs

default risks can only be extended but not diminished. The rising amounts of unproductive capital not only result in huge overcapacity but may also heighten the financial burden given the growing interest.

3.3 Alternative Funding and Bond Issuance

A more permanent solution to the debt troubles is issuance of local government bonds.[37] China's domestic bond market of US$4 trillion is the world's fourth largest after the US, Japan and France, and is even larger than Shanghai's equity market of US$2.4 trillion. China's bond market remains small compared to the size of its economy even though it is growing at a rate of 30% per year, with 1.2 trillion yuan in debt sold in 2012, double the amount sold in 2011.[38] The bond market, however, is less liquid due to the fact that (i) the majority of bonds are held by domestic investors; and (ii) the market is dominated by treasuries and bonds issued by a small group of large state-owned and policy issuers. In addition, the

[37] Some local governments turned to trust companies and other sources of funding.
[38] Wynne Wang, "China Firms Scrapping Debt Sales", *The Wall Street Journal,* 27 March 2014, C2.

issuance of bonds is subject to a time-consuming, repetitive and costly approval process involving multiple regulators including the PBOC, CBRC, NDRC, MOF and China Securities Regulatory Commission (CSRC).

Local governments have been prohibited from raising funds through direct bond issuance since 1994. Chinese law bans local governments from selling debt directly so as to restrain their borrowings. The MOF sold bonds on behalf of local governments with a full sovereign guarantee. Local governments were allowed to allocate funds collected from the sale of bonds issued by the MOF under special circumstances. If so, they were also responsible for repaying the interest and capital to the bondholders.

The central government wants local governments to borrow directly by issuing bonds in the bond market. At the initial stage, the Chinese government allowed bond sales by four local governments including Shanghai, Guangdong, Zhejiang and Shenzhen (which were hand-picked due to their financial strength) in a pilot scheme. Allowing local government bond issuances would greatly improve transparency of local governments' financial status. Disclosure requirements impose a hard budget discipline on local governments and officials. Shanghai became the first local government in China to directly issue bonds in the past two decades.[39] Bank of Communications, Bank of Shanghai and China Development Bank were appointed to underwrite the debt sale.[40] The Shanghai government sold bonds in equal amounts of three- and five-year bills: RMB 3.6 billion of three-year bonds at a yield of 3.1% and RMB 3.5 billion of five-year bonds at 3.3%. As of today, only 10 local governments are allowed to issue bonds,[41] and the local government bond pilot programme remains tiny compared with the scale of local government financing needs.

The National People's Congress legalized local governments' bond sales by amending the Budget Law in August 2014.[42] The amended Budget

---

[39] China has launched a high-yield bond market. There are also plans for the country's domestic commodities exchange to begin trading crude oil futures soon. Reuters, "Financial Reformers Adapt Communist Party Rhetoric", *South China Morning Post*, 13 November 2012 (online).

[40] Daniel Ren, "Shanghai Moves Closer to Bond Sale", *South China Morning Post*, 8 November 2011, B1.

[41] Ministry of Finance, "Pilot Rules of Self-issuance and Repayment of Local Government Bonds in 2014", 21 May 2014.

[42] PRC Budget Law was first promulgated 20 years ago, and the amendments were initiated 10 years ago. The newly amended Budget Law is now double the size of the old one, with changes in 82 areas, many of which are worth highlighting. Just to mention a few, the most important achievement of the amended Budget Law is its compliance with the framework set out by the CCP's Third Plenum's

Law now ends the direct borrowing ban and allows local governments to issue bonds directly for "public-welfare capital expenditure",[43] providing a legal basis for the formalization and expansion of the pilot scheme. The Standing Committee of the NPC imposed a 600-billion-yuan limit on the direct debt local governments are allowed to run up in 2015, which would be on top of 15.4 trillion yuan owed by local governments by the end of 2014.[44] With bond issues, the debt structure will be changed: local governments may borrow little money. Instead, they would finance through the open bond market. However, as banks are predominantly the major buyers of bonds, the systemic risk is still trapped in the banks, exposing them to high risks of defaults. Eventually, it may be the Chinese government that needs to bail out its provinces and cities, which would add to its own debt stock.

Partial statistics on local government fundraising show that they sold RMB 1.66 trillion worth of bonds in 2014, compared with RMB 900 billion in each of the two previous years. Allowing bond issues does not wipe off the debts.[45] Instead, the current debts just change hands from commercial lenders to investors. In other words, bond issuance is not an ultimate solution to reduce debts. Given the fact that the central government's liabilities are less than 17% of GDP,[46] one possible solution is for the central government to take on some of the local debt by issuing long-term sovereign bonds.

3.4 Municipal Bankruptcy and Defaults

Municipal bankruptcy is a possible solution for local government debts in some jurisdictions. However, it is not a feasible option under Chinese law as the bankruptcy regime, centred on the Enterprise Bankruptcy Law, does not include clear legal procedures for resolving municipal insolvency. An overhaul of China's fiscal system may be necessary and is now spearheaded by a leading group on economic reform. Premier Li

---

reform blueprint. The Budget Law has strengthened oversight by the legislatures at all levels. This is in line with the Third Plenum's call for a law-based and transparent budgeting system. The shift is reflective of the ruling party's changing attitude towards budgeting, which is no longer a private matter to the government.

43 Budget Law, Article 35.

44 Carlos Tejada, "Lawmakers Place Cap To Rein In Local Debt", *The Wall Street Journal*, 31 August 2015, p.5.

45 Jamil Anderlini, "China: Overborrowed and Overbuild", 30 January 2015 (online).

46 "Debt Relief for China's Local Governments", *International New York Times*, 15 September 2015, p.20.

Keqiang indicated in an early March 2014 speech that some debt defaults are hard to avoid in a challenging economic environment. In addition, he proposed that China set up procedures for troubled borrowers, including local governments, "to be orderly restructured"[47] though it is unclear what "restructuring" refers to.

Allowing a default can be used as a valid instrument to step up credit-risk monitoring, inject more discipline into the market and create a "knock-on" effect,[48] thereby raising yields and slowing down borrowing at a time when fixed assets investment growth is slowing. The government appears comfortable with modest-size defaults, which may lead to capital efficiency and a reduction of the moral hazard problem after years of bailout.[49] Widespread moral hazard across borrowers and lenders is one of the reasons that credit growth in China has spiralled out of control, with total debt rising sharply from 130 to 210% of national income in the past five years. The government is likely to allow more debt defaults.[50]

Given the political reality of China's financial system, it is unlikely that the Chinese government would allow a large number of LGFVs to default, as there could be a chain reaction. As a matter of fact, no bond has ever publicly defaulted in China, making investment in LGFVs akin to a one-way bet.[51] The unintended effect would be deteriorating confidence in the

---

[47] Lingling Wei, "China Tries Allowing Defaults", *The Wall Street Journal*, 26 March 2014, C3.

[48] Some commentators argued for an all-out panic, a market psychology that Chaori's failure may naturally trigger. Joseph Sternberg, "China's Quiet Lehman Moment", *The Wall Street Journal*, 13 March 2014, A13.

[49] It is reported that Shanghai Chaori avoided a default one year ago after a local government in Shanghai persuaded the bank to defer claims on overdue loans. Lingling Wei, "Corporate Default Heading to China", *The Wall Street Journal*, 6 March 2014, C3. But the difficulty for investors is to quantify the risk of default. In other words, it is hard for investors to rely on conventional tools of corporate financial analysis and economic forecasting to assess risks. Largely, it will be a guessing game about which distressed company will be allowed to default based on what factors such as the size, industrial sector and political connections of the company. The usual deciding factors such as capital pricing and allocation may not have sufficient business merit.

[50] This is also consistent with the market expectation. According to the IMF's Global Financial and Stability Report, problematic corporate loans could increase as much as US$750 billion and many companies may be forced to default. Landon Thomas Jr, "I.M.F. Warns of Risk from Emerging-Market Corporate Debt", *New York Times*, 10 April 2014, B3.

[51] Henry Sanderson and Michael Forsythe, *China's Superbank: Debt, Oil and Influence – How China Development Bank is Rewriting the Rules of Finance* (Singapore: John Wiley & Sons Publishing 2013) p.26.

solvency of a wide range of borrowers, which may in turn result in a credit squeeze and more defaults. In China's financial system, determining which borrower to default is a political process which may end up making decisions based on principles other than the fittest borrowers to survive, that is prioritizing private borrowers for defaults first.[52] Politically, enforcing market disciplines could lead to a political backlash as retail investors come into the market based on an implicit understanding that the government may eventually bail out the failed lenders.

The market, however, will play its role in the defaulting process. The lenders may lose patience and take more proactive measures. Mr Yan Jiehe, the president of China Pacific Construction Group, China's largest private infrastructure construction company,[53] and China's seventh richest man with a fortune estimated at US$14.2 billion, has shown his intention to sue six municipal and county governments for overdue payments on infrastructure contracts.[54] This would be a rare legal action, the first lawsuit of this type, but highlights the risks of unpaid debts cascading through China's economy. As Mr Yan claimed, suing local governments for unpaid debts will help strengthen the rule of law in China. Apart from this, the lawsuit may set a precedent for other creditors to follow suit. In effect, Mr Yan will have the first-mover advantage in the litigation as he basically has the priority to obtain assets owned by the local governments. Economically, local defaults could spark a full-blown financial crisis as other creditors may follow Yan's suits.

---

[52] It was reported that the PBOC, China Construction Bank and the government of Fenghua, a town in eastern China with a population of 500,000 bailed out Zhejiang Xingrun Real Estate Co, a defaulting real estate developer in Zhejiang, with Renminbi 3.5 billion. The company took deposits from individuals who were offered annual interest rates of between 18 and 36%. Jamil Anderlini, "China Weighs State Rescue of Developer", *Financial Times*, 19 March 2014, p.2. The company claimed its inability to repay US$600 million of bank loans. Grace Zhu, "Chinese Banks Increase Write-offs", *The Wall Street Journal,* 1 April 2014, C3.

[53] In 2014, it was ranked 166th on the Forbes 500 list of the world's largest companies, with US$60 billion in annual revenues.

[54] Tom Mitchell, "Yan Jiehe, CPCG: the Chinese Billionaire Turned Debt Collector", *Financial Times,* 1 February 2015 (online). CPCG did not reveal the total amount of money CPCG was owed. It mentioned two local governments. One is Jinning county in Yunnan province owed Renminbi 95 million for four infrastructure projects completed two years ago. Ningjin county in Hebei province owed Renminbi 83 million for 16 completed projects. Tom Mitchell and Gabriel Wildau, "Chinese Tycoon Sues Local Governments for Late Payment", *Financial Times*, 26 January 2015 (online).

3.5 Debt Swap Scheme

The MOF has recently introduced a debt swap program to restructure the liabilities of local governments. Local governments are allowed to swap RMB 1 trillion of their maturing high-interest debts for lower-cost bonds. The 1 trillion yuan local bonds will replace, as reported, 53.8% of the 1,858 trillion yuan debt falling due in 2015.[55] The current stock of debt is largely in the form of bank loans and trust loans borrowed through around 100,000 LGFVs.[56] Each province is given a quota for the debt-for-bond swap. Anhui province, for example, among the first batch of provinces, is allowed to swap 32.2 billion yuan. Anhui is to use the funds to repay debt due to mature in 2015. Chongqing received a 33 billion yuan quota in the swap scheme. But it has outstanding liabilities of 590 billion yuan.[57] Jiangsu in May 2015 completed a bond sale in the amount of RMB 52.2 billion with a coupon rate slightly higher than equivalent sovereign Treasury rates.[58] The MOF plans to give local governments a total of 3 trillion yuan quota for refinancing.

(a) Benefits of the scheme

The debt-for-bond scheme itself is designed to help ease the massive debt burden on local governments without crippling the broader economy. Given the huge size of local government debts, the debt swap and new debt issuance[59] may only cover a small portion of the overall debt liabilities. The scheme does have some benefits though.

The primary benefit of this debt-for-bond swap scheme is to help lower the financing costs of these local government debts. Local governments are paying interest rates 4–5 percentage points above the prevailing treasury yield on the debts. The swap scheme therefore may save 40–50 billion yuan in a single year on interest costs. This suggests that the swap scheme itself does not solve the debt problem as the outstanding debt is still there.

---

55 "Debt-Swap Plan of Local Government Set To Be Expanded", *China Daily*, available at http://www.ecns.cn/business/2015/03-28/159758.shtml.

56 The figure was released by the Ministry of Finance through the finance minister in a conference. Ibid.

57 Ibid.

58 Jamil Anderlini, "China Province Completes Landmark Bond Sale", *Financial Times*, 19 May 2015, available 29 February 2016 at http://www.ft.com/intl/cms/s/0/03296f56-fdf2-11e4-9f10-00144feabdc0.html#axzz3jXYM2uZQ.

59 Previously, local governments were restricted to issue bonds. The central government issued bonds on behalf of local governments. Under the new Budget Law, local governments can issue bonds. The 2015 budget calls for 600 billion yuan in bond issues to cover local government debt.

It is estimated that local debts have reached as high as 30 trillion yuan, and a 3 trillion yuan swap still leaves the remainder more exposed to default risks. What is partially solved is to lower the interest payment so that the interest costs are not inexorably adding to leverage.

Bond securities can be more easily sold and are more liquid. Compared with bank loans, bonds usually have a longer term. The swap scheme may also effectively extend the maturity from 3 or 5 years to 7 or 15 years, thereby reducing current principal payments by RMB 800 billion to RMB 1 trillion per year. While lowering debt service costs, the scheme is likely to bring much needed relief to local finance and improve debt sustainability. It is also a sensible means to deleverage at an acceptable pace. Deleveraging too fast would cause stagnation in the property and other overheated sectors.

The bond market is certainly more disciplined than the lending market. Local governments have to disclose their financial situation to the public and get approval from the central government if they want to issue debt. The swap scheme is a strong credit enhancement measure as local governments have to budget for the repayments. This can increase transparency for local borrowing and spending. Issuance of debt backed by the local government's revenue streams offers little room for abuse compared to LGFVs.

The swap scheme is technically different from quantitative easing unless the central bank is to buy bonds outright. Without the central bank's involvement, the swap scheme is, in nature, a debt restructuring and asset securitization. In other words, this may not result in asset bubbles. But on the other hand, there is no guarantee that the central bank will not take the opportunity to implement a large-scale easing program. The central bank allows commercial banks to use local-government bail out bonds that they purchase as collateral for a wide variety of low-cost loans from the central bank.[60] The goal is apparently to promote bond sales and provide Chinese banks with more funds to make new loans.

The swap scheme may also help upgrade and expand China's bond market. Currently, the interbank bond market accounts for 95% of the total bond market in China. The municipal bond market is estimated to grow 1,000% to 12.1 trillion yuan by 2020, which is larger than the current size of the entire treasury market.[61] The debt-bond deal is a market-oriented way to neutralize the shadow banking sector.

---

[60] Lingling Wei, "China Stimulus Aims at Restructuring Trillions in Local-Government Debt", *The Wall Street Journal*, 13 May 2015, available 29 February 2016 at http://www.marketwatch.com/story/china-stimulus-aims-at-restructuring-trillions-in-local-government-debt-2015-05-13-71035643.

[61] Nathaniel Taplin, "Explosive Local Government Debt Issuance

(b) Who are investors?

The swap scheme itself does not help solve the debt problem as the purchasers of these bonds will largely be Chinese commercial lenders, who will suffer losses because their high-yielding assets are exchanged for lower-yielding bonds. This was the reason that the initial issuance of the bonds was not well received which forced the provincial governments to postpone the sale.[62] The Chinese government was unable to sell all the bonds offered at an auction in April 2015, which raised a concern about the market demand.[63] Commercial lenders are the main investors in the Chinese bond market. Due to the political connection with the government, commercial lenders are pressured into accepting lower-yielding bonds and lose interest revenue. The central government issued administrative orders, guarantees and preferential policies to convince state-owned banks to buy the bonds.

The trade-off is that government bonds may guarantee repayment. Holding lower-risk bond assets helps banks reduce capital charges, increase the capital adequacy ratio, and improve their asset quality and liquidity. However, the central bank may be under pressure to provide commercial banks with more liquidity support as these commercial banks will need more funds to make loans.

Meanwhile, the State Council, China's cabinet, unveiled measures to expand the investment scope of the country's social-security fund to include local government bonds and other financial instruments. The social-security fund is now allowed to invest up to 20% (from the previous 10%) of its portfolio in local government debt and corporate bonds, and up to 10% (an increase from 5% previously) in trust loans. In order to contain potential risks, the portfolio investment used to be confined to bonds, bank deposits, stock and mutual funds.[64] The increase of local government holding from 10 to 20% makes it possible for the social

Threatens China Central Bank's Easing Efforts", Reuters Economy, 22 May 2015, available 29 February 2016 at http://in.reuters.com/article/2015/06/22/china-bonds-cenbank-idINKBN0P20MP20150622.

[62] Gabriel Wildau, "China Treasury Bond Auction Failure Raises Concerns on Debt Plan", *Financial Times*, 24 June 2015, available 29 February 2016 at http://www.ft.com/intl/cms/s/0/00129228-1a3c-11e5-a130-2e7db721f996.html#axzz3jXYM2uZQ.

[63] Simon Rabinovitch, "China Bond Auction Failure Reinforces Slowdown Concerns", *Financial Times*, 11 April 2014 (online).

[64] The social security fund can now invest in interbank certificates of deposit and in affordable housing, a government-led program for lower-income households. Apart from the state-owned enterprises, it can now take direct stakes in private companies.

security fund to purchase an extra RMB 300 billion–400 billion in local government bonds.

(c) Persistent uncertainties

The bond market effectively provides a market-oriented platform for the debt problem. However, there are some technical uncertainties. First, if the local government defaults on its repayment, will the central government provide bail outs? Second, can a local government enter bankruptcy in the event of debt defaults if the central government does not bail it out? It appears that a bail out program may be the final solution.[65]

China's clean-up operation is only a minor step. The MOF has indicated its plan to expand the program to 3 trillion yuan[66] to alleviate the debt-repayment burdens of local governments. In June 2015, the Ministry of Finance granted another 1 trillion yuan quota to provinces and brought a quota first issued in March 2015 to 2 trillion yuan.[67] Even though the total swap program was recently expanded from RMB 2 to 3.2 trillion, it is still too small to make a difference.[68]

4. CAUSES OF LOCAL GOVERNMENT DEBTS: LAW AND GOVERNANCE PERSPECTIVES

The local government debt in China is on the verge of a cliff and the causes of increasing local government debts are multi-faceted.

4.1 China's Fiscal System under the Budget Law

The underlying problem with local government debts is rooted in China's fiscal system – a lack of revenue generating capacity or borrowing capacity at the local level. China's old Budget Law entirely prohibited local governments from engaging in debt financing, including issuance of local

---

[65] Lynette Ong, "Local Government Debt: Another Bail-out Job", (2006) *China Economic Quarterly* 48–52.

[66] "China Prepared to Expand Local Government Debt Swap If Needed", *The Economic Times*, available 29 February 2016 at http://economictimes.indiatimes.com/topic/China-Prepared-to-Expand-Local-Government-Debt-Swap-If-Needed.

[67] Bloomberg Business, "China Doubles Local Government Debt Swap Quota to Ease Risks", 10 June 2015, available 29 February 2016 at http://www.bloomberg.com/news/articles/2015-06-10/china-grants-additional-1t-yuan-quota-for-local-govt-debt-swap.

[68] "Debt Relief for China's Local Governments", *International New York Times*, 15 September 2015, p.20.

government bonds and public fund-raising.[69] Under the Budget Law, local governments are under legal obligations to abide by the principle of balancing revenue and expenditures and not to run fiscal deficits.[70] The Budget Law used to make no mention of a clear delineation of spending responsibility between central and local governments. The MOF draws a rough line of dividing spending responsibilities: central expenditure items include defence, armed police, capital investment, central administration, central level institutions and debt services; local expenditure items cover local administration, institutions, locally sponsored capital investment and technical renovation, aid to agriculture, urban maintenance and construction, price subsidies and others.[71]

As the World Bank report correctly pointed out, "over the past two decades there has been a considerable devolution of expenditures to local governments, which are responsible for day-to-day government administration and the provision of social services while at the same time the tax sharing system has re-centralised revenue assignments".[72] Figure 6.2 indicates a percentage split of expenditures between the central and local governments in the period from 2008 to 2012. In reality, local governments bear far more responsibilities than the central government in terms of providing public services to the general public.

In order to meet increasing spending demands, local governments have been heavily reliant upon land sales and fiscal transfers from the central government.[73] It has been estimated that local governments rely on sales of land for 35% of their revenues.[74] The flaws in the fiscal system were

---

[69] Budget Law (before the 2014 amendments), Article 28.

[70] Budget Law, Article 35.

[71] Christine P.W. Wong, "Central-Local Relations in an Era of Fiscal Decline – The Paradox of Fiscal Decentralization in Post-Mao China", (1991) 128 *The China Quarterly* 703–706.

[72] World Bank, *National Development and Sub-national Finance – A Review of Provincial Expenditures* (Beijing: Poverty Reduction and Economic Management Unit, East Asia and Pacific Region, World Bank 2002).

[73] Another incentive for local officials to sell land is to create glamorous projects to aid their chances of promotion, which will be discussed in the later part of this section.

[74] Jamil Anderlini, "China: Overborrowed and Overbuilt", *Financial Times*, 30 January 2015 (online) (citing research from Deutsche Bank). As a matter of fact, local governments are dominant buyers of land in the past several years. Previously, financing vehicles were set up for the purpose of borrowing money. As real estate sales have slumped and demand for land from commercial developers has evaporated, these financing vehicles are now used to purchase land from themselves using credit from lenders. This attempt may help boost short-term growth and flag fiscal revenues. However, this attempt is not sustainable.

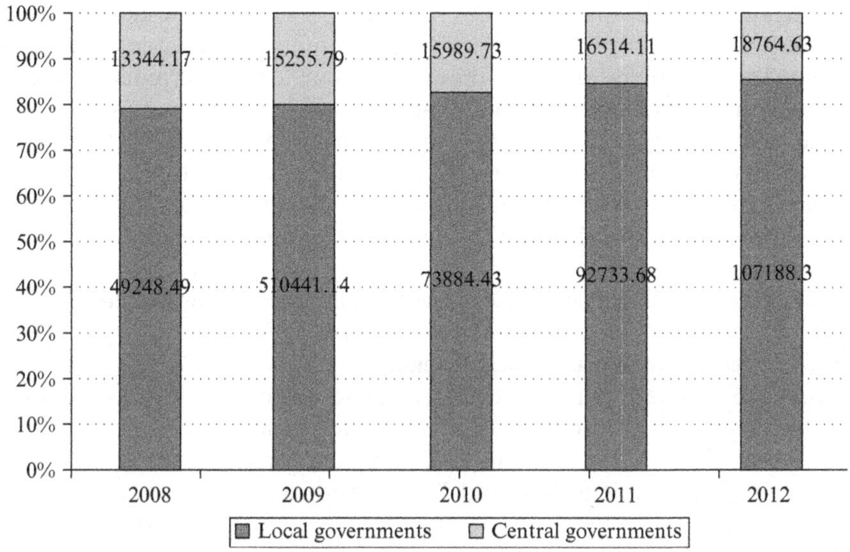

Source: Compiled by the author.

Figure 6.2 Split of total expenditures between central and local governments (2008–2012, RMB 100 million)

exposed when China introduced a large stimulus package in response to the 2008 financial crisis. The stimulus package was largely implemented through local governments which do not have funding and are not allowed to borrow money from banks.[75] The revenue gap was understandably filled by China's growing shadow banking system where companies and individuals feed their savings into white elephant projects as well as public services.

The institutionalized budgeting process is not yet able to effectively constrain policymaking. In reality, there exists a severe separation between policymaking and budgeting. The higher-level government often exerts its discretion to determine the allocation of spending responsibilities. Arbitrary shifting of responsibilities to a lower-level government has been in existence and sometimes routine due to the lack of a clear-cut assignment of expenditure responsibilities. Higher-level government or the China Communist Party (CCP) leader may initiate new policies that are likely to result in new

75 This does not take into account local governments' responsibility for retirement income and health care for local residents.

expenditures. In response to uncertainties in executing the budget, local governments usually have to reserve a large amount of revenue when compiling the annual budget.[76] For the same reason, local governments have to levy an array of charges to finance various tasks handed down from above. The lack of a detailed division of expenditure responsibility in the Budget Law appears a key shortcoming in executing governmental spending and budgetary activities. Due to the importance of a country's fiscal policy, this lack showcases the backwardness of China's governance regime.

4.2 Vertical Imbalances between Central and Local Governments

(a) Vertical imbalance of fiscal revenues

The other related cause of the local government debts is the vertical imbalance of tax revenue between the central and local governments.[77] Up until 1993, China had a self-financing regime for both central and local government, occupying 30% and 70% of budgetary revenue respectively. Since the fiscal reform in 1994, local governments' share of the tax revenue has decreased to 40% but at the same time their responsibility for public expenditures spiked at 70 to 80%. This change showed the central government's tendency to strengthen its ability to reallocate financial resources and collect revenue thereby possessing stronger macroeconomic regulatory capacity and control over local governments.[78]

Table 6.1 shows a split of revenue collected by the central and local governments. During the period from 2007 to 2012, local governments' revenues steadily remained at the level of 46–50% of the total revenues.

Taking year 2010 from the above table as an example, fiscal revenue of local governments accounted for 48.9% of nationwide fiscal revenue, but local governments assumed 82.2% of nationwide fiscal expenditures. The immediate consequence is that the local financial deficit climbed up to RMB 3,327.1 billion.[79] The gap between budgetary income and total

---

[76] Jun Ma and Yinlin Zhou, "Policymaking and Budgeting Process in China's Provincial Budgeting", (2005) 5 *Comparative Economic and Social System* 64–72.

[77] This has been at the centre of academic attention in the 1990s. The more important publications include Michael Oksenberg and James Tong, "The Evolution of Central-Provincial Fiscal Relations in China, 1971–1984: The Formal System", (1991) 125 *The China Quarterly* 1–32; World Bank, *China: Revenue Mobilization and Tax Policy* (Washington DC: World Bank 1990).

[78] World Bank, "Urban Policy and Economic Development: An Agenda for the 1990s: A World Bank Policy Paper" (Washington DC: World Bank 1990) p.26.

[79] NAO, "Auditing Reports of Local Government Debts Nation-wide (No. 35 2011)", available 29 April 2016 at http://www.audit.gov.cn/n1992130/n1992150/n1992500/2752208.html.

Table 6.1 *Split of fiscal revenue between central and local governments (2005–2012, RMB 100 million)*

	2005	2006	2007	2008	2009	2010	2011	2012
Total Fiscal Revenue	3,164.929	3,876.020	5,232.178	6,133.035	6,851.830	8,310.151	10,387.443	11,725.352
Central Government	1,654.853	2,045.662	2,774.916	3,268.056	3,591.571	4,248.847	5,132.732	5,617.523
%	52.29%	53.01%	53.04%	53.29%	52.42%	51.13%	49.41%	47.91%
Local Governments	1,510.076	1,830.358	2,357.262	2,864.979	3,260.259	4,061.304	5,254.711	6,107.829
%	47.71%	46.99%	46.96%	46.71%	47.58%	48.87%	50.59%	52.09%

Source: Compiled by the author. Data from China Statistics Yearbooks 2008–2013.

expenditure of local governments further widened after the mid-1990s and remains at around 45%. The figures in Table 6.2 demonstrate that local government-generated revenues declined after 1994, and can only cover roughly 55% (on average) of their expenditures between 2007 and 2012. Year 1994 saw the introduction of fiscal system reform, witnessing a fundamental change and since then, the local governments' own revenues were no longer sufficient for their own expenditures.

There were widespread complaints by the local governments of fiscal shortage.[80] The rural tax reforms in the early 2000s to reduce exactions from the farmers and to abolish agricultural taxes further undermined local governments' ability to raise funds and provide public services.[81] The division of enterprise and personal income tax between the central and provincial governments, a further modification to the tax-sharing system, since 2002, has also worsened the fiscal shortage at the local level.[82]

(b) Bureaucratic inefficiency in revenue transfer and allocation

Revenue collection is an essential instrument to maintain political integration, regulate economic activities and provide public goods. The concentration of revenue collection is important to both federal and central governments. In the unitary system, fiscal resources are transferred along with responsibilities of different levels of government. China is a unitary country with a more powerful central government evidenced by the fact that the central government's share of disposable revenue is higher than that of federal government in other federal countries. However, the allocation of funds is not necessarily efficient due to the distorted implementation mechanisms and politically oriented fiscal institutions.

To address the problem of fiscal inadequacy, an institutionalized intergovernmental fiscal transfer system was introduced by the central government in 1994 with the aim of sustaining sufficient and equitable public services. The objective of the system was to change the budgetary positions of the central and local governments. Starting from 1994, the central

---

80 Jean C. Oi and Zhao Shukai, "Fiscal Crisis in China's Townships: Causes and Consequences", in Elizabeth J. Perry and Merle Goldman (eds), *Grassroots Political Reform in Contemporary China* (Cambridge, MA: Harvard University Press 2007).

81 John James Kennedy, "From the Tax-for-Fee Reform to the Abolition of Agricultural Taxes: The Impact on Township Governments in North-West China", (2007) 189 *The China Quarterly* 43–59.

82 State Council, Circular on the Publication of the Reform Plan for the Sharing of Income Tax Revenue, Guofa No. 37 (2001).

Table 6.2 Share of local governments' expenditures financed with own revenues (1978–2012)

Year	Local Government-owned Revenues (Billion Renminbi)	Local Government Expenditures (Billion Renminbi)	Self-owned revenues as % of Expenditures (%)
1978	95.6	59.0	162.13
1979	91.5	62.7	146.01
1980	87.5	56.2	155.77
1981	86.5	51.3	168.64
1982	86.5	57.8	149.69
1983	87.7	65.0	134.93
1984	97.7	80.8	121.01
1985	123.5	120.9	102.17
1986	134.4	136.9	98.18
1987	146.3	141.7	103.28
1988	158.2	164.6	96.13
1989	184.2	193.5	95.21
1990	194.5	207.9	93.53
1991	221.1	229.6	96.32
1992	250.4	257.2	97.36
1993	339.1	333.0	101.84
1994	231.2	403.8	57.24
1995	298.6	482.8	61.83
1996	374.7	578.6	64.76
1997	442.4	670.1	66.02
1998	498.4	767.3	64.96
1999	559.5	903.5	61.92
2000	640.6	1,036.7	61.79
2001	780.3	1,313.5	59.41
2002	851.5	1,528.1	55.72
2003	985.0	1,723.0	57.17
2004	1,189.3	2,059.3	57.75
2005	1,510.1	2,515.4	60.03
2006	1,830.4	3,043.1	60.15
2007	2,357.3	3,833.9	61.48
2008	2,865.0	4,924.8	58.17
2009	3,260.3	6,104.4	53.41
2010	4,061.3	7,388.4	54.97
2011	5,254.7	9,273.4	56.66
2012	6,107.8	10,718.8	56.98

Source: Compiled by the author. Data from China Statistics Yearbooks 2008–2013.

government funded about 40% of local government expenditure. There has been no clear rule as to how the tax rebate should be calculated.[83] Fiscal transfers can be roughly divided into three categories: tax returns,[84] financial-capacity subsidies and earmarked subsidies. All these transfers follow divergent distributive mechanisms and serve different purposes. From 1994, provincial governments switched to be more dependent on transfers from the central government for the purpose of financing one-third of their expenditure. The transferred revenue from the central to local governments remains at the level of 44.6% (on average) from 2008 to 2012. The percentage of transferred revenue and expenditures ranged from 42 to 49% during the period from 1996 to 2012.[85] The inter-governmental transfer system, however, underfunded the local expenditures.[86]

(c) Tax sharing scheme

The tax sharing system, also implemented in 1994 to replace the previous revenue-sharing system, was aimed at increasing the central government's share of revenues to enable it to regain regulatory power over local finance and to have greater autonomy in redistributing revenue across regions. More local revenues were then reallocated by the central to local governments in the form of tax rebates or transfer payments.[87] In order to raise the budgetary revenue-to-GDP ratio and the central government's share ratio in revenue collection, taxes are divided into three categories according to the recipient of their revenue. Taxes are categorized as central taxes, central-local shared taxes and local taxes. The shared taxes account for the

---

[83] World Bank, "National Development and Sub-national Finance – A Review of Provincial Expenditures" (Beijing: Poverty Reduction and Economic Management Unit, East Asia and Pacific Region, World Bank 2002).

[84] Tax returns from the central government include the returns of value-added taxes, consumption taxes, and individual and company income taxes as well as export debates.

[85] Fiscal Yearbook of China (1994–2011), available 29 February 2016 at http://tongji.cnki.net/kns55/Navi/YearBook.aspx?id=N2013020024&floor=1; 2012 data available 29 February 2016 at http://yss.mof.gov.cn/2012qhczjs/201307/t20130715_966263.html, http://www.gov.cn/gzdt/2013-06/28/content_2436129.htm.

[86] Maria Edin, *Market Forces and Communist Power: Local Political Institutions and Economic Development in China* (Uppsala: Uppsala University, Department of Government 2000).

[87] Transfer payment is a horizontal fiscal equalisation arrangement to address economic dislocation, political disharmony and capital movements. Jon Craig, "Horizontal Equalization Grants" in Ethisham Ahamd, Gao Qiang and Vito Tanzi (eds), *Reforming China's Public Finance* (Washington DC: International Monetary Fund 1995) p.270.

largest portion of revenue and include VAT (which is split as 75% for the central government and 25% for localities), resource tax (100% of offshore oil resource tax revenue for the central government while other resource taxes are for local governments), securities trading stamp tax (which is divided between the central and provincial governments) and consumption tax (100% of which belongs to the central government). As part of this tax-sharing scheme, the central government made a compromise to guarantee the revenue level of provincial governments by adopting a special transfer payment mechanism, termed as a tax repayment system. The reform is a pro-central-government one with the aim of striking a new balance between central and provincial governments. While the largest beneficiary of this reform was the central government, provincial governments' interests were also taken into consideration being ranked after the central government.

It has been widely recognized that there has been a fiscal decline in China since 1994,[88] and that the revenue-sharing system was the partial cause of this decline. Thus, the revenue sharing system was often viewed as a revenue reducing system. As a matter of fact, the "two ratios", the ratio of budgetary revenue to GDP and the ratio of central budgetary revenue to total budgetary revenue, encouragingly rose in the years after the reform was implemented in 1994, which solidified the central government's claim of success for the reform. For example, the share of central government revenue collection ratio rose to 57% of total budgetary revenue in 1994 and reached 52.17%, 55.6% and 56.5% in 1995, 1996 and 1997 respectively.[89] The ratio of the budgetary revenue to GDP also experienced a rising trend in the next several years. The other consequential result of this redistribution of tax collection power and a change to the revenue-sharing system, as planned, was a substantial rise of tax revenue from 22% in 1993 to 55.7% in 1994 for the central government.[90] By contrast, the local governments' share of tax revenue dropped from an average of 70.2% to 48%. As expenditure responsibilities remained unchanged, there emerged

---

[88] But some research casts doubt on this conclusion given the fact that China's state budget does not include extra-budgetary funds and extra-establishment funds. Le Yin Zhang, "Chinese Central-Provincial Fiscal Relationships, Budgetary Decline and the Impact of the 1994 Fiscal Reform: An Evaluation", (1999) 157 *The China Quarterly* 115, 125–126.

[89] Le Yin Zhang, "Chinese Central-Provincial Fiscal Relationships, Budgetary Decline and the Impact of the 1994 Fiscal Reform: An Evaluation", (1999) 157 *The China Quarterly* 115, 134–135.

[90] World Bank, *National Development and Sub-national Finance – A Review of Provincial Expenditures* (Beijing: Poverty Reduction and Economic Management Unit, East Asia and Pacific Region, World Bank 2002).

a large fiscal gap of revenue and expenditure at local levels. Local government debts are heavy compared with the taxes they raise. For example, direct debts of Yunnan and Qinghai amounted to over 260% and 370% of their budget revenues in 2012.[91]

4.3 Fiscal Reforms on Township Governments' Fiscal Situation

The township fiscal system was set up in 1983 based on the principle that "each level of government has its own budget". Various reforms were carried out in the 1980s and 1990s including the fiscal contracting system in 1988, the tax sharing system in 1994 (which divided all revenues into central and local entitlements and imposed a standard formula on all localities)[92] and the tax-for-fees policy in 1998, all of which, however, worsened local governments' financial status.

The notion of tax-for-fee first appeared in a joint document issued by the State Commission of Restructuring Economy, Ministry of Construction, MOF and eight other ministries and commissions in 1995.[93] The idea of tax-for-fee was put forward as a measure to tackle the problems of chaotic fund-raising and excessive charges in rural areas. Grassroots governments in these areas imposed heavy financial burdens on the farmers to collect fees and levies, causing a long festering crisis in the relations between farmers and governments. Abolishing abusive local levies and charges and extending formal fiscal control into the rural grass-roots level not only decreased peasant burden but also enhanced fiscal discipline. To sustain the reform, the central and provincial governments provided extra financial subsidies to underwrite the decrease of collected revenues suffered by township administrations under the reform scheme.

Replacing local charges and fees with formal taxation entails budgetary approval, scrutiny and control as well as more rigorous reporting and monitoring mechanisms. While this reform dismantled parochial dominance over local financial management, it increased the level of predictability and transparency. The insufficiency of fiscal distribution undermined the goal of reform and the central government's desire to have more effective regulation and control. As far as local governments are

---

[91] "Bridging the Fiscal Chasm", *The Economist*, 22 February 2014 (online).

[92] Pak K. Lee, "Into the Trap of Strengthening State Capacity: China's Tax-assignment Reform", (2000) 164 *China Quarterly* 1007–24; Tsang Shu ki and Cheng Yuk shing, "China's Tax Reforms of 1994: Breakthrough or Compromise?", (1994) 36(9) *Asian Survey* 769–788.

[93] Document Relaying the Opinion on the Test Point of Comprehensive Reform of Small Towns.

concerned, collection of fees is extra-budgetary but secured entitlement, over which local governments have more discretionary power to exert.

Nevertheless, the reform to abolish the collection of various fees and charges from rural residents further strained the grassroots governments' financial status. The central government's strategy was to strengthen its control over and surveillance of these funds. According to the *Notice on the Promulgation of the Method for Implementing the Management of Extra-budgetary Funds*, issued by the State Council on 18 November 1996, the extra-budgetary funds were subject to a new and more stringent monitoring regime, so-called "separate management of income and expenditure". Under this regime, the extra budgetary funds are included into the budget but spending is still determined by the administrative authorities that collect the funds. This regime effectively makes this part of budgetary revenue separate from normal government expenditure. Reforming fees to taxes, envisaged to reduce financial burdens on farmers, however, further shrunk the grassroots governments' coffers and dried up their limited revenue sources. Fiscal revenue shrank along with the phasing in of the tax-for-fee reform in the late 1990s.[94] The latest blow was the phasing out of agricultural tax by 2009 while the key policy aim of this reform, first announced in 2004, was to lift the living standard of the rural residents.

4.4 Dry-up of Local Government Revenues

Local governments are under obligations to provide basic social welfare and benefits to local residents, for example, a compulsory nine-year education scheme, basic infrastructure projects and facilities, township enterprise financing, and so on and their hands can be tied especially with rather limited sources of revenues. Local governments also need to fulfil the tax quota required by higher level authorities. Corruption, misconduct and plundering of public resources further waste financial resources.

Local governments, faced with constrained money-denominated budgets, resort to any means they can make use of in a desperate scramble for funds, so-called off-budget revenues. In some provinces, off-budget revenues were worth more than 30% of GDP in 2012. In Qinghai, that percentage exceeded 50% while the percentage has gone down to 8–10% in Guangdong and Shandong.[95] Local governments across China derive

[94] Lynette Ong, "The Political Economy of Township Government Debt, Township Enterprises and Rural Financial Institutions in China", (2006) 186 *China Quarterly* 377, 393.

[95] "Bridging the Fiscal Chasm", *The Economist*, 22 February 2014 (online).

between 20 to 90% of their income from selling arbitrarily or even violently expropriated land.[96] The sale of land has become the main source of income in some cities. Land sales now account for an average of 40% of local government revenue, 10% higher than a decade ago.[97] As in other countries, governments will allocate resources inefficiently if they can obtain certain goals off-budget.[98] The income, however, has been in a decline due to the unavailability of land[99] and the property bubble. The central government's efforts to push down property prices may also risk more defaults of bad debts.[100]

Local governments also heavily relied upon collective enterprises, which generate a not insignificant portion of extra-system funds (or quasi-public funds). At the township level, township enterprises were operated and used as local governments' financing vehicles. The fiscal decentralization policies in the 1980s incentivized local governments to develop and make use of collective enterprises because tax revenues collected from them could be kept at the township government level[101] and did not need to be shared with higher authorities. Fiscal decentralization is a remedy to the highly centralized system of remitting all funds to the central government and then disbursing them among subordinate governments. Local governments need to be assigned with more stable sources of revenues so as to be equipped with more decision-making powers to dispose of their shares of revenues. To this end, local governments are given freer rein in tapping

---

96 Koh Gui Qing, "Beatings, Evictions, Demolition: The Ugly Side of China's Local Debt Pile", *South China Morning Post*, 3 September 2013 (online).

97 Andrew Collier, "A Crash in the Making?", *South China Morning Post*, 23 July 2013, A13.

98 Mark Kelman, *Strategy or Principle? The Choice between Regulation and Taxation* (Ann Arbor: University of Michigan Press 1999) 79.

99 Land is not an endless resource and the revenue from land sales will sooner or later come to an end. The research indicates that the average tract of land sold was 50% farther from the city centre by 2007 than it had been four years earlier. Andrew Collier, "A Crash in the Making?", *South China Morning Post*, 23 July 2013, A13 (citing a study by the National University of Singapore).

100 In response to the slowing economy, 36 cities have recently eased home purchase restrictions. But this policy change has not averted a broad-based slide in valuation at local government land sales. It is reported that revenue from land sales in 300 cities dropped 15% from June to July 2014. Sandy Li, "China Land Sale Revenue Falls Despite Easing of Home Purchase Curbs", *South China Morning Post*, 6 August 2014 (online).

101 Yingyi Qian, "Reforming Corporate Governance and Finance in China", in Masahiko Aoki and Hyng ki Kim (eds), *Corporate Governance in Transition Economies: Insider Control and the Role of Banks* (Washington DC: The World Bank Press 1995) pp.215–222.

off-budget resources so as to make up for their budgetary shortfalls. The collapse of collective enterprises contributed negative effects on the township's fiscal status. This source of revenues vanished with the collapse of numerous enterprises. Without this source of revenues, township governments lost the flexibility of mobilizing financial resources locally. As said above, local fiscal responsibilities were shared by grassroots governments as well as local township enterprises. Now, grassroots governments, having no way to find alternative revenue sources to fill the vacuum left by the collective enterprises' contribution, have to play their "public" role on their own. Grassroots governments are hardly able to function well on their own, let alone repay the existing debt. To most township governments, revenue only accounts for a small proportion of expenditures and is insufficient to pay for the major expense items.

5. POLITICAL ECONOMY INTERPRETATION OF LOCAL GOVERNMENT DEBTS

Political economy interpretation demands a deeper understanding of the true causes of local government debts as well as "other needs" of local government officials.

5.1 Spending Pattern of Local Governments

Performance evaluation of government officials is primarily based on indicators of economic growth in their jurisdictions, without due regard to the resource and environmental costs. This encourages officials to focus more on the growth of GDP, and less so on sustainable economic growth, environmental protection, societal development and ecological conservation. Figure 6.3 reflects a general spending pattern of the Chinese government, which confirms that the majority of expenditures, that is more than 80% in 2012, were devoted to economic construction and government administration (including foreign affairs, national defence and public security).

The Chinese government's spending on economic construction, historically, was the largest expenditure category in the national budget from 1978 to 2005. In 2006, the expenditure on public goods for the first time exceeded that on economic construction. Yet, China's expenditure on economic construction as a share of total budgetary expenditure is still rather high.[102]

[102] OECD, *Challenges for China's Public Spending: Toward Greater Effectiveness and Equity* (Paris: OECD 2006) pp.60–63.

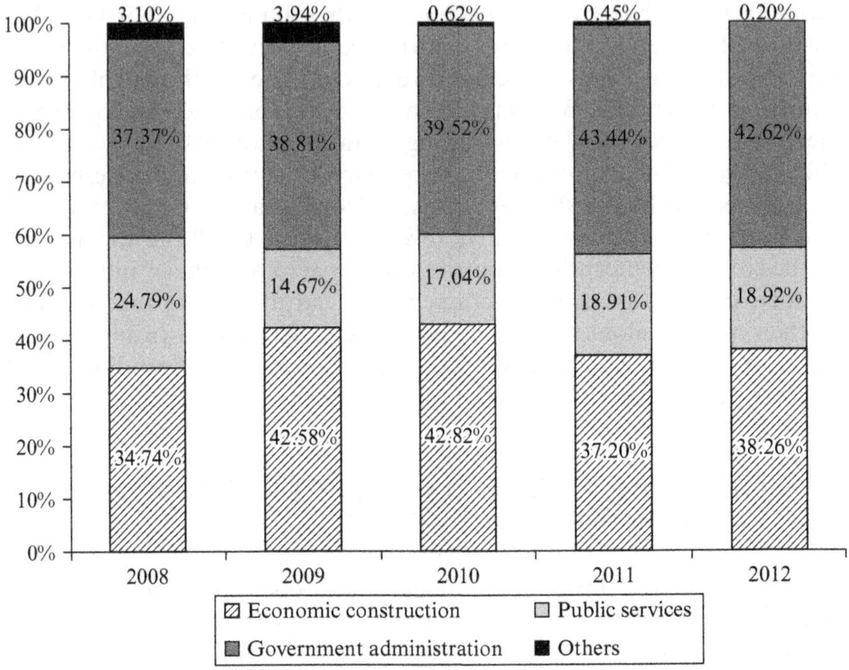

Source: Compiled by the author.

Figure 6.3 Composition of governmental expenditures (2008–2012)

Administrative spending follows a different logic. Governments have self-interests to maximize the budget due to the involvement of the salary and prestige of the bureaucrats.[103] The Chinese government makes no exception and has shown the same tendency of prioritizing administrative expenditure. Some early empirical research looking into local governments' spending behaviours in Shanxi province during the period from 1994 to 2005 confirmed some key features of local governments' spending activities. First, administrative expenditure accounted for at least a quarter of total expenditure and slightly declined over time. Expenditures on economic constructions were on average 11%. Thirty per cent of total expenditure was spent on public goods and services. Second, other expenses accounted for the largest share, representing 30% of total

[103] William A. Niskanen, *Bureaucracy and Public Economics* (Aldershot, UK and Brookfield, VT, USA: Edward Elgar 1994).

expenditure,[104] and the murky nature of this category tells of a low level of institutionalization and transparency of local governments' public finance. More significantly, most expenditure was made on an *ad hoc* basis and could not be categorized.

The figures in Figure 6.3 demonstrate a competing relationship between these spending categories. The expenditure on government administration was on average 40.35% from 2008 to 2012, which was almost 2.1 times the spending on public goods and services. In essence, Figure 6.3 suggests that what evolved in China is a system which may be described as the "minimal welfare state".[105] China may be characterized by a somewhat paradoxical hybrid regime combining heavy public involvement in financing and provision of public goods, especially educational and general infrastructures and maintenance of comparatively high overall government spending (compared to revenues) at the same time.

Economic growth is critically important as that is the factor the CCP, as the ruling party, can rely on to strengthen its legitimacy for ruling. Local government debts help the government complete investment projects and achieve high rates of growth even in the immediate aftermath of the global financial crisis. Excessive investment by local governments in recent years, however, has created serious overcapacity and lowered investment efficiency. Most of the funds borrowed from banks were short-term loans for potentially unprofitable or redundant long-term projects, as part of China's infrastructure-focused stimulus package. Despite such risks, local government officials continue to devote resources to boost investment and projects. Consequently, financial institutions' exposure to LGFVs has been growing rather than declining.

5.2 Dysfunctional Cadre Management System

Local governments at the county level are the primary providers of public services and shoulder the majority of responsibilities of providing compulsory education, health care and social security.[106] County-level governments' level of determination and sufficiency of resources to deliver pubic

104 Haiyan Duan and Jing Vivian Zhan, "Fiscal Transfer and Local Public Expenditure in China: A Case Study of Shanxi Province", (2011) *The China Review* 57, 66–67.

105 See generally, James A. Mirrlees, *Welfare, Incentives, and Taxation* (Oxford: Oxford University Press 2006).

106 Christine Wong and Deepak Bhattasali, *China: National Development and Sub-National Finance: A Review of Provincial Expenditures* (Washington, DC: World Bank 2002) p.27.

goods and services determines the quality of social welfare and security provided to local residents. On the other hand, the central government lacks the capacity to enforce its development objectives due to its limited economic and fiscal resources. The cadre appointment and management system provides the levers for upper-level governments to control low-level governments. While the management of cadres is more decentralized, the central government is not prevented from moulding a new and evolving system to oversee the appointment, evaluation, promotion and dismissal of local cadres in a more decentralized setting. Among others, the target responsibility system is a set of criteria that not only dispense the various tasks to their subordinates but also shape the behavioural model of local cadres.

The motives of local cadres are largely channeled into ventures that ultimately account for the spectacular economic performance at the localities. Economic performance is a politically driven concept. Local governments have more incentives to invest more on economic construction instead of public goods or services.[107] Economic construction projects are easier to use to demonstrate the "achievements" made by local officials to their superiors so as to increase local officials' chances of promotion. Spending on public services, however, cannot showcase local officials' managerial achievements. Therefore, local officials are keener to spend more on projects as the spending on projects can more easily boost the local GDP.

The target responsibility system took its current shape in the mid-1980s after local experimentations. Gradually, the system is a wider scope of tasks and targets including fertility control, the attainment of nine-year compulsory education and the eradication of illiteracy, environment protection, suppression of inflation, grain production and the promotion of agriculture-related projects. According to a formal set of performance criteria published by the Central Organisation Department in 1995, local cadres are evaluated in accordance with three major sets of tasks and each of them is further broken down into sub-categories and sub-tasks. Among others, the first category is economic construction and the first and arguably paramount sub-category is "economic aggregates, their growth rates

[107] Christine P. W. Wong and Richard M. Bird, "China's Fiscal System: A Work in Progress", in Loren Brandt and Thomas G. Rawski (eds), *China's Great Economic Transformation* (New York: Cambridge University Press 2008) pp.429–66; Mingxing Liu and Ran Tao, "Regional Competition, Fiscal Reform and Local Governance in China", in Vivienne Shue and Christine Wong (eds), *Paying for Progress in China: Public Finance, Human Welfare and Changing Patterns of Inequality* (London: Routledge 2007) pp.166–189.

and per capita levels" followed by the sub-category of "state taxation and local fiscal capacity".[108] In order to reflect the differentiated importance of a large number of tasks and criteria, formal weighting schemes are systemically introduced into the target responsibility system with points attached to various tasks and heavy importance assigned to economic construction and growth. The performance of local governments and cadres is ranked in accordance with the points based on weighting schemes. Needless to say, economic growth is one of the most important factors in this technical and sophisticated cadre performance evaluation system.

Through these targets, upper level governments reduce local cadres' autonomy in the disposition of local revenues. Meanwhile, local cadres have more incentives to exert efforts on those tasks to which upper level governments attach more importance and which are more measurable at the expense of other less measurable tasks with less weight attached. Effectively, the target responsibility system is a hierarchical multi-task principal-agent model[109] as well as a top-down target-based vertical control mechanism. In this system, local cadres are accountable to the upper levels of governments and are confronted with the problem of allocating their efforts and fiscal resources with the aim of maximizing the benefits of local bureaucracy as well as promoting their own career paths. Under such a system, local cadres are induced to allocate their fiscal resources in ways commensurate with the preferences of the central government. Since local cadres are assessed in accordance with important tasks and corresponding targets laid down by superior governments, higher-level governments are able to take from the off-budget coffers of local governments even without actually controlling these resources. This explains why fiscal resources are often misallocated.

China's economy is more investment-driven rather than consumption-driven. Public goods and services are never prioritized as the top criterion in cadre performance evaluation. The side effect of this evaluation system is that local governments tend to allocate more resources onto short-sighted projects. As local officials at various government levels are not put in their positions through democratic elections, they pay less attention to public needs at the grassroots level. Although village elections and transparency in village financial management have been put in place allowing

---

[108] Central Organization Department, the Notice on the Strengthening and Perfection of Performance Evaluation Pertaining to the Leadership Group of the County (City) Party Committee and Government, No. 10, 31 August 1995.

[109] Bengt Holstrom and Paul Milgrom, "Multitask Principal-Agent Analyses: Incentive Contracts, Asset Ownership, and Job Design", (1991) 7 *Journal of Law, Economics and Organization* 24–52.

villagers to resist illegal exactions, the cadre management and political systems undermine the central government's determination to cut burdens and change local governments' spending patterns. Without effective disciplinary and whistle-blowing mechanisms, local cadres' interests will not be aligned with those of the local communities. Likely, cadres, central or local, driven by the local government performance evaluation system, may prioritize their careers and the interests of local bureaucracies over public interest. As a result, the GDP-driven mindset will remain.[110]

6. FURTHER DEEPENING REFORMS

The IMF called on the Chinese government to continue tax reform and revamp the framework for local government borrowing and spending.[111] The so-called land fiscal system is an unhealthy and unsustainable method for local government's public financing.[112] The central government should put in place a revenue collection system for local governments so that they can maximize the revenue generating capacity. Correspondingly, spending burdens should also be fairly distributed between the central and local governments. Local governments should implement a property tax and should be allowed to issue municipal bonds. In addition, local governments may need to map out a market-orientated system to facilitate land sales. To facilitate these changes, local governments should have separate balance sheets, using their asset size to set the limits for how much they could borrow. These instruments may not only help make local government debt more transparent but also enhance local governments' fiscal capacity.

---

110 There have been some news reports saying that some changes to the evaluation system are underway. A focus on public well-being and environment protection is to replace the GDP-obsessed assessment. This however has not been formalised and widely applied. *Xinhua News*: "China Focus: China's Reformed Official Assessment Hailed as Landmark", available 29 February 2016 at http://www.sme.gov.cn/web/assembly/action/browsePage.do?channelID=1085219651121&contentID=1386721022055 (last visited 10 October 2014).

111 Victoria Ruan, "IMF Warns China of Risks in Investment Binge", *South China Morning Post*, 30 May 2013 (online).

112 It has been reported in a China Finance 40 Forum that half of two-thirds of construction funds in many cities were raised from land sales, and that around 40% of government debt at the end of 2010 needed to be repaid by land sales revenues. In the past decade, around 2.42 million hectares of good quality rural land was allocated for urbanization which hurt China's grain sufficiency. Victoria Ruan, "Debts Weigh down New Vision for Urban Push", *South China Morning Post*, 6 June 2013 (online).

Apart from furthering fiscal reforms, the key aim of public spending should be improving the supply and quality of public goods and services. For the sake of macroeconomic stability, the role of public expenditure guaranteeing many basic capabilities and social benefits must be placed within a broad framework of social objectives.[113] To this end, financial overspending needs to be constrained to the greatest extent so as to avoid fiscal indulgence and irresponsibility. Government should be downsized. Given the fact that China's budgetary system is very path-dependent, the management of fiscal transfers must be strengthened and made transparent to prevent leakage and diversion of funds to unintended use. In order to support public services and lower local governments' fiscal burden, local governments may consider introducing private funds into education, health care and low-cost housing industries.[114] Public investments in infrastructure projects need to be reflective of some market considerations and, as said, can be only effectively financed through progressive taxation.

The severity of local government debts directs attention to the crucial issue of China's state capability to rule, administer and govern.[115] The local government debt crisis is a symptom of a more pertinent problem of weakening state capacity of redistributing financial resources and systemic weaknesses in political and administrative systems as a whole. As far as the vast rural areas are concerned, given the lack of local industries, flexible and arbitrary extra-budgetary financing vehicles seem to be the only solution. Looking at the larger picture reveals that the local government debt crisis is a reflection of the inability of the Chinese government to adapt its fiscal structure to the dynamically changing political/economic structure. Apparently, institutional insufficiencies contribute to the paucity of financial resources for local governments. The government faces a daunting task of finding the subtle balance between maintaining stability and financing modernisation. The resolution of the local government debt crisis does not merely hinge upon tightened regulation; it requires full-scale institutional reforms.

Local governments are supposed to be more decentralized and autonomous but the system of vertical bureaucratic control is more potent than the paradigm of market-preserving federalism may explain. China still has

---

113 Amartya Sen, *Development as Freedom* (New York: Anchor Books 1999) p.141.

114 Joseph E. Stiglitz, *The Price of Inequality* (London: Penguin Books 2013) p.144.

115 Treda Skocpol, *States and Social Revolution* (Cambridge: Cambridge University Press 1979); Charles Tilly, *From Mobilization to Revolution* (Reading, MA: Addison-Wesley 1978).

a top-down and more centralized central-local governance structure even in the reform era.[116] The degree of centralization (or decentralization) is somewhat off-set by the vertical control through the target responsibility system, evidenced by the proliferation of unfunded mandates and arbitrary charges. The World Bank called for the re-assignment of taxes and expenditure responsibilities between the central and local governments to address vertical imbalances.[117] The remedial measures must be designed to tackle the root cause of the dysfunctional governance structure. As long as the target-based vertical control system remains intact and cadres prioritise their career concerns over public interests, local governments' spending behaviours will not change. Local governments should be given more responsibilities and a freer rein to tap local resources so that they are more accountable to local residents than upper level governments. A bottom-up decision-making process must be put in place for the provision of public goods to be bolstered by voice[118] and exit as disciplining devices; this may be the long-term solution. The relaxation of the household registration system and the opening of the rural land market can be seen as an exit route. Strengthening the voice and exit option can be conducive to credible decentralization. These sideline measures can make the tax-for-fee reform or the re-design of the central-local fiscal system more effective and functional.

Economically, China's growth model must be transformed. The status quo is that the focus is exclusively placed on the ability to drive economic growth, which has led to an investment-driven but debt-laden economic model.[119] The government must introduce more comprehensive governance and market programs to tackle endemic social justice deficiencies in

---

116 Huang Yasheng, "Administrative Monitoring in China", (1995) 143 *The China Quarterly* 828–842; Huang Yasheng, *Inflation and Investment Controls in China: The Political Economy of Central-Local Relations During the Reform Era* (Cambridge: Cambridge University Press 1996) Ch 4.

117 World Bank, "China: National Development and Sub-National Finance", Report No. 22951-CHA, 9 April 2002.

118 See generally, Robert A. Pastor and Qingshan Tan, "The Meaning of China's Village Elections", (2000) 162 *The China Quarterly* 490–512; Jean C. Oi and Scott Rozelle, "Elections and Power: The Locus of Decision-making in Chinese Villages", (2000) 162 *The China Quarterly* 513–539.

119 This appears a strategy to stimulate the economy, the underlying principle of which is based on the doctrine called the balanced-budget multiplier. The government simultaneously increases taxes and expenditure in order to stimulate the economy. Stiglitz, *The Price of Inequality*, p.272. Nevertheless, China is a different case as the deficit also increases but the tax rates are already high and cannot be increased any more.

China.[120] In a policy pronouncement from the ruling elite, a verbose communiqué at the conclusion of the Third Plenum of the CCP's 18th Central Committee in late 2013 reinforced the reformist rhetoric, signalling an eventual end to the state-influenced economy. The Third Plenum draws a picture for tackling these grassroots problems: shoring up the finance of local governments, clearing up their dangerous debts, giving farmers more secure legal rights over their land, and reforming the nationwide *hukou*, or household registration system.[121] According to the Third Plenum, local governments will levy a property tax. Conversely, local governments' ability to raise funds by expropriating land will be curtailed as landowners' property rights are strengthened. The long-awaited reform pushes at reducing reliance on massive investment to drive economic growth and to wean the country off a diet of easy credit and breakneck expansion which leaves troubled local governments in a vulnerable position.

7. CONCLUSIONS

The EU sovereign debt crisis in 2010 involving Greece and a number of Eurozone countries demonstrates the serious consequences of fiscal mismanagement and unsustainably high levels of public debts.

The World Bank warned in January 2015 that "the slowdown in China could turn into a disorderly unwinding of financial vulnerabilities with considerable implications for the global economy". The financial vulnerabilities are particularly concentrated at the local government level. Local officials continue to ignore budget constraints and a ban on borrowing to indulge in a credit and construction binge even though the central government has forbidden local governments from raising excessive amounts of money. Path dependency theory explains why local government borrowing still surges with more infrastructure investment while local officials are still tasked with propping up growth.

---

[120] China's official Gini-coefficient figure (which measures income inequality in a society) was 0.474 in 2012 (having peaked at 0.491 in 2008), above the international danger line of 0.4 and a big jump from 0.3 almost 25 years ago. "Inequality", *The Economist*, 26 January 2013. Comparable (World Bank) figures for the UK and USA are 0.34 (2005) and 0.45 (2007) respectively.

[121] China scraps urban-rural distinction in "hukou" household registration system. Citizens will be classified as "residents" rather than "agricultural" or "non-agricultural" workers. Therefore, around 100 million migrant workers are expected to have their hukou transferred to cities by 2020. See State Council's Opinions to Further Promote the Reform of the Household Registration System, 24 July 2014.

Attributing China's local government debt crisis solely to a weakening central government or a disorderly borrowing by local governments simplifies the complexity of this issue. The fact that there has been an explosion of local government debts indicates the dynamics of a variety of economic, social, legal and political factors such as the worsening performance of the state-owned sector, poor public finance system and weak enforcement and political struggles between central and local governments. Apart from some critical fiscal and financial solutions, the economic growth model must be slower, less resource-intensive and more balanced. The country's governance regime, including the fiscal management, must move towards a process that is people-oriented and democratic. The medicine for the local government debt crisis is a raft of full-bodied measures to address the many legal, financial, social and political flaws and related hazards which China's current governance framework generates.

7. Optimizing the regulation of internet lending: from popularity to risks

P2P lending, internet lending or person-to-person online lending,[1] involves individuals or "peers" who use online platforms without the involvement of a financial institution as a middle man. The platforms originate the loans by matching lenders and borrowers, who usually are individuals and small business owners. P2P lending enables individuals and small firms to lend to each other over the internet, thereby cutting banks and other financial institutions out of the lending process. According to the International Organization of Securities Commission, the size of the global P2P sector's loan originations reached US$2.8 billion in 2013.[2] Together with equity crowdfunding, the capital origination reached US$6 billion in 2014.[3] The development of the online lending market also brought out not only new products and commercial needs but also regulatory challenges and uncertainties in the online business environment.

P2P lending centred internet finance is popular both globally and domestically, and represents a new wave of internet revolution. The emergence of P2P lending as a popular credit alternative to mainstream lending represents a regulatory challenge to the financial regulators not only in China but also abroad. Some regulatory moves have been made in a number of jurisdictions. For instance, "operating an electronic system in relation to lending" has been added into the activities regulated by the UK's Financial Services and Markets Act 2000 since 1 April 2014. Accordingly, the P2P lending platforms within section 36H need

---

1 It is also termed as marketplace lending or loan-based crowdfunding, one subcategory of crowdfunding. Other subcategories of crowdfunding include donation-based crowdfunding, rewards-based (or pre-payment) crowdfunding and equity (or investment-based) crowdfunding. Both P2P lending and equity crowdfunding are collectively referred to as financial return crowdfunding. Eleanor Kirby and Shane Worner, "Crowd-funding: An Infant Industry Growing Fast", Staff Working Paper of IOSCO Research Department [SWP3/2014], p.4.

2 Tracy Alloway and Arash Massoudi, "P2P Lenders Install 'Speed Bumps'", *Financial Times*, 11 February 2014, p.20.

3 Kirby and Worner, "Crowd-funding: An Infant Industry Growing Fast", p.12.

to comply with prudential and other standards affecting their structure and operation as well as conduct of business rules affecting their deals with lenders and borrowers.[4] In the US, the Securities and Exchange Commission (SEC) has asserted jurisdiction over P2P lending by requesting the platform to be registered as a public company with the SEC and to sell notes through a prospectus with an effective registration statement.[5] In New Zealand, the Financial Markets Conduct Act 2013 was enacted to specifically deal with P2P lending with the aim of facilitating financial market activity by promoting the confident participation of businesses, investors and consumers in financial markets and the development of fair, transparent and efficient capital markets.[6]

Internet lending or P2P lending is excessively popular in China compared to other economies. However, this sector is still completely free from regulatory oversight. A consequence is that P2P platforms lack sufficient supervision and information disclosure and involve high-risk loan business with sometimes fraudulent activities. The fact that P2P lending is currently unregulated presents a puzzling question – why an interventionist government such as the Chinese government has been less proactive this time?[7] Does this suggest a more encouraging approach taken by the Chinese government to tackle lending platforms?[8] This chapter attempts to understand this business phenomenon as well as these puzzling legal issues in the Chinese context, with a particular focus on the causes, effects, potential risks and possible regulatory movements.

This chapter investigates China's growing P2P platforms and the

---

[4] Emily Reid and James Black, "The Future for Peer-to-peer (P2P) Lending: the Proposed Regulatory Framework for Lending Platforms", (2014) 29(1) *Journal of International Banking and Financial Law* 37–39.

[5] Andrew Verstein, "The Misregulation of Person-to-Person Lending", (2011) 45 *U.C. Davis Law Review* 445–530.

[6] Financial Markets Act 2013, section 3(a) and (b); section 390.

[7] China is not the only jurisdiction which lacks regulatory oversight over P2P lending. In Brazil, Ecuador, Egypt, South Korea, the United Kingdom and Tunisia, either the regulation has classified P2P lending as an exempt market or there is a lack of definition in legislation. Kirby and Worner, "Crowd-funding: An Infant Industry Growing Fast", p.32.

[8] A more encouraging approach is being adopted by various governments in order to enable funds for small businesses and individuals to be raised in internet-based market places. See the New Zealand Government, Building Capital Markets Report part of the Business Growth Agenda, available 1 March 2016 at http://www.mbie.govt.nz/info-services/business/business-growth-agenda/2012/building-capital-markets/?searchterm=Building%20Capital%20Markets%20Report*.

dangers if this new form of lending is left unregulated. Regulators need to take a coordinated approach tackling potential risks endogenous in this sector. The chapter proceeds as follows. Section 1 gives a brief account of the P2P lending sector followed by the introduction of China's P2P lending sector in Section 2. Section 3 looks into the causes behind the popularity of China's P2P lending business followed by an investigation of potential risks in this business in Section 4. Further, Section 4 looks into various regulatory options necessary to combat the potential risks in China's P2P lending business. Section 5 makes sense of the market trend of involving conventional industrial sectors in the P2P lending sector. Section 6 points out the impact the P2P sector is bringing to China's banking system. A conclusion briefly rationalizes China's tolerant attitude towards the P2P lending sector.

1. GLOBAL POPULARITY OF P2P LENDING

P2P has gained popularity in advanced economies in the wake of scaled-back lending from traditional banks since the outbreak of the latest financial crisis. In January 2014 in the UK, Lendinvest, a UK-based P2P lender, coordinated hundreds of private investors in making the world's largest P2P loan by lending £4 million to a property developer in the south London suburb of Croydon.

LendingClub.com and Prosper.com are the two largest platforms in terms of loan volumes. These two websites essentially bring together the people who can lend and the people who need money. LendingClub, for instance, differs from traditional lenders in that many of its loans are funded by individuals who buy portions of each loan. The two dominant US P2P lending sites originated US$2.4 billion in new loans in 2013, up from US$870 million in 2012.[9] LendingClub.com, the leading US-based P2P lender, expanded its loan book at an annualized rate of 150% in 2013. It has issued US$4 billion in loans since 2006[10] and reached a valuation of US$2.3 billion in late 2013[11] and US$3.8 billion after its completion of the major acquisition of Springstrone.[12] It transitioned from a start-up

---

[9] Andrew Blackman, "Who's Your Banker? Who Isn't?", *The Wall Street Journal*, 10 February 2014, R2.

[10] Telis Demos, "LendingClub Raises Infusion of Capital", *The Wall Street Journal*, 18 April 2014, C5.

[11] Elaine Moore and Arash Massoudi, "P2P Group Zopa Secures £15m", *Financial Times*, 30 January 2014, p.15.

[12] Telis Demos, "LendingClub Raises Infusion of Capital".

company worth a few million dollars to a public company worth US$8.9 billion, in a few short years.[13]

Crowdfunding platforms like Kickstarter, Seedrs and Indiegogo, notably, have used the power of the internet and social networks to create a place where people can contribute or donate money to start-ups and other projects. Different from P2P lending, crowdfunding allocates stock equity to investors with the financial return generated in the form of dividends and/or capital growth. They are developing momentum and are providing investors with potential hefty returns, with the support of new US regulation and the advances of modern technology. Crowdfunding platforms represent the democratization of a financial sphere previously reserved exclusively for professional investors. Crowdfunding can be viewed as a new paradigm, in which incumbent financial institutions provide new opportunities.

In cases in which a myriad of loans, as well as debt and land purchases are up for grabs, the crowdfunding possibilities are limitless. The leading crowdfunding platforms have helped investors and campaigners raise billions of dollars for projects. The New York City Opera, a 70-year-old Manhattan institution, turned to crowdfunding to raise US$1 million through a 22-day Kickstarter campaign.[14] Crowdfunding platforms featuring lending, rather than offering equity, are more effective for projects offering a cheap product and related intangible benefits to donors. The product's popularity makes crowdfunding useful for investors, but its limitations are also apparent. The money collected through the crowdfunding platform may not be sustainable for startups, which usually need active and continuous investment in order to stay afloat. Unlike private equity and venture capital investment, crowdfunding platforms are unable to offer skills and managerial supports which are also crucial to startups.

Other platforms offer different services. SoFi.com specializes in student loans from alumni. LoanBack.com allows users to create legally binding loan agreements to lend to friends or family. Kiva.org enables lending to needy entrepreneurs in developing countries. Springstone lends money to individuals seeking elective medical procedures and to parents paying for private school education.[15]

Internet finance, P2P *per se*, satisfies its customers' needs through

---

[13] Tracy Alloway and Eric Platt, "Investors Bank on Lending Club Success", *Financial Times*, 15 December 2014 (online).

[14] Doing a successful crowdfunding campaign involves lots of work including creating a compelling video, building a prototype, and bringing the investor's own network.

[15] Telis Demos, "LendingClub Raises Infusion of Capital".

increased convenience, customer service, resource and incentives. Standardized and automated lending or funding processes built upon digital technology help reduce marketing, distribution and transaction costs. However, the popularity of the P2P sector has disrupted the world of traditional bank and credit card lending. The key innovation behind the P2P platforms is their efficient method of matching borrowers and lenders. The P2P platforms directly match borrowers with lenders without the involvement of the banks acting as a credit intermediary, enabling them to extend credit at lower rates than those charged by banks and financial institutions. To some extent, these platforms are really speciality finance companies even though they would characterize themselves as technology disrupters who disrupt the conventional financial sector. The existence of crowds in this sector means self-vetting and transparency without credit intermediation. With more P2Ps in the marketplace, the banking sector becomes more competitive[16] and marginalized.[17] These loans are priced so competitively that they can compete with loans offered by the banks in the market. Financial industry professionals are hopeful that the longer-term disintermediation by P2P platforms will complement the existing business rather than disrupt it.

2. P2P'S POPULARITY IN CHINA

In China, P2P platforms have gained popularity and market recognition in recent years. The first P2P lending platform was established in 2007. Pandai, a major peer-to-peer lending website, was also established in 2007, enabling individuals with surplus funds to lend to others who want money. The number of P2P platforms has increased since then. The P2P lending industry explosion began in 2013, when there was a surge in the number of P2P platforms. Approximately 150 platforms were set up in 2013, accounting for 50% of the total number of P2P platforms in China. The P2P sector continued to mushroom in 2014; about 900 platforms were set up in 2014, which constituted a record. More than 2,000 platforms were

---

16 "P2P Lending: Peer Less", *Financial Times*, 24 January 2013 (online).

17 The blurb of Lending Club says: Lending Club is an online marketplace that facilities loans to consumers and businesses and offers investors an opportunity to fund the loans. Our goal is to transform the banking industry to make it more cost efficient, transparent and consumer friendly. We replace traditional bank operations with an online marketplace that uses technology and a more efficient funding process to lower operational costs and deliver a better experience to both borrowers and investors.

now in operation by mid-2015, with loans outstanding reaching RMB 209 billion.[18] Online payments are expected to hit RMB 11.8 trillion by 2015, up from RMB 8.1 trillion in 2014.[19]

The underground lending crisis in Wenzhou did not lead to a halt in P2P lending. In response, P2P micro-finance platforms have promoted lending through the non-banking system. However, P2P loans of all type still only comprise a tiny fraction of the RMB 65 trillion outstanding in the formal banking system.

In 2013, more than 200,000 people lent a total of 105.8 billion yuan on approximately 800 P2P lending platforms. In 2014, there were 1.16 million investors and 0.63 million borrowers involved in the P2P lending sector. Compared to 2013, this means a 364% and 320% increase respectively for participating investors and borrowers on a yearly basis. More than 1,500 P2P online platforms in China are currently involved in matching lenders and borrowers. Loans via P2P platforms reached RMB 252.8 billion by the end of 2014, which totaled 2.39 times the transactional volume in 2013.[20] The Chinese market now accounts for 28% of the global market, right after the US which makes up over a half at 51%, and before the UK at 17%. China and South Korea make up 95% of the total Asian market. The conservative estimated market value for China is half of the US, that is, US$1.8 billion.[21]

As a middleman bringing people who want to borrow money together with those who want to lend, the lending platforms obtain their revenues through origination fees collected from the matchmaking business. P2P players in China usually set up and register themselves as consultancy firms and may charge service fees ranging from 1 to 10%. P2P platforms primarily get their profits from charging service fees. In China, P2P platforms' fees consist of three parts: fees paid by the lenders, fees paid by the borrowers, and fees charged from the assignment of debts between lenders. Fees paid by the borrowers occupy 70% of the revenues generated from the lending business. However, only the fees paid by the lenders are transparent; the exact nature of the other two types of fees is unknown to industry outsiders. This portion of fees is composed of contribution fees, withdrawal fees, VIP fees and management fees. More than 80% of P2P

---

18 Gabriel Wildau, "China Seeks to Tame Online Finance Risks", *Financial Times*, 27 July 2015 (online).

19 Ibid.

20 The statistics were from the Online Lending House, a web portal that tracks the industry.

21 Kirby and Worner, "Crowd-funding: An Infant Industry Growing Fast", pp.14–15.

platforms do not charge contribution fees from lenders.[22] Actually, some platforms charge for account management fees based on the number of registered users (or investors) apart from the service fees paid by both borrowers and lenders.

3. CAUSES OF P2P'S POPULARITY IN CHINA

Consumers maximize utility based on such desired attributes as cost and convenience, within constraints relating to wealth, time, importance and the availability of payment instruments and related infrastructure. Furthermore, consumers, being responsive to market signals, make rational choices. The fact that investors are rushing to online investment products exposes weaknesses in China's financial system, where investors have fewer options than in Western countries. The implication is that consumers are not arbitrarily predisposed to cash, cheques, or credit cards or disposed against debit cards, e-cash and smart cards. Rather, consumers are driven by the attractiveness of the financial instruments or products.

P2P's popularity results largely from China's unbalanced financial and economic system. The wide use of P2P companies is a result of combined factors such as the need of capital-starved small- and medium-sized businesses, the lack of funding from the state-owned banks and the existence of the underground lending market.[23] Technology has allowed downtrodden banking customers to slip the shackles of large financial institutions and deal directly with each other as lenders and borrowers. P2P platforms used this narrative to market themselves as modest community operations with sound underwriting and low defaults. Both the borrowers and lenders benefit from the P2P sector and contribute to its booming status.

3.1 Alternative Financing

P2P can provide a vital source of funding to cash-starved small businesses and individuals, which always encounter tremendous difficulty in borrowing money from the state-owned banks, partly due to the limited scale of collateral assets and in part because of the banks' tendency to lend money to better connected state-owned enterprises. Obtaining sizable and stable

---

22 China's Internet Lending Business Annual Report 2014.

23 In the US, P2Ps are used to borrow money to consolidate debt or pay off their credit cards. Lending Club for example reported that 83% of borrowers using loans to do so. Andrew Blackman, "Who's Your Banker? Who Isn't?", *The Wall Street Journal*, 10 February 2014, R2.

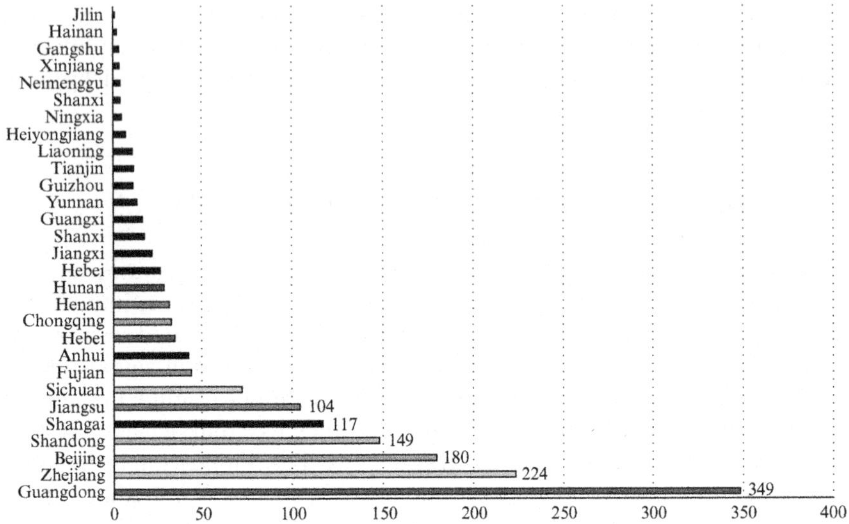

Source: Compiled by the author. Information available in China's Internet Lending Business Annual Report 2014.

Figure 7.1 Number of P2P platforms in each province

loans from commercial lenders involves a complicated and costly vetting process, an extended approval and waiting period and demanding lending standards. In addition, commercial banks are usually less keen to lend money to private enterprises due to their lack of valuable assets for collateral purposes. These practical difficulties push away private enterprises, which have had to turn to other means for funding. The growth of the P2P sector satisfies the financing needs of small- and medium-sized enterprises.

The positive correlation between P2P platforms and entrepreneurship can be illustrated by P2P platforms' geographic distribution in China. By the end of June 2014, the P2P platforms were widely dispersed across 30 provinces in China. Figure 7.1 indicates the number of P2P platforms in each province.

Tibet and Qinghai are the only two provinces that do not yet have P2P platforms. Guangdong province hosts 349 platforms, accounting for 22.15% of the total platforms in China, far outpacing other provinces, and followed by Zhejiang, Beijing, Shandong, Shanghai and Jiangsu. The P2P platforms incorporated in these six provinces accounted for 71.3% of the total platforms. Guangdong and Zhejiang are well known for their strong private sectors. Accordingly, they are known as private sector hubs. One

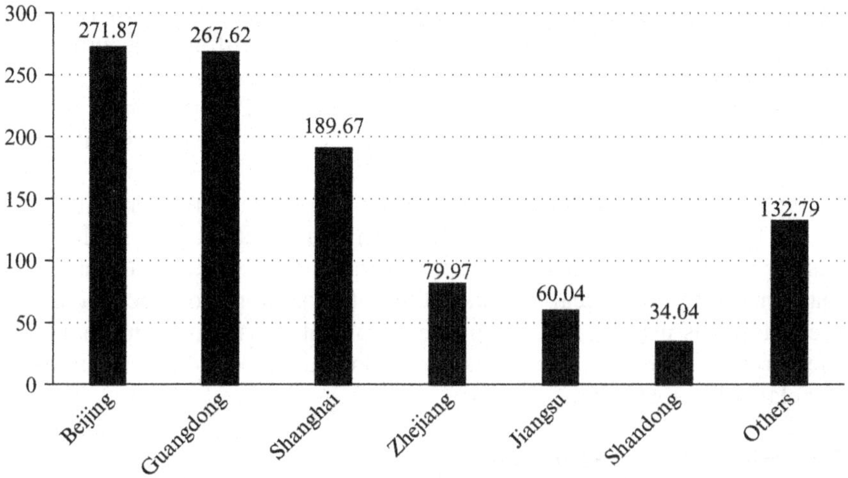

Source: Compiled by the author. Information available in China's Internet Lending Business Annual Report 2014.

Figure 7.2 Outstanding loans of P2P platforms in key provinces (Renminbi 100 million, 2014)

feature that private enterprises possess is their small size and hunger for funding. Logically, these two provinces have naturally become the hub for P2P platforms as well. In contrast, the northeastern and western parts of China have relatively fewer online platforms, due in part to the domination of the local economies by state-owned enterprises.

Figure 7.2 further indicates outstanding loans with P2P platforms in key provinces in 2014. The fact that the value of outstanding loans incurred in Beijing was much larger than that in Guangdong and Zhejiang, considering that more P2P platforms are being operated in Guangdong and Zhejiang, means that P2P platforms in Guangdong and Zhejiang probably serve more small- and medium-sized enterprises than those in Beijing and the borrowing size of these enterprises from the platforms is relatively small. This again confirms the business model of P2P platforms in China, which is largely used to help finance private enterprises and entrepreneurs.

The lending services P2P platforms are engaged in are more diversified even though these platforms may mainly target individuals and micro-enterprises as their clients. People usually borrow money from the P2P websites for consumer financing or sometimes merely for extra capital. As indicated by the 300 lending platforms carefully monitored by Rong 360, the lending platforms can be categorized into five types in terms of their key services: personal credit (targeting individual borrowers), micro credit (targeting small- and medium-sized enterprises), automobile mortgage loans, housing mortgage loans, and mixed businesses.

It has been estimated that 53% of loans via the P2P platforms in July 2014 were less than RMB 50,000. The loan amount per individual varies significantly depending on the business scope of each platform. A real estate affiliate of Ping An Insurance offers loans for up to 36 months and boasts that a borrower can receive funds in as little as five hours. The business scope of the platform also decides the level of risks. P2P platforms may encounter manageable risks if they offer personal or micro loans as the amount is usually in a small size. Those platforms offering loans for the purchase of houses or cars may be opposite as the lending amount may be relatively substantial.

3.2 High Return in Short Term

The P2P model offers new options to financial consumers due to slender costs. P2Ps do not involve regulatory costs as they are exempt from regulatory oversight. The technological advancement makes market-based P2P lending viable through reducing transaction costs associated with providing financial services. Cutting out the middleman, consumers (that is, lenders and borrowers), can save costs and secure better and more competitive interest rates. It is the market practice that the interest rate is higher than the savings rate available to the lender but lower than a traditional loan available to the borrower, depending on the borrower's evaluated risk. Therefore, while returns for lenders are satisfactory, costs for borrowers are also acceptable. In the US, for instance, both LendingClub.com and Prosper.com demonstrate that historic annual returns range from 5% (for the safest loans) to 10% (for riskier loans).[24]

Although the investment yield of the P2P platforms varies, the relatively high level of average returns goes to explain why P2P lending platforms have been so attractive to investors. Figure 7.3 shows the average annual yield of P2P platforms in China. More than sixty per cent of China's P2P platforms have their average annual yields in the range between 12 and 18% or between 18 and 24%, which are much higher than through using traditional avenues of credit provision such as banks. This reaffirms the strong demand side of borrowers for funding as well as their difficulty in obtaining financing from conventional banks. Those platforms with insurance companies being the majority shareholders have an average annual

---

[24] Andrew Blackman, "Who's Your Banker? Who Isn't?".

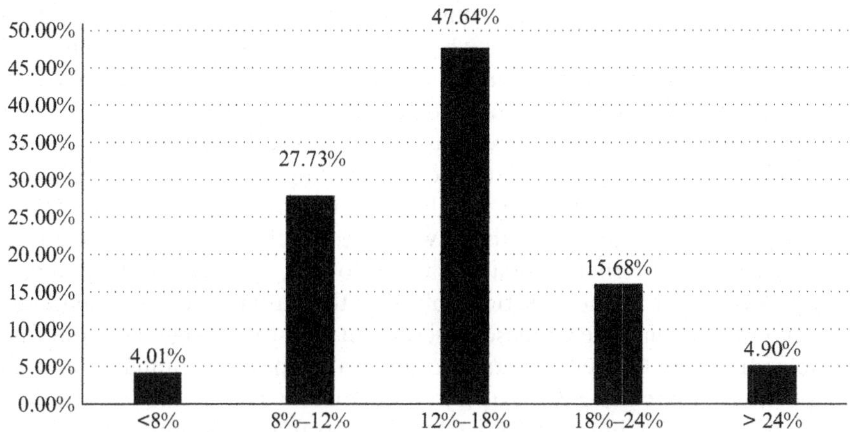

Source: Compiled by the author. Information available in China's Internet Lending Business Annual Report 2015.

Figure 7.3 Yield of P2P platforms

yield of 8.61%, lower than the whole industry. Similarly, the platforms involving state-owned companies as shareholders have an average annual yield of 9%, lower than the whole industry. These two lower yields may suggest that institutional investors may not necessarily bring positive returns to the sector, probably due to their insensitivity or remoteness to the P2P lending market. Privately-held platforms have a much higher average annual yield of 15.57%. In any event, even the lowest annual yield is higher than the deposit rate offered by the commercial banks and the capital markets.

Nonetheless, there has been a decline of monthly yield since March 2014 despite the fact that average annual yield stood at 17.86% in 2014. The last month of 2014 saw a 16.08% yield. Currently, the interest rate of main P2P platforms vacillates between 12 and 14%.[25] More than 36% of platforms decreased their high interest rates in 2014 compared to previous years.

---

[25] These interest rates were much higher than those offered by Prosper and LendingClub, which reported that lenders received average net annualized returns exceeding 11% and 9% for loans respectively. Lenders have the potential to earn higher returns than their returns for savings accounts and certificates of deposit. US Government Accountability Office, Report to Congressional Committees: Person-to-Person Lending, New Challenges Could Emerge as the Industry Growth (July 2011), p.9 (footnote 22) and p.18.

The number of platforms, utilizing relatively high rates to attract popularity, decreased as well. Meanwhile, following a series of scandals and "closures", investors become more sceptical and less enthusiastic towards those platforms offering higher rates, and have turned their investment to other platforms with safer returns and more established brand names.

High yields are closely related to the lending rates in the P2P sector. Annualized lending rates are roughly maintained at the rate of 15% in the small-loan sector, more than twice the benchmark bank loan rates. Large Chinese internet companies are following suit and offering higher returns than Yu'E Bao, a serious blow to the banking sector, one of the crucial instruments the Chinese government uses to manage the economy. The winners are Chinese savers who now earn up to 7% annually on cash deposits compared to 3.3% paid by commercial banks. However, after the People's Bank of China (PBOC), China's central bank, loosened its grip on the interbank market as its effort to push down the currency, yields have fallen as more cash has flooded into the market. The decline shows the mounting complexity of the regulators' efforts to control China's financial system, making it harder for money funds to lock in competitive yields.

The largest group of borrowers are small- and medium-sized enterprises, which make use of the P2P lending platforms to arrange short-term financing in order to fill the financing gaps for their business operations. Figure 7.4 shows the portion of lending transactions according to a variety of lending terms. The majority of lending transactions have a short term of between one and three months. Very few loans were granted in a longer term of more than 12 months. In this sense, P2Ps are alternative investment platforms for investors.

Lending terms are gradually being extended.[26] In the first half of 2014, the average term for P2P lending was 4.75 months. Still, over half of the lending transactions had a shorter term of three months or less. Due to the involvement of larger platforms in the lending business, more longer-term loans may be offered. Lufax.com, renrendai.com and Jimubox.com are the main players to offer longer-term loans in the market.

The average lending term in 2014 was 6.12 months. The average lending term increased from 5.37 months in January 2014 to 6.88 months in December 2014. With the exception of February and December, the trend in 2014 was to see longer-term loans offered in the market. The availability of longer-term loans in the market depends on various factors. Loan term is usually interconnected with not only the loan amount but also the interest rate. Sohu's P2P platform offers loans as small as RMB

---

[26] Ibid.

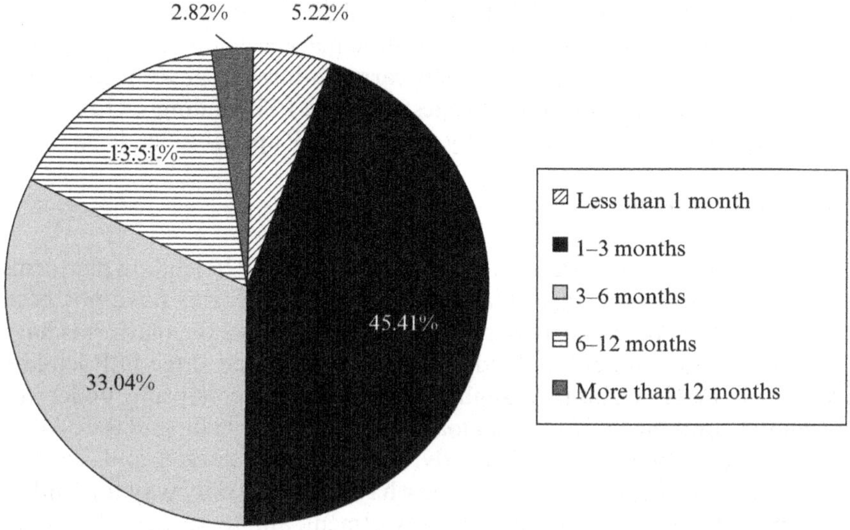

Source: Compiled by the author. Information available in China's Internet Lending Business Annual Report 2015.

Figure 7.4 P2P platforms' range of lending terms

30,000, at rates as high as 12%. Sina's platform offers interest rates of 7.5–8% for 12-month loans ranging from RMB 200,000 to RMB 500,000. Sohu's platform also allows lenders to resell their loans before maturity to other investors, increasing the liquidity of their products. Along with the declining interest rate, the platforms are likely to increase the lending requirements for longer term loans. The increasing borrowing costs may also affect the lending term.

4. POTENTIAL RISKS AND REGULATORY MOVES

Because a default affects the P2P borrower's credit score, borrowers have every single incentive to repay their debts. Default rates among small Chinese lenders are low, only about 1% of their total loan books, which is much lower than the overall default rate in the range of 0.2 to 7% in the US.[27] Disputes over defaults may end up in courts, which are often hostile

[27] Kirby and Worner, "Crowd-funding: An Infant Industry Growing Fast", p.23.

to the enforcement of private loans with higher interest rates. P2P funds are mainly used as a replacement for grey-market lending. Investors are under no illusion that these products carry an implicit government guarantee. However, this does not suggest that the P2P lending sector is risk free. Higher defaults could quickly diminish P2P appeal to lenders.

4.1 Scandals in the Market

Dealing directly with strangers carries its own risks. P2P lending platforms started to mushroom in China in 2006. These platforms have not been well regulated. When borrowers renege, the owners of the platforms have to step in and compensate lenders. Scandals involved three P2P lending platforms in Hangzhou, Shanghai and Shenzhen, collapsing under the weight of combined outstanding loans of 231 million yuan, and the owners fleeing their obligations.[28] Recently, defaults have surged and sparked concerns over social unrest as protests have been the only way for lenders to express their anger over their lost investment, and to attract the government's attention for a possible rescue scheme. Increasingly, reported cases of fraud and huge losses have led to calls for tighter regulation.

In the past two years, there have been more reported cases that some platforms were experiencing "run-away" or "closure" in which the owners of platforms ran away without leaving any trace or the platform had to be closed due to cash shortage, poor management or even fraud. In 2014, the number of "in-trouble" P2P platforms reached 275.[29]

Among others, these "in-trouble" platforms encounter such problems as cash shortage, fraud, run-away and shut-down. Run-away (or flight) is close to a "bank run", in which the owners of the platform run away leaving the platform behind which in turn is no longer able to pay off outstanding debts or to continue to serve clients. Most "in-trouble" platforms are short of cash, owing to the fact that the platforms themselves were invested with small capital contributions as indicated in Figure 7.5. Fraud also exists in this sector and some owners may use the platforms to solicit money without having any intention of staying in the lending business. 74% of the P2P platforms in 2013 reported "operational difficulties, cash squeezes or owners' run-away" and, more importantly, 1.2 trillion yuan of their money was lost.[30] 184 platforms were in trouble in 2014,[31] and 115

---

28 *National Business Daily*, 21 January 2014.

29 China's Internet Lending Business Annual Report 2014.

30 Jane Cai, "Online Lending Risks Escalate on Mainland China Amid Scandals", *South China Morning Post*, 10 February 2014 (online).

31 *Jiefang Daily*, 15 January 2015, p.9.

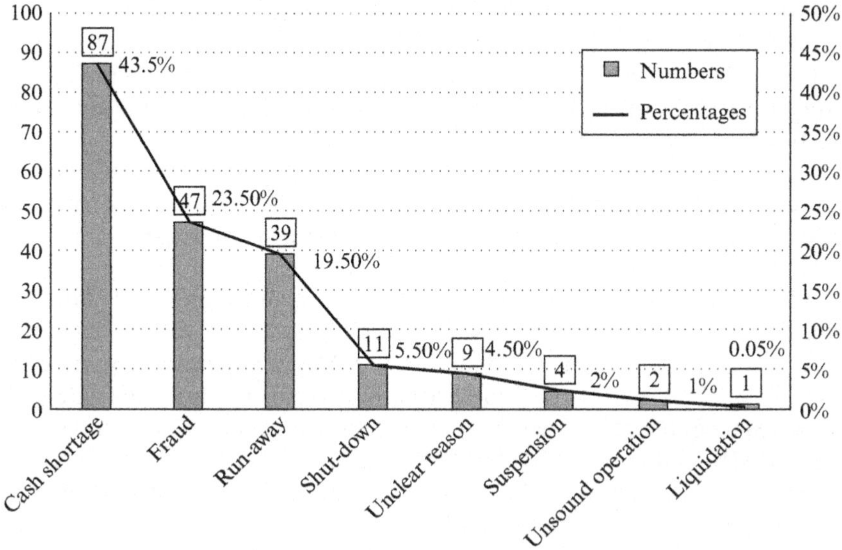

Source: Compiled by the author. Information available in China's Internet Lending Business Annual Report 2014 as well as some newspapers.

Figure 7.5 "In-trouble" P2P platforms (2011–2014)

P2P companies were reported to have gone bust in 2014, compared with 1,438 still in operation.[32]

Fraud seems to be a major risk in this sector. The inherent anonymity of internet offers and heavier reliance on internet portals or websites in this sector create a higher chance of fraud. Likely, the sector may encounter such fraudulent activities as identity theft, consumer privacy and data protection violations. More traditional loans – such as credit cards – are typically originated, managed and serviced by a single entity, retaining the risks and balancing costs and benefits from longer-term relationships. This helps to promote more consistent underwriting and collateral performance, particularly in stressful economic conditions. The whole P2P structure is built around getting investors to do the due diligence themselves owing to the transparency provided by the platforms in the first place. Although the platforms verify the identities of borrowers and

[32] Gabriel Wildau, "China Online Lenders Offer Mortgage Loans", *Financial Times*, 19 October 2014 (online).

control the process, monitoring the lending practices is not sufficient. As P2P lending is conducted online, as Standard & Poor's point out, fraud is a key significant risk. Therefore, the ongoing concern relates to the quality and consistency of the loan underlying process as well as to the substance of the data that such systems collect and maintain.

One of the main reasons why the platforms are not able to fence off potential risks is their small capitalization. Shareholders merely contribute a small amount of registered capital into the platforms, most of which are incorporated as limited liability companies.

Up to mid-2014, the average registered capital of China's P2P platforms was RMB 23.7 million. The majority of China's P2P platforms have registered capital between RMB 5 million to RMB 20 million, accounting for 63% of all P2P platforms. Some earlier platforms fall into this category. For instance, the registered capitals of paipaidai.com and renrendai.com were RMB 10 million and RMB 6.16 million respectively. Platforms with large registered capital are rare in the market. The largest platform, in terms of its registered capital, is Lufax.com, one of its key shareholders is Ping An Group, which owns China's insurance giant, Ping An Life Insurance. Lufax.com's registered capital is RMB 837 million.

The small capitalization is reflective of the involvement of relatively smaller investors in this sector, different from the conventional banking sector which features large state-owned enterprises. This also shows the function of the P2P lending sector which is used to finance small- and medium-sized enterprises or private enterprises. In response to the small capitalization, one possible regulatory instrument taken up by the regulators is to impose an "aggregate limit" on the lending amount incurred by the platform. For instance, a platform in New Zealand may not raise more than NZ$2 million from the public in any 12-month period.[33] In the US, there is also a limit placed by the JOBS Act on the percentage of an investor's money allowed in any particular loan.[34]

However, there has been a trend of increasing P2P platforms' registered capital. Among 900 platforms which were incorporated in 2014, their average registered capital was RMB 27.84 million, which was almost double the average registered capital of those P2P platforms incorporated in 2013. Around 61% of platforms set up in 2014 had registered capital in the range of RMB 10 million and 50 million. Among them, 48 platforms

---

33 FMC Regulations, reg. 186(1)(g).

34 SEC. 302 (a) (6) (B). OSC Consultation Paper on Exempt markets, 2012, available 1 March 2016 at http://www.osc.gov.on.ca/documents/en/Securities-Category4/sn_20121214_45-710_exempt-market-review.pdf.

had more than RMB 100 million in registered capital. This matches the market trend that more state-owned enterprises, private equity firms and financial institutions are gradually becoming involved in the P2P lending sector by investing into the P2P platforms.

4.2 Regulatory Vacuum and Responses

In China, P2P lending is currently unregulated. P2P platforms cannot be easily classified as conventional commercial lenders as their main function is to facilitate lending by providing credit-related information rather than credit itself. Therefore, requirements relating to the form and content of lending agreements and provisions under the Commercial Banking Law and the General Lending Provisions do not apply. As a result, platforms do not need to be licensed credit-brokers.

The P2P sector at least raises significant investor (or financial consumer) protection issues, particularly in relation to retail investors who do not have a sufficient level of understanding and experience. As P2Ps have been supportive to small- and medium-sized businesses, the government has been tolerant and encouraging. The government believes that internet finance may have the potential to force the state-owned banks out of their lethargy. The immediate consequence is that P2P platforms lack sufficient supervision and information disclosures and involve high-risk loan business and occasionally fraudulent activities. Investors usually do not know where their money is being placed and are vulnerable to theft of personal information. There is a possibility that tens of billions of dollars have been flowing into largely unregulated and untested investments. As part of shadow banking, P2P lending also brings systemic risks to the formal banking sector.

Regulators are well aware of the potential risks that are likely to arise from uncontrolled growth of P2P platforms. However, they have not crafted detailed policies on regulating theP2P lending sector. The major potential pitfall is credit risk, the management of which relies upon the vast amount of digital information. Few platforms have grasped the vast data or the technology or methods to apply borrowers' data for their creditability appraisal. In theory, the technology can help assess the repayment capability based on the track record of consumption, payment and other historical transactional behaviours. The technology can even help calculate the possibility of default. Most platforms, however, still rely on traditional means to do business. Another difficulty is the lack of uniform business rules on the borrower's assets and liabilities and loan-grant in the marketplace, which reduce the online loan quality.

Other possible risks include the potential for money laundering and fraud, poor administration and/or platform failure (closure), illiquidity and cyber-attack. Some risks are unique to the P2P lending sector. The illiquidity risk, for example, refers to the non-existence of a credible secondary market on which investors can sell their loan portfolios. Nor is there a secondary market for shares in start-ups through equity crowdfunding. The illiquidity risk makes loan portfolios or equity stakes illiquid and then creates a barrier for investors to liquidate positions. The investors therefore are locked into a contract and have no effective way to get out of it unless they accept a significant discount to the face value. This illiquidity risk is technically different from the liquidity risk in the conventional banking sector. Bank liquidity is affected or constrained by various monetary policy movements and regulatory changes such as capital adequacy rules.

The regulation of P2Ps across the world is in flux. In the UK, the Financial Conduct Authority began oversight in April 2014. This move encourages more interest from investors and borrowers. In the US, most states allow borrowers to participate in P2P lending, but the rules for investors vary. Residents of some states are not allowed to participate while other states have minimum-income or net-worth requirements.[35] Both LendingClub.com and Prosper.com are required to register by SEC. However, treating P2P lending as issuing securities may encounter several obstacles in China. The biggest one is that the statutory types of securities are limited under the Securities Law and the P2P loan cannot be characterized as any of them.

The good news is that some initiatives have been put forward. The PBOC has made suggestions to the State Council that all P2P firms should set up capital custody systems. A deputy to the Shenzhen People's Congress has called for legislation to regulate P2P companies. The regulation can govern P2Ps' business scope and risk control measures.[36] China's banking regulator, the China Banking Regulatory Commission (CBRC), has warned Chinese banks of the mounting risks surrounding this popular P2P lending and indicated its regulatory outline to the public. Circular No. 107 divides internet finance businesses into two categories. The first type refers to financial institutions that conduct their business through internet technologies and platforms. The restriction is placed on the business scope and they are allowed to exceed their business scopes through technological advancement. The second type covers non-financial institutions which

---

[35] Andrew Blackman, "Who's Your Banker? Who Isn't?".

[36] Jane Cai, "Online Lending Risks Escalate on Mainland China Amid Scandals", *South China Morning Post*, 10 February 2014 (online).

establish internet payment platforms, internet financing platforms and internet credit platforms. These institutions are not allowed to use internet technologies to engage in financial businesses, which otherwise violates the law.[37]

4.2.1 Potential risks

P2P lending provides some benefits into the market including the availability of more channels for capital-raising, the spreading of risk, the higher return for low cost capital and the boost to the real economy via encouraging the growth of entrepreneurship and small- and medium-sized enterprises. All these benefits justify and determine the continuous growth of P2P firms. Nevertheless, as far as the Chinese market is concerned, P2P lending may evolve into illegal financial institutions that may illegally take deposits and make loans, crossing the boundary set by the CBRC. Without effective risk controls, 70 to 80% of the existing P2P players may go bust in the next several years.

Investor protection is a thorny topic in relation to P2Ps. There is no deposit insurance for P2P investors. Nor are there capital reserve requirements or any other equivalent rules with which P2P lending platforms have to comply. Lenders and borrowers, however, face similar risks that are currently overseen by a complex regulatory regime in the conventional banking sector. Lenders risk losing their principal and interest on their investments while borrowers may suffer from unfair lending and collection practices, such as potentially unclear or misleading lending terms, predatory or discriminatory credit decisions, and abusive or deceptive servicing acts. In addition, borrowers may face some privacy issues unique to the P2P lending platforms. Meanwhile, lenders are exposed to operational risks associated with the platform's screening of loan applicants and service and enforcing collection of the loans.

Some P2P lenders hold "provision funds" to cover losses arising out of various risks such as credit risk, liquidity risk, operational risk, market risk and legal risk. However, there are two-pronged limitations. First, contingency funds for loan-based platforms may not provide as much security as investors reasonably expect if the default rate dramatically increases and ultimately exhausts the fund.[38] Second, as the use of these funds is entirely at the full discretion of the organizers of the P2P platforms,

---

[37] Circular No. 107, Article 3(7).

[38] UK Financial Conduct Authority, "The FCA's Regulatory Approach to Crowdfunding over the Internet, and the Promotion of Non-readily Realisable Securities by Other Media, Feedback to CP 13/13 and Final Rules", (14 March 2014) p.14.

the risk is beyond control. The possible regulatory instrument is to have higher capital (or financial resources) requirements for firms operating contingency funds or have the entire sector voluntarily covered by the financial service compensation scheme (given the regulatory and compliance costs and economies of scale) in order to help platforms withstand financial shocks and relevant risks.

More importantly, the money acquired from the banks can easily flow to the grey market through the P2P platform, which may accumulate systemic risks. It has been estimated that three trillion yuan of bank loans have been channeled into underground lending in Jiangsu and Zhejiang Provinces.[39] Some players are like loan sharks as they use the platforms to raise funds while lending to businesses and individuals at lofty interest rates. The annualized interest rate on the P2P platforms could hit as high as 15%, five times the benchmark rates recommended by the PBOC.[40]

In a larger context, private loans through P2P platforms are largely channeled into the property market and energy-guzzling industries other than the real economy. This is also the case in the UK. For example, 75% of LendInvest's £26 million loan portfolio goes to property developers.[41] In the US, 83% of LendingClub.com's loans are used to refinance other loans rather than new companies.[42] In China, the property and other industries are heavily monitored by the Chinese government. Any change to government policy in these sectors may severely escalate systemic risks to a higher level.

The internet financial products have the potential to topple the Chinese financial system into the abyss and could pose risks to China's debt-laden economy. But both interest rate liberalization and deregulation of China's monopoly in the financial sector would be beneficial for China's economic reform. Therefore, the State Council pledges to promote the healthy development of internet banking. Technically, this policy means that all the benefits P2P lending brings to the market must be balanced with the risks posed by this innovative industry.

4.2.2 "Firewall" approach

The CBRC has recommended that Chinese banks take cautious measures to strengthen internal controls by setting up "firewalls" or ring fencing to

---

[39] Jane Cai, "Banks Warned on Risk of Underground Lending," *South China Morning Post*, 15 September 2011, B3.

[40] Daniel Ren, "Non-bank Lenders Back in the Game," *South China Morning Post*, 16 December 2013, B2.

[41] "P2P Lending: Peer Less", *Financial Times*, 24 January 2013 (online).

[42] Ibid.

isolate themselves from P2P companies. The firewall may cut the channeling of bad loans into the banking system when borrowers in the underground market default. In China, it is inevitable that lending standards may slip as competition intensifies via new entrants.

Having "firewalls" is of great importance under the current circumstances, for some Chinese P2Ps are venturing into mortgage loans with the aim of drawing mainstream investors into an industry often viewed as the domain of speculators and hucksters. These P2Ps are partnering with real estate developers and financial institutions to offer loans to homebuyers so that the latter can satisfy the 30% down payment requirement[43] in order to obtain a commercial bank mortgage. Regulations forbid conventional banks from offering down payment loans. P2P platforms are not under legal obligations to enforce this 30% rule due to the fact that they are not classified as financial institutions. The same freedom from legal obligations applies to inter-personal lending and micro-lending.

4.2.3 Information or credit intermediary?

The CBRC has also attempted to crack down on intermediary lending with the goal of removing the grey market in the end. The possible rule is a so-called "red-line" approach distinguishing the credit intermediary and information intermediary.

The CBRC seems to allow P2P platforms to act as information intermediary only without being engaged in the credit business. In other words, under this "red-line" regime, any P2P platform engaged in transmitting credit is to be equated with crossing the line and violating the existing banking regulations, which do not allow a non-bank or financial institution to conduct lending or banking business. Therefore, if implemented, being information intermediaries, P2P platforms can only act as business consultancy firms by introducing and transmitting lending information and matching lenders and borrowers. As the P2P platforms may channel funds into various sectors, regulators may need to take a coordinated stand.

This regulatory movement may affect the P2P platform's safety mechanisms. Internet finance bears credit and other risks. Although the online deposits are promoted as if they were savings accounts that carry risk, the principal is not guaranteed. This suggests that if consumers were to begin to suffer losses, there could be a floor of redemptions. When coming to the

---

[43] China's central bank requires commercial lenders to enforce a 30% down payment requirement for standard mortgage loans. This requirement becomes a major hurdle for most homebuyers.

safety mechanisms, the P2P platforms in China choose a totally different approach from that in the overseas markets. The P2P platform itself will not be involved in shouldering responsibilities if a bad loan appears. If the CBRC's design is implemented, the question will arise whether an information intermediary is able and entitled to continue to rely on the existing safety models in the marketplace.

In overseas markets, both LendingClub.com and Prosper.com look at potential borrowers' credit histories and other factors and assign them risk scores. Then two sites decide the interest rate of the loan. For instance, on Prosper.com, someone with the best rating, AA, could get a three year unsecured loan with an annual percentage rate as low as 6.73%. A low-rated borrower could pay more than 20%.[44] After borrowers get a rating, they create a listing on the site explaining why they need the loan and detailing their financial situation. Potential investors browse and choose which loans to invest in. The funds are transferred to the borrower's bank account within a few days after a loan is completely funded.

P2P platforms effectively provide investors with a new type of asset in the form of uncollateralised debt. This innovation enables investors to diversify their portfolios, which in turn reduces the possibility of a build-up of systemic risk. However, unsecured loans do not give lenders any distribution preference under the bankruptcy law when the debt goes wrong. The nature of an unsecured loan calls for a variety of security mechanisms that the platforms need to put in place. Some platforms involve outside institutions for debt collection so as to offer some protections to lenders. Other mitigating methods include a pooled insurance fund that provides compensation in the event of a borrower default.

P2P platforms in China have different safety models, the underlying rationale of which is to reduce business risks. These platforms can be grouped into the following safety modes: non-advance payment mode, security mode, risk-deposit mode and security plus risk deposit mode. Figure 7.6 indicates that the security mode is the most popular safety scheme taken by most P2P platforms in relation to investor protection. The risk deposit mode ranks next. Few platforms will prefer the non-advance mode, which is apparently not safe to protect investors and lenders.

The security model is operated in a variety of ways. Under Jimubox.com's business model, no transactions can be conducted without a loan guarantor. The use of the guarantor incurs extra costs on the borrowers as they have to pay the guarantor's fees. This arrangement may help rule out the possibility of defaults. Since it started operation in August 2013, it

---

44 Andrew Blackman, "Who's Your Banker? Who Isn't?".

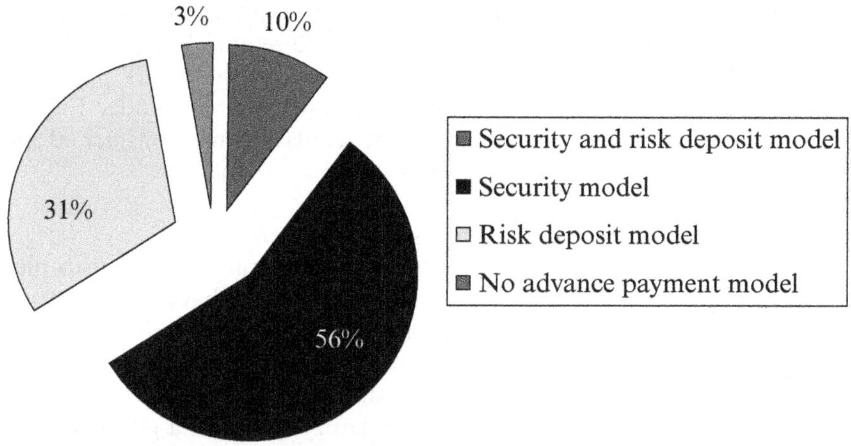

Source: Compiled by the author. Information available in China's Internet Lending Business Annual Report 2014.

Figure 7.6 P2P platforms' major safety mechanisms

has conducted total lending business worth more than 100 million yuan. Its main targets in 2014 were businesses worth more than one billion yuan. Customers with collateral can borrow at lower rates.

Down payment loans offer lenders lower yields than other P2P products. The trade-off is that such loans offer enhanced risk protection. For example, Sina participated in this new campaign by offering loan products guaranteed by insurance companies, micro-lenders, and real estate developers themselves. Different from other types of P2P loans, which typically are for three to six months and carry interest rates of at least 10%, down payment loans offer lenders a greater sense of security. This is so because those companies offering down payment loans have to have a trustworthy reputation or a well-established brand. Otherwise there would be no lenders willing to offer long-term funds at such low cost.

For safety, leading platforms have introduced custody systems under which clients' money is deposited in a third-party account to minimize the chance of fund embezzlement. Creditors may rely on debt collection companies for the repayments. Therefore, loans in default are passed to an external collection agency.[45] These safety mechanisms are quite different from those in the US or the UK.

---

45 Andrew Blackman, "Who's Your Banker? Who Isn't?".

It would be advisable for P2P platforms to establish an independent depository system for clients' funds. This would require P2P platforms to provide clients' funds to independent, third-party custody. P2P platforms would also bear liability to investigate the third parties. Under English law, a third party must be a bank. Chinese regulators may consider adopting similar rules.

4.2.4 Information monitoring and disclosure system

Information intermediary is the role a P2P platform is expected to play in the internet lending business sector. Accordingly, what a P2P platform can do is merely to disseminate information and not assume any credit risk itself. It would therefore be reasonable to expect a minimum level of regulation with a focus on information disclosure. In order to obtain relevant information and also fulfil its regulatory function, a proportionate regime for the risks associated with lending platforms should be devised and accordingly the P2P platforms should file their basic information with the regulators.

Information disclosure is also the regulatory instrument employed by some regulators in other jurisdictions to address concerns about how to promote the transparency of novel internet finance and ensure adequate protection for borrowers and lenders without stifling business innovation. For instance, the UK Consumer Credit Source Book requires P2P platforms to extend to borrowers the key protection they would have had if the credit had been provided under a regulated agreement. Accordingly, a platform must, among other things, provide adequate explanations of the key features of the credit agreement to borrowers, assess the creditworthiness of borrowers, provide notices and information sheets to borrowers in arrears or default and a specific risk-warning if the loan is secured against the borrower's home. The chief purpose of these disclosure rules is to allow investors to make informed investment decisions.[46] Similarly, under the New Zealand Financial Markets Conduct Regulations 2014, a disclosure statement for a P2P service must contain a description of the nature of the service provided; how investors apply for, and obtain, access to the facility and the eligibility criteria that apply; how issuers apply for, and obtain, access to the facility and the eligibility criteria that apply; how investments are made and financial

---

[46] The P2P platforms are likely to be involved in a conflict of interests as they not only need to satisfy consumers but also to guarantee rewards for finding investors. Therefore, information asymmetry may be a key concern arising out of the information disclosure regime. The pure disclosure regime may not work if the information is not scrutinized by a specific regulator.

products are issued under the service; and how investor money is received and dealt with.[47]

Regular reporting requirements can also help regulators monitor the market. The P2P platforms also need to provide regular reports to the regulatory agencies. These regular reports need to contain such information as the financial position, client money held and details of loans arranged each quarter. For example, in the UK, the platforms are required to submit a summary report regularly to the regulator and the reported information includes financial statements, customer funds status, complaints, litigation and detailed information regarding quarterly loan arrangements. In addition, the platform has notification obligations when the total lending amount experiences a fluctuation of 25% or more. The benefits of the reporting requirements need to outweigh the costs, which can be further lowered if the reporting can be conducted via the online reporting system.[48] The diversity of business models across the market may not justify uniform requirements on the form and content of those disclosures. Instead, the regulators or firms should consider multiple factors such as the nature and risks of the investment, and the information needs of their customers.

In the market, investors fully rely on the efficacy of the platforms and the value of their internal creditworthiness. Therefore, P2P platforms should vet borrowers in order to avoid fraudulent transactional information. They should also possess certain technical conditions to ensure the smooth exchange of information and network safety. Due to this requirement, the regulator could even set a minimum capital rule requiring a P2P platform to maintain a minimum level of capital.

Disclosure only makes information available to borrowers and lenders. However, it does not guarantee investors' awareness of risks. As far as retail investors are concerned, the innovative nature of P2P lending tends to be difficult to understand and the high attribution rate of investments therein incomprehensible. Retail investors, in particular, those with learning difficulties, the elderly and young investors, are more vulnerable in the sense that they are more susceptible to emotive advertising highlighting headline rates of return compared to lower interest rates on deposit accounts or to social network promotion of platforms. Against this background, the regulatory objective is to ensure fair, clear and non-misleading communications to these vulnerable investors.

---

47 FMC Regulations, reg. 215(1).

48 UK Financial Conduct Authority, "The FCA's Regulatory Approach to Crowdfunding over the Internet, and the Promotion of Non-readily Realisable Securities by Other Media, Feedback to CP 13/13 and Final Rules" (14 March 2014) p.33.

P2P platforms should not only disclose information regarding interest, duration, fees and charges but also warn the lenders and investors of potential risks including the credit risk, the borrowers risk of default, and the risk that is covered by the deposit protection scheme. For instance, the New Zealand Financial Markets Conduct Regulations 2014 imposes an obligation on the platform to make a warning statement available. The required boilerplate points out that "investment in these types of businesses is very speculative and carries high risks", and suggests investors "ask questions, read all information given carefully, and seek independent financial advice before committing yourself".[49] This type of hard information is necessary to solve the information asymmetry issue in P2P lending by helping in the prediction of default, and improve the overall investment prospects.

An effective disclosure regime can also achieve the purposes anti-fraud and fair-dealing policies are supposed to achieve. At a minimum, publicly available and readily accessible information about the platform, investors and borrowers may allow the counterparties to check the identities of various transacting parties thereby assessing, rating and screening these parties' creditworthiness. An adequate disclosure system may help ensure a fair, orderly and transparent system for the new lending services.

4.2.5 Is rating P2P a valid regulatory tool?

Credit rating agencies, together with lawyers, accountants and other professionals, are viewed as the gatekeepers helping financial regulators monitor the players in the financial market given their expertise and experience in providing rating services to public investors. They are regarded as reputational intermediaries and third party monitors with the capacity to prevent misconduct by withholding support from wrongdoers.[50] It has been argued that it is the gatekeeper failure in serving as a watchdog for the public that led to an array of financial scandals.[51] Therefore, part of

---

[49] FMC Regulations, reg. 196(1) and (2).

[50] Reinier H. Kraakman, "Corporate Liability Strategies and the Costs at Legal Controls", (1984) 93(5) *Yale Law Journal* 857–898; Ronald J. Gilson, "Value Creation by Business Lawyers: Legal Skills and Asset Pricing", (1984) 94 *Yale Law Journal* 239–313; Ronald J. Gilson and Reinier Kraakman, "The Mechanism of Market Efficiency", (1984) 70 *Virginia Law Review* 549–644; Reinier H. Kraakman, "Gatekeepers: The Anatomy of a Third-Party Enforcement Strategy", (1986) 2(1) *Journal of Law, Economics & Organization* 53–104; Stephen Choi "Market Lessons for Gatekeepers", (1986) 92(4) *Northwest University Law Review* 916–966.

[51] John C. Coffee Jr., "The Acquiescent Gatekeeper: Reputational Intermediaries, Auditor Independence and the Governance of Accounting", (2001)

the solution to cure the financial crisis or corporate failure is to improve the regulatory regime governing gatekeepers and their operational behaviours, which in turn improves corporate governance and financial regulation. Seen in this vein, the importance of rating activities and regulating rating agencies in financial markets is not disputed. The question relevant to the key theme of this chapter is whether rating agencies can be relied upon to apply their business models to the growing world of P2P loans. Standard & Poor's believes the novelty of this sector, and its wide range of players, present unique challenges in assessing the overall risks in future P2P loan securitizations. In its statement, Standard & Poor's claims that:

> We monitor developments in this nascent sector from a cross-sector vantage point and draw upon our experience in rating various types of consumer, commercial, and structured debt.
>
> P2P lending is evolving, and it is still too early to know what the industry will look like in its more mature state. As with any young and untested market, we believe there are issues that need to be addressed before we can assign ratings. Some of these issues are P2P companies' lack of performance histories through full economic cycles, uncertainty about their long-term commitment to the business, and their financial stability, operational risks, servicing quality, and loan credit performance in a downturn. We also consider the unproven ability and capacity to comply with new and ongoing regulatory and legislative requirements.

P2P is more like a retail version of securitization. S&P's main concern seems to be that the asset class has not been tested in a full economic cycle yet. Besides, the risk is still evolving and unique even though P2P loans exhibit some similar features like other types of securitized debt. As these loans are not intermediated by the platforms but rather by users of the platforms themselves, investors do not need a third party's view of the risk. The counter argument may be that there is a need for an intermediary to do the bulk of the work on risk assessment. By declaring the P2P sector rateable, Standard & Poor's is legitimizing the P2P lending trend, thereby opening the door to larger institutional flows into the sector. There is

---

(Ctr. for Law & Econ. Studies, Columbia Law Sch., Working Paper No. 191, 2001), available 1 March 2016 at http://papers.ssrn.com/paper.taf?abstract_id=270944; John C. Coffee Jr., "Understanding Enron: It's About the Gatekeepers, Stupid", (2002) 57 *Business Lawyer* 1403–1420; John c. Coffee Jr., "Gatekeeper Failure and Reform: The Challenge of Fashioning Relevant Reform", (2003) (Ctr. for Law & Econ. Studies, Columbia Law Sch., Working Paper No. 237), available 1 March 2016 at http://papers.ssrn.com/sol3/papers.cfm?abstract_id=447940; John C. Coffee Jr., "The Attorney As Gatekeeper: An Agenda for the SEC", (2003) 103 *Columbia Law Review* 1293–1316; John C. Coffee Jr., *Gatekeepers: The Professions and Corporate Governance* (New York: Oxford University Press 2006).

another technical difficulty. The credit rating industry in China is still at a preliminary stage, which does not seem sophisticated enough to monitor the financial market by sending reliable rating information to the market.

4.2.6 Latest online finance rules

The Chinese government unveiled the *Guidelines Concerning the Promotion of Healthy Development of Online Finance* (the guidelines) to govern the rapidly growing internet finance sector on 18 July 2015. The guidelines, to a certain extent, legitimize the online finance sector, which has been operating in a vacuum. The chief purpose of the guidelines is to maintain market order and transparency. Although the guidelines indicate the government's positive attitude towards the development of the internet finance sector, they also reflect the government's traditional and long-standing support for incumbent banks.

The guidelines draw a clear line between P2P lending and banking. P2P platforms must clearly disclose to customers that they are intermediaries between borrowers and lenders and are forbidden from taking deposits or providing guarantees. P2P platforms are not allowed to raise funds for their own projects. This restrictive line is drawn up in favour of incumbent financial institutions.

The guidelines apply to wide range of services, including loans, investments and other financial products offered online. The guidelines support the growth of online financial services such as online payments,[52] P2P lending,[53] crowdfunding equity finance,[54] online asset management,[55] online insurance,[56] online trust[57] and online consumer financing[58] by creating a clear regulatory framework under which they operate.

The guidelines give the priority to risk control. For instance, the so-called custodians would be chosen to oversee the security of assets invested online. Although many third-party payment companies working closely with P2P lending platforms have hoped to win the right to serve as custodians for the funds that investors deposit on the platforms, the guidelines only give this privilege to the banks.[59] There are pros and cons for this exclusivity. Giving the banks the exclusive right to act as custodian

---

52 Guidelines, Article 7.
53 Ibid, Article 8.
54 Ibid, Article 9.
55 Ibid, Article 10.
56 Ibid, Article 11.
57 Ibid, Article 12.
58 Ibid, Article 12.
59 Ibid, Article 14.

obviously does not match the reality of the online lending business. It may be detrimental to the growing sector. On the other hand, reserving fund custody for banks is necessary to protect investors. These measures may help ensure that the funds are safe.

In addition, businesses in this sector would be required to fully disclose information about their operations. Further, a system of "qualified institutions" would be set up to ensure high standards of governance in the industry. With more rules in place, the online financing operations will be standardized. Due to the increasing compliance costs, weaker players may find it harder to meet more stringent requirements and the entire market may be more consolidated than before. The increasing operational costs will raise barriers to entry but benefit larger and more dominant players in the market.

5. P2P LENDING'S NEW TRENDS

The P2P market is not uniform. Rather, it is still evolving and expanding. The alternative finance sector has also been drawing a positive response from institutional investors. Hedge funds, pension funds and other large investment companies are rapidly becoming involved in the sector due to the high yields on offer from the loans. Indiegogo, the world's largest crowdfunding platform, announced it had raised US$40 million from investors to fund expansion.[60] Eaglewood Capital, an investment firm, bundled together US$53 million of P2P loans and sold them in tranches to institutional investors.[61]

There has been a tendency that the P2P platforms are falling back into the arms of the formal banking. Notably, some of the largest US P2P platforms have abandoned their retail focus and institutional investors have directly been involved in the lending business. In the US, more than 60% of the P2P loans are now purchased by institutional investors.[62] LendingClub and Prosper are tracking the growing institutional interest. John Mack, the former Morgan Stanley chief executive, has been appointed onto the board of LendingClub.[63] Prosper recruited Stephan Vermut, its chief

[60] "Startups Turn To Crowdfunding Sites Kickstarter, Indiegogo for Guinea Pigs", *Financial Post*, 29 August 2013, available 1 March 2016 at http://business.financialpost.com/2013/08/29/startups-turn-to-crowdfunding-sites-kickstarter-indiegogo-for-guinea-pigs/?__lsa=adc1-2508.

[61] "Wall Street vs 2P", *Financial Times*, 15 November 2013, p.8.

[62] Alloway and Massoudi, "P2P Lenders Install 'Speed Bumps'".

[63] Tracy Alloway and Arash Massoudi, "Wells Fargo Reverses P2P Loan Ban", *Financial Times*, 12 March 2014, p.15.

executive, from Wells Fargo, where he headed the bank's prime brokerage business.[64] The participation of institutional investors into the P2P platforms may eventually change the nature and features of P2P platforms. Larger investors seek large numbers of loans so as to bundle them into securitized bonds, which can be further sold to more investors. This may drag the P2P sector back into the formal banking system. Institutional investors can purchase best loans much faster than individual investors as they have more sophisticated computer programs to plug directly into the P2P platform. As a consequence, LendingClub has placed limits on the amount of loans investors can purchase and has installed technology that is designed to allow individual investors time to scan the site and give them a chance to compete for loans. Prosper installed speed limits to deter trading firms from buying up its loans by using multiple servers and rapid-fire computer software.

Wells Fargo reversed its internal policy toward the budding alternative lending sector and dropped a ban on its employees making loans with their own money on P2P platforms. Wells Fargo claimed that, after review of the P2P market, loans made by its staff on the platforms were not "inconsistent with its code of ethics". The U-turn follows the fact that Wells Fargo had deemed making loans on for-profit P2P platforms such as LendingClub and Prosper a "competitive activity that poses a conflict of interest" given the bank's bread-and-butter business of lending.[65] Wells Fargo's changing stance is a sign that the P2P lending sector may become a mainstream competitor to conventional lenders.

The increased participation of institutional versus individual investors may result in a dramatic growth of the P2P sector.[66] The immediate consequence is the stronger interconnectedness of the P2P lending sector with the broader financial sector. However, this may likely increase system-wide concerns about the shift of credit risks back from individual lenders to banks and non-depository lenders, thereby exposing other financial sectors to the risk of default inherent in P2P lending. The rapid growth of P2P lending may eventually materialize systemic risk. In addition, the involvement of institutional investors in the P2P lending sector may further worsen market concentration due to the limited number of established players in the market. High concentration is a key feature in the P2P lending sector not only in China but also abroad where most active

64 Ibid.

65 Ibid.

66 US Government Accountability Office, Report to Congressional Committees: Person-to-Person Lending, New Challenges Could Emerge as the Industry Growth (July 2011), Foreword.

platforms are of a small size. Regulation can be designed to protect investors from concentration risk, which could be a systemic risk if the market were to become sizeable.

In China, many investors have been showing their great interest and appetite for the P2P lending business since 2007. Many of them enter into the industry including traditional financial institutions such as banks, insurance companies and listed companies. The involvement of these investors has changed the landscape of the P2P lending sector. In 2014, venture capital firms, banks, state-owned companies and listed companies have continued to venture into this sector. It appears that banks, state-owned enterprises, venture capital/private equity, and listed companies have shown a great interest in investing in the P2P lending sector in 2014.[67]

Large P2P platforms have been planning initial public offerings (IPOs), which may also change the landscape of the P2P sector. The listing of some P2P platforms not only shows a publicized sector but also a return of the technology sector into the spotlight. The cooperatives of equal customers are re-classifying the P2P platform into the two-tier structure of retail and institutional clients. LendingClub's listing on 11 December 2014 in New York with a valuation of US$9 billion already (even though it had just US$160 million in revenues in 2013)[68] paid off for early investors, who include a range of venture capital firms such as Canaan Partners and Morgenthaler Ventures. Its board members include Lawrence Summers, the former US Treasury Secretary, and John Mack, the former Morgan Stanley CEO.[69] This change increases the borrowing costs to retail customers even though smart and cheap technology may also improve returns. For banks and institutional investors, investing in P2P will not harm their brands and bring risks and creates additional costs for marketing to individuals. It will be interesting to see if these global changes will also be reflected into the Chinese P2P lending market.

P2P lending, together with equity crowdfunding, has clear securities market implications. Along with some P2P platforms' public listings is the securitization of P2P unsecured loans, which not only opens the market to new investments but also the rest of the financial market to exposure to packaged loans. Some P2P lenders started to securitize loan bundles and sell them to other financial entities or P2P platforms in the form of asset-backed securities. P2P platforms may purchase these loan portfolios at face value less fees and then consolidate and sell them to third parties

---

67 China's Internet Lending Business Annual Report 2014.

68 "Lending Club: Peer Position", *Financial Times*, 12 December 2014 (online).

69 Alloway and Platt, "Investors Bank on Lending Club Success".

in different credit tranches.[70] As these packaged loans are predominately unsecured in nature, this securitization may deepen the financial market and increase systemic risks.

6. P2P's IMPACT ON CHINA'S BANKING SECTOR

6.1 Mixing with Social Media Platforms

The internet finance market is destined to arise, in part, as a result of enhancements in digital technology. The substantial growth of crowd-funding and P2P lending is deeply associated with the technological innovation of so-called Web 2.0 applications on the internet, which allows users of the internet to participate in the creation of content hosted on stable websites.[71] The online platform has a social-networking aspect with the capability of involving a large number of users, thereby increasing the potential reach of financing opportunities or capital-raising facilities.

Internet finance in China is interconnected with social media platforms, for example, WeChat. WeChat or Weixin in Chinese, similar to WhatsApp, an American messaging service, is known mostly for private chatting and innocuous photo-sharing among small circles of friends. It has become the showcase product for Tencent, China's internet giant, with more than 272 million active users. Tencent has aggressively promoted WeChat in China and abroad, effectively boosting the number of active monthly users to 355 million at the end of 2013, up 9% from the end of September 2013.[72] WeChat has one of the largest user bases in the world for a messaging app.

Tencent has recently been branching out into ecommerce, payments and gaming.[73] In this sense, it is more diversified than Sina.[74] Recently,

---

[70] Tracy Alloway, "P2P Lenders to Turn to Securitisation Deals", *Financial Times*, 1 October 2013 (online).

[71] Tim O'Reilly, "What Is Web 2.0: Design Patterns and Business Models for the Next Generation of Software", (2007), available 1 March 2016 at: http://mpra.ub.uni-muenchen.de/4578/1/MPRA_paper_4578.pdf.

[72] Juro Osawa and Paul Mozur, "Marketing Costs Hit Tencent", *The Wall Street Journal*, 20 March 2014, B7.

[73] Sarah Mishkin, "Sina Weibo Growth Slows", *Financial Times*, 26 February 2014, p.18.

[74] Sina focuses on mobile and social space. Its Twitter-like Sina Weibo has been listed in New York. It made money from advertising and selling data on user behaviour. The number of daily average users grew 4.2% from about 59 million in September to 61.4 million in December 2013. Sarah Mishkin, "Sina Weibo

WeChat has integrated online-payment functions. Customers can do their banking through WeChat and a wealth-management service has been launched as well. Tencent announced a plan to improve its mobile offerings with the hope of making money by means of fees charged through payment transactions, in which users buy goods with their phones.[75] The downside of the use of social media is that fixed rates of returns may put lenders in a less advantageous position.

Alibaba bought a minority stake in Weibo from Weibo's parent company Sina,[76] valuing Weibo at US$3.3 billion.[77] Alibaba used Sina Weibo, a microblogging service in China, to launch its most recent push into innovative finance, or a form of crowdfunding for Chinese movies, in March 2014. The investment product is called Yu Le Bao in Chinese, or Entertainment Treasure. Investors are offered an opportunity to be involved in the film-making industry by making suggestions regarding what films should be made and who should direct and star in them. Investors can have an expected annual interest rate of 7% for putting up as little as 100 yuan. There will be four projects initially targeting 73 million yuan in total.[78] By offering a 7% return rate, Alibaba's novel online investment projects have amassed a substantial share of China's household savings. The money raised through crowdfunding will be channeled into insurance and wealth management products that were being offered by Guohua Life Insurance, based in Shanghai, and will then be invested in the entertainment industry.

Customers, through a smartphone app, can stash 20,000 yuan in Alibaba's money-market fund, called Yu'E Bao (or "leftover treasure"). The account pays the customer a 4.8% interest rate, compared with the

---

Growth Slows", *Financial Times*, 26 February 2014, p.18. Since Weibo's launch in 2009, it had grown to 144 million monthly active users as of March 2014. Paul Mozur, Telis Demos and Matt Jarzemsky, "After Slow Start, Weibo Gains 19%", *The Wall Street Journal*, 18 April 2014, B2. Weibo's IPO in New York received warm welcomes. Shares of Weibo surged 19% in their first day of trading. Michael J. de la Merced, "Shares of Twitter-like Weibo Surge on Opening Day, as China IPOs Mount", *New York Times*, 18 April 2014, B3.

[75] Osawa and Mozur, "Marketing Costs Hit Tencent", *The Wall Street Journal*, 20 March 2014, B7.

[76] Weibo, as a matter of fact, accounts for the bulk of Sina's market value. Aaron Back, "China's Weibo Sends Message in Tech Selloff", *The Wall Street Journal*, 8 April 2014, C8. Weibo was listed in the US, fetching 21 times sales. In this sense, Weibo's IPO only gives employees some liquidate gains.

[77] Michael J. de la Merced, "Shares of Twitter-like Weibo Surge on Opening Day, as China IPOs Mount", *New York Times*, 18 April 2014, B3.

[78] Neil Gough, "Alibaba to Make Movies with Crowdfunding Idea", *New York Times*, 27 March 2014, B10.

0.35% from a savings account with a state-owned bank. By early February 2014, around 81 million people, more than the total number of equity investors in China,[79] had signed up for Yu'E Bao, which now has US$40 billion in assets under management and is the largest money market fund in China.[80] Alibaba also plans to sell mutual funds through its Taobao electronic-market platform. Since its launch in June 2013, Yu'E Bao, the deposit-like money market fund, has attracted 400 billion yuan in assets under management, which is already more than the customer deposits held by the five smallest listed mainland banks.[81] Similar online products from Baidu and Tencent contributed to a fall of one trillion yuan in bank deposits in January 2014.[82] Baidu Inc. is offering its own money-market-like investment product. The upstart lenders are stepping into areas that Chinese banks traditionally ignored. This constitutes an important sector if China is to sustain growth by empowering consumers and small businesses, and to move away from its dependence on big infrastructure projects funded by state-owned banks.[83]

China's internet companies and investment firms are a powerful combination given the fact that there are about 600 million internet users in China, nearly twice the population of the US, according to the China Internet Network Information Centre.[84] Chinese internet companies have demonstrated astonishing growth. Baidu reported a 43% jump in sales while Tencent posted a 38% rise in revenue in 2013.[85] The funds owe their success to a combination of good timing and the failings of China's creaky financial system. Nonetheless, they also have to face a slowing economy, a weakened yuan and declining interest rates.

Crowdfunding is often viewed as having a material impact on promoting overall economic performance.[86] This is also the case in the Chinese context as the capital for innovative enterprises is scarce and the needs of

---

[79] Henny Sender, "Tech Groups Transform How Finance Is Done in China", *Financial Times*, 16 April 2014, p.12.

[80] David Barboza, "Web Banks, Offering High Interest Rates, Rise in China", *New York Times*, 3 March 2014, B1.

[81] "Chinese Banks Call for Cap on Online Interest Rates", *South China Morning Post*, 28 February 2014 (online).

[82] Ibid.

[83] Paul Mozur and Dinny McMahon, "Alibaba Affiliate Strides Onto Bankers' Turf", *The Wall Street Journal*, 7 November 2013, C3.

[84] Michael J. de la Merced, "Shares of Twitter-like Weibo Surge on Opening Day, as China IPOs Mount".

[85] Ibid.

[86] The Corporations and Markets Advisory Committee (in Australia), *Crowd Sourced Equity Funding Report* (November 2013).

innovative enterprises are not sufficiently met by the conventional funding channels such as banks. Nevertheless, there is a lack of regulatory accommodation. Although it is true that regulation of or legislation on crowdfunding is still new and even some advanced jurisdictions such as Australia have no legislation in place to facilitate crowfunding,[87] the regulatory vacuum may not only substantially reduce competition in the crowdfunding market but also reduce small- and medium-sized enterprises' access to credit.

6.2 Break-up of the Conventional Banking System in China

Internet finance like P2P is envisioned as a possible vehicle that can eventually break the monopolies of the state-dominated banking system in China, as it disrupts the traditional bank payment systems and takes away the charges and fees the banks have gleaned from such monopolistic services. Alibaba, for example, has dominated the internet money-fund market. Within its first ten months, it has hauled in more than 400 billion yuan in assets.[88] Tencent Holdings has attracted 50 billion yuan to its Licaitong fund.[89] State-owned banks are used to lending money to the state-owned sector, which, compared to small businesses, is seen to have the necessary financial strength to repay loans. These market players can serve their customers better than most banks as they have a whole ecosystem which facilitates their communications and transactions with e-commerce customers. This intimacy also lowers transaction costs. Lenders can diversify across many borrowers while borrowers get quicker approvals than they would if forced to go through the bank's internal approval process.

Large state-owned banks have moved to cap the amounts depositors can transfer into online products.[90] For instance, China Construction Bank imposed a cap of 5,000 yuan per transaction and a total of 50,000 yuan a month for deposits transferred to Alibaba's Yu'E Bao fund. The

---

87 Terence Wong, "Crowd funding: Regulating the new phenomenon", (2013) 2 C. & S.L.J. 89 and Tim Heasley, "Law Changes to Crowdfunding Needed to Kickstart Australian Innovation", 29 October 2014, available 1 March 2016 at http://www.smh.com.au/it-pro/it-opinion/law-changes-to-crowd-funding-needed-to-kickstart-australian-innovation-20141028-11d4on.html.

88 Chao Deng, "China's E-Money Funds Lose Buzz", *The Wall Street Journal*, 7 March 2014, C2.

89 Ibid.

90 Paul Mozur and Grace Zhu, "Beijing to Put Limits on Mobile Spending", *The Wall Street Journal*, 25 March 2014, C3.

Table 7.1 Balance sheet of Yu'E Bao (31 December 2013, Renminbi)

Assets		Debts	
Bank deposit	175,541,071,053.14	Sale of repurchase Financial assets	4,949,996,640.00
Trading financial assets		Remuneration payable to manager	39,100,241.16
Including: bond investment	12,762,005,913.59	Payable trust fee	10,426,730.96
Purchase of resale financial assets	1,580,737,687.37	Payable sales service fee	32,583,343.31
Interest receivable	492,025,474.79	Payable transactional fee	101,301.04
		Payable interest	1,327,955.44
		Total debt	5,033,770,402.91
		Paid-in fund	185,342,015,725.98
Total assets	190,375,786,128.89	Total debts and owner's equities	190,375,786,128.89

limit of 10,000 yuan per transfer and 50,000 yuan a month is imposed on Tencent's online product.[91] Chinese banks' restrictions on the depositors' capital transfer again showed their monopolistic positions in the market which harm depositors' interests.

Banks are lobbying regulators to tighten rules governing online products as they felt marginalized due to the 20% capital reserve requirements and other regulatory restrictions, which increase transaction costs. The Chinese Banking Association, a government-backed industry group, is lobbying regulators to cap the yields on online money market funds and reserve requirements as banks have felt a threat from online financial products.[92] If adopted, online money market products would be subject to the same regulatory cap that governs conventional term deposits.

An immediate consequence is the elimination of online products' competitive advantage. Currently, Yu'E Bao and other similar products invest most of their funds in interbank deposits, which are not subject to the cap governing retail deposits. Table 7.1 is the balance sheet Yu'E Bao publicized at the end of 2014 showing that the major source of income was actually from the interest from commercial lenders. No wonder commercial banks always complained that Yu'E Bao indeed is the banks' vampire.

The structural model allows Alibaba to pass on higher interbank yields

[91] Ibid.

[92] "Chinese Banks Call for Cap on Online Interest Rates", *South China Morning Post*, 28 February 2014 (online).

which, however, hurts bank profits by reducing their supply cost deposits and increasing their reliance on relatively expensive funding from the interbank market. The rates on commercial bank deposits are subject to a cap of 10% above the benchmark set by the PBOC. The current benchmark is 3% for one-year deposits. By contrast, the annualized yield on Yu'E Bao is 6.09%.[93] Convenience is another advantage. Investors in Yu'E Bao and other similar products can withdraw cash at any time without being subject to any penalty. By contrast, premature repayment may trigger monetary penalty on the borrowers in conventional bank loans.

Commercial banks in China are now tackling various challenges and competitive pressure from internet finance. For instance, ICBC is steadily promoting IT-based banking businesses by exploring ways to apply the big data technology, and expedite the building of a modern information platform meeting transformation and development demand.[94]

Since 2007, many investors have been showing their great interest and appetite in the P2P lending business. Many of them enter into the industry including traditional financial institutions such as banks, insurance companies and listed companies. The involvement of these investors has changed the landscape of the P2P lending sector. In 2015, more venture capital firms, banks, state-owned companies and listed companies continue to venture into this sector. Figure 7.7 indicates the number of P2P platforms which were incorporated in 2015 with various institutional investors. It appears that banks, state-owned enterprises, venture capital/private equity, and listed companies have shown a great interest in investing in the P2P lending sector in 2015.

7. TENTATIVE CONCLUSIONS

Internet lending is booming in China while conventional banks cut back on lending to small- and medium-sized businesses and individuals. As previously discussed, commercial lenders in China are barred from lending money to these borrowers at interest rates that bankers lend to state-owned enterprises and large players in the market. In practice, banks may be less interested in these customers due to the lack of proven cash flows and collateral. Being part of shadow banking, P2P lending is filling the

---

93 It has been reported that the yields were around 7%, double what banks offer. Chao Deng, "China's E-Money Funds Lose Buzz", *The Wall Street Journal*, 7 March 2014, C2.

94 Zhang Hong, "ICBC Profit Climbs 10.2 Percent on Fees, High Net Interest Margins", *South China Morning Post*, 28 March 2014 (online).

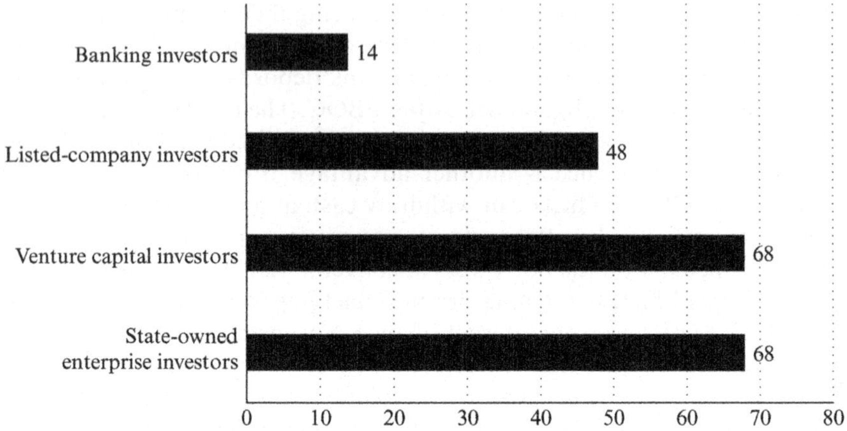

Source: China's Internet Lending Business Annual Report 2015.

Figure 7.7 Number of P2P platforms with institutional investors in 2015

vacuum by offering new types of loans. Currently, P2P lending is only a small portion of all social financing. Nevertheless, it is fair and reasonable to expect a surge in P2P lending, which is likely to be a bigger part of the financial landscape.

For years, Chinese policymakers tried to liberalize interest rates but made no progress due to lobbying efforts made by Chinese banks and other state-owned financial institutions. P2P indeed brings a new opportunity for interest rate liberalization as savers can get around the regulation while getting a higher yield on their savings by depositing in P2P platforms. Therefore, P2P can help shake up China's banking and financial sector. Seen from this angle, the government's tolerance of internet companies' offering a wide range of investment and financial products is an effort to create alternatives to state banks and to loosen interest rate controls.

P2Ps provide great opportunities to grow a powerful lending business in the future. The P2P platforms may have a bright future if the money is channeled into the real economy and regulators gradually loosen their grip over the tightly controlled financial system. The Chinese government's online finance guidelines, unveiled on 18 July 2015, aimed at steering growth of lending and investment over the internet with the hope of generating more growth and increasing funding and investment in the mainland's "new normal" economy. The PBOC's regulatory move is a strong indicator of the Chinese government's commitment to overhauling state-run enterprises as subjecting protected state-controlled sectors to more direct competition is an effective means of putting China's economy on a healthier footing. These moves are part of the larger "internet plus" strategy the Chinese government has been deploying to foster new ideas and growth in the economy. P2P lending platforms and other market players offering other internet-based financial products have gone a long way to democratizing finance through their online money market funds, online lending and other innovations. Such platforms are destined to play a critical and innovative role in China's transition to a domestic demand driven and consumption oriented economy. The P2P lending sector may help realize some key domestic initiatives including broadening the financial markets, aiding in the long-term financing of the real economy, and promoting wider stability within the financial system.

Although there have been different views as to the appropriate roles of regulators and the effective regulatory instruments that can be employed, the general consensus is that P2P lending warrants regulation. The Chinese government therefore should put an adequate and facilitative framework in place. There are two options for regulating P2P lending. One option is to rely upon the current financial regulatory system to protect lenders and borrowers. The current regulatory system provides borrowers and lenders with protections consistent with those afforded to conventional bank borrowers and lenders. However, the drawback is that the current system does not have goals and agency responsibilities that are specific to the sector. The latest example is the online finance guidelines which were drawn up and issued by ten central government ministries and regulators including the central bank, the CBRC, the CSRC and the Ministry of Finance. Although the government's role is identified in these guidelines, the functions of each regulator and ministry involved in drawing them up are defined in a fragmented manner. The guidelines merely specify which agencies are responsible for regulating which types of internet financial institutions. The other option is to consolidate legal protections under a single regulator with a sector-wide focus. The downside of this regulatory option is the uncertainties about the efficiency and effectiveness of a new regime. The choice between these two regulatory approaches depends on regulatory flexibility, efficiency and effectiveness. In any event, even in the formative stage, the regulatory system needs to have broad goals – ensuring adequate consumer protections, monitoring the safety and soundness of institutions and overseeing the integrity and fairness of markets. A lack of regulatory accommodation is likely to continue to disadvantage start-ups and small- and medium-sized enterprises vis-à-vis their counterparts in the state-owned sectors.

8. Removing underground lending markets out of the shadows

The informal or underground lending market is made up of private money lenders, loan sharks or pawnshops, which provide an additional source of capital for households or entrepreneurs. These financing institutions are not licensed or supervised by a regulatory or supervisory authority, which distinguishes them from formal lending institutions. Serving households and small enterprises is a high-risk and high-cost business for banks for their higher transaction costs, unstable income streams or low capabilities to repay the debt. As a result, lending to these borrowers may involve higher default risks due to the lack of sufficient collateral or credit information. However, the strong demand from these borrowers to gain access to capital creates a demand-side of the informal lending market which deepens market segmentation and pushes up higher interest rates. The informal lending sector is large in some emerging Asian economies. In India, the underground lending market is as large as 36% of GDP while the formal banking sector accounts for 52% of GDP. In Thailand, the formal and informal lending sectors are 118% and 47% of GDP respectively.[1]

This chapter focuses on the informal (or underground) lending market, which not only supplements the formal financial system by serving the lower end of the market but also accumulates the potential risks further eroding the efficient financial market. The rest of the chapter proceeds as follows. Section 1 analyses the basic concepts of underground lending and informal lending along with their economic justifications. Underground lending is a severe economic phenomenon in China and the on-the-ground reality, in particular, the recent runaway crisis caused by the serious defaults in the underground lending market will be discussed. Section 2 tries to understand the nature of risks involved in the underground lending market and the government responses to such risks. The government's traditional approach can be understood through a study of the Wu Ying

---

[1] Apanard Prabha and Minoli Ratnatunga, Underground Lending: Submerging Emerging Asia? (Santa Monica, CA: Milken Institute April 2014), p.6.

case. Underground lending businesses can easily be caught upon by the criminal liability of illegal fundraising, which was crafted based on the financial repression doctrine. Section 2 analyzes the logic of criminal liability attached to illegal fundraising. Section 3 and Section 4 focus on two new responses to the runaway crisis caused by the frequent defaults in the underground lending market. The government makes an attempt to legitimize and formalize part of the underground lending market through local experimentation in Wenzhou. Meanwhile, the Supreme People's Court is liberalizing its previous rigid judicial attitudes towards contract-based interest rates in private lending. These two responses are important to understand the liberalizing trend in China, switching its financial market from financial repression to financial liberalization. Section 5 is a brief section discussing China's open-up of its financial market to private investors. A short conclusion ends in Section 6.

1. UNDERGROUND LENDING: FROM CONCEPT TO ON-THE-GROUND REALITY

1.1 Concepts of Underground Lending and Informal Lending

Underground lending, informal lending and illegal lending are different concepts but can be grouped under the umbrella of informal finance. Informal lending is opposite to formal lending, which is mainly composed of deposit-taking and credit-granting banks. Legally speaking, underground lending is not exactly the same as informal lending but these two concepts have an overlap. In this chapter, the terms underground lending and informal lending are used interchangeably.

Beside underground lending, informal finance includes some credit guarantee companies, microfinance or small loan companies, trust companies and leasing companies, all of which possess the credit-issuing function. The key differences between formal and informal finance lies in three perspectives. First, while banks are heavily regulated in China, informal financing institutions are quasi regulated or even unregulated. Informal financing firms are mainly monitored by some government authorities other than banking regulators. In other words, some informal financing entities are not even included in the banking regulatory space. Second, informal financing institutions are not allowed to take deposits, which distinguishes them from banks. This probably explains why they are excluded from the banking regulatory regime as they are unable to mobilize savings deposits from the public. As a result, they are only monitored as regular firms instead of banks or financial institutions. Third, in terms of credit-granting, informal lending institutions are subject to the legal restriction that they are not allowed to charge interest rates more than four times the benchmark lending rates set by the PBOC. This restriction is used to curb potential risks involved in the informal lending sector.

The underground lending market connects China's army of savers with mostly small borrowers unable to access formal lenders and who can end up paying exorbitant annual interest rates. As informal financing institutions are not viewed as formal banks, the informal lending market has not been targeted by the national or international financial regulatory reform efforts. This, however, does not suggest that the risk is minimal and there is no systemic risk. As a matter of fact, the risk of informal lending is mounting in China while the government intensifies its efforts to discipline risky lenders and calm exuberant credit growth with the purpose of pushing away borrowers from informal lenders. Due to the lack of regulatory oversight and uncertainty of the macroeconomic environment, the underground lending market can be the most vulnerable sector in China's shadow banking sector, and is thus viewed as the largest risk to China's financial stability.

Underground lending can be divided into grey and black forms of financing. The grey market, encompasses a large number of microfinance firms,[2] trust and investment companies, pawnshops and credit guarantee companies, and may be economically beneficial to some innovative activities and cash-constrained market players. They play a gap-filling role in providing financial services that would otherwise be provided by the bank-centered financial system.[3] This gap-filling function justifies the existence of shadow banking, which can be viewed as a market response to financial exclusion. The black market, on the other hand, has detrimental effects only. However, there is not a clear line drawn between grey and black markets. For instance, some of China's credit guarantee agencies have moved beyond their intended business scope and effectively become banks, taking deposits and providing loans. Some investment brokers and private fund managers have also used their capital to provide illegal commercial and personal loans. Pawnshops can be offering some banking services to individuals and firms.[4]

Banks are not necessarily risk free from both grey and black financing

---

[2] Ling Wang, "Microfinance Play Seeks Macro Boost", *The Standard*, 5 January 2015, available 1 March 2016 at http://www.thestandard.com.hk/section-news.php?id=152860&story_id=43633307&d_str=20150105.

[3] William Vlcek, "From Road Town to Shanghai: Situating the Caribbean in Global Capital Flows to China", (2014) 16 *British Journal of Politics and International Relations* 539–540; World Bank, *Enterprise Survey China* (2012).

[4] Michael F. Martin, "China's Banking System: Issues for Congress",

markets as banks are somehow involved in the credit chain (or financial (re-)intermediation chain), upstream or downstream. Some foreign investors seeking entry into China's financial market are also attracted to credit guarantee agencies, thereby turning themselves into financial intermediaries. When a business faces debt service challenges in a reciprocal loan guarantee network, bank loans guaranteeing or guaranteed by that business may be at risk. Certainly, the black lending market may be more distant than the grey one from the banking system and may pose limited systemic risk to the banking system.

1.2 On-the-Ground Reality in China

It is technically difficult to accurately estimate the size of the underground lending market as most informal lending is executed through private negotiations and contracting. There is no formal reporting or filing system for informal lending. The People's Bank of China (PBOC), Ministry of Finance (MOF) or the China Banking Regulatory Commission (CBRC) do not release official statistics on informal lending. Occasionally, there are news reports quoting officials' comments, which may disclose some relevant information, which drew an incomplete picture about the underground lending market for whatever messages such information is trying to deliver.

The underground credit market is estimated by the PBOC and private sector analysts at 2 to 4 trillion yuan (US$325 to US$650 billion),[5] or as much as 7% of total lending.[6] In some areas, informal lending exceeds that of official banks.[7] It has been estimated that such informal lending amounts to about US$630 billion (or even US$2.6 trillion)[8] a

---

20 February 2012, available 1 March 2016 at http://fas.org/sgp/crs/row/R42380.pdf, p.6.

5 BBC, "China to Control Shadow Banking and Private Lending", 19 October 2011.

6 Zhao Hongmei and Koh Gui Qing, "China's Runaway Bosses Spotlight Underground Loan Market", 29 September 2011, available 1 March 2016 at http://www.reuters.com/article/2011/09/29/china-economy-runaway-bosses-idUSL3E7KS1B120110929. In March 2010, PBOC estimated that the underground lending market was worth 2.4 trillion yuan, or 5.6% of China's total lending.

7 Joe McDonald, "China's Unofficial Lending Falters, Savers Protest", available 1 March 2016 at http://www.businessweek.com/ap/financialnews/D9T11K7O0.htm.

8 Sunanda Sen, "Finance in China After WTO", (2005) 40(6) *Economic and Political Weekly* 565–571.

year, or the equivalent of about 10% of China's GDP,[9] while the formal lending market offers 135% of GDP as of 2012. Comparatively, the underground lending market in China is smaller than in India (26% of GDP) and Thailand (47% of GDP).[10] Some sources notice that the size of undergrounding lending in China accounted for 33% of the entire shadow banking sector in 2011.[11] Unlike other major sources of funding for shadow banks, an assessment of what underground lenders get up to is an intelligent guess at best as informal lenders are the least transparent of the market players in China's shadow banking system.[12]

After the financial crisis in 2008, the Chinese government tried to tighten monetary policies in order to clamp down on a credit boom, combat inflation and cool its overheated economy after 4 trillion yuan was pumped into the economy in response to the crisis. During the economic downturn, the credit tightening has been hurting China's 7.5 million or so non-state small- and medium-sized companies (SMEs). State-owned banks cut the small amount of private sector lending they were doing while continuing support to the state-owned sector. Many cash-strapped firms are unable to borrow from banks amid a credit clampdown by the government while struggling with slumping global demand, and some of them have had to turn to China's underground lending market – which pools money from individuals and firms.

SMEs and farmers are generally poorly served by the larger state-owned banks and frequently have no option but to turn to these informal lending firms. State-owned enterprises (SOEs), however, find it easier to secure funding from the state-owned banks. Large SOEs are able to obtain over

---

9 David Barboza, "In cooling China, Loan Sharks Come Knocking", *New York Times*, 13 October 2011 (citing UBS's estimation), available 1 March 2016 at http://www.nytimes.com/2011/10/14/business/global/as-chinas-economy-cools-loan-sharks-come-knocking.html?_r=0.

10 Prabha and Ratnatunga, *Underground Lending: Submerging Emerging Asia?*, p.7.

11 Mao Junhua and Luo Jing, "An Analysis of China's Underground Lending", (2011) 11 *Capital Markets* (in Chinese).

12 Almost half of families in China have been involved in private lending, according to a survey of more than 28,000 families published in January 2014 by the Survey and Research Center for China Household Finance at the Chengdu-based Southwestern University of Finance and Economics. The figures show that about 49% of families in China's western regions had participated in private lending, around 46% in central China and 38% in eastern China. Nearly 320,000 households in western regions offered high interest loans totaling 100 billion yuan in 2013. Chen Yang, "Wenzhou to Legalize Private Loans", *Global Times*, 18 February 2014, available 1 March 2016 at http://www.globaltimes.cn/content/843104.shtml.

75% of loans from state-owned commercial banks[13] at a 7.2% interest rate, compared with the one-year benchmark interest rate of 6.56%. Through third-party companies such as financing firms, they can then lend the money on at higher rates, ranging from 36% to 60%, to SMEs.[14] SMEs have been severely marginalized by the state banking system. In 2011, only 19% of bank lending went to small businesses, while total loans fell 6% from 2010 to 7.5 trillion yuan (US$1.2 trillion).[15] In 2013, 23.2% of bank loans, in which 4.7% of short-term working capital loans, were extended to SMEs.[16] The World Bank's survey confirmed that, during the period from 2011 to 2013, only 25% of SMEs obtained bank credits and 90% used internal financing.[17] The general estimation was that 10% of SMEs have access to formal bank loans while they account for 65% of the workforce and 60% of China's GDP.[18]

SMEs have thus been forced to resort to non-banking sources of credit due to structural constraints on their borrowing from state-owned banks. Underground lending firms provide as much as a third of the loans to SMEs and 55% of the loans to farmers.[19] Against this backdrop, informal lending has been surging while the state has been trying to reduce legitimate lending to cool the economy. Its popularity reflects widespread desperation for an alternative financing source to China's banking sector, which pays low deposit rates that fail to keep up with inflation and channel savings.

Entrepreneurs and private firms face barriers in accessing credit, which is an enduring structural feature in both advanced and emerging economies.[20] Research concludes that SMEs are financially more

---

[13] Chris Leung, "It's Far From Enough to Only Adjust Stock Structure of SOEs", available 1 March 2016 at http://money.163.com/14/0811/15/A3CI99HS00254TFQ.html.

[14] Olivia Chung, "China Squeeze Drives Boom in 'Black' Banks", *Asia Times*, 26 August 2011, available 1 March 2016 at http://www.atimes.com/atimes/China_Business/MH26Cb02.html.

[15] Joe McDonald, "China's Unofficial Lending Falters, Savers Protest", available 1 March 2016 at http://www.businessweek.com/ap/financialnews/D9T11K7O0.htm.

[16] CBRC, "CBRC Vice Chairman Yan Qingmin Attended Small- And Micro-Sized Financial Service Sub-forum of Boao Forum for Asia", available 1 March 2016 at: http://www.cbrc.gov.cn/Chinese/home/docView/C1B3D38F6C61440B024B7FABEAD15A57.html.

[17] World Bank, *Enterprise Surveys: China* (2012).

[18] Prabha and Ratnatunga, Underground Lending: Submerging Emerging Asia?, p.13.

[19] "Chinese Lenders: Black Market Banking", *The Economist*, available 1 March 2016 at http://www.economist.com/node/9622318.

[20] OECD, Financing SMEs and Entrepreneurs 2014, p.35.

constrained than large companies in both developed and developing countries.[21] Serving small enterprises can be a high-risk, high-cost business for banks as such borrowers have neither stable revenue streams nor repayment capabilities. Small, short-term and unsecured loans do not economically justify the extension of credit from formal banks to SMEs. Borrowers usually do not have sufficient collateral assets and credit information, increasing not only the default risk of lending to them but also the transaction costs for banks. Small enterprises, unable to meet the lending criteria set out by banks, may prefer informal lending as the loan approval process is much more straightforward. The difficulty in financing for SMEs is more severe in China. SMEs are more limited to financial resources than large companies in China[22] as well as their counterparts in other Asian countries. The World Bank's survey shows that on average, Chinese SMEs receive 12% of their working capital from bank loans, compared to 21% in Malaysia, 24% in Indonesia, 26% in Korea, and 28% in Philippines.[23]

In the Chinese context, this structural bias against SME financing not only has an economic logic but also reveals political priority. Compared to SMEs, SOEs and larger firms usually have stronger connections with the government, which provides an implicit guarantee or subsidy to the bank credit. The logical development of limited access to the formal lending market is the increasing reliance on underground lending markets by SMEs. Financial exclusion worsens the equilibrium between demand and supply of financial resources. Commercial bank branches and ATMs per 100,000 adults are two key measures of financial outreach, evidencing a lack of access to formal finance. In China, there are only eight commercial bank branches per 100,000 adults, lower than 19 worldwide and 35 in G7 countries, and 38 ATMs per 100,000 adults, lower than 43 worldwide and

---

[21] Allen N. Berger and Gregory F. Udell, "The Economics of Small Business Finance: The Roles of Private Equity and Debt Markets in the Financial Growth Cycle", (1998) 22 *Journal of Banking and Finance* 613; Thorsten Beck and Aslı Demirgüç-Kunt, "Small and Medium-Size Enterprises: Access to Finance as A Growth Constraint", (2006) 30 *Journal of Banking and Finance* 2931.

[22] Justin Yifu Lin and Yongjun Li, "Promoting the Growth of Medium and Small-sized Enterprises through the Development of Medium and Small-sized Financial Institutions", (2001) 1 *Economic Research Journal* 11; Hongshui Xu, "Financing Gap and Minimization of Transaction Cost: Why SMEs Have Problems in Financing and How to Improve the Policy", (2001) *Journal of Financial Research* 11.

[23] David Dollar, et al., "Improving the Investment Climate in China, Investment Climate Assessment", available 1 March 2016 at http://info.worldbank.org/etools/docs/library/113671/madagascar/english/china_climate.pdf.

135 in G7.[24] China has a small microfinance penetration rate compared with other Asian countries, evidenced by the number of active borrowers from microfinance institutions. In 2011, China only recorded 0.57 million active borrowers, far less than 26.49 million borrowers in India, and 20.88 million in Bangladesh, only slightly more than 0.46 million borrowers in Indonesia.[25]

The popularity of underground lending is closely connected with the higher return it offers to investors. A thriving underground lending market has bloomed amid depositors' zeal to place their money for higher returns or better use. As much as 90% of underground lending is used for speculative trades in financial markets.[26] Interest rates on loans provided by China's underground lending institutions are often 10% per month or even higher.[27] Some have offered annual interest rates as high as 100%, 180%[28] or even 200%.[29] Chinese banks were offering lending rates between 7% and 8% for commercial loans. China's one-year deposit rate stands at 3.5%, under the PBOC's 2011 inflation target of 4% and below actual inflation which recently has exceeded 6%. Higher interest rates attached to underground loans may be justified by high administration costs to secure repayment, and higher rates of default. Informal lenders are not under downward pressure from formal banks to lower their interest rates as the demand side is guaranteed by the financing needs of SMEs.

Most underground lending businesses are not truly illegal or prohibited. In jurisdictions where there is an interest rate cap, underground lending offering a higher interest rate above the cap is then prohibited. A closed financial market imposing restrictions on market entry also disallows underground lending, which operates outside of the formal banking sector without regulatory approval and regulatory oversight. These happen to be the restrictions in China. An excessive size of underground lending market impedes a country's economic development. Lack of access to credit is identified as one of the major constraints for entrepreneurial activities in developing economies,[30] and an obstacle to economic growth

---

24 IMF, *Financial Access Survey* (2014).

25 Nan Zhang and Perry Wong, "Sustainable Microfinance in Asia: Landscape, Challenges, and Strategies" (Santa Monica, CA: Milken Institute January 2014), p.11.

26 "Chinese Lenders: Black Market Banking".

27 Martin, "China's Banking System: Issues for Congress", p.6.

28 Ma Guangyuan, "What Do We Have For Wenzhou's Rescue", *China-US Focus*, 16 November 2011.

29 "China's Economy: Bamboo Capitalism", *The Economist*, 10 March 2011.

30 Beck and Demirgüç-Kunt, "Small and Medium-Size Enterprises: Access to Finance as a Growth Constraint".

and development. Empirical work confirms a correlation between the lack of credit access and poverty.[31] Formal financing, as empirical research confirmed, plays a larger role in enhancing productivity and economic growth.[32] Higher interest rates, heightened costs of borrowing, and coercive measures for debt collections lead to larger household debt and massive social disruption. Therefore, social risks and impacts become the main concerns over the informal lending market.

1.3 Runaway Crisis

The private lending craze has fueled an economic bubble, and the "runaway episode" in Wenzhou, China's entrepreneurial capital, a city of about 9 million people on the eastern coast of Zhejiang province. Wenzhou is considered a bellwether for the growth of SMEs and private businesses in China. It is a city famed for its savvy, risk-taking merchants, and well-known for its strong entrepreneurial activities and underground banking industry. A PBOC survey reported that 60% or so of local businesses and 89% of households in Wenzhou had loans from underground banking in some form.[33]

The global financial crisis which began in 2008 caused falling overseas orders, rising raw material costs and a firmer yuan. Weak demand and surging labour costs also dragged down many SMEs. A thriving underground banking system has begun to fracture, exposing new fault lines in China's economy. The staggering rates, at more than 15 times China's benchmark lending rates, have pushed some firms to the limit.

Starting in 2011, the state media reported that nine bosses of small-sized firms in Wenzhou had skipped town after realizing that they could not repay their corporate loans. Corporate failures in Wenzhou sparked a series of suicides and runaways of some entrepreneurs who were making their interest payments of as much as 7% a month to informal lenders in order to keep their businesses afloat.[34] A string of Chinese entrepreneurs

---

[31] Patrick Honohan, "Cross-Country Variation in Household Access to Financial Services", (2008) 32(11) *Journal of Banking and Finance* 2493–2500.

[32] Meghana Ayyagari, Aslı Demirgüç-Kunt and Vojislav Maksimovic, "Formal Versus Informal Finance: Evidence from China", (2010) 23(8) *Review of Financial Studies* 3048–3097.

[33] Martin, "China's Banking System: Issues for Congress", p.6.

[34] Bloomberg, "Private Lending 'Legal' in Wenzhou", *South China Morning Post*, 3 March 2014, available 1 March 2016 at http://www.scmp.com/business/banking-finance/article/1438786/private-lending-legal-wenzhou.

have gone into hiding to avoid repaying loans.[35] During the credit crunch in 2011, many private business owners in Wenzhou were reported to have disappeared, committed suicide or been declared bankrupt.[36] Two heavily indebted Wenzhou-based entrepreneurs jumped to their deaths and nearly 100 business owners fled their factories, leaving piles of unpaid loans behind.[37] This caused a surge in the number of lawsuits concerning private lending disputes in Wenzhou to 19,446 in 2012 from 2,896 in 2007.[38] Some media even reported that there were more than 80 suicides or bankruptcies by indebted businessmen in a four-month period in late 2011.[39] The runaway crisis highlighted a credit squeeze on private firms and the dangers of steep interest rates in China's vast and growing informal lending market.

2. NATURE OF RISK AND POLICY RESPONSES

2.1 What Risks are Involved? What Nature?

There is a misperception about the nature of risks associated with informal financial intermediation in China. There are several risks which deserve attention.

The risk of default is real. Lending to SMEs carries a higher perceived risk of payment delays, if not defaults. Lending savings to firms is more lucrative than putting money in banks that give negative returns. Interest rates can be as high as multiple times of banks' lending rates, which trap households and entrepreneurs in a cycle of debt and predatory lending practices. Borrowers cannot afford such sky-high rates. There is a high likelihood of seeing a high default risk at the end of this debt cycle.

---

[35] Zhao Hongmei and Koh Gui Qing, "China's Runaway Bosses Spotlight Underground Loan Market", Reuters, 29 September 2011, available 1 March 2016 at http://www.reuters.com/article/2011/09/29/china-economy-runaway-bosses-idUSL3E7KS1B120110929.

[36] Ibid.

[37] David Pierson, "Shaky Underground Banking System Raises Fears in China", *Los Angeles Times*, 14 October 2011, available 1 March 2016 at http://articles.latimes.com/2011/oct/14/business/la-fi-china-wenzhou-debts-20111014.

[38] Chen Yang, "Wenzhou to Legalize Private Loans", *Global Times*, 18 February 2014, available 1 March 2016 at http://www.globaltimes.cn/content/843104.shtml.

[39] Luo Jun and Sheridan Prasso, "Testimony before the US-China Economic and Security Review Commission: China's Banking System and Access to Credit", 7 March 2013, available 1 March 2016 at http://www.uscc.gov/sites/default/files/3.7.13_Sheridan%20Prasso_Written%20Testimony.pdf.

Speculative private lending is outside the banking system and such loans are generally embedded in an excessively lengthy credit chain even though they are not necessarily used to fund speculative businesses. The government always sends a comforting message that there are no large-scale collapses among small firms in the country and that SMEs do not face extreme credit shortages. However, private lending can create various risks such as credit risk and systemic risk. Credit woes faced by one small firm can affect its peers through "debt triangles". This is the case when a firm that is short of cash delays payments to its suppliers, causing suppliers to suffer cash flow problems which in turn can affect others higher up the supply chain. To this specific firm, the risk is a credit risk but involves operational risk management. In other words, management of business processes[40] can influence the probability of a failing event occurring[41] even though credit risk is exogenous while operational risk is endogenous.[42] In a larger picture, the risk is that a major default of an underground loan could trigger a domino effect threatening the wider financial system. Then, credit risk of a firm, apart from its risk-rewarding consideration, can easily turn to systemic risk of the entire financial system. Among anecdotal evidence of the growth in loan sharking, media reports said Inner Mongolia saw an "explosion" in the number of court disputes over underground loans in 2013 – as many as 43,000[43] – which indicates a connection among lenders and borrowers in the underground lending market.

Banks are not entirely insulated. Savers' reluctance to put their money in banks has sparked a "war for deposits". Banks are said to be part of the underground lending market by positioning and channeling capital into the underground lending market.[44] The collapse of the underground

---

[40] Basel II lists seven event types and one of them is called clients, products, business practices. Basel III however focuses on other risks and additional capital requirements without touching upon operational risk. Andreas A. Jobst, "The Treatment of Operational Risk under the New Basel Framework: Critical Issues", (2007) 8 *Journal of Banking Regulation* 316.

[41] Michael Power, "The Invention of Operational Risk", (2015) 12 *Review of International Political Economy* 577.

[42] For a comparison of operational risk and credit risk, Réne Doff, "Why Operational Risk Modelling Creates Inverse Incentives", (2015) 1(2) *Journal of Financial Regulation* 284, 286–287.

[43] Jon Woo, "China's Loan Sharks Circle in Murky Shadow Bank Waters", *Chicago Tribune*, 30 January 2014, available 1 March 2016 at http://articles.chicagotribune.com/2014-01-30/business/sns-rt-us-china-loans-underground-20140130_1_shadow-bank-underground-banking-underground-loans.

[44] Zhang Bing, Zheng Fei and Zhao Jingting, "Cash Crash for Wenzhou's Private Loan Network", Caixin, 11 October 2011.

banks threatens to spread to the formal banking system. Underground banks are seen as a major conduit for the illegal flow of overseas capital in China given the existence of two money markets due to the differentials in exchange rates of renminbi and foreign currencies.

As far as the government is concerned, social stability remains a leading concern for the country. Financial stability is an essential component of an overarching society goal. Rising defaults threaten to aggravate social tensions, lending to social problems and criminal activity. The social instability risk lies in the government's potential inability to effectively intervene in the underground lending market if the default risk elevates to a larger scale because there is no centralized pool for the funding as in a bank bailout or bail-in.[45] The other related risk is the central bank's inability to implement effective monetary policy if a large scale of lending takes place outside of the formal banking system. Consequently, it will become more difficult for the government and financial regulators to manoeuvre the levers of the economy such as fiscal stimulus and controlling inflation. The risk will become a real one should there be a fiscal or economic crisis.

The absence of a balanced financial sector itself presents a risk to the economic growth. The market does not play a decisive factor in forming interest rates and other lending terms. Interest rate ceilings or floors and other restrictions in the financial market inhibit the banks from pricing loans to reflect the trade-off between profit and risk, which leads to allocative inefficiency. The fact that the scale of shadow banking assets is close to the value of assets in regular banks itself presents a risk for the financial market, and shows the severity of this distortion. The strategy to mitigating this risk is to balance the distorted financial sector through market-oriented approaches.

2.2 Government Attitudes and Market Situation

China's Ministry of Finance and the State Administration of Foreign Exchange have been cracking down on underground banks since 2002. The Chinese authorities have shut down over 500 underground banks with over 100 cases involving more than 20 billion yuan in illegal funds.[46] Leaders including the ex-Premier Wen Jiabao and other top economic

---

[45] The bail-in process is superior to bailouts in the case of idiosyncratic failure but is still possible to entail risks. Emilios Avgouleas and Charles Goodhart, "Critical Reflections on Bank Bail-ins", (2015) 1(1) *Journal of Financial Regulation* 3–29.

[46] Xinhua, "China Shuts Down 500 Underground Banks in 8 Years: Ministry", 22 November 2010.

officials repeatedly promised more credit for small companies.[47] The government allowed the underground lending market to grow over the past decade, apparently seeing it as necessary to support entrepreneurs.

Zhejiang province alone has about 2.4 million non-state companies with an output valued at more than 1.5 million yuan, and abounds with underground banks for cash-strapped small businesses. About 80% of the SMEs in Zhejiang are using underground banking loans to fund their businesses, despite the fact that the black market interest rates in the province have surged as high as 10% monthly. About 600 billion yuan flows through the province's underground banking system a year.[48] In 2011, Wenzhou's underground lending market amounted to 110 billion yuan, which was 20% of the whole city's banking loans.[49]

Underground lending markets often trap households and entrepreneurs in a cycle of debt with high interest rates and predatory lending practices, leading to social problems and criminal activity. More than 7,300 companies in Zhejiang were forced to close from January to April in 2011 due to the central government's monetary tightening measures.[50] The number of civil cases involving underground lending disputes rose dramatically after 2008, increasing to 747,809 cases in 2012 from 488,301 cases in 2008. The caseload of underground lending disputes was around 10.22% first instance civil cases in 2012, or 48% of disputes arising out of loan agreements.[51]

2.3 Crime of Illegal Fundraising: Wu Ying Case

Across the country, borrowers have been arrested after failing to repay loans running to billions of yuan (hundreds of millions of dollars). In Zhejiang province on the southeast coast, an export centre hit by an avalanche of bankruptcies, 11 people have been sentenced to death since 2009 on charges of "illegal fundraising".

---

[47] McDonald, "China's Unofficial Lending Falters, Savers Protest".

[48] Empirical research shows that the largest amount of bank financing funded to private firms is in the coastal (23.3%) and southwest (26%) regions which were said to have an investment climate that facilitates access to formal sources of external finance. Ayyagari, Demirgüç-Kunt and Maksimovic, "Formal Versus Informal Finance: Evidence from China". This may suggest that Wenzhou probably is not the worst place to see a large amount of informal lending compared to other surveyed areas in China.

[49] Wu Guolian, "An Investigation into the Current Underground Lending Market", (2011) 8 *Zhejiang Finance* (in Chinese).

[50] "China Squeeze Drives Boom in 'Black' Banks", *Asia Times*.

[51] Tong Ji, "An Analysis of Underground Lending Case Data in Recent Five Years in Court Nationwide", *Legal Daily*, 19 February 2014, p.9 (Chinese).

Among them was a 31-year-old woman, Wu Ying, who once was praised by state media as one of China's most successful businesswomen. Wu Ying, probably China's best known underground lender was jailed for life in 2012 for raising 770 million yuan (US$120 million) from investors from 2005 to 2007. She was said to have invested in over 700 shops and 20 cars, including four BMWs and one Ferrari. This 31-year-old woman was convicted of illegal fund-raising. Wu Ying began her career at 15 working in her aunt's beauty salon in Zhejiang. She went on to establish a business empire. Her business included the Zhejiang-based Bense Group, which runs hotels, wedding planners, laundry shops, a logistics company and other investments. Amazingly, in 2006, aged just 25, she was named China's sixth-richest woman by Hurun Report, a wealth research magazine.

Wu Ying was arrested in February 2007 and was held for two years before she faced charges of embezzling nearly 380 million yuan from 11 people in what the China Daily described as "one of the country's biggest financial frauds committed by a woman". Initially, she was charged with illegal fundraising, which carried a maximum penalty of 15 years in prison and would have been heard at a district-level court. As investigations proceeded, the charges were altered so that she was accused of fundraising fraud when the case eventually came to trial. In spite of her denial that she had cheated anyone and that all the money she had borrowed had been invested rather than used for personal use, she was sentenced in 2009 by the Jinhua City Intermediate Court in Zhejiang Province to death on charges of fraud and "illegal fundraising", violating the Criminal Law aimed at fighting underground banking, financial improprieties and loan-sharking.[52] She was stripped of her political rights and all her possessions confiscated. She later lodged an appeal within the 10-day period for appealing her sentence. On 7 April 2009 judges from the Zhejiang Higher People's Court presided over an appeal hearing in the No. 2 courtroom of Jinhua City Intermediate Court. In the appeal, she switched her plea on the lesser charge of "illegally collecting deposits from the public" to guilty.

Since 2007 China has required that all death sentences be reviewed and confirmed by the Supreme People's Court, which was Wu's final chance of reprieve. Due to public outcry, in an apparent effort to mollify critics, Wu Ying was re-sentenced by the Supreme People's Court to death with a two-year reprieve, which usually is commuted to a long prison term.

---

[52] "Death Sentence for Business Woman Arouses Opposition in China", *Los Angeles Times*, 18 February 2012, available 1 March 2016 at http://articles.latimes.com/2012/feb/17/world/la-fg-china-death-penalty-20120218.

Technically, she still faces the death penalty, but the two-year reprieve means it will probably be commuted to a life term if she is deemed to have reformed. Public support for the death penalty for non-violent crimes was falling. Apparently, public opinion affected what it coyly called "judicial independence" in the case of Wu Ying.

The case has unleashed a grey area about illegal fundraising and private financing. Private fundraising is illegal but common in China, especially in Zhejiang and other provinces where the private sector is strong. There are two crimes that an individual could be accused of. One is the crime of fraud in fundraising under Article 192 of the Criminal Law, and the other is the crime of illegally taking deposits from the general public under Article 176 of the Criminal Law. The maximum sentence of the second crime is only ten years. Illegal fundraising is composed of the following key elements: (i) absorbing funds without approval from the relevant government department in accordance with the law; (ii) making use of public means of solicitation such as the media, promotion conferences, leaflets and text messages on mobile phones; (iii) engaging in undertakings to repay the principal and interest or to pay a return in the form of currency, property in kind, or equity within a certain timeframe; or (iv) absorbing funds from the general public, that is, non-specific targets in society.[53] Illegal fundraising crime may be disguised in other forms as long as the above elements are satisfied.[54] Among these four elements, raising funds from the general public is the most important condition illustrating the scale of damage the crime can bring to the financial system.

Wu Ying was initially charged with illegally taking deposits from the general public, but those charges later escalated to fraud in fundraising as a private lender. Obviously the first instance court, considering the severity of the case, has referred to the first. However, what is unusual is that, if it is a fraud concerning hundreds of millions of yuan, there ought to be a lot of victims. The indictment said she had raised money illegally from 11 people, with unreasonably high interest rates promised and never delivered. There is no evidence that Wu Ying's activities caused harm to

---

[53] The Supreme People's Court's Interpretations on the Specific Application of Laws in the Trial of Criminal Cases of Illegal Fundraising (Fa Shi [2010] No. 18), issued in 2010.

[54] Other disguised acts targeted by law enforcement include fraud in share or bond issuance (Article 160 of the Criminal Law), establishing a financial institution without approval (Article 174 of the Criminal Law), issuing shares or bonds without approval (Article 179 of the Criminal Law), organizing or legal pyramid sale schemes (Article 224 of the Criminal Law), and illegal business operation (Article 225 of the Criminal Law).

anyone, except possibly some rich investors. The Criminal Law stipulates that financial deals can be punishable by death if the money involved is "an especially large sum", which, however, is not explicitly specified.

The fact that no such widespread appeals for compensation appeared in the media suggested that Wu Ying should not be charged with violating Article 192 of the Criminal Law but rather Article 176. Wu's lawyer insisted that she did not swindle funds from the public, but raised money from friends and did not use it for illegal purposes or personal indulgence.[55] The court may have just placed more emphases on the amounts involved, and the prosecutor felt obligated to go beyond the sentencing constraints of Article 176 and purse Wu Ying on the other charges.

Wu Ying's fundraising activities clearly violated the Criminal Law. However, the law concerning illegal fundraising is itself controversial and criticized not only by the general public but also academics. The Criminal Law is meant to regulate the financial market that has a substantial impact on the society and to safeguard the financial sector, as the government advocated, in the best interest of financial stability. Accordingly, the criminal liability is meant to be a deterrent towards criminal behaviour. The death sentence, however, may be excessively harsh if its sole purpose is to deter crime as the impact on the financial sector of this type of "crime" is less severe than crime which deserves the death penalty. The supreme penalty therefore is meted out with the goal of suppressing informal finance, which benefits the official financial channels.

State-owned enterprises can borrow money from (state-owned) banks, whereas private businesses are often left to fend for themselves in an informal market of moneylending, such as the one in which Wu Ying thrived. Without strong political connections, entrepreneurs have to work around a banking system that favors SOEs.[56] The existence of these unofficial financing avenues is the tragic result of the systemic or structural problems that plague the country's financial system. The "crime" of "illegal fundraising" as defined by the law not only sets a strict ceiling for private enterprises, but stunts their development and the development of the entire private financial sector, the law is a direct denial of society's needs. The

---

[55] Kenneth Rapoza, "A China Millionaire's Brush With Death", Forbes, 21 April 2012, available 1 March 2016 at http://www.forbes.com/sites/kenrapoza/2012/04/21/china-millionaire-escapes-death-sentence/.

[56] However, it has been argued that private economic actors must have succeeded in striking the political bargains that are needed to conduct business given the rapid growth of the private sector and entrepreneurship unfriendly business environment. Kellee S. Tsai, *Back-Alley Banking: Private Entrepreneurs in China* (Ithaca and London: Cornell University Press 2002) 246.

Wu Ying case stirred debate about the unfairness of the economic system, and demonstrated the inadequacy of China's financial system for SMEs.

In Jiangsu, north to Shanghai, businesswoman Gu Chunfang was sentenced in October 2013 to effective life in prison for illegally amassing 17.68 million yuan with promises of annual returns of 40%. Some of the money was invested in coal mines. The ruling was rendered on the grounds of multiple crimes of financial fraud, contract fraud and capital flight. The death sentence was suspended for two years, deprivation of political rights, lift and confiscation of all personal property.[57] The 1,449 people imprisoned were among a total of 4,170 people convicted since 2011 of violating rules on loans outside the state-run banking system.[58] These 1,400 or so people were sentenced to prison terms of at least five years for involvement in underground lending in a crackdown on a financing practice widely used by China' entrepreneurs. People netted in the crackdown were convicted of violations including public advertising to find lenders and promising excessively high rates of return.

In China, "illegal fundraising" outlaws various kinds of investment schemes. There were differences between illegal fundraising and private lending, but no distinct boundaries were clearly drawn by laws. The charge has been used to sentence private lenders. The purpose of the Criminal Law and the imposition of criminal liability on illegal fundraising is not only to discourage the informal credit market but also to protect state-owned banks. The side effect is an apparent attack on the entrepreneurial sector at the grassroots level, which can no longer fund itself through informal means and personal savings.

2.4 Understanding Criminal Penalties on "Illegal Fundraising": Financial Repression v. Financial Liberalization

Stronger or more favourable protection of the state-owned banking sector helps the government secure less expensive sources of funding and steer domestic savings to politically-favoured investment projects or industrial sectors. This is a clear example of financial repression, which is used through coercive power in the form of policy, law or regulations to bolster myriad government policies.[59] Financial repression is composed of a package of political-legal policies, measures and rules,

---

[57] "Ten Events in 2013", available 1 March 2016 at wenku.baidu.com/link?url.

[58] *Jamaica Observer*, "China Jails Over 1,400 in Loan-Shark Crackdown", 27 April 2013, available 1 March 2016 at http://www.jamaicaobserver.com/news/China-jails-over-1-400-in-loan-shark-crackdown_14159514.

[59] Carmen M. Reinhart and Kenneth S. Rogoff, "A Decade of Debt", (2011)

which shift the benefits of consumer capital from the individual to the state, thereby ensuring lower costs of financing. These measures are put in place to provide SOEs or policy-biased industries to have subsidized credit. Without financial repression and contingent cheaper funding, the mushrooming public debt and low-efficient state-owned sectors may deteriorate faster. The by-products of financial repression include a weaker private sector, a monopolistic banking sector and an unhealthy consumer finance system. Consequently, the financial system is not market-based as the banks are unable to price loans properly and are heavily influenced by the government's invisible hands. Financial repression is a shadow taxation redistributing capital and financial resources through policies instead of the market itself. Without an invisible hand, credit is misallocated,[60] increasing the instability and uncertainty of the financial systems.[61] Financial repression is invisible to financial consumers even though it has the same effect on consumers as direct taxation.

Financial repression, as a financial market development model or governance framework, was once popular among developed countries after World War II when these countries tried to secure cheaper funding to reduce war debts.[62] Nowadays, financial repression is more often seen in developing countries while most developed countries have switched their financial development strategy towards financial market liberalization or a liberalized financial system.[63] There are various forms of financial repression.[64] Developed countries may practice a light form of financial

---

NBER Working Paper No. 16827, available 1 March 2016 at http://www.nber.org/papers/w16827.

[60] Ronald I. McKinnon, *Money and Capital in Economic Development* (Washington DC: Brookings Institution 1973).

[61] Apanard P. Angkinand, Wanvimol Sawangngoenyang and Clas Wihlborg, "Financial Liberalization and Banking Crises: Cross-Country Analysis", (2010) 10(2) *International Review of Finance* 263–292.

[62] Seppo Honkapohja, "Lessons from the Financial Liberalization in the Nordic Countries in the 1980s", in Wing Thye Woo, Yingli Pan, Jeffrey David Sachs and Junhui Qian, *Financial Systems at the Crossroads: Lessons for China* (Singapore: World Scientific Publishing 2014) Ch 4.

[63] It has been pointed out that liberalization in developed economies has been uninterrupted and mature financial markets are on average less regulated than emerging economies. Graciela L. Kaminsky and Sergio L. Schmukler, "Short-Run Pain, Long-Run Gain: The Effects of Financial Liberalization", (2003) NBER Working Paper No. 9787, available 1 March 2016 at http://www.nber.org/papers/w9787.

[64] David O. Beim and Charles W. Calomiris, *Emerging Financial Markets* (New York: McGraw-Hill 2001) pp.47 and 119 (listing six aspects to define a jurisdiction as a repressed or liberalized one: interest rate ceiling on bank deposits,

repression by imposing some restrictions on the players in the financial market. After the latest financial crisis, there has been a revival of financial repression in the developed countries where the governments used explicit or implicit caps on interest rates, tighter regulation on cross-border capital movements, and more directed lending to government by captive domestic investors. These measures are put in place to reduce debt rollover risks and curb rising interest expenditures. Developing countries, on the other hand, often practice financial repression heavily.[65] Typical measures include the market entry restriction, cross-border capital flow restriction, deposit interest cap, compulsory purchase of government bonds and favourable policies towards a monopolistic position of banks or SOEs in the lending market.

China is characterized as a highly financially repressive regime,[66] imposing controls on credit, interest rates, exchange rates, capital flow and market entry. Credit controls require state-owned lenders to grant loans to borrowers based on imposed quotas or favoured policies with the aim of achieving broader economic, social and political objectives. As quotas or policies, other than economic criteria, are used or relied on to allocate credit, formal lenders are more likely to accumulate non-performing loans and suffer from undesired economic outcomes. In China, credit controls are reflected in policy lending, which often pursues policy goals instead of economic returns. Interest rate controls in China are formulated in the form of a ceiling on the deposit rate, the purpose of which is to limit the cost of borrowing. Banks, however, charge higher lending rates, which guarantee their profit margin and in turn reduce competition in the financial market. As the benchmark interest rate set by the central bank guides and determines both deposit and lending rates, the pricing of credit is less transparent and does not reflect the market price.

Through the suppression of interest rates below market rates, depositors' savings are transferred through the banks to subsidize SOEs (including state-owned banks) and some policy-favoured industries.[67] This explains

---

high bank reserve requirements, government credit and direction of bank credit, government ownership and micromanagement of banks, restrictions on foreign bank and domestic non-bank entry, and restrictions on capital flows).

65 Reinhart and Rogoff, "A Decade of Debt".

66 Ken Miller, "Coping With China's Financial Power", (July/August 2010) *Financial Affairs* 96–109.

67 Michael Pettis, *Avoiding the Fall: China's Economic Restructuring* (Washington DC: Carnegie Endowment for International Peace 2013); Nicholas Lardy, *China's Unfinished Economic Revolution* (Washington DC: The Brookings Institution 1998).

the Big Five's (the Big Four plus the Bank of Communications) extraordinarily high profitability during the latest financial crisis. The Big Five's combined profit rose to 674 billion yuan (US$108 billion) in 2011 from 121 billion yuan (US$19.4 billion) in 2005.[68] The economic contribution made by the private sector and SOE sector is in a stark contrast. Privately owned companies account for 70% of total employment on the mainland and 60% of China's GDP.[69] By contrast, SOEs account for two-fifths of GDP, and employ one-tenth of China's workforce.[70] Reliant on state support and inexpensive capital, the SOEs have far lower returns on equity than private enterprises. Since the onset of the global financial crisis, SOEs (excluding banks) have delivered virtually no earnings growth while the private sector profit growth was in double digits,[71] at an average 18% growth rate. The average return on assets for SOEs was at about 4.6% in 2014, compared with 9.1% for private businesses.[72] SOEs apparently remain a drag on growth due to the mismatch between their earnings and cost of capital,[73] indicating that SOEs are inefficient in terms of capital allocation and utility.

In a financially repressed regime, the financial sector is not designed to serve consumers' needs. Rather, the financial sector, in particular, the banking sector, is utilized as a political-legal tool for the government to pursue broader political, economic and policy goals at the expense of financial consumers. Although financial repression preserves China's fast-speeding economic growth and social harmony, it makes financial market liberalization and reform more difficult due to the current supplementary institutional structures supporting the heavily financially repressed regime. Structural changes are likely to cause severe financial losses and encounter the prohibitively high switching costs due to path dependency. In addition, financial market liberalization may be blocked by some fractions which are beneficiaries of financial repression. Both commercial law and banking regulation should be crafted to reduce the number of legal restrictions necessary to regulate private enterprises and allow greater financial and entrepreneurial freedom.

---

68 Jun and Prasso, "Testimony before the US-China Economic and Security Review Commission: China's Banking System and Access to Credit".

69 Some statistics claim that China's SMEs absorb 80% of urban employment. Ibid.

70 "Chinese SOEs: Hope and Experience", *Financial Times*, 15 September 2015, p.14.

71 Ibid.

72 Gabriel Wildau, "Beijing's Overhaul of State Groups Faces Compromise", *Financial Times*, 15 September 2015, p.6 (citing Gavekal Dragonomics data).

73 Nicholas Lardy, "China's Rise is a Credit to Private Enterprise Not State Control", *Financial Times*, 16 September 2014 (online).

3. REGULATORY RESPONSES TO THE RUNAWAY CRISIS: WENZHOU PRIVATE LENDING REGULATIONS

In response to Wenzhou's blight, and with fears that Wenzhou's economic stumble could reverberate throughout the rest of China, the Chinese government in 2012 launched a pilot scheme to funnel more money to private enterprises in Wenzhou, a business hub in east China rife with under-the-counter lenders. A pilot project was approved by the central government allowing private lenders in Wenzhou to register as private institutions that can operate with the blessing of the State.

Wenzhou passed the Private Financing Regulations to legalize underground lending that had previously led to a local financial crisis. The Wenzhou Private Financing Regulations, passed at the 6th session of the 12th Standing Committee of the Zhejiang Provincial People's Congress in November 2013, are the first of their kind in China, aimed at turning underground lending into acceptable credit and benefit SMEs that find it difficult to obtain loans from banks. The Regulations, effective as of 1 March 2014, with 7 chapters and 50 clauses, specify regular private financing operations, risk control measures and legal liabilities.

The Regulations essentially legalize the underground lending market allowing it to be part of the formal financial institutions. This move reflects efforts by both national and local authorities to increase the transparency of private lending and discourage regulatory arbitrage in the wake of a crisis that broke out in 2011. The financial reform in Wenzhou underscores the central government's recognition of the plight of small businesses, which have been sidelined in its credit binge in the past few years. It was the first piece of local regulation in China to turn grey-market lending into acceptable credit to support cash-thirsty SMEs while reducing financial risks.

Private financing developed extremely fast following China's 4 trillion yuan stimulus package in 2009, and became rampant when the country adopted a tightening monetary policy in 2011. SMEs then turned to underground lending to raise money. It is said that 89% of households and 57% of firms in Wenzhou were involved in private financing, with total capital estimated at 110 billion yuan.[74] In 2012, nearly 26,000 lawsuits relating to private loans were filed in Wenzhou, almost six times the number of suits

---

[74] Chen Yang, "Wenzhou to Legalize Private Loans", *Global Times*, 18 February 2014, available 1 March 2016 at http://www.globaltimes.cn/content/843104.shtml (citing a 2011 survey by the PBOC).

in 2011, with the aggregate amount in dispute of approximately US$7.5 billion.[75] Private loan defaults started to soar in 2011 and increased from 0.37% in early 2013 to 4.31% in late 2013.[76] The Regulations legalize private lending channels for 400,000 local SMEs to obtain finance in Wenzhou and helps individual investors to gain investment returns.

Private lending has a high degree of heterogeneity, opacity and diversity in terms of business models and lending patterns. Technically, this shadow banking subsector is hard to monitor or regulate. Circular No. 107 divides the private lending sector into two categories. First, underground financing which is largely unregulated. The second is petty-loan companies, pawn shops and financing leasing companies, and the regulation of these micro-finance firms needs to be improved. These micro-finance firms are not allowed to take deposits, make shark loans or collect loans through illegal means.[77] Petty loan companies are supposed to use self-owned funds for lending and can obtain finance from commercial banks[78] while pawn shops and financing leasing companies are not regarded as financial institutions in nature and their business scope is strictly regulated.[79] In addition, pawn shops must not increase leverage and financing leasing companies must not on-lend bank loans and relevant assets.[80]

3.1 Key Objectives

The strategy applied by the Private Lending Regulations is to formalize the private lending market by paving the way to convert underground loan companies into local banks servicing SMEs. The key objective of the Private Lending Regulations is to guide the regulation of healthy development of private lending. Bringing private lenders under the regulatory umbrella should help prevent and dissolve the risks of private lending, curb systemic risks, and promote better allocation of funds in economic and social development.

---

75 "Regulating China's Shadow Banking System Isn't Easy", *Bloomberg News* (25 April 2013).

76 "Wenzhou Banks' NPL Ratio Hit 28-month High, Paper Says", EJI Insight (3 December 2013).

77 Circular No. 107, Article 3(5).

78 Ibid.

79 Ibid.

80 Ibid.

3.2 Definition of "Private Financing"

Private financing is defined by the Regulations as financing activities that take place between individuals and non-financial institutions and organizations through private lending, bonds issuing or private placement.

3.3 Types of Lenders

Enterprises in need of funds can borrow private loans via three kinds of intermediary agencies, including private capital management firms, private financing information service firms (engaged in funds-matching and financial products promotion) and private lending public service institutions (serving as a government resource for private lenders and borrowers), which are still not part of the formal financial system elsewhere in China.

The registered capital of a private fund management firm must be no less than RMB 50 million and is required to be paid in monetary capital.[81] The registered capital requirement serves the same function as the capital reserve requirement for a bank. This is put in place to provide a safety net for depositors by providing them with confidence so that there will be no bank run type of collapse. The downside is the increase of transaction cost and barriers to entry for establishing such a fund.

This RMB 50 million capital requirement serves as a barrier to prevent small investors from entering into the business. Certainly there is an assumption that larger private fund management enterprises are less likely to commit fraud or unethical behaviour towards consumers. In addition, larger private fund management may be more powerful to counter systemic risk but may also easily possess a monopolistic position in the market place. Free competition helps drive down prices or interest rates. Rational consumers with choices will choose the best and most valuable option for their projects.

Wenzhou's lending service institutions emerged in 2012, when the State Council approved a broad package of financial reforms allowing Wenzhou to serve as a test bed for liberalizing private lending, which had grown into a colossal underground industry, powered by the robust growth of the city's private economy. There are currently seven such service centers in Wenzhou. By 12 December 2013, they had registered private capital of 7 billion yuan, with 2.5 billion in outstanding loans. These institutions keep records of lenders who lend over 3 million yuan in a single private loan and collective loans with a combined value of over 10 million yuan.

---

81 Wenzhou Private Financing Regulations, Article 6.

Wenzhou also has 11 private capital management firms, which specialize in offering financial services from private placement to project investment. By December 2013, they had directed 2 billion yuan into private funding for investment in 618 commercial projects.[82]

Civil servants from local financial management departments are disallowed from participating in private financing activities, which helps prevent abuses of power by rent-seeking. Due to the resources public servants may possess, if they are allowed to enter the private lending market, they would be able to translate those resources into profits, which is unfair to other market players.

Lenders are required to establish a confidential information protection system to avoid the disclosure of business secrets and personal privacy of parties concerned in private financing.[83] Information protection and security is a must in the world of private financing. The lenders will be collecting sensitive data from all parties. This requirement should go beyond the establishment of a confidential information protection system and mandate an up-to-date cyber security system for all enterprises involved in private lending. However, it is worth noting that the dissemination of private information is not a prevalent problem for shadow banking clients.

When an enterprise is ineligible to carry out private bond financing or private fund raising, the local financial management authority has the authority to fine it not less than 1% but not more than 5% of the funds it has raised and may order it to refund the funds raised.[84] A refund does a much better job than a fine because a fine may be an indirect cost to consumers. A potential fine may push up the costs if the fund raiser wants to ensure returns.

3.4 Mandatory Filing Requirement

A private fund management enterprise shall file the duplicate of its business license with the local financial management authority of Wenzhou City for record within 15 days after the date of company registration.[85]

---

[82] "China Legalizes Private Lending in Wenzhou", *Xinhua News*, 28 February 28, 2014, available 8 March 2016 at http://www.china.org.cn/business/2014-02/28/content_31637420.htm; and Jasmin Sasin, "Wenzhou Given Approval to Legalize Private Lending", *Shenzhen Standard*, 13 March 2014, available 8 March 2016 at http://www.shenzhen-standard.com/2014/03/13/wenzhou-given-approval-to-legalize-private-lending/.

[83] Wenzhou Private Financing Regulations, Article 11.

[84] Ibid, Article 42.

[85] Ibid, Article 6.

An enterprise which conducts private bond financing or a private fund management enterprise which conducts private fundraising shall apply for registration with the local financial management authority in Wenzhou City,[86] and report financing conditions to the registration authority in writing within 20 days after the completion of financing.[87] Borrowers are required by the Regulations to file with the local financial management authority or private lending registration service centre if a single loan exceeds 3 million yuan (US$494,400),[88] multiple loans total over 10 million yuan,[89] or when more than 30 people are involved as lenders.[90] The Regulations also incentivize lenders to record private lending contracts by prioritizing recorded materials as evidence having higher probative force and being an important basis on which the legality of private lending is determined by the court or arbitration institutions when private lending cases are handled.[91]

Mandatory registration of private lending has a two-pronged effect. It strengthens information disclosure by ensuring that the borrower engaging in certain private lending transactions is on the radar. It is meant to enhance the safety of lending by resolving the information asymmetry that exists between lenders and borrowers in the shadow banking sector. This information-sharing rule tries to expose the privacy of transacting parties. Then the lenders can optimize their lending decisions with complete information about the creditworthiness of borrowers. This is a useful step for China to develop its credit information sharing scheme. More things can be done. For instance, Circular No. 107 requires the establishment of a credit checking system covering both institutions and individuals.[92]

The government will review private financing to check the money is legal, and they will have to share the information with the local industrial and commercial administration, tax bureau and public security bureau to prevent potential fraud and protect all parties' interests. This requirement is to protect consumers. The government is put in place to solve the information asymmetry problem by checking the accuracy and completeness of financial information. The caution is that the procedural requirement can be cumbersome. The other option is random audits which can ensure a thorough reporting of authentic information.

86 Ibid, Articles 20 and 26.
87 Ibid, Article 26.
88 Ibid, Article 14.
89 Ibid.
90 Ibid.
91 Ibid, Article 17.
92 Circular No. 107, Article 5(3).

The local financial management authority is to monitor private investment and to instruct private lenders to establish corporate government systems, codes of conduct, disclosures, credit archives and risk controls.[93] It also has power to supervise the fulfilment of information disclosure obligations by the enterprise conducting private bond financing and a private fund management enterprise.[94] This is to promote risk disclosure and ensure that investors are adequately informed of risks and that all disclosed information is accurate.[95] Failure to file and submit written reports, or providing counterfeit materials for filing and reporting trigger legal liability to a private fund management enterprise, a private financing information service enterprise, or the borrower in a private lending, or an enterprise conducting private bond financing needs to make corrections under the order of the local financial management authority. Unrecorded private fund management enterprise, private financing information service enterprise and private lending activity shall be publicized and a fine will be imposed.[96] Public shaming is an effective tactic. There is a certain element of fear when companies face fines that are astronomically high and will directly affect the firm's bottom line.

Where an enterprise conducting private bond financing or a private fund management enterprise fails to fulfill the obligation of advance registration, the local financial management authority has power to order it to make corrections. In a case where no funds have been raised, the enterprise shall be fined not less than 50,000 but not more than 100,000 yuan, or else, it shall be fined not less than 1% but not more than 5% of the funds it has raised.[97]

Where the enterprise conducting private bond financing and a private fund management enterprise provide counterfeit registration materials, they shall, within a prescribed limit of time, make corrections under the order of the local financial management authority, or else they shall be punished.[98]

Where an enterprise conducting private bond financing and a private fund management enterprise fail to fulfill the obligation of information disclosure as agreed, or disclose information containing counterfeit records, misleading statements or material omissions, they shall make corrections under the order of the local financial management authority and be fined not less than 10,000 yuan but not more than 100,000 yuan; in

93 Wenzhou Private Financing Regulations, Articles 28–29.
94 Ibid, Article 27.
95 Ibid.
96 Ibid, Article 41.
97 Ibid, Article 43.
98 Ibid.

case of a serious offence, they shall be fined not less than 100,000 yuan but not more than 200,000 yuan.[99] A higher level of penalty deters institutions from committing wrongful acts, thus protecting the consumer interest while dissolving risks in the private lending industry.

Wenzhou set up an administrative system to regulate private financing activities. It is composed of a financial management bureau, a financial arbitration institution, a financial crime investigation team and a court.

3.5 Lending Practice

Firms are allowed to issue bonds, in a non-public way, to a maximum 200 qualified investors, for each issue[100] over a period of one year or longer and the coupon rate capped at three times the official benchmark lending rate, as long as the firm satisfies such conditions as operating well, having the ability to repay financial principal and interest, a financing term over one year, and, most importantly, an asset-liability ratio lower than 70% after financing.[101] These requirements lay out a high threshold allowing fewer firms access to a private bond market. The side effect of such eligibility restrictions on private bond financing and fundraising will limit the demand for credit and increase the cost of credit for borrowers. The sheer fact that the investors are qualified means that they are presumed to be financially savvy enough to make an intelligent investment decision. Qualified investors here refer to natural persons with proprietary financial assets of over 300,000 yuan or enterprises or other organizations with net assets of over 1 million yuan, all of which have corresponding risk identification and undertaking capabilities.[102] By restricting the pool of investors, the Regulations may hamper the ability of potential investors to invest in bond financing or fund raising, as well as increasing the price of credit and forcing bonds to offer higher returns.

A private fund management firm is allowed to conduct private fundraising. The preconditions the firm needs to satisfy are to have sustainable profitability and to have net assets of RMB 20 million or more, of which at least 20% must be registered capital.[103] In addition, there is a loan-to-asset ratio cap on the amount of total funds this private fund management firm can raise, that is, eight times the net assets of the firm.[104] Requiring

---

[99] Ibid, Article 44.
[100] Ibids, Article 19.
[101] Ibid, Article 20.
[102] Ibid, Article 24.
[103] Ibid, Article 22.
[104] Ibid, Article 23.

sustainable profitability, a certain amount of net assets, a percentage of registered capital and a maximum loan-to-asset ratio is to reduce risk and protect such firms from being too detrimentally affected by defaults since more financial resources can ensure financial soundness and stability. However, the cap on the maximum amount the firm can raise is expensive due to the opportunity cost, which may effectively rule out the possibility of an overly profitable Ponzi scheme. In addition, these requirements restrict the supply of credit to the financial system.

In addition, the total funds raised by the firm shall be under the custody of a financial institution with conditions prescribed by the state authority in Wenzhou.[105] The private fund management firm is required to make a contribution of no less than 10% of funds raised by it every time. Privately raised funds shall be used in the production and operation project determined at the time of fund raising. With the consent of qualified investors with over two-thirds of privately raised funds at that time, idle project funds may be used as short-term private lending (no more than six months) in Wenzhou; however, the amount shall not exceed 30% of the total of privately raised funds at that time.[106] This is a paternalistic requirement with the aim of protecting consumers.

A written contract is required to be signed in the case of lending between natural persons and between natural persons and non-financial enterprises and/or other organizations to meet the needs of production and operation, or temporarily regulatory lending between non-financial enterprises. The local financial management authority of Wenzhou City may make a sample contract on private lending for use by parties concerned in private lending.[107] The fact that the government authority may propagate a sample contract (a boilerplate contract)[108] is a good way not only to reduce transaction costs but, more importantly, regulate private lending.[109] While this requirement improves transparency, it may stifle innovation. There is no way the government or regulator can police the lending by making the parties form written contracts.

Any lender is only allowed to lend its self-owned funds[110] and may not "illegally absorb public funds to do so in disguised form, or fraudulently

---

105 Ibid.

106 Ibid, Article 23.

107 Ibid, Article 12.

108 Ibid.

109 Stephen J. Choi and G. Mitu Galti, "Contract as Statute", in Omri Ben-Shahar (ed.), *Boilerplate: The Foundations of Market Contracts* (Cambridge: Cambridge University Press 2007) Ch 11.

110 Wenzhou Private Financing Regulations, Article 12.

obtain credit funds from a banking institution to make illegal incomes through lending them".[111] This requirement is put in place with the purposes of decreasing leverage and reducing the way in which these institutions intertwine and rely upon one another.

The interest on a loan may not be deducted from the principal in advance. Where the interest is deducted from the principal in advance, the loan shall be returned and the interest thereon shall be calculated based on the actual amount of loan. These rules are to avoid some illegal fundraising activities.

3.6 Lending Rate

Unlike the preliminary draft, the Regulations do not specify the ceiling of the rate in a private lending. The Regulations make the interest rate provision default rule by stipulating that the private lending rate will be set based on negotiations between the borrower and lender as long as it does not violate national regulations.[112] This sets a good precedent, by acknowledging the importance of market-oriented interest rate formation mechanism as well as leaving the government or regulators the ability to override the market when they choose to do so. Currently, private lending is capped at four times the benchmark official lending rate. Private financing has thrived in Wenzhou and many other places in China as small firms often have no access to bank loans and State-dominant banks prefer lending to large state-owned enterprises backed by local government credit. Considering that China's shadow banking system emerged out of a desire to circumvent tight regulation that restricts the flow of credit, the fact that the Regulations delegate a fair amount of control to the market, rather than the state or regulators, is a positive change.

A private fund management enterprise and a private financing information service enterprise may not promise a return to any party concerned in private financing.[113] This provision tries to eliminate the practice of guaranteeing a fixed return and decrease risky behaviour on the part of investors. However, where informal lending is being formalized, the lenders may have a misperception that there is implicit guarantee return for their loans.

---

[111] Ibid.
[112] Ibid, Article 13.
[113] Ibid, Article 10.

3.7 Liability

Violation of the Regulations will be subject to fines ranging from 10,000 yuan up to 500,000 yuan.

Where an enterprise conducting private bond financing and a private fund management enterprise fails to fulfill the obligation of information disclosure as agreed, or disclose information containing counterfeit records, misleading statements or material omissions, they need to make corrections under the order of the local financial management authority and be fined no less than RMB 10,000 but no more than RMB 100,000; in case of a serious offence, they shall be fined not less than RMB 100,000 but no more than RMB 200,000.[114]

Small firms are willing to invest less in compliance to avoid a higher penalty. By contrast, large firms are willing to pay these small fines to get away with misleading statements or material omissions because the revenues they generate from said wrongdoings will outweigh the modest fines. Raising the fines can deter more institutions from committing wrongful acts, thus protecting the interest of the state and consumers while dissolving risks in the private lending industry.

Privately raised funds and benefits thereof shall be independent of proprietary properties of private funds management enterprises. Liabilities that shall be borne by proprietary properties of a private fund management enterprise shall not be borne by privately raised funds and benefits thereof. Collective fund properties shall be accounted for every time and bear risks independently.[115] The enterprises therefore are required to create separate funds to curb liabilities. This protects consumers by providing them with a veil to shield them from the liabilities the enterprises may take on without investor permission.

The Regulations explicitly prevent some non-bank institutions from taking public funds or doing so in disguised form as a means to provide illegal private loans, specifically mentioning guarantee companies, investment consulting companies, pawn shops and consignment shops.[116] The upside of such limits is to reign in the complexity of the dynamic arrangement in shadow banking and leave little space for coming up with practical and innovative solutions to solve for credit issues in China. Those that do so are subject to investigation, fines of up to RMB 200,000, confiscation

---

114 Ibid, Article 44.
115 Ibid, Article 25.
116 Ibid, Article 34.

of gains and other criminal penalties.[117] Enterprises' illicit activities such as illegally carrying out private bond financing or private fund raising will result in a fine of "not less than 1% but not more than 5% of the funds raised, and the possibility of being forced to refund the funds raised".[118] This fine functions more like a tax, deterring potential fund raisers and bond financiers. Private lenders and borrowers that do not submit accurate records or fail to disclose required information to the local financial management authority are subject to fines of up to RMB 100,000.[119] These provisions are crafted to encourage private lending in a controlled manner, weeding out some of the high-risk investments that have plagued the domestic financial system, and providing more transparency and government oversight in order to maintain financial safety.

Where a private financing public service institution discloses or illegally provides the filing information for private lending, it shall make corrections under the order of the local financial management authority and be fined not less than 10,000 yuan but not more than 100,000 yuan; in case of a serious offence, it shall be fined not less than 100,000 yuan but not more than 200,000 yuan, and the directly responsible supervisor and any other staff directly responsible for the offence shall be fined not less than 10,000 yuan but not more than 50,000 yuan; if there are illegal gains, the gains shall be confiscated.[120]

Where a party concerned in private financing or any other institution such as a guarantee company, investment consulting company, pawnshop or consignment shop, illegally absorbs public funds or does so in disguised form, or provides loans illegally, it shall be ordered to stop the unlawful activities and fined not less than 500,000 yuan but not more than 100,000 yuan by the local financial management authority; in the case of a serious offence, it shall be fined not less than 50,000 yuan but not more than 200,000 yuan; if there are illegal gains, the gains shall be confiscated.[121]

3.8 Local Authority's Role

The local financial management authority is required to monitor, calculate, analyse, manage, supervise and check private financing.[122] It is charged with the task of instructing financing institutions to establish

---

[117] Ibid, Articles 35, 40 and 46.
[118] Ibid, Article 42.
[119] Ibid, Articles 41, 43 and 44.
[120] Ibid, Article 45.
[121] Ibid, Article 46.
[122] Ibid, Article 28.

management systems to monitor risk control.[123] It is also granted a fairly broad power to ensure compliance with the risk prevention elements of the Regulations, in particular, in terms of its ability to investigate potential violations[124] as well as supervise the fulfillment of disclosure obligations.[125]

The local financial management authority has the power to order a staff member of a private financing public service institution, who makes use of the convenience of its position to participate in private financing, or a practitioner of a private fund management enterprise or a private financing information service enterprise making use of the convenience of its position to participate in private financing in the enterprise to seek improper interests, to make corrections, give a warning to him, confiscate his illegal gains and fine him not less than 10,000 yuan, but not more than 100,000.[126]

3.9 Experimental Nature of the Regulations and Deeper Reform

Frequently, the Regulations and such like expose the tension between encouraging growth and limiting instability in finance and credit markets. Clearly, the Regulations seek to legalize formerly underground lending institutions, thereby allowing for regulation, while creating a system of registration, disclosure and obligations that are meant to improve transparency and discipline – both between the government and private lenders, and between lenders and borrowers. The former should make oversight easier while the latter should decrease risky investment and borrowing. With this said, there is much action that the government could take in order to curb the risks. The most glaring deficiency is the failure to liberalize and marketize interest rates, a measure that would likely be the simplest and most effective way of curbing illegal lending. This can effectively increase the use of formal banking and decrease the widespread regulatory arbitrage.

The Regulations in Wenzhou are significant because these rules bring Wenzhou back from the brink and set a good example for other cities and provinces where underground banking is active to follow. The local government may have a better sense of the economic needs and may be privy to local information that the State is not aware of. The local government is in a better position to monitor and regulate systemic risks

---

123 Ibid, Article 29.
124 Ibid, Article 35.
125 Ibid, Article 27.
126 Ibid, Article 47.

involving private financing businesses. The local experimental nature of these Regulations will not be ignored given China's unitary regime and centralized-governance model. The Regulations are supposed to embrace underground lending rather than eliminating it completely, and mend the inefficiencies of financial institutions in Wenzhou. The solution deployed in Wenzhou's Private Lending Regulations is to formalize informal lending markets, which is used as a means to provide financial access to the private sector and inject more competition into the closed financial market. The Regulations are likely to play an active role in standardizing private lending. However, it is far from a comprehensive solution. The Regulations try to address many issues in relation to underground lending, but not many of the issues that caused the popularity of underground lending. It is unlikely to totally solve the problems, such as small firms which face financing difficulties. A shift in government policy for commercial banks would go a long way towards decreasing the need for underground lending. Clearly, deeper financial reform is necessary.

4. 4-TIMES INTEREST RATE RULE AND INTERCOMPANY LENDING REGULATIONS

Private lending and borrowing activities among individuals and firms are not just subject to regulation. PRC law addresses loan-related interest in a gradualist manner.

4.1 Party Autonomy Principle

The Supreme People's Court in the early 1980s provided that:

> Parties can agree on interest-free loan. However, if the debtor intentionally delays repayment over a long period of time and the creditor requests for interest, the applicable interest rate can refer to the national bank's interest rate for loans. For loans with interest, parties may agree on an interest rate suitably higher than national bank's interest rate for loan. However, if the creditor takes advantage of the debtor's perilous state or reaps exorbitant profits from extremely high interest rate loan, that loan is not protected.[127]

The last sentence of this ruling shows that a high interest loan should be regarded as a forbidden form of exploitation. What is unclear is the

---

[127] Supreme People's Court's Opinions on the Implementation and Enforcement of Some Civil Policies and Laws, 30 August 1984, Article 69.

level of interest that the PRC courts may consider to be "suitably higher" than the national bank's interest rate for loans or "extremely high" rate of interest.

4.2 Interest on Loans under Contract Law

Interest on loans is codified in the Contract Law's Chapter 12 on Contracts for Loan of Money. It is specified that interest on the repayment of loans in arrears be charged according to the parties' agreement or relevant state provisions.[128]

As far as a loan agreement between natural persons is concerned, the interest rate agreed between natural persons needs to comply with the state provisions on the limits to the level of interest to be charged.[129] Where the agreement is silent or ambiguous on the payment of interest, it is then identified as an interest-free loan.[130]

One example is the agency agreement under which the principal pays the agent's expenses to conduct the mandate of the principal in advance, and pays these expenses back to the agent together with interest if the agent pays out necessary expenses on behalf of the principal. However, the Contract Law is silent on how to calculate the interest rate. Then, relevant state provisions will be applied.

The other example is the consumer's contract. According to the Consumer Protection Law, consumers can recover interest from a business supplier of goods or services who is obliged to refund the price a consumer paid in advance.[131] Interest here in nature is restitution of benefits for the protection of consumers. However, the Consumer Protection Law does not provide for the commencement of interest accrual. Likely the relevant provision in the Contracts for the International Sale of Goods (UN) (CISG) applies: a seller must pay interest on the price from the date on which the price was paid if the seller is bound to refund the price.[132] The court may use the CISG as a relevant international convention to fill the gap in the Contract Law concerning the awarding of interest.

---

128 PRC Contract Law, Article 207.
129 Ibid, Article 211.
130 Ibid.
131 PRC Consumer Protection Law, Article 47.
132 CISG, Article 84(1).

4.3 Interest under the Secured Interest Law

Interest is also governed by the Secured Interest Law. The parties are allowed to agree to a payment of a deposit as guarantee.[133]

When a party who accepts the deposit as a guarantee fails to perform his or her obligations, he or she should refund double the deposit paid. The party paying the deposit fails to perform his obligations under the contract; such party has no right to demand for the return of the deposit.[134]

The amount of deposit that can be agreed upon by parties as a security should not exceed 20% of the total value of the main contract.[135]

4.4 Calculation of Interest

In principle, in the absence of the parties' agreement, the court may refer to the interest rate for the late repayment of loans charged by financing institutions as fixed by the PBOC. The court may adjust that interest rate in accordance with any adjustments made by the PBOC from time to time.[136]

After the promulgation of the Contract Law, Chinese courts are more consistent in calculating interest rate by reference to the lending rate of the PBOC.

In contrast to the CISG, the Contract Law does not use interest as a remedy to recover the amount of damages caused by the breach, including loss of profit. Under the CISG, interest is recoverable independently from damages. As the PRC is a party to the CISG, the CISG is a source of law in China, and may apply when domestic laws contradict the CISG.

4.5 Judicial Interpretations

The Supreme People's Court issued the second piece of judicial interpretation in relation to the Contract Law in February 2009.

This piece of judicial interpretation came into force on 13 May 2009. Article 2 provides that, in addition to the primary debts, the obligator/debtor shall bear the interest and the expenses to realize the obligee's/creditor's rights. Chinese courts accordingly have the authority to award interest on pre-judgment debts. The interpretation explicitly provides

---

[133] PRC Contract Law, Article 115.

[134] Ibid.

[135] PRC Secured Interest Law, Article 91.

[136] Supreme People's Court's Reply on How to Calculate Late Repayment Penalty, issued in 1999 and revised in 2000.

an obligation to pay interest independently from penalties or damages, without regard to fault or proof of loss. It is reasonable to assume that interest on damages for non-performance of non-monetary obligations may be recovered. However, the judicial interpretation still fails to address the method of calculating the interest to be awarded.

Lending rates in excess of four times the benchmark interest rate are illegal.

4.6 Private Lending Regulations – Latest Judicial Movement

On 6 August 2015, the Supreme People's Court issued the *Regulations on Application of Laws to Certain Issues For Hearing of Private Lending Cases* (Fa Shi [2015] No. 18) (the Private Lending Regulations), which came into effect on 1 September 2015. The Private Lending Regulations are introduced at a time when the increasing financing needs of SMEs cannot be fully satisfied by the banking system, and alternative financing solutions (including funding provided by an online peer-to-peer network, which is also covered by the Regulations) are being developed.

The Private Lending Regulations provide a much needed legal framework for regulation of the increasing onshore lending activities undertaken by non-bank entities, and present new opportunities and structuring options for both investors and lenders. The Private Lending Regulations apply to lending activities between natural persons, corporates and other organizations, but exclude loans made by financial institutions.[137] In this section, the focus is placed on the provisions of the Private Lending Regulations which change the legal regime on intercompany loans, and how such change may impact the way financing transactions involving PRC companies are structured.

(a) Key changes

Prior to the Private Lending Regulations coming into force, the making of intercompany loans directly between PRC companies is not allowed. Article 61 of the General Principles for Lending, promulgated by the People's Bank of China in 1996, prohibits any direct or de facto intercompany loan. The PRC Supreme People's Court confirmed, in a reply letter dated 23 September 1996, that any intercompany loan agreement should be null and void. In view of these legal restrictions, a PRC company wishing to borrow from, or lend to, another PRC company would need to enter into an entrustment loan arrangement with a domestic bank, where

---

[137] Private Lending Regulations, Article 1.

the domestic bank acts as the funding conduit between the two PRC companies and charges a fee.

The position is changed under the Private Lending Regulations, which make clear that, subject to limited exceptions, an intercompany loan agreement entered into for production or operating purposes is valid and will be recognized by the courts.[138] That said, the validity of an intercompany loan agreement can still be challenged if the lender (not being a financial institution) regularly carries out lending business or if money-lending activities have become its main income source, as in such cases the lender's entry into an intercompany loan agreement may not be for production or operating purposes. This suggests that a non-financial-institution lender can only lend money on an *ad hoc* basis.

Under the Private Lending Regulations, interest, default interest and other fees can be charged. As a rule of thumb, any interest rate on an intercompany loan not exceeding 24% per annum will be upheld by the courts.[139] The detailed rules are as follows. Where the interest rate agreed upon by the borrower and the lender exceeds the annual interest rate of 36%, the agreed interest on the excessive part shall be null and void. If the borrower requests the lender's return of the paid interest on the part exceeding the annual interest rate of 36%, the court will support such as request.[140]

The working of 0%, 24% and 36% is indicated in Figure 8.1.

Where the borrower and the lender include the interest after the settlement of the principal and interest of the loan at the earlier period in the principal of the loan at the later period and issue a new certificate of creditor's right, if the interest rate at the earlier period does not exceed the annual interest rate of 24%, the amount indicated in the newly issued certificate of creditor's right may be determined as the principal of the loan at the later period; and the interest on the excessive part shall not be included in the principal of the loan at the later period. If the interest rate agreed upon exceeds the annual interest rate of 24%, and the party claims that the interest on the excessive part cannot be included in the principal of the loan at the later period, the people's court shall support such a claim.[141]

The sum of principal and interest payable by the borrower after the loan term expires that is calculated based on the preceding paragraph shall not exceed the sum of the principal of the initial loan and the interest during the entire loan term calculated based on the principal of the initial loan at

138 Ibid, Article 11.
139 Ibid, Article 26.
140 Ibid.
141 Ibid, Article 28.

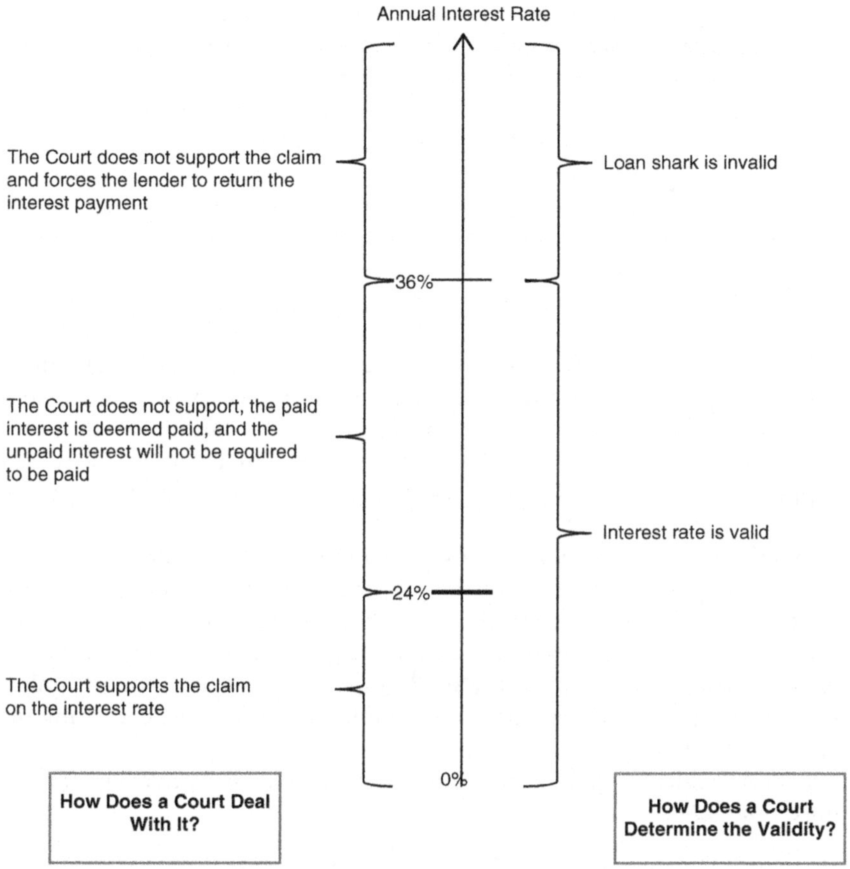

Figure 8.1 The Supreme People's Court's judicial interpretation on interest rates

the annual interest rate 24%. If the borrower requests the lender's payment of the excessive part, the court shall not support such a request.[142]

Where the interest rate on an overdue loan is agreed upon by the borrower and the lender, such interest rate shall prevail, but it shall not exceed the annual interest rate of 24%.

Where the interest rate on an overdue loan is not agreed upon or clearly agreed upon by the borrower and the lender, the court may handle the situation based on different circumstances:

---

142 Ibid.

(1) Where neither the interest rate within the loan term nor the interest rate on an overdue loan is agreed upon by the parties, and the lender claims the borrower's payment of interest as of the overdue date at the annual interest rate of 6% during the period when the funds are occupied, the court shall support such a claim.
(2) Where the parties only agree on the interest rate within the loan term, but fail to agree on the interest rate on an overdue loan, and the lender claims the borrower's payment of interest as of the overdue date at the interest rate within the loan term during the period when the funds are occupied, the court shall support such a claim.[143]

Where the lender and the borrower agree on both the interest rate on an overdue loan and the liquidated damages or other expenses, the lender may claim the interest on the overdue loan, the liquidated damages or other expenses, or claim them as a whole, but the court shall not support the claim on the part exceeding the annual interest rate of 24%.[144]

Where the borrower voluntarily pays the interest not agreed upon, or voluntarily pays the interest or liquidated damages exceeding the agreed interest rate without harming the interest of the state, the collective or the third party, if the borrower requests the lender's return under the excuse of unjust enrichment, the court shall not support such a request, unless the borrower requests the return of the interest on the part exceeding the annual interest rate of 36%.[145]

An intercompany loan agreement will be held invalid under the following circumstances:[146]

(1) a lender uses funds borrowed from financial institutions for on-lending to a borrower at an "excessive" interest rate, where the borrower has prior knowledge of such arrangement or should have knowledge of such arrangement;
(2) a lender uses funds borrowed from other corporates or its employees for on-lending to a borrower for profit-making purposes, where the borrower has prior knowledge of such arrangement or should have knowledge of such arrangement;
(3) a lender makes available a loan to a borrower for funding illegal

---

143 Ibid, Article 29.
144 Ibid, Article 30.
145 Ibid, Article 31.
146 Ibid, Article 14.

activities, where the lender has prior knowledge of such arrangement or should have knowledge of such arrangement;

(4) the loan arrangement is in contravention of social order and good custom; or

(5) other circumstances involving a breach of law or mandatory provisions of regulations.

For the purposes of paragraph (1) above, the meaning of an "excessive" interest rate is not defined in the Private Lending Regulations.

(b) Practical implications

(1) Rationalising funding arrangement Prior to an intercompany loan being legalized, as an alternative funding arrangement, a PRC company may obtain funding by way of equity, or by entering into certain "quasi" lending arrangements, such as a joint development agreement or cash pooling, in order to address its capital needs. Some funding arrangements between PRC companies may be booked as receivables and payables. Typically, those receivables and payables are not documented. Some of those arrangements seek to achieve the commercial effect of a loan but there may be some uncertainties under Chinese law.

The Private Lending Regulations now provide for a legal framework for an intercompany loan to be recognized. It offers legal protection and commercial certainty to the parties. This also enhances the bankability of a financing structure if the repayment cash flow under an intercompany funding arrangement is a key part of the credit.

(2) Security and subordination arrangement made possible The legal recognition of an intercompany loan will enable any properly documented intercompany loan receivable to be pledged or assigned, and a subordination arrangement to be put in place in respect of such liabilities.

(3) Streamlining fund flows In a structured lending transaction, lenders will typically require to closely monitor the fund flow between the borrowing vehicle and any company ultimately using the loan proceeds. The use of a direct intercompany loan without a third party entrustment bank as an intermediary enhances the ability of lenders to monitor their debt and remove any credit and performance risk of the entrustment loan bank, and also saves on transaction time and costs. This, together with the possibility to put in place any security or subordination arrangement in connection with an intercompany loan, increases structuring options for structured financing with PRC companies.

(4) Flexibility on capitalisation Capitalization of a foreign invested enterprise (FIE) may be done by way of equity or debt. In the case of a Sino-foreign joint venture enterprise, an injection of capital by the domestic joint venture party using direct debt was not legally feasible because of the restrictions on the intercompany loan. The injection of additional equity, on the other hand, is subject to regulatory approval, which may take time to obtain. According to the Regulations, a PRC domestic joint venture party may choose to lend an intercompany loan to an FIE without going through any approval in order to address any urgent funding needs of that FIE. Similarly for a domestic enterprise, the making of a direct loan by its shareholder will be a more streamlined process as any capital increase will be subject to the amendment of its constitutional documents and filings with the relevant authorities.

The flexibility in providing funding by way of debt will be useful where a PRC sponsor has given a cost overrun funding undertaking, or a completion undertaking, in respect of the obligations of another PRC company. This is common in real estate finance or project finance transactions. With an intercompany loan being feasible, funding can be promptly made available by the sponsor to the project company by way of debt in case the relevant undertaking is being performed.

The intercompany loan structure offers more options to put in place funding arrangements between PRC companies. For any domestic and multinational group which has multiple subsidiaries in the PRC, there is more flexibility on intra-group liquidity by way of intercompany loans among themselves without setting up a cash pool with a bank.

(c) Impact on cross-border loans and security

The Private Lending Regulations are silent on whether they apply to cross-border intercompany loans. Until any new rules are promulgated by the relevant authorities, it could be reasonably expected that the current legal regime for cross-border lending, administrated by the State Administration of Foreign Exchange (SAFE) and the PBOC, remains unaffected. For example, a PRC company (other than a financial institution) may not convert the foreign currency proceeds of a foreign debt it borrows to renminbi for on-lending to another domestic company under the current SAFE regulations. Accordingly, notwithstanding the Regulations, a PRC company still cannot downstream the proceeds of a foreign debt to its ultimate operating companies onshore by way of intercompany loans. Similarly, the making of an intercompany loan by a PRC company to an offshore company which is not its offshore subsidiary is beyond the scope permitted under SAFE Circular 59, and is not expected to be permitted by reason of the Regulations.

Now that a PRC company may pledge its receivables under an intercompany loan in favour of an onshore lender, there is no reason why a PRC company cannot pledge its receivables under an intercompany loan agreement in favour of an offshore lender, or such pledge be registrable with SAFE (if registration is required under the "*nei bao wai dai*" regime).

(d) Summary

The Private Lending Regulations recognize the existence and necessity of intercompany lending, and provide more funding options for PRC companies. The explicit recognition of intercompany loans provides more flexibility for a PRC company in managing its cash flow and capital structure. The Private Lending Regulations are important for the development of the onshore financing market, as it is the first time that the legality of intercompany loan agreements has been recognized by the PRC judiciary.

5. PRIVATE BANKING AND INNOVATIVE FINANCE

Reliance on the Big Four or other state-owned banks to solve the underfinance problem for SMEs is not a solution. Loan competence of stateowned banks at the district level is fairly low and cannot be used to satisfy local-based SMEs' capital demand.[147] Besides, state-owned banks do not have natural intimacy with SMEs. The solution should be crafted to strengthen the supply side, and more specialized small- and medium-sized banks can be set up to support SMEs. These banks have greater information advantages to provide financing for SMEs.[148]

There are two types of private commercial banks in China: 12 Chineseowned joint-stock commercial banks and a growing number of foreignowned banks. Among others, China Minsheng Bank is the largest and first Chinese joint stock commercial bank. In the Chinese market, there are wholly foreign-owned banks, foreign joint-venture banks and wholly foreign-owned finance companies. A large number of foreign banks have chosen to open branches of their home bank in China. However, the market share of foreign banking establishments is small, merely 1.83% of

[147] Yanzhong Wang, "Financing Difficulties and Structural Characteristics of SMEs in China", (2004) 12 *China & World Economy* 34, 45.

[148] Lin and Li, "Promoting the Growth of Medium and Small-sized Enterprises through the Development of Medium and Small-sized Financial Institutions".

total banking assets in China, even though the combined assets of these establishments was valued at US$1.74 trillion yuan.[149]

The CBRC approved China's first privately held bank, as part of reforms intended to open the country's financial sector to private investors. Shandong Yucheng Rural Commercial Bank obtained approval from the CBRC, with its largest shareholder Shenzhen-listed Baolingbao Biology Co, according to a statement filed with Shenzhen Stock Exchange on Friday. Baolingbao, a private firm in Shandong, is the largest shareholder with an 8.21% stake in the rural commercial bank, and four other major shareholders are also private firms. Baolingbao's share price soared by almost 10%.

China is to allow qualified private investors to set up small- and medium-sized financial institutions in an effort to open up the state-dominant sector, according to a recent road map that charts the future course of the world's second largest economy. More than 20 listed companies, including air conditioner maker Gree Electric Appliances Inc, home appliance retailer Suning, and personal computer maker Lenovo have expressed interest in banking business. The approval of the bank marks a step forward for policy implementation.

The rapid development of shadow banking including internet banking has lead to *de facto* interest-rate liberalization. Allowing banks to compete on interest rates would boost lending rates because banks would be forced to fight for customers by offering higher interest rates on deposits and in turn, charging more for loans. Freeing China's banking market is another policy option. Shang Fulin, the head of the CBRC, said the government will allow privately owned banks to be set up in the wealthier regions of Tianjin, Shanghai, Zhejiang and Guangdong so that these lenders can provide financing for cash-strapped small and private businesses. Both Alibaba and Tencent are among the companies that won regulatory approval to take part in this pilot program.

At the same time, innovative finance continues to grow and will change the landscape of entrepreneurship, finance and innovation in China. Alibaba Group Holding has aggressively been lending, through its affiliate, Alibaba Small & Micro Financial Services, to small businesses and has taken deposits from savers while maintaining its dominance in the online shopping sector in China. Alibaba, in collaboration with money managers, has expanded beyond its usual e-commerce and texting businesses into the world of money-market funds. Alibaba's internet money-fund market has hauled in more than 400 billion yuan in assets, and had topped 81

---

149 PWC, *Foreign Banks in China*, May 2010.

million investors by the end of February 2014 (comparing with 77 million equity trading accounts in China).[150] This fund sold US$16.3 billion of its money-market-like investments and amassed loans totaling US$2 billion by the end of 2013. It became the fourth largest fund in the world.[151] Other big five funds include Vanguard Group and Fidelity Investments. Tencent Holdings has attracted 50 billion yuan to its Licaitong fund.[152] Alibaba and Tencent are two of a number of new financial offerings stepping onto the turf of Chinese banking sector.

Technology companies are also trying to break into China's taxi market. Alibaba, Baidu and Tencent is developing mobile payments, similar to a system originally developed in Europe, where consumers are able to pay for merchandise via their cell phone, and in which the payment is charged either to a bank account or to the telephone operator's billing system.[153] Tencent in 2013 added an electronic payment function to WeChat. In 2014, Tencent started allowing users to invest their savings in a money market fund.[154] Alibaba is expanding the mobile-payment and financial services it offers through its Alipay electronic-payment affiliate.[155] Baidu also ramped up investment in smartphone taxi apps through taking a stake in Uber, a US car-haling company, in an effort to expand its user base. Alibaba-backed Kuaidi Dache and Tencent-backed Didi Dache had 54.4% and 44.9% of market share respectively.[156]

The prize is more than taxi customers for the internet companies, which are keener to promote more widespread use of their online payment systems, one of the most lucrative mobile businesses. Alibaba's taxi app allows smartphone users to access the Kuaidi taxi-hailing service by selecting it from a menu in Alipay Wallet, the mobile version of its electronic-payments service. Passengers pay for rides by scanning a QR code on a driver's handset, and then the amount is automatically deducted from the

---

[150] Jamil Anderlini, "Alibaba Fund Soars to 81m Investors", *Financial Times*, 11 March 2014, p.1.

[151] Ibid.

[152] Chao Deng, "China's E-Money Funds Lose Their Buzz", *The Wall Street Journal*, 7 March 2014, C2.

[153] Carol Power, "Bank-Telecom Alliance Trend Said on Way to U.S.", (2001) 166(81) *American Banker* 10.

[154] Juro Osawa and Paul Mozur, "Marketing Costs Hit Tencent", *The Wall Street Journal*, 20 March 2014, B7.

[155] Ibid.

[156] Kana Inagaki, "SoftBank Invests in Chinese Taxi App", *Financial Times*, 15 January 2015 (online) (citing Analysis Inernational's research results as well as reporting the Chinese government's ban on drivers of private cars offering unlicensed taxi services via mobile-phone apps).

riders' Alipay accounts. However, the Shanghai government has recently limited the use of taxi hailing apps in the city and banned their use at the rush hour. The Shanghai government limited their use on the grounds that apps' marketing and function, allowing premium prices to be charged, have disturbed the fair market order. Shanghai banned the use of Fast Taxi or Beep Beep Call a Cab during rush hours. It also blocked the use of taxi-hailing apps by private vehicles licensed for hire, which may affect Google-backed Uber. Beijing took a similar step with the rationale that the apps may unduly disrupt taxi services.

Apps that help users hail and pay for cabs on their smartphones have become the battleground in a proxy war for dominance in the lucrative mobile payments market. The taxi-app is the next frontier in China's internet-services market and competitors are seeking to win over 500 million smartphone-wielding consumers and tap the massive revenue they control. Apps backed by local internet groups, Tencent and Alibaba, offer subsidies to users in moves designed to grab a larger share of the market. Globally, taxi hailing apps have sparked contention between tech startups and regulators. A major concern is the high fares that apps can charge and their impact on the livelihoods of taxi drivers that do not use them. For various reasons, Paris for example, banned or limited the apps' reach. For internet companies such as Alibaba and Tencent, both of which have payment networks similar to PayPal, taxi-hailing apps give them a larger presence in mobile commerce markets. WeChat's mobile-payment function now has tens of millions of users.[157] Mobile internet payments in China nearly quadrupled between the first half of 2012 and 2013 to RMB 130 billion,[158] or 70% of transactions by value.[159]

6. TENTATIVE CONCLUSIONS AND POLICY APPROACHES

Availability of finance is of great importance for SMEs and poor households in the sense that credit can strengthen their capability to produce, innovate and expand their small businesses, thus boosting productivity and increasing income. In the long run, as evidenced by the empirical

[157] Mozur and Osawa, "Can Alibaba's Taxi App Be New Growth Driver?".

[158] Sarah Mishkin, "China's Curb on Taxi Apps a Blow in Proxy Payments War", *Financial Times*, 28 February 2014, p.16.

[159] Mozur and Osawa, "Can Alibaba's Taxi App Be New Growth Driver?".

cross-country studies, the availability of credit is likely to protect SMEs from financial vulnerability, and to stimulate overall economic and social development.[160] The power of credit lies in its inherent force to distribute income opportunities more evenly and effectively among various constituents in the community. The significance of equal access to finance has been well recognized. Securing access to finance is perceived as a catalyst for attainability of the Millennium Development Goals[161] and has been closely associated with the WTO Doha round of negotiation on international trade liberalization.[162]

The dominant view in the law and finance literature is that informal financial institutions play a complementary role to the formal financial system. The informal financial system cannot replace the formal financial system due to their incompatible monitoring and enforcement mechanisms. China has been often singled out as a counter-example to the law and finance literature's focus on the formal financial system and its contribution to economic development.[163] As confirmed by empirical work, it is alternative financing and governance mechanisms that strongly support China's fast growing private sector firms albeit weaker legal protections and poorer access to finance.[164] The large underground lending in China is one of such informal financing sources and involves several hundred billion dollars in bank deposits.[165] However, economically, as empirical findings also confirm, firms which rely on informal external financing do not grow faster or have higher productivity growth than firms that are

---

160 Thorsten Beck, Aslı Demirgüç-Kunt and Ross Levine, "Finance, Inequality and Poverty: Cross-Country Evidence", (2004) NBER Working Paper No. 10979, available 1 March 2016 at http://www.nber.org/papers/w10979.

161 All the country members of the United Nations in 2000 signed up to a set of Millennium Development Goals (General Assembly Resolution 55/2), available 1 March 2016 at http://www.un.org/millenniumgoals/. UN Human Development Report, "Millennium Development Goals: A Compact among Nations to End Human Poverty" (2003).

162 UN, "Doha Declaration on Financing for Development: Outcome Document of the Follow-up International Conference on Financing for Development to Review the Implementation of the Monterrey Consensus", (2008), available 1 March 2016 at www.un.org/esa/ffd/doha/documents/Doha_ Declaration _FFD.pdf.

163 Franklin Allen, Jun Qian and Meijun Qian, "Law, Finance and Economic Growth in China", (2005) *Journal of Financial Economics* 77, 57–116.

164 Katherine Connor Linton, "Access to Capital in China: Competitive Conditions for Foreign and Domestic Firms", (2006) *Journal of International Commerce and Economics*, available 1 March 2016 at ssrn.com/abstract=1031223.

165 Diana Farrell, et al., "Putting China's Capital to Work: The Value of Financial System Reform", (2006) McKinsey Global Institute Report.

bank financed.[166] This suggests that informal financing is not an effective substitute for formal financing channels in promoting economic growth. The broader policy implication is that informal financing should not be used as an ultimate solution to the financing gap problem the private sector faces in China. In addition, the informal financing market, as part of the least regulated shadow banking sector, involves various risks.

Some market-based approaches have been offered to mitigate the negative aspects of informal lending practices.

- Increasing access to formal funding sources, including microcredit institutions charging lower interest rates that make continued operation sustainable.
- Lowering the cost of serving target populations.
- Improving the availability of financial records to lower the cost to formal banking institutions of serving target populations.
- Increasing transparency and competition among formal loan providers by standardizing the advertised total cost of loans to allow for easier comparisons of providers and highlighting the gap between formal rates and those offered by informal lenders.
- Increasing competition to drive down interest rates to market rates.
- Reducing restrictions on interest rate controls to make cost recovery on smaller, unsecured, shorter-term or higher-risk loans possible for formal lenders.

These policies are put in place to address the concern over the lack of access to formal finance. Partially formalizing the underground lending market in Wenzhou through legislative moves, allowing private investors to set up commercial banks, liberalizing interest rates are all targeting the lack of access to formal finance. While these policy moves are important and will remedy some negative effects of underground lending, the extent of the problem, the role of government and the range of sophistication in the financial systems may affect the efficacy of these solutions. For instance, formalizing underground lending firms may increase the bureaucratic and monitoring costs, which negatively affect both borrowers and lenders. Lowering interest rates will shrink the lender's profitability margin, leading to a cut in total lending by the lenders. This again turns borrowers to the underground lending markets.

Without proper policy actions, the negative impacts on private firms

---

166 Ayyagari, Demirgüç-Kunt and Maksimovic, "Formal Versus Informal Finance: Evidence from China".

could potentially cause deeper economic distress and unexpected political unrest. The policy should place more emphasis on the supply side of the financial market by offering more formal funding. Some market economy approaches can help strengthen the supply side. Microfinancing can be one solution as it brings broad access to credit. Good examples are Building Resources Across Communities and Grameen Bank in Bangladesh.[167] To make microcredit firms work, government support or public funding is a must. In a larger context, China needs to turn its financial market from a repressed one to a liberalized one. With credit controls and interest rate controls in place, the state-owned sector, large firms, favoured industries and well-connected clients are more likely to secure more formal bank lending at more favourable terms and conditions, that is, a lower interest rate. By contrast, small firms and start-up firms will have to pay higher interest rates or be subject to less favourable terms in lending transactions. Equilibrium can be adjusted or rebalanced through the relaxation of financial controls and increasing of market competition.

In the foreseeable future, the informal lending market in China may continue to grow owing to the facts that (i) the demand for informal finance may grow more rapidly than the supply; and (ii) the solutions to address the imbalance between demand and supply may have no immediate effect. Given the benefits of financial repression and the huge size of non-performing loans and local government debts, maintaining the status quo may make sense so as to ease the repayment of growing debts in the face of a potential debt bomb. Financial repression, even in a weaker form, can be used to maintain and drive up consumer deposits, as a stable and less expensive source of revenue and funding, which is necessary to keep China's economy moving and growing. Getting a handle on debt without disrupting economic stability and societal harmony probably needs China to continue to practice its opaque financial repression as the preferred approach to minimize side effects of its slowing economy instead of a sudden switch to a financial market liberalization strategy. Nevertheless, in the long run, China needs to reform its financially repressed regime, which is not compatible with a modern consumer finance industry. Empirical work has unveiled a link behind the economic development that the more concentrated financial resources tend to be in a national economy, the higher the country's level of poverty.[168] Access to finance

---

[167] "A Tale of Two NGOs: Bangladesh's Grameen Bank and BRAC", available 1 March 2016 at https://www.smu.edu.sg/perspectives/2012/06/26/tale-two-ngos-bangladeshs-grameen-bank-and-brac.

[168] Stijn Claessens and Enrico Perotti, "The Links between Finance and

can be used as a device to improve the imbalanced governance structure which favours some constituents over others. Widening the channels to funding can be achieved through the opening-up and strengthening of the capital markets or the reform of the existing financial system eroding the vested power of the incumbent elite groups.[169] Deeper financial market reform requires an effective institutional structure, which China does not possess right now. A top-down reform is needed to have a liberalized and bottom-up consumer financial regime, which not only presents citizens with more economic benefits but also economic and political rights.

Inequality: Channels and Evidence", (2005) World Bank Report, available 1 March 2016 at https://openknowledge.worldbank.org/handle/10986/9227.

[169] Raghuram Rajan and Luigi Zingales, *Saving Capitalism from the Capitalists* (Princeton University Press, 2nd edn, 2004).

9. Credit crunch and liquidity supply in China's banking sector

China recently experienced the most severe cash crunch since the 2008 financial crisis, which was evidenced by a credit crunch in mid-June 2013. Lenders rushed to raise funds from the market in order to meet capital requirements, pushing the interbank lending rate up to as high as 28%. The sudden cash squeeze shocked the global markets. This chapter tries to understand why the credit crunch took place in 2013 and why China's central bank, unlike what it has often done through "credit easing", refused to inject any credit liquidity into the market on this occasion.

Sections 1 and 2 offer an overview of the credit crunch in general and in China, respectively. Section 3 explains the reason for no credit crunch in China even in the latest financial crisis. Section 4 focuses on the credit crunch episode in 2013 and unveils the central bank's no-action policy towards this credit crunch. A discussion of various economic and institutional factors is offered in Section 5 to explain why this no-action strategy is not sustainable in a long run. Section 6 wraps up the chapter by looking into the possible macroeconomic policy change which may affect the central bank's monetary policymaking.

1. CREDIT CRUNCH: OVERVIEW

A credit crunch is also known as a credit squeeze. Often, a credit crunch may be followed by a credit crisis. A credit crunch is accompanied by a reduction in the general availability of loans (or credit) or a sudden tightening of the conditions required to obtain a loan from the banks. Sometimes, a credit crunch appears together with a rise in official interest rates. The other way of interpreting the correlation between credit crunch and interest rate is that credit becomes less available at any given official interest rate.

There are a number of reasons why we may witness a credit crunch. A credit crunch is often caused by a sustained period of careless and inappropriate lending which results in losses for lending institutions and investors in debt when the loans turn sour and the full extent of bad debts becomes known. Other causes may include an anticipated decline in the value of the collateral used by the banks to secure the loans; an exogenous change in monetary conditions (for example, where the central bank suddenly and unexpectedly raises reserve requirements or imposes new regulatory constraints on lending); the government imposing direct credit controls on the banking system; or even an increased perception of risk regarding the solvency of other banks within the banking system, which in turn causes panics and fears in the market place.

A financial crisis may be triggered by a variety of factors, but is always typically connected with a collapse in credit.[1] The global financial crisis of 2008 was another vivid and repeated example of the collapse of the money supply and the exacerbated credit crunch that resulted in such severe consequences on the banks and other financial markets.[2]

2. CREDIT CRUNCH IN CHINA

Overall, credit crunch in China is rare as a financial phenomenon. However, credit crunch or credit squeeze may take place as a consequence of the central bank's monetary policy.

Central banks in many countries are set up to help commercial banks survive financial panics as a last resort. The origins of the PBOC were different. For a long time after it was set up, PBOC was the sole lender of any sort, collecting the nation's funds and allocating the funds according to economic planning. Now, it is a national financial administrative organ and no longer a commercial lender.

Currently, the key task of the PBOC is to determine the size and rate of growth of the money supply, which affects interest rates. This is the major content of the PBOC's function of formulating and implementing monetary policy. The PRC Law of the People's Bank of China (the "PBOC Law") states that the objectives of monetary policy are to maintain monetary stability, and in this way to promote economic growth.[3]

The control of inflation is PBOC's stated objective though it is termed in the language of "maintaining the stability of the value of the currency". Price stability is also an indicator used to measure monetary stability even though neither the central bank law nor the commercial law clarifies the meaning

---

[1] Gordon Brown, *Beyond the Crash: Overcoming the First Crisis of Globalisation* (Simon & Schuster 2010) p.35.

[2] Nouriel Roubini and Stephen Mihm, *Crisis Economics: A Crash Course in the Future of Finance* (New York: The Penguin Press 2010) pp.19, 23, 28 and 49.

[3] PBOC Law, Article 3.

of "price stability". Inflation generally tends to be a self-fulfilling prophecy as an expectation of price rises will result in a demand for higher wages and higher prices, which means that other economic factors come into the picture simultaneously. The PBOC Law appears to suggest that monetary stability is a primary objective for monetary policy while economic growth is a secondary one, which is more closely connected to the governmental function of the central bank. This explains why credit crunch is rare in China as the PBOC in any event is supposed to rescue the banks and the market.

Different from its counterparts in other free market economies, PBOC is more sensitive to deviations from its targets than to turbulence in the markets. PBOC needs to take into account the control of unemployment, economic growth and the balance of payments between trading states in formulating its monetary policy. The role of monetary policy has emerged as a key instrument adjusting economic performance while central planning becomes less important. Major mechanisms and monetary instruments used by PBOC in pursuing its monetary policy goals include implementing a reserve requirement ratio, setting a central bank base interest rate, engaging in central bank lending and conducting open market operations as well as the use of other policy instruments specified by the State Council, China's cabinet. This also explains why credit crunch is rare. The PBOC, together with the Chinese government, is bound to stabilize the financial market in the case where the banks are hungry for credit.

While the use of open market operations has grown rapidly over time, it is no secret that the PBOC more often uses reserve requirements to influence the volume of funds commercial banks have available to lend. Further, it maintains annual (and typically binding) bank-by-bank caps on credit growth, and uses official "window guidance" to influence the direction of bank lending. Last but not least, PBOC regulates retail interest rates,[4] which it typically moves in conjunction with other monetary

---

[4] The PBOC previously had set both a floor for lending rates and ceiling for deposit rates, which guaranteed a sizeable net interest margin but mispriced credit. A floor for lending interest rates provides an artificial subsidy to financial institutions so that they can borrow less expensively and then invest in higher yielding safe assets such as government bonds and property market. By offering interest rates that exceed the benchmark deposit rate and providing more wealth-management products, Chinese banks can secure more funds, which however may accumulate risks in the financial system. By contrast, a system of "financial repression" caps the deposit interest rates on offer, which are much lower than the higher returns promised by wealth management products, a "domestic" form of shadow banking in China. The lender in a shadow banking system, built on a lattice of interlocked credit, usually borrows money from banks and other private lenders with the aim of arbitraging interest rates. A mandatory ceiling on deposit rates (interest rates)

policy instruments. Despite this array of instruments, Chinese monetary policy relies heavily on quantity-based instruments (that is, through annual credit caps) and administrative measures such as reserve requirements and window guidance.

3. WHY NO CREDIT CRUNCH IN CHINA EVEN IN THE FINANCIAL CRISIS?

Chinese banks did not experience any credit crunch in the latest financial crisis. In order to fend off the financial crisis gripping the US and most of Europe, China powered through the global financial crisis in large part thanks to an explosion of credit, either through its formal banking system or a series of "shadow banks" and off-balance-sheet vehicles. The PBOC had consistently injected enough cash into the banking system through its regular bond auctions so as to maintain its money market and lending rates within its target range.

In late 2008, China started its massive economic stimulus package,[5] equivalent to about 27% of China's economy.[6] Chinese banks have extended huge amounts of loans to local borrowers, a legacy of the lending spree in 2009 that helped fund China's 4-trillion-yuan stimulus package. The PBOC released the data on its official webpage showing that total lending is to exceed RMB 8.5 trillion in 2012, up from RMB 7.47 trillion in 2011.[7] New loans extended by Chinese banks in the first half of 2013 totaled 5.08 trillion yuan, 221.7 billion yuan more than in the same period

---

deprives savers of the market return on their money. Inflation in China which in most cases surged past official interest rates made savers suffer losses.

[5] Reuters, "Lending to Local Banks to Decline: ICBC Chief", *South China Morning Post*, 1 June 2011, B3. The latest estimate is that total bank loans to local governments reached 14.4 trillion yuan. Lulu Chen, "Regulator Clears Bids to Raise Capital", *South China Morning Post*, 27 July 2011, B3. A large-scale of economic stimulus program was to ensure an 8% growth. Jamil Anderlini, "China Comfortable with Weaker Growth", *Financial Times*, 18 October 2012 (online).

[6] Based on the first national audit of regional finances published by Beijing on 26 June 2011. Robert Cookson, "Resilient Asia More Vulnerable to a Global Crisis", *Financial Times*, 28 July 2011, p.23.

[7] Reuters, "China Loans Slow But Economic Recovery on Track", *South China Morning Post*, 11 December 2012 (online). It was pointed out that credit growth, as measured by total social financing, may have peaked in the second half of 2012 and may decline in 2013. Jane Cai, "Mainland Banks Face Mounting Loan Dangers", *South China Morning Post*, 16 January 2013 (online).

of 2012.[8] Chinese credit issuance has risen to more than 22% year-on-year (at the time of writing) in 2013 while nominal gross domestic product growth has dipped below 10%.[9] China's banking sector assets would have risen by nearly US$14 trillion since 2008, which is almost equal to replicating the entire US commercial banking sector in just five years.[10] Monetary stimulation has seen the mainland's broad money supply, or M2, balloon by 21.1% annually over the past 27 years, fuelling a long period of inflation and widening wealth disparity.

The side effect of this credit spree or "quantitative easing" tactic was a remarkable increase of leverage: the overall credit to gross domestic product ratio has shot up from about 115% to nearly 173% over the past five years.[11] These financial strains are all of the government's own making. This again confirms the basic closed nature of the Chinese banking system which is controlled by the state, to a significant extent, by the credit crunch. The credit of the Chinese government forms the backdrop of the entire Chinese financial system.

Instead of quickly raising the interest rate to cool down the overheating economy, Chinese regulators have been more accustomed to imposing quotas on the amount of credit banks could extend. To smother inflation in 2011, for example, the PBOC's first tightening action was to withdraw as much as RMB 900 billion from lenders' hands. And, administrative measures can have prompt healing effects against economic problems. For instance, the government's tight grip on lending yielded fast results in pressing inflation rates – consumer inflation fell to 6.1% in September 2011 from its peak of 6.5% in July 2011.[12] Although inflation in China edged lower in December 2011, the pace of decline levelled off and food prices picked up.[13]

---

8 Jane Cai, "Merchants Bank Cash Call Sparks Sector Sell-off", *South China Morning Post*, 25 July 2013, B3.

9 Simon Rabinovitch, "China's Central Bank Assures Financial Markets", *Financial Times*, 28 June 2013 (online).

10 Victoria Ruan, "Tough Tasks Await Next PBOC Head", *South China Morning Post*, 30 November 2012 (online).

11 Gavin Davies, "China Faces a Different Credit Bubble Workout", *Financial Times*, 8 July 2013 (online).

12 "Cutback on Lending Puts Chinese Businesses in a Bind," *International Herald Tribune*, 9 November 2011, p.14. The Chinese government's full-year target in 2011 was 4%. The official data was not reliable somehow because consumer prices were rising at double-digit rates in so many products and services. Robert Cookson, "Chinese Equities Recover as Beijing Battles Inflation," *Financial Times*, 14 April 2011, p.22.

13 Simon Rabinovitch, "Chinese Inflation Falls But Anxiety Remains," *Financial Times*, 13 January 2012, p.4.

Yet, administrative measures are not without weaknesses – they are easier to be manipulated or circumvented. During a credit squeeze, lending had been flowing from the banking system into an informal "shadow" market. To curb explosive lending, policymakers need to raise interest rates so as to change the nature of cheap capital for business.

The PBOC's monetary policy, aiming to deal with the recent rapid growth in off-balance sheet activity, however, has strong side effects. The central bank's higher reserve requirements help accumulate unusable cash. The PBOC reserves rose to US$2,100 billion in 2011, one-third more than the reserve balance of the US Federal Reserve.[14] The more rigid reserve requirements would squeeze commercial banks' profitability. With a higher lock up ratio, Chinese banks' earnings were just 1.62% in the same year.[15] In addition, reserve requirements also prevent Chinese banks from allocating a larger share of their portfolios to higher yielding investments. Even worse, there can be a regressive tax and it can disproportionately hurt small banks with weak deposit bases as well as small- and medium-sized enterprises facing a worse cash squeeze than during the global financial crisis in 2008.[16]

4. CREDIT CRUNCH EPISODES AFTER THE FINANCIAL CRISIS

However, more recently we saw a credit crunch in China while the global financial crisis has been gradually moving out of our sight.

4.1 Credit Crunch Episode in 2013

Here is what happened in June 2013 in China, a crisis-like episode. Credit had been growing at 20% plus, which is more than double the rate of economic growth.[17] The overall credit-to-gross domestic product ratio in China has jumped from roughly 120% in 2008 to closer to 200% in mid-2013,[18] which indicated a rising leverage throughout the economy.

---

[14] "People's Bank of China", *Financial Times*, 24 May 2011, p.16.

[15] Ibid.

[16] Simon Rabinovitch, "China Repo Rate at 3-year High", *Financial Times*, 23 June 2011, p.13.

[17] "China's Banks: Of Liquidity and Credit", *Financial Times*, 19 June 2013 (online).

[18] Simon Rabinovitch, "Echoes of Mao in China Cash Crunch", *Financial Times*, 20 June 2013 (online).

Put differently, this ratio suggested that the stock of outstanding credit has been rising faster than GDP, and much lending is not pooled into the real economy. Money rates began to rise and anxious Chinese banks stopped lending to each other. The PBOC this time refused to inject any extra cash into the system. Money market rates jumped to unprecedented levels above 20%. At that point, China had a feel of a financial system on the brink: its interbank lending market froze. Concerns have mounted that defaults in the interbank market could trigger a crisis in China's financial sector and cause social chaos across the country. Each time China's economy faces any difficulty, talk of a collapse tends to surface. This time, the question is whether China's stretched bank credit will lead to a financial crisis.

The PBOC established the first unified national interbank lending market in January 1996. However, lending in this market often violated interest rate caps and occurred with unauthorized participants. Then, the PBOC formed a new market, that is, the China Interbank Offered Rate (CHIBOR) market. Meanwhile, the PBOC increased monitoring (all trading between members was made electronic through the China Foreign Exchange Trading System), and set new rules for loan maturities, membership, and on the use of interbank funds raised. Banks can borrow from each other in the interbank markets to meet temporary shortfalls in funding. Banks usually find themselves running low on cash in mid-year due to corporate tax payments, holiday withdrawals, and their need to keep cash on their balance-sheets to pass mid-year regulatory inspections for the satisfaction of the deposit reserve requirements. Banks nevertheless were prohibited from participating in other funding markets, and were also explicitly forbidden from using the interbank market to fund fixed asset or other investments. This new national market was primarily for settling temporary discrepancies in accounts and working capital loans, with the majority of lending for periods up to one week, but then was extended to other instruments and maturities. Of the two types of interbank lending, uncollateralized lines of credit and collateralized repos, repos are more important. This type of lending is very short term, ranging from overnight to seven days, even though transactions with maturity of up to one year are possible. There are clear structural liquidity imbalances, with the large state commercial banks being the major supplier of liquidity in the repo market, and other financial institutions (principally insurers, securities firms, and fund managers), foreign banks and, to some extent, other commercial banks net recipients. Among other factors, administered interest rates, as proved by empirical research, are the key determinants of both the level and volatility of the market determined interbank rates. Accordingly, open market operations and direct instruments that influence base interbank liquidity have no immediate impact on the interbank rates.[19]

The cash crunch, to a certain extent, reflected the fragile state of China's banking sector. The cash crunch was caused by a variety of factors, *inter alia*, the tighter regulatory deposit reserve requirement, a crackdown on hot money inflows, an imploding financial crisis fuelled by off-balance-sheet local government financing vehicles, a ballooning property bubble and massive wealth management products. From a monetary policy perspective, a slower M2 growth in June 2013 was consistent with the expected outcome of macroeconomic adjustments and prudent monetary policy. The complexity of multiple causes of the cash crunch again confirms China's pressing need to address the root cause of market distortions.

4.2 Central Bank's No-action and Market Reactions

From the beginning, the PBOC rebuffed pleas to inject more cash into the financial system to alleviate market stress when commercial lenders have been overstretched. Short-term money market rates surged to all-time highs. The seven-day bond repurchase rate, a key gauge of liquidity in China, jumped 270 basis points to 12.45% on 20 June 2013, roughly triple where it stood in early June 2013.[20] Interbank lending rates were also pushed higher to 28%. The stock market also felt the pain. The Shanghai Composite Index, China's main stock index, fell 5.3% to 1,962, the lowest level in the past four and a half years. The pain spread to the bond market. China Development Bank, a state-owned policy bank, pulled a RMB 20 billion debt offering.[21]

As a result, the Bank of China's equity was unlikely to be received well in the market. Hong Kong listed mainland shares completed their longest losing streak since the 1990s on 11 June 2013 amid deepening worries over the bad news on export growth and industrial output on mainland China. Investors also feared that interest rate liberalization would squeeze lenders' margins and that the Chinese government's tighter control over wealth management products would hurt their profitability.

---

[19] Nathan Porter and Teng Teng Xu, "What Drives China's Interbank Market", (2009) IMF Working Paper WP/09/189.

[20] The overnight Shanghai Interbank Offered Rate surged to 13.44% on 20 June 2013. Daniel Ren, "China Central Bank Boss Vows to Maintain Stability After Its Credit Squeeze", *South China Morning Post*, 5 June 2013 (online).

[21] Simon Rabinovitch and Josh Noble, "PBOC Plays Hard Ball Over Cash Crunch", *Financial Times*, 24 June 2013 (online).

Consequently, the Bank of China and other Chinese lenders were sold off. Bank of China shares lost 3% down to HK$3.26.[22]

The credit crunch also brought an impact on Hong Kong's banking sector, which experienced rapid lending growth. In June 2013, loans grew at the highest rate since January 2011. According to the Hong Kong Monetary Authority, Hong Kong's *de facto* central bank, mainland companies accounted for most of the rapid loan growth[23] as they had difficulty securing loans from lenders on the mainland because of tightening liquidity. The loan-deposit ratio, in US dollars, rose to 85% from 80% in May 2013, and 40 to 50 mainland firms had taken out loans amounting to HK$133 billion from Hong Kong-based banks.[24]

Regulatory experience shows that an overly aggressive tightening could have severe consequences. If the policy squeezing lasts too long, lending rates in the real economy could spiral up, which may result in a further steeper slowdown. The PBOC has a number of tools to deal with excessive tightening in money markets. It can allow maturing bill transactions to provide gradual relief, inject liquidity to banks individually or via the open market, and lower reserve requirements if it thinks fit. However the PBOC refrained from repurchases and other operations in the face of shortages.

4.3 Central Bank's U-turn Move

The PBOC took an abrupt U-turn in the late stages of the episode and agreed to provide liquidity support to cash-strapped banks in a bid to ease the fears of investors rattled by the credit crunch. The PBOC pumped in fresh liquidity for selected "prudent" lenders that faced temporary cash squeezes,[25] and added 12 billion yuan in rediscounted loans for banks to support small businesses, which led to an easing of the seven-day repurchase rate to 5%.[26] The shortage of yuan liquidity also eased a little in early July 2013: one-week onshore yuan interbank rates declined to 3.65% on 8 July 2013 from between 6 and 7% at the end of June 2013. The seven-day

---

[22] Jeanny Yu, "Mainland Chinese Companies Continue Slide in Hong Kong", *South China Morning Post*, 12 June 2013 (online).

[23] Kanis Li, "Lending Growth to Slow as Liquidity Returns to China, Says HKMA", *South China Morning Post*, 11 August 2013 (online).

[24] Ibid.

[25] PBOC in its statement made it clear that its assistance only is provided to banks that act in line with the government's "macro-prudential requirements". Simon Rabinovitch, "PBOC Hints at New Status Quo for China's Banks", *Financial Times*, 26 June 2013 (online).

[26] Victoria Ruan, "China Credit Squeeze Puts Brakes on Factory Growth", *South China Morning Post*, 5 July 2013 (online).

bond repurchase rate, a key gauge of short-term liquidity in China, fell to 3.98%. Meanwhile, the one-month interbank rates dropped to 4.3% from between 7 and 8%.[27] Even so, short-term liquidity and interbank borrowing rates were roughly twice as high as their pre-crunch levels.

4.4 Why was this Time Different?

The soaring interbank rates punished lenders who had used their privileged access to the stable, central bank-controlled interbank market to fund purchases of risky and high-yielding bonds. The central bank's concern was a balance-sheet mismatch. Many smaller banks had taken advantage of stable interbank funding to borrow short-term from other banks and lend long. These banks simply rolled over their borrowings while the interbank rates remained stable, resulting in an oversized balance sheet.[28] Moreover, a spike in interbank lending costs threatened to spill over into real financing costs for businesses, which put pressure on profits of already struggling private sector manufacturers. As a consequence, concerns were growing that China's export-oriented manufacturers were facing a credit squeeze that put an already flagging economic recovery at risk of future decline. China's manufacturing sector has suffered a prolonged downturn in demand. Order book growth shrank while borrowing costs continued to surge. The financial squeeze also put more pressure on some industrial sectors. Banks cut excess capacity across a range of sectors including shipyards which were already suffering from sluggish demand and a supply glut. For instance, banks in some cases cut credit lines and moved to recover outstanding loans.[29] In addition, banks asked yards to charge as much as 30% in upfront payments from their clients. These measures echoed the government's efforts to cut off credit so as to force consolidation in industries plagued with overcapacity.[30] These measures were useful to strengthen the weakly implemented regulations and forced

---

27 Kanis Li, "Hong Kong Lenders Pay More for Yuan Deposits", *South China Morning Post*, 9 July 2013 (online).

28 "Financial Reforms: Re-education Through Shibor", *The Economist*, 29 June 2013 (online).

29 Reuters, "Credit Squeeze Adds to Pressures on Shipyards", *South China Morning Post*, 25 July 2013, B2 (citing the China Association of the National Shipbuilding Industry's source).

30 China rivals South Korea as the world's top shipbuilder. However, the ships built on the mainland are less complex technologically and mostly of lower value. The order book of mainland yards stood at US68.5 billion, second to South Korea's US$102.5 billion, though China's order book in tonnage terms exceeded South Korea's. Reuters, "Credit Squeeze Adds to Pressures on Shipyards",

banks to channel less of their assets into risky-off-balance-sheet vehicles. Borrowers, especially local governments, state enterprises and investors had flocked to shadow financing to bypass tighter regulations in the formal banking sector. For example, the interbank market was used by some banks and intermediaries to fund lending or offload loans from balance sheets. The three-month Shanghai Interbank Offered Rate or SHIBOR had leapt to 5.8% from around 3.9% in a period of two-weeks.[31] On 20 June 2013, it peaked at 13.4% for overnight loans.[32] However, private firms borrowed well above that rate. This was a blunt warning to overstretched lenders that they must bring risky lending under control.

The credit squeeze signaled the PBOC's intention to contain credit expansion and rein in riskier forms of lending. The turmoil in the market and volatility in the overnight bank rate were the result of the PBOC and the government's desire to rein in the shadow banking sector.[33] The PBOC clearly requires banks to "prudently control the liquidity risks that arise from excessively rapid expansion of credit".[34] This in effect amounted to an order to commercial banks to rein in credit growth and curb their appetite for risky business practices such as shoveling deposits into off-balance-sheet "shadow banking" vehicles. The fact that large enterprises continue to invest in wealth management products, that capital is still in search of speculative investment opportunities and that private lending continues to be strong seems to suggest that China's credit crunch was not real. Essentially, the so-called "credit crunch" was a result of structural funding constraints caused by a misallocation of funds. The PBOC, as well as the government, was willing to sacrifice economic growth and short-term market gains for fiscal reform and discipline among banks and trust firms. The short term gain was that money could better serve the real economy.

Amid the current financial climate, the PBOC was not willing to pump liquidity on demand into the money market. It was apparent that China

---

South China Morning Post, 25 July 2013, B2 (citing data from Clarkson Research Services).

[31] Nick Edwards, "China Firms Face Fresh Credit, Export Crunch", *South China Morning Post*, 21 June 2013 (online).

[32] "Financial Reforms: Re-education through Shibor", *The Economist*, 29 June 2013 (online).

[33] Kathrin Hille, "Crackdown on Shadow Financing Caused Cash Crunch, Says China", *Financial Times*, 23 June 2013 (online) (citing Xinhua News Agency's argument in its commentary that the broad money supply M2 had still expanded by 15.8% compared with the same period in 2012, new loans were high and total social financing aggregate, a broad liquidity measure, continued to grow in the first five months of 2013).

[34] Rabinovitch, "PBOC Hints at New Status Quo for China's Banks".

was at a turning point again in monetary policy. This time, the PBOC was not likely to use as fast money supply growth as in the past so as to promote economic growth. In other words, PBOC was to control the pace of money supply growth, which may push banks to better manage their own balance sheets. Unlike the cash crunch that occurred in developed markets, the squeeze in China was almost entirely self-inflicted, a deliberate move by the central bank. It first refused to provide the expected short-term liquidity injections that were needed to stabilize money market rates. When share prices plunged sharply and the credit market momentarily froze up, the PBOC stepped in. The PBOC remained on the sidelines of the market and refused to conduct repo business at a scheduled auction.[35] By doing so, it sent a warning signal to commercial banks and other credit issuers that unchecked credit expansion, particularly through the shadow banking system, would not be accommodated. It was also a signal of official determination to cool rapid credit growth, and to limit funds to a vast informal loan market. The PBOC's goal of taking a laid-back stance was to prevent the leverage ratio from reaching an even higher level, and, hopefully, to bring the rate of credit growth down to about 17 or 18%, and to limit the leverage that had built up in the economy.[36] However, the consequences of the regulatory tightening were still hard to predict because of the growing complexity of Chinese financial markets. The PBOC's move was also in line with the policy suggestion made by the Bank for International Settlements (often known as the central bankers' bank), which encourages central banks to head for the exit and not to spur a global economic recovery.[37]

On the other hand, in order to soothe market concerns about tighter monetary conditions, PBOC had pledged to adjust banking liquidity to ensure steady credit growth. The movement was to "use a mix of price and quantitative policy tools to adjust liquidity in the banking system and guide steady and appropriate growth in money, credit and social financing". The new pledge came after new statistics had been released showing that the total social financing aggregate, a broad measure of

---

[35] Simon Rabinovitch, "PBOC Dashes Hopes of China Liquidity Boost", *Financial Times*, 20 June 2013 (online).

[36] There has been some speculation that PBOC's position is reflective of some political calculations. PBOC ordered a thorough implementation of the new "mass line education" campaign launched by President Xi Jinping to fight against "four winds" of formalism, bureaucracy, hedonism and extravagance. Rabinovitch, "Echoes of Mao in China Cash Crunch".

[37] Claire Jones, "Central Banks Told To Head For Exit", *Financial Times*, 23 June 2013 (online).

liquidity conditions that includes bank loans and bond sales, fell to 1.04 trillion yuan in June 2013.[38] The falling social financing was a reflection of the government's efforts to crack down on shadow banking, forcing banks to scale back their balance-sheet lending.

The freeze-up in China's interbank lending market reflected a symptom of a more chronic disease. The burden of bad debt requires more credit which, however, generates less growth. Overall credit growth at the rate of 22% suggests China's dependence on debt for economic growth. It may take several years for China to tackle the combination of excess credit and over-investment that has followed the RMB 4 trillion stimulus package of 2008. The credit explosion massively increased the debt service ratio in the economy, an indicator which the Bank for International Settlements' states "reliably signal[s] the risk of a banking crisis".[39] It also triggers a re-thinking of monetary policy. The central bank governor claims that the PBOC would "make comprehensive use of policy tools and administrative measures to adjust liquidity to ensure overall market stability", and "the monetary policies are aimed at smooth operation of the financial markets and healthy economic growth".[40]

The current leadership in China appears more determined than its predecessors to guide China onto a path of slower and more sustainable growth. The cabinet headed by Premier Li Keqiang has diverged from the policy of its predecessor by refraining from injecting fresh liquidity into the economy to ease a credit crunch on the interbank market, which is a sign that the government is no longer keen to chase short-term growth. Rather, the government is in an attempt to force banks to curb lending and issuance of controversial wealth management products. The focus of the economic policy is on structural reform to the economy in which the wealth gap has been widening and where rapid industrial growth has come at the expense of overcapacity and pollution. The government is trying to walk a fine line between job creation and structural reform.[41] The PBOC's

---

[38] Reuters, "China to Adjust Liquidity, Keep Credit Growth Steady", *South China Morning Post*, 16 July 2013 (online).

[39] BIS Quarterly Review, September 2012. The Bank for International Settlements is of the opinion that the danger point for the debt service ratio is around 20 to 25% and increases in the ratio of five percentage points or more would be problematic. Official figures for China cannot be found. It is estimated to stand at 30% of GDP. A soft landing requires single digit credit growth for a long period of time.

[40] PBOC website.

[41] The decline of the export-driven economy is crucial to the policymakers while grappling with a looming decision to get back on track with long-delayed financial reforms, or push the panic button to underwrite jobs and stability in the

hands-off strategy in monetary policy is a reflection of that overall policy strategy – China will not let the credit bubble get out of control and will not use the credit crunch to push up GDP growth. The government may be prepared for a bigger financial deficit. It is time for China to address financial risks that have built up in the banking system even if it may lead to a steep economic slowdown.

An optimistic interpretation of the cash squeeze is that the Chinese government has an appetite for short term pain to favour more sustained growth and to change the economic structure, hopefully a gain of a sounder growth model in the long term. Reining in credit expansion may help curb overcapacity and bad debt. However, cracks in the Chinese economic model have begun to show. Nominal GDP growth has slipped below 8% with a decline in investment returns.[42] The refusal of the current leadership to ease the credit crunch and boost liquidity has translated into slower growth in the real economy. Take one example, China's official purchasing managers' index slipped to 50.1 in June 2013, showing that the world's second largest economy is weakening.[43] The HSBC China Purchasing Managers Index fell to 48.2 in June 2013, down from 49.2 in May 2013, showing operating conditions deteriorating at the quickest pace since September 2012.[44]

---

near future. The slower economic growth rate is a looming test of the policymakers' tolerance for a slowdown in growth. Economists doubt the government can do the heavy lifting to turn the entire economy around. Meanwhile, foreign investors are anxiously waiting for the restart of a reform effort stalled in part by the financial crisis and partly by the 4 trillion yuan stimulus program unleashed by the ex-cabinet. The new leadership has steadily made encouraging noises and rhetoric of long-term reform.

42 For the first time in the past 13 years, the rate of GDP growth was only 7.5% in 2012, the slowest year of growth. The Chinese government seems more comfortable with a slower growth. In the current five-year plan, the government only forecast a 7% average annual growth for the period of 2011–2015, against the 10% average growth delivered over the past three decades. Barclays warned of "an increasingly likely downside scenario" and a temporary "hard landing", with quarterly growth falling to 3% over the next three years before bouncing back rapidly. Ruan, "China Credit Squeeze Puts Brakes on Factory Growth".

43 Ruan, "China Credit Squeeze Puts Brakes on Factory Growth".

44 Different from HSBC Index, with a heavy weight in small businesses, the official PMI data compiled by the National Bureau of Statistics, covering a wider range of companies, was at 50.1 in June, down from 50.8 in May and only slightly above the threshold of 50 that indicates an expansion instead. Ruan, "China Credit Squeeze Puts Brakes on Factory Growth".

5. THE PBOC'S NEW MOVE: BACK TO THE OLD DAYS?

The PBOC pumped RMB 17 billion into the money market via seven-day reserve repurchase agreements on 30 July 2013. This was the first time PBOC had conducted this kind of liquidity injection since February 2013. The amount was small but the intention was clear: to prevent cash rates from drifting too high and to avoid a repetition of the June credit squeeze. The impact was immediate: the seven-day bond repurchase rate fell 14 basis points to 4.98% and the Shanghai Composite Index jumped nearly 1%.[45] Simultaneously, credit expansion in Hong Kong also slowed down as fewer mainland companies may need urgent loans from Hong Kong banks while liquidity on the mainland returns to normal levels.[46] The easing of demand for credit helps to mitigate banks' risks associated with mainland exposure amid weakening economic growth.

After the June 2013 squeeze, lending remained strong but off-balance-sheet credit issuance slowed. The PBOC's strategy to use the squeeze to warn lenders to do a better job of managing their liquidity and to rein in overall credit growth was largely successful. The PBOC since then has refused to conduct any market-wide liquidity injections except allowing older bills and repurchase agreements to mature, thereby providing banks with some additional cash. The PBOC set the seven-day repo rate at 4.4%, which suggested that the cost of capital had risen in China. This may mark an end to the era of ultra-loose and easy money. The credit crunch appeared to be a short-term problem. The root cause of this pain was the new policy transitions, combined with slower economic growth.

However, it has been clear that the PBOC's no-action approach to the credit crunch is not sustainable for various deep-down economic and structural reasons.

The financial markets are usually under pressure for the second term in each year. In the second part of 2013, interbank rates and bond yields rose steadily for several weeks and spiked when the PBOC abstained from accommodating seasonal demand for cash. The interbank market is an important conduit for the build-up in non-financial and financial leverage and liquidity needs, and is central to the expansion of loan assets outside the conventional remit of loan regulation. However, short-term interbank

---

45 Simon Rabinovitch, "China Injects Funds into Money Markets, Quelling Fears", *Financial Times*, 30 July 2013 (online).

46 Kanis Li, "Lending Growth to Slow as Liquidity Returns to China, Says HKMA", *South China Morning Post*, 11 August 2013 (online).

lending rates cannot be used as an independent indicator of macroeconomic or financial conditions given the close connection between the regulated interest rates and interbank rates.[47]

Liquidity is traditionally tight in China at the end of the year. The reason is the seasonal demand for funds and banks' preparation for regulatory assessment. The demand for cash rises and banks rush to book deposits on their balance sheets. Then the competition for deposits has been compounded by the growing array of bank-like institutions that offer higher-yielding alternatives for savers. Other factors such as the build-up in government deposits in the banking system to finance government spending growth, financial liberalization creating funding demand for IPOs in the equity market, and accumulated deposits in the wealth management industry which originates higher yielding, short-maturity financial products also contributed to the tightening of financial market conditions. There is a mid-term policy struggle.

Borrowing costs for Chinese companies are rising strongly,[48] which may indicate weaker corporate profits, slower economic growth and possible defaults by indebted companies in China. According to JP Morgan Chase, China's corporate debt was 124% of GDP in 2012, up from 111% in 2010 and 92% in 2008.[49] Standard & Poor's says that Chinese companies had amassed an estimated US$12.1 trillion of debt by the end of 2013.[50] The high leverage in the corporate sector poses a latent risk to the entire economy. The risks are mounting when the government tightens credit and investors demand higher interest rates to fund borrowers. High corporate debt not only hurts companies but also puts Chinese banks into a vulnerable status as Chinese lenders tend to hold loans on their balance sheets and are the biggest buyers of corporate bonds. Chinese policy banks asked their international clients to postpone drawing down previously committed credit lines, which highlights the strains on the country's financial system. The China Banking Regulatory Commission (CBRC) has been trying to rein in rapid credit growth by making it harder for banks to move assets off their balance sheets and by pushing up the cost of borrowing

---

[47] Porter and Xu, "What Drives China's Interbank Market".

[48] Banking institutions, SOEs and local government financing vehicles are less insensitive to higher interest rates and bond yields.

[49] Shen Hong, "Risks Mount as Debt Costs Rise in China", *The Wall Street Journal*, 11 February 2014, C2 (reporting that corporate debt in emerging economies is 40% to 70% of GDP, while in the US the figure is 81%).

[50] Shen Hong, "Perils Mount As Debt Costs Swell in China", *The Wall Street Journal*, 11 February 2014, C1 (also reporting that the US businesses had US$12.9 trillion debts).

in the money market. The aim is to crack down on the shadow banking sector. China Development Bank and Export-Import Bank of China have been more willing to put international borrowers into bankruptcy and sell their assets on the global market in an attempt to recover value from failed loans. Raising interbank rates is the effective way of enforcing the lending cuts and loan management.[51] Chinese banks charged each other nearly 9% to borrow cash in a near doubling of rates from the previous week. The central bank provided targeted money to cash-strapped lenders but did not provide any liquidity via its open-market operations. Cash crunch abated after the central bank reassured investors that it wanted to avoid deeper turmoil by making its first market-wide money injection in the amount of RMB 29 billion via open-market operations (in the form of a seven-day reverse bond repurchase agreements). The immediate result is that the seven-day bond repurchase rate, a key gauge of short-term funding, fell 344 basis points to 5.4%.

The larger concern is about China's financial market, in particular, the credit cycle and economic reforms. China's credit boom is in full swing. Total credit in the economy (total social financing) showed a 40% rise in November 2013 over the prior month. The whole year was on course for growth in 2013 of almost 20%. The credit to GDP ratio is 215% in 2013.[52]

The PBOC is not experienced in managing complex financial markets, which are now more market-driven than before. Financial markets in China are now more opened up to market forces and external impulses. The dilemma the PBOC often falls into is how to deploy its tools between targeting interest rates while bringing down the rate of credit expansion. A higher debt burden and non-performing loans may result in a possible solvency crisis. But a controlled credit expansion may be accompanied with more volatile interest rates. Then it may turn into a full-blown liquidity crisis, which is a huge cost to economic growth.

Chinese financial institutions issued 624.6 billion yuan worth of new yuan loans in November 2013, from 506.1 billion yuan in October. The total social financing rose to 1.23 trillion yuan in November 2013, from 856.4 billion yuan in October 2013. New trust loans, or loans from a type of wealth-management company, rose to 101.8 billion yuan from 40.4 billion yuan.[53] These data showed that the central bank actually did not

---

[51] Henny Sender, "Chinese Credit Squeeze Felt Overseas", *Financial Times*, 10 February 2014, p.1.

[52] George Magnus, "China Cash Crunch Symbolises Central Bank Policy Quandary", *Financial Times*, 23 December 2013 (online).

[53] "China Banks Stepped Up Lending Last Month," *The Wall Street Journal*, 12 December 2013, p.20.

tighten the monetary policy as many had thought and the demand for credit was strong after the economy showed signs of rebounding in the third quarter. The PBOC may still maintain its monetary stance in order to support the growth rate of 7.5%. A rise in interest rates seems to suggest that the PBOC may want to keep a tight rein on credit. The benchmark seven-day weighted average repo rates stood at around 4.9% at the end of November and dropped to 4.43% in early December. Interest rates have long been in the range of 2% and 3%. However the interest rates have been more volatile since the June 2013 cash crunch. The rise in rates was partly due to increased competition among banks for funds as China moves to gradually ease its controls on the lending markets. China's broadest measure of money supply, M2, was up 14.2% by November compared with one year earlier.[54] Higher interest rates in China and the appreciation of the yuan against other currencies have created an incentive to borrow money abroad and invest it onshore. The government has shown a signal to tighten its grip on credit. The consequence of this monetary policy move is higher borrowing costs for banks and their customers.

Money market rates spiked as a result of heavy demand for cash ahead of the lunar new year holiday. Cash was also needed to meet month-end regulatory requirements. The central bank then made a brief statement saying that it had offered funds to the largest commercial banks. The central bank offered 75 billion yuan worth of seven-day reverse repurchase agreements, short-term loans to commercial lenders, as well as 180 billion yuan worth of 21-day reverse repos via tis routine open-market operations. It provided cash via the so-called standing lending facility, or SLF, a tool it had launched a year earlier to discreetly provide funds. The central bank's pumping in an unusually large amount of funds into the money markets was intended to pre-empt a potential liquidity crisis as demand for cash rose ahead of the lunar new year holiday. This was an unusual move as the central bank held off from providing cash until the squeeze became much worse in most cases. More surprisingly, the central bank made an advance disclosure of its intention to further inject more money into the financial system via reserve repos. These measures helped to reduce the liquidity risk in the interbank market and the default risk in the corporate sector. The weighted average of the seven-day repurchase agreement rate, the benchmark cost of short-term loans among banks, fell to 5.55% from 6.59%. The Shanghai Composite Index reacted to the move by rising 0.9%.[55]

---

54 Ibid.

55 Shen Hong, "China Moves Early to Avoid Credit Crunch," *The Wall Street Journal*, 21 January 2014, C3.

The PBOC drained 48 billion yuan from money markets, which indicated its concern with the boom in lending in early 2014. PBOC withdrew the cash by issuing 14-day bond repurchase agreements, the first time using repos to drain liquidity from the money market after the credit crush in June 2013.[56] The Shanghai Composite, China's main stock index, fell 0.8%. A jump in bank and shadow bank lending was witnessed in January 2014. New local currency loans reached 1.32 trillion in January 2014, tripling December's total, 200 billion yuan more than market expectations and the highest monthly total since January 2010. Although it is customary for banks to lend most heavily at the beginning of the year, it is still unusually strong even accounting for seasonal patterns. The June crush and a smaller echo in December 2013 demonstrated the government's willingness to rein in credit. However, the subsequent injections ran in the opposite direction. The credit withdrawal again showed the PBOC's intent to tighten liquidity and to maintain tight liquidity conditions. In a monetary policy report in mid-February 2014, the PBOC called for financial institutions to be prepared for greater interest rate volatility as a reform to reduce regulatory control of the economy. By making rates more volatile, the Chinese government is trying to make it harder for the banks to funnel cash into off-balance-sheet assets by generating more uncertainty about their cost of funding.

6. HEADING TOWARDS A NEW ECONOMIC GROWTH MODEL?

The IMF has warned that time is running short for China to implement economic reforms as the government, banks and companies come under mounting strain from rapid but unbalanced growth. In its annual report on China's economy, IMF suggested China take "decisive measures" to shift away from a growth model which relies heavily on credit and investment. This model, in a long run, is not sustainable but raises vulnerabilities. From the IMF's viewpoint, the immediate priority was to "rein in broader credit growth and prevent a further build-up of risks in the financial sector".[57] China's entire social financing (credit) in the economy has increased by more than 60% since the start of 2009. This not only indicates

---

56 Simon Rabinovitch, "China Central Bank Drains $7.9bn from Money Markets", *Financial Times*, 17 February 2014 (online).

57 Simon Rabinovitch, "IMF Urges China to Implement Critical Economic Reforms", *Financial Times*, 17 July 2013 (online).

a rising leverage that weakens the balance sheet but also creates a source of funding for the shadow banking sector.

China's priority is a shift to broader platforms of growth so as to put economic growth on a more concrete footing while its margins of safety are falling amid growing domestic problems. Currently, China's economy has been underpinned by a mix of investment, fiscal stimulus and credit which, however, is not a sustainable pattern of growth. A package of reforms is needed to secure more balanced and sustainable growth and to contain the growing risks so that China's economy can be put on a more consumer-based, inclusive and environmentally friendly path. Rebalancing the Chinese economy towards more consumption could lift private households' appetite for cars and luxury goods. The risk in this direction of rebalancing is a potential drop of investment before consumption picks up the baton, turning a slowdown into a Chinese slump. The new leadership has shown its tolerance for a slower growth rate in order to wean the economy off a reliance on exports and investment and to boost consumption.[58] In the near term, a priority is to rein in broader credit growth and prevent a further build-up of risks in the financial sector, in particular, the shadow banking sector.

The IMF suggested the Chinese government should not make a new round of stimulus plans.[59] Instead of deploying a gargantuan stimulus package, the Chinese government recently rolled out a number of fiscal and investment measures to boost its sluggish economy. The three-pronged measures constitute a "mini-stimulus" package with the aim of "arousing the energy of the market" as the government tries to achieve. First, the State Council temporarily scrapped all value-added and sales taxes on businesses with monthly sales of less than RMB 20,000. This tax cut will help more than 6 million enterprises which hire tens of millions of employees. Second, the government plans to streamline customs

[58] Li Keqiang said in a business seminar that 7.5% GDP growth, with a 3.5% inflation rate, is not the bottom line but a 7% growth is needed to achieve the goal of doubling GDP by 2020 and building a middle-class society. This suggests that a GDP growth rate below 7% will not be acceptable. Ayishah Ma, "Economic Support Measures Vital and Timely, Say Experts", *Hong Kong Economic Journal*, 26 July 2013, B10. This also suggests that the government may resort to a short term stimulus if growth is too close to 7%. Shirley Yam, "Li Keqiang Speech Leak Reflects Sensitivity of Growth Slowdown", *South China Morning Post*, 27 July 2013, B8. However, it is worth noting that a Chinese economy growing at an annual rate of 7.5% still makes a great contribution to global demand growth than expansion in any other economy. Chris Giles, "Slower but Steady", *Financial Times*, 24 July 2013, p.6.

[59] Rabinovitch, "IMF Urges China to Implement Critical Economic Reforms".

procedures and reduce administrative costs for exporting companies. In particular, the government will temporarily cancel inspection fees for commodities exports and streamline customs inspections of manufactured goods. Third, private investors will be invited by the government to be involved in railway projects. For this purpose, new bond products will be issued. The government will accelerate the building of railways in underdeveloped central and western regions.[60] Investment in low-income housing is also accelerated. Chinese banks are also implementing this semi-stimulus plan by injecting some liquidity into the market. In the latest economic downturn, CDB has extended a huge amount of loans to local governments such as Hebei, Jiangsu and Qinghai as a semi-stimulus package (or unofficial stimulus program). CDB agreed to fund massive infrastructure borrowing by three provincial governments; it seems that the Chinese government is to prop up growth with targeted bursts of lending. According to CDB's Memorandums of Understanding with these three provincial governments, CDB will offer financial support for a variety of local projects, ranging from a new airport to public housing. CDB's loan to the Jiangsu government will be used to improve Jiangsu's urban infrastructure and upgrade the regional transport network. Qinghai is granted the loan for road, railway and waterway construction projects. Hebei plans to use the loan to tackle the redevelopment slum areas and construction for its new airport zone. 2013 may have witnessed the lowest GDP growth in the past 23 years but the Chinese government, while being unwilling to launch a nation-wide stimulus program, still wants to maintain a stable path of growth.[61] The major concern is additional financial risks may add to the stimulus plan. These measures are on the supply side which may generate more efficient results.

There are various ways of interpreting these measures. First, China is in a deepened downturn and the government fears a further slowdown. The slowdown in the rate of deflation can be taken as further evidence of a possible stabilization of the economy.[62] The Chinese government appears

---

[60] Victoria Ruan and Reuters, "New Growth Measures Revealed As PMI Dips", *South China Morning Post*, 25 July 2013, B1.

[61] George Chen and Jane Cai, "China Development Bank Loans Point to Stealthy Economic Stimulus", *South China Morning Post*, 15 August 2013 (online).

[62] China's industrial output rose 9.7% in July 2013 while retail sales rose 13.2%, exports rose 5.1% in July 2013, and inflation steadied (with a 2.7% rise in consumer prices). The consumer prices rise is well below 3.5% upper annual limit targeted by the Chinese government at the beginning of 2013. However, producer prices remained in deflationary territory for the 17th consecutive month, falling 2.3% in July from one year earlier, compared with a 2.7% drop in June 2013. Agencies in Beijing, "Rise in Factory Output, Retail Sales May Give Beijing More

ready to intervene to pull the economy out of its instability, even though it seems more acceptable to see a slowdown as it rebalances the economy to become more consumption-driven. Second, the government is trying to help small firms and exporters to generate momentum in the economy that has slowed in nine of the past ten quarters. Third, the government is cautious to deploy effective measures and to direct public money towards more productive ends as growth slows.[63] Against this background, the government has ruled out the possibility of implementing any large-scale stimulus to revive the economy.

The financial reforms should be accelerated and the package could include a revamp of local government finances, a more market-based currency exchange rate, a liberalization of the capital account, and an open market for competition. The recent credit crunch, though rare, may show us a new direction towards which the Chinese economy is heading.

Leeway", *South China Morning Post*, 9 August 2013 (online). Jamil Anderlini, "Muted China Inflation to Spark Rate Cut Calls", *Financial Times*, 9 August 2013 (online). But, it may be too early to conclude if China's economy is on the track of rebounding.

[63] The State Council decreed a ban on 24 July 2013 on the construction of all new government buildings for the next five years. The ban was part of the campaign by Xi Jinping, to rein in ostentatious spending by the government which has been a major source of public discontent.

10. Interest rate reform: full or partial liberalization?

The PBOC has put China on course to free up interest rates on bank deposits in the past several years. The impact is multifaceted. First, this would force commercial lenders to compete for customers by offering the best terms. As commercial lenders are under pressure to more carefully evaluate risks, they are likely to lend more to privately owned firms. Second, this may offer more protection to depositors. The risk is also clear. The removal of interest rate restrictions may lead to the sharp growth and then collapse of a number of savings-and-loan firms. This took place in the US, which eased the rules on interest rates in the 1980s followed by many savings-and-loan firms' collapse. The main reason for this side effect is due to the fact that banks compete for funds, pushing up their costs and leading them to make risky loans that end up badly. Third, interest rate liberalization is the key to solving the problem of financing small businesses. On the other hand, a surge in interest rates could put further pressure on local governments, real-estate developers and other companies already struggling to repay debt. Banks' inability to offer higher deposit rates has fueled the growth of less regulated informal lenders that are willing to pay more.

This chapter looks into China's recent path of reforming its interest rate formation mechanism. Section 1 briefly outlines the current interest rate formation mechanism, followed by Section 2 which unveils the connection between this formation mechanism and commercial lenders' high profitability. Imposing restrictions on interest rates is a key aspect showing that the nature of China's financial system is a repressed one. Section 3 explains this perspective in detail. Section 4 moves to China's efforts to liberalize its interest rate formation regime while Section 5 focuses on China's latest reform approaches and limitations. A conclusion follows in Section 6.

1. INTEREST RATE FORMATION MECHANISM

Interest rates in China comprise a mix of both market determined interest rates (interbank rates and bond yields), and regulated interest rates (lending and deposit rates). This mixture of both market and regulatory forces in fixing the interest rates reflects China's gradual process of interest rate liberalization.

The base interest rate is set by the PBOC, upon which all other lending or savings interest rates are based. The increase or decrease of the base interest rates would increase or decrease the financing cost of a financial institution, whether from the central bank or from the market. Commercial lenders would raise or lower their lending interest rates accordingly, resulting in a reduction or expansion in lending demand and money supply.

Previously, PBOC had set both a floor for lending rates and a ceiling for deposit rates, which guaranteed a sizeable net interest margin for banks but mispriced credit. A floor for lending interest rates provides an artificial subsidy to banks so that they can borrow less expensively and then invest in higher yielding safe assets such as government bonds and property market. By offering interest rates that exceed the benchmark deposit rate[1] and providing more wealth-management products, Chinese banks can secure more funds which, however, may accumulate risks in the financial system. By contrast, a system of "financial repression" caps the deposit interest rates on offer, which are much lower than the higher returns promised by wealth management products, a "domestic" form of shadow banking in China. The lender in a shadow banking system, built on a lattice of interlocked credit, usually borrows money from banks and other private lenders with the aim of arbitraging interest rates. A mandatory ceiling on deposit rates (interest rates) deprives savers of the market return on their money. Inflation in China which has often surged past official interest rates has made savers suffer losses.

The interest rate forming mechanism in the US is a different one. The US Federal Reserve sets out the federal funds rate, which is the rate at which banks borrow from one another using funds held at the Federal Reserve. One possibility of reforming China's interest rate system is to use interbank rate as the benchmark rate. To do so, the PBOC has to stabilize interbank market rates, which are, however, now often used by the central bank to

---

1 Keynes appeared to encourage the government to reduce interest rates, and if it is reduced, the ultimate target level should be "zero". Hunter Lewis, *Where Keynes Went Wrong . . . And Why World Governments Keep Creating Inflation, Bubbles, And Busts* (Mount Jackson, VA: Axios Press 2011) p.19. Low rates do not necessarily increase the supply of credit. Risk aversion and higher returns on capital would encourage banks to eschew loans so that they can put more money in government securities or property market. This is also the case in the US where banks are holding more cash and government securities than the outstanding volume of commercial and industrial loans.

bounce around to achieve its policy goals. In June 2013, for instance, the PBOC pushed the rates as high as 25% to discipline shadow banks and non-bank financial institutions that depend on the interbank market for borrowing. With a market-driven interbank market rate, commercial lenders are then free to charge what they like for deposits and loans.

2. INTEREST RATE AND PROFITABILITY OF BANKS

It is worth noting that the rise or reduction of interest rates, as a monetary instrument, may have little impact on Chinese banks, which remain profitable as they can earn almost all of their income from government-set interest rate margins. Stable net interest margins and steady credit charges may guarantee Chinese banks' profit growth. Net interest margin at the mainland's 3,800 lenders contracted to 2.75%[2] in the fourth quarter from 2.77% in the third quarter in 2012.[3] China Construction Bank's (CCB) net interest income, which represents 76% of its operating income, rose 15.9% year on year to 353.2 billion yuan in 2012, while its net fee and commission income increased by 7.49% to 93.5 billion yuan.[4] Liberalizing interest rates has been ongoing. As a result of interest rate liberalization, net interest margin (NIM), the difference of loan income to funding cost relative to interest-bearing assets, is in compression because of competition for loans and deposits among banks. It may be reasonable to expect that the profitability of Chinese lenders may continue to decline along with the continuing interest rate deregulation which introduces competition in the deposit and loan businesses. The gradual deepening of interest rate liberalization may further intensify competition in the financial market.

In addition, Chinese banks, due to their monopolistic positions in the market place, may make profits by charging higher fees in providing financial services to end customers. This was the case in the period from October 2010 to April 2011. The PBOC raised interest rates four times since October 2010 but the Big Four continued to be profitable in the first quarter of 2011, ranging from 27.7% (for Bank of China) to 36% (for the

---

[2] This performance measure is the difference between interest income and cost of funds, as a ratio of interest-bearing assets.

[3] Jane Cai, "China Banks See Bad Loans Rise for Fifth Quarter", *South China Morning Post*, 2 March 2013 (online).

[4] Ray Chan, "CCB Says Greater Competition Set to Hurt Growth", *South China Morning Post*, 25 March 2013 (online).

Agricultural Bank of China (ABC)).[5] Jiang Jianqing, the chairman of the Industry and Commerce Bank of China (ICBC), admitted in an interview that the impact of rising interest rates on ICBC would be "neutral" simply because any drop in borrowing demand was offset by higher income from interest margins.[6] By contrast, increases in the reserve requirement ratio may have been more effective in changing banks' operational behaviours because the required portion of overall deposits banks are required to keep in reserve at the central bank would affect a bank's profitability. It was said by the president of ICBC that every 0.5 percentage point increase in banks' reserve requirement ratio could reduce a bank's (that is, ICBC's) interest income by roughly RMB 700 million.[7]

Largely due to the government controlled interest rate regime, the Big Four and other commercial banks enjoyed huge profits from the spread between deposit and lending interest rates. The margins between deposits and loans are quite sizeable. A vast nationwide network can easily help these banks collect deposits and secure large loan transactions due to their close connection with state-owned firms. Besides, these banks do not face any severe competition from private or foreign players as the market entry requirements are too high to be easily satisfied by the private players.

More recently, profits of China's listed banks have been poised to grow by less than 10% in 2014, for the first time since at least 2005,[8] in the face of a slowing economy, financial reform and the challenge from internet newcomers. Net profits of China's largest banks have grown at more than double-digit percentage rates since the first of them was listed in 2005, buoyed by a balance sheet clean-up that involved the sale of billions of dollars of bad loans, and by large capital injections from the government. Chinese banks are now under pressure from the rising costs of deposits due to rate deregulation and disintermediation caused by shadow banks.

3. INTEREST RATE AND FINANCIAL REPRESSION

Low interest rates have been the key to China's rapid economic growth and its domestic imbalances. The role of financial repression has been

---

[5] Jamil Anderlini, "Strong Profits at China Lenders Despite Tightening," *Financial Times*, 29 April 2011, p.16.

[6] Ibid.

[7] Ibid.

[8] Paul J. Davies, "Profits Hit For Listed Lenders in China", *Financial Times*, 21 January 2014, p.14.

widely recognized in the Chinese growth model – manipulating the financial system to divert money from savers to producers. The general rule of thumb is that rewards of growth can be efficiently and effectively distributed to savers and users of capital when nominal lending rates are largely in line with nominal gross domestic product growth rates. In China, the case is opposite. Interest rates are intentionally kept low; household depositors as net lenders pay a hidden subsidy to net borrowers such as state-owned enterprises, manufacturers and real estate developers. The longstanding cap on bank deposit rates has ensured a plentiful supply of low-cost capital for state-owned enterprises and public infrastructure projects. But this has caused wasteful investment and spiraling debt. This subsidy also pushes irresponsible borrowing and forces down household income. Any liberalizing reform of interest rates will be good for the rebalancing of the economy as well as reducing the amount of wasteful investment.

Here is the dilemma in China: the faster China reduces the gap between the nominal growth rate and the nominal lending rate,[9] the more painful it will be for existing borrowers, in particular, those most irresponsible banks and state-owned enterprises (SOEs), which are reliant upon the subsidy. By contrast, the slower the PBOC cuts rates, the more debts will be accumulated to the overstretched balance sheets. This is true especially of the least efficient banks. Then it would become more difficult to make any adjustment to the current interest rate system.

By eliminating the hidden transfer from household depositors to borrowers, the government can boost growth in household income even as output growth slows. This will allow China to move more quickly towards developing a healthy balance between consumption and investment while preventing slower economic growth from undermining the income of ordinary households. Freeing interest rates may increase bad debt. Not doing so, however, may worsen the imbalance of the economy. The government has shown tremendous restraint as it wants to maintain GDP growth at around 7–7.5%. A less expensive source of funding is still important to sustain China's economic growth. Interest rate liberalization faces resistance from state-owned lenders which do not want to competitors to poach depositors by offering better rates. The benefit of

---

[9] In the five years from 2006 to 2011, nominal GDP growth averaged about 18% or more whereas the official lending rate averaged around 7%. In 2011 and 2012, the nominal GDP growth rate has fallen to below 10% while the lending rate rose to 7.5%. The gap between the two has been closed quite substantially. Michael Pettis, "China Has a Choice – Short-term Growth or Sustainability", *Financial Times*, 2 September 2013 (online).

such a resistance is that the overall debt can be reduced but rebalancing may be slower.

Eliminating government control over interest rates is a crucial step in shifting China's growth model away from state-directed investment and forcing banks to allocate funds more efficiently. Cheaper deposit funding has discouraged banks from seeking smaller borrowers willing to pay high interest rates as lenders are guaranteed to have large margins even on conservative loans. The goal of increasing efficiency forces banks to lend more to companies that can generate higher returns.

4. INTEREST RATE LIBERALIZATION

The PBOC has been taking steps towards allowing market forces to set the price of money. The deposit-ceiling remains fixed by the government after the PBOC removed the floor on bank lending rates in 2013. Bond and money-market interest rates can now float freely.

Interest rate liberalization means tougher competition, and could hurt the Big Four's future income growth. Ongoing interest rate liberalization will put an end to the good days when Chinese banks could simply sit on lucrative interest rate spreads. The competition may even become more intensive as both non-bank financial institutions and shadow banks intervene in banking businesses, including wealth management, payment and settlement. Apparently, interest rate liberalization is slowly eating into Chinese commercial banks' margins, and is lessening their dependence on loan income with fee-based services. The Big Four's net interest margin is likely to go further downward as new loans have been repriced at cheaper rates in the first quarter of 2013, following the Chinese central bank's cuts to benchmark lending and deposit rates in 2012. For instance, CCB's net interest margin, which measures the spread between funding costs and lending income, edged up 0.05 percentage points to 2.75% in 2012, while return on equity, a measure of profitability, fell 0.53 percentage points to 21.98%.[10] These figures suggest that the bank may face mounting pressure from slowing interest income and increases in provisions amid deteriorating asset quality. Earnings growth of Chinese banks can continue to slow from the skyrocketing pace of the past few years while the economy cools.

PBOC has been relaxing its control over interest rates gradually,

---

[10] Ray Chan, "CCB Says Greater Competition Set to Hurt Growth", *South China Morning Post*, 25 March 2013 (online).

giving new impetus to plans to unshackle the tightly controlled yuan (see Table 10.1). PBOC granted banks more flexibility in June 2012 to set interest rates by raising the ceiling for deposit rates to 1.1 times benchmark interest rates and allowed lending rates to float as much as 20% lower than the benchmark levels.[11] The new rules now allow deposit rates to be set as high as 110% of the benchmark rate while the rate on new loans can be as low as 70% of the official borrowing cost. In a larger context, to free the interest rates market is a critically important component of the much needed financial reform as rightly pointed out in PBOC's 2012 third quarter monetary policy report.[12] The next step is probably to remove the ceiling for deposit rates and the floor for lending rates.[13] The deposit rate is subject to tight control. Any change to the deposit rate may have a greater impact on the cost of capital for banks and borrowers. The removal of a lending rate floor appears aimed at lowering lending costs for small companies. It may take longer than that of the lending rate.

Allowing more flexibility to set the interest rate can help to create an environment to allow banks to compete with each other by setting rates based on their own risk assessments. While the reduction in the officially guaranteed spread between lending and deposit rates hurts bank profitability, this move may help create a better financial market as the corporate reliance on bank loans for funding will be decreased in favour of equity and bond financing, which is crucial to sustaining economic growth. In this sense, interest-rate liberalization lies at the heart of China's financial reforms. It can be expected that liberalizing interest rates will encourage banks to introduce more consumer credit services, insurance

---

11 Victoria Ruan, "PBOC 'Has Scope to Widen' Yuan Band", *South China Morning Post*, 12 March 2013 (online).

12 Reuters, "PBOC to Prioritise Economic Growth, Recovery", *South China Morning Post*, 2 November 2012 (online).

13 However, Wu Xiaoling, a former vice governor of the central bank, indicated that the ceiling control over the deposit rate should remain unchanged for a while. Meanwhile, the PBOC may allow a wider upfloating range for deposit rates slowly. The underlying rationale of this policy recommendation is to "avoid excessive competition among financial institutions". Reuters, "China Central Bank Facing Pressure for Aggressive Easing", *South China Morning Post*, 17 December 2012 (online). A full opening of the interest rate market may lead to a price war for capital among Chinese banks if the policy is to rush to allow fully competitive and differentiated rates. This perception is supported by the recent fierce competition in the sector of wealth management products in recent years. The sector pays higher rates of interest than regular deposits and allows banks to use the funds for lending. The more fierce competition in this sector worries the ratings agencies and regulators as the competition may make the sector more risky than before.

Table 10.1 Roadmap of interest rate liberalization (2004–2015)

Time	Action
Lending rate	
2004	To relax its interest rate control policy by allowing banks to set their loan rates at discount of 10% of the official base rate fixed by the central bank
2006	Lower limit of mortgage loan rate is set at 85% of the benchmark rate
2008	Lower limit of mortgage loan rate is set at 70% of the benchmark rate
June 2012	To allow a discount of 20% (lower limit of lending rate is lowered to 80% of the benchmark rate)
July 2012	To allow a discount of 30% (lower limit of lending rate is lowered to 70% of the benchmark rate)
July 2013	To abolish the lower limit on the lending rate
October 2013	To allow nine commercial banks to submit the lending rate they charge their best quality clients each day as the basis for a loan prime rate, and China's interbank funding center will calculate a weighted average rate based on the submissions[14]
June 2015	To allow nine banks to issue large-scale negotiable certificates of deposit on the interbank market, and the interest rate of this batch of certificates of deposit float upwards by 40% from benchmark interest rate at most[15]
Deposit rate	
2004	To remove the lower limit of deposit rates
June 2012	To allow the deposit rate to be higher than the official base rate by up to 10%
2020	PBOC promised to remove the deposit rate ceiling by 2020

Source: Compiled by the author.

products and mutual funds.[16] The government is to allow market forces to play a larger role in setting interest rates. The de-regulation of interest rates is one of the key steps necessary for full capital account liberalization, which in turn helps the internationalization of the yuan.

[14] "Rules for Banks to Write Off Bad Loans Relaxed", *China Daily*, 23 January 2014, available 2 March 2016 at http://www.ecns.cn/business/2014/01-23/98311.shtml.

[15] Muyan Cai, "Nine Banks to Issue China's First Certificates of Deposit", 12 June 2015, available 2 March 2016 at http://www.chinadaily.com.cn/business/2015-06/12/content_20986491.htm.

[16] Meanwhile, fast-growing wealth management products and trust loans, which offer higher returns, have aroused concern about risks.

The PBOC is facing a dilemma: on the one hand, it prefers to use more bank loans and greater financial support for economic growth, and on the other hand, it needs to keep a close eye on the risks in the shadow banking system. One of the major concerns to the PBOC is aggregate financing – a measure of funding that includes loans, stock and bond sales, in particular, a surge in shadow bank lending over the past two years, the default of which may lead to social unrest. The PBOC and other financial regulators may tighten control on the quality and quantity of credit supply, particularly through non-bank channels such as trust loans. The PBOC introduced aggregate financing as an indicator designed to capture broader funding sources in the economy with such money raised through trust investment products and bond and stock sales. PBOC tries to have a "stable and appropriate growth" of aggregate financing other than a "reasonable scale" of financing the PBOC claimed previously. Yuan-denominated bank loans accounted for 45.8% of aggregate financing in November 2012, down from 58.8% in the same month in 2011. Meanwhile, the share of trust loans rose from 7.5% to 17.5% in the same period of time.[17] New loans extended by mainland banks as well as non-bank entities grew more than anticipated in March 2013, indicating the PBOC's desire to keep liquidity ample. Banks doled out 1.06 trillion yuan in March 2013, 51.5 billion yuan more than one year earlier. Aggregate financing or total social financing, including bank and shadow bank credit as well as bond and equity issuances, amounted to 2.54 trillion yuan in March 2013, 673.9 billion yuan more than one year ago.[18] These figures have drawn us a picture not only showing us a strong recovery, but also a mixture of fears about inflation, property bubbles, government debt and shadow banking.

5. LATEST INTEREST RATE REFORM

Interest rate liberalization could take place in two ways. First, allowing banks partial freedom to set interest rates on deposits and loans would likely reduce the margin the banks earn from lending. Accordingly lenders

[17] Bloomberg, "China's Central Bank to Focus on Controlling Risks in Financial System", *South China Morning Post*, 30 December 2012 (online).

[18] In the first quarter of 2013, bank loans accounted for 44.7% of aggregate financing, 18.6 percentage points lower than one year ago. The proportion of aggregate financing made up of trust loans increased by 8.8 percentage points to 13.4% during the quarter, with the amount of new trust credit surging 360% year on year. Jane Cai, "Boost To China's Money Supply Brightens Outlook", *South China Morning Post*, 16 April 2013 (online).

need to change their business strategy. For example, banks can expand their businesses into higher margin products to maintain profits but credit risk may likely increase. Second, increasing the volatility of interest rates makes it more difficult for banks to manage the balance sheets. This impact will bring huge pressure to Chinese banks. Small- and medium-sized banks would be more vulnerable to the change, owing to their less developed network and branding. They have difficulty in expanding into new business lines and attracting new customers. Correspondingly, large banks can adapt themselves to new business models and internal financial management mechanisms. China's latest decision to let banks set lending rates freely by removing an artificial floor was another gesture from the current leadership to deepen economic reform without touching upon vested interest groups.

5.1 Relaxing the Cap on Lending Rates

The PBOC moved a step closer to letting markets set the price of credit after scrapping a key rule governing bank lending rates. Effectively from 20 July 2013, mainland lenders were allowed to charge rates on loans below the official benchmark lending rate. The floor on lending rates, previously set at 30% below the benchmark rate, was scrapped. Besides, the cap on credit union lending rates which was set at 2.3 times the benchmark rates was also abolished. These have been the biggest changes to the interest rate regime since 2004 when the PBOC scrapped the ceiling on the interest rates banks are allowed to charge. Previously, commercial banks had the freedom to set their lending rates no higher than 70% above the PBOC base rate. Accordingly, all the commercial banks were allowed a downward movement of Renminbi deposit interest rates within the corresponding tranches. On 28 October 2004, in order to ensure the country's economic expansion, the PBOC raised the base lending and deposit interest rates for the first time in more than nine years and broadened the floating range of lending rate. The base rate for one year Renminbi loans was hiked by 0.27% from 5.31 to 5.58%, while the one year Renminbi deposit rate was raised by the same magnitude from 1.98 to 2.25%, both of which were raised to 6.12 and 2.52%, respectively, on 19 August 2006.[19]

The PBOC tweaked lending rules in 2012, enabling banks to offer up to 30% off the benchmark rate, which sat at 6%. The least a bank could charge was 4.2%. This move, however, has not been that effective given the market responses. The statistics showed that only 11% of loans in the

[19] Zhongfei Zhou, *Banking Laws in China* (Alphen aan den Rijn: Kluwer Law International 2007) para.7–7.

first quarter of 2013 were priced below the benchmark rate,[20] and almost none of them were priced at a 30% discount. Indeed, the effect of this reform on lending rates was marginal simply because no bank charges less than 5.4% on loans. Although the move was originally designed to benefit the private sector, the easing of control over credit costs may still largely benefit the state-owned sector because of their larger bargaining power in the marketplace.

Major banks were allowed to charge prime rate based on lending to favoured customers. The PBOC eased its control over interest rates with the introduction of prime loan rates based on lending reports by Chinese major banks. Accordingly, lenders would be allowed to price their loans based on the prime rates. The weightings of the banks in setting the prime rate would vary based on each lender's share of the total loans outstanding in the past quarter. This was another step towards interest rate liberalization. The prime loan rates would be determined based on the daily reporting of nine commercial banks on the lending rates offered to their best corporate clients. The nine banks participating in the reporting system were China's largest lenders by assets, comprising the Big Four, Bank of Communications, and four joint-stock banks including China Citic Bank and China Merchants Bank. Meanwhile, the PBOC would continue to publish benchmark lending rates to guide banks in setting reasonable rates during the transition period. By taking this move, the PBOC effectively gave up the benchmark lending rates as policy rates. This means that the central bank is more cautious with the concrete move to liberalize deposit rates, which is a more crucial step towards a market-based pricing system.

The latest move was a follow-up step in interest rate liberalization and Renminbi internationalization. Chinese propaganda called this liberalizing move a "courageous" step.[21] This was a step along the road from centrally commanded to market-driven rates. From an economic perspective, this was a critically important reform measure that could lead to the markets setting the price of credit as it creates a market in which banks can discount lending for lower-risk investments and charge higher rates to projects carrying greater risk. From a macroeconomic perspective, this was also a stimulus to the real economy as state-owned entities would face a lower effective borrowing rate. In the economic downturn, the PBOC's conventional policy tools of loan quotas and lending directives

---

[20] Kwong Man-ki and Victoria Ruan, "Chinese Banks Given Freedom to Set Lending Rates", *South China Morning Post*, 20 July 2013 (online).

[21] Reuters, "Liberalising of the Yuan Courageous, Says Xinhua", *South China Morning Post*, 22 July 2013, B1.

have no longer been able to deliver stable growth, evidenced by the fact that GDP growth has fallen for two consecutive quarters in 2013. Apparently, this was evidence of the diminishing marginal efficiency of debt financing, showing the problem of diminishing marginal returns on investment. This growth fatigue indicated that China's credit model had reached a boiling point and needed a regime change from a tight control to a more market-driven model.

Therefore, this can be viewed, in a larger picture, as part of the economic rebalancing agenda which can more efficiently allocate resources as the mispricing of a large pool of funds makes for inefficient use and misallocation of capital on a grand scale. By doing so it shows the Chinese government's intention to tackle the difficult financial reforms that are needed to keep the Chinese economy on track. At least, the reform shows the Chinese government's determination to forge ahead with capital markets reform to remove conditions that helped fuel the property-led credit bubble. China's new leadership appears committed to pushing ahead with financial reforms. The reform in this sense keeps the idea of reform alive. Reform of the state-owned banking system is urgent since easy credit combined with tight restrictions on the formal financial sector have spawned a thriving shadow banking sector.

The market reaction to this deregulation move was a drop in Chinese bank shares on the Hong Kong stock exchange[22] as investors worried about the potential drag on profitability after the PBOC abolished the floor for lending rates. Banks' ability to set their lending rates may naturally intensify competition which in turn drives down interest income and causes them to lower credit standards. The deregulation may decrease net interest margin which is a measure of loan profitability. The decrease of net interest margin will be caused by the falls of interest earned on loans when interest paid on deposits remains unchanged. This is especially the case for medium-sized banks which often target small- and medium-sized enterprises and face more competition for high quality borrowers.

Liberalizing tightly controlled lending rates is a moderate measure. Scrapping the lending rate floor is not equivalent to an interest rate cut. In a strict sense, removing the floor may not be relevant at all because the rate floor has never been a binding constraint on lending. In reality, for one-year loans, the floor had been set at 4.2% – a sizable discount to the PBOC's benchmark rate of 6%. Chinese banks made almost 90% of their

[22] Kanis Li, "Bank Shares Tumble After Freeing of Lending Rates", *South China Morning Post*, 23 July 2013, B3.

loans at or above the benchmark rate.[23] Banks resisted lending at the floor rate because the spread between the floor rate and banks' funding cost (for example, interbank rate and saving deposit rate) was only about 100 basis points. According to an estimate made by Capital Economics, the average bank lending rate in the previous month of the reform was 8%, a full 2 percentage points above the benchmark and almost double the floor rate.[24] In addition, very few loans were extended at the floor rate in the last year. The PBOC's data showed that two-thirds of bank loans were made at a premium over the benchmark rate.[25] These data suggest that scrapping the minimum rate is less effective in reducing lending rates.

Nevertheless, fiddling with lending rates had little impact due to the fact that bank credit was allocated according to government-determined quotas. State-owned banks may not take advantage of this opportunity. Rather, they were likely to continue to lend the bulk of their quotas to well-connected state-owned companies regardless of rates simply because they could easily secure the source of funding from the government. The private sector, on the other hand, may continue to be shut out of the formal financial system and have to rely on the shadow banking market, where the lending rates were running at a crippling 20%.

The reform is still incomplete in the sense that the banks are not allowed to set deposit rates. Currently, the PBOC maintains the ceiling, at 10% higher than the benchmark deposit rates.[26] In other words, Chinese banks are not allowed to pay more than 1.1 times the benchmark deposit rate as set by the PBOC. The base rate for a one-year deposit is 3%, so no bank can pay more than 3.3%. The cap on the demand deposits is set a whisker below 0.4%. Most of China's 44 trillion household savings deposits are kept in the demand deposits.[27] Owing to this cap and a 2.7% consumer inflation rate, China's savers are losing roughly 1 trillion yuan a year by keeping their money in Chinese banks.

---

[23] Reuters, "Rate Reform May Serve Interests of State Companies", *South China Morning Post*, 22 July 2013, B5. Deutsche Bank said in a report that less than 12% of new loans were priced below benchmark rates in the first quarter of 2013. Kanis Li, "Bank Shares Tumble After Freeing of Lending Rates", *South China Morning Post*, 23 July 2013, B3.

[24] Tom Holland, "Beijing's Latest Rate Reform Makes No Difference At All", *South China Morning Post*, 22 July 2013, B14.

[25] Chi Lo, "Deposit Rate Reform Already Happening with Shadow Banking", *Hong Kong Economic Journal*, 25 July 2013, B10.

[26] Kanis Li, "Bank Shares Tumble After Freeing of Lending Rates", *South China Morning Post*, 23 July 2013, B3.

[27] Vivian Chung, "The Truth About Record-breaking Chinese Bank Deposits", *Hong Kong Economic Journal*, 23 July 2013, B12.

PBOC's scrapping of the rural credit unions' lending rate cap may help price credit by market forces because this can relax small- and medium-sized enterprises' budget constraint. The impact should not be overestimated as credit unions' lending accounts for less than 13% of total credit.

Chinese lenders issued RMB 682 billion in certificates of deposit to companies and individuals in June and July 2015.[28] For the first time, Chinese commercial lenders sold certificates of deposit to the public at unregulated interest rates. This marked a milestone in pushing to let market forces set the price of money. Certificates of deposit require a minimum investment of RMB 30,000 for individuals and RMB 10 million for companies. The high threshold is designed to limit their mass-market appeal so that it can avoid an abrupt rise in banks' funding costs as customers switch from regulated to unregulated deposits. These thresholds may be gradually lowered.

Promoting certificates of deposit achieves partial marketization and prepares for full liberalization of deposit rates. It is worth noting that large-denomination certificates of deposit are often used by many countries as an important means for pushing ahead with interest rate marketization reform. The central bank has cut benchmark interest rates four times since November 2014 with the purpose of boosting the slowing economy. Meanwhile, it granted banks increased freedom to set actual deposit rates above the benchmark. Deposit rates are allowed to float as much as 50% above the benchmark, up from only 10% before November 2014. In practice, nevertheless, the PBOC instructed large banks not to raise deposit rates by the legal limit. The intention is to not prevent large banks from passing on higher funding costs to borrowers.

PBOC explained in a statement the main reason for not removing caps on interest rates for deposits: PBOC felt that scrapping controls on savings rates would have far-reaching impact, and the risks of implementing it were much higher.[29] State-owned banks are the main opponents of deposit-rate liberalization because their profits are largely generated from the spread between artificially low deposit rates and lending rates. Large state-owned banks are the key lobbyists to the PBOC to delay the liberalization. The

28 PBOC Monetary Policy Report.

29 The source of information outlines a roadmap for the deregulation of the deposit rate. The cap on deposit rate is expected to be lifted to 1.2 times the benchmark in early 2014 from the current 1.1 times. Then it will be further raised to 1.3 times the benchmark afterwards. The rate cap on long-dated deposits will be removed by 2015 while that for short-dated ones should be cancelled by 2017. Jeff Pao and Ayishah Ma, "Call for Depositor Protection", *Hong Kong Economic Journal*, 23 July 2013, B12.

deregulation move may have a larger impact on large state-owned banks as they have relatively large exposure to big state-owned firms that are able to secure lower lending rates. The market showed their concern over the profitability of large banks.[30] The profitability of Chinese banks largely depends on the spread between the interest rate they charge borrowers and what they pay on deposits. A narrow spread between the deposit rate and lending rate as well as the capital-consuming nature of lending may erode the financial strength of Chinese banks. ChinaScope Financial, a Hong Kong-based research firm, estimated that Chinese banks need to raise US$5 billion to US$10 billion over the next two years in order to keep capital ratios at current levels.[31]

The rationale of the government's cautious stance towards reforms is to avoid stirring up unwanted competition among banks so as to pursue stable economic growth amid a downturn. Likely, Chinese banks would quickly jack up their savings rates to compete for deposits. Keeping a rule that caps deposit rates is viewed as a measure to constrain the banks' ability to truly set the price of money circulating in the economy. Limiting the banks' ability to control deposit rates means that banks are unlikely to slash lending rates because that could trigger a squeeze on their own lending margins. While banks are not in the position to lower lending costs immediately, they are safe to secure profit margins. For instance, CCB enjoys a net interest margin of 3.4%, three times what European giant Commerzbank marks despite the recent credit crunch pushing up financing costs.

5.2 Broader Implications of Interest Rate Reform

This half-done interest rate liberalization process may be even more damaging to the financial sector. Without removing caps on deposit rates, the shadow banking sector may still grow as a plethora of entities, which are somehow connected with state-owned banks, and are able to enter the financial market by selling trust products, wealth management products and other financial instruments which can offer higher interest rates than tightly controlled traditional bank deposits. A slower pace of interest rate reform may delay economic rebalancing. The cap on deposit rates also depresses consumption simply because many lower-income families rely

---

[30] Kanis Li, "Bank Shares Tumble After Freeing of Lending Rates", *South China Morning Post*, 23 July 2013, B3.

[31] Jane Cai, "Merchants Bank Cash Call Sparks Sector Sell-off", *South China Morning Post*, 25 July 2013, B3.

on interest income to supplement their earnings.[32] Liberalizing deposit rates would boost personal income by at least five percentage points as a share of Chinese gross domestic product and play a constructive role in the long-awaited pro-consumption rebalancing. The poor cannot afford to invest in these products and are forced to put their savings into deposit accounts offering artificially suppressed interest rates that are barely above the rate of inflation. The rich, however, can enjoy the benefits of this liberalization as they may borrow even cheaper.

Although the move to liberalize lending rates is part of the whole process of easing the flow of capital, the PBOC's grip on lending quotas may indicate that capital is not in a free flow. There is a major concern to taking a further step. Giving markets free rein to set the price of bank lending and to allocate the funding only to the most promising projects would risk turning off the cash taps to a vast web of state-owned enterprises. The majority of bank loans flowing from the Big Four go to the state-owned sectors on a PBOC-enforced quota basis. As a result, that practice has concentrated lending to projects and companies on the basis of connections and influence, rather than on prospects for profit. This practice has led to massive overcapacity in some favoured industrial sectors and a dependence on yet more lending to sustain diminishing returns on growth. Technically speaking, liberalizing bank lending rates may help address the concern over possible loan defaults and ultimately relieve heavily-indebted state firms and local government financing arms as they are more able to get lower interest rates. The timing of the reform – coming roughly a month after the PBOC cracked down on lending in the shadow banking sector – demonstrated that the reform would be more about keeping old loans from going into default.

Deepening financial reforms is an initiative which can ensure a better distribution of resources in the market and correct distortions caused by a pricing system that is dominated by state-owned enterprises. However, freeing control over deposit rates requires a more sophisticated legal infrastructure. The bankruptcy law may need to be further amended to define the rights of depositors so that due protection can be offered to depositors in the liquidation of any failed financial institution. In the normal bankruptcy proceeding, the liquidated assets will be used to pay staff costs, social security fees and tax, followed by general creditors and

---

[32] According to the PBOC's statement on its website on 14 July 2013, total deposits in commercial banks were 100.9 trillion by the end of June 2013. However, this 100-trillion deposit includes all kinds of deposit accounts, not only individual but also corporate accounts and government accounts.

shareholders. In the case that a bank is liquidated, without any rules in place, depositors will fall into the category of general creditors. In contrast to secured creditors, general creditors are unsecured and therefore rank behind secured creditors, administrators, employees and the tax authority. In other words, when the liquidated assets are distributed, general creditors do not have any priority right to these assets. Also, there is a need for the introduction of a deposit insurance scheme because some small banks may be at risk of going bankrupt. Without a deposit insurance scheme, depositors may be easily disadvantaged in the liquidation process. Currently, China does not have a deposit insurance scheme to protect savers if a bank becomes insolvent. The PBOC has made a plan to set up a scheme in the near future.[33] The next sensible move in a short term may be to widen the floating range for deposit rates. It was reported that the rate ceiling may be lifted for all deposits in early 2014, followed by the removal of the rate cap on long-dated deposits such as three and five year investments.[34]

Interest rate liberalization is a necessary precondition for eventual full convertibility of Renminbi. Removing the floor on lending rates suggests a freer Renminbi as the market can now play a larger role in valuing Renminbi against major currencies. The interest rate curve is one of the most important inputs into the exchange rate. A freer interest rate is also a prerequisite to activate the domestic foreign exchange market. A freer interest rate can help the PBOC to widen Renminbi's trading band against US dollars. The current trading limit impedes the global use of Renminbi even though it protects Renminbi from excessive volatility. Interest rate liberalization will help China to eventually loosen its tight restrictions on

---

[33] Jeff Pao and Ayishah Ma, "Call for Depositor Protection", *Hong Kong Economic Journal*, 23 July 2013, B12. The depositor protection scheme is a mechanism of immediate crisis resolution which can support confidence in times of crisis. Increasing numbers of jurisdictions have been turning to this scheme or deposit insurance. Any form of depositor protection can either be implicit or explicit. No depositor insurance system implies an implicit government guarantee, at least for depositors of the large financial institutions. China has in place implicit guarantees. Explicit systems take two forms: an explicit blanket guarantee of all depositors, and an explicit limited-coverage system of deposit insurance. An explicit blanket guarantee scheme can take either a formal legal form such as ones in Japan, Mexico and Turkey or a government pronouncement or policy such as the ones in Malaysia, Thailand and Sweden (1992–1996). Explicit deposit insurance is a guarantee limited to "preferred creditors", that is, insured depositors, and meanwhile expose general creditors, uninsured depositors, shareholders, managers, subordinated debt holders to more risks.

[34] Jeff Pao and Ayishah Ma, "Call for Deposit Protection".

cross-border capital flows. China prohibits yuan movement across the Chinese border as part of capital account controls against external shocks. The restrictions are being gradually removed to promote the currency in offshore centres such as Hong Kong, Singapore, London and Taiwan. A free-floating exchange rate would speed up China's entry to the IMF's special drawing rights (SDR), the reserve currency preferred by most reserve managers, cementing China's reputation as a global leader.

6. POLICY DESIGN FOR A FULL LIBERALIZATION

The IMF has hailed China's progress on financial reform and pointed out that China lags behind rivals on key metrics that determine whether the fund will formally endorse the redback as a reserve currency. Renminbi's inclusion in the composition of the IMF's special drawing rights – a global reserve asset – serves as recognition of the currency's rising global status and a signal to the world that Renminbi assets are a solid investment. IMF already recognized Renminbi's widespread use and trading.

Across a range of factors, financial market development, further opening of the capital account, and greater exchange rate flexibility are some of the key elements for determining Renminbi's inclusion in the SDR basket. The IMF calls on China to increase foreign access to its onshore stock and bond markets. Germany, France and the UK have expressed support for adding Renminbi while the US has urged more progress in deregulation of Chinese cross-border investment flows and domestic interest rates before IMF endorsement of Renminbi.[35]

While the market is eager to see the Chinese government move forward by taking more aggressive reform measures, we also need to be aware of the difficulty and complexity of implementing various macroeconomic policy tools regardless of the fact that the world is awash with easy money from the US and Japan. A more aggressive move towards a freer Renminbi may cause a significant loss to low-end manufacturers operating at a low profit margin. Hot money flows in and out of China could paralyse the country's macroeconomic policy tools. China must be cautious about the severe economic shock that currency reform may bring. "To allow more flexibility for China's yuan is easier said than done."[36]

The IMF warned that time is running short for China to implement

[35] Gabriel Wildau, "IMF Alert to Snags in Renminbi's Progress", *Financial Times*, 6 August 2015, p.2.

[36] Reuters, "Liberalising of the Yuan Courageous, Says Xinhua".

economic reforms as the government, banks and companies come under mounting strain from rapid but unbalanced growth. In its annual report on China's economy, the IMF suggested China take "decisive measures" to shift away from its growth model which relies heavily on credit and investment. This model, in a long run, is not sustainable but raises vulnerabilities. From the IMF's viewpoint, the immediate priority was to "rein in broader credit growth and prevent a further build-up of risks in the financial sector".[37] China's entire social financing (credit) in the economy has increased by more than 60% since the start of 2009. This not only indicates a rising leverage that weakens the balance sheet but also creates a source of funding for the shadow banking sector.

China's priority is a shift to broader platforms of growth so that China can put economic growth on a more concrete footing while its margins of safety are falling amid growing domestic problems. Currently, China's economy has been underpinned by a mix of investment, fiscal stimulus and credit which, however, is not a sustainable pattern of growth. A package of reforms is needed to secure more balanced and sustainable growth and to contain the growing risks so that China's economy can be put on a more consumer-based, inclusive and environmentally friendly path. The purpose of further reform is to steer the economy from a reliance on debt-fueled investment to a more balanced model driven more by consumption, services and innovation.[38] Rebalancing the Chinese economy towards more consumption could lift private households' appetite for cars and luxury goods. The risk along this direction of rebalancing is a potential drop of investment before consumption picks up the baton, turning a slowdown into a Chinese slump. The new leadership has shown its tolerance for a slower growth rate in order to wean the economy off a reliance on exports and investment and to boost consumption.[39] In the near term,

---

[37] Simon Rabinovitch, "IMF Urges China to Implement Critical Economic Reforms", *Financial Times*, 17 July 2013 (online).

[38] Reuters, "Communist Party's Yu Zhengsheng Vows 'Unprecedented' Reforms", *South China Morning Post*, 26 October 2013 (online).

[39] Li Keqiang said in a business seminar that 7.5% GDP growth, with a 3.5% inflation rate, is not the bottom line but a 7% growth is needed to achieve the goal of doubling GDP by 2020 and building a middle-class society. This suggests that a GDP growth rate below 7% will not be acceptable. Ayishah Ma, "Economic Support Measures Vital and Timely, Say Experts", *Hong Kong Economic Journal*, 26 July 2013, B10. This also suggests that the government may resort to a short term stimulus if growth is too close to 7%. Shirley Yam, "Li Keqiang Speech Leak Reflects Sensitivity of Growth Slowdown", *South China Morning Post*, 27 July 2013, B8. However, it is worth noting that a Chinese economy growing at an annual rate of 7.5% still makes a great contribution to global demand growth

a priority is to rein in broader credit growth and prevent a further build-up of risks in the financial sector, in particular, the shadow banking sector.

The IMF suggested the Chinese government not make a new round of stimulus plan. The government ruled out the possibility of implementing any large-scale stimulus to revive economy. The major concern is that additional financial risks may add to the stimulus plan. Instead of deploying a gargantuan stimulus package, the government in April 2014 announced a series of "mini-stimulus" measures to offset recent slippage in trade and industrial production and to boost its sluggish economy.

The three-pronged measures constituted a "mini-stimulus" package with the aim of "arousing the energy of the market". First, the State Council temporarily scrapped all value-added and sales taxes on businesses with monthly sales of less than RMB 20,000. This tax cut was to help more than 6 million enterprises which hire tens of millions employees. Second, the government planned to streamline customs procedures and reduce administrative costs for exporting companies. In particular, the government was to temporarily cancel inspection fees for commodities exports and streamline customs inspections of manufactured goods. Third, private investors would be invited by the government to be involved in the railway projects. For this purpose, new bond products would be issued. The government would accelerate the building of railways in underdeveloped central and western regions. Investment in low-income housing has been accelerated. These measures were on the supply side which may generate more efficient results. There are various ways of interpreting these measures. First, China is in a deepened downturn and the government fears a further slowdown. The slowdown in the rate of deflation can be taken as further evidence of a possible stabilization of the economy. The government appears ready to intervene to pull the economy out of its instability even though it seems more acceptable to see a slowdown as it rebalances the economy to become more consumption-driven. Second, the government is trying to help small firms and exporters to generate momentum in an economy that has slowed in nine of the past ten quarters. Third, the government is cautious to deploy effective measures and to direct public money towards more productive ends as growth slows.

While the US is paring back its easy-money policies (or quantitative easing), other countries including China and Japan are still relying on monetary policy and currency depreciation to buffer short-term growth. The financial reforms should be accelerated and the package can include

---

than expansion in any other economy. Chris Giles, "Slower but Steady", *Financial Times*, 24 July 2013, p.6.

a revamp of local government finances, a more market-based currency exchange rate, a liberalization of the capital account, and an open market for competition.

China's move towards a full market-based interest-rate system is part of a broader liberalization of its economic policies, which also include overhauling its financial system, giving the market a greater say in valuing the yuan and permitting more investment in China by foreigners. Currently, the PBOC maintains a cap on the rate banks can pay depositors, which acts as an implicit tax on savers and a subsidy to borrowers. The cap on the deposit interest rates has left Chinese households poorly compensated, as deposit rates often fall short of the rate of inflation. Banks are permitted to charge a rate on loans 10% higher than the benchmark deposit rate, which is now 3%. Large lenders channel inexpensive loans to SOEs, often seen as riskless borrowers, giving the borrowers a big advantage in competition with Chinese private firms and foreign competitors. Large banks have profited for years by paying very low rates for deposits and charging higher rates for lending. The liberalization of deposit rates would be the final step in the whole liberalization process.

The IMF has urged the PBOC to sequence the financial reform by allowing a full liberalization of longer-term deposits. Market-based interest rates are a key criterion that the IMF will use to decide whether it will endorse Renminbi as an official reserve currency in late 2015. The PBOC has indicated its plan to lift the deposit rate cap by the end of 2015. To open up the deposit rate, the PBOC may first introduce certificates of deposit, under which interest rates could be negotiated. The PBOC can also establish a deposit insurance scheme and bankruptcy law for financial institutions. Eventually, the PBOC may adopt the Shanghai interbank offered rate as the rate-setting benchmark.

11. Renminbi's ongoing exchange rate reform

Given the fact that Chinese currency, renminbi or yuan, is not freely convertible in the international foreign exchange market, foreign exchange is still heavily controlled in China even though major reforms swept the Chinese foreign exchange control regime in 2005. Whilst the foreign exchange liberalization reform has been underway, uncertainties exist and the market has to have a second guess at how further reform moves forward and whether the government will have a policy U-turn at a certain point. These uncertainties increase transaction costs and hinder China's deeper financial reform.

1. HISTORICAL REVIEW OF CHINA'S EXCHANGE RATE REGIME

China's foreign exchange policies after its economic opening in 1979 can be roughly divided into three phases. From 1979 to 1994, there were exchange controls on both current and capital transactions, and on both exports and imports as a result of which any economic transactions with foreign partners had to be conducted through state-owned trading companies. There was a two-tiered exchange system, that is, the official and swap markets. Until 1994, China had two official foreign exchange systems with different rates: an unfavourable one for foreigners and a better one for qualified Chinese enterprises. This created a thriving black market along with the formal market. The 1994 reform unified the two official foreign exchange systems by establishing an interbank foreign exchange system,[1] which signalled China's efforts to bring local practice into line with international standards. In this uniform system, the rate is set for foreigners at roughly the same level used internally by Chinese enterprises on swap markets. From 1994, as part of its financial reform, China abolished the

[1] The Further Restructuring the Foreign Exchange Control System Notice, promulgated by the PBOC in 1993.

exchange controls on current-account transactions. By 1996, China had formally satisfied the International Monetary Fund's Article VIII on current account convertibility. Up to date, China had basically achieved currency convertibility in the direct investment account, meaning strict restrictions in most cross-border funds payments and remittances were no longer needed. The new consolidated official exchange rate was set at RMB 8.7 per US dollar in 1994. Effectively, China devalued its currency by 33%. However, this sharp decline had little effect on global markets. At that time, China was relatively unimportant in world finance and Renminbi was not a major currency. Domestically, the 10-year fixed Renminbi 8.28 per dollar exchange rate was a successful instrument of implementing monetary policy and stabilizing the national economy. The third stage roughly started in the new century.

Renminbi has been the highest profile and longest-running subject of controversy between China and its trade partners, especially the US and EU. China was accused of intentionally manipulating renminbi's exchange rate to the US dollar in order to gain a competitive advantage and keep its export artificially cheaper. As to how much Renminbi was misaligned, substantial disagreement appeared in various pieces of research, ranging from 1 to 56% undervaluation.[2] There are also proponents against the idea that China should alter its exchange rate.[3]

The undervalued Renminbi, as often asserted by the US, EU and others, was said to be the key reason for China's growth in its foreign exchange reserves, rising from US$170 billion in January 2001 to more than US$3.2 trillion by mid-2014,[4] and the transformation to the "world's

---

2 W.L. Chou and Y.C. Shih, "The Equilibrium Exchange Rate of the Chinese Renminbi", (1998) 26(1) *Journal of Comparative Economics* 165–174 (claiming that renminbi was about 10% undervalued at the beginning of the 1990s); Morris Goldstein, "Adjusting China's Exchange Rate Policies", (2004) Institute for International Economics Working Paper 04-1 (arguing that renminbi is undervalued by at least 30–35%); Ernest H. Preeg, "Exchange Rate Manipulation to Gain an Unfair Competitive Advantage: The Case Against Japan and China", in C. Fred Bergsten and John Williamson (eds), *Dollar Overvaluation and the World Economy* (Washington DC: Institute for International Economics 2003) pp.267–284 (estimating that renminbi exchange rate undervaluation is about 40%).

3 Ronald McKinnon and Gunther Schnabl, "China: A Stabilizing or Deflationary Influence in East Asia? The Problem of Conflicted Virtue", (2004) available 2 March 2016 at http://scid.stanford.edu/publications/china-stabilizing-or-deflationary-influence-east-asia-problem-conflicted-virtue.

4 China's current account surpluses began to rise exponentially after 2003, and went up from 2% to 11.4% of its GDP by 2007. The surplus fell sharply to 2.9% by 2011. Martin Wolf, "Two Cheers for China's Rebalancing", *Financial Times*, 3 April 2012, p.11. By the end of the first quarter of 2014, China's foreign

manufacturing powerhouse" as well as the source of job losses and trade deficits in other countries. In the global financial crisis, Washington and Brussels identified undervalued Renminbi as a prime cause of global macroeconomic imbalances, and claimed that the appreciation of Renminbi is an important tool of the rebalancing, which will help increase consumer spending in China by raising purchasing power and allowing deficit countries such as the US to expand net exports. General principles of international law recognize the sovereign right of a country to issue currency, determine and change the value of the currency, and regulate the use of its own currency and any other currency within its territory.[5] A country, however, at least in theory, is bound by the Articles of Agreement of the IMF which modifies these general principles.[6] The WTO is not a conventional forum for the issue of currency. But currency is perceived to be an effective vehicle for a country to gain dominance in international trade. More importantly, the WTO is an institution with more effective enforcement mechanisms. Under international law, it can be argued either way whether or not China has manipulated its currency according to the Articles of Agreement of the IMF, and by its exchange action frustrated the intent of the WTO.[7]

Due to constant political pressure from the US, EU and Japan,[8] the Chinese government appreciated Renminbi by 2.5% on 21 July 2005. On the same date, the Chinese government announced to re-peg Renminbi

---

exchange reserves reached US$3.94 trillion. The figure almost doubled in the past five years. See China's State Administration of Foreign Exchange Balance Sheet for the First Quarter of 2014.

[5] This is a so-called "reserved domain" approach which fixes a domain of state activities where the jurisdiction of the state is not bound by international law. Accordingly, assumed by some jurists, there is a list of topics recognized as within the reserved domain including among others immigration and nationality. However, this has been claimed to be a misleading approach since some purely domestic subjects, depending on the precise facts and legal issues arising therefrom, cannot be fixed within the reserved domain when they are placed on the international plane. Ian Brownlie, *Principles of Public International Law* (Oxford: Oxford University Press, 5th edn. 1998) 293. For instance, a country's immigration policy may be subject to international refugee law and practice.

[6] Articles IV(1) and IV(1)(iii) of the Articles of Agreement of the IMF. The former tries to achieve a stable exchange rate system while the latter allows the IMF to exercise firm surveillance over the exchange rate policies of members.

[7] See generally, Michelle Oliel, *Undervalued and Manipulated? – Evaluating China's Foreign Exchange Arrangements under the International Monetary Fund and the World Trade Organization* (The Netherlands: Wolf Legal Publishers 2011).

[8] Martin Wolf, "Two Cheers for China's Rebalancing", *Financial Times*, 3 April 2012, p.11.

to the US dollar and allowed it to float within a band. Since then, the exchange rate of Renminbi has appreciated against the US dollar by about 25%.[9] Nevertheless, even after its abandonment of its hard currency peg, China is still under growing international pressure to let the currency rise by abandoning Renminbi's link to the US dollar.[10]

Since 21 July 2005, China has implemented a new foreign exchange rate regime termed as "a market-based managed floating exchange rate system", where the exchange rate is adjusted on the foundation of "market supply and demand with reference to a basket of currencies", though "in accordance with China's needs for reform and development". In simple economic terms, China scrapped the Renminbi's fixed peg to the US dollar in favour of a steady and crawling appreciation. The policy was formulated much earlier than 2005. China planned as early as in 1993 to liberalize foreign exchange policy gradually and made Renminbi fully convertible.[11] In 2003, China further planned to "selectively, and in steps, deregulate restrictions on cross-border capital transactions and gradually establish renminbi's convertibility on the capital account, provided that risks can be effectively guarded off".[12] This was the first time that China specifically mentioned the capital account convertibility as its official goal.

In theory, the level of current account surpluses and deficits are voluntary decisions to save and invest: countries with a deficit import capital while countries with surplus savings such as China export capital. As a

---

[9] Renminbi has risen still more steeply against a trade-weighted basket of currencies, and by about 50% against the Japanese yen. IMF no longer finds the renminbi undervalued. Henny Sender, "A Currency Skirmish That Was Not Made in China", *Financial Times*, 19 August 2015, p.7.

[10] Martin Feldstein, "Why the Renminbi Has to Rise to Address Imbalances", *Financial Times*, 30 October 2009, p.11 (complaining of renminbi being pegged at a fixed rate and Chinese policy of keeping renminbi weak); Martin Wolf, "Grim Truth Obama Should Have Told Hu in Beijing", *Financial Times*, 18 November 2009, p.12 (expressing the concern that China's decision to depreciate renminbi along with US dollars makes a healthy global economic recovery less likely); Peter Garnham, "Reminbi Keeps Analysts Guessing", *Financial Times*, 20 January 2010, p.23 (reporting that Chinese premier said in December 2009 that he would "absolutely not yield" to pressure for a stronger renminbi albeit a greater tension between China and other major economic powers on this issue).

[11] See "The Resolutions of the Central Committee of the Chinese Communist Party on Several Issues concerning Building a Socialist Market Economy", *People's Daily*, 15 November 1993.

[12] See *"The Resolutions of the Central Committee of the Chinese Communist Party on Several Issues concerning Building a Socialist Market Economy", People's Daily*, 22 October 2003.

result, surplus countries like China enjoy a higher return on savings but deficit countries such as the US enjoy a lower cost of investment. There is no reason to question the wisdom of the underlying choices. The reason China has been blamed for global imbalances is its interventionist (or mercantilist) monetary policies resulting in the explosion of China's surpluses. The US may also deserve blame for global imbalances as it proved incapable of using its capital inflows wisely. China, on the opposite, suffers from its own policies. While it has a huge investment boom, its consumption is repressed and savings encouraged. Private consumption fell from 46% of GDP in 2000 to 36% in 2007. During the same period, gross saving jumped. A large part of these savings was invested in low-yielding foreign assets at great cost: China's external reserves are US$2,300 for every man, woman and child, or as much as 40% of GDP. The sensible way of changing this imbalance, internal and external, is a huge expansion in consumption relative to investment.

By 2006, China's bilateral trade surplus reached 1.1% of the US GDP, which is twice as large as Japan's. Therefore, politicians in the US expressed their great concerns.[13] US lawmakers, led by Senators Charles Schumer and Leslie Graham, threatened to sanction China by imposing a 27.5% tariff on Chinese imports in order to pressure China to raise the value of Renminbi.[14] Senator Schumer continued to lead the charge to force Beijing to let Renminbi appreciate and introduced yet another version of his legislation on 17 January 2011 to allow the US to restrict imports on grounds of currency misalignment. However, Senator Schumer's interventions looked more like bluster than threat.[15] Meanwhile, the EU refused to grant China market economy status partly because of the undervalued Renminbi.[16] Japan's Ministry of Finance called for a Renminbi appreciation in order to stop China from exporting its price deflation to the rest of the world.[17] Policymakers, economists and analysts, however, all calculate the Renminbi's fair value. China's current account surplus over five years dropped from 10% of gross domestic

---

13 Ronald McKinnon and Gunther Schnabl, "China's Exchange Rate Impasse and the Weak US Dollar", (September 2006) CESifo Working Paper Series No. 2386.

14 "US Lawmakers Turn up Yuan Beat", *The Standard* (Hong Kong), 13 June 2007.

15 Alan Beattie, "Renminbi Issue Is Put on the Back Burner", *Financial Times*, 20 January 2011, p.6.

16 "Surplus Fuels EU-China War of Words", *Financial Times*, 13 June 2007 (online).

17 Haruhiko Kuroda and Kawai Masahiro, "Time for a Switch to Global Reflation", *Financial Times*, 1 December 2002 (online).

product in 2007 to 2.1% in 2013.[18] This change suggests that Renminbi may be close to its equilibrium.

2. OPERATION OF NEW FOREIGN EXCHANGE REGIME

The operation of this new foreign exchange rate regime, said to be a reform in "a self-initiated, controllable and gradual manner", is very much mixed with China's foreign trade policy. The long-term strengthening of Renminbi's real exchange rate is a combined effect of deep historical forces, such as China's rapid economic growth, stronger labour laws, and shrinking working age population. A more balanced trade would be to address the main source of disruption in China's trade relations with the US and would promote the Chinese currency to appreciate at a faster pace against the dollar. Amid the global economic downturn, the rise in Renminbi has slowed to a crawl as a drop-off in demand in more advanced economies hit Chinese exports.

The Chinese government has made commitments not to deliberately pursue a trade surplus,[19] which, as a matter of fact, was set to decline in recent years. For instance, the trade surplus in 2011 was about half the size of the record US$298 billion in 2008, which would amount to less than 3% of GDP.[20] To China, the corollary of a cheap currency is a large current-account surplus. China's surplus narrowed to less than 2.8% of GDP in 2011, the smallest size since 2002. In absolute terms, the $201 billion surplus was also the smallest since 2005.[21] China's narrower surplus reflects an unsustainable rise in investment rather than in consumption. These data indicated that China's trade relationship with the rest of the world is increasingly balanced. While China's external imbalance has narrowed, a big internal imbalance remains. For example, private consumption grew less quickly than the economy as a whole from 2001 to 2010.[22]

While appreciation of Renminbi is an incremental and irreversible trend, the Chinese government has also been carrying on its promise to make the Renminbi exchange rate a volatile and two-way trade. Renminbi

---

18 Delphine Strauss and Josh Noble, "Investors Take a Pace Back from Renminbi", *Financial Times*, 18 March 2014, p.18.

19 Kathrin Hille and Simon Rabinovitch, "Hu Commits Beijing to More Balanced Foreign Trade Relations," *Financial Times*, 12 December 2011, p.1.

20 Ibid.

21 "The Incredible Shrinking Surplus", *The Economist*, 18 February 2012.

22 Ibid.

was allowed to float within a band, up or down 1% from a daily reference rate against the dollar that is set by the People's Bank of China (PBOC).[23] Previously, Renminbi only moved one way. Renminbi was better priced by the market after it was allowed to flow in a band.[24] The PBOC doubled the trading band from 0.5% to 1% on either side of the bank's daily reference rate in April 2012. A widened band can give traders greater leeway to push the yuan up or down.[25]

After June 2010, the Chinese government allowed Renminbi to start rising again. At the same time, the government expanded its Renminbi trade settlement scheme so that eligible firms in China could pay for imports and exports of goods and services in their own currency rather than the US dollar.[26] The currency has been rising at an annualized rate of 6% since then. However, high Chinese inflation makes the real appreciation more than 10% a year.[27] Renminbi, together with other Asian currencies, soared to new highs against the US dollar, reflecting broad weakness in the greenback amid a political stalemate in Washington over the US Government's multi-trillion dollar debt. Renminbi hit 6.4375 in Shanghai on 27 July 2011, its strongest since 1993.[28] China allowed Renminbi to appreciate to a 19-year high on 13 October 2012 against the US dollar, right before the US presidential election. On the other hand, Renminbi, as it is said, only appreciated by over a tenth on a trade-weighted basis even though it appreciated by a fifth against the dollar in the previous five years. While the currency is appreciating, the growth of China's foreign currency reserves is flattening.[29]

A widened trading band was supposed to allow market forces to play a larger role as it encourages two-way volatility and avoids the one-way bet on the yuan strengthening. However, the widening of the band would not necessarily lead to a strengthening of the yuan. The past several year records showed that the band indeed played a distinctly secondary role to

---

23 Simon Rabinovitch, "China Steers Renminbi Two-way Trade", *Financial Times*, 26 October 2012 (online).

24 Enoch Yiu, "London Pushes Ahead with Yuan Ambitions", *South China Morning Post*, 3 December 2012 (online).

25 Jane Cai, "PBOC Poised to Widen Trading Band of Yuan", *South China Morning Post*, 24 April 2013 (online).

26 Large Chinese companies used letters of credit to take out foreign currency loans offshore as part of the scheme.

27 Alan Beattie, "Renminbi Issue is Put on the Back Burner", *Financial Times*, 20 January 2011, p.6.

28 Yonnex Li, "US Debt Logjam Lifts Yuan", *Hong Kong Economic Journal*, 28 July 2011, p.1.

29 "Renminbi – Yuan Direction", *Financial Times*, 15 October 2012 (online).

the daily fixing in determining the yuan's value. Largely, the value was up to the central bank.

The spot yuan closed on 4 June 2013 at 6.1287 per dollar in Shanghai. It had been hitting 19-year highs frequently in the previous few months and had strengthened about 1.7% against the dollar since April 2013. That already suppressed the 1.03% appreciation for the whole of 2012 while capital unleashed by quantitative easing in developed countries flooded into China, betting on robust economic growth and greater financial reforms.

The yuan could reach another key psychological level in 2013 to trade at 6 to the US dollar as the Chinese regulators seem included to ease the reins on the currency further. It is possible for the spot dollar-yuan to fall below the 6 figure. However, the yuan's persistent appreciation is not supported by economic fundamentals. China's trade surplus totaled US$43 billion in the first quarter of 2013 but the surplus adjusted for overstated exports to Hong Kong was only US$2.4 billion.

The exchange rate between Renminbi and US dollars reached a peak in February 2013. Thereafter, Renminbi fell nearly 2% against the US dollar. Compared to other currencies' downward moves and Renminbi's stability and strength, the drop of Renminbi's exchange rate was minimal. Renminbi has been the only one out of the eight currencies that JPMorgan surveys in its Global Data Watch on which investors would have made money than the dollar. The Chinese government appeared tolerant to Renminbi's relative strength even though both export growth and the current account were sharply slowing. This tolerant approach underscored the Chinese government's commitment to further reforms at the expense of economic growth. The Chinese government made no secret of its intention for Renminbi to eventually become a reserve currency, as an alternative to the dollar. Seen from this angle, the continuous appreciation of Renminbi is a sign of China's ambitions that are both economic and geopolitical. If China does implement reforms, the quality of economic growth will improve and the economic trajectory will be put on a more sustainable path.

With the current account surplus set to narrow and the growth of foreign direct investment likely to slow as the Chinese economy gears down, further gains in the yuan should be quite limited. The IMF, however, estimates the actual value of the yuan was 4.214 to the dollar in 2012, based on the purchasing power parity.[30] The yuan closed trading

---

[30] Jane Cai, "Yuan Heads for Key Level Against Dollar", *South China Morning Post*, 5 June 2013 (online).

on 27 May 2013 at 6.12 to the dollar, 35% stronger than its June 2003 rate.[31] The surge in Renminbi's normal exchange rate is puzzling as it comes at a time of disappointing growth, falling inflation and flagging exports.

According to the data, China's foreign exchange reserves reached US$3.66 trillion at the end of the third quarter of 2013, up from US$3.5 trillion at the end of the second quarter. The further expansion of foreign exchange reserves suggests there have been capital inflows back into China due to the recent recovery in China's economic growth as well as faster gains in Chinese property prices. The quick accumulation of reserves is also evidence showing that yield-hungry international capital continued to favour China while other emerging markets are experiencing sell-offs in stocks and currencies in recent times. The yuan gained 2.1% against the US dollar in 2013, compared to a 1% rise in 2012.[32] The capital inflows, however, signalled a wary central bank as it tried hard to keep Renminbi weak. The PBOC purchased US$70 billion from the market in September 2013, compared with US$16 billion in both July and August 2013, indicating that the PBOC does not want Renminbi to rise too fast. The PBOC's frequent and large-scale purchases of dollars also indicated its eagerness to strengthen the foundation of the economic recovery. The PBOC is apparently uncomfortable with allowing market forces to determine the exchange rate at times of uncertainty.

China has gradually scaled back its interventions in the foreign exchange market while it holds trillions of dollars in US Treasury bonds, bought with proceeds from export sales as part of China's effort to manage its currency. The rise in labour costs made Chinese products less competitive. Meanwhile, there has been a pickup in US job growth. These factors took the wind out of Washington's sails even though the US trade deficit with China grew to a record US$315 billion in 2012. Second, the US was faced by anger from other countries which are more eager to ease monetary policy and to drive down the dollar, a change that puts the US in a tough spot from which to criticize China. The US Federal Reserve's extraordinary easing of monetary policy is yet another factor cooling the US's appetite for criticizing China. Third, the US administration is shifting its focus to issues such as increased market access for US manufacturing firms and financial institutions that want to do business in China and better protection of intellectual property rights. Fourth, US

---

31 "The Cheapest Thing Going is Gone", *The Economist*, 15 June 2013.

32 Shen Hong, "Beijing Steps in to Tame Currency", *The Wall Street Journal*, 16 October 2013, C2.

preoccupation with its own fiscal problems also may have helped push China off the US political agenda.

The US, however, was unsatisfied with the pace of Renminbi's appreciation. In November 2012, given China's foreign currency reserves, trade surplus[33] and other factors, the US Treasury claimed that the rise of Renminbi over the previous two years had been insufficient even though it decided not to call China a currency manipulator.[34] Meanwhile, it was recognized by the US Treasury that China "has substantially reduced the level of official intervention in exchange markets since the third quarter of 2011", and taken "steps to liberalise controls on capital movements, as part of a broader plan to move to a more flexible exchange rate regime".[35] The US Treasury in its semi-annual currency report to the US Congress in November 2012 estimated that Renminbi gained 9.3% against the dollar (in nominal terms) between June 2010 and November 2012, and 12.6% (in real terms) if inflation is taken into account.[36] The US Treasury would pay "particular attention" to the pace of the yuan appreciation and "press for policy changes that yield greater exchange-rate flexibility, improve transparency, level the playing field for American workers and businesses, and support a strong, sustainable, and balanced global economy".[37]

Meanwhile, Renminbi reached a record high on 15 April 2013 when the PBOC fixed its midpoint against the US dollar at the strongest level ever: 6.2506 yuan per US dollar.[38] The yuan rate in the spot market touched 6.1903 per dollar on 15 April 2013, the highest since 1994.[39] The PBOC let the yuan appreciate 2.36 basis points between 12 to 17 April, setting record highs, compared with a rise of 1.54 basis points for all of 2012. These dates spanned the publication of the US Treasury currency report, a visit to China by US Secretary of State John Kerry and the G20 meeting, all of which served as platforms for criticism of China currency controls. The renminbi had approached equilibrium after appreciating 34% since the central bank scrapped a decade-old peg of 8.27 yuan per

---

33 The US ran a US$295.4 billion trade deficit with China in 2011, around an 8% increase above the 2010 level.

34 Agence France-Press, "China Rebuts US Claim that the Yuan is Still Significantly Undervalued", *South China Morning Post* (online).

35 Bloomberg, "China Not a Currency Manipulator, US Says", *South China Morning Post*, 28 November 2012 (online).

36 Ibid.

37 Ibid.

38 Jane Cai, "Yuan Reaches Record High Against the US Dollar", *South China Morning Post*, 16 April 2013 (online).

39 Ibid.

US dollar in July 2005.[40] China has indicated that a full convertibility of the yuan would be the next step in an overhaul of the exchange rate system.[41]

After years of grabbing the spotlight in US-China economic relations, while some lawmakers in the US continue to argue that a weak Chinese yuan was robbing jobs from the US, the US concern over the value of Renminbi seem to be fading and more substantial actions to force a change seems unlikely, giving ground to newer issues such as cyber-security, trade secret theft and North Korea.[42] Talk of currency manipulation has more or less ceased in Washington.[43] There are several reasons for this. First, China has allowed its currency to appreciate a significant amount. According to the US Treasury, since mid-2010, China's exchange rate, adjusted for inflation rates in the US and China, has risen 16% against the dollar.[44] Based on the US Treasury's calculation, Renminbi has appreciated 33% on a trade-weighted, priced-adjusted basis against major trading partners since July 2005 when it embarked on currency reforms. A conservative calculation is that the yuan has appreciated on a trade-weighted basis by 25% since 2007.[45] There has been a big drop in China's global trade surplus (measured by the current account). China's current account surplus, the broadest measure of its trade with the rest of the world, fell from a peak of 10.1% in 2007 to a preliminary reading of 2.6% in 2012.[46] Since mid-2011, Renminbi has moved up nearly 20% on a trade weighted basis and nearly 10% in 2013 alone.[47] For many of the small manufacturers, dealing with the rising Renminbi is hard because they cannot hedge against currency fluctuation. It was reported by *China Daily* in October 2013 that 17,000 companies in Guangdong had been

---

40 Jane Cai, "PBOC Poised to Widen Trading Band of Yuan", *South China Morning Post*, 24 April 2013 (online).

41 Ibid.

42 Cary Huang, "Xi Jinping and US Treasury Secretary Jack Lew Vow to Strengthen Sino-US Ties", *South China Morning Post*, 25 March 2013 (online).

43 Niall Ferguson and Mortiz Schularick, "The U.S. and China Both Need Economic Rehab", *The Wall Street Journal*, 6 November 2013, A15.

44 IMF in its first published estimate in July 2012 said that China's yuan was undervalued by 5 to 10%, much less than 25 to 40% figures touted by many US lawmakers for years.

45 Ferguson and Schularick, "The U.S. and China Both Need Economic Rehab".

46 Reuters, "US Concern on China Currency Fades as Yuan Grinds Higher", *South China Morning Post*, 11 March 2013 (online).

47 Henry Sender, "All China's Roads Lead to A Lower Renminbi", *Financial Times*, 4 March 2014 (online).

encouraged to conduct transactions in Renminbi since 2009.[48] But most foreign traders do not have offices in China and have no capability to generate Renminbi.

Yuan surged to a record high of 6.2187 versus the US dollar (after the central bank's strongest fixing of daily midpoint at 6.2712) in early January 2013, indicating the PBOC's increasing tolerance for appreciation amid strong export and inflation data. Throughout 2013, Renminbi rose to the strong side of its daily 1% band when China was under pressure to strengthen the currency.[49] Renminbi traded in a straight line, inclined softly upwards, with few bumps along the way. Renminbi moved in the same pattern even after the trading band was widened. China's motives have not been entirely altruistic. A rising Renminbi forced Chinese manufacturers to move upmarket. China is increasingly making its own capital goods instead of importing them from Germany or Japan. Manufacturers in China can challenge Samsung and other Korean markers on everything. Through a rising currency, the economy can rely more on value-added manufacturing and a shift to domestic consumption and spending on services. A consumption-based economy also depends on workers earning more and having more income to spend.

PBOC's stronger fixings have mainly acted as a restraint against what the authorities might consider excessive appreciation rather than the cause of such appreciation. Demand from companies and banks bumped Renminbi up against the strong-side limit as these marker players fear delaying the purchases of Renminbi may mean paying a higher price when Renminbi is further appreciated. The market events suggested that the PBOC's intervening to strengthen Renminbi was not a pure response to anti-China rhetoric in the US. The key to exchange-rate reforms is making the yuan pricing system more flexible to better reflect market dynamics instead of small amendments.

The PBOC in rare circumstances resorted to direct intervention to control the yuan's value. It could directly sell dollars and buy yuan to keep the Chinese currency from plummeting. The PBOC was said to spend more than US$40 billion of China's roughly US$3.6 trillion foreign exchange on the currency intervention.[50] PBOC was cautious about direct intervention

---

[48] Demetri Sevastopulo, "Chinese Manufacturers Feel Squeeze of Stronger Renminbi", *Financial Times*, 5 November 2013, p.2.

[49] However, the yuan rarely moves to either the top or bottom end of the trading band. Anjani Trivedi, "Companies Caught in Yuan Riptide", *The Wall Street Journal*, 18 March 2014, C4.

[50] Lingling Wei, "China Plans to Boost Liquidity", *The Wall Street Journal*, 24 August 2015, p.3.

and monetary measures. The concern was that liquidity would prop up share prices and result in a surge in lending to financing institutions. But the loans did not go to the real economy.[51] Besides, the liquidity pushed up inflation and created asset bubbles.

3. RENMINBI'S DEPRECIATION: A COURSE OF REVERSAL?

A technical question is when Renminbi appreciates to an optimal level, or whether Renminbi will depreciate at a certain point in the course of appreciation. In 2014 and 2015, Renminbi dramatically depreciated twice, which triggered strong market reactions.

3.1 Sudden Decline of Renminbi's Exchange Rate in 2014

In the third week of February 2014, during the final three trading sessions of the week, Renminbi dropped as much as 1.4% against the US dollar to renminbi 6.14.[52] Renminbi was 0.6% weaker against the dollar than it was at the start of 2014. This was the yuan's steepest weekly fall against the US dollar since China reformed its exchange rate system in 2005. Renminbi's decline to the lowest level in the previous seven months appears a reversal of the practice for most of the time in the past several years. Renminbi's depreciation not only reflects an adjustment of trading strategy by major market participants but also highlights the PBOC's concern about currency speculation. In the month of February, Renminbi became less predictable and suffered more than 1% loss, marking an abrupt shift from its steady appreciation in 2013, during which period yuan gained 2.9%.[53] The dollar was trading at 6.1587 yuan in early trading on 17 March 2014, making Renminbi weakened by 1.7% against the US dollar.[54]

After nearly a decade of ultra-low volatility due to the well-managed peg against the dollar, Renminbi has been considered as the subject of large and highly leveraged positions for investors viewing it as an effective one-way bet. The yuan has been carefully managed by the PBOC

[51] Alex Frangos, "Chinese Developers Get Easy Financing", *The Wall Street Journal*, 24 August 2015, p.28.

[52] Josh Noble and Ralph Atkins, "Renminbi's Fall Marks Seismic Shift", *Financial Times*, 28 February 2014 (online).

[53] Lingling Wei and Nicole Hong, "Yuan Trading Band Doubled", *The Wall Street Journal*, 17 March 2014, C3.

[54] Ibid.

and the exchange rate was set by the PBOC on a daily basis. More often than not, the China Foreign Exchange Trade System assigned a value to the currency slightly stronger than it had finished the previous day.[55] As Renminbi is tightly controlled by the government, it is the least volatile of Asian currencies. The near-guaranteed appreciation makes the yuan a popular and lucrative bet. The market feels that the US dollar and Chinese yuan pair was fixed much higher than expected.[56]

Seen from this angle, the yuan's decline is a seismic shift. Renminbi has further risen 10% against the US dollar since 2010 when China further loosened controls on the exchange rate. The steady appreciation was backed by rising capital flows, strong economic growth and the general market consensus that China had become a global powerhouse. Small- and medium-sized businesses and wealthy investors leveraged bets on the yuan's further appreciation. They bought products that magnified profits from gains in the yuan. Borrowers are certain about the lack of any risk when they buy dollars offshore and sell Renminbi onshore so their investment strategy has been bold by not hedging their currency exposure, which means they do not buy contracts that guarantee them dollars at an agreed-upon price in the future when they need to repay the loans. On a risk-adjusted basis, it was more rewarding to leverage up the yen (which is driven down by the Japanese government) and invest in the yuan due to little volatility in the yuan. In January 2014 alone, Chinese banks bought a net US$73 billion of foreign currency in the onshore market from clients who wanted Renminbi.

The speculation is apparent, evidenced by huge inflows of capital in recent months as well as a sharp increase in lending into mainland China by Hong Kong banks while clients try to profit from the mainland's high interest rates. A surge in loans from Hong Kong to mainland Chinese companies from outside the country has contributed to large inflows of cash into mainland China and some of them are short-term and speculative. Foreign-currency lending by banks in Hong Kong to mainland China rose to a record of HK$2.9 trillion by the end of 2013.[57] In 2013, fund inflows into China amounted to US$500 billion or so.[58] UBS estimates

---

[55] Neil Gough, "In China, Shaking Up Currency's Strength", *New York Times*, 17 March 2014, B1.

[56] Lingling Wei and Aniani Trevidi, "China: Liberalized Rates Are Coming", *The Wall Street Journal*, 11 March 2014, C4 (quoting comments made by Scotiabank in Hong Kong).

[57] Enda Curran and Prudence Ho, "Hong Kong Bank Lending is Worry", *The Wall Street Journal*, 28 February 2014, C3.

[58] Henry Sender, "All China's Roads Lead to a Lower Renminbi", *Financial Times*, 4 March 2014 (online).

that banks in Hong Kong and Singapore lent Chinese companies more than US$200 billion in 2012 and that US$170 billion were sent back to mainland China.[59] UBS further estimates that inflows amounted to more than US$150 billion in 2013 and US$76.3 billion in January 2014.[60] At least part of such money was further injected into the shadow banking sector and real estate market, the favourite destination of speculative capital. For example, 87% of the total debt of China Overseas Land and Investment, one of China's largest property companies, was from the offshore market.[61] Over-lending makes Hong Kong banks vulnerable and could fuel a spike in bad loans.

3.2 Rational Policy Interpretations

The Chinese government claimed that the decline was a result of market forces. But it can be viewed as a result engineered by the regulators, in particular, the PBOC, to stamp out currency speculation. Indeed, the US complained of the lack of transparency of China's monetary policy, and made a request that China disclose its intervention in the currency market more regularly so as to "increase the creditability of its monetary policy framework and to promote exchange-rate and financial-market transparency".[62] As a matter of fact, the yuan is still a tightly managed currency. There are various more comprehensive ways of interpreting the PBOC's movement.

The PBOC's push-down of yuan's exchange rate may be a means to increase domestic liquidity when stress within the financial system is rising.[63] It also helps to reduce demand for offshore loans as a softer yuan would make foreign currency borrowing more expensive. This sharp move follows a period of time in which the offshore Renminbi rate has been trading at an increasing premium to the onshore rate, due to China's tight control on the capital accounts. Chinese exporters are big buyers of derivatives because they allow them to hedge against the rising yuan. The yuan's appreciation makes exporters' goods more expensive to

---

[59] Simon Rabinovitch, "Fall in Renminbi Leads Investors and Companies Towards Caution", *Financial Times*, 28 February 2013, p.2.

[60] Shen Hong, "Beijing's Move to Weaken Yuan Floods China With Cash", *The Wall Street Journal*, 4 March 2014, C2.

[61] Ibid.

[62] William Mauldin and Eric Morath, "U.S. Raps China Over Currency Moves", *The Wall Street Journal*, 16 April 2014, A9.

[63] Liquidity was under pressure each time when the regulators introduced regulatory measures to curb arbitrage.

sell overseas and exporters' revenues, which come in foreign currencies, shrink.

More fundamentally, this can be a signal of a shift in Chinese currency policy. The sudden drop of Renminbi's exchange rate is part of the PBOC's strategy to prepare a possible change to the existing foreign exchange regime,[64] that is, turning the tightly tethered yuan for wider trading and changing Renminbi's label as a two-way bet. The PBOC guided the onshore currency weaker through higher fixes. The PBOC's action is intended to dampen appreciation expectations by introducing more two-way volatility into the market. The PBOC is also trying to widen the daily trading band, and bringing the onshore and offshore rates together is a precondition to achieving the goal of widening the daily trading band. A wider trading band may make the yuan less stable. Introducing more volatility is therefore necessary before the PBOC widens the trading band.

The exchange rate decline laid the groundwork for allowing the currency to trade more freely. The market expects the PBOC to expand the range in 2014 by allowing the currency to move up or down by 2% daily.[65] The PBOC's heavy intervention was so effective that a chastened market dutifully took the yuan even lower when the PBOC widened the trading band. A wider band would be in keeping with the PBOC's intention to gradually free up the yuan. A more freely traded yuan is part of the Chinese government's new reform package. A freer yuan would give Chinese consumers more flexibility in terms of spending and investment as it can be more easily converted into foreign currency. The PBOC's intervention is two-fold. First, it set a weaker benchmark against which the yuan can trade. Second, it directed Chinese banks to buy dollars, pushing up the price of the dollar against the yuan.

The PBOC set the daily reference rate at 6.1312 to the US dollar on 10 March 2014, compared with 6.1201 to the US dollar on 7 March 2014, the largest one-day move in the rate since July 2012.[66] By guiding the yuan weaker, the PBOC intends to thwart short-term speculators betting on a continued rise of Renminbi and to introduce greater two-way volatility into its trading. Mounting speculative flows into the currency,

---

64 Josh Noble, "Renminbi's Sharp Fall Signals Policy Shake-up, Say Analysts", *Financial Times*, 26 February 2014, p.22.

65 Lingling Wei, "China's Central Bank Engineered the Recent Move Lower by Yuan", *The Wall Street Journal*, 27 February 2014, A8; Kwong M-Ki, "Yuan Suffers Its Biggest Fall on Record Amid Speculation over Widening of Trading Band", *South China Morning Post*, 4 March 2014 (online).

66 Lingling Wei and Aniani Trevidi, "China: Liberalized Rates Are Coming", *The Wall Street Journal*, 11 March 2014, C4.

as estimated by Deutsche Bank, stand at US$500 billion.[67] The so-called hot money inflows make managing domestic liquidity and money supply more difficult. The speculators in the offshore Renminbi market should be squeezed out. However, neither the PBOC nor the SAFE acknowledged any role in guiding the Renminbi. The PBOC made an official statement on the sudden weakening of the yuan saying that the sell-off was a reflection of market forces and should not be over-interpreted while the SAFE confirmed that the recent movement is a result of market players' adjustment of their near-term trading strategies.[68] But economists and analysts had a different view and saw the PBOC's tight grip on the exchange rate. When the currency started falling, the PBOC steadily lowered its daily reference rate. to the contrary, banks and companies continued to trade Renminbi at a stronger level.

The yuan's decline was mixed with a slower economy and a rapid outflow of capital as economic conditions worsened. The market expects a longer-term process of Renminbi appreciation, which is still possible and remains intact. But it is also apparent that the days of low volatility are coming to an end. It has been asserted that the yuan is overvalued and should trade at a lower level. Higher volatility enables the PBOC to set interest rates higher to curb credit growth in the economy. On the other hand, the sharp drop of Renminbi serves a notice that China is opening up a new front in its battle to reduce risks in a highly volatile financial system. Certainly, a sharp drop of Renminbi may make exporters suffer big losses as most products to hedge against dollar earnings were sold to Chinese export businesses.[69]

The PBOC said in a statement on its website that beginning on 17 March 2014, the daily trading band on the Chinese currency, Renminbi, would double to 2% above or below a fixed rate the government sets each day, a move that could lead to wider daily price fluctuations. This move would give market forces a larger role in determining the exchange rate, and send a strong signal to the market that bolder moves are imminent. However, a wider band is not sufficient to make Renminbi freely tradable. What is needed is the PBOC's step-aside from managing the currency on a daily basis. Other hard currencies, or freely convertible currencies, such as the yen and the euro, rarely rise or fall by more than 1% against the dollar

---

[67] Jeanny Yu, "Yuan Depreciation Raises Investment Risks", *South China Morning Post*, 10 March 2014 (online).

[68] Simon Rabinovitch, "China Denies Direct Role in Renminbi's Decline", *Financial Times*, 27 February 2014, p.1.

[69] Alex Frangos, "Crossing China's Big Red Currency Line", *The Wall Street Journal*, 21 March 2014, C12.

in one day. Technically, a 2% daily range is tantamount to setting yuan free. Given the past two-year exchange rate record, the band-widening since 2012 has not heightened exchange rate volatility, which means a technical flexibility would not change market behaviour except making the yuan less of a guaranteed source of return for many investors. This is largely true due to the PBOC's practice. Presently, the PBOC continues to set the reference rate each morning and pushes the currency around by buying dollars or selling yuan. The PBOC may still drag the yuan back by setting the reference rate even if trading moves the full 2% in either direction.

The drop in Renminbi's rate should be interpreted as part of a broader effort by the central bank to overhaul the financial system. There has been a market theory that the Chinese government is easing monetary policy to cushion the slowing economy[70] simply because a weaker yuan could help Chinese exporters by lowering the price for their goods internationally. Currently, the influx of speculative capital has complicated China's efforts to manage the economy, contributing to property bubbles and excess cash into the financial system.

The PBOC's move weakened Renminbi by 4% in 2014,[71] making it the worst performing currency in Asia against the US dollar. This ended a four-year period during which Renminbi appreciated almost 12%. It certainly alerted the US which closely looks at whether Renminbi's devaluation represents a shift in policy that could start a new round of competitive devaluations.[72] The concern, as stated in the US Treasury Department's semi-annual report on currencies in April 2014, is whether the Renminbi is moving away from China's publicly stated policy of scaling back intervention to have a more market-determined exchange rate.[73] Deeper down, the US is apparently also concerned about a more balanced global trade, as Jack Lew, the US Treasury secretary expressed in his visit to China in mid-May 2014.[74] Apart from the concern over currency manipulation, the US is also concerned with the negative impact a weaker Renminbi may bring

---

[70] Simon Rabinovitch, "Renminbi Range Move Fuels Doubts", *Financial Times*, 17 March 2014, p.4.

[71] Tom Mitchell, "US Calls on China to Do More to Overhaul Exchange Rate Policy", *Financial Times*, May 13, 2014 (online).

[72] William Mauldin and Bob Davis, "Treasury Warns on China's Currency", *The Wall Street Journal*, 8 April 2014, A11.

[73] William Mauldin and Eric Morath, "U.S. Slams China's Currency Moves", *The Wall Street Journal*, 16 April 2014, A1.

[74] Tom Mitchell, "US Calls on China to Do More to Overhaul Exchange Rate Policy", *Financial Times*, 13 May 2014 (online).

to the recovery of the US economy.[75] The engineered monetary policy may help China to increase competitiveness and boost exports. The PBOC has indicated that it will not make the Renminbi even higher as part of the PBOC's job is to maintain stability in Renminbi's exchange rate and a sharp decline of Renminbi could destabilize the country's economy.

PBOC has powerful instruments to dictate the yuan's daily movements. The PBOC can guide the yuan lower using the so-called central parity rate, a fixing the PBOC sets daily. By fixing the midpoint of Renminbi's trading band, the PBOC can play a crucial signalling role. The currency can slide further. The PBOC set the central parity rate at 6.1460 yuan to the dollar on 20 March 2014. The decline leaves the loss for 2014 at 2.8%, which is almost the same as the entire 2013 gain of 2.9%.[76] Gradually, companies become the largest force to drive Renminbi lower as they made a decisive shift in trading the renminbi. Market expectation has changed. State-owned oil companies and private sector exporters were strong believers that Renminbi's depreciation would be short-lived. But they are now positioning themselves for a weaker currency for longer.

3.3 Unexpected Consequences and Unsolved Dilemma

While the PBOC is determined to dispel the notion that Renminbi will always continue to appreciate, there are always unintended consequences to significant changes in fiscal and monetary policies. The sudden slide of the yuan raised concern that the yuan is nearing levels that could trigger an unwinding of billions of dollars in highly leveraged bets on its appreciation. Net foreign-currency purchases by the PBOC and financial institutions, a key proxy for inflows of foreign capital, fell to 128.25 billion yuan in February 2014.[77] The sudden decline of Renminbi's exchange rate, with the aim of curbing heavy inflows of money from abroad, pushed a sharp increase in cash flowing into the financial system. As the drop of Renminbi may signal a further slowdown of the Chinese economy,[78] which in turn reduces the demand for Renminbi, the investors take this as a cue to sell yuan and buy US dollars. As a result, yuan flooded into China's money markets thereby adding liquidity into the financial system

---

[75] Robin Harding and Josh Noble, "Concerns Raised over Renminbi's Fall", *Financial Times*, 9 April 2014, p.3.

[76] "All Eyes on Beijing as Yuan Keeps Sliding", *The Wall Street Journal*, 21 March 2014, C3.

[77] Ibid.

[78] A broad range of economic indicators, ranging from trade, consumer spending to industrial production, have showed a slowing economy.

and plummeting the yuan's short-term interest rates. The use of Renminbi in global payments also declined, which was evidenced by an 8.5% fall of transactional value in February from January 2014. According to the data from the Society for Worldwide Interbank Financial Telecommunication (or Swift), this pushed Renminbi down to the eighth most used currency from the seventh position.[79]

A sudden fall in the value of the yuan means a rising cost to repay foreign currency loans, putting more pressure on corporate balance sheets that are already suffering as China's economy slows and external demand for exports shrinks. Soaring interest rates increase the benchmark cost of short-term loans among banks, making the weighted average of the seven-day repurchase agreement rate higher. The measure for dealing with hot-money inflows is implemented at the expense of achieving long-term goals. The PBOC may have prioritized hot-money inflows before other policy objectives.

The changing balance of inflows and outflows of Renminbi casts a shadow on the PBOC's policy of maintaining the borrowing costs at a reasonable level with the aim of rebalancing a credit-driven economy and reining in risky financing, in particular, the shadow banking sector. The dilemma is related to the competing objectives: interest rate and liquidity. A weakened currency goes hand in hand with a higher liquidity while higher interest rates are always in existence with tight liquidity. This dilemma well explains the complexity of managing the macroeconomy and financial system at the same time. Renminbi's recent depreciation is just a sign showing that China's policymakers are facing a challenging job and complicated economic outlook with many moving pieces.

Renminbi's decline has a broader impact on Chinese companies that had placed bets on an appreciating yuan to guarantee steady revenue from exports as the currency's value climbed steadily against the dollar. While losses on yuan bets will be offset by the benefits of a weaker currency, some companies borrow money to make these trades, magnifying gains when the yuan rises. The renminbi's fall also opens them up to big losses. Paper losses on target redemption-forward products

---

[79] Anjani Trivedi, "Global Use of Yuan Fell in February", *The Wall Street Journal*, 27 March 2014, C3. This ranking is based on the payment value exchanged over the Swift Network. The global payment provider's data are based on commercial payments and financial flows through this system. In the past three years, yuan overtook 22 currencies and entered the ranks of the 10-most-used currencies globally. Yuan currently has a 1.42% share of global payment activity in February 2014.

hit US$2.3 billion.[80] For now most losses remain on paper as investors have not sold their positions. However, banks may ask these investors to provide more collateral. The added volatility in the exchange rate may give some investors pause. If the currency appreciation is no longer clearly guaranteed, the result is likely to be that there will be less foreign portfolio investment in China. Some hedge funds are closing up positions.[81] A weaker yuan led to a loss of competitiveness for emerging-market manufacturers, and subsequently caused the exchange rate depreciations in Asia and elsewhere.[82]

Renminbi's decline also affected the derivatives market in other regions. A local bank in Taiwan sold complex derivatives to companies and billions of dollars of these leveraged products bet on Renminbi. The selling bank misled clients into overinvesting in so-called target redemption forwards for high commissions. Sales of these products surged in the past two years as the investors bet on the yuan's one-way appreciation.[83] According to Deutsche Bank's estimates, US$250 billion worth of these contracts were traded in 2013 when the products were first launched, and between US$80 billion and US$100 billion have been traded.[84] These products were originally designed to help with hedging against currency fluctuations but were later instead used to speculate on the yuan's gains. Taiwanese investors have been major buyers betting on the one-way appreciation of Renminbi but the unexpected slide of Renminbi has turned many investors into heavy paper losses for holders. Taiwan's financial regulator, the Financial Supervisory Commission, decided to penalize the local bank. The regulator has instructed local banks to be more prudent in selling these products by limiting the amount based on clients' risk tolerance and ensuring the money-losing potential of the products is understood. Meanwhile, the Australian dollar also strengthened against the US dollar due to the fact that Australia is a heavy supplier of resources.[85]

---

80 Anjani Trivedi, "Companies Caught in Yuan Riptide", *The Wall Street Journal*, 18 March 2014, C1.

81 Ibid.

82 Michael J. Casey, "Dollar's Moment Is Here", *The Wall Street Journal*, 27 March 2014, C4.

83 Anjani Trivedi and Fanny Liu, "Taiwan Takes Aim at Yuan Products", *The Wall Street Journal*, 18 April 2014, C3.

84 Ibid.

85 William Mauldin and Eric Morath, "U.S. Slams China's Currency Moves", *The Wall Street Journal*, 16 April 2014, A9.

3.4 Depreciation in 2015

China devalued its currency in August 2015, which drew comparisons to the 1997–1998 Asian crisis sparked by Thailand. The PBOC made an announcement on 11 August 2015 that it had devalued Renminbi against the dollar by nearly 2% overnight by setting the guidance 1.9% weaker, the biggest one-day fall since the set-up of China's modern foreign exchange market in 1994. The PBOC then raised the daily reference rate for dollar/RMB 1.6% to RMB 6.3306. Renminbi fell 3.3% in total against the US dollar over the three days after the PBOC's announcement.[86]

The PBOC said the move was a one-time adjustment to reflect changes in the way it calculates the daily fix – the rate at which the central bank sets the currency every morning from which the currency is allowed to move as much as 2% points in either direction. The quotes in the future, as the PBOC said, reported to it by market makers should be "in conjunction with demand and supply in the foreign exchange market and exchange rate movement of the major currencies".[87] The daily fix, as the PBOC pointed out, will refer to the closing rate of the interbank foreign exchange market on the previous day.

The PBOC issued a statement reiterating its promise to give the market a larger role in setting the exchange rate. It also dismissed concerns that China was embarking on a campaign to weaken its currency in the face of stalling economic growth. In the statement, it was said that: "in view of both domestic and international economic and financial condition, currently there is no basis for persistent depreciation of [the] renminbi". "Recently, major economic indicators stabilized and showed good signs, which provides a favourable macroeconomic environment for a stable renminbi".

The devaluation was necessary to boost the economy at a time when economic growth is slowing. To outsiders, the devaluation was framed as a liberalizing step towards a more market-oriented and freely tradeable Chinese currency and a more market-based onshore foreign exchange

---

[86] Jamil Anderlini, "Rare Defence by Chinese Central Bank Reassures Jittery Markets on Renminbi", *Financial Times*, 14 August 2015, p.1. With this margin of decline, the renminbi still outperformed other currencies of emerging markets. For example, the Russian ruble is down 9% and the Colombian peso down more than 6%. Jeff Sommer, "A Short Step in China's Long Advance", *International New York Times*, 24 August 2015, p.13.

[87] Jennifer Hughes, Patrick McGee and Jamil Anderlini, "China Risks Clash with US as 1.9% Devaluation Surprises Markets", *Financial Times*, 12 August 2015, p.1.

regime. This move can kill two birds with one stone. This can help prevent competitive devaluations[88] while convincing the IMF to include Renminbi in a basket of reserve currencies.[89] As far as Renminbi is concerned, China's action created a two-way environment, and the transition phase is always volatile. In a larger picture, China is no longer able to be a primary engine of the global economy.[90]

However, to the outside of the world, China's currency devaluation had a domino effect across the region, and would export the deflationary woes of China's manufacturers, even though it was not the big by the standards of emerging market devaluations. China's position as the world's largest trading power ensured that its action would distribute deflationary pressures throughout its global supply chain, thereby intensifying pressure on competitors to seek their own currency depreciation. Renminbi's decline caused the S&P 500 index to drop by 1% and the FTSE Eurofirst 300 to fall by 2.7%. Stock markets slid across Asia[91] and even the world.[92] The devaluation hit commodity prices and mining company shares hard. Broader US and Eurozone equity markets fell.[93] The currencies of nations that export to China were caught up in the first round of reaction. The Australian dollar fell 1.4% against the US dollar while the New Zealand dollar fell 1%. South Korea's won weakened 1.8%. Nations competing with China's exporters came under pressure. The Japanese yen slipped

[88] Proponents of the reform interpretation argued that the PBOC is not increasing money and selling into the market. The previous central bank intervention had held in check. Since November 2014, the spot rate has traded weaker than the central bank's guidance every day. This was clear evidence that market forces have weighed on the renminbi but that the PBOC's strong reference rate prevented depreciation. Foreign exchange traders detected signs that the PBOC was buying renminbi in order to slow the currency's decline. This suggests that the PBOC wants to strike a balance between permitting moderate devaluation while preventing depreciation expectations from become entrenched. Josh Noble, "China Seeks to Calm Global Nerves Over Renminbi Fall", *Financial Times*, 13 August 2015.

[89] The IMF made a recommendation that the renminbi be included in the SDR basket as the fifth currency along with the US dollar, euro, yen and sterling in mid-November 2015. "The Renminbi Receives a Symbolic Seal of Approval", *Financial Times*, 17 November 2015 (online).

[90] Roger Blitz, "China's Devaluation Triggers Dramatic Falls in Emerging Markets Currencies", *Financial Times*, 21 August 2015, p.1.

[91] Josh Noble, "China Seeks to Calm Global Nerves Over Renminbi Fall", *Financial Times*, 13 August 2015, p.1.

[92] Dave Shellock, "Investors Head for Safety as Fresh Fall for Renminbi Sows Uncertainty", *Financial Times*, 13 August 2015, p.19.

[93] Jennifer Hughes, Patrick McGee and Jamil Anderlini, "China Risks Clash with US as 1.9% Devaluation Surprises Markets", *Financial Times*, 12 August 2015, p.1.

0.2% and Taiwan dollar weakened by 1.8%.[94] Nations like Kazakhstan and Vietnam devalued their currencies as well.

A slowing China economy and a devalued Renminbi are a twin blow to Japan and the Eurozone,[95] which have been indirectly pushing their currencies weaker to bolster exporters with big trading relationships with China. Since April 2013, the Bank of Japan, the central bank in Japan, has ploughed 170 trillion yen into a radical quantitative easing program.[96] However, inflation remains barely above zero. The rising costs of the program include the potential for asset bubbles, and the distortion to markets, especially the government bond market, which is increasingly dominated by the Bank of Japan. The program may also let the government off the hook on fiscal reform. China's devaluation exposes an undefended flank in its efforts to jolt its flagging economy out of decades of deflation, which rely heavily on a solid pickup in overseas demand. The devaluation can be a cause of a "currency war" waged by government planners desperate to rescue a spluttering economy.[97] Asian countries are expected to follow suit – setting up a cascade of tit-for-tat devaluations.[98] American cries of "currency war" directed at emerging economies for loosening monetary policy and manipulating exchange rates' fall are no more justified than when those countries did the same to the US during the Federal Reserve's (the Fed) execution of the quantitative easing program. Global monetary policy appears to be a zero-sum game in a system of inflexible exchange rates. The Fed has the capacity to respond to the dollar strengthening by keeping interest rates lower than they might otherwise have been. More recently, the Fed has been reluctant to raise interest rates due to a blast of deflationary pressure from China as well as China's uncertain economic growth.[99]

---

94 Michael Hunter, Peter Wells and Patrick McGee, "Australia and NZ Hit by Renminbi Move", *Financial Times*, 12 August 2015, p.22.

95 Roger Blitz and Leo Lewis, "Beijing Turns Up the Heat on Yen and Euro", *Financial Times*, 18 August 2015, p.24.

96 "BOJ Worry About Fallout From Yuan Devaluation", *The Business Times*, 21 August 2015, p.23.

97 For a general account of "currency wars", see James Rickards, *Currency Wars – The Making of The Next Global Crisis* (New York: Portfolio/Penguin 2011).

98 Technically, China is a newcomer to the currency skirmishes. Central banks in developed economies have held interest rates at close zero and used freshly minted cash to buy financial assets in huge quantities. This quantitative easing is an instrument to drive their currencies down and their exports up. Japan embarked on its own quantitative easing program in April 2013, and the Japanese yen has fallen 33% against the US dollar since then.

99 John Authers, "Look to China for Clues on When the Fed Will Raise Rates", *Financial Times*, 19/20 September 2015, p.18.

The US, as usual, accused China of manipulating its currency by making it artificially cheap. But the market is saying that Renminbi is not cheap enough. The Chinese government has been trying to keep Renminbi from falling more sharply.[100] As a matter of fact, the PBOC has been under pressure to devaluate the yuan for a while. The PBOC has frequently bought the yuan and sold the US dollar to prevent the Chinese currency from falling too much. It spent more than US$40 billion of China's US$3.7 trillion foreign exchange reserves.[101] It had resisted the action largely because of its desire to turn the yuan into a global currency. A weaker yuan will hurt its appeal to international business and investors. But the sharp slowdown of the economy left the PBOC with few options.

Capital outflows have put downward pressure on the exchange rate. Capital outflows in July reached US$70 billion.[102] Data showed that foreign exchange purchases by banks exceeded Renminbi purchases by US$43 billion in July 2015.[103] Increasing signs of capital outflow are hitting investor confidence. Diminished confidence in the macroeconomy can fuel a panicky flight of foreign and domestic capital and generate a currency crisis. Intervention can help prevent the currency falling further. Giving market forces a greater role to a certain extent helps reform efforts but will affect the domestic economy. It may not drastically affect the exchange reserves of US$3.65 trillion. The short-term dangers of devaluation are clear: capital cannot flee easily but the sneaked-out money will deplete the

---

[100] The renminbi has dropped less than 3% against the dollar since the close of trading on 10 August. The next day, China announced a technical change in its rules that market forces would begin to play a bigger role in renminbi price-setting. It set the renminbi less than 2% lower against the dollar. The currency's declines over the next two days were smaller. By 14 August 2015, the Chinese central bank's intention to stabilize the renminbi become clearer, and the currency started to flat-line on the foreign-exchange charts. Jeff Sommer, "A Short Step in China's Long Advance", *International New York Times*, 24 August 2015, p.13.

[101] Lingling Wei, "PBOC Frees Up Credit as Economic Slowdown Worsens", *The Wall Street Journal*, 26 August 2015, p.13.

[102] Neil Gough, "Stock Slide Extended Amid Doubts about China", *International New York Times*, 25 August 2015, p.15.

[103] Gabriel Wildau, "Stocks Rout Puts Beijing Rescue Effort in Doubt", *Financial Times*, 19 August 2015, p.18. It is worth noting that a flood of capital gushing out of emerging markets is a widespread phenomenon. The capital outflow reached US$ 1 trillion from July 2014 to 2015, double the amount that left during the financial crisis of 2008–09. Total net capital outflows from the 19 largest emerging market economies reached US$940.2bn in the 13 months to the end of July 2015. James Kynge and Roger Blitz, "Emerging Markets Rocked by $1tn Capital Flight As Confidence Slumps", *Financial Times*, 19 August 2015, p.1.

pile of reserves,[104] which could have been used to support China's indebted businesses. Depreciation is likely to intensify capital flight. The surprising devaluation prompted investors to sell the yuan both on the mainland and in the Hong Kong offshore market in expectation that Renminbi would go even lower.[105] One of the long-term benefits is a more volatile trading environment for Renminbi.

Chinese regulators have been gradually loosening capital controls. The pace is unfixed and complicated by the need to introduce other reforms at the same time, such as interest rate deregulation. According to the PBOC's new rules, the currency could rise or fall by as much as 10% over the course of a week. Relaxing exchange controls means greater volatility, which in turn justifies lower asset prices.

4. RENMINBI ARBITRAGE AND SHADOW BANKING

Mainland banks set their own exchange rates for the yuan against the US dollar for the first time in early July 2014 in deals with retail clients. Daily rates for retail banking clients could experience some fluctuation as banks start to set their own rates. This could lead to move volatility in daily rates for retail banking customers. Exchange rates on retail deals will be guided by interbank market rates which are subject to controls such as the midpoint trading rate set each day by the central bank. The midpoint trading rate is set by the regulators rather than the market. This is part of a series of piecemeal reforms that are pushing banks to compete more actively for foreign currency deposits. The mainland previously lifted retail yuan exchange controls involving currencies other than the dollar. The PBOC removed the cap on deposit rates for foreign currency accounts in Shanghai, allowing banks to set the rate according to market terms.

Between February and May 2014, Renminbi fell almost 4% in both onshore and offshore markets, ending years of steady appreciation that had led many investors and companies to view it as a one-way bet – in contrast to the uncertain returns offered by more volatile emerging markets currencies. Currency depreciation could cause credit stress and a rise in

---

[104] A sudden devaluation was preferred over a slow-motion slide as the latter risks entrenching long-term depreciation expectations, which might create a vicious cycle of capital outflows.

[105] Lingling Wei, "PBOC Frees Up Credit as Economic Slowdown Worsens", *The Wall Street Journal*, 26 August 2015, p.13.

investors' perceived risk premiums, which can lead to higher market interest rates and reduce the effectiveness of PBOC monetary easing.

The depreciation, engineered by the PBOC, through its daily fixing and outright intervention in the market, was widely seen as a warning to speculators, especially those companies in China who had bet heavily on Renminbi continuing to rise, instead of hedging currency exposure. Large net hot-money outflows, which tend to occur in tandem with market expectations of CNY/USD depreciation, can push the balance of payments into a deficit. Chinese corporates have significantly increased their foreign currency borrowing in recent years. Chinese companies have tried to build up dollar deposits, and investors have become much more nervous of betting on long-term appreciation. The currency is under pressure in offshore markets. The PBOC's fixings suggest that it favours a stable exchange rate even though the broad-based dollar rally would make it easy to guide the currency weaker. This appreciation in the face of weak growth and a dollar rally is "doubly dangerous".

Firms may make a profit because of the hedges. The derivatives that underlie some structured-products are based on the offshore yuan and are bought mostly in Hong Kong and Taiwan. The most popular among the derivative products is the so-called "target redemption forward". In 2013, the first year of executing these derivative products, contracts in the value of US$250 billion were signed.[106] The product is a leveraged bet that pays out every month in which the currency keeps rising. Losses, however, can begin to mount quickly when the yuan falls to a specific level. The steady gains promoted investors to take large positions in the yuan.

Renminbi is now traded on both onshore and offshore markets. The Hong Kong version of Renminbi is better known as CNH. The offshore trades mainly take place on the Hong Kong Interbank Market,[107] and trade without the restrictions imposed onshore by the Chinese authorities. In addition, the offshore trading of the yuan is not subject to the strict movements set by the PBOC for yuan trades on the mainland. This means that the offshore Renminbi can trade freely and is the focus of international investors. The onshore trading, known as CNY, takes place through the China Foreign Exchange Trade System, which is managed by

---

[106] "Yuan's Sharp Fall Threatens Hedges", *The Wall Street Journal*, 26 February 2014, C4.

[107] CNH is often traded at a premium to its onshore equivalent, CNY. The premium has swung to a discount. Up to 7 December 2011, CNH was trading at 6.3745 against the dollar, 0.15% weaker than the onshore rate of 6.3651 dollar. Simon Rabinovitch and Robert Cookson, "Renminbi Hit Amid Economy Fears", *Financial Times*, 8 December 2011, p 22.

the PBOC. In mainland China, investors use the official onshore rate, or CNY, which however is limited by a daily trading band. The PBOC sets a fixing daily rate against the dollar around which the onshore Renminbi is permitted to fall or gain 1% a day. CNH is often traded at a premium to its onshore equivalent, CNY. As a result, both interest and exchange rates can vary hugely between Hong Kong and the mainland, which provides an opportunity to market players for arbitrating the two markets.[108]

Partly due to the wild fluctuations in the offshore Renminbi exchange rate, the Hong Kong Monetary Authority (HKMA)[109] is increasing scrutiny over foreign exchange deals under the Shanghai conversion window, a mechanism by which the Bank of China (HK), the designated Renminbi clearing bank in Hong Kong, can purchase or sell Renminbi to other banks at the mainland exchange rate to support genuine trade flows from its corporate customers. The Real Time Gross Settlement System was upgraded from the Renminbi Settlement System in June 2007.[110] The banks would be forced to unwind deals with the Renminbi clearing bank if the underlying transaction is found to be a "non-eligible trade transaction." In addition, banks that square more than RMB 20 million of positions with the clearing bank in a month are required to supply the HKMA with evidence of their top 10 Renminbi cross-border transactions to verify compliance with the rules.[111]

Interest rate disparities between Hong Kong and mainland China have played a large role. The gap can reach as much as three percentage points on three month interbank rates. For money borrowed in Hong Kong and invested in China's shadow banking system, the differential can be much wider. US or Hong Kong dollars borrowed at 2.5% can yield almost 2%

---

[108] Robert Cookson, "Banks Warned on HK Renminbi Trade" *Financial Times*, 10 November 2011, p.24.

[109] HKMA is a de facto central bank in Hong Kong. However, Hong Kong does not have real control over its monetary policy. From a policy point of view, Hong Kong may be a colony of the US thanks to Hong Kong's currency peg to the US dollar, being at the mercy of US interest rates for decades. Similarly, Hang Seng index is linked intrinsically to what's going on in the US. For instance, Hong Kong is also experiencing a classic credit bubble in the latest financial crisis because of the fact that $130 billion has flowed into Hong Kong since the first round of quantitative easing was announced in 2008, and has resulted in more than twice that amount of credit growth. Josh Noble, "Poor-performing Hong Kong Stocks are Slaves to US Policy", *Financial Times*, 10 June 2013 (online).

[110] Gary Cheung, "Yuan Clearing Beats Volume in Hong Kong Dollars", *South China Morning Post*, 17 June 2013 (online).

[111] Robert Cookson, "Banks Warned on HK Renminbi Trade", *Financial Times*, 10 November 2011, p.24.

more if invested in wealth management products in China, and 6% more in riskier trust products.[112] A rising Renminbi can push those returns up further. Over-invoicing for exports from mainland China to Hong Kong has operated as an important channel guiding these financial flows into China. It is natural to see that exports to Hong Kong have surged to the highest level since 1995. The Chinese government has been trying to bring the over-invoicing under control. New banking rules in China also stipulate a reduction in the ratio of foreign currency loans to foreign current deposits. Domestic banks are likely to buy US dollars in order to satisfy these rules. The risk is that inflows turn quickly to outflows given the fact that the US dollar is likely to strengthen against other major currencies, which could contribute to a liquidity crisis in China's fragile shadow banking system.

The depth and size of the onshore Chinese debt market has been increasingly attractive to large institutional investors. Compared to the dim sum bond market, which is subject to international legal and regulatory standards and offers much simpler tax and repatriation rules for those seeking to exit investments, onshore markets have better liquidity and higher yields. Domestic bond markets have a larger pool of bonds and far longer durations. Even with a booming debt market, Chinese borrowers still rush to offshore markets for borrowing. Moody's has restated its negative outlook on Hong Kong's banking system, citing concerns about risks to lenders from rapidly expanding exposure to mainland borrowers.[113]

Chinese companies then bet on a stronger Renminbi by borrowing dollars offshore, mainly in Hong Kong, and then remitted dollars into mainland China. Some Chinese companies may be using trade finance as a way to borrow money more cheaply offshore, evading strict restrictions on lending at home. Chinese regulators cracked down on credit growth by preventing financial institutions from disguising corporate loans as interbank loans. A Chinese company can circumvent the capital control rule by getting a yuan-denominated letter of credit from its Hong Kong subsidiary, and using the proceeds to obtain a loan in Hong Kong for a lower interest rate. China's benchmark interest rate is 6% and the rate in Hong Kong is 0.5%. Savvy Chinese businesses are using letters of credit as a way to borrow at a lower rate outside of China.

Global investors take bets on Renminbi through Hong Kong. The

---

112 "China Money Flows: the Ins and Outs", *Financial Times*, 6 June 2013 (online).

113 Joyce Ng, "HSBC Backtracks on Occupy Central as Reason for Downgrading Hong Kong's Outlook", *South China Morning Post*, 7 July 2014 (online).

yuan's appreciation makes eventual repayment easier and offshore interest rates lower than Chinese rates. The widening gap between the CNH rate and the CNY rate, even though both are tied to each other, may have prodded the PBOC into action. It is an effective means to make investors more cautious before betting on sustained appreciation. Caution itself is a good means to slow Renminbi's rise. By making Renminbi regain volatility, the PBOC is forcing people borrowing offshore to hedge their risk. Speculators would have to unwind one-way bets on Renminbi's continued appreciation, and showed reluctance to pile into the yuan. Some investors have started to bet against the yuan through the options market.[114] Ultimately, this will work against Renminbi's endless appreciation.[115]

After the devaluation of Renminbi in August 2015, Renminbi's value in Hong Kong has been persistently weaker than the more tightly controlled rate on the mainland. The Hong Kong rate is 0.5% lower against the dollar than the onshore Renminbi rate. The offshore Renminbi market has been used by the PBOC as a way of stimulating the currency's international status. According to the Bank of International Settlements, daily turnover in the spot offshore market was 70% of the US$20 billion a day onshore market.[116] Two Renminbi markets work well when both exchange rates rise in value against the dollar. Chinese exporters are then willing to have offshore dollars exchange for Renminbi onshore. Similarly, holders of offshore Renminbi deposits and Renminbi-denominated bonds are also willing to own assets in an appreciating currency. The situation can be very different when the offshore Renminbi is weak. Chinese importers are more willing to sell Renminbi onshore in order to have hard currency. The Renminbi devaluation may align the two exchange rates. But the real effect is that the devaluation chokes offshore liquidity to kill speculation and triggers capital flight.

This round of currency decline is more closely connected to the persistence of higher interest rates in China than elsewhere. Benchmark interest rates in Shanghai have long been three to five percentage points higher than similar rates in London. This in turn promotes short-term capital to flow back to China, much of which is disguised as export earnings. The PBOC has largely accommodated the yuan's rise within its daily

---

114 Lingling Wei and Nicole Hong, "Yuan Trading Band Doubled", *The Wall Street Journal*, 17 March 2014, C3.

115 Currently, Chinese companies have heavily hedged in covering their exposure to dollar earnings. Exporters are actively buying derivatives as they earn dollars but pay costs in yuan.

116 "China's Currency Problem in Hong Kong", *International New York Times*, 22 September 2015, p.18.

band by raising its morning reference rate by a similar amount. Chinese government's tolerance of a stronger Renminbi may reflect its larger reform ambitions. The Chinese government is planning to work out an operational plan for easing capital controls. An undervalued yuan can attract a destabilizing influx of foreign money under a loosened capital control regime. In this sense, a stronger yuan is a necessary precondition for looser controls.

Cutting the interest rate may be of limited efficacy. Rather it may lead to more capital outflows, which is a monetary tightening indeed. To the contrary, the reserve-requirement reduction is the means to keep capital from leaving the country and to boost market liquidity. China's capital controls can prove more porous than expected. Foreign exchange reserves fell by US$315 billion in one year up to July 2015.[117] The central bank even took a step toward interest rate liberalization by removing the upper limit on interest rates for fixed-term deposits of more than one year.[118] Apparently, China has entered into a stage of deflation in its economic downturn. To maintain economic stability in the short run, the central bank inevitably needs to ease credit. However, the central bank still refrained from fully giving up its control on deposit rates for fear of driving up interest rates and prompting more risk-taking behaviour by banks amid a slowing economy.

The exchange rate manoeuvering in August 2015 was backfiring. The long-term strengthening of China's real exchange rate reflects deep historical forces, such as China's rapid economic growth, stronger labour laws, and shrinking working age population. The yuan closed trading on 27 May 2013 at 6.12 to the dollar, 35% stronger than its June 2003 rate.[119] The latest surge in Renminbi's normal exchange rate is puzzling as it comes at a time of disappointing growth, falling inflation and flagging exports. According to the Bank for International Settlements, the yuan has become 15% less competitive on a trade-weighted basis since 2010.[120] The yuan appreciation engineered by the PBOC shifts the balance between exports and imports. While the reform may accelerate the drive towards domestic demand through the services sector as opposed to export demand in the manufacturing sector, the further reform may also

---

[117] Martin Wolf, "China Risks An Economic Discontinuity", *Financial Times*, 2 September 2015 (online).

[118] Neil Gough, "Stock Slide Extended Amid Doubts about China", *International New York Times*, 25 August 2015, p.15.

[119] "The Cheapest Thing Going is Gone", *The Economist*, 15 June 2013.

[120] Nick Edwards, "China Faces Test of Nerve on Reform", *South China Morning Post*, 16 July 2013 (online).

have some negative consequences: higher currency costs making it harder to dump excess capacity overseas, the yuan's gain against currencies in other emerging economies eroding China's currency advantages.[121] As a matter of fact, a rise in the value of the yuan against a wide swathe of currencies from countries that compete with mainland manufacturers as well as customers for the goods their production lines churn out makes the shift of economic growth model more painful and difficult. The credit crunch is just one simple example showing that China is now experiencing pains brought about by domestic economic restructuring.

5. INTERNATIONALIZATION OF RENMINBI

In the short term, allowing Renminbi to trade more freely appears to be a step that could help China to liberalize its interest rates. From China's viewpoint, the yuan is approaching its fair market value as the country's trade surpluses continue to shrink.[122] However, the US disputed the notion that the currency is at equilibrium.[123] In the long run, Renminbi is on the path of appreciation as long as China is able to generate current account surpluses, attract large net foreign direct investment flows and accumulate excessive reserves.[124] The newly injected volatility and uncertainty over the yuan is one area where China is a pushing ahead with a campaign of wide-ranging financial overhauls, which are likely to redefine the nation's state-driven growth model and to reverberate in economies far beyond China's borders.

Renminbi's exchange rate regime needs to be put in the context of Renminbi's internationalization. The fact that China sits in the centre

---

[121] It has been calculated that the yuan's rally against the Indonesian rupiah and the Japanese yen had reached about 23% and 33% respectively since late 2011. Nick Edwards, "China Faces Test of Nerve on Reform", *South China Morning Post*, 16 July 2013 (online).

[122] It is however estimated by Lombard Street Research that the renminbi is between 15 and 25% above fair value. Diana Choyleva, "Weaker Renminbi Could be China's Subprime", *Financial Times*, 8 April 2014, p.22.

[123] William Mauldin and Eric Morath, "U.S. Raps China Over Currency Moves", *The Wall Street Journal*, 16 April 2014, A9 (citing the US report "The Chinese authorities have been unwilling to allow an appreciation large enough to bring the currency to market equilibrium, opting instead for a gradual adjustment which has now been partially reversed").

[124] This may suggest that more weakness of yuan could be lethal for arbitrage and leverage strategies based on expectations that the currency was certain to keep rising.

of a globalized production, supply and container cargo network should theoretically help consolidate the status of Renminbi. The rise of Renminbi heralds a major change in the global financial system. Renminbi will be an important international transaction currency in the next decade and may become a significant reserve currency alongside the dollar and other developed currencies.[125] According to Arvind Subramanian of the Peterson Institute for International Economics, there are now more currencies that move in tune with Renminbi, eclipsing the US dollar as the world's *ipso facto* reference currency.[126] In the next 30-odd years to 2040, China may achieve the internationalization of Renminbi through a 3-step strategy. The first step is to push the rise of the yuan in neighbouring countries. Then Renminbi will be extended to other Asian countries. The last step is a full convertibility of the currency.[127]

China is taking steps to internationalize Renminbi by broadening the use of Renminbi among international investors. Dominance of the global economy goes hand-in-hand with dominance of the global monetary system. In a global context, the changes in the international reserve currency also represent the shifts in global powers. Recently, US dollars, the yen and Australian dollars have become directly exchangeable with Renminbi. Given China's rise to be the world's largest economy, it is in its strategic interest to press ahead with full currency convertibility. Controls on the capital account are being liberalized to enable Renminbi to emerge as a global rival to the dollar. Along with China's economic growth, Renminbi will attain reserve currency status sooner rather than later. However, whether China will obtain reserve currency status for Renminbi will be a long journey. China may accomplish basic or partial capital account convertibility in the near future, followed by a full convertibility.

Dismantling the protection under Renminbi's non-convertibility on the capital account is not an easy task. A reserve Renminbi will be fully convertible on both capital and current accounts, which may expose China to global capital as well as global financial crisis. The protection served

---

125 The BRICS emerging powers sought a deal on setting up an infrastructure-focused development bank that would rival Western-backed institutions such as the World Bank. This can be a way of tapping China's vast financial resources. Aside from the development bank, the group will try to establish a foreign exchange reserve pool worth as much as US$240 billion to be drawn on in times of financial crisis. "BRICS Nations Seek to Establish Rival to World Bank", *South China Morning Post*, 29 March 2013 (online).

126 Andrew Leung, "A Fully Convertible Yuan Is Possible By 2020, But Only If Reforms Can Succeed", *South China Morning Post*, 22 July 2013, A13.

127 Reuters, "China Adviser Sees Yuan Supplant US Dollar in 30 Years: Paper", *South China Morning Post*, 27 May 2013 (online).

China well during the Asian financial crisis in 1997–98 and the recent financial crisis. Free capital flows may also destabilize domestic banks, create liquidity bubbles in a good economy or choke off the credit supply when the economy deteriorates. To a certain extent, a freely convertible Renminbi may be a source of economic volatility. The government may lose control over Renminbi as maintaining a currency peg in the face of massive capital inflows is technically difficult. Meanwhile, the increasing demand for Renminbi may push up its value and make export-oriented growth model less sustainable.

Whilst China is moving faster to globalize Renminbi, the currency only accounts for less than 1% of the global currency trade (compared with 86% for the US dollar).[128] Renminbi is only the world's 14th most widely used currency with a market share of 0.57%.[129] In 2013, the yuan has jumped to the ninth-most-traded international currency,[130] leaping to the ninth place from 17th in 2010.[131] Daily trading in the yuan tripled to US$120 billion in the same period.[132] Internationalization of Renminbi is a clear policy and irreversible direction of the Chinese government. It was pledged by the ruling Communist Party in its 18th National Congress in November 2012 to further promote free movement of capital in and out of China for investment purposes and make the exchange rate more market based.[133] The PBOC has outlined its plan to focus on the reform of convertibility.[134] Likely, as part of the Renminbi exchange rate formation mechanism, the foreign exchange policy needs to be further liberalized, with the daily trading band for the yuan gradually widened and then eventually eliminated, and the capital account increasingly open with the bond market leading the way.[135] Similarly, China will steadily push forward market-based libersalization of interest rate. Renminbi's internationalization,

---

[128] The Bank for International Settlements Report. Alice Ross, "CCB Issues 'Dim-Sum' Bonds in London", *Financial Times*, 30 November 2012 (online).

[129] Reuters, "Yuan Transactions Tail Off in US, Flat Growth for Year", *South China Morning Post*, 23 January 2013 (online).

[130] Brian Spegele, "UK, China to Increase Yuan's Role", *The Wall Street Journal*, 16 October 2013, C2.

[131] Nicole Hong, "Yuan Hits Milestone in Trade Deals," *The Wall Street Journal*, 4 December 2013, C1.

[132] Ibid.

[133] Bloomberg, "More Convertible Yuan Next Goal, China's Central Bank Chief Says", *South China Morning Post*, 18 November 2012 (online).

[134] Ibid.

[135] Credit Agricole Report, cited in Toh Han Shih, "Winds of Change 'to Blow Through' China's Economy", *South China Morning Post*, 27 November 2012 (online).

that is, the yuan's convertibility, is more likely to be dependent on China's own speed of liberalizing its financial and currency markets.[136] The more quickly China liberalizes its currency, the more quickly Renminbi would broaden its horizon.[137]

The PBOC Governor, Zhou Xiaochuan, indicated in a sideline conference to the annual assembly of the National People's Congress in early 2014 that the internationalization of Renminbi is a long and gradual process, and its acceptance as a world currency is up to the international market.[138] The market on the other hand expects the yuan to continue to appreciate up to 6.000 by the end of 2014.[139]

Nevertheless, Renminbi will not become a global currency if China's financial market remains out of sync with international norms. This is why the reform of the Chinese financial market and its regulatory regime has been given great importance in *China 2030*, a World Bank report jointly undertaken with the Development Research Centre of China's State Council. Open and well-regulated markets, transparent governance and a solid banking system are needed to make Chinese currency rise to dominate. To get its currency generally accepted around the world, China needs more than a widespread international trade network. In the past several decades, investors and trade partners relied on a "Beijing put", a policy option that provides assurance that a minimum level of growth will be attained. In order to achieve a high growth rate to ensure it remains on track, the government took an intervening approach to cure the economic pains: freeing up credit, introducing subsidies, and investing in large projects. It must have deep, sophisticated and well-regulated capital markets, which are freely open to foreign investors. It must have a credible and transparent governance structure, with policymakers that can demonstrate a track record of successful financial management. It must have solid economic prospects and a strong and stable banking system. However, currently, China' capital markets are underdeveloped and

---

136 It has been reported that the State Council is working on an operational plan to achieve full convertibility, and the plan will outline steps towards a market-based exchange rate system and capital account liberalisation. Jane Cai, "Yuan Heads for Key Level Against Dollar", *South China Morning Post*, 5 June 2013 (online).

137 Some market observers estimated that a full convertibility of renminbi is likely within five years. "Dim Sum Bond Sales Double as New Elite Back Global Yuan", *South China Morning Post*, 30 November 2012 (online).

138 Lingling Wei and Aniani Trevidi, "China: Liberalized Rates Are Coming", *The Wall Street Journal*, 11 March 2014, C4.

139 "All Eyes on Beijing as Yuan Keeps Sliding", *The Wall Street Journal*, 21 March 2014, C3.

closed to outsiders and its banking system and economy are fragile. The government maintains tight control over large aspects of the economy, including interest rates and exchange rate. The state's heavy-handed role is distorting prices, intensifying inefficiencies and giving an unfair advantage to state-run enterprises, government-backed banks and exporters. If the yuan cannot be relied upon to fix and maintain its value in the marketplace, the yuan's eventual internationalization may be imperiled. Viewed thus, Renminbi internationalization is a tool to help force through reforms in China by opening the country's capital account, and later on, financial markets.

12. "A tale of three zones" and financial reforms

After the Communist Party of China's (CCP) Third Plenum of the 11th Congress in 1978, the Chinese government instituted some political changes: four special economic zones were established in 1979, the development of the coastal region was set forth as national policy in the Sixth Five-Year Plan (1981–1985),[1] 14 coastal cities were opened in 1984; three deltas, the Lower Yangtze delta, the Pearl River Delta and the Xiamen-Zhangzhou-Quanzhou Triangle, were declared as Coastal Economic Development Zones, and Hainan was established as a special economic province.[2] These measures of selective territorial deregulation including special economic zones, coastal open cities and central economic cities allowed more than two dozen sub-provincial cities to implement more autonomous and preferential economic policies.

The key objective of the set-up of special economic zones is to attract foreign investment, capital and technology. A series of preferential policies has been granted to the special economic zones in the past three decades so that they can attract more foreign investment, advanced technology and managerial skills. The underlying rationale of the economic zone model is a "trickle-down" strategy not only diffusing growth but also governance or policymaking experience from the coastal to other areas. Therefore, these zones are labeled as "windows" to implement more liberal and deregulatory economic policies, and are used as "corridors" through which developmental ideologies and experiences can be diffused into other localities.

Since the outbreak of the latest financial crisis, China has established

1 *The Sixth Five-Year Plan of the People's Republic of China for Economic and Social Development* (1981–1985) (Beijing: Foreign Languages Press 1984).

2 There are numerous economic and technological development zones, bonded zones, high-tech science parks, state-approved tourism and leisure zones, export-oriented industrial processing zones in China. They play different roles. For example, high-tech parks are devoted to manufacturing industries such as electronics, machinery and biochemical products and these products are more for domestic sales and technology transfer. The state tourism and leisure zone is empowered to provide lower tax rate (24%) for tourism enterprises located in the zone and to approve projects on golf clubs and foreign-invested department stores.

three new zones in Wenzhou, Zhejiang Province, Qianhai, Shenzhen and Pudong New Area and Shanghai respectively. Different from the old-generation special economic zones, these three new zones are armed with a new task of deepening financial reforms in these areas. This chapter looks into new financial policies adopted in these three zones, and analyses some pitfalls while more liberal policies are being implemented. Sections 1 to 3 will respectively study the comprehensive financial reform zone in Wenzhou, Qianhai economic zone in Shenzhen, and the pilot free trade zone in Shanghai. A conclusion follows in Section 4.

1. COMPREHENSIVE FINANCIAL REFORM ZONE IN WENZHOU

Wenzhou, well known for its widespread and successful private sector based on family and hometown networks, came into the spotlight in 2012. Systemic risks in underground banking system have turned into a so-called "runaway" debt crisis – at least 80% business people were reported to have disappeared, committed suicide or been declared bankrupt in early 2012 after borrowers' failing to repay loans or operators of underground banks being unable to repay deposits.[3] The debt crisis underscores the fragility of private-sector finances as well as unregulated shadow financing system across the nation.

The shadow banking system in Wenzhou played an important role in flourishing private businesses, the strength of which has won Wenzhou a reputation as being a national hub for private businesses and a hotbed of entrepreneurship. Zhejiang Province itself is an economically developed region, and the key feature of its economy is the high proportion of privately owned enterprises. In 2010, for example, privately owned enterprises accounted for 73.7% of Zhejiang's GDP, the highest percentage in all provinces in China. This percentage is even higher than that in Shanghai (47.8%) and Guangdong (41.1%).[4]

According to the Chinese government's estimate, the total outstanding loans to underground banks in Wenzhou were 110 billion yuan.[5]

---

[3] Jane Cai, "Bad Loan Rate Adds to Woes in Wenzhou", *South China Morning Post*, 5 November 2011, B3.

[4] Bureau of Statistics of Zhejiang Province, A Comparative Study of the Development of Privately Owned Enterprises in Zhejiang Province (24 February 2011).

[5] Daniel Ren, "Zhejiang Helps Lenders Aid Small Firms", *South China Morning Post*, 9 November 2011, B1.

This eventually made them strapped for cash in the entrepreneurial hub. The non-performing loan ratio of financial institutions in Wenzhou rose 0.18 percentage points to 0.55% in September 2011 from August 2011.[6] The non-performing loan balance in local financial institutions reached about RMB 1.1 billion in October 2011.[7] This month-on-month pickup in the past ten years underscores the difficulty private businesses are encountering in financing their businesses.

China's efforts to tighten credit in the financial crisis have starved small enterprises and entrepreneurs of badly needed finance. More private businesses found difficulty in raising funds from state-owned banks which have been reluctant to lend due to the lack of collateral from small firms. The macroeconomic status forced private firms to finance their business through the local underground lending market that usually charges usurious rates of interest. Private savers, pushed away by negative interest rates, are lending directly in the underground market, investing in structured notes and other shadow banking products at higher return rates.

Among others, rising borrowing costs (including soaring black market interest rates), skyrocketing operational costs (including rentals, raw material prices and labour costs),[8] the strengthened yuan, slackening external demand (that is, declining exports to the US and Europe) as well as the Chinese government's sudden tighter monetary policy are the root cause of a collapse in the underground financial system. As export growth dropped sharply and the economy turned slower, the situation became even worse, which resulted in the close-down of many enterprises. When the borrowers defaulted on loans, declared bankruptcy or simply disappeared, the shadow banking system was severely hit. As the underground banking system in essence is a private network of individual savers or private investors, the worsened situation may escalate the debt problem into chaos and eventually threaten social stability.

Chinese business people have a long tradition of borrowing money

---

[6] It was reported that Wenzhou's non-performing loan ratios were three times above the national average."China's Leadership – Appearance and Reality", *Financial Times*, 16 November 2012 (online).

[7] Jane Cai, "Bad Loan Rate Adds to Woes in Wenzhou", *South China Morning Post*, 5 November 2011, B3.

[8] High inflation rates made export-product industries suffer huge pressure. It was said that rising labour costs, rentals and raw material prices would make manufacturers easily suffer losses of 10 to 20% on taking up orders from foreign purchasers. Other export-orientated areas such as Guangdong Province also encountered similar problems and saw exports plunge, poor profit figures, and slow economic growth rates. He Huifeng and Fiona Tam, "Slowdown in Shenzhen Mirrors National Gloom", *South China Morning Post*, 29 March 2012, A7.

from family-and-friend pools. The informal lending market has fed many entrepreneurial businesses which may not be able to finance from banks due to their low creditworthiness according to official standards. Take one example. Rotating savings and credit associations is a basic finance system at the grassroots level. The associations are popular in China given the limited access for private entrepreneurs to the formal financial system. For instance, in 1998, only 0.4% of all loans were extended by the formal banking system to the private sector. The percentage only slightly increased to 0.8% if loans extended by officially sanctioned non-banking financial institutions to "private and independent businesses" are included.[9] Empirical research has attributed the relative popularity of micro-financing associations to the structure of the local economy and demographic trends in these localities. These localities often experienced relative economic success in the reform period and hosted impressively performing township and village enterprises. The similarity of these southern coastal cities is a strong private sector compared to other localities.

The popularity of underground lending is a market reaction to the need of capital-starved firms underserved by banks as well as the affluence of idle funds owned by capital-rich firms or individuals. Nevertheless, the legality of these private lending institutions or pools is uncertain under Chinese law depending on the source of funding and arrangement of interest rates. The funding in these pools is evolving all the time with new deposits coming to cover interest to earlier investors.

The underground lending market has more severe systemic risks compared to conventional bank lending. In usual bank lending, the systemic risks are easier to contain as cash flow can be seen from the lender to the customer. In the informal lending market, once the loan is out, the lender will lose control of cash flow as the loan will continuously flow from one borrower to the other and there will be a long chain of debt. Any borrower's failure to repay may bring about a Pandora effect to the entire chain of debt. Besides, the lender in an informal lending business, built on a lattice of interlocked credit, is usually a pool of local residents or firms, borrowing money from banks and other private lenders with the aim of arbitraging interest rates. These lenders are only pursuing a higher return rate. Underground lenders often demand annual interest of from 20 to 40% or higher, many times the official lending rate of 6.56% a year. The rate may even rocket when the new bank loans decrease. In order to repay

[9] "Fourth Quarter Financial Statistics", *Jinrong Shibao*, 25 January 1999, p.1.

the loan, the borrower may have to borrow new loans to pay interest and roll over the principal.

Tighter credit and falling housing prices in Wenzhen have further led to a wave of mortgage defaults. Mortgage loans in Wenzhou, as reported, totaled 247.7 billion yuan by the end of July 2013 and non-performing loans totaled 5.29 billion yuan.[10] Speculation drove up local property prices, triggering a government clampdown with the aim of stabilizing the market. The loose credit environment in the past several years caused many people in Wenzhou to be excessively leveraged. In August 2013, new-home prices in 70 Chinese cities rose at their fastest pace since January 2011, according to official data. At its peak, average home prices in Wenzhou were almost at par with cities such as Beijing and Shanghai and 160% above second-tier cities. Known for abundant lending fueled by trust-based financing networks without collateral, Wenzhou has posted declines in housing prices every month since August 2011 as a result of the liquidity crunch and government curbs on multiple home purchases. This made Wenzhou the only city among the 70 cities included in the office price survey whose housing prices declined in the previous two years. In the economic downturn, some people are then forced to sell off their assets. The price drop suggests that those who heavily borrowed to make purchases may owe more than the houses are worth. In the last resort some may to give up their properties. It is reported that homeowners in Wenzhou have abandoned 580 homes and there are an additional 15 cases of mortgage in default.

Wenzhou's problems indeed took place in other parts of China since private enterprises heavily rely on underground borrowing rather than banks to operate. It has been estimated that outstanding private loans stand at 4 trillion yuan or 8% of total lending in the mainland.[11] 6,555 mircocredit firms had outstanding loans of 653.7 billion yuan by the end of March 2013.[12] The situation may turn worse along with the tightening policy on the real estate market as most of the informal lending was pumped into a nationwide property boom that is showing signs of slowing. The bad-loan problem is far more serious among private credit firms than formal banks because of looser risk control and larger exposure to small companies. When the economy grows slowly and liquidity is not

---

10 Esther Fung, "Debt-Laden Homeowners Bolt in Chinese City", *The Wall Street Journal*, 27 September 2013, C3.

11 Bloomberg, "A City Built on Borrowed Time", *South China Morning Post*, 11 November 2011, B10.

12 Jane Cai, "China Microlenders Get Death Threats as They Try to Recover Bad Loans", *South China Morning Post*, 8 June 2013 (online).

plentiful, microcredit firms' businesses are severely hit. Microcredit firms' reluctance or inability to provide fresh loans to small- and medium-sized firms would endanger them and dent employment. The increased mistrust among informal lenders or roadside lenders may push for a credit squeeze and eventually more widespread bankruptcies of small firms.

The collapse of the shadow banking system and a wave of large-scale bankruptcies in Wenzhou have shaken social stability, about which the Chinese government and the CCP, the ruling party in China, are the most concerned. Though small in size or economic significance, private companies indeed account for 60% of economic output and 80% of jobs. To rescue the private sector from collapse is critically important to the Chinese economy.

The central government has lent some support to embattled companies. Ex-Premier Wen Jiabao pledged stronger financial support to troubled businesses on his visit to Wenzhou on 4 October 2011, urging banks to lend more to small companies,[13] and in April 2012 voiced criticism that "our banks make profits far too easily".[14] Thereafter, the State Council, China's cabinet, has been trying to reform or even overhaul the banking sector and curb shadow banking (that is, avoiding a large amount of domestic deposits being steered from bank loans into opaque, off-balance-sheet and risk-laden vehicles) by allowing Wenzhou to test how to channel more funding to the private sectors.[15]

Wenzhou became a pilot area for financial reform in China. In March 2012, the State Council approved Wenzhou as the pilot city of a financial reform, through which it hopes to tame the underground lending market and act as a laboratory for national implementation. Wenzhou since then has been advancing efforts to build a "comprehensive financial reform zone" to legalize the local underground banking system. The policy options include encouraging local entrepreneurs to set up small financial firms and alleviate the cash crush, buying into local banks and investing into other financial products such as private equity firms,[16] channeling private money into local businesses through formal institutions, mainly small credit firms, to stem a surge in bad loans, implementing a trial program that would allow individuals to make direct overseas investment

---

13 "Fearful Symmetry", *The Economist*, 19 November 2011.

14 Simon Rabinovitch, "Chinese Banks Face Scrutiny Over Profits", *Financial Times*, 31 October 2012 (online).

15 Reuters, "Shadow Bank Reform Needed to Fight Bubbles", *South China Morning Post*, 12 January 2012, B3.

16 Daniel Ren, "Fears Wenzhou Reforms Could Increase Risks", *South China Morning Post*, 30 April 2012, B3.

in yuan, offering easier access to bank loans, imposing a cap on private-lending interest rates in Wenzhou and a crackdown on violent *gaolidai* (a Chinese term for a loan shark).

In addition, Wenzhou wants to set up a financial exchange through which borrowers and lenders can do their matching exercises. A 5 billion yuan emergency fund was launched by the Wenzhou government to help private businesses.[17] The other initiative is to allow the establishment of a private bank, which will be an experiment to formalize the large number of illegal underground banks in Wenzhou that were lending at usurious rates to cash-starved private business.[18]

Wenzhou Private Finance Index was launched in December 2012 to increase transparency around the private capital market. The Index makes it easier to compare and monitor the interest rates charged on informal loans registered with the Wenzhou financing service centers. The Index tracks local private financing interest rates. The first index released on 7 November 2012 showed that the private financing interest rate in the last week of November was at 21.43%;[19] it remained at 19.91% in December 2013, down 1.12 percentage points from the beginning of 2013, because of growing competition among private lenders and banks increasing support to micro- and small-sized firms. The Index will be updated weekly and is to complement a similar index announced by the PBOC in May 2013.

Zhejiang Province took more concrete steps to ease restrictions on microcredit companies so as to bolster lending to cash-dry small firms. Meanwhile, local governments are gradually allowing providers of small loans to raise more capital for loans. Small lenders are allowed to borrow as much 100% of their own capital to fund lending businesses. Previously, this percentage was 50%.[20] These measures are aimed at relaxing the controls on small-loan firms so as to help them function well in sustaining a healthier financial system. However, these measures do not seem adequate to address the difficulties microcredit firms face. The China Banking Regulatory Commission (CBRC), China's banking regulator, did allow domestic firms and residents to set up microcredit firms in 2006 and these firms could have offered petty loans to clients. According to the PBOC, the mainland had 3,366 microcredit firms by the end of June 2011 with

---

[17] Daniel Ren, "Zhejiang Helps Lenders Aid Small Firms", *South China Morning Post*, 9 November 2011, B1.

[18] Simon Rabinovitch, "China's Stores Check out Chance to Try Banking", *Financial Times*, 15 October 2013, p.18.

[19] Reuters, "Wenzhou Launches Private Lending Index", *South China Morning Post*, 10 December 2012 (online).

[20] Daniel Ren, "Zhejiang Helps Lenders Aid Small Firms".

outstanding loans of 287.5 billion yuan in total.[21] Although this was a bold step in liberalizing the lending market, small-loan firms are required to comply with some rigid rules such as having a registered capital of no less than 50 million yuan, taking no deposits from residents or firms and offering loans at interest rates a maximum of four times rates set by the central bank. These rules make the operation of Zhejiang's 134 small-loan firms (with total net assets of 23 billion yuan)[22] technically difficult. Under the more relaxed rules, small-loan firms can borrow 11.5 billion yuan to replenish their lending businesses.[23] However, some economists expressed suspicion about the real effect of these measures taken by central and local governments. This is largely because the banking system is dominated by state-owned banks which are seen as biased against privately owned businesses and are always reluctant to extend credit to these firms.

As part of its efforts to legalize the underground banking system and liberalize capital outflow, Wenzhou published a long-awaited guideline to further financial reform. According to the new rules, Wenzhou is to create a registration system for private capital through which private firms and individuals can participate in the so-called "sunshine private lending" scheme. This may improve liquidity in the capital market and more private capital could be lent out to individuals and businesses.[24] The Wenzhou government also set up intermediary firms that will act as "matchmakers" for borrowers and lenders. This is a very substantial move which effectively relaxes the rigid financial rules that only financial institutions can take deposits and lend. The new rules also touch upon some aspects of the capital control regime. For instance, Wenzhou residents are encouraged to undertake "direct investments" abroad under a looser foreign exchange control, which is currently subject to the rigid foreign exchange control rules. The relaxation of capital control rules may lead to misuse of the funds and money can be poured into Hong Kong stock market since some of the H-shares are less expensive but more profitable than the mainland's yuan-denominated A shares. If these rules were effectively implemented, the new guideline may eventually transform Wenzhou into the nation's financial services center. Wenzhou's success in legalizing underground credit would help China's fast-track legislation on private lending.

These measures seem similar to those currently taken in the EU.

---

21 Jane Cai, "Banks Warned on Risk of Underground Lending", *South China Morning Post*, 15 September 2011, B3.

22 Daniel Ren, "Zhejiang Helps Lenders Aid Small Firms".

23 Ibid.

24 Daniel Ren, "Underground Banking May Become Thing of the Past in Wenzhou", *South China Morning Post*, 24 November 2012 (online).

Some banks in the EU, including UBS and Royal Bank of Scotland, have discussed with specialized loan funds how banks might give those funds access to the corporate client base. Given the likelihood of sharp "deleveraging" across the banking sector in the EU, banks would only act as lending intermediaries. In other words, these banks would help to pool small- and medium-size enterprise (SME) loan exposures to the funds and provide credit assessments in return for a fee of up to 3% for the banks. The loan funds then provide SMEs with a combination of senior debt and higher-priced mezzanine loans to achieve a compromise between a borrowing company's need for low funding costs and a fund's return expectations.[25]

Nevertheless, economists and jurists cast doubt on the effect of these initiatives. The liberalizing efforts in the financial sector may encourage speculation in funds on properties and land rather than productive investment into the real economy. It is uncertain whether the financial reform in Wenzhou will really rescue troubled Wenzhou or spearhead a reform nationwide.[26] As a matter of fact, the pilot scheme was hindered partly by the eurozone debt crisis since the local economy in Wenzhou was export-oriented and heavily reliant upon exports to the European market.[27] In order to accumulate more experience and test for further reform in the financial sector, China has designated areas including Shanghai, Tianjin and the Pearl River Delta to trial reforms in the financial services industry.[28] The plan is that the central government would assess changes initiated by local governments in formulating the overall reform plan nation-wide.

2. SPECIAL FINANCIAL TEST ZONE IN QIANHAI, SHENZHEN

In June 2012 China established a special test zone to experiment with freer currency convertibility in Qianhai, Shenzhen. Qianhai is known as a Shenzhen-Hong Kong cooperative service industry zone, with total registered capital of more than 37.2 billion yuan. By January 2013, at least

---

[25] Daniel Schafer and Patrick Jenkins, "Banks Look to Farm out Portion of SME Loans," *Financial Times*, 4 May 2012, p.13.

[26] Daniel Ren, "Fears Wenzhou Reforms Could Increase Risks," *South China Morning Post*, 30 April 2012, B3.

[27] Bloomberg, "More Convertible Yuan Next Goal, China's Central Bank Chief Says", *South China Morning Post*, 18 November 2012 (online).

[28] Ibid.

302 enterprises had been approved to enter Qianhai. Qianhai in Shenzhen, Henqin in Zhuhai and Nansha in Guangzhou are the three key projects supported by the central government to boost Guangdong economic development and cooperation with Hong Kong and Macau. The plan is to turn Qianhai into the "Manhattan of the Pearl River Delta", a high-level, high-quality and high value-added modern service industrial zone.[29] In particular, Qianhai is designed to be a testing ground showing the Chinese leadership's determination to carry on the financial reform with a focus on Renminbi's internationalization.

Renminbi or yuan, is not freely convertible in the international foreign exchange market;[30] capital flow either in foreign exchange or in Renminbi is still heavily controlled in China even though major reforms swept the Chinese foreign exchange control regime in 1994. Amid the financial crisis and its foreign exchange rate reform,[31] China has taken more substantial steps to internationalize Renminbi since the outbreak of the recent financial crisis. The mid-term policy strategy is to make inflow and outflow of Renminbi easier, and to boost the use of Renminbi in international trade and finance so as to reduce its reliance on the US dollar. One way to achieve this mid-term objective is to internationalize Renminbi by broadening the use of Renminbi among international investors.

The experiments in Qianhai include allowing Hong Kong banks to lend Renminbi directly to companies in Qianhai Bay, a 15-square-kilometer

---

29 Minnie Chan, "Qianhai Experimental Zone Won't Be Expanded, Says Shenzhen Mayor", *South China Morning Post*, 28 January 2013 (online).

30 In the foreign exchange control regime, China makes a distinction between two types of transactions: current account items and capital account items. By 1996, China had formally satisfied the IMF's Article VIII on current account convertibility.

31 China has adopted a new foreign exchange rate regime termed as "a market-based floating exchange rate system", where the exchange rate is adjusted on the foundation of "market supply and demand with reference to a basket of currencies", though "in accordance with China's needs for reform and development". The policy was formulated much earlier than 2005. China planned in 1993 to liberalise the foreign exchange policy gradually and made Renminbi fully convertible. See the *Resolutions of the Central Committee of the Chinese Communist Party on Several Issues concerning Building a Socialist Market Economy*, *People's Daily*, 15 November 1993. In 2003, China further planned to "selectively, and in steps, deregulate restrictions on cross-border capital transactions and gradually establish Renminbi's convertibility on the capital account, provided that risks can be effectively guarded off". See the *Resolutions of the Central Committee of the Chinese Communist Party on Several Issues concerning Building a Socialist Market Economy*, *People's Daily*, 22 October 2003. This was the first time that China specifically mentioned the capital account convertibility as its official goal.

peninsula across the water from Hong Kong.[32] Fifteen banks in Hong Kong were granted permission in late January 2013 to offer a combined 2 billion yuan in loans to 26 companies in Qianhai for construction work.[33] While Chinese lenders must adhere to official lending rates, the Qianhai lending scheme allows the parties to negotiate loan rates,[34] which is also an experiment for the mainland's interest rate reform. These moves will further energize cross-border yuan lending and create a new channel for Renminbi held overseas to flow back to mainland China, since Hong Kong banks currently can only lend money to companies in Hong Kong but not in mainland China.

These moves can be viewed as a relaxation of China's tight capital account controls and a new business opportunity for Hong Kong lenders to deploy Renminbi funds and promote Renminbi circulation between the two sides. The experiment is a further step following a series of steps taken by the Chinese government to dismantle capital controls and internationalize Renminbi, making it a freely convertible currency in the future. In the past several years, Chinese companies have been able to settle most of their international trade in Renminbi and flow Renminbi abroad in large volumes. Meanwhile, foreign institutions have also been given limited opportunities to invest Renminbi they may hold such as in the dim sum bond market and in a program to buy Chinese securities.

Qianhai is a milestone for opportunities to remove capital controls on the mainland, boosting the two-way flow of funds and making the mainland currency more convertible. The government will back the development of Hong Kong's offshore Renminbi business, encourage innovations in cross-border Renminbi businesses, allow banks operated in Qianhai

---

[32] 37 Hong Kong and Japanese banks and financial firms including HSBC, Hang Seng Bank, the Bank of East Asia and Sun Hung Kai Financial, Bank of Tokyo-Mitsubishi UFJ, Sumitomo Mitsui Banking Corporation and ICBC signed a deal to invest in Qianhai in July 2012. Sandy Li, "Hong Kong Banks May Extend Yuan Loans to Firms in Shenzhen's Qianhai Zone", *South China Morning Post*, 28 December 2012 (online).

[33] The 15 banks include HSBC, Standard Chartered, Bank of China (Hong Kong), Bank of East Asia, Wing Lung Bank, Nanyang Bank, Hang Seng Bank, and Hong Kong arms of ICBC, ABC and CCB. Enoch Yiu, "Banks Get Green Light for 2b Yuan in Cross-border Loans for Qianhai", *South China Morning Post*, 29 January 2013 (online); Reuters, "Qianhai Cross-border Loan Scheme Starts with 2b Yuan", *South China Morning Post*, 29 January 2013 (online). Meanwhile, Hong Kong brokers have urged the Shenzhen government to allow them to set up joint ventures with mainland counterparts in Qianhai.

[34] In the scheme, a bilateral agreement is signed between a bank and a Qianhai enterprise, which negotiate the structure, term and interest rate of the loan. Ibid.

to extend Renminbi loans across the border and issue yuan-denominated bonds.

Any measures employed in Qianhai would give Hong Kong banks more opportunities to expand yuan currency lending apart from existing channels such as interbank lending and dim sum bond investments. Hong Kong's yuan deposit pool will grow fast due to the qualified domestic institutional investor scheme II (QDII2) and Renminbi qualified domestic institutional investor scheme (RQDII). Financial reforms in the Qianhai special economic zone effectively spur a surge in yuan deposits in Hong Kong, pushing them to 30% of the city's deposit base from the current 10%.[35] Given the wide spillover effect special economic zones have brought about, the impact of Qianhai will spread to all connected areas.

More recently, some players in the Hong Kong financial sector suggest the Chinese government allow those Qianhai-incorporated firms to invest in Hong Kong markets so that the cross-border securities trade can be boosted. One possibility is that a QDII3 (qualified domestic institution investors) scheme may help trading from the special economic zone. Under a QDII scheme (which is to remove restrictions on capital control), mainland investors can invest overseas by buying fund products designed by mainland banks and fund houses, which are granted quotas to invest in Hong Kong or overseas markets.[36] Chinese regulators in 2012 considered introducing QDII2, allowing individuals to trade Hong Kong securities directly. Nevertheless, the plan has not yet materialized. A QDII3 scheme may allow firms set up in Qianhai to invest a certain amount of money in Hong Kong securities or bond markets. QDII3 is a new concept to make Qianhai a gateway for mainlanders investing overseas.

The success of Qianhai's Special Test Zone, however, depends more on China's further easing of its control of interest rates and deepening of its domestic bond market while tackling the risk of opening its capital account restrictions.[37] Mainland China has capital controls under which only institutional investors can invest overseas and then only through the original QDII scheme, which gives local institutions quotas to invest outside China in equities and fixed-income products. The returns of QDII

---

[35] Jeanny Yu, "Hong Kong RMB Deposits Seen Surging on Qianhai Reforms", *South China Morning Post*, 20 July 2013 (online).

[36] Enoch Yiu and Jeanny Yu, "Industry Players Want Qianhai Trade Zone Firms to Invest in Hong Kong", *South China Morning Post*, 13 July 2013 (online).

[37] "China State Council Approves Special Financial Test Zone in Qianhai", available 2 March 2016 at http://english.caijing.com.cn/2012-07-04/111927931.html.

funds have outpaced the Chinese market in recent years. QDII funds struggle to attract assets.[38]

The Shenzhen government set a target for the zone's gross domestic product of 150 billion yuan by 2020. Recent developments seem to suggest that the Chinese government supports the zone's role as a testing ground for yuan convertibility. Different from Pudong New Area where the Shanghai Pilot Free Trade Zone is located, Qianhai however is only an empty plot of land. The other inefficiency of Qianhai is that its policies are too narrow to derive significant benefits for foreign investors. Most international players who are keen on entering Qianhai need a clearer picture on how to transfer funds in and out. China's closed capital account means funds cannot flow freely in and out. In addition to free yuan convertibility in the form of loans, it has also been indicated that private equity funds can invest in Qianhai companies.[39] However, details are still not clear: can private equity funds based outside Qianhai take advantage of the privileged funds status afforded under the regulations? If not, can foreign funds which set up in Qianhai have free flow of funds and currency convertibility in Qianhai only or also into China? Fund houses want to know when and how they can transfer funds out of the country after the investment.

3. PILOT FREE TRADE ZONE IN SHANGHAI

A free trade zone was set up in Shanghai by the Chinese government in September 2013, a major step towards China's long-term ambition of turning Shanghai to be a leading international trading and financial hub.[40] The free trade zone, the newest and most advanced type of special economic zone, originally spanned 28.78 square kilometres in Waigaoqiao, Yangshan port, and Pudong New Area in Shanghai. Starting from 1 March 2015, the SPFTZ has been expanded to cover Lujiazui Financial District, Zhangjiang High-tech Park and Jinqiao Export Processing Zone in Pudong, Shanghai.

---

[38] Ellen Kelleher, "Shanghai Free-trade Zone Lifts Expectations", *Financial Times*, 29 September 2013 (online).

[39] Enoch Yu, "Investors Want More Details on Qianhai", *South China Morning Post*, 19 July 2013, B3.

[40] Currently, Shanghai has three bonded areas in Shanghai: Yangshan bonded port area, Waigaoqiao bonded area and Pudong Airport bonded area. The total volume of the three bonded areas was US$100 billion in 2012. Alice Yan and Enoch Yiu, "Shanghai Plans Free-trade Zone", *South China Morning Post*, 28 January 2013 (online).

The free trade zone is viewed by the business community as the Chinese government's most important policy move for economic reform in more than a decade. Both internal and external factors are pushing for a deeper reform of China's legal and regulatory regime and a substantial change in China's economic growth model. At home, soaring wages and an ageing workforce are forcing China to move towards a "middle-income" trap. Abroad, rivals are rushing into regional free-trade deals such as the Trans-Pacific Partnership and the Transatlantic Trade and Investment Partnership without involving China. Both forces put pressure on China. Inefficient and cosseted services sectors must be further opened up in a global competitive game. If China wants to continue to remain a trustworthy trade partner, secure its economic model and distribute its prosperity across the nation, it needs to take into account this set of parameters.

The free trade zone is a landmark one, similar to the creation of the Shenzhen special economic zone nearly four decades ago. The new pilot free trade zone has been touted as the successor to the special economic zone set up in Shenzhen in the 1980s by Deng Xiaoping when he embarked on a series of market experiments. This zone is used as a controlled laboratory to experiment with loosened regulations on key economic reform initiatives ranging from interest rates to foreign investment approvals. If the planned result can be achieved, the zone will be tasked to spark wider market reforms. Progressive geographical expansion of free trade zones within countries is largely viewed as an effective means to further trade liberalization as long as these countries have strong administrative control mechanisms.

3.1 Key Reforms in the Free Trade Zone

The free trade zone in Shanghai has a multi-layered mission. China's State Council highlighted six areas of focus for the free trade zone: financial services; shipping and logistics; commercial trade; professional services such as law and engineering; culture and entertainment; and social services including education and healthcare. These six areas of industries, as listed in Table 12.1 below, are to be opened within the three years.

The proposed set of rules could contain as many as 21 initiatives to attract foreign investment, covering sectors as diverse as financial services, commodities trading and culture-based businesses.

The reform plan for the free trade zone included 18 new policy initiatives, reducing restrictions on the above six key industries. The overall goal is to promote trade, upgrade financial services and improve governance as well as introducing measures to encourage foreign investment in

Table 12.1 Key sectors opening for investment in Shanghai's free trade zone

Industry	Subsector
Financial	Banking
	Health insurance
	Leasing
Shipping	Ocean shipping and management
Commercial	Value-added telecoms services
Professional	Legal services
	Credit investigations
	Travel agencies
	Investment management
	Construction services
Cultural	Entertainment venues
Social	Educational and vocational trading
	Medical services

18 sectors in China's highly regulated service industry, including shipping, engineering and law.

Trade and logistics

The free trade zone was initially directed at the logistics sector such as lowering tariffs on traded goods. The zone is designed to become a hub for logistics firms and cargo operators and will be attractive for the bonded warehousing of commodities and raw materials, which can be used in trading or as loan collateral, and export manufacturers.[41]

The plan as released, however, indicates an ambition to use the zone to experiment with a wide-ranging series of reforms. The plan is to turn the free trade zone into a Hong Kong-like zone, or a free port, which is an area where customs authorities allow the flow of goods with zero tariffs on imports. This would promote cross-border commodity and capital flow. In a bonded duty free area, goods can be imported, processed, manufactured, altered and re-exported without interference from customs; and it is expected that import duties and value-added tax (VAT) will not be levied.

The free trade zone will eventually cut red tape by simplifying and

41 Article 16 (Shipping Hub Function), Procedures for the Administration of China (Shanghai) Pilot Free Trade Zone, promulgated by Decree No. 7 of Shanghai Municipal People's Government on 29 September 2013 (Hereinafter "Admin SPFTZ").

speeding up imports and exports. This will not only save firms' costs but also give benefits to Shanghai which can then compete with Hong Kong and Singapore to be a regional hub for Asian retail markets. The geographical limitations of the free trade zone will nevertheless restrict the latter while the emphasis of the plan appears to favour service industries in line with overall national focus towards higher value-added businesses, including foreign human resources firms and international trade agents.

In the free trade zone, foreign companies would be allowed to participate in commodities trading. Foreign commodities exchanges and trading companies could own warehouses.[42] Setting up futures delivery warehouses in the Shanghai free-trade zone could replace the functions of those warehouses in South Korea's Busan and Singapore to a very large extent. It could help reduce the trading costs of Chinese enterprises. As commodities trading in the Shanghai free trade zone would be considered offshore trading, setting up futures delivery warehouses in the zone would not have an impact on domestic futures trading or delivery and pricing systems. Nor would it have any negative impact on the stability of domestic financial markets.

Tax

As a general rule, businesses located in free trade zones are eligible for benefits such as duty and tax exemptions on goods based on the fact that they are physically located within the zones but are outside the customs territory of the host country. The free trade zone is supposed to offer a more preferential tax rate. The free trade zone was once said to have cut its business taxes to a 15% corporate tax for qualifying investors.[43] This seems more preferential compared to Hong Kong's 16.5% corporate tax rate. Some corresponding moves may include a cut in individual income tax rates. Currently, the top band rate is 45% for individual income tax. However, the national taxation authority did not make this move, which certainly disappointed the business community. Corporate tax rates are still held at 25%, as in the rest of China, compared with 15% in Hong Kong.

Some but limited preferential tax treatments are granted. Investors injecting capital in the form of non-monetary assets into their companies in the free trade zone may average their asset appreciation premium over

---

[42] George Chen, "Shanghai Free-trade Zone May Just be the Start of Something Bigger", *South China Morning Post*, 4 September 2013 (online).

[43] Benjamin Robertson, "Shanghai Free-trade Zone a Proving Ground for Wider Reforms", *South China Morning Post*, 29 September 2013 (online).

a period of five years for corporate income tax and individual income tax purposes. Professionals may enjoy preferential individual income tax treatment on gains derived from awards under share-based payment schemes granted in the free trade zone, which is currently only available in Zhongguanchun, a high-tech zone in Beijing. Financial leasing companies in the free trade zone are granted an export value-added tax refund, which is currently only available to domestic companies in Tianjin's Binhai New District. The limited scope of preferential tax treatments indicates the special nature of the free trade zone which is not designed to be used as a testing ground for energizing export-oriented industries.

Foreign investment

More industrial sectors are planned to be opened up to foreign investors in the free trade zone. Foreign-owned performing arts agencies and medical institutions will be allowed. The sale of video game consoles, which are banned in China, will also be allowed, pending approval from authorities of individual games and systems. Another field is to allow foreigners to set up joint venture talent management agencies with local partners. These opening up measures will be applicable to companies that are registered in the zone.[44]

The free trade zone welcomes bids from foreign telecoms companies for licenses to provide internet services within the zone. Currently, the Chinese market is dominated by the "Big Three" players, that is, China Mobile, China Unicom and China Telecom. Allowing foreign telecoms companies to compete with state-owned telecoms enterprises is a long-awaited breakthrough that would be welcomed by several major foreign players. But there has been little progress in the past partly due to domestic political pressure.

China has lifted a 14-year ban on the sale of foreign-made video game consoles. When China implemented the ban in 2000, the Chinese government cited concerns about the harmful effects that violent video games might have on the country's youth. The relaxation of the restrictive measures was formalized on 7 January 2014, allowing foreign invested enterprises (FIEs) to ship their products into Shanghai's free trade zone. The relaxation allows Microsoft, Nintendo and Sony to gain the chance to enter China's multibillion-dollar video game market.[45]

---

[44] Associated Press, "China Launches Its First Free-trade Zone in Shanghai", *South China Morning Post*, 29 September 2013 (online).

[45] The ban failed to dent the rapid rise of PC, internet and mobile gaming in China. The existing ban has been largely circumvented by the market players. Microsoft's Xbox, Nintedo's Wii, and Sony's PlayStation consoles became

As part of the blueprint for the zone, Shanghai-based China Eastern Airlines obtained approval for a cross-border e-commerce business in the free trade zone that allows it to sell upmarket items and food directly to mainland shoppers. Airlines are major beneficiaries of the free trade zone. China Eastern Airlines' e-commerce services are based in the zone's business-to-customer section.[46]

The tax breaks may eventually spark a surge of purchases by locals of foreign products ranging from luxury handbags and clothes to seafood. Currently, half of Chinese citizens' purchases of luxury goods are made abroad due to higher prices at home amid steep import duties.[47] It is likely that air freight will become one link in the chain of comprehensive logistics businesses. China Eastern's e-commerce business will eventually be allowed to deliver imported items to mainland customers outside the free trade zone. The plan is that China Eastern will buy goods abroad, transport them to mainland China and then sell them to mainland shoppers through the e-commerce site.[48] Rising income and an appetite for luxury goods amongst mainland Chinese indicates a business potential.[49]

The Chinese government is considering lifting a ban on internet access to Facebook, Twitter and news websites such as the *New York Times* within the free trade zone to attract foreign investors and professionals to the zone.[50] These websites are not open to the public at the moment as they are viewed as politically sensitive. The Chinese government keeps tight control over the media by blocking access to several internet websites through the Great Firewall of China, the colloquial name for the Golden Shield project which is operated by the Ministry of Public Security.

The Chinese authorities have published a keenly awaited "negative

---

available to buyers in China, as many units were smuggled into China. Lenovo unveiled its own home entertainment console, which it marketed as a family exercise device or "sports machine" to circumvent the equipment import ban. The device was priced at more than US$600, twice the cost of a comparable Xbox. Most of the world's most popular consoles are already made in China – by contract manufacturers, for export. Such operations offer another potential source of leakage into the market.

46 Currently, the e-commerce sector is dominated by some privately owned enterprises such as Alibaba and Tencent.

47 Luxury goods are now sold on mainland China at a premium of up to 40% over the price in Europe.

48 Daniel Ren, "Shanghai Free-trade Zone Spurs China Eastern's Plans", *South China Morning Post*, 12 September 2013 (online).

49 According to McKinsey, China accounted for a third of the US$175 billion global luxury market by 2015.

50 George Chen, "China to Lift Ban on Facebook – But Only Within Shanghai Free-trade Zone", *South China Morning Post*, 29 September 2013 (online).

list" of sectors, similar in concept to the US-led Trans-Pacific Partnership Agreement, establishing which business lines will be closed to foreign companies in the zone, while all others will be open. The move is expected to give foreign investors much more freedom. A short list banning guns, drugs and pornography is theoretically investor-friendly. Currently, the negative list contains over 2,000 banned areas, slapping hundreds of restrictions on investments in 18 industries, including media and publishing, real estate and telecommunications. In June 2014, the government trimmed 51 items including real estate, oil exploration technology, and chemicals. Among 139 items in the negative list, 110 items are restricted and 29 prohibited.[51] Compared to the negative list used by the US government, the free trade zone's version is still too long to be utilized. The foreign investment community has complained of the tiny and incremental progress made so far. There are virtually no businesses or investment projects permitted in the zone that are not allowed in the rest of China.[52]

Chinese regulators in the free trade zone have decided to give quotas of US$50 million each to Citadel, Man Group, Oaktree, Och-Ziff, Winton Capital and Canyon Partners as part of a pilot investment program.[53] Other foreign fund managers are lobbying aggressively for the qualified domestic limited partner program (QDLP) licenses. QDLP is one of four main cross-border investment schemes that allow either Chinese to invest outside China or foreign to invest on mainland China. A similar program is set to be launched in Qianhai, Shenzhen as well. There are no real offerings of hedge funds in China, with the exception of vehicles with limited capacity. The program represents a fledgling step in opening China's capital account and breaking down the blockades that divide the country from global markets. The program offers a way for the government to allow people to invest in uncorrelated strategies. Chinese institutions, for example, are given the chance to offer exposure to alternative investment strategies from arbitrage and options to shorting.

It has been challenging for foreign managers to establish an onshore presence in China. Therefore, the QDLP will be an attraction for western fund managers as it scraps some of the burdens they face when setting up shop in China. Joint ventures, for example, require foreign managers to hold a 49% stake when foreign managers partner with local partners. The QDLP offers flexibility to foreign fund houses which will enjoy more

---

51 *Jiefang Daily*, 1 July 2014, p.5.

52 Jamil Anderlini, "New China Free Trade Zones to Lift Growth", *Financial Times*, 14 December 2014 (online).

53 Ellen Kelleher, "Shanghai Free-trade Zone Lifts Expectations", *Financial Times*, 29 September 2013 (online).

control over fund distribution. Another motivating factor driving the push to broaden the repertoire of investments on offer is that China is facing a pension funding gap of as much as Renminbi 18.3 trillion. If a range of alternative investments are added to the asset mix, the shortfall might be addressed better.

Financial liberalization

The plan for the free trade zone goes far beyond greater liberalization of trade to take in investment and financial services, and throws long-protected areas of the economy directly into the path of efficient global competitors. The free trade zone needs better financial services such as cross-border financing businesses and international trade settlement. Therefore, reforms in the financial sector including foreign-denominated offshore bank accounts and financial leases are on the agenda. The key experiments are in freeing foreign exchange markets and liberalizing domestic interest rates.

The major policy initiatives include allowing foreign banks to set up wholly owned subsidiaries or joint venture operations in the free trade zone. Qualified foreign banks are allowed to operate in the zone directly. Currently, foreign banks can only operate representative offices for at least two years before they can establish a branch, wholly-owned subsidiary or majority-controlled subsidiary with Chinese business partners in the region within a shorter time period. Foreign banks currently have a very limited impact on the onshore banking system given their size of capitalization and the scale of retail banking businesses.

HSBC and Bank of East Asia won approval to set up a presence in the free trade zone. These two banks set up a sub-branch in the zone. HSBC has initially focussed on international banking services targeting corporate customers in the zone. Likely it may expand its service scope as the regulatory framework for the pilot free trade zone evolves.[54] Other banks are still awaiting clearer rules. The current plan allows foreign banks to skip long and bureaucratic approving processes when setting up their wholly owned units in the free trade zone. In the past, it often took a few years for a foreign bank to first set up a symbolic representative office in China and then upgrade it to a full-scale service branch. Now, foreign banks and insurance firms should have a fast track route to opening branches in the zone.

The other key initiative is to allow all domestic banks, if they meet

[54] Kanis Li, "HSBC and BEA Approved to Operate in Shanghai Free-trade Zone", *South China Morning Post*, 13 October 2013 (online).

certain capital requirements and have operations within the zone to provide offshore banking services. Up to now, the Shanghai Pudong Development Bank has an offshore banking certificate for a trial business. The free trade zone welcomes privately funded financial institutions.[55] The zone can be a testing ground for Chinese commercial banks to explore how they can manage the risks of offshore banking and then build up a system.

The most valuable part of the free trade zone plan is to allow individuals to directly invest into overseas capital markets. Those investments will no longer be restricted by quotas under the qualified domestic institutional investor scheme (QDII). This move is to change the current regime in which Chinese nationals can invest overseas only in a limited number of funds that have been cleared by regulators to exchange a certain amount of yuan into foreign currency. The PBOC unveiled a blueprint to make it easier for businesses and individuals in the free trade zone to invest abroad by relaxing restrictions on investment flows that apply elsewhere in China. This measure can partially increase flows of yuan into and out of China. Although the PBOC claims to be "reform and innovation-minded" and wants to carry out trials in the zone, it has made it clear that it would not let the free trade zone become a back door to circumventing financial restrictions throughout China. A Chinese Wall will be erected around the free trade zone so that money will be prevented from seeping out of the zone into the rest of China. Even in the zone, the PBOC will continue to tightly manage Renminbi's value as it does elsewhere in China. The PBOC will not allow the market to set exchange rates. Any experimentation with deposit rates will be limited to foreign currency accounts.

Among the most significant changes the PBOC is to carry out are those that concern investment in securities. Presently, the PBOC has limited funds entering and leaving China for financial investments. Foreign capital can be invested into mainland securities in the zone. Foreign financial institutions in the free trade zone with a free trade account can also invest or trade in the Shanghai Stock Exchange or Shanghai Future Exchange and are exempt from quotas under the qualified foreign institutional investor scheme (QFII).

PBOC crafted the guidelines governing cross-border yuan businesses in the zone. Banks in the zone are encouraged to ease their clients' setting up of trade deals by simplifying business procedures. Firms will be able to centralize their yuan payment businesses for current account items,

---

[55] Agence France-Presse, "HKMA Chief Warns Against Complacency Over Shanghai Trade Zone", *South China Morning Post*, 6 September 2013 (online).

a move to aid yuan settlements. The plan indicates the government's stepped-up effort to internationalize its currency while giving a boost to Hong Kong as more Chinese companies are now seeking yuan borrowing in Hong Kong.

Foreign financial institutions in the zone will be allowed to borrow yuan from overseas. This is different from elsewhere in China where foreign banks are hobbled by tight quota limits on how much they can borrow from overseas to lend domestically. This relaxation allows foreign banks in the zone to compete against local banks. PBOC set out the rules for offshore yuan borrowing in the free trade zone, which is a long-heralded liberalization of the yuan's capital account in the zone. According to new rules, Chinese companies are allowed to conduct offshore yuan borrowing, which is an initial step towards drastic financial liberalization inside the high-profile testing ground for further economic reforms on the mainland. Companies in the zone are allowed to borrow as much as 1.5 times their registered capital from abroad. Approval for offshore yuan borrowing is not a groundbreaking move since the PBOC allowed Qianhai to conduct such business in early 2013.

The Chinese government made a promise to make the yuan fully convertible in the zone thereby facilitating cross-border fund flows and reinforcing Shanghai's efforts to transform itself into an international financial centre. One internal document indicates that "on the condition risks can be controlled, firms can undertake convertibility of the yuan on the capital account on a first-to-do and first-to-try basis within the zone".[56] The free trade zone, as planned, will pioneer wider convertibility of the currency and freer market-oriented interest rates. It is appropriate to improve the yuan's convertibility on the capital account so that foreign currency can be channeled into China and be exchanged at market rates for yuan, and vice versa.

A liberalized capital account would be significant to the Chinese financial system. The State Administration of Foreign Exchange (SAFE), China's foreign exchange watchdog, took a preliminary step towards liberalizing the yuan capital account in the zone by easing controls on foreign currency conversions for foreign direct investment (FDI) while attracting multinational companies to establish foreign exchange assets pools inside the zone. According to the new rules, foreign investors can park foreign currencies in advance in the zone before clarifying the use for the money as further FDI on the mainland. Investors with bank accounts in the zone are

[56] George Chen, "Shanghai to Lead on Yuan Reform", *South China Morning Post*, 6 September 2013 (online).

entitled to do conversions between the yuan and foreign currencies whenever they want. This is different from the current rule under which there is a rigid approval procedure for FDIs which cannot be conducted unless investors receive approval from SAFE to exchange the foreign currencies into the yuan before using them to set up production facilities or buy local assets. The investors are required to state clearly the use of the funds and the exact amount of investment into each of the FDI projects before going through SAFE's review procedure. This move marks a reform to make the yuan convertible under the capital account. Yet, the measures do not make the yuan fully convertible.

Many economists see interest rate deregulation as a precursor to a freely tradeable yuan because proficiency in doing this domestically would prepare banks better for global market fluctuations when the capital account is fully opened. However, largely due to the great concern over the full convertibility on the capital account and the ensuing excessive money inflows and outflows, the Chinese government appears cautious about the potential risks of greater convertibility even within the zone. The PBOC now allows banks in the zone to pay corporate and individual clients as much interest as they want from March 2014 on foreign currency deposits worth no more than US$500,000. In the rest of China, foreign-exchange deposits of less than US$500,000 are subject to the PBOC's guided maximum rates. The lifting of the ceiling on foreign exchange deposits is a significant step towards implementing a complete, market-based system for setting interest rates. The PBOC is cautious about implementing the policy due to potential risks.

The China Securities Regulatory Commission (CSRC), China's securities regulator, indicated that it would allow parent companies of companies domiciled in the free trade zone to issue Renminbi bonds in the domestic Chinese market. Other possibilities include experimentation with banking deposit rates determined by the market, a crude oil futures trading centre allowing domestic and foreign investors to participate in over the counter (OTC) derivatives, and issuance of bonds from offshore holding companies with subsidiaries in the free trade zone.

The free trade zone in Shanghai is designed to test the viability of freer yuan movement. Without free cross-border capital flows, there is no way Shanghai can become a global financial centre. Table 12.2 below summarizes the most critically important areas for financial liberalization in Shanghai's free trade zone.

If all these policy initiatives are implemented, it would be tantamount to a full opening of the capital account, which will effectively place foreign and domestic banks on a level playing field at least within the free trade zone. The weight placed on the financial liberalization in the free trade

Table 12.2 To-do list of financial liberalization in Shanghai's free trade zone

Area	Status Quo	Objectives	Benefits
Interest rates	Cap on deposit rates and the floor on lending rates	Both the cap and the floor to be abolished Price risk into interest rates	Create an equal footing for foreign banks to attract deposits
Renminbi convertibility	Not freely convertible	Fully convertible in the zone and at least to foreign banks	Allow foreign banks to attract needed deposits and broaden their range of product offerings
Reserve ratio	Higher reserve ratio for foreign financial institutions	Same reserve ratio requirements	To eliminate the foreign currency debt and investment quotas

zone distinguishes it from all other types of economic development zones in China in two key respects. First, it is more like a financial experiment zone with the aim of opening up the tightened financial sector and market. Although the State Council listed six key areas for market open-up, the focus is financial reforms. This is a distinguishing feature of the Shanghai free trade zone, as the majority of special economic zones in China and abroad concern a long-established strategy to promote export-oriented industries and international trade. Second, further financial liberalization is China's unilateral and more liberal move to offer foreign investors more preferential and flexible market entry conditions. This distinguishes the Shanghai free trade zone from other economic development zones or areas which often offer incentives or measures inconsistent with the WTO rules, notably export subsidies and import substitution or domestic content subsidies. These incentives or measures are directly prohibited or subject to challenge under the WTO's Agreement on Subsidies and Countervailing Measures.[57] In principle, the free trade zone will take the lead in China's long-awaited reform of foreign exchange and interest rates. The free trade zone can accommodate substantial interest rate liberalization and

[57] Some measures and incentives offered by the special economic zones such as exemptions from duties and taxes on goods exported from these zones are consistent with the WTO rules.

exchange rate restructuring. This may change the course of the yuan's internationalization.

3.2 Hurdles in Implementing the Free Trade Zone Plan

The free trade zone plan lays out the Chinese government's ambition to use the zone as a vehicle to more deeply integrate the country in globalization. The target is to build this zone up to international standards for the facilitation of trade and investment, currency convertibility, effective and convenient regulation as well as standardized legal environment. The Chinese government is eager to see the zone as a testing ground for wider and deeper financial reforms. The Chinese government wants to copy the Shanghai model to the rest of the country if the zone proves to be successful. However, the so-far released plan only outlined the reforms in mostly skeletal terms and left many questions unanswered. Specific rules are still vague with no sign of "big bang" reforms from the Shanghai launch. Domestically, the government faces serious and open resistance from entrenched interest groups.

The free trade zone plan is generally promising. But some terms are less practical. Trade is more visible but finance is less visible. A free trade zone pushes for a deeper liberalization of the financial sector but cash flow in and out of the zone is hard to monitor. Given the fungible nature of money, the greatest challenge will be controlling the flow of capital between the free trade zone and the rest of China. If capital account liberalization takes place, the different interest rates and exchange rates will create trading distortions and arbitrage opportunities for traders on both sides of the zone.[58] Without effective controls and further reforms of the Chinese banking system, there is a danger that leakage from the free trade zone may destroy the country's financial stability. Some analysts warned that a rush to financial liberalization might precipitate a crisis similar to that experienced by the banking systems in Asian countries in the 1990s before their collapse in the Asian financial crisis in 1997, due to the two channels of contagion, that is, cross-linkages and common shocks.[59] At this stage, banks may need to build control systems to ensure money is not being misused outside the zone.

The plan outlines a more open business environment to the foreign

---

[58] Dubai and Hong Kong succeeded in part because they do have defined controls and regulatory structures.

[59] Carmen M. Reinhart and Kenneth S. Rogoff, *This Time Is Different: Eight Countries of Financial Folly* (Princeton and Oxford: Princeton University Press 2009) pp.242–247.

investment community. The financial services sector in the free trade zone would be fully open to foreign institutions and foreign companies would be allowed to participate in commodities trading. However, implementing rules are expected to be crafted and released to gauge what is really permitted. Without detailed rules, investors may get hold of assets that might benefit from the free trade zone, which creates another sort of regulatory arbitrage. The plan to set up the zone itself was short of specifics, which Chinese regulators are now trying to flesh out. The PBOC's blueprint came months after the set-up of the zone. The PBOC and other regulators were initially against the idea of setting up a free trade zone, reasoning that the zone might reduce regulatory effectiveness. Allowing changes in the zone to spill over into the rest of China would amount to haphazard liberalization.

The free trade zone will be a proving ground for further liberalization of the mainland's capital account and financial services. Changes are to include interest rate reform and exchange rate convertibility.[60] There are plans to experiment with the convertibility of China's tightly controlled currency, and let market forces rather than regulators set interest rates. There is no fixed timeline for the reform to make Renminbi fully convertible. Rather, the full convertibility of Renminbi is only declared "the final step", to be taken at an unspecified time. Likely, rules in the zone will be introduced over a three-year period. Implementation would be combined with restrictions on "speculative" capital flows and short-term foreign borrowing. Given the slow-down of the national economy and uncertainty of global economic recovery, China is unlikely to impose "big bang" reforms in the near future.[61] That is to say, full integration may be indefinitely delayed. This is a sensible policy taking into account the benefits and risks of financial "reform and opening" for China and the world. The toughest tasks, such as breaking the state monopoly over the internet, data transmission and storage business are still under discussion. It is still uncertain how far the government is willing to go.

The PBOC is working on a detailed operating guide on major financial liberalization in the zone, including full convertibility of the yuan and a market-based interest rate mechanism.[62] CBRC may also adjust the loan-to-deposit ratios and other regulatory requirements so that banks

---

60 Malaysia's Labuan is also a distinct geographical zone with separate monetary policies from the rest of the country.

61 Simon Rabinovitch and Robert Cookson, "China Unlikely to Impose 'Big Bang' Reforms", *Financial Times*, 24 February 2012, p.3.

62 Daniel Ren, "Beijing Reassures Hong Kong on Shanghai Free-trade Zone", *South China Morning Post*, 30 September 2013 (online).

will have a freer hand to operate. Banks in the zone are allowed to receive deposits from abroad.[63] The government left itself plenty of wriggle room in the way it worded its plan. In the plan, it is claimed that risks would have to be controlled as a precondition for capital account convertibility and interest rate liberalization. Nevertheless, the Chinese government did not commit itself to full convertibility or rate liberalization. The central bank has not made announcements on the long-heralded liberalization of the yuan's capital account in the zone. Rather, the plan claims that the zone would only be used to experiment with these reforms ahead of other parts of China.

A first batch of 36 firms, including Citibank and DBS, has received approval to set up business inside the zone.[64] Overseas banks, however, have given the free trade zone a chilly reception. Citibank and DBS are the only foreign banks that will begin operations in the new zone for the time being. Citibank plans to open a sub-branch in the zone to handle trade financing and cash management for clients. This sub-branch may benefit from yuan convertibility and interest rate liberalization, the two biggest reform promises. It has been reported that very few applications had been submitted and virtually all of the banks that had applied were accepted.[65] The tepid reaction of foreign financial institutions so far reflects widespread confusion and uncertainty about the how the zone will be operated. Many foreign banks have made enquiries but they are trying to understand what the zone will involve and whether it is worth setting up a branch there. Some foreign banks are confused about whether to apply to establish sub-branches connected to their existing Chinese operations or to incorporate entirely new subsidiaries. Larger subsidiaries are more willing to forge ahead into a more uncertain regulatory environment due to the more limited resources they have in China and the less relevant experience others have (they may only have experience in setting up a domestic branch locations). Citibank and DBS received approval to establish sub-branches.

In the field of financial services, the zone is to host a wide range of banking services, and therefore a freer foreign exchange regime and market-oriented interest rate reforms would take root in the zone. The Chinese government's move to eliminate the bureaucratic approval process to encourage foreign banks to open branches in the free trade zone

---

[63] Ibid.

[64] Ibid.

[65] Simon Rabinovitch, "Banks Cautious on Shanghai Free-trade Zone", *Financial Times*, 30 September 2013 (online).

has met with a lukewarm response. Ten or so banks have applied for and received permission to open branches in the zone but only two are foreign ones. Foreign banks' major concern is whether they need to have a separate branch in the zone, independent from those they have in Shanghai. The CBRC's requirement is that foreign banks in the zone should have completely distinct systems of internal compliance, risk management and human resources from their existing operations in the rest of the mainland China. This requirement causes additional costs, which may not be justifiable from their headquarters' perspective. HSBC, Standard Chartered and United Overseas Bank are all awaiting more detailed rules to be released.[66] In particular, rules about how capital will flow into and out of the zone and how banks in the zone will be allowed to set interest rates that are different from those outside the zone would be critically important.

However, there is a big question mark as to whether the reform can be eventually implemented and the target achieved. More importantly, it appears that some of the rules drafted for the free trade zone were not in line with current Chinese financial regulations and laws. The national legislature needs to approve amendments to existing laws to legalize some experimental policies. There has been some open opposition against the idea of using Shanghai's free trade zone to spearhead liberalization of the interest rates paid on yuan bank deposits to avoid providing opportunities for speculators to exploit the difference with interest rates outside the zone.[67] The government is trying to fill in the loopholes which could be taken advantage of by foreign investors to challenge the legitimacy of these new policy initiatives or drag the government into the dilemma over whether national or local rules should be obeyed. But the legal and regulatory structures in place for the zone are not fully functioning. Like all previous economic experiments, the free trade zone is to work in progress, subject to constant refinement. In terms of regulation and governance, the zone can be a test ground to improve the quality and predictability of regulation and governance. The management committee in the free trade zone should help coordinate the actions of various regulators to ensure that the zone is administered in a transparent, predictable and coordinated fashion. Regulators also need to get rid of their bad habit of being obsessed with control.

According to the Shanghai government, fewer than 3% of the firms

---

66 George Chen and Jeanny Yu, "Foreign Banks Shun China's Shanghai Free-trade Zone Amid Uncertain Rules", *South China Morning Post*, 10 October 2013 (online).

67 Jane Cai, "Ex-central Bank Official Wary of Interest-rate Deregulation", *South China Morning Post*, 15 September 2013 (online).

that had registered at the zone since its opening in September are foreign funded. Domestic firms account for most of the approximately 1,400 companies setting up shop in the zone.[68] The reason that the foreign business community's response has been lukewarm is the lack of specifics. Foreign firms want to know why they need to be in the zone before making a move.

It is said by the Shanghai government that companies in the free trade zone will receive business licenses in as little as four days, down from the 29 days it normally takes now. Foreign companies registered in the free trade zone may also be allowed to sell their shares to raise capital. This gives these firms the opportunity to tap the world's fourth largest stock market by capitalization. Currently, foreign firms are not allowed to issue shares in China. The platform can be an over-the-counter market,[69] likely the Shanghai Equity Exchange, 29% owned by the Shanghai Stock Exchange, and will be a test for the long-awaited international board for the Shanghai Stock Exchange. If a trial of a fully convertible yuan capital account in the free trade zone is implemented, an easing of controls that bar foreign firms from raising capital through IPOs can be put in place. The State Council's plan is to support equity exchanges for unlisted firms to set up all-round financial service platforms in the zone. If China allows full convertibility of the Chinese currency in the free trade zone, it would enable foreign and domestic firms registered in the zone to raise funds via private share placements as well as derivative trading via the planned share-sale platform. However, China needs to draw up the structure of shareholders of the platform, the amount of registered capital of the platform, and rules governing the operation of the marketplace before foreign firms can sell shares via the platform.

Although economists, jurists and policymakers portray the zone as a unique experiment, the Chinese authorities still scrutinize the investors' intention and ask the applicants why they come to the zone. This suggests that how the concept of the free trade zone works remains mysterious. There is a mismatch between high expectations in the investment community and low regulatory transparency. For instance, when an investor registers a company, he must propose a corporate name with three Chinese characters. The company registry may reject the choices if any two of the characters appear in the name of another already-registered company in

---

[68] Daniel Ren, "Foreign Firms Shun Shanghai Zone", *South China Morning Post*, 29 November 2013 (online).

[69] Local governments are eager to buoy employment rates have been forming over-the-counter stock markets. These markets enable small businesses that do not meet the Shanghai and Shenzhen stock exchanges' listing requirements to raise capital.

Shanghai. It is reported by the Shanghai government that 36,314 would-be applicants were dealt with by the licensing office in the first month, including 3,172 people checking a potential name but only 218 companies were registered. The registration also requires a business address while the landlord may offer a "virtual" address at the price of US$3,380.[70] The registration procedure seems similar to that for regular companies in non-free-trade zone.

The requirement that overseas manufacturers must base factories in the free trade zone means that they cannot redirect their current output to China's domestic market, and take advantage of existing economies of scale. Meanwhile, the State Council indicated that the ban was temporary in nature and consoles manufactured in the zone would be subject to "content" examinations by cultural departments. These factors may push away foreign investors. The approval from the culture department is seen to be the most challenging obstacle. The PBOC signaled fresh support for financial experimentation in October 2015 in Shanghai's free trade zone. New reform initiatives include allowing some firms and individuals to trade derivatives and futures in the domestic and overseas markets, as well as allowing more foreign and private investment in financial services. Other moves include making it easier for citizens in the zone to make outbound investments[71] and allowing foreign issuance of onshore yuan-denominated bonds by companies in the FTZ. Some investment firms, in particular, hedge funds, have taken advantage of easier registration environment to create companies that can raise funds in China and then trade on Chinese exchanges in cooperation with domestic partners. Financial regulators have thus begun moving more quickly to resume liberalizations to the foreign exchange market and capital account.

4. CONCLUSION

China's economic growth and development in an imbalanced manner are no longer desirable and are heavily hindered by a pattern of monetary imbalances. As rightly pointed out: "China's negative deposit rates impose a high implicit tax on households, which are large net depositors in the banking system, and lead to excessive investment in residential housing.

---

[70] James T. Areddy, "Name Game in Shanghai Trade Zone", *The Wall Street Journal*, 12 December 2013, A11.

[71] Citizens currently can only make overseas investments through third parties including banks and securities firms.

Negative real lending rates subsidize investment in capital-intensive industries, thus undermining the goal of restructuring the economy in favor of light industries and services."[72] The distorted financial market and regulatory regime in China has a wide range of side effects including repressing consumption, promoting investment and exports, saving taxes, all of which in turn trigger aggressive interventions in foreign currency markets and vast accumulations of foreign currency reserves. Both China and the world have a huge interest in a healthy and gradual shift of China's economy towards a more balanced growth model. China's economic and monetary policies do not matter for China alone as it is in the global interest to see Chinese economic policies would make the global economy more balanced.

In contrast to China's other special economic zones which were set up more than three decades ago, the three zones discussed in this chapter are more financial reform oriented with a larger emphasis on financial liberalization other than manufacturing or export sectors. These three zones are armed with different tasks and objectives. While the Wenzhou zone is set up to deal with the pressing shadow banking crisis, Qianhai zone and Shanghai free trade zone are more relevant to financial liberalization reforms, in particular, capital accounts and interest rate reforms. Apparently, the scale of reforms and functions of these three zones are different in degrees. In particular, Shanghai free trade zone is to carry on more comprehensive financial reforms while the Qianhai zone focuses on the yuan's inflows and outflows in the cross-border context (see Table 12.3).

The free trade zone in Shanghai gives the hope that it may be followed by a "big bang" reform ranging from an opening of the country's closed capital account to relaxation of strict internet censorship. The free trade zone will be a testing ground for major policy reforms as part of a plan to boost the service economy and cut reliance on exports. This well explains why, unlike other special economic zones, more liberal policy and regulatory measures are introduced into the free trade zone. These initiatives will throw long-protected areas of the economy directly into the path of efficient global competitors. A freer economy will reduce the economy's reliance on investment and boost consumption while the government reduces its control over the allocation of key productive resources. If all these reforms are implemented, the zone no doubt will open a new phase in China's financial, economic and social reform process, bringing greater

---

[72] Nicholas Lardy, *Sustaining China's Economic Growth After the Global Financial Crisis* (Washington, DC: Peterson Institute for International Economics 2012).

Table 12.3 Comparison among zones in Wenzhou, Qianhai and Shanghai

	Wenzhou	Qianhai	Shanghai
Similarity	• Further liberalize banking sector and financial market • Internationalize Renminbi		
Target	Underground lending market	Renminbi's internationalization	• Financial liberalization • Burdensome governance regime
Policies	• Partially legalize underground lending market • Set up "emergency fund" to rescue bankrupt private firms • Allow private firms to invest into the banking sector • Remove restrictions on the operation of microcredit firms	• Relax restrictions on capital flows between Qianhai and Hong Kong • Allow Hong Kong banks to lend directly to mainland borrowers	• Further open up banking sector to foreign investors • Open up capital account transactions • Liberalize interest rates • Further open up capital markets to foreign investors • Allow domestic investors to invest overseas
Challenges	• Strict lending policies by state-owned banks to private firms • Tightened credit lending policy • Slowing economy • Global economic downturn • Semi-closed financial market • Strict administrative and governance system • A less pro-private investment macro-economic environment	• Being an "empty plot" as the scope of its financial reform objectives is narrower than that of Shanghai free trade zone	• Systemic risks in and outside of the zone • Non freely convertible currency

flexibility and fresh options to the heart of China. The whole purpose of setting up a free trade zone is to facilitate the freer flow of cross-border capital and commodity flow, which may further integrate China into the global economy.

All these reforms are not risk free. This may explain why there is no detailed plan for the yuan's free convertibility, and why the free trade zone only adopts a piecemeal approach to tackle a wide range of pressing problematic areas. When it comes to controlling hot money, the idea of a free trade zone only works if there is a tight border between the zone and the rest of China. In this sense, the PBOC's cautious plan to gradually relax the capital control regime makes great sense. The more capital outflows the less accumulated foreign currency reserves will be. On the contrary, the higher the interest rate, the more savings and current account surpluses might be. As a result, it would worsen China's external imbalances. These challenges remind us of two opposite directions of further policy moves. One cautious view is that reforms that work well in the zone will be rolled out to elsewhere. But the true reformists may argue that the whole point of having this zone is to spark broader liberalization. Otherwise the free trade zone may become another Qianhai which has not been highly regarded by market players and policymakers simply because few things have yet taken place. No matter which prevails, one thing is correct: the reforms of the zone are irreversibly linked to plans for national economic liberalization. In a larger context, the landmark plan for a free trade zone in Shanghai is the clearest sign that China's leadership is determined to deliver long-delayed economic reforms. The leadership must deliver on economic reform or risk seeing three decades of high speed growth slip into reverse, sowing the seeds of social discontent that could cause the ruling party to lose its grip on power.

The objectives of these three zones are all difficult to achieve. Open and well-regulated markets, transparent governance and solid banking systems are needed to make China's financial system more market-oriented. China must have a deep, sophisticated and well-regulated capital market, which is freely open to foreign investors. It must have a credible and transparent governance structure, with policymakers that can demonstrate a track record of successful financial management and reform. It must have a strong and stable financial system and solid economic prospects. Renminbi will not become a global currency if China's financial market remains out of sync with international norms. However, currently, China's capital markets are underdeveloped and closed to outsiders; its governance regime is a black-box, and its banking system and economy are fragile. The fulfilment of the Shanghai free trade zone's comprehensive reforms, hopefully, may substantially overhaul China's macroeconomic governance and regulatory regime, thereby boosting China's economy in the years to come.

13. Is China's new deposit insurance scheme a panacea? A functional analysis

China's recent implementation of a deposit insurance scheme brings deposit insurance to the centre of the debate on regulatory policy in financial markets. Deposit insurance, as one of the three pillars of the financial safety net, serves to protect depositors in banking crises and limit the disruption and fiscal costs caused by them. It largely focuses on consumer protection and depositor confidence, unlike the other two pillars that concern capital adequacy requirements (focusing on solvency) and lender of last resort (which helps banks facing liquidity problems). While deposit insurance systems have proliferated rapidly around the world, designing and operating these systems is much less straightforward. Moreover, deposit insurance is not the only possible solution; other regulatory options, such as the capital adequacy rule enshrined in the Basel Accords and restrictions on banks' investment opportunities, may likewise substitute deposit insurance and in fact function more effectively to curb systemic risks.

Against this background, this chapter is structured as follows. Section 1 investigates key features of China's new deposit insurance scheme, while Section 2 offers a brief comparative study of deposit insurance globally. Setting aside the notion of best practices, Section 3 aims to understand why China changed its implicit deposit insurance regime to an explicit one from a functional perspective. Conventional wisdom holds that deposit insurance is introduced only when the banking sector is sound or as a policy response to financial crisis. This chapter explains China's rationale in adopting deposit insurance at this juncture while the economy is slowing down and non-performing loans and local government debts are mounting. Section 4 investigates the immediate impact that deposit insurance may bring to the banking sector. The long-term significance of deposit insurance in the context of deepening financial reform is further discussed in Section 5. Section 6 concludes this chapter by looking into one of the most important elements in building up an effective deposit insurance scheme – that is, the contracting environment.

1. BASIC FABRIC OF CHINA'S DEPOSIT INSURANCE SCHEME

The Deposit Insurance Regulations were passed by the State Council on 29 October 2014 and came into effect on 1 May 2015. The Deposit Insurance Regulations contain 23 provisions in total.

1.1 Scope of Deposit Insurance

The deposit insurance scheme is a compulsory one. Commercial banks, rural commercial banks and rural credit cooperatives are required to participate in the scheme.[1] Banks and cooperatives must set aside funds to cover liabilities should they take deposits.[2] Newly established banks and cooperatives must participate in the deposit insurance scheme within six months after their establishment.[3] China's deposit insurance scheme has a wide coverage including all deposit-taking financial institutions.

The compulsory membership requirement increases the size of the insurance pool, and more importantly, avoids adverse selection – that is, a bank's selecting out of the scheme. If the scheme is a voluntary one, big banks tend not to participate in the scheme so as to avoid subsidizing weaker and smaller banks.

1.2 Coverage Limit

The deposit insurance fund management institution will pay maximum compensation of 500,000 yuan (US$81,500) per depositor if a bank suffers insolvency or bankruptcy.[4] The coverage limits are much lower than the starting level or current level in most countries with a deposit insurance system. It is well below the US$250,000 ceiling in America, A$250,000 in Australia, and the EU's €100,000 per depositor.[5] It is just above the Hong Kong's guarantee of HK$500,000,[6] and Singapore's S$50,000 cap.[7] The International Monetary Fund (IMF) once recommended one or two times per capita GDP as the benchmark for countries to adopt as an

---

1 Deposit Insurance Regulations, Article 2.

2 Ibid, Article 8.

3 Ibid, Article 8.

4 PRC Deposit Insurance Regulations, Article 5.

5 Directive 94/19/EC of 30 may 1994 on deposit-guarantee scheme, [1994] OJ L135/5.

6 http://www.dps.org.hk/en/coverage.html (available 2 March 2016).

7 https://www.sdic.org.sg/ (available 2 March 2016).

appropriate limit for deposit insurance coverage.[8] However, at close to 12 times annual per capita GDP, China's cap is more generous than the prevailing international standard of two to five times.[9] Few jurisdictions offer full coverage, except Germany, France, Hong Kong and Singapore, which temporarily lifted the coverage limit after the financial crisis. However, these were only temporary measures that have since been done away with.

The People's Bank of China (PBOC) pointed out in a statement that the financial impact of this coverage limit on depositors is small, as 99.6% of Chinese depositors have account balances below RMB 500,000. This level of coverage seems to strike a balance between preventing bank runs and enforcing effective market discipline on banks by limiting their risk-taking appetite.

This level of coverage is high enough to maintain depositors' confidence, and is consistent with the public policy objective of protecting depositors. It is higher than Brazil's 98.9%, which used to be the highest level among surveyed jurisdictions by the Financial Stability Board (FSB). However, the level of coverage is also limited so as to maintain market discipline. BNP Paribas SA has estimated that a system of the type planned may cover 46% of deposit balances, based on past PBOC data. This means that the level of coverage may not be good enough for the 1%. Accounts with more than 500,000 yuan – which make up 50% of total deposits – will be left unprotected. For those jurisdictions without figures on the proportion of depositors fully covered, the average percentage of eligible deposit accounts fully covered was 97%, with the highest being Mexico (99.9%) and the lowest being Turkey (88.7%). China's coverage percentages for deposit account and total value of deposit liabilities are close to Canada's. Canada's deposit insurance scheme fully covers an estimated 97% of eligible deposit accounts but only 35% of the total value of deposit liabilities. Certainly, there is another way to justify this level of coverage. Instead of offering a blanket guarantee that is freighted with adverse effects, limited coverage may rather help to avoid moral hazard.

Adequate compensatory controls are needed to ensure a proper

---

[8] Nicholas J. Ketcha Jr., "Deposit Insurance System Design and Considerations", in *Bank for International Settlements, Strengthening the Banking System in China: Issues and Experience*, BIS Policy Paper No. 7 (1999) 221, 231, available 2 March 2016 at http://www.bis.org/publ/plcy07.htm.

[9] This is probably an accepted way to standardize the coverage ratio by dividing the amount of deposits covered by per capita GDP. By this measure, many high-income countries only extend deposit insurance to amounts that are equal to or less than their per capita GPD. Developing countries offer more generous coverage.

balance between financial stability and market discipline. Banks still need to improve their performance and operation in order to attract and comfort those depositors with accounts of more than RMB 500,000. Limited coverage also incentivizes depositors to monitor the bank's risk profile by exposing those wealthier depositors to some potential losses.

The 500,000 yuan ceiling covers both the principal and interest of deposits in all insured deposit accounts owned by the same depositor at the same bank. Banks will cover losses of more than 500,000 yuan with their own assets. The portion in excess of the maximum amount of coverage is to be paid with the liquidated property of the failing bank.[10] This is similar to the path of Indonesia, charging an additional premium to the depositor for all deposits over 500,000 yuan. Once the insured deposit is paid to the depositor, the deposit insurance fund management institution acquires the depositor's claim against the bank in the same order of liquidation.[11]

1.3 Deposits Covered by Deposit Insurance

One way of limiting deposit insurance coverage is to exclude particular types of accounts or account holders. China's deposit insurance scheme covers both local and foreign-currency deposits.[12] This can guarantee the full coverage of retail and small business depositors and avoid them from adverse selection.

But countries do not always cover deposits denominated in foreign currency.[13] Foreign lenders' branches in China and Chinese banks' overseas units are not covered by the deposit insurance scheme.[14] The exemption of domestic banks' overseas branches is understandable as they may be subject to regulatory oversight in a foreign jurisdiction. The exemption of foreign banks' China branches may cause regulatory arbitrage. Countries are divided on whether local branches of foreign banks and foreign branches of domestic banks are covered by the deposit insurance

---

[10] PRC Deposit Insurance Regulations, Article 5.

[11] Ibid, Article 5.

[12] Ibid, Article 4.

[13] Aslı Demirgüç-Kunt, Edward J. Kane and Luc Laeven, "Deposit Insurance Design and Implementation: Policy Lessons from Research and Practice", in Aslı Demirgüç-Kunt, Edward J. Kane and Luc Laeven (eds), *Deposit Insurance Around the World: Issues of Design and Implementation* (Cambridge, MA and London, England: The MIT Press 2008) p.9.

[14] PRC Deposit Insurance Regulations, Article 2(2).

scheme. As far as foreign branches of domestic banks are concerned, they are not covered in Argentina, Brazil, Canada, India, Japan and Russia but are covered in the US, the UK, Spain, Korea, Italy, and Germany. The deposit insurance schemes in the US, Japan, Australia and Brazil do not cover local branches of foreign banks while other countries like France, Germany, India, Italy and Korea do.[15] Member states in the EU differed in their treatment of foreign branches and depositors,[16] which led to regulatory competition and regulatory arbitrage.[17] In the EU context, both race to the bottom and race to the top appeared. Member states tried to attract international depositors with lower insurance premiums or unlimited state deposit guarantees.[18]

Interbank deposits by financial institutions and deposits by senior bank executives in their own banks are not insured in China's deposit insurance scheme.[19] Likewise, most schemes exclude interbank deposits.[20] Low- to middle-income countries, however, choose to guarantee such deposits.[21] Excluding interbank deposits from the scope of deposit insurance is an appropriate arrangement, which can discourage banks from monitoring one another.

The Deposit Insurance Regulations do not make a distinction between time deposits and ordinary deposits.

---

[15] FSB: *Thematic Review on Deposit Insurance Systems – Peer Review Report* (2012).

[16] European Commission, Report: Investigating the Efficiency of EU Deposit Guarantee Schemes (May 2008, available 2 March 2016 at ec.europa.eu).

[17] Robert A. Eisenbeis and George G. Kaufman, "Cross-Border Banking and Financial Stability in the EU", (2008) 4 *Journal of Financial Stability* 168; Harry Huizinga, "The EU Deposit Insurance Directive, Does One Size Fit All?", in Demirgüç-Kunt, Kane and Laeven (eds), *Deposit Insurance Around the World* p.253.

[18] Nikolay Nenovsky and Kalina Dimitrova, "Deposit Overinsurance in EU Accession Countries", in Demirgüç-Kunt, Kane and Laeven (eds), *Deposit Insurance Around the World* p.281.

[19] PRC Deposit Insurance Regulations, Article 4.

[20] Aslı Demirgüç-Kunt and Edward J. Kane, "Deposit Insurance Around the Globe: Where Does It Work?", in Demirgüç-Kunt, Kane and Laeven (eds), *Deposit Insurance Around the World* p.180.

[21] Aslı Demirgüç-Kunt, Edward J. Kane and Luc Laeven, "Deposit Insurance Design and Implementation: Policy Lessons from Research and Practice", in Demirgüç-Kunt, Kane and Laeven (eds), *Deposit Insurance Around the World* p.9.

1.4 Funding

Adequate funding is the essential prerequisite to a modern and effective deposit insurance scheme.[22] There are two options: a public-funded deposit insurance scheme and a scheme financed solely through premiums paid by insured financial institutions. A combination of both can also be a design choice. A scheme financed through premiums solves the alignment issue.

A public-funded deposit insurance scheme lends more credibility to the scheme due to government backing. The privately funded scheme relies on premiums, which secure a stable source of funding and relieves the government's commitment. In the UK, the deposit protection scheme is financed through a levy on all authorized institutions in proportion to their deposit base.[23]

The sources of the deposit insurance fund include:

- insurance premiums paid by institutional policyholders;
- property distributed in the liquidation of institutional policyholders;
- proceeds gained in the use of the deposit insurance fund by the deposit insurance fund management institution; and
- other legal income.[24]

The above seems to suggest that premiums paid by banks are the chief source of funding for the deposit insurance fund management institution, which will not have any financial support from the government. Having a stake in the bank motivates the deposit insurance fund management institution to closely scrutinize a bank's financial stability, and vice versa. This is a market-based self-policing arrangement, effectively aligning the interests of both banks and the deposit insurance fund management institution. But this arrangement is a harsh one for the banking sector given the fact that China had implicit deposit guarantee for such a long time, and both banks and depositors were accustomed to relying on the state for financial stability. It also shows the government's determination to switch a government-monitored banking sector to a more market-oriented one. But this arrangement encounters a technical challenge. As the deposit insurance agency will have to pay for losses by the bank when

---

22 Mark Hsiao, *International Banking and Finance Law: Principles and Regulations* (Hong Kong: Sweet & Maxwell 2011) p.334.

23 Rosa Maria Lastra, *Central Banking and Banking Regulation* (FMG of LSE, 1996) 130.

24 PRC Deposit Insurance Regulations, Article 6.

a bank fails, the deposit insurance agency itself may run into bankruptcy if government agencies do not inject further funds. The solution is the timely intervention by the regulators. The difficulty faced by the regulator is then to distinguish bank runs caused by sudden liquidity problems from bank failures caused by bad investment decisions. The regulator must determine whether early withdrawals by depositors are a pure coordination problem causing short-term liquidity problems for the bank, or a rational reaction to a pending failure of the bank's investment. Seen from this angle, deposit insurance can be an effective protective measure if outside funds are injected in the case of bank failure. The costs of such a protective measure depend on the distortion created by raising the additional funds other than premiums contributed by banks.

1.5 Use of Funds

The deposit insurance funds are to be held by and under the control of the central bank.[25] Funds will be invested in government bonds, PBOC notes, high-rated debentures or other channels approved by the State Council.[26] This suggests that the deposit insurance fund management institution is owned and run by the government.

The institution may, in the interest of depositors and based on the cost minimization principles, use the deposit insurance fund in various ways:

- directly pay insured deposits within the limit;
- engage other qualified institutional policyholders to pay insured deposits for it within the limit;
- provide guarantees, loss sharing or financial support for other qualified institutional policyholders to facilitate their acquisition or assumption of all or part of the businesses, assets, and liabilities of institutional policyholders to be taken or cancelled or applying for bankruptcy.[27]

Research underscores the importance of building in capacity and incentives for deposit insurance managers to adapt dynamically to financial changes. One core principle advocated by the scholarship is to involve the private sector in overseeing the scheme.[28] It is not clear in the regulations

---

25 Ibid, Article 11.
26 Ibid, Article 11.
27 Ibid, Article 18.
28 Demirgüç-Kunt, Kane, and Laeven (eds), *Deposit Insurance Around the World*.

how the agency is to operate the deposit insurance scheme and whether this role is a hybrid mixture of public and private sectors. Likely, the new agency will make detailed rules on how to manage the fund and set insurance premium rate for different banks based on how riskily they run their business.

1.6 Premium

Premiums are an important factor in the deposit insurance program to maintain adequate financial capacity for the deposit insurance fund management institution. There is no uniform practice for the fixing of premiums. The US, for example, applied a flat-rate system for almost 60 years. A flat rate does not consider the size and quantity of risks taken by the insured bank. The flat-rate premium regime provides greater incentives to banks to invest in riskier projects, thereby resulting in the waste of financial resources and economic inefficiency. A more market-based approach is the risk-related premium system, which encourages banks to be more cautious about some risk-taking activities. In theory, the deposit insurance scheme should adopt a risk-based premium regime, incorporating incentive-compatible and risk-sensitive factors, to align deposit insurance premiums with the level of risk passed on by the insured bank. Nevertheless, charging risk-rated premiums is a challenge owing to the technical difficulty in assessing the banking sector's level of risk. The general view is that a risk-based premium system reflects the banking sector's risks and eliminates risk-shifting, but the efficacy of this system is widely questioned. Consequently, the risk-related premium system has been adopted by a minority of states and is said to be only in the experimental stage.[29]

It is not yet clear how annual premiums are determined in China's deposit insurance program. The deposit insurance fund management institution is able to charge two insurance rates of deposits: the standard rate and risk-based differential rate.[30] It is only specified that the standard rate is to be determined and adjusted by the deposit insurance fund management institution on the basis of factors such as economic and financial situation, deposit structure, and accumulation of the deposit insurance fund, subject to approval by the State Council.[31] The regulations are silent on how the risk-based differential rate is fixed.

---

29 Ketcha, "Deposit Insurance System Design and Considerations".
30 PRC Deposit Insurance Regulations, Article 9.
31 Ibid, Article 9.

1.7 Deposit Insurer and its Mandate

A deposit insurance fund management institution, acting as the deposit insurer, will be set up by the State Council[32] to manage money and set premium rates.[33]

A clearly defined mandate for the deposit insurance fund management institution is necessary to achieve the policy objectives of the deposit insurance scheme. At a minimum, the deposit insurance fund management institution needs to be equipped with the power to finance reimbursements, enter into contracts, set internal operating budgets and procedures, and access timely and accurate information. Meanwhile, it needs to be pointed out the scope of mandates is determined based on the local economic, financial and social conditions, and there is no one-size-fits-all type of practice. One apparent perspective of diversity is that national deposit insurance schemes are equipped with a variety of mandates. A survey of mandates of various deposit insurance schemes is outlined in Table 13.1.

After the financial crisis, more countries have been transforming their deposit insurance to a "loss minimizer" model. This switch is beneficial to global coordination on effective resolution planning and depositor reimbursement.

The scope of mandates for the deposit insurance fund management institution under the Deposit Insurance Regulations includes:

- to develop and publish rules relating to its performance of duties;
- to develop and adjust deposit insurance rates and submit them to the State Council for approval;
- to determine the insurance rates applicable to each institutional policyholder;
- to collect insurance premiums;
- to manage and use the deposit insurance fund;
- to take early corrective actions and risk disposal measures;
- to pay the insured deposits of depositors timely within the limit set by the law; and
- other duties approved by the State Council.[34]

---

32 Ibid, Article 7.

33 Pricing the deposit insurance is affected by design features of the scheme. There are two ways to price the deposit insurance scheme: the option pricing model and the expected loss pricing approach. Using a market-based model is vital due to the ability to create estimates of actuarially fair deposit insurance premiums for banks.

34 PRC Deposit Insurance Regulations, Article 7.

Table 13.1 Scope of mandates in various deposit insurance programs

Type	Systems	Mandates	Jurisdictions
1	"Paybox" mandate (or narrow mandate)	The deposit insurance scheme is only responsible for the reimbursement of insured deposits.	Australia, Hong Kong, India, Netherlands, Singapore, Switzerland, Germany
2	"Paybox plus" mandate	The scheme has additional responsibilities such as bank resolution/insolvency functions.	Argentina, Brazil, UK
3	"Risk minimizer" mandate	The scheme has comprehensive risk minimization functions such as resolution powers and prudential oversight responsibilities.	Korea, US
4	"Loss minimizer" mandate	The scheme engages in the selection from a full suite of appropriate least-cost resolution strategies.	Canada, France, Indonesia, Italy, Japan, Russia, Spain, Turkey

Based on the wording, the deposit insurance system here is not just a pure "paybox". It may play some other functions. For example, under certain circumstances, the depositors have the right to require the deposit insurance fund management institution to pay for the insured deposits where it acts as an institution to take over the insured bank and conducts the liquidation of the insured bank.[35] This means that the deposit insurance fund management institution could be involved in a failing bank's restructuring, liquidation or resolution proceedings. The scope of mandates is structured in a relatively wider sense but still narrower than the role a "loss minimizer" or "risk minimizer" may play in other jurisdictions. A clear difference is that the scope of mandates does not involve a wide range of responsibilities such as preventive action and loss or risk minimization/management. Unlike the US's Federal Deposit Insurance Corporation, the institution is not equipped with additional supervisory oversight for the troubled banks.

To ensure fairness and efficiency, the institution should be operationally independent, transparent, accountable and insulated from undue political and industrial influence so that it can deploy the resources needed to carry out its mandate. It appears that the responsibilities of the deposit

[35] Ibid, Article 19.

insurance fund management institution in China's deposit insurance scheme overlap with certain functions played by the financial regulators.

The institution has been delegated the power to:

(a) inspect matters relevant to the calculation of insurance rates where any change in the risk status of the insured bank is likely to result in an adjustment of its insurance rates;
(b) inspect the size, structure, and veracity of the bank's deposits where the premium base of the insured bank is likely to be doubtful;
(c) inspect the veracity of the information and materials filed by the insured bank.[36]

The institution is under a legal obligation to report its material findings to the China Banking Regulatory Commission (CBRC), the banking regulator.[37] In addition, the institution is allowed to participate in the coordination mechanism for financial supervision and administration and shall establish information sharing mechanisms with the PBOC, the CBRC and other financial regulatory authorities or institutions.[38]

The uncertainty lies in the relationship between the institution, the PBOC and the CBRC. As the institution is to be set up by the State Council, it is likely to be parallel to the PBOC and the CBRC, which is similar to the parallel relationship between the Financial Services Compensatory Scheme Ltd and the Financial Conduct Authority in the UK. The key here is how to ensure that the institution maintains a certain level of independence from the PBOC and the CBRC while still being accountable to the State Council. Relevant to this is the governing body and organizational structure of the institution, which has not been clarified.

The various forms of deposit insurance scheme, with numerous characteristics, have several key functions in common. First, they are to provide payment to depositors when there is a bank run. They are equivalent to a safety gate for all types of commercial banks that are able to take deposit business. When a bank meets the threat of sudden economic crisis or financial panic, a deposit insurance scheme will serve as the bank's insurance company. Second, they are to oversee the operation of the banks by disciplining the way they are operated. Third, they are to be a financial institution taking charge of, disposing of and resolving market failure in the banking sector. It is a key component in the bank resolution scheme.

---

36 Ibid, Article 13.
37 Ibid, Article 13.
38 Ibid, Article 14.

2. COMPARATIVE LAW AND ECONOMICS STUDY IN A GLOBAL CONTEXT

The deposit insurance scheme is intended to make bank failures less likely. A regulatory agency will first collect mandatory contributions from financial institutions covered by the scheme, and then use the accumulated funds to pay back deposit claims in case of a bank run or failure. It was first adopted in America during the Great Depression, when nearly half the country's 24,000 banks failed.[39] The US launched a deposit insurance scheme in 1934 to restore confidence in the banking system. Economists claimed that the adoption of deposit insurance reflected the political capture of regulatory form. Similar schemes, which aim to deter bank runs by indemnifying savers from losses up to a certain level if their bank goes bust, spread through Europe in the wake of financial crises in the 1970s.[40] Both the World Bank and the IMF encouraged member states to establish a deposit insurance program. The World Bank recommended deposit insurance to the member states as a component in the adjustment program while the IMF provided technical and policy advice on system design.[41] The number of countries adopting explicit deposit insurance rose from 20 in 1980 to 87 by the end of 2003. Twenty-one out of 24 FSB members have established an explicit deposit insurance scheme with objectives clearly and formally specified in law or regulations. The economic justification of the expansion of the government-sponsored deposit insurance scheme accounts for the frequency and severity of banking crises in modern times.[42]

Since the 1930s, 112 countries have adopted deposit insurance, in full or in part, explicitly or implicitly, saving depositors from losses caused by a bank's inability to pay its debts when due.[43] Most OECD countries

---

[39] Joseph F. Sinkey Jr., "Regulatory Attitudes Toward Risk", in Richard C. Aspinwall and Robert A. Eisenbeis (eds), *Handbook for Banking Strategy* (New York: Wiley 1985) p.349.

[40] The EC adopted the Directive on Deposit Guarantee Schemes on 30 May 1994 to ensure "a harmonized minimum level of deposit protection wherever deposits are located in the Community". Members were required to develop such a scheme in compliance with the Directive.

[41] IADI, 2011/2012 Annual Report; IMF, *Financial System Soundness*, available 2 March 2016 at http://www.imf.org/external/np/exr/facts/banking.htm.

[42] Charles W. Calomiris, "Banking Crises Yesterday and Today", (2009) NBER Working Paper.

[43] Some research affirms that holdouts outnumber adopters albeit a rise of deposit insurance worldwide in recent decades. See generally Demirgüç-Kunt, Kane, and Laeven (eds), *Deposit Insurance Around the World.*

feature some form of explicit depositor protection. All G20 members have adopted such a scheme, except South Africa, Saudi Arabia and – until recently – China. Australia adopted the scheme after the latest financial crisis. In the financial crisis, many countries expanded deposit insurance by providing explicit guarantees for many non-deposit liabilities.[44] Seventy-five per cent of high-income countries offer deposit insurance while only 16% of low-income countries do.[45]

In contrast to the United States and European countries, China did not have a deposit insurance scheme until recently. Rather, China had an implicit guarantee system largely because commercial banks' creditworthiness in China was virtually endorsed by the government. Chinese banking laws and regulations offered a certain level of comfort to the depositors. For instance, the Regulations Governing Deposit and Savings provide that: "the government shall protect the ownership and other legitimate rights of household deposit and savings".[46] The PBOC may take appropriate measures to stabilize the deposit base and to protect the depositors' interest.[47] The Commercial Banking Law provides that "a commercial bank shall guarantee the payment of the principal and the interest of every deposit and shall not delay or refuse the payment thereof".[48] It further states that "at the time of bankruptcy or liquidation, a commercial bank shall give priority to paying the principal and interests of savings deposits after paying the liquidation fees and staff wages and labor insurance fees in arrears".[49] Nevertheless, it is not clear what priority right depositors may have in a failing bank's resolution proceedings. These provisions are not the same as a deposit insurance scheme. In essence, these provisions merely provide some symbolic protection to the depositors but fail to clarify the priority the depositors have in the bank's bankruptcy proceeding.

China's implicit deposit insurance scheme was merely comprised of conservative prudential regulations and proactive supervision. The scheme is not consistent with the G20's call to national authorities to make feasible the resolution of financial institutions without severe systemic disruption

---

44 Aslı Demirgüç-Kunt and Harry Huiziga, "Are Banks Too Big to Fail or Too Big to Save? International Evidence from Equity Prices and CDS Spreads", (2010) The World Bank Policy Research Working Paper 5360.

45 Demirgüç-Kunt, Kane and Laeven, "Deposit Insurance Design and Implementation: Policy Lessons from Research and Practice" p.8.

46 Regulations Governing Deposit and Savings, Article 5.

47 Ibid, Article 7.

48 PRC Commercial Banking Law, Article 33.

49 Ibid, Article 71.

and without exposing taxpayers to loss. China's implicit deposit insurance system was once implemented from the top to the bottom with the government's implicit backing.[50] The strongest form of protection rested with the fact that commercial banks in China are owned by the state. Depositors know that the government will not let state-owned banks fail. With this implicit scheme in place, the government was likely to maintain a hands-off approach and leave banks to manage risks.

There have been arguments in favour of implicit deposit insurance. The primary justification is that it lowers costs to taxpayers if a failing bank can be stabilized without a large deposit payout. It is less procedurally burdensome to the government or banking regulator, as this route avoids building up the institutional structure to get an explicit deposit insurance up and running. In the same vein, operational costs can be saved. In particular, state ownership of commercial banks helps achieve the same objective as explicit deposit insurance since the state has every incentive to ensure financial stability and bank soundness. Even though the government does not directly guarantee the repayment of deposits to depositors when a bank fails, state ownership offers a blanket guarantee to depositors.

There are proponents of the idea that an explicit deposit insurance scheme works better for China's banking sector. Replacing implicit deposit insurance with an explicit one can help lower the rescue costs of the government for a failing bank as explicit deposit insurance can set a cap on the coverage of insured deposits. While it makes sense to argue in favour of or against having explicit deposit insurance, quantifying these benefits or costs is impossible. The deposit insurance scheme is viewed as one of the pillars of modern financial safety nets. The benefits of adopting deposit insurance are obvious. In the short term, this is a costless instrument to reduce the risk of a bank run as the adopting country does not need to book any budgetary expenditure.

However, it is also recognized that the deposit insurance scheme is not a panacea for financial instability. On the eve of the financial crisis, there were no uniform views on the operational rules and design features of deposit insurance.[51] In particular, the scheme has been viewed by

---

[50] Lawrence J. Lau, "The Macroeconomy and Reform of the Banking Sector in China", in *Strengthening the Banking System in China: Issues and Experiences* p.74.

[51] The Financial Stability Forum in 2000 formed a Working Group on Deposit Insurance and tried to identify good international practices. Guidance for Developing Effective Deposit Insurance Systems, available 2 March 2016 at http://www.fsb.org/wp-content/uploads/r_0109b.pdf. IADI was established in 2002 to

financial economists and economic historians as the primary source of the unprecedented financial instability that we have seen across the globe over the past three decades.[52] As far as the real function the deposit insurance scheme can play is concerned, both the theoretical and empirical effects are mixed. Theoretically, full deposit insurance helps the banking system avoid bank panics.[53] Meanwhile, it increases the moral hazard issue in the banking industry. The general equilibrium result is not straightforward due to its vague welfare effects in a framework where the market structure of the banking industry is endogenous.[54] Some empirical work proved a link between the existence of explicit deposit insurance and banking fragility[55] while it was also empirically proved that deposit insurance increases the stability of the banking system and reduces the duration of banking crises.[56]

Poorly designed deposit insurance schemes are widely seen partly due to the fact that these poor designs are installed during crisis circumstances or in response to external pressures to emulate other countries. There is scant empirical data on what factors determine the adoption and design of deposit insurance or their impact on financial stability, market discipline and economic development. Establishing explicit deposit insurance is often included in the policy package on financial architecture that outside experts present to developing countries undergoing financial reform.[57] It can be a useful part of a country's overall system of banking regulation and financial markets. A deposit insurance scheme can be a politically correct policy choice. It can be packaged as a tool to prevent wasteful liquidations of bank assets caused by bank runs. On the other hand, the

---

formulate guidance so as to enhance the effectiveness of deposit insurance systems at the international level.

[52] James R. Barth, Gerard Caprio Jr. and Ross Levine, *Rethinking Bank Regulation till Angels Govern* (Cambridge: Cambridge University Press 2008).

[53] Douglas W. Diamond and Philip H. Dybvig, "Bank Runs, Deposit Insurance, and Liquidity", (1983) 91(3) *Journal of Political Economy* 401–419.

[54] Carmen Matutes and Xavier Vives, "Competition for Deposit, Fragility, and Insurance", (1996) *Journal of Financial Intermediation* 184–216.

[55] Aslı DemirgÄuc-Kunt and Enrica Detragiache, "Does Deposit Insurance Increase Banking System Stability? An Empirical Investigation", (2002) 49 *Journal of Monetary Economics* 1373–1406.

[56] Fulbert Tchana Tchana, "The Empirics of Banking Regulation", (2014) 19(3) *Merging Markets Review* 49–76.

[57] David Folkerts-Landau and Lindgren Carl-Johan, *Toward a Framework for Financial Stability* (Washington, D.C.: International Monetary Fund 1998); Gillian Garcia, "Deposit Insurance: A Survey of Actual and Best Practices", (1999) IMF Working Paper No. 99/54, available 2 March 2016 at http://www.imf.org/external/pubs/ft/wp/1999/wp9954.pdf.

deposit insurance scheme may induce risk-taking by financial institutions. Empirical evidence on the efficiency of deposit insurance systems in the real world is scarce.

Due to the lack of a global regulatory framework and more prescriptive guidance, national deposit insurance schemes exhibit diverse characteristics in terms of the scope of mandates, coverage level, funding structure, risk-based premiums and access to emergency funding sources. Conventional wisdom is that the effectiveness of deposit insurance lies in the institutional environment, and depends on a particular jurisdiction's domestic circumstances, settings and structures.[58] Some interrelated elements that are outside the deposit insurance system but may have a direct and combined effect on the functioning of deposit insurance include the condition of the economy and banking system, the sound governance of agencies comprising the safety net, prudential regulation and supervision, legal framework and the accounting and disclosure regime.[59] The policy implication of this line of thinking is that deposit insurance should be used together with other banking regulatory instruments. For instance, eligible banks can be given membership in the deposit insurance scheme as part of the licensing process. Deposit-taking financial institutions should be subject to robust regulation and supervision, and should be financially viable when they become members of a deposit insurance system. When the deposit insurance membership is terminated, there should be arrangements to provide for coordination in withdrawing the banks' operating licenses. The deposit insurer should be further provided with the power to seek legal redress or initiate legal proceedings against those parties (such as officers, directors, managers, auditors) at fault in a bank failure on the grounds that it is a creditor of the failed bank for the reimbursement of losses and costs it incurs. Some of these moving pieces are transplanted into China's deposit insurance scheme.

3. WHY DID CHINA ADOPT A SCHEME AT THIS TIME?

China used to be the only major economy in Asia, even in the world, without an explicit deposit insurance scheme. The Chinese government started to mull over the establishment of a deposit insurance scheme as

---

[58] Basel Committee on Banking Supervision: Core Principles for Effective Deposit Insurance Systems: A Methodology for Compliance Assessment (2010).

[59] Ibid. p.11.

Table 13.2 Total domestic deposit base in key economies

Country	Total Domestic Deposit Base (US$ billion in 2013)	GDP (US$ billion in 2013)	% (Deposit/GDP)
US	2,736.12[1]	16,768[2]	16.32
China	4,784.69[1]	9,490.6[2]	50.42
Australia	425.36[1]	1,560.37[2]	27.26
Canada	420.87[1]	1,838.96[2]	22.89
Japan	899.68[1]	4,919.56[2]	18.29

Notes:
1. Worldbank.org, http://search.worldbank.org/data?qterm=Gross+domestic+savi ngs+2013.
2. Worldbank.org, http://data.worldbank.org/indicator/NY.GDP.MKTP.CD.

early as 1993 and promised to set up such scheme in an ambitious reform plan released in November 2013, after 20 years of deliberation. The IMF has recently urged the PBOC to sequence the change by first putting in place a bank deposit-insurance system and a mechanism for handling banks that go broke after they have greater freedom to chase deposits through higher interest rates. This may have pushed China to speed up the process of adopting deposit insurance.

One reason for this delay was due to China's deposit base: it has one of the largest deposit bases in the world. In 2010, Chinese bank deposits were 119.4% of GDP. In comparison, bank deposits outstanding in Indonesia and Mexico were only 39.4% and 17.3% respectively in 2010. Excluding city-states like Singapore and Hong Kong, the only large country comparable in Asia is Japan in which outstanding bank deposits were at 126.4% of its GDP when the country launched its limited explicit deposit insurance scheme in 1971 (they are now 202.3% of GDP). Table 13.2 gives a comparison of key economies' deposit bases and their corresponding proportion of GDP.

A larger deposit base certainly makes an explicit deposit scheme expensive, even though it has a trade-off by capping the government's future commitments to depositors of insolvent financial institutions. The large deposit base may affect the design of deposit insurance scheme. Japan moved in and out of full guarantee deposit insurance in response to the crisis between 1996 and 2002.[60]

[60] To address this concern, some countries have managed to phase into a limited deposit insurance scheme over time by gradually reducing the coverage.

The funding of deposit insurance can come from an official source, a private source or a combination of the two. Chile is the only country that provides an official source of funding for the deposit insurance scheme. The most common way to administer a deposit insurance scheme is an official administration. It would be a large administrative burden to run a deposit insurance scheme of this size in China. In addition, deposit insurance may increase budgetary costs by running an insurance enterprise, and if this latter enterprise is state-owned as is the case in China, there may also be additional compliance and administrative pressure on the government. The complexity of deposit insurance requires the regulators' capacity to manage transparency, accountability and deterrence, and involves additional resources and costs for the government. Uncontrolled moral hazard embedded in deposit insurance rewards bad bankers and penalizes good ones, thence imposing unexpected obligations on the national treasury and risking new and deeper crises in years to come. In deposit insurance, the insurer will pay out large claims to depositors of a failed bank in the event of a bank run. Given the state shareholding of the insurer, this may trigger a large amount of central bank borrowing and result in a present, not contingent, danger of inflation.[61]

Any explicit deposit insurance scheme will certainly cover less than depositors might expect and it could be difficult to convince depositors that deposits in large state commercial banks are just as safe as city commercial banks or rural commercial banks. For example, if launched in 2003, a deposit insurance fund equal to 1.35% of all deposits (the same coverage target as the Federal Reserves in the US) would have taken 10 years and cost RMB 1.1 trillion. The ROA of the domestic banking sector would have dropped 14% from 1.13 to 0.97% as a consequence. The fund would then be large enough to cover the failure of larger city commercial banks, such as Bank of Beijing (which accounts for 0.8% of the national total), but still not be enough to cover a bank such as Minsheng Bank with deposits accounting for 2% of the national total, let alone enough to cover one of the Big Four like China Construction Bank with deposits accounting for 12.2% of all deposits in the banking sector.

Some commentators speculate that China could get around this program with deposit insurance coverage more limited than most other countries. Many countries have a deposit insurance scheme covering a similar share of deposit accounts but few countries have accounts as large as China.

---

[61] Geoffrey P. Miller, "Deposit Insurance for Economies in Transition", in Rosa M. Lastra and Henry N. Schiffman, *Bank Failures and Bank Insolvency Law in Economies in Transition* (The Hague and Boston: Wolters Kluwer 1999) p.43.

Table 13.3 Deposit account value covered by deposit insurance

Jurisdiction	Share Value (%)
United States	79
Japan	71
Indonesia	61
Mexico	58
Canada	35
India	33
Argentina	29
Singapore	19

Chinese bank accounts at or less than RMB 500,000 only represent 46% of the value of deposits. The close equivalent, as indicated in Table 13.3, is Mexico where 99.9% of deposit accounts are covered but only account for 58% of the value of all outstanding deposits. If this were the coverage level for China over 50% deposits today would no longer be insured. Then, the key objective of having a wider coverage of bank stability and security fails.

The low coverage level would make it easier to launch a credible deposit insurance fund. If China follows a path similar to that of Argentina with a premium rate of 30 bps and a fund target of 5% of all covered deposits, they could have a fund capable of covering bankruptcy of one of China's large state-owned banks in 20 years. The current pace could not be quickened as the source of funding for the deposit insurance fund management institution is largely from premiums. It might be better if the Ministry of Finance were to inject start-up capital.

What would happen to the banking system as a result of the low coverage? The question is more relevant to those who hold accounts in individual banks larger than RMB 500,000. China has large income inequality with some wealthy individuals holding large amounts of money in bank accounts. Due to financial market distortions favouring real estate, the middle-class traditionally saves large sums of money in order to afford the purchase of a home with little or no down payment. Non-financial enterprise deposits accounted for 35% of the value of all outstanding deposits in 2012.

If high net-worth individuals and enterprises were to remove their funds from the banking system in response to the change in coverage rules, then all banks could struggle. Even with a low coverage rule banks are going to be negatively impacted by deposit insurance. A rough estimate is that with a 0.5% reserve target and an 8 pbs premium on covered deposits, a medium-sized bank such as China Minsheng Bank will suffer a loss of 1.15% of its profits in 2014. The effect would certainly be worse if banks had to contend with an eroding deposit base. A high coverage level is supposed to reduce the incentives for depositors to run. Adequate controls are needed to ensure a proper balance between financial stability and market discipline.

If the implicit deposit insurance system worked and having an explicit one is troublesome, one is left to ask why China set up an explicit deposit insurance regime at all. Adopting deposit insurance is usually a response to the financial crisis or collapse. In other words, it is a crisis management strategy to avoid future financial instability. Without a financial crisis, the best practice is to introduce deposit insurance when the country's banking sector is sound.[62] Against this backdrop, does the fact that deposit insurance is brought into China provide evidence of a sound banking sector?[63]

China needs the deposit insurance scheme if the government is now less reluctant to let banks fail. In the past, commercial banks were described as "too big to fail" as the government has always bailed out troubled financial institutions or banks and made sure investors got their money back. The government has implicitly guaranteed the entirety of the money the depositors put in banks, and offered its full support in the event of bank failures. The government set this precedent in 1998, when Hainan Development Bank failed due to a real estate market collapse. At the time the bank's deposits only accounted for 0.06% of all deposits in China. But the PBOC bailed out all depositors when they transferred the failed bank's liabilities to ICBC. The underlying rationale was that anything short of a complete bailout of depositors could have led to bank panics throughout the country.

This implicit guarantee from the government encouraged banks to make bad loans, and investors to buy the riskiest products around as both could count on a government rescue. Even investments offered by the massive shadow banking system have been considered safe as state-owned banks and financial institutions have been deeply involved.

One efficient way to fix this moral hazard problem is for China to embrace bank failure or default, allowing the market to play a larger

---

62 Garcia, "Deposit Insurance: A Survey of Actual and Best Practices", p.23.

63 Sound financial system is important for both domestic and international economic and financial stability. But sound financial system is a high standard as a country's financial system includes its banking sector, securities market, pension and mutual funds, insurance sector, central bank and regulatory authorities. With increasing connectivity among financial sectors, problems in one sector may easily cause a spread to other sectors, thereby exacerbating economic downturns.

role in the economy, and introducing more risk into the banking system. Therefore, the launch of a deposit insurance program is a clear message to the effect that unlimited bailouts have come to an end. It is a two-pronged message. The deposit insurance scheme will hold financial institutions responsible for their own losses and profits. Meanwhile, it makes depositors and investors more aware of the risks they face and, by extension, apt to exercise greater caution about them. This can lower the possibility of a run on a bank and contain financial contagion.

The new deposit insurance scheme comes as the halcyon days of Chinese banks seem to be drawing to a close. New financial platforms with higher return promises, including internet-based financing and wealth management products from Alibaba and Tencent, have prompted Chinese depositors to withdraw their money from banks and invest directly through other non-bank channels, resulting in a decline in deposits. Affected by this financial disintermediation and the economic slowdown, Chinese banks are reporting rising non-performing loans and squeezed profit margins.

In a financial system where shadow banking investment is often protected, the deposit insurance scheme represents a great leap of faith. The risk comes down to how the half of deposits – and the entire bond market as well as the shadow banking investment market – that are unprotected will react to the implementation.

4. DEPOSIT INSURANCE'S MULTIPLE-FACETED IMPACT

The set-up of deposit insurance will not be sufficient to guarantee macroeconomic stability. The deposit insurance scheme, by and large, is just one instrument in the entire financial safety net, and complements other macro-prudential regulatory tools such as prudential regulation and lender of last resort. Three pillars in a financial safety net can be seen in Figure 13.1 in Section 6 below. The purpose of deposit insurance is to step up supervision of banks, prevent systemic risks in the financial sector, and protect the public interest. While the deposit insurance scheme is meant to diminish the threat of bank runs and create social benefits, it also involves large fiscal costs, which justify regulatory oversight and government intervention. Crafting a financial safety net involving a deposit insurance scheme is an exercise in incomplete contracting. Likely, it is also prone to moral hazard, or excessive risk taking by participating banks as the banks may take for granted that taxpayers share the downside costs. If the scheme is a voluntary one, it can cause adverse selection, leaving high-risk banks as members in the scheme without the participation of better banks.

The scheme can become burdensome and ineffective due to regulatory forbearance, poor oversight, moral hazard and under-funded insurance. This is the partial reason that it is termed as a risk-taking tool. Protecting banks from financial crises and economic shocks can indirectly subsidize banks' risk-taking activities and waste considerable financial and fiscal resources due to inefficient borrower investment.[64] Based on some empirical studies, it is asserted that deposit insurance distracted banks from market discipline and prudential practices and could become the single greatest source of banking instability.[65] Mitigating moral hazard can be achieved through good corporate governance, risk-adjusted based premiums, effective resolution of failed banks by the deposit insurer, market discipline and prudential regulation.[66]

China needs deposit insurance now because the mainland economy is less robust and there is, implicitly, a greater risk of small banks having a liquidity crisis. The scheme is a market-based exit strategy for troubled banks as well as a means to promote the establishment of market-based risk prevention and resolution mechanisms.

While Chinese banks are largely state-owned and almost never go bankrupt, recent years have still seen rare runs on smaller financial institutions, including rural cooperative banks that have mismanaged their cash. For example, in March 2014 a rumour sparked a three-day bank run in the small city of Yancheng that led banks to pile stacks of cash behind teller windows to reassure depositors they were liquid.

These unusual incidents suggest that the launch of the deposit insurance scheme in China inverts the usual logic. China's financial system could hardly be more stable. It has been nearly 20 years since a big bank failed. Even without an explicit deposit insurance program, the government made a full payment to cover household deposits of failing financial institutions such as the China Agricultural Trust and Investment Company, Hainan Development Bank, Guangdong International Trade and Investment Corporation (GITIC), and other financial institutions.[67]

---

[64] Demirgüç-Kunt, Kane and Laeven, "Deposit Insurance Design and Implementation: Policy Lessons from Research and Practice" p.5.

[65] Gerard Caprio, and Daniela Klingebiel, "Bank Insolvencies: Cross Country Experience", (1996) The World Bank Working Paper No. 1620; Demirgüç-Kunt and Detragiache, "Does Deposit Insurance Increase Banking System Stability?".

[66] Basel Committee on Banking Supervision: Core Principles for Effective Deposit Insurance Systems: A Methodology for Compliance Assessment (2010) pp.16–17.

[67] Joseph Lam, "The Insolvency of GITIC", (1999) 14(6) *Journal of International Banking Law* 193–197.

GITIC's US$4.7 billion bankruptcy case was the largest ever in China.[68] In these bank failure cases, local governments, through other banks, repaid the principal owed to individual depositors. Apparently, the aim of the deposit insurance scheme is to shake things up – to add risk to a banking sector that relies on the government for financial rescue.

The launch of the scheme marks a step back from the current assumption that the state will stand behind all financial institutions at all costs. At the end of the 1990s, when bad loans accounted for one-third of banks' assets, the government injected foreign exchange reserves into the Big Four.[69] More recently the support has even extended to some commercial lenders' off-balance-sheet businesses. When an investment product sold by the Industrial and Commercial Bank of China was on the verge of defaulting in 2015, the CBRC and local governments orchestrated a bailout.[70] This has fueled capital misallocation as bankers shrug off risk, counting on the government to rescue them if they find themselves in a pinch.

China's depositors had piled up 112 trillion yuan in deposits as of 31 October 2014, while non-performing loans had climbed to a six-year high, suggesting increasing stress within the financial system. Meanwhile, in the past five years, borrowing by businesses and households as a percentage of gross domestic product rose nearly 60% in China, according to Goldman Sachs. From 2010 to 2012, shadow lending doubled to 36 trillion yuan, according to analysts at J.P. Morgan. Bank loans totaled just 53% of all lending in China in the first ten months of 2013, down from 72% in 2010 and 92% in 2002, according to figures from the PBOC.[71] The total debt-to-GDP ratio, including government, corporate and household debt, was set to reach 218% of GDP by the end of 2013, up 87 percentage points since 2008, Fitch estimated in 2013.[72] The dominance of state-controlled lenders has

---

68 Vincent A. Pace, "The Bankruptcy of the Zhu Kuan Group: A Case Study of Cross-border Insolvency Litigation Against A Chinese State-owned Enterprise", (2006) 27(2) *University of Pennsylvania Journal of International Law* 517–599.

69 Shen Wei, "Healthy or Unhealthy? That Is A Problem – Unveiling the Myth of Chinese Banks' Success", (2013) 28(2) *Journal of International Banking Law and Regulation* 81–88.

70 Shen Wei, "Wealth Management Products in the Context of China's Shadow Banking: Systemic Risks, Consumer Protection and Regulatory Instruments", (2015) 23(1) *Asia Pacific Law Review* 55–85.

71 "Loan Sharks Smell Blood In China Waters", *The Wall Street Journal*, available 2 March 2016 at http://www.wsj.com/articles/SB10001424052702304579404579236001885224902.

72 "China's Loan Sharks Circle in Murky Shadow Bank Waters", *Chicago Tribune*, available 2 March 2016 at http://articles.chicagotribune.com/2014-01-30/

left depositors believing in an implicit government guarantee. The deposit insurance system can help to prevent bank runs. At the same time, by acknowledging the possibility of bank failures, the plan may encourage depositors with balances exceeding RMB 500,000 in accounts with small lenders to shift their accounts to larger banks seen as more stable.

A credible deposit insurance scheme might indeed benefit small banks. On the face of it, the scheme may lead to a depositor shift from small banks to large- and medium-sized banks in the short term. Smaller banks face the risk of withdrawals by corporate depositors to counterparts with strong capital bases and extensive distribution networks. Besides liquidity risk, smaller lenders may have to bear higher funding costs to keep customers, putting pressure on their earnings.

Introducing the deposit insurance system, however, promotes competition among commercial banks, thereby improving efficiency in allocating funds through the market mechanism. This serves as a cost-effective way to limit the government's financial commitment to depositors. The scheme will significantly improve the competitiveness of medium- and small-sized banks as the insurance will assure depositors of the safety of their savings. Therefore, it will help create a fair environment for all financial institutions. Small banks are given more opportunities by the insurance scheme to compete with large banks for deposits as the potential concern about the fragility of small banks is alleviated to a certain extent.[73] The deposit insurance system will enhance smaller banks' credibility and competitiveness and create a fair environment in which they can compete. China's largest banks have long enjoyed an advantage in attracting deposits because customers view them as having an implicit state guarantee. By extending a guarantee to deposits at all banks, the government theoretically erodes that competitive edge.

While the scheme is designed to protect savers and is probably one of the least contentious banking reforms, it may also expose Chinese banks to uncertainty. Banks will need to be cautious about their risk-taking capacity from now on. Any person or company with more than RMB 500,000 in his or her account will want to make sure that his or her bank is well run. Banks will receive no insurance coverage for their off-balance-sheet vehicles. These high-yielding pseudo-deposits will look less attractive. Assuming premium rates of 0.05% to 0.11% for different

business/sns-rt-us-china-loans-underground-20140130_1_shadow-bank-underground-banking-underground-loans.

[73] It has been claimed that the insurance scheme exposed taxpayers to loss from risk-taking at insured financial institutions. Edward J. Kane, *The S&L Insurance Mess: How Did It Happen?* (Washington, DC: Urban Institute Press 1989).

types of banks, the deposit insurance system may reduce Chinese banks' 2015 earnings by 1.53% and their net interest margin by 26 basis points on average. Introducing deposit insurance and allowing banks to fail could significantly increase the chance of a severe financial crisis if not managed deftly. It may exacerbate a liquidity shortage at smaller banks and boost their chance of failure as savings shift to the biggest lenders.

As in the US and many other places, the deposit insurance scheme will be funded by a levy on banks' assets. If banks mismanage their books, they will be put on notice. Banks that are classified as bigger risks will have to pay extra to secure protection. Moreover, if their capital falls too low or their leverage rises too high, regulators could order their closure, transferring their assets to other institutions.

The concern is that, perversely, the scheme may cause trouble for rural credit cooperatives, because the notion that any bank might be allowed to fail will prompt savers to move their deposits to bigger institutions, the insurance notwithstanding. The other concern is that the scheme will be too small to make a difference. With the levy expected to be no more than 0.05% of deposits, it will take a decade to accumulate a trillion yuan, barely enough to cover the deposits of a middling bank. The government may solve this problem by issuing a bond to give the insurance fund a cushion of cash from the outset.

The bigger concern is that the government will continue to stand behind uninsured deposits. The 0.4% of accounts that are not fully covered contain more than half of all money on deposit. Much of this belongs to state-owned enterprises, the country's richest firms. The government has no appetite to let them go bust, nor does it want to see the collapse of the banks managing their cash. Thus the implicit, blanket guarantee for state firms and good-sized banks may endure. Nevertheless, too-big-to-fail would be progress of a kind for the Chinese financial system. It suggests the government would at least be willing to let small banks bite the dust.

5. LONG-TERM SIGNIFICANCE TO FINANCIAL LIBERALIZATION REFORM

The deposit insurance scheme clears the way for China to deregulate savings rates. The deposit insurance scheme is considered a precondition for China to free up deposit rates – the last and most important step of interest rate liberalization. Interest rate liberalization has been high on the financial reform agenda. By completing a safety net for the banking sector, the deposit insurance scheme sets the stage for the eventual deregulation of interest rates on deposits, which will allow banks to compete more vigorously. The PBOC has indicated that it is very likely to ease its grip on banks' deposit rates in 2015 or 2016.

Chinese banks currently operate under a rigid system under which they take deposits and extend loans according to the PBOC's guiding rates, which allows them to rake in large profits due to the gap between the lending and deposit rates. Deposit rates in China have been partially liberalized: banks can set their actual deposit rate at up to 1.3 times the official benchmark rate. On 22 November 2014, the PBOC decided to raise the deposit rate ceiling to 120% of the one-year benchmark deposit rate, from 110%. This means banks are able to price loans more freely.

The move is considered one of a number of preconditions for China to free up deposit rates, the last step in its interest rate liberalization. China has many accomplishments in liberalizing its interest rates over the past several years, and it is very close to the last step of fully liberalizing interest rates, namely scrapping the upper limit of deposit rates. Banks and clients have wider options to choose from the different prices the banks set based on different conditions.

Large banks have for the most part been content to let deposit yields stay steady or fall since the central bank granted greater flexibility in November 2014. Big banks have been loath to try to use higher rates to attract savers, given that the central bank is determined to push lending rates down; as a result, raising deposit rates would only compress profit margins. This may persist even after liberalization.

In China's banking sector, smaller banks are not competitive in absorbing deposits. Rising competition for deposit interest rates will drive depositors away from China's 198 small- and medium-sized depository institutions into five large state-owned banks. China has made process in reducing the share of deposits held by the largest five state-owned banks from 71.1% in 2002 down to 51.3% in 2012 but depositors still view these banks as too big to fail.

The risks of rising interest rate competition for small- and medium-sized banks may be mitigated with an explicit insurance program design to reimburse depositors in the event of bank failure. Small banks have more latitude to raise deposit rates, since they often lend to riskier borrowers and so their lending rates are also much higher. There is an incremental move on interest rate liberalization whenever there has often been a bigger reaction from the small banks. Indeed, some have already begun doing so since the first in a series of central bank rate cuts in November 2014.

The smaller banks have carved out a niche lending to riskier and/or more productive enterprises at higher rates. For at least some savers, higher returns outweighed safety, suggesting a possible effect of the rate liberalization. Small banks need to strike a balance between high deposit rate incentives and their own investment management to secure a proper profit margin.[74] Rules were put forward in 2014 to lower reserve requirements for banks with heavy business with small companies, encourage development of guarantee agencies, and improve performance assessment for banks to correct their preference for large deals. These rules are immediately beneficial to small businesses which are unable to acquire loans from large banks because of the small deal size and the lack of guarantees.

The establishment of the deposit insurance scheme is critical to deepening the financial reform. If deposit rates are liberalized, banks can fight back with rate hikes to win over more depositors. In this sense, the deposit insurance scheme allows smaller banks to compete on the basis of deposit yields. Therefore, the market, instead of the state, is able to set the price of capital and risk. With more autonomy in deciding deposit rates, many banks tended to lure deposits with high return promise and invest in risky projects. While the deposit insurance scheme improves funding efficiency, it will restrict them from going too far and keep risks under control.

Although financial liberalization is considered crucial to correct the inefficiency of funds when interest rates are tightly controlled, revamping deposit rates is the "riskiest" part of liberalization. Conditions for liberalization are maturing when banks are able to adapt to differentiated deposit rates, and a market-based benchmark rate can take a good shape based on the interbank seven-day repurchase rate.

6. WILL DEPOSIT INSURANCE ACHIEVE ITS PURPOSE?

Empirical work has proved that deposit insurance is not a panacea for financial crisis and financial instability. Indeed, deposit insurance reduces banking stability in countries whose contracting environment is underdeveloped.[75] It is contended that deposit insurance involves a multiparty principal-agent contract problem.[76] Banks, depositors, regulators, politicians and taxpayers are all important in ensuring the proper functioning of deposit insurance. Just to mention a few examples: a poorly performing

---

[74] The PBOC however pointed out that small banks now usually offer the ceiling rate while large banks would raise their rate by about 10%.

[75] Demirgüç-Kunt and Detragiache, "Does Deposit Insurance Increase Banking System Stability?", (2002) 49 *Journal of Monetary Economics* 1373–1406.

[76] Edward J. Kane, "Three Paradigms for the Role of Capitalization Requirements in Insured Financial Institutions", (1995) 19(3–4) *Journal of Banking and Finance* 431–459.

banking regulator can cause huge costs to taxpayers due to the financial and economic disruption of a mounting banking crisis; offering deposit insurance allows the government to negotiate more rights to participate or intervene in the affairs of insolvent banks; a deposit insurance scheme assigns a substantial role to the private parties in loss control.

A more effective contracting environment not only favourably affects the level and volatility of financial activities[77] but also serves to mitigate moral hazard incentives generated by the deposit insurance scheme. In the same vein, countries with weak contracting environments are apt to suffer adverse consequences from installing a deposit insurance scheme. The contracting environment, or an institutional infrastructure which consists of reliable institutions for loss control and failure resolution, limits the contribution that deposit insurance may bring to the financial market and macroeconomic growth. There have been discussions on the improvement of the financial safety net by adding an effective failure resolution mechanism.[78] The financial safety net should not only include an effective regulatory structure regulating key aspects of systemic risk but also a contract-based resolution regime involving major stakeholders whose interests can be aligned to ensure financial order and stability. The interplay between three pillars in the financial safety net and failure resolution can be seen in Figure 13.1. More importantly, all components of the financial safety net must be designed to work in an integrated manner.[79]

Bringing explicit deposit insurance into a weak contracting environment is likely to undermine market discipline, and banks tend to have a larger appetite for risk-taking activities. China has been studying the adoption of deposit insurance for decades. Even with a large number of non-performing loans, China's implicit deposit insurance scheme worked and sustained its long-term economic growth. This makes great economic and political sense in a broader institutional context which rests its strength on the financially repressed banking market, the underlying theory is for

---

[77] Robert Cull, Lemma W. Senbet and Marco Sorge, "Deposit Insurance and Financial Development", (2005) 37 *Journal of Money, Credit and Banking* 43–82.

[78] Mads Andenas and Iris H-Y Chiu, *The Foundations and Future of Financial Regulation – Governance for Responsibility* (London and New York: Routledge 2014) pp.315–317; Douglas W. Diamond and Philip H. Dybvig, "Bank Runs, Deposit Insurance, and Liquidity", (2000) *Federal Reserve Bank of Minneapolis Quarterly Review* 14–40.

[79] Mario Giovanoli, "Preface", in Mario Giovanoli and Gregor Heinrich (eds), *International Bank Insolvencies: A Central Bank Perspective* (London: Kluwer 1999) p.xv.

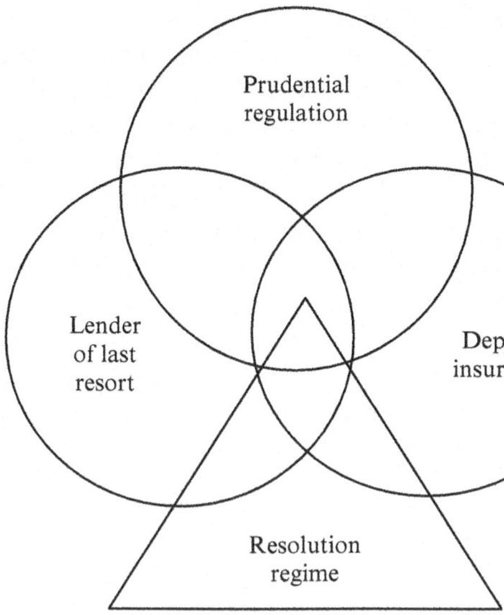

Figure 13.1 *Improved financial safety net*

China to secure less expensive financing to sustain its rapidly growing economic development.

What is a more important and relevant question here is why China is adopting an explicit deposit insurance at this point. Replacing its implicit deposit insurance scheme with an explicit one sent a strong signal to the banking sector that the government's unconditional bail out scheme for insolvent banks comes to an end. There are at least two messages being carried by this signal. First, the market should be aware that the government should not be counted on to rescue troubled banks all the time. Second, it shows the government's concerted efforts to rely more on a market-oriented approach to relieve pressure on the government for the heavily indebted banking sector. This is a sensible move in the midst of mounting debts and a slowing economy. Switching to explicit deposit insurance indicates the government's changing policy towards deteriorating non-performing loans for the commercial banks and accumulating debts for local governments by relying more on market discipline to monitor banks' behaviours.

The global experience has showcased the importance of the contracting environment. Weaknesses in the institutional environment or financial safety net need to be addressed while deposit insurance is instituted for the local financial market. Therefore, it is advisable to eliminate bank insolvencies, foster informative accounting standards, and establish reliable procedures for contract enforcement before the deposit insurance scheme is set up.[80] As far as China is concerned, one institutional weakness that requires immediate attention is the lack of explicit responsibility for resolving bank insolvencies. Aside from the deposit insurance scheme, China needs to put in place a more market-based failure resolution scheme for commercial banks.[81] Private ordering and bonding between the bank and depositors are also critically important to shape banks' lending patterns that may increase or decrease financial fragility. While regulatory supervision is weak, private monitoring can be used to overcome weakness in financial regulation. Without a strong contracting enforcement, deposit insurance may reduce the incentive of depositors to monitor the riskiness of banks, thereby distorting, rather than correcting, market and regulatory failures.

80 Demirgüç-Kunt, Kane, and Laeven (eds), *Deposit Insurance Around the World.*

81 Such a scheme can be a rescue package, financial assistance, merger or acquisition, liquidation and pay-off. Douglas W. Arner, *Financial Stability, Economic Growth, and the Role of Law* (Cambridge: Cambridge University Press 2007) p.218.

14. No conclusion yet: bringing China's shadow banking into the light

In the aftermath of the latest global financial crisis, there has been a surging shadow banking sector both in China and abroad. An econometric analysis demonstrates some market forces behind this growth of shadow banking: tight banking regulation, low interest rates and investment return rates, limited channels for funding, and a large institutional demand for assets. These are the common factors China shares with other economies. What is unique about China's shadow banking is its highly repressed financial market and system in which banks and state-owned sectors possess a much more predominant and monopolistic position in terms of allocation of financial resources and assets. The institutional infrastructure, including the interest rate and exchange rate formation mechanism as well as monetary policies, has been put in place to facilitate this financial repression strategy. While this strategy has successfully secured a stable and less expensive source of funding to sustain economic growth, it also distorts the supply and demand sides. As a result, the market response is to create a shadow banking sector to fill in this gap between supply and demand.

Defining (the scope of) shadow banking is not merely an academic exercise. It is highly relevant to regulatory design and regulatory efficacy. While there is not a uniform definition of shadow banking accepted by both regulators and academics, some attempts have been made to clarify the understanding of shadow banking. A break-down approach is often adopted to set the boundaries for shadow banking. For example, the Financial Stability Board (FSB) breaks the shadow banking system down into three sectors and nine subsectors, that is, the fund-related sector (money market funds, hedge funds and other investment funds), country-specific sector (Dutch special financial institutions, US funding corporations, and US financial holding companies), and finance-type sector (broker-dealers, finance companies, and structured finance vehicles).[1] The commonality of these sectors and subsectors is their financial intermediary

[1] FSB, "Global Shadow Banking Monitoring Report 2013", (2014) p.14.

function and non-bank characteristics, which differentiate them from banks and financial institutions. This is also the reason that the FSB term them as "other financial intermediaries".[2] Apart from its technical value, the FSB's way of drawing the boundary of shadow banking has a limitation. It may overlook the domestic conditions each country has in its financial market.

As far as China is concerned, shadow banking shares some features in common with other countries' shadow banking sectors. The defining feature is its credit intermediary function outside the banking system. Therefore, P2P lending and underground lending are two key shadow banking subsectors in China. However, credit intermediation outside of the banking system does not exclude banks and financial institutions. The participation of banks and financial institutions in shadow banking is common, caused by regulatory arbitrage. Given the predominant position banks occupy in China's financial market, the involvement of banks in shadow banking activities and services is inevitable. In this vein, wealth management products (WMPs) offered by or through banks and local government financing vehicles borrowing money from banks can be fairly included into the ambit of shadow banking. It is worth noting that the focus on these four shadow banking subsectors in this book is not meant to be exhaustive. Shadow banking should be an open-ended system through which funding can be channeled without relying on the bank's typical credit intermediation function.

The benefits of shadow banking are multi-faceted. Shadow banking broadens access to credit, which enlarges the supply side to feed cash into the cash-starved private sector and real economy. A growing shadow banking sector itself is a natural product of the deepening of financial markets,[3] which deserves positive policy or regulatory treatment. Lending by shadow banks contributes to the entire social financing (total lending) in China. As shadow banking makes a refinement to the distorted supply-demand equilibrium, it effectively improves the efficiency of the financial system and remedies market failure. From the policy perspective, shadow banking can be utilized as a strong market force pushing for deeper financial reform for market liberalization, owing to the fact that regulatory arbitrage is one of the key causes for a sizeable shadow banking sector in China.

---

2 Ibid, p.7.

3 IMF, "Risk Taking, Liquidity, and Shadow Banking – Curbing Excess While Promoting Growth", (October 2014) Global Financial Stability Report, p.67.

Intermediating credit through shadow banks provides additional sources of funding to the real economy. However, the downside of shadow banking is the possibility of systemic risk not only to the shadow banking system but also the regular banking sector, given their close interconnection. The connection between the shadow and regular banking sectors easily creates a contagion channel as well as a cross-sector spillover effect. Consequently, the stress in one sector can be transmitted to the other and can be amplified back through feedback loops.

Shadow banking exhibits risk characteristics such as excess leverage, liquidity mismatches, and vulnerability to runs, which involves, in a sequence, credit risk, liquidity risk, and systemic risk. These risks warrant regulatory intervention and monitoring regardless of the classification of shadow banking or the benefits which shadow banking generates. Apparently, different shadow banking subsectors are associated with different types of risk, which requires a sector-based (or functionally) differentiated approach to each subsector.[4] Risk velocity (meaning the speed at which a risk can materialize) is the key factor that has been used to assess the risk[5] and design responsive regulatory techniques and measures. In addition, one fundamental (or ultimate) purpose of regulatory design is to mitigate the build-up of systemic risk and avoid financial crises. Risk characteristics of shadow banking vary across countries as well. Therefore, country or regulatory context may also shape the perception and regulatory focus. In China's context, risk needs to be evaluated in light of China-specific conditions. More specifically, societal safety or broader social concern needs to be addressed and minimized while risks in financial market in other advanced economies may be merely constrained and assessed in the financial regulatory setting in modern times.

There are several paradoxical perspectives regulators and policymakers have to appreciate when they come to regulate shadow banking.

---

[4] A sector-focused approach differs from micro-prudential regulation, which is the hallmark of pre-emptive governance in financial regulation. On the term of micro-prudential supervision, see Jan J. Dalhuisen, *Transnational and Comparative Commercial, Financial and Trade Law*, Vol III (Oxford: Hart Publishing, 5th edn, 2012) Chs 1 and 2. A comparison of macro-prudential and micro-prudential approaches can be found in Dirk Schoenmaker and Jeroen Kremers, "Financial Stability and Proper Business Conduct: Can Supervisory Structure Help To Achieve These Objectives?", in Robin Hui Huang and Dirk Schoebnmaker (eds), *Institutional Structure of Financial Regulation – Theories and International Experiences* (London and New York: Routledge 2015) pp.29, 32.

[5] Thomas H. Stanton, *Why Some Firms Thrive While Others Fail – Governance and Management Lessons From The Crisis* (New York: Oxford University Press 2012) p.112.

Regulating shadow banking requires identifying and taking into consideration risks in the banking sector and making subsequent adjustments for assets and liabilities of banks. The purpose and objective of regulating shadow banking is to ensure the banking system's stability and soundness. Likewise, responsive policies dealing with the defects and inefficiency in the banking sector eventually help solve the problems and mitigate risks in the shadow banking system. At the technical level, bank-like regulatory tools or instruments are the key devices for the regulation of shadow banking. Regulating shadow banking eventually is all about the regulation of banks. These paradoxical linkages between the shadow and regular banking sectors is a mirror-effect connection, or so-termed a bank-centric misperception of shadow banking.[6] In China's context, a clear example is the regulation of WMPs issued by commercial banks or by trust or securities companies (broker-dealer) through commercial banks. The China Banking Regulatory Commission (CBRC) on 24 September 2005 issued the *Provisional Measures of Administration of Individual Wealth Management Business by Commercial Banks* to regulate these products and cast the regulatory net over off-balance-sheet products issued by commercial banks. The ambiguously drawn line between shadow and regular banking challenges both sectors. For instance, the mixture of trust companies and commercial lenders in issuing WMPs raises a true sale concern that is discussed in the context of securitization where off-balance-sheet treatment of underlying assets or bankruptcy remoteness of the sponsoring entity often creates a regulatory challenge.[7] Corresponding to this murky line between the shadow and regular banking sectors, a network approach may be employed to regulate banks and shadow banks on an aggregate basis, which fills in the gap created by such factors that contribute to interconnection risks. This network approach not only reflects the interconnection of the shadow and regular banking sectors but also matches a macro-prudential supervisory framework[8] in a systemic stability context.

---

[6] Tri Vi Dang, Honglin Wang and Aidan Yao, "Chinese Shadow Banking: Bank-centric Misperceptions" (September 2014) Hong Kong Institute for Monetary Research Working Paper No.22/2014.

[7] Yingmao Tang, "Shadow Banking or 'Bank's Shadow': Re-conceptualizing Global Shadow Banking Regulation", in Ross P. Buckley, Emilios Avgouleas and Douglas W. Arner (eds) *Reconceptualising Global Finance and Its Regulation* (Cambridge: Cambridge University Press 2016) pp.326, 332.

[8] Mads Andenas and Iris H-Y Chiu, *The Foundations and Future of Financial Regulation – Governance for Responsibility* (London and New York: Routledge 2014) Ch 15.

Regulating shadow banking is a new challenge to financial regulators. The analyses of four key shadow banking subsectors in China highlight the complexity of regulating shadow banking as a whole. In most cases, regulatory tools tackling these shadow banking subsectors are typical ones to banks; just to list a few: disclosure rules, accounting and rating procedures, reserved capital restrictions, and loan quota. However, the effect of choosing these bank-type regulatory instruments is not yet clear. For instance, disclosure rules may not create the desired effect in ameliorating the risks in relation to WMPs when the investors lack expertise or incentives to digest disclosed information.[9] Limiting the proportion of certain illiquid assets to 35% of total assets under management is unlikely to prevent the withdrawal of liquidity during periods of acute market uncertainty.[10] Without a liquidity backstop, the WMP market is vulnerable to financial instability owing to market uncertainty and liquidity constraints. Regulating local government financing vehicles (LGFVs) requires market discipline. Both the State Council and the CBRC required banks to grant loans for profitable projects only, and mandated that loans to LGFVs each year should not exceed the previous year's amount.[11] Nevertheless, market disciplines do not satisfy the local governments' financing demands. Further, the tightened credit policy plunged local governments into deeper financial distress. Possibly, local governments would continue to seek funding if there were no structural change to the budgetary system. In terms of P2P lending, regulatory authorities have not taken any measures. Whether P2P lending involves systemic risk and justifies a large scale of regulation itself is debatable. The opacity of underground

---

9 Omri Ben-Shahar and Carl E. Schneider, *More Than You Wanted To Know – The Failure of Mandated Disclosure* (Princeton and Oxford: Princeton University Press 2014) (claiming that mandated disclosure, though being a lawmaker's panacea, rarely works).

10 CBRC's Interim Measures for the Administration of Commercial Banks' Personal Financial Management Services; the CSRC's Notice on Enhancing Regulation on Wealth Management Business for Specified Customers Conducted by Fund Companies and Their Subsidiaries (Zheng Jian Ban [2014] No. 26); Guidance of the General Office of the CBRC on the Regulation of Risks of Trust Companies (Yin Jian Ban Fa [2014] No. 99); CBRC's Notice on Regulating the Investment Operations of the Wealth Management Business of Commercial Banks (Yin Jian Fa [2013] No. 8).

11 Relevant regulations and notices include the Notice of the State Council on Issues Concerning the Administration of Local Government Financing Vehicles (Guo Fa [2010] No.19); the Notice of the CBRC on Controlling Loan Risks of Local Government Financing Vehicles (Yin Jian Fa [2011] No. 34); Guiding Opinions of the CBRC on Strengthening the Control over Loan Risks of Local Government Financing Vehicles (Yin Jian Fa [2013] No. 10).

lending is bound to be a headache to regulators which are keen to build up a regulatory mechanism for this purely private business arena. Regulation can only be used as substitutionary or gap-filling rules improving market conditions for this arena. These regulatory devices are not mutually exclusive, and constitute a regulatory net. However, the difficulty in effectively regulating the entire shadow banking system requires a reconceptualization of the financial market and financial regulation.

Shadow banking has grown sizeably globally. In China, shadow banking has already reached a not insignificant share of the economy and the entire financial system. Shadow banking clearly poses some types of risks to financial stability. The interconnection between the formal and shadow banking sectors can generate systemic risk. Segments of the shadow banking sector are subject to regulatory oversight with varying levels of intensity, thereby leading to regulatory arbitrage and undermining the effectiveness of tighter prudential regulation on the banking sector. On the other hand, shadow banks have become an important alternative source of funding to the real economy. Some categories of loans fill the gap created by bank retrenchment.[12] This reminds policymakers and regulators of the importance of striking a balance between curbing potential risks and promoting trade-offs.

Bringing shadow banking under the regulatory umbrella appears to be a clear regulatory response to the sizeable shadow banking sector. The underlying rationale of such a move is to prevent systemic risk from being spread, damaging financial stability and economic growth. Legislating away financial fragility through various laws and rules may not be enough. Policymakers should work toward a regulatory regime for shadow banking. If the growth of shadow banking is caused by regulatory arbitrage, removing regulatory gaps and reversing regulatory changes can be a possible regulatory choice leading to a smaller shadow banking system in some countries such as China. However, a negative attack on such arbitrages is not a sensible response. The objective of the regulatory policy is to strengthen, rather than harm, financial services for the weak areas in society such as small- and medium-sized firms. Besides, reversing financial regulation (or re-regulation) is a radical course which is not an endogenous response and may trigger undesired switching costs. The side effect of this reversal course is to drive shadow banking into a new unregulated darkness. The feasible solution to the rapid rise of shadow banking

---

[12] Erik Feyen, Katie Kibuuka and Inci Otker-Robe, "Bank Deleveraging: Causes, Channels, and Consequences for Emerging Market and Developing Countries", (2012) World Bank Policy Research Working Paper No. 6086.

should be a full package of policies and regulatory tools addressing some, if not all, of the root causes that give rise to regulatory arbitrage.

The details need to be worked out in conjunction with the regulation of the banking sector, with which they would be closely intertwined. Setting new rules for shadow banking is likely to make new demands of regulators and these demands are analogous to those needed to set rules for banks. There are no private-sector solutions to ensure the safety of the financial market. In other words, leaving shadow banking under the invisible hands of the market is not a wise solution, and the role of regulators remains essential. The visible hands of the government have to take a hands-off approach towards the market and let the market play a constructive or even "decisive" role.

The benefits of shadow banking justify a dedicated reconciliation approach towards shadow banking – regulators need to work out how to reconcile the financing demands satisfied by shadow banking and the desire to have a sound and safe financial market. Apart from regulating shadow banking in order to curb systemic risk, the other policy option is to legitimate or legalize some shadow banking subsectors. This is recognition of the importance of shadow banking in financing the economy. In the UK and the euro area, supporting and facilitating non-bank lending has been included as part of the public initiatives.[13] Legal hurdles for non-banks to engage in lending activities are being lifted in other jurisdictions.[14] Legitimating some shadow banking subsectors is effectively to bring them into the light so as to fill the regulatory gap and avoid regulatory arbitrage. Back to China, legitimating or formalizing the undergrounding lending market is a similar policy initiative deployed to achieve the same objective. The key for China is to regulate its shadow

---

[13] These initiatives included the UK government's Business Finance Partnership scheme and the European Central Bank's initiative to promote a functioning market for asset-backed securities collateralized by loans to non-financial corporations. The Business Finance Partnership scheme's two strands include an investment in fund managers who lend to medium-sized businesses with turnover of up to £500 million. The first six funds have now been set up and together they manage £863 million of government investment alongside over £1 billion from private investors. The second strand invests in fund managers and non-traditional lenders that provide an alternative source of lending for small businesses with turnover up to £75 million. UK Department for Business Innovation and Skills and HM Treasury, "Policy Paper 2010–2015 Government Policy: Business Enterprise", (2015), Appendix 2; Reuters, "ECB Launches Programme to Buy Asset-backed Securities", 22 November 2014, available 2 March 2016 at http://finance.qq.com/a/20141122/007018.htm.

[14] FSB, "Global Shadow Banking Monitoring Report 2013", (2013) p.43.

banking sector to the extent that it ensures stability throughout the financial system, but without intervening to the extent that it causes market distortions. However, this balanced policy option must be used with caution. For example, the CBRC tends not to allow P2P platforms to act as credit intermediaries, which is equated to opening the banking business to non-banks without any hurdles. This means that regulators may have to prioritize the source of funding for economic growth, rather than containing the financial market. The benefits of shadow banking, especially in a time of economic downturn, justify a laid-back (or light-regulatory) approach to at least some shadow banking subsectors.

In the Chinese context, the difficulty of combining regulatory tightening and restricted liquidity is the risk of miscalculation or an accident that might trigger the instability the regulators have been trying very hard to avoid. Another layer of complexity lies in the hybrid nature of the shadow banking sector. While it poses various challenges to financial regulations, the emergence of the shadow banking sector reflects a market demand for diversified financial products. Simply, the role of the shadow banking system cannot be denied. Rigid rules may curb financing for smaller and weaker firms, thereby hurting the economy. Regulators should explore "the most appropriate" way of supervision that could control risks in shadow banking while enhancing financial services to the weakest sectors in the real economy. To minimize the potential hazards, regulators should strike a balance between effective regulation and gentle de-regulation.

A variety of regulatory tools, instruments, techniques, and policy responses, touching upon capital, liquidity, activity restrictions, business operations and governance, have been put forward by regulators, legislators, policymakers and scholars. Regulators and policymakers are keen to rely on rules and guidance documents sending strong signals to the market. Meanwhile, efforts have been devoted by regulators to enhance enforcement aiming to fix the loopholes, level the playing field and reduce regulatory arbitrage. The PBOC and CBRC's regulatory measures can basically be grouped into four categories.

(a) The regulation of shadow banking has been tailored to partially target banks' exposure to shadow banks with the purpose of disconnecting the interconnection of the shadow and regular banking sectors.
(b) The financial safety net has been extended to cover some shadow banking markets or entities either because the interconnection is hard to remove or due to the fact that shadow banking subsectors have merged into the banking regulatory ambit. Extending the regulatory boundary or implicit government guarantees of shadow banks

may create a similar effect. Accordingly, the regulatory or policy net needs to be wide enough not only to integrate the vehicle, activity and market dimensions of shadow banking but also to avoid stagnation.

(c) The causes of shadow banking are addressed through some regulatory instruments under a macro-prudential framework dealing with the supply-demand disequilibrium. Applying bank-like regulatory tools such as capital requirements, restrictions on leverage and maturity or liquidity transformation under the macro-prudential framework helps curb regulatory arbitrage. Under extreme circumstances, it is conceivable to extend the lender-of-last-resort function to some shadow banking subsectors or vehicles to protect the financial system against liquidity shocks.[15]

(d) As a backup, consumer protection rules including reporting requirements are designed and deployed so that weaker financial consumers can be well protected if they are disadvantaged in their transactions with shadow banks.

All of these efforts are relevant, either pragmatically or technically. Chinese regulators have recently declared a partial victory over shadow banking. According to the PBOC's data in January 2015, credit creation from all sources fell 6% in 2014 from one year earlier, only the third annual decline since collection of data on "total social finance" started in 2002.[16] This fall, the PBOC claims, is attributable to the slowing growth or shrinking of non-bank lending.

Given the complexity of shadow banking, the entire architecture of financial regulation may need to be revisited and redesigned given the dynamic and complex nature of shadow banking.[17] In terms of China's shadow banking sector, it is worth noting and enhancing both demand and supply sides of shadow banking. Shadow banking emerges, survives and grows in supply-demand (dis)equilibrium. When regular banks fail to function as a credit intermediary responsible for credit, maturity and liquidity transformation, and become unable to meet the financing

---

[15] Tamim Bayoumi, Giovanni Dell'Ariccia, Karl Habermeier, Tommaso Mancini-Griffoli and Fabrián Valencia, "Monetary Policy in the New Normal", (2014) IMF Staff Discussion Note SDN/14/3.

[16] Gabriel Wildau, "China Shadow Bank Regulation Shows Results", *Financial Times*, 2 February 2014 (online).

[17] Steven L. Schwarcz, "Regulating Financial Change: A Functional Approach", (2015) 100 *Minnesota Law Review* 1441–1494, available 2 March 2016 at http://scholarship.law.duke.edu/cgi/viewcontent.cgi?article=5995&context=faculty_scholarship.

demands of businesses, shadow banks quickly kick in and fill the vacuum left by regular banks. While technological innovation and regulatory arbitrage lend convincing force to the explanation of the popularity of shadow banking in China's financial market, financial repression is a theoretical framework laying down a solid foundation for more effective regulatory design and policy responses.

Financial regulation is always mixed with increased financial innovation, which in turn evolves with and affects the risk allocation function of the financial system.[18] Chinese regulators have been tolerant for the financial sector to experiment with new products or off-balance sheets, allowing the system gently to displace state allocation of capital through decreed interest rates, loan quotas, loan-to-deposit ratios and specific credit restrictions. However, regulators disapprove of banks and financial institutions taking advantage of financial innovation and bypassing administrative and regulatory measures governing capital adequacy and loan-to-deposit ratios.

In order to secure the least expensive source of funding to sustain long-term economic growth, China has been applying more favourable monetary policies and regulatory devices, mainly in the form of interest rates and exchange rates, to state-owned banks. The consequence of such a financial repression model is two-fold. First, state-owned banks are able to secure the least expensive source of deposit, and ensure a sizeable profit margin.[19] Related to this is the commercial banks' lending behaviour in favour of state-owned sectors and discriminating against non-state players in the market. Second, the private sector, including start-up firms and privately-owned enterprises, has difficulty in financing their business and expansion, creating the demand side of shadow banking. Viewed thus, regulating shadow banking at a technical level is insufficient to contain the growth of shadow banking. Rather, the government and regulators have to adopt a more holistic solution or scheme to deal with both the supply and demand sides of financing. It has been proposed that the holistic solution should include better demographic, industry and urban planning.[20]

---

[18] Dwight B. Crane et al., *The Global Financial System: A Functional Perspective* (Boston, MA: Harvard Business School Press 1995) p.153.

[19] The real sources of the high profitability of Chinese banks revealed by some empirical research not only include the managed interest system but also unsustainable low staff costs. It appears that the high net interest margin alone did not guarantee the "windfall" profits for Chinese commercial banks. Horst Löchel and Helena Xiang Li, "Understanding the High Profitability of Chinese Banks", (2011) Frankfurt School of Finance and Management Working Paper Series No. 177, available 2 March 2016 at www.frankfurt-school.de.

[20] Li Guo and Daile Xia, "In Search of a Place in the Sun: The Shadow Banking System with Chinese Characteristics", (2014) 15(3) *European Business*

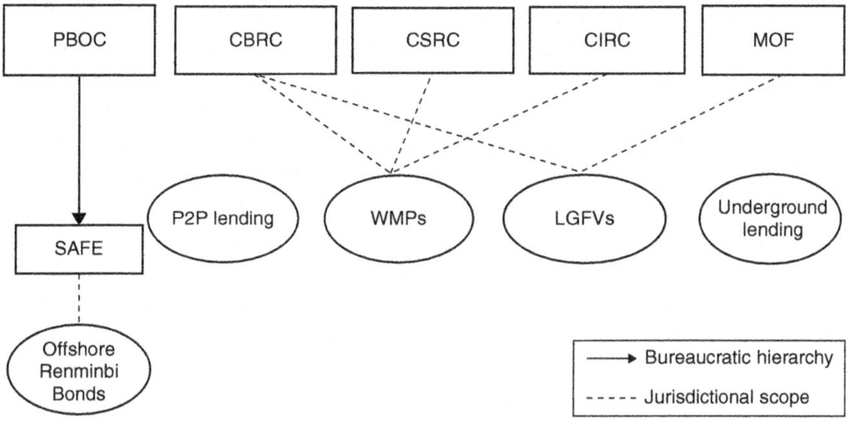

Figure 14.1 Shadow banking's regulatory space

What can be achieved through this holistic solution appears to ensure that all of the parts of the financial market (whatsoever they may be labeled) that perform economically equivalent functions are, to the fullest extent possible, subject to functionally equivalent forms of prudential regulation. In this author's view, this holistic solution (howsoever it may be conceived) is merely to address the narrow scope of the regulatory net, but yet tackle the fundamental flaw in market-disequilibrium. Seen from this angle, as far as China's shadow banking is concerned, a "visible" device is to rely on the "invisible hand" by injecting more competition into the financial market and removing restrictions on market entry, interest rate and exchange rate so that the market can shape the equilibrium of demand and supply sides[21] in an efficient and cost-effective manner.

In order to diminish the motivation for arbitrage, the proposal has been made to reform the existing financial regulatory regime. In China's current sectoral (or sector-based) regulatory regime, it is easy to create regulatory arbitrage as the financial regulatory framework has been segmented to respond to each fragmented financial sector. While this sectoral regulatory regime guarantees a higher level of responsiveness, specialty and relevance, regulatory arbitrage and regulatory loopholes are natural by-products of such a regulatory architecture. As Figure 14.1 indicates, some major shadow banking subsectors span a number of regulatory

---

Organization Law Review 387, 417.

[21] Peter C. Carstensen, "Antitrust Law and the Paradigm of Industrial Organization", (1983) 16 *UC Davis Law Review* 487.

arenas while others may fall outside the entire regulatory space of the financial market. Circular No. 107, China's key regulatory and policy response to shadow banking, presents a clear example showing the limitation of the sectoral regulatory model, the effectiveness of which relies on the implementing rules each financial regulator may have in the future.

Transforming China's current sectoral regulatory model to the twin-peaks structure, as some have suggested, is something the Chinese government may consider in order to revamp the financial infrastructure and cure regulatory failure.[22] In light of the latest global financial crisis, the institutional structure of financial regulation is a hotly debated subject of academic and practical interest. Both the sole-regulator model and twin-peaks model have been extensively analysed and compared as well as tested and improved in various major advanced economies. They have both strengths and weaknesses compared to China's sectoral regulatory model. They both appear to strike at the root and consequence of regulatory arbitrage as both models target bringing the whole financial market under one regulatory umbrella instead of a fragmented framework. However, the belief that these institutional structures are able to contain the size of shadow banking and eventually to mitigate systemic risk related to shadow banking[23] may be an over-simplistic approach, as prohibitively high switching costs may be involved in overhauling China's current sectoral model to one of the other two regulatory structures, more specifically, the twin-peaks model. The unworkability of this proposal is chiefly due to the fact that institutional change, in most cases being the result of either a political choice[24] or evolutionary development,[25] may only address regulatory failure but leave market failure[26] uncorrected and even untouched.

---

22 Robin Hui Huang, "The Regulation of Shadow Banking in China: International and Comparative Perspectives", (2015) 30 *Banking & Finance Law Review* 481.

23 Ibid.

24 Eílis Ferran, "The Break-up of the Financial Services Authority in the UK", in Robin Hui Huang and Dirk Schoenmaker (eds), *Institutional Structure of Financial Regulation – Theories and International Experiences* (London and New York: Routledge 2015) pp.109, 136.

25 Richard Scott Carnell, Jonathan R. Macey and Geoffrey P. Miller, *The Law of Banking and Financial Institutions* (New York: Wolters Kluwer, 5th edn, 2013) Ch 1 (claiming that "the world of banking is a world in upheaval").

26 Steven L. Schwarcz, "Regulating Shadow Banking", (2012) 31 *Boston University Review of Banking & Financial Law* 619; Steven L. Schwarcz, "Shadow Banking, Financial Risks, and Regulation in China and Other Developing Countries" (unpublished paper on file with the author) (both claiming that shadow banking involves information failure, rationality failure, principal-agent failure, and incentive failure).

A functional perspective remains flexible and adaptable to the possible institutional configuration.[27]

The new proposal to merge the PBOC, CBRC, China Securities Regulatory Commission (CSRC) and China Insurance Regulatory Commission (CIRC) emerged in the CCP's 18th Congress's Fifth Plenum and may materialize in the period of China's implementation of its 13th Plan. This may be different from the sole-regulator model in the sense that an overarching mega-regulatory (coordinative) body on top of the PBOC, CBRC, CSRC and CIRC will be established to coordinate, instead of completely substitute, the current "one-central-bank-and-three-commissions" structure.[28] This new structure may facilitate the reduction of coordination (or collective action) problems among these four institutions. The benefits of this super regulatory (or coordinative) structure arise more from applying the broad principles of regulation consistently to all financial sectors than in applying the details of any particular sector slavishly. A clear example is that the same principle applies to other sectors if off-balance sheet activities require capital in the banking sector.

Market theory is conditioned on numerous assumptions. So is market efficiency, which relies on rational individuals with the aim of maximizing utility, their stable and ordered preferences informing their maximizing behavior, and their supply and demand equilibrium.[29] It has been well recognized that market failure may be caused by lack of sufficient information,[30] moral hazard or externalities. Neoclassical economists posit that free markets are the engines of progress and function as efficient allocators of resources.[31] The widely accepted tenet of the functioning of market systems is that the government can be the worst force to encumber the working of the market. This explains the ineffectiveness of the holistic solution full of regulatory instruments and tools. A more relevant medicine to cure market failure in China is to reformulate market policies, not only

---

[27] Guo and Xia, "In Search of a Place in the Sun: The Shadow Banking System with Chinese Characteristics", p.418.

[28] Ifeng.com News, available 2 March 2016 at http://finance.ifeng.com/a/20151113/14068185_0.shtml (in Chinese).

[29] Gary Becker, *The Economic Approach to Human Behaviour* (Chicago, IL: University of Chicago Press 1978).

[30] Giandomenico Majone, "The New European Agencies: Regulation by Information", (1997) 4 *Journal of European Public Policy* 262.

[31] James W. McKie, "Regulation and the Free Market: The Problem of Boundaries", (1970) 1 *Bell Journal of Economics and Management* 6, Frederic M. Scherer, "Conservative Economics and Antitrust: A Variety of Influences", in Robert Pitofsky (ed.), *How the Chicago School Overshot the Mark* (Oxford: Oxford University Press) pp.30–39.

transforming the market but, more fundamentally, correcting government failure,[32] the cause of market failure in the context of China's shadow banking. The government failure in China has been reflected into China's interventionist approach toward both banking regulation and broader macroeconomic policy[33] and its top-down governance hierarchy, in stark contrast to the bottom-up market-oriented macroeconomic structure. Freeing the market therefore is probably a much more effective policy prescription.

A comparative study of shadow banking in different countries indicates both differences and similarities. The size of shadow banking in advanced and emerging economies varies. So does the speed of growth of shadow banking sector in these countries. Although the financial markets in all countries differ in terms of the level of deepening financial markets and the degree of complexity of financial system, the key drivers and growth patterns of shadow banking in these countries are very similar. The driving forces behind a growing shadow banking sector are: a strong demand for funding, an increasing appetite for higher yield,[34] regulatory arbitrage, complementarities with the regular banking sector,[35] and the availability of innovative financial products and services such as structured finance and trust and special purpose vehicles. Shadow banking benefits the economy by channeling more funding to the real

---

[32] Rent-seeking is one theoretical ground to explain government failure. Gerald M. Meier and James E. Rauch, *Leading Issues in Economic Development* (New York and Oxford: Oxford University Press, 7th edn., 2000) p.434.

[33] Dan Awrey, "Law and Finance in the Chinese Shadow Banking System", (2015) 48 *Cornell International Law Journal* 1.

[34] There is a search-for-yield-effect caused by the demand of funding on the demand side and the supply of assets on the supply side, and shadow banking satisfies both sides. Thomas Goda, Photis Lysandrou and Chris Stewart, "The Contribution of US Bond Demand to the US Bond Yield Conundrum of 2004 to 2007: An Empirical Investigation", (2013) 27 *Journal of International Financial Markets, Institutions and Money* 113–136; Thomas Goda and Photis Lysandrou, "The Contribution of Wealth Concentration to the Subprime Crisis: A Quantitative Estimation", (2014) 38(2) *Cambridge Journal of Economics* 301–327.

[35] Caroline Fohlin, "Does Civil Law Tradition and Universal Banking Crowd Out Securities Markets? Pre-World War I Germany as Counter Example", (2007) 8(3) *Enterprise & Society*, 602–641; Thierry Tressel and Enrica Detragiache, "Do Financial Sector Reforms Lead to Financial Development? Evidence from a New Dataset", (2008) IMF Working Paper WP/08/265 (arguing that large fiscal deficits may lead to macroeconomic instability and may crowd-out private investment); Samah Shetta and Ahmed Kamaly, "Does the Budget Deficit Crowd-out Private Credit from the Banking Sector? The Case of Egypt", (2014) 16(2) *Topics in Middle Eastern and African Economies* 251–279.

economy, injecting competitive force in the financial market, and deepening the financial market. It has been advocated that the difference between China's shadow banking and the US's is built upon the notion of information insensitivity vs. financial engineering relevant to China and the US respectively. In summary, the information insensitivity theorem refers to information asymmetry deeply embedded in China's less developed financial market, which captures the eagerness of investors (that is, depositors and non-bank institutions) and borrowers (that is, state-owned enterprises and private enterprises) in China for less information-sensitive funding,[36] akin to bank deposits. In contrast, a sizeable shadow banking sector in the US is due to the strong capital markets, which allow the application of computational techniques and methods for financial engineering activities. This analytical model is claimed to capture the fundamentally dynamic differences between these two countries' shadow banking sectors.[37]

This book, however, suggests a financial repression (primarily in the form of limits on interest rate, exchange rate, capital flow, market entry and business scope) vs. financial liberalization framework to explain opposite theories (roots) for the same economic phenomenon. China is a heavily repressed and closed financial market which forces both banks (financial institutions) and investors to circumvent tighter regulation through non-bank intermediation.[38] In the US, UK, Germany and EU, among others, financial markets have been liberalized allowing more financial innovation and alternative financing channels,[39] which is said to be the most original aspect of recent times.[40] Consequently, shadow banking grows from the demands of institutional cash pools for alternatives to insured

---

[36] Lack of transparency has been recognized to be the primary problem in as well as the key cause of China's shadow banking system. "Shadow Banking in China: Battling the Darkness", *The Economist* (10 May 2014).

[37] Tri Vi Dang, Honglin Wang and Aidan Yao, "Chinese Shadow Banking: Bank-centric Misperceptions", (September 2014) Hong Kong Institute for Monetary Research Working Paper No.22/2014.

[38] Dimitri Vittas, *Financial Regulation – Changing the Rules for the Game* (Washington DC: World Bank 1992).

[39] Eílis Ferran, "The Liberalisation of Financial Markets: The Regulatory Response in the United Kingdom", Rainer Grote, "The Liberalization of Financial Markets: The Regulatory Response in Germany", John K.M. Ohnesorge, "Perspectives on US Financial Regulation", and Volker Röben, "The Regulation of Financial Services in the European Union", in Rainer Grote and Thilo Marauhn, *The Regulation of International Financial Markets: Perspectives for Reform* (Cambridge: Cambridge University Press 2006) Chs 2, 3, 4 and 5 respectively.

[40] Youssef Cassis, *Capitals of Capital: The Rise and Fall of International Financial Centres 1780–2009* (Cambridge: Cambridge University Press 2010) p.248.

deposits and safe assets.[41] The comparison of these two models is a pair of differences between environments of dry liquidity vs. ample liquidity or between the development stages of financial constraints vs. financial innovation. This analytical framework can also be applied to explain a host of general and structural differences between shadow banking sectors in developed and developing countries.

A balanced policy framework has been proposed by the FSB to achieve two objectives: ensuring financial stability and promoting financial and economic development. National regulators must appreciate the importance of shadow banking in filling a credit void, broadening access to finance and deepening the financial market. More importantly, shadow banking is valuable in promoting financial inclusion, which hints towards the "democratization" of finance. The state of the financial services industry is highly institutionalized insofar as it comprises of highly organized and politically focused economic actors.[42] Corresponding to this institutionalization of finance is a regulatory framework with greater hierarchy and vested interest. Shadow banking is a viable agent of the "democratization" of finance[43] as it mitigates the dominance of traditional institutional actors such as banks in the financial industry and economic development.[44] Seen through this lens, shadow banking optimizes the distribution of financial resources, thereby improving economic efficiency and increasing social welfare. This is particularly relevant to China which is a heavily repressed financial market. Shadow banking is a result of financial repression and can be relied on to improve the financial market.

A broader policy package needs to be designed and deployed to address this wide financial repression scheme. The CCP pledged in its Third Plenum in November 2013 to give markets a "decisive" role in resource allocation.

---

41 Zoltan Pozsar, "Institutional Cash Pools and the Triffin Dilemma of the US Banking System", (2011) IMF Working Paper 11/190.

42 Susanne Soederberg, "The New International Financial Architecture (NIFA): An Emerging Multi-level Structure of Neo-Liberal Discipline", in Andrew Baker, David Hudson and Richard Woodward (eds), *Governing Financial Globalization: International Political Economy and Multi-Level Governance* (London and New York: Routledge 2005) p.189.

43 Robert J. Shiller, "The Democratization of Banking", available 2 March 2016 at http://www.theglobalist.com/the-democratization-of-banking-nobel/.

44 Wendy Dobson and Anil K. Kashyap, "The Contradiction in China's Gradualist Banking Reforms", (2006) 2 *Brookings Papers on Economic Activity* 103–62, available 2 March 2016 at http://www.frbsf.org/economic-research/publications/working-papers/wp2014-07.pdf (claiming that the fact that 90% of financial assets flows through the banking system is a truly striking feature of China's financial system).

This landmark agenda included liberalizing interest and exchange rates, liberalizing the flow of investment funds in and out of China, and putting privately-owned companies on a par with state-owned enterprises (SOEs). These policy initiatives were put in place to improve the allocation of financial resources and correct distortions in the economy, putting China on a secure footing for several more decades of rapid growth. Restrictions on capital controls which prevent Chinese citizens from moving funds abroad and contribute to wasteful domestic investment are to be gradually relaxed. Without a cap on bank deposit rates, borrowing costs will not be kept artificially low, and investment and loan pouring into infrastructural and manufacturing sectors will be discouraged. Demand, therefore, would be affected either way. Freer capital flows would create opportunities for foreigners, especially overseas asset managers which will enjoy increased access to mainland capital markets. These reforms will aid not only short-term destabilization but also long-term growth. However, these reforms are likely to cause risks, uncertainties and vulnerabilities for China's stability-obsessed leadership. Financial liberalization could lead to excessive lending and place pressure on credit quality and banks' profitability. Once banks are forced to compete for depositors' money, interest rates will rise. It will be painful for SOEs and local governments. Rising rates increase the cost of servicing debt, sparking a wave of defaults among highly-indebted corporate borrowers. Freer capital flows will open the door to capital flight if investors lose confidence in the economy. Both local and international experience affirms the importance of heightened regulation and supervision.

Regulators should avoid over-regulation of shadow banking. This shows the importance and relevance of local peculiarities and circumstances, that is, the stage of financial development and the level of financial innovation, which need to be taken into account to warrant policy relevance and efficacy. The regulators and policymakers instead need to prioritize risk prevention and continuously stress that financial innovation should serve the needs of the real economy. Implementing these large-scale economic and financial reforms will take years. Apart from mounting concern over the sizeable shadow banking sector (indeed a potential debt-fuelled crisis), it is in China's own best interests to improve the breadth and sophistication of financial markets and implement its "mass entrepreneurship and innovation"[45]

[45] Xinhua News, "China Eyes Mass Innovation, Entrepreneurship as New Engine", 28 January 2015, available 2 March 2016 at http://www.globaltimes.cn/content/904599.shtml (last visited on 25 November 2015), and "China Boots Mass Entrepreneurship and Innovation", 16 June 2015, available 2 March 2016 at http://english.gov.cn/policies/latest_releases/2015/06/16/content_281475128473681.htm

scheme or the idea of "inclusive economy",[46] which will help avoid the economy's hard landing, and more importantly, drive Chinese economic and societal growth in future.

(reporting that the government is determined to innovate its institutional mechanisms to facilitate mass entrepreneurship and innovation).

[46] Inclusive growth is imperative not only for achieving the equity objective but also for sustaining the growth momentum. The major policy to achieve inclusive growth is to encourage easier and affordable access to financial services. China, together with other developing countries, has been including inclusive growth into the policy package. See generally, Shafei Moiz Hali, "APEC 2015 Lays the Foundations for Inclusive Economies", 23 November 2015, available 2 March 2016 at http://www.china.org.cn/opinion/2015-11/23/content_37133786.htm; Fu Peng, "China to Foster 'Inclusive Development' with Britain: Premier Li", available 2 March 2016 at http://news.xinhuanet.com/english/bilingual/2014-06/18/c_133417232.htm; Usha Thorat, "Inclusive Growth – The Role of Banks in Emerging Economies", (2008) *RBI Monthly Bulletin* 411–424.

Select bibliography

Acharya, Viral V., "Governments as Shadow Banks: The Looming Threat to Financial Stability", (2012) 90 *Texas Law Review* 1745.

Acharya, Viral V. and S. Viswanathan, "Leverage, Moral Hazard, and Liquidity", (2011) 66 *Journal of Finance* 99.

Aitken, Michael and Carole Comerton-Forde, "How should Liquidity Be Measured?", (2003) 11 *Pacific-Basin Finance Journal* 45.

Allen, Franklin, Jun Qian and Meijun Qian, "Law, Finance and Economic Growth in China", (2005) 77(1) *Journal of Financial Economics* 57–116.

Andenas, Mads and Iris H-Y Chiu, *The Foundations and Future of Financial Regulation – Governance for Responsibility* (London and New York: Routledge 2014).

Angkinand, Apanard P., Wanvimol Sawangngoenyang and Clas Wihlborg, "Financial Liberalization and Banking Crises: Cross-Country Analysis", (2010) 10(2) *International Review of Finance* 263.

Arner, Douglas W., *Financial Stability, Economic Growth, and the Role of Law* (Cambridge: Cambridge University Press 2007).

Ashcraft, Adam B. and Til Schuermann, "Understanding the Securitization of Subprime Mortgage Credit", (2007) 2(3) *Foundations and Trends in Finance* 191.

Avgouleas, Emilios, *Governance of Global Financial Markets: The Laws, The Economics, The Politics* (Cambridge: Cambridge University Press 2012).

Avgouleas, Emilios, "The Vexed Issue of Short Sales Regulation When Prohibition Is Inefficient and Disclosure Is Insufficient", in Kern Alexander and Niamh Moloney, *Law Reform and Financial Markets* (Cheltenham, UK and Northampton, MA, USA: Edward Elgar 2011).

Avgouleas, Emilios and Charles Goodhart, "Critical Reflections on Bank Bail-ins", (2015) 1(1) *Journal of Financial Regulation* 3.

Awrey, Dan, "Law and Finance in the Chinese Shadow Banking System", (2015) 48 *Cornell International Law Journal* 1.

Ayyagari, Meghana, Aslı Demirgüç-Kunt, and Vojislav Maksimovic, "Formal Versus Informal Finance: Evidence from China", (2010) 23(8) *Review of Financial Studies* 3048.

Bar-Gill, Oren, "The Law, Economics and Psychology of Subprime Mortgage Contracts", (2009) 94 *Cornell Law Review* 1073.

Barth, James R., Chen Lin and Clas Wihlborg, *Research Handbook on International Banking and Governance* (Cheltenham, UK, Northampton MA, USA: Edward Elgar 2012).

Barth, James R., Gerard Caprio Jr. and Ross Levine, *Rethinking Bank Regulation till Angels Govern* (Cambridge: Cambridge University Press 2008).

Barth, James R., R. Dan Brumbaugh Jr. and Robert E. Litan, *The Future of American Banking* (London: Sharpe 1992).

Beck, Thorsten and Aslı Demirgüç-Kunt, "Small and Medium-Size Enterprises: Access to Finance as A Growth Constraint", (2006) 30 *Journal of Banking and Finance* 2931.

Becker, Gary, *The Economic Approach to Human Behaviour* (Chicago, IL: University of Chicago Press 1978).

Bell, Ian and Petrina Dawson, "Synthetic Securitization: Use of Derivative Technology for Credit Transfer", (2002) 12 *Duke Journal of Comparative and International Law* 541.

Ben-Shahar, Omri and Carl E. Schneider, *More Than You Wanted To Know – The Failure of Mandated Disclosure* (Princeton and Oxford: Princeton University Press 2014).

Berger, Allen N. and Gregory F. Udell, "The Economics of Small Business Finance: The Roles of Private Equity and Debt Markets in the Financial Growth Cycle", (1998) 22 *Journal of Banking and Finance* 613.

Bliss, Robert R. and George G. Kaufman, "U.S. Corporate and Bank Insolvency Regimes: A Comparison and Evaluation", (2007) 2 *Virginia Law and Business Review* 143.

Boyd, John and Mark Gertler, "US Commercial Banking: Trends, Cycles, and Policy", in Oliver Blanchard and Stanley Fischer (eds), *NBER Macroeconomics Annual 1993* (Cambridge, MA: MIT Press 1993).

Brunnermeier, Markus K. and Lesse Heje Pedersen, "Market Liquidity and Funding Liquidity", (2009) 2(6) *Review of Financial Studies* 2201.

Bryan, Lowell L., *Breaking Up the Bank: Rethinking an Industry under Siege* (Homewood IL: Dow Jones-Irwin 1988).

Bryant, John, "A Model of Reserves, Bank Runs, and Deposit Insurance", (1980) 4 *Journal of Banking & Finance* 335.

Calomiris, Charles W., "The Subprime Turmoil: What's Old, What's New, and What's Next", (2009) 15 *Journal of Structured Finance* 6.

Calomiris, Charles W., "Financial Innovation, Regulation and Reform", (2009) 29 *Cato Journal* 65.

Calomiris, Charles W., "Is Deposit Insurance Necessary? A Historical Perspective", (1990) 50 *Journal of Economic History* 283.

Calomiris, Charles W. and Gary Gorton, "The Origins of Banking Panics: Models, Facts, and Bank Regulation", in R. Glenn Hubbard (ed.),

Financial Markets and Financial Crises (Chicago: University of Chicago Press, 2nd edn., 1991) 109.

Carmichael, Jeffrey and Michael Pomerleano, *The Development and Regulation of Non-bank Financial Institutions* (Washington DC: The World Bank 2002).

Carnell, Richard Scott, Jonathan R. Macey and Geoffrey P. Miller, *The Law of Banking and Financial Institutions* (Austin: Wolters Kluwer, 5th edn, 2013).

Carstensen, Peter C., "Antitrust Law and the Paradigm of Industrial Organization", (1983) 16 *UC Davis Law Review* 487.

Cassis, Youssef, *Capitals of Capital: The Rise and Fall of International Financial Centres 1780–2009* (Cambridge: Cambridge University Press 2010).

Choi, Stephen J., "Market Lessons for Gatekeepers", (1986) 92(4) *Northwest University Law Review* 916.

Choi, Stephen J. and G. Mitu Galti, "Contract as Statute", in Omri Ben-Shahar (ed.), *Boilerplate: The Foundations of Market Contracts* (Cambridge: Cambridge University Press 2007) Ch 11.

Coates, John C., IV, "Cost-Benefit Analysis of Financial Regulation: Case Studies and Implications", (2015) 124 *Yale Law Journal* 926.

Coffee, John C., Jr., *Gatekeepers: The Professions and Corporate Governance* (New York: Oxford University Press 2006).

Coffee, John C., Jr., "The Attorney as Gatekeeper: An Agenda for the SEC", (2003) 103 *Columbia Law Review* 1293.

Coffee, John C., Jr., "Understanding Enron: It's About the Gatekeepers, Stupid", (2002) 57 *Business Lawyer* 1403.

Craig, Jon, "Horizontal Equalization Grants" in Ethisham Ahamd, Gao Qiang and Vito Tanzi (eds), *Reforming China's Public Finance* (Washington DC: International Monetary Fund 1995).

Cranston, Ross, *Principles of Banking Law* (Oxford: Oxford University Press, 2nd edn, 2000).

Cull, Robert, Lemma W. Senbet and Marco Sorge, "Deposit Insurance and Financial Development", (2005) 37 *Journal of Money, Credit and Banking* 43.

Dalhuisen, Jan J., *Transnational and Comparative Commercial, Financial and Trade Law*, Vol III (Oxford: Hart Publishing, 5th edn, 2012).

Dam, Kenneth W., "The Subprime Crisis and Financial Regulation: International and Comparative Perspectives", (2010) 10 *Chicago Journal of International Law* 581.

Davis, E. Philip, *Pension Funds – Retirement-income Security and Capital Markets: An International Perspective* (Oxford: Clarendon Press 1995).

Demirgüç-Kunt, Aslı, and Enrica Detragiache, "Does Deposit Insurance

Increase Banking System Stability? An Empirical Investigation", (2002) 49 *Journal of Monetary Economics* 1373.

Demirgüç-Kunt, Aslı, Edward J. Kane and Luc Laeven (eds), *Deposit Insurance Around the World: Issues of Design and Implementation* (London: The MTI Press 2008).

Diamond, Douglas W. and Philip H. Dybvig, "Bank Runs, Deposit Insurance, and Liquidity", (2000) 24(1) *Federal Reserve Bank of Minneapolis Quarterly Review* 14.

Diamond, Douglas W. and Philip H. Dybvig, "Bank Runs, Deposit Insurance, and Liquidity", (1983) 91(3) *Journal of Political Economy* 401.

Doff, Réne, "Why Operational Risk Modelling Creates Inverse Incentives", (2015) 1(2) *Journal of Financial Regulation* 284.

Duan, Haiyan and Jing Vivian Zhan, "Fiscal Transfer and Local Public Expenditure in China: A Case Study of Shanxi Province", (2011) 11(1) *The China Review* 57.

Edin, Maria, *Market Forces and Communist Power: Local Political Institutions and Economic Development in China* (Uppsala: Uppsala University, Department of Government 2000).

Eichberger, Jürgen, and Ian R. Harper, *Financial Economics* (Oxford: Oxford University Press 1997).

Eisenbeis, Robert A. and George G. Kaufman, "Cross-Border Banking and Financial Stability in the EU", (2008) 4 *Journal of Financial Stability* 168.

Ennis, Huberto, and Todd Keister, "Bank Runs and Institutions: The Perils of Intervention", (2009) 99 *American Economic Review* 1588.

Ferran, Eílis, "The Break-up of the Financial Services Authority in the UK", in Robin Hui Huang and Dirk Schoenmaker (eds), *Institutional Structure of Financial Regulation – Theories and International Experiences* (London and New York: Routledge 2015) p.109.

Ferran, Eílis, "Examining the UK's Experience in Adopting the Single Financial Regulator Model", (2003) 28 *Brooking Journal of International Law* 257.

Fohlin, Caroline, "Does Civil Law Tradition and Universal Banking Crowd Out Securities Markets? Pre-World War I Germany as Counter Example", (2007) 8(3) *Enterprise and Society* 602.

Freixas, Xavier, and Jean-Charles Rochet, *Microeconomics of Banking* (Massachusetts Institute Technology, 2nd edn, 2008).

Gamble, William B., *Investing in China: Legal, Financial and Regulatory Risk* (Westport, CT and London: Quorum Books 2002).

Garbade, Kenneth D., "The Evolution of Repo Contracting Conventions in the 1980s", (2006) 12(1) *Federal Reserve Bank of New York Economic Policy Review* 27.

Gilson, Ronald J., "Value Creation by Business Lawyers: Legal Skills and Asset Pricing", (1984) 94 *Yale Law Journal* 239.

Gilson, Ronald J., and Reinier Kraakman, "The Mechanism of Market Efficiency", (1984) 70 *Virginia Law Review* 549.

Goda, Thomas, and Photis Lysandrou, "The Contribution of Wealth Concentration to the Subprime Crisis: A Quantitative Estimation", (2014) 38(2) *Cambridge Journal of Economics* 301.

Goda, Thomas, Photis Lysandrou and Chris Stewart, "The Contribution of US Bond Demand to the US Bond Yield Conundrum of 2004 to 2007: An Empirical Investigation", (2013) 27 *Journal of International Financial Markets, Institutions and Money* 113.

Gordon, Jeffrey N., "The Empty Call for Benefit-Cost Analysis in Financial Regulation", (2014) 43(2) *Journal of Legal Studies* 351.

Gorton, Gary B., *Misunderstanding Financial Crises: Why We Don't See Them Coming* (Oxford: Oxford University Press 2012).

Gorton, Gary B., and Andrew Metrick, "Securitized Banking and the Run on Repo", (2012) 104 *Journal of Financial Economics* 425.

Gorton, Gary B. and George Pennacchi, "Financial Intermediaries and Liquidity Creation", (1990) 45 *Journal of Finance* 49.

Gorton, Gary B. and Nicholas S. Souleles, "Special Purpose Vehicles and Securitization", in Réne M. Stulz and Mark Carey (eds), *The Risks of Financial Institutions* (Chicago: University of Chicago 2006) p.549.

Gorton, Gary B., and Andrew Winton, "Financial Intermediaries", in George M. Constantinides, Milton Harris and Réne M. Stulz (eds), *Handbook of the Economics of Finance* (Elsevier Science Ltd 2003) p.431.

Greenbaum, Stuart I. and Anjan V. Thakor, "Bank Funding Modes: Securitization Versus Deposits", (1987) 11 *Journal of Banking and Finance* 379.

Greene, Edward F. and Elizabeth L. Broomfield, "Promoting Risk Mitigation, Not Migration: A Comparative Analysis of Shadow Banking Reform by the FSB, USA and EU", (2013) 8(1) *Capital Markets Law Journal* 6.

Grote, Rainer and Thilo Marauhn, *The Regulation of International Financial Markets: Perspectives for Reform* (Cambridge: Cambridge University Press 2006).

Guo, Li and Daile Xia, "In Search of a Place in the Sun: The Shadow Banking System with Chinese Characteristics", (2014) 15(3) *European Business Organization Law Review* 387.

Hirtle, Beverly, "Credit Derivatives and Bank Credit Supply", (2009) 18 *Journal of Financial Intermediation* 125.

Holmström, Bengt and Paul Milgrom, "Multitask Principal-Agent Analyses: Incentive Contracts, Asset Ownership, and Job Design", (1991) 7 *Journal of Law, Economics and Organization* 24.

Holmström, Bengt and Jean Tirole, "Private and Public Supply of Liquidity", (1998) 106 *Journal of Political Economy* 1.

Honohan, Patrick, "Cross-Country Variation in Household Access to Financial Services", (2008) 32(11) *Journal of Banking and Finance* 2493.

Howson, Nicholas Calcina, "China's Restructured Commercial Banks: Nomenklatura Accountability Serving Corporate Governance Reform?" in Zhu Min, Cai Jinqing and Martha Avery (eds) *China's Emerging Financial Markets: Challenges and Global Impact* (Singapore: John Wiley and Sons 2009) 123.

Howson, Nicholas Calcina, "China and WTO Liberalization of the Securities Industry: Le Choc des mondes or L'Empire immobile?", (2007) 3 *Asia Policy* 151.

Huang, Robin Hui, "The Regulation of Shadow Banking in China: International and Comparative Perspectives", (2015) 30 *Banking & Finance Law Review* 481.

Huang, Robin Hui and Dirk Schoenmaker (eds), *Institutional Structure of Financial Regulation: Theories and International Experiences* (Oxford and New York: Routledge 2015).

Huang, Yasheng, *Inflation and Investment Controls in China: The Political Economy of Central-Local Relations during the Reform Era* (Cambridge: Cambridge University Press 1996).

Huang, Yasheng, "Administrative Monitoring in China", (1995) 143 *The China Quarterly* 828.

Hudson, Alastair, *The Law of Finance* (London: Sweet & Maxwell 2009).

Jensen, Michael C. and William H. Meckling, "Theory of the Firm: Managerial Behavior, Agency Costs, and Ownership Structure", (1976) 3 *Journal of Financial Economics* 305.

Jobst, Andreas A., "The Treatment of Operational Risk under the New Basel Framework: Critical Issues", (2007) 8 *Journal of Banking Regulation* 316.

Johnson, Christian A., "Exigent and Unusual Circumstances: The Federal Reserve and the US Financial Crisis", in Kern Alexander and Niamh Moloney, *Law Reform and Financial Markets* (Cheltenham, UK and Northampton, MA, USA: Edward Elgar 2011) p.269.

Kane, Edward J., "Three Paradigms for the Role of Capitalization Requirements in Insured Financial Institutions", (1995) 19(3–4) *Journal of Banking and Finance* 431.

Kane, Edward J., *The S&L Insurance Mess: How Did It Happen?* (Washington, DC: Urban Institute Press 1989).

Kelman, Mark, *Strategy or Principle? The Choice between Regulation and Taxation* (Ann Arbor: University of Michigan Press 1999).

Kennedy, John James, "From the Tax-for-Fee Reform to the Abolition of Agricultural Taxes: The Impact on Township Governments in North-West China", (2007) 189 *The China Quarterly* 43.

Kindleberger, Charles P., *The World in Depression, 1929–1939* (Berkeley, CA: University of California Press 1973).

Kindleberger, Charles P. and Robert Aliber, *Manias, Panics, and Crashes* (Basingstoke: Palgrave Macmillan, 5th edn, 2005).

Kraakman, Reinier H., "Gatekeepers: The Anatomy of a Third-Party Enforcement Strategy", (1986) 2(1) *Journal of Law, Economics and Organization* 53.

Kraakman, Reinier H., "Corporate Liability Strategies and the Costs at Legal Controls", (1984) 93 *Yale Law Journal* 857.

Lam, Joseph, "The Insolvency of GITIC", (1999) 14(6) *Journal of International Banking Law* 193.

Lardy, Nicholas, *China's Unfinished Economic Revolution* (Washington DC: The Brookings Institution 1998).

Latimer, Paul, "Regulation of Over-the-Counter Derivatives in Australia", in Michael C.S. Wong (ed.), *The Risk of Investment Products – From Product Innovation to Risk Compliance* (Singapore: World Scientific 2011).

Lee, Emily, "Basel III and Its New Capital Requirements, as Distinguished from Basel II", (2014) 13(1) *Banking Law Journal* 27.

Lee, Pak K. "Into the Trap of Strengthening State Capacity: China's Tax-assignment Reform", (2000) 164 *China Quarterly* 1007.

Levine, Ross, "Financial Development and Economic Growth: Views and Agenda", (1997) 35 *Journal of Economic Literature* 688.

Lin, Justin Yifu and Yongjun Li, "Promoting the Growth of Medium and Small-sized Enterprises through the Development of Medium and Small-sized Financial Institutions", (2001) 1 *Economic Research Journal* 11.

Liu, Mingxing and Tao Ran, "Regional Competition, Fiscal Reform and Local Governance in China", in Vivienne Shue and Christine Wong (eds), *Paying for Progress in China: Public Finance, Human Welfare and Changing Patterns of Inequality* (London: Routledge 2007).

Lo, Wai Chung, "A Retrospect on China's Banking Reform", in Hung-Gay Fung and Kevin H. Zhang (eds), *Financial Markets and Foreign Direct Investment in Greater China* (Armonk, NY and London: M.E. Sharpe 2002) p.38.

Ma, Jun, and Yinlin Hou, "Policymaking and Budgeting Process in China's Provincial Budgeting", (2005) 5 *Comparative Economic and Social System* 64.

Majone, Giandomenico, "The New European Agencies: Regulation by Information", (1997) 4 *Journal of European Public Policy* 262.

Matutes, Carmen and Xavier Vives, "Competition for Deposit, Fragility, and Insurance", (1996) 5 *Journal of Financial Intermediation* 184.

McKie, James W., "Regulation and the Free Market: The Problem of Boundaries", (1970) 1 *Bell Journal of Economics and Management* 6.

McKinnon, Ronald I., *Money and Capital in Economic Development* (Washington DC: Brookings Institution 1973).

Meier, Gerald M. and James E. Rauch, *Leading Issues in Economic Development* (New York and Oxford: Oxford University Press, 7th edn, 2000).

Meltzer, Allan H., "Financial Failures and Financial Policies", in George G. Kaufman and Roger C. Kormendi (eds), *Deregulating Financial Services: Public Policy in Flux* (Cambridge, MA: Ballinger 1986) p.79.

Miller, Geoffrey P., "Deposit Insurance for Economies in Transition", in Rosa M. Lastra and Henry N. Schiffman, *Bank Failures and Bank Insolvency Law in Economies in Transition* (The Hague and Boston: Wolters Kluwer 1999) p.43.

Miller, Ken, "Coping with China's Financial Power", (2010) 89(4) *Financial Affairs* 96.

Mirrlees, James A., *Welfare, Incentives, and Taxation* (Oxford: Oxford University Press 2006).

Niskanen, William A., *Bureaucracy and Public Economics* (Aldershot, UK and Brookfield, VT, USA: Edward Elgar 1994).

North, Douglass C., "Economic Performance through Time", (1994) 84(3) *American Economic Review* 359.

Norton, Joseph J., C.J. Li and Yangxin Huang, *Financial Regulation in the Greater China Area: Mainland China, Taiwan and Hong Kong SAR* (The Hague, London and Boston: Kluwer Law International 2000).

Oatley, Thomas and W. Kindred Winecoff, "The Domestic Rooting of Financial Regulation in an Era of Global Capital Markets" in Phoebus Athanassiou, *Research Handbook on Hedge Funds, Private Equity and Alternative Investments* (Cheltenham, UK and Northampton, MA, USA: Edward Elgar 2012) p.474.

OECD, *Challenges for China's Public Spending: Toward Greater Effectiveness and Equity* (Paris: OECD 2006).

Oi, Jean C. and Scott Rozelle, "Elections and Power: The Locus of Decision-making in Chinese Villages", (2000) 162 *The China Quarterly* 513.

Oi, Jean C. and Shukai Zhao "Fiscal Crisis in China's Townships: Causes and Consequences", in Elizabeth J. Perry and Merle Goldman (eds),

Grassroots Political Reform in Contemporary China (Cambridge, MA: Harvard University Press 2007).

Ong, Lynette "The Political Economy of Township Government Debt, Township Enterprises and Rural Financial Institutions in China", (2006) 186 *China Quarterly* 377.

Pace, Vincent A., "The Bankruptcy of the Zhu Kuan Group: A Case Study of Cross-border Insolvency Litigation Against A Chinese State-owned Enterprise", (2006) 27(2) *University of Pennsylvania Journal of International Law* 517.

Pastor, Robert A. and Qingshan Tan, "The Meaning of China's Village Elections", (2000) 162 *The China Quarterly* 490.

Pettis, Michael, *Avoiding the Fall: China's Economic Restructuring* (Washington DC: Carnegie Endowment for International Peace 2013).

Posner, Richard A., *A Failure of Capitalism: The Crisis of '08 and the Descent into Depression* (Cambridge, MA: Harvard University Press 2009).

Posner, Richard A., *The Crisis of Capitalist Democracy* (Cambridge, MA: Harvard University Press 2010).

Power, Carol, "Bank-Telecom Alliance Trend Said on Way to U.S.", (2001) 166(81) *American Banker* 10.

Power, Michael, "The Invention of Operational Risk", (2015) 12 *Review of International Political Economy* 577.

Qian, Yingyi, "Reforming Corporate Governance and Finance in China", in Masahiko Aoki and Hyng ki Kim (eds), *Corporate Governance in Transition Economies: Insider Control and the Role of Banks* (Washington DC: World Bank 1995).

Rajan, Raghuram and Luigi Zingales, *Saving Capitalism from the Capitalists* (Princeton: Princeton University Press, 2nd edn, 2004).

Reid, Emily and James Black, "The Future for Peer-to-peer (P2P) Lending: the Proposed Regulatory Framework for Lending Platforms", (2014) 29(1) *Journal of International Banking and Financial Law* 37.

Reinhart, Carmen M., and Kenneth S. Rogoff, *This Time Is Different: Eight Centuries of Financial Folly* (Princeton and Oxford: Princeton University Press 2009).

Ricks, Morgan, "Regulating Money Creation after the Crisis", (2011) 1 *Harvard Business Law Review* 90.

Romano, Roberta, "For Diversity in the International Regulation of Financial Institutions: Critiquing and Recalibrating the Basel Architecture", (2014) 31 *Yale Journal on Regulation* 1.

Roubini, Nouriel and Stephen Mihm, *Crisis Economics: A Crash Course in the Future of Finance* (New York: The Penguin Press 2010).

Scherer, Frederic M., "Conservative Economics and Antitrust: A Variety of Influences", in Robert Pitofsky (ed.) *How the Chicago School Overshot the Mark* (Oxford: Oxford University Press) p.30.

Schoenmaker, Dirk and Jeroen Kremers, "Financial Stability and Proper Business Conduct: Can Supervisory Structure Help To Achieve These Objectives?", in Robin Hui Huang and Dirk Schoenmaker (eds), *Institutional Structure of Financial Regulation – Theories and International Experiences* (London and New York: Routledge 2015) p.29.

Schwarcz, Steven L., "Regulating Shadows: Financial Regulation and Responsibility Failure", (2013) 70 *Washington and Lee Law Review* 1781.

Schwarcz, Steven L., "Controlling Financial Chaos: The Power and Limits of Law", (2012) 3 *Wisconsin Law Review* 815.

Schwarcz, Steven L., "Regulating Shadow Banking", (2011) 31 *Review of Banking and Financial Law* 619.

Schwarcz, Steven L., "Protecting Financial Markets: Lessons from the Subprime Mortgage Meltdown", (2008) 93(2) *Minnesota Law Review* 373.

Schwarcz, Steven L., "The Alchemy of Asset Securitization", (2008) *Stanford Journal of Law and Business* 531.

Sen, Amartya, *Development as Freedom* (New York: Anchor Books 1999).

Shen, Wei, "Wealth Management Products in the Context of China's Shadow Banking: Systemic Risks, Consumer Protection and Regulatory Instruments", (2015) 23(1) *Asia Pacific Law Review* 55.

Shen, Wei, *The Anatomy of China's Banking Sector and Regulation* (Hong Kong: Wolters Kluwer 2014).

Shen, Wei, "Healthy or Unhealthy? That is a Problem – Unveiling the Myth of Chinese Banks' Success", (2013) 28(2) *Journal of International Banking Law and Regulation* 81.

Shen, Wei, "Shadow Banking System in China – Origin, Uniqueness and Governmental Response", (2013) 28(1) *Journal of International Banking Law and Regulation* 20.

Shen, Wei, "Wealth Management Products in China: Recent Scandals and Regulatory Loopholes", (2013) 28(5) *Journal of International Banking and Financial Law* 303.

Shetta, Samah and Ahmed Kamaly, "Does the Budget Deficit Crowd-out Private Credit From the Banking Sector? The Case of Egypt", (2014) 16(2) *Topics in Middle Eastern and African Economies* 251.

Shin, Hyun Song, "Securitization and Financial Stability", (2009) 119 *Economic Journal* 309.

Sinkey, Joseph F., Jr., "Regulatory Attitudes Toward Risk", in Richard C.

Aspinwall and Robert A. Eisenbeis (eds), *Handbook for Banking Strategy* (New York: Wiley 1985) p.349.

Skocpol, Treda, *States and Social Revolution* (Cambridge: Cambridge University Press 1979).

Soederberg, Susanne, "The New International Financial Architecture (NIFA): An Emerging Multi-level Structure of Neo-Liberal Discipline", in Andrew Baker, David Hudson and Richard Woodward (eds), *Governing Financial Globalization: International Political Economy and Multi-Level Governance* (New York: Routledge 2005) p.189.

Stanton, Thomas H., *Why Some Firms Thrive While Others Fail – Governance and Management Lessons from the Crisis* (New York: Oxford University Press 2012).

Stein, Jeremy, "Securitization, Shadow Banking and Financial Fragility", (2010) 139 *Daedalus* 41.

Stiglitz, Joseph E., *The Price of Inequality* (London: Penguin Books 2013).

Tang, Yingmao, "Shadow Banking or 'Bank's Shadow': Re-conceptualizing Global Shadow Banking Regulation", in Ross P. Buckley, Emilios Avgouleas and Douglas W. Arner (eds) *Reconceptualising Global Finance and its Regulation* (Cambridge: Cambridge University Press 2016).

Tchana, Fulbert Tchana, "The Empirics of Banking Regulation", (2014) 19(3) *Merging Markets Review* 49.

Tilly, Charles, *From Mobilization to Revolution* (Reading, MA: Addison-Wesley 1978).

Tsai, Kellee S., *Back-Alley Banking: Private Entrepreneurs in China* (Ithaca and London: Cornell University Press 2002).

Tsang, Shu-Ki, and Yuk-Shing Cheng, "China's Tax Reforms of 1994: Breakthrough or Compromise?", (1994) 36(9) *Asian Survey* 769.

Verstein, Andrew, "The Misregulation of Person-to-Person Lending", (2011) 45 *U.C. Davis Law Review* 445.

Vittas, Dimitri, *Financial Regulation – Changing the Rules for the Game* (Washington DC: World Bank 1992).

Vries Robbé, Jan Job de, *Structured Finance: on from the Credit Crunch – The Road to Recovery* (Austin: Wolters Kluwer 2009).

Wang, Yanzhong, "Financing Difficulties and Structural Characteristics of SMEs in China", (2004) 12 *China and World Economy* 34.

Wong, Christine (ed.), *Financing Local Government in the People's Republic of China* (Hong Kong: Oxford University Press 1997).

Wong, Christine P.W., "Central-Local Relations in an Era of Fiscal Decline – The Paradox of Fiscal Decentralization in Post-Mao China", (1991) 128 *The China Quarterly* 703.

Wong, Christine and Deepak Bhattasali, *China: National Development and Sub-National Finance: A Review of Provincial Expenditures* (Washington, DC: World Bank 2002).

Wong, Christine P.W. and Richard M. Bird, "China's Fiscal System: A Work in Progress", in Loren Brandt and Thomas G. Rawski (eds), *China's Great Economic Transformation* (New York: Cambridge University Press 2008).

World Bank, *China: National Development and Sub-national Finance – A Review of Provincial Expenditures* (Beijing: Poverty Reduction and Economic Management Unit, East Asia and Pacific Region 2002).

World Bank, *National Development and Sub-national Finance – A Review of Provincial Expenditures* (Beijing: Poverty Reduction and Economic Management Unit, East Asia and Pacific Region, World Bank 2002).

Xu, Hongshui, "Financing Gap and Minimization of Transaction Cost: Why SMEs Have Problems in Financing and How to Improve the Policy", (2001) *Journal of Financial Research* 11.

Zhang, Leyin, "Chinese Central-Provincial Fiscal Relationships, Budgetary Decline and the Impact of the 1994 Fiscal Reform: An Evaluation", (1999) 157 *The China Quarterly* 115.

Zhao, Yingwei, "A Comparison of Shadow Banking Credit Risk Aggregation from the Perspective of Global Financial Crises in the Past", (2013) 11 *Finance and Economics Science* 24.

Zhou, Zhongfei, "Banking Regulatory Law Reforms in China: A Long Way to Go Towards International Standards" in James R. Barth et al., *Financial Restructuring and Reform in Post-WTO China* (Alphen aan den Rijn: Kluwer Law International) p.45.

Zhou, Zhongfei, *Banking Law in China* (Alphen aan den Rijn: Kluwer Law International 2007).

Index